Foundation PHP 5 for Flash

David Powers

Foundation PHP 5 for Flash

ISBN (pbk): 1-59059-466-5

Printed and bound in the United States of America 9 8 7 6 5 4 3 2

Distributed to the book trade in the United States by Springer-Verlag New York, Inc., 233 Spring Street, 6th Floor, New York, NY 10013, and outside the United States by Springer-Verlag GmbH & Co. KG, Tiergartenstr. 17, 69112 Heidelberg, Germany.

In the United States: phone 1-800-SPRINGER, e-mail orders@springer-ny.com, or visit www.springer-ny.com. Outside the United States: fax +49 6221 345229, e-mail orders@springer.de, or visit http://www.springer.de.

For information on translations, please contact Apress directly at 2560 Ninth Street, Suite 219, Berkeley, CA 94710. Phone 510-549-5930, fax 510-549-5939, e-mail info@apress.com, or visit www.apress.com.

The source code for this book is freely available to readers at www.friendsofed.com in the Downloads section.

Credits

Lead Editors
Steve Rycroft
Chris Mills

Technical Reviewer
Sham Bhangal

Editorial Board
Steve Anglin, Dan Appleman, Ewan Buckingham, Gary Cornell, Tony Davis, Jason Gilmore, Jonathan Hassell, Chris Mills, Dominic Shakeshaft, Jim Sumser

Associate Publisher
Grace Wong

Project Manager
Beckie Stones

Copy Editor
Nicole LeClerc

Production Manager
Kari Brooks-Copony

Production Editor
Katie Stence

Compositor
Dina Quan

Proofreader
Elizabeth Berry

Indexer
Michael Brinkman

Artist
Kinetic Publishing Services, LLC

Cover Designer
Kurt Krames

Manufacturing Manager
Tom Debolski

CONTENTS

About the Author ix

About the Technical Reviewer x

Acknowledgments xi

Introduction xiii

Chapter 1: Getting Ready to Work with PHP 1

- Accessing external data with Flash 2
  - Choosing the right technology 2
  - What PHP, Apache, and MySQL have to offer 4
  - How everything fits together 5
- PHP and ActionScript: Distant cousins 7
- Installing the necessary software 9
  - Setting up on Windows 9
  - Setting up on Mac OS X 27
- Setting up your work environment 38
- Getting a first taste of the power of PHP 43

Chapter 2: Flash Breaks Free 45

- Communicating with external sources 46
- Taking first steps in PHP 51
  - How PHP fits into web design 51
  - The basic grammar of PHP 52
- Sending feedback from Flash by email 64
- Progress so far 82

Chapter 3: Calculations and Decisions 85

- Performing calculations with PHP 86
  - Working with arithmetic operators 87
  - Useful math functions 91
  - Performing calculations in the right order 93
  - Combining calculations and assignment 95
- Making decisions with PHP 96
  - Using if... else conditional statements 96
  - Using comparison operators 97

Testing more than one condition 99
Using switch for long decision chains 102
Using the conditional operator 103
Flash application: A multiconverter 104
Planning the conversion script 105
Building the Flash interface 110
Summing up 127

Chapter 4: Of Strings and Things 129

Manipulating strings with PHP 130
How PHP outputs strings 130
Changing case 135
Working with substrings 138
Modularizing code with functions 144
Understanding where PHP functions run 145
Why roll your own? 146
Understanding how PHP and ActionScript functions handle variables 147
Returning a value from a function 150
Deciding where to put functions 151
Completing the multiconverter script 151
Formatting the main measurement units 152
Handling gallons, pints, and liters 155
Dealing with kilograms, pounds, and stones 160
Handling meters to feet and yards 161
Reviewing the multiconverter project 162
Taking the project further 163
Dealing with user input 164
Trimming leading and trailing whitespace 164
Stripping HTML tags 165
Removing backslashes 165
Using regular expressions to identify patterns 166
Fine-tuning the feedback application 171
A pause for breath 174

Chapter 5: Working Smarter with Arrays and Loops 177

Understanding the basics of arrays and loops 178
Organizing items in arrays 178
Grouping similar items in multidimensional arrays 179
Using loops for repetitive tasks 180
Creating arrays in PHP 180
Indexed arrays: Organizing by number 181
Associative arrays: Organizing by name 184
Array length: Key to understanding the difference between PHP and ActionScript arrays 188
Multidimensional arrays: Nesting arrays 189
Zipping through repetitive tasks with loops 191
Looping through arrays with foreach 191

Using the versatile for loop . . . 192
Simple loops with while and do . . . 194
Breaking out of loops . . . 195
Nesting loops . . . 196
Passing information securely with $_POST . . . 198
Why register_globals is so important . . . 199
Manipulating arrays . . . 201
Slicing and splicing arrays . . . 202
Sorting arrays . . . 206
Building an RSS feed aggregator . . . 209
What an RSS feed does . . . 209
Taking a look inside an RSS feed . . . 210
Parsing an RSS feed with MagpieRSS . . . 212
Displaying the merged RSS feed in Flash . . . 223
Eliminating HTML entities that Flash cannot handle . . . 229
Deploying the feed aggregator on the Internet . . . 230
Progress report . . . 231

Chapter 6: PHP and Databases: Packing Real Power Behind Your Applications . . . 233

Why MySQL? . . . 234
MySQL's shortcomings . . . 234
MySQL's strengths . . . 236
Choosing the right version of MySQL . . . 237
Choosing the right license and cost . . . 239
Considering SQLite as an alternative . . . 239
SQLite's strengths . . . 239
SQLite's shortcomings . . . 240
Choosing the right database system . . . 240
Installing MySQL on Windows . . . 241
Changing the default table type on Windows Essentials . . . 253
Starting and stopping MySQL manually on Windows . . . 255
Launching MySQL Monitor on Windows . . . 257
Configuring MySQL on Mac OS X . . . 259
Working with MySQL Monitor (Windows and Mac) . . . 261
Creating your first database in MySQL . . . 263
Loading data from an external file . . . 272
Using MySQL with a graphical interface . . . 275
phpMyAdmin: A golden oldie . . . 275
MySQL Administrator and MySQL Query Browser: Smart new kids on the block . . . 280
Looking ahead . . . 282

Chapter 7: Playing with Words . . . 285

Building the game's graphical elements . . . 286
Using PHP to communicate with the database . . . 291
A touch of class to emulate mysqli on all setups . . . 292

Using the mysqli object-oriented interface . . . 292
Building and using PHP 5 classes . . . 308
Naming and declaring classes . . . 309
Creating class properties . . . 309
Using the constructor function . . . 310
Setting class methods . . . 312
Accessing public methods . . . 313
Refining the word selection with SQL and PHP . . . 313
Building a scoring mechanism that remembers . . . 322
Introducing the Flash SharedObject . . . 323
Other ways to enhance the game . . . 326
Handling database failures . . . 327
Setting different skill levels . . . 330
SQLite: An alternative database system . . . 331
SQLite basics . . . 331
Making sure SQLite has the right permissions . . . 333
Rewriting the Hangman PHP script for SQLite . . . 341
Comparing MySQL and SQLite . . . 343
Ever onward and upward . . . 343

Chapter 8: Creating a User Registration Database . . . 345

Understanding database types . . . 346
Keeping things simple with flat-file databases . . . 346
Gaining greater flexibility with relational databases . . . 348
Understanding MySQL storage formats . . . 353
Choosing the right column type . . . 354
Column types in MySQL . . . 354
Default values and NULL . . . 358
Choosing the right language settings . . . 358
Building a user registration system . . . 359
Registering users with MySQL . . . 359
What if it doesn't work? . . . 384
Time to take stock . . . 385

Chapter 9: Protecting Your Data with Sessions . . . 387

Keeping track with PHP sessions . . . 388
The Web is a stateless environment . . . 388
How sessions work . . . 390
PHP session basics . . . 392
Using sessions to restrict access . . . 393
Other uses for sessions . . . 405
Summary . . . 405

Chapter 10: Keeping Control with a Content Management System 407

The four essential SQL commands 408
SELECT 408
INSERT 410
UPDATE 410
DELETE 411
Building a simple content management system 411
Building the content management interface 412
Scripting the application 419
Securing the content management system 466
Adding an extra column to a table 468
A solid foundation has been laid 470

Chapter 11: Working with Dates 473

How ActionScript, PHP, and MySQL handle dates 474
Navigating the minefield of incompatible timestamps 475
Creating a timestamp 477
Formatting dates in PHP 483
Working with dates in MySQL 486
Using dates in calculations 486
Finding and creating records based on temporal criteria 493
Handling dates in user input 494
Formatting dates from text input 495
Checking a date's validity with PHP 495
Building a Flash date selector for MySQL 498
Nearly there 510

Chapter 12: Working with Multiple Tables and XML 513

Designing the table structure 514
Deciding the basic requirements 514
Normalizing the tables 515
Preparing to build the bookstore database 518
Getting an overview of the project 521
Completing the database structure 523
Creating the content management system 529
Deciding the basic structure 529
Activating the forms with PHP 545
Retrieving data from more than one table 569
Avoiding ambiguous column references 569
Using a full join 569
Using a left join to find an incomplete match 572
Completing the content management system 574
Managing existing book records 574
Deleting records from more than one table 585
Maintaining referential integrity on deletion 587
Updating multiple records 594

Using SimpleXML to parse an XML feed 596
Securing your CMS 601
Displaying the database contents in Flash 601
Getting the database ready 601
Communicating with the database through PHP 602
Building the Flash interface 608
Creating the ActionScript to load results from the database 609
A long road traveled 616

Appendix A: When Things Go Wrong with PHP and MySQL 619

Appendix B: Converting Applications to ActionScript 1.0 641

Appendix C: Installing Older Versions of MySQL on Windows 647

Appendix D: Using Languages Other Than English in MySQL 657

Appendix E: Essential MySQL Maintenance 667

Index 684

ABOUT THE AUTHOR

David Powers is a professional writer who has been involved in electronic media for more than 30 years, first with BBC radio and television, and more recently with the Internet. A mild interest in computing was transformed almost overnight into a passion, when he was posted to Japan in 1987 as a BBC correspondent in Tokyo. With no corporate IT department just down the corridor, he was forced to learn how to fix everything himself. When not tinkering with the innards of his computer, he was reporting for BBC radio and television on the rise and collapse of the Japanese bubble economy.

It was back in the UK as Editor, BBC Japanese TV, that David started working with web design. He persuaded the IT department to let him have free run of a tiny corner of the BBC's Internet server; and he built and maintained an 80-page Japanese and English website—first, coding by hand, and then trying all variety of HTML editors, good and bad. He decided to set up his own independent company, Japan Interface (`http://japan-interface.co.uk`) in 1999, and he is actively involved in the development of an online bilingual database of economic and political analysis for Japanese clients of an international consultancy.

This is David's third book for friends of ED/Apress. He co-authored *Foundation Dreamweaver MX 2004* (friends of ED, ISBN: 1-59059-308-1) and *PHP Web Development with Dreamweaver MX 2004* (Apress, ISBN: 1-59059-350-2). David was also the technical reviewer for the highly successful second edition of *Cascading Style Sheets: Separating Content from Presentation* (friends of ED, ISBN: 1-59059-231-X) and *Web Designer's Reference* (friends of ED, ISBN: 1-59059-430-4). He has also translated several plays from Japanese, most recently *Southern Cross*, the final part of a war trilogy by Keita Asari.

ABOUT THE TECHNICAL REVIEWER

Sham Bhangal has written for friends of ED on new media since the imprint's inception over five years ago. In that time, he has been involved in the writing, production, and specification of just under 20 books.

Sham has considerable working experience with Macromedia and Adobe products, with a focus on web design and motion graphics. Creating books that teach other people about his favorite subjects is probably the best job he has had (ignoring the long hours, aggressive deadlines, lost manuscripts, and occasional wiped hard drives). If he was doing something else, he'd probably be losing sleep thinking about writing anyway.

Sham currently lives in the north of England with his longtime partner, Karen.

ACKNOWLEDGMENTS

Writing books is a lonely business, pounding away at the keyboard night and day for months on end, but it's not something you can achieve all on your own. Every member of the editorial and production team deserves thanks for guiding, encouraging, and cajoling me from the initial concept through to completion: Steve Rycroft for planting the original idea for this book in my brain and seeing it through the early stages; Chris Mills and Beckie Stones for putting up with my sometimes interminable phone calls when I needed help in sorting out the forest from the trees; Nicole LeClerc for her sensitive and perceptive copy editing; plus, of course, all the others.

Special thanks must go to Sham Bhangal for the superb job he has done as technical reviewer, subjecting both the text and the code to scrutiny, not only for accuracy, but also for ease of use. On many occasions, he suggested that something buried deep in a chapter would make more sense if brought to the front—and he was right. I originally learned ActionScript from Sham's books, so it was a particular honor to have him work on my first Flash-related book.

I'm also grateful to Al Sparber of Project Seven (`www.projectseven.com`) for allowing me to adapt his Uberlink CSS concept for the navigation menu in Chapter 12.

The unsung heroes to whom we should all be grateful are the development teams behind PHP, MySQL, and Flash. Without them, the Web would be a much duller place and there would have been no book to write.

The biggest thanks of all must go to you, the reader, who makes it all worthwhile. If you have just bought this book, I hope it lives up to your expectations. If you have borrowed this book, I hope you enjoy it enough to want to go out and buy a copy of your own.

INTRODUCTION

Back in 2001, friends of ED published *Foundation PHP for Flash*. It was very popular, but it has long been out of print, and is now very much out of date. It was written in the days of Flash 5, PHP 4.0, and MySQL 3.23. Since then, a lot of water has passed under the bridge. The release of ActionScript 2.0 in September 2003 and of PHP 5 ten months later represents a significant milestone in the evolution of both languages. Both now have a formal object-oriented programming (OOP) syntax, turning them from being merely useful tools into essential assets for developing rich, interactive web applications. MySQL, the world's most popular open source relational database, has also been making rapid strides. It has gone through two major upgrades (the current version is MySQL 4.1), and work is moving apace on the development of MySQL 5.0, which will add more of the advanced features currently associated with much more expensive commercial systems.

Consequently, *Foundation PHP 5 for Flash* is not a new edition of an old book. It is completely new from the first page to the last. Although it touches only briefly on OOP, the emphasis is on laying a solid foundation of good coding practice, so that when you move on to a more advanced level, you won't have to unlearn any bad habits.

Using the latest standards, but remaining version neutral

Software developers often move at a rapider pace than administrators with the responsibility for deploying software. Also, not everyone can afford to upgrade every time a new version comes out. So, in writing this book, I have taken particular care to use the latest standards, but to keep them version neutral wherever possible. Where something works only in PHP 5 or MySQL 4.1, I say so clearly and suggest alternative ways of achieving the same result. A special feature of this book is the set of `Database` classes in Chapter 7 that enable you to use exactly the same code to communicate with a database, whether your hosting company is using the latest versions of PHP and MySQL or it's still stuck in the past with PHP 4 and MySQL 3.23. All the ActionScript is written using ActionScript 2.0, but Appendix B gives advice on how to adapt it to work in Flash MX, and the download files (available from `www.friendsofed.com`) include special versions rewritten in ActionScript 1.0 and saved in Flash MX format.

Who this book is for

Although this book is part of the Foundation series, it's not aimed at beginners taking their first steps with Flash. It's a book about integrating PHP and MySQL with Flash, so you need to be comfortable moving around the Flash authoring environment. Ideally, you'll also have some experience of ActionScript. You don't need to be able to recite the contents of the ActionScript Dictionary in your sleep, but your progress will be a lot swifter if you have a reasonable grasp of the main concepts, such as working with loops, arrays, and so on. If you have worked through the ActionScript chapters in *Foundation Flash MX 2004* by Kristian Besley and Sham Bhangal (friends of ED, ISBN: 1-59059-303-0), you should have no difficulty.

Even if you don't have much experience of ActionScript, don't worry. Everything is explained in detail. Rather than just throw a chunk of code at you and tell you to get on with it, my approach is to get you to understand what's happening and why. The other main feature of this book is the way it highlights the differences and similarities between PHP and ActionScript. Both languages use the same basic concepts and structures, but there are often subtle differences that catch out the unwary. So, even if your knowledge of arrays is shaky, by the time you have finished Chapter 5, you should have a firm grasp of how they're used in both PHP and ActionScript.

If you're looking for a half-dozen lines of code that will solve the problems of the universe, then this isn't the book for you. PHP is not a point-and-click language. You need to roll up your sleeves and code by hand. Similarly, the only way to get the best out of a database—not just MySQL—is to learn the basics of database design and Structured Query Language (SQL), the language used to interact with databases. But don't let that put you off. Neither PHP nor MySQL is particularly difficult to learn—that's one reason they're so popular. Creating the code yourself puts great power and flexibility at your fingertips. Instead of being shoehorned into a rigid and, perhaps, inappropriate solution, you gain the freedom to create your own solutions.

If you're still using Flash MX, and you recoil in horror at the thought of Expert Mode in the Actions panel, you're in for a bit of a shock. The dialog boxes in Normal Mode were removed in MX 2004, and it became Expert Mode or nothing. Again, don't worry. By the time you've worked through a couple of chapters, you'll realize that typing in the code directly is much faster. You'll also notice that I don't sprinkle ActionScript all over the place; most of the time it goes on frame 1 of a layer reserved solely for ActionScript. In the projects toward the end of the book, this produces long scripts that may look off-putting at first glance. Take a closer look and you'll quickly realize that they're made up of short code blocks. Keeping them in one place makes updating and maintenance far, far easier than playing "hunt the script" for an action buried in a movie clip nested three levels deep.

What if you're someone with a fair knowledge of PHP, but you're looking for ways to integrate it with Flash? Although I don't set out to teach ActionScript, your knowledge of programming combined with reference to the ActionScript Dictionary in Flash (Help ➤ ActionScript Dictionary) should make the transition relatively painless. Welcome on board.

What you need

First of all you need a copy of Flash. Ideally, you should be using MX 2004 or later, but the minimum requirement is Flash MX (see Appendix B for details on how to convert ActionScript 2.0 to work with MX). You also need the Apache web server, PHP, MySQL, and a copy of a graphical interface for MySQL called phpMyAdmin—all available for download free of charge over the Internet. If you're using Mac OS X, Apache and PHP should already be installed on your computer, although you may need to enable them. Installation isn't difficult, but the correct configuration seems to cause problems for many beginners, so I've given detailed instructions for both Windows and Mac in Chapters 1 and 6, highlighting points that seem to trip up many people. The size of downloads varies with your operating system, but some are as big as 20MB, so give yourself plenty of time if you're on a dialup connection.

The only other software needed is a text editor or, preferably, a dedicated script editor. PHP scripts need to be saved as plain text files (but with a `.php` filename extension), so Notepad or TextEdit are perfectly adequate. Your life will be made a lot easier, though, by a script editor that displays line numbers and uses syntax coloring. I find working in Code view of Dreamweaver MX 2004 the most convenient, but other script editors you might wish to consider are TextPad or SciTEFlash (Windows), or BBEdit (Mac). For more information, including where to obtain these programs, see the section "Using a script editor to reduce syntax errors" in Appendix A.

What you'll get out of this book

First of all, I hope you get a lot of fun. Although the book is project driven, I've structured each chapter around a particular aspect of PHP or working with a database, such as string manipulation, arrays, or joining tables. Hands-on projects are a good way to learn new skills, but it can be a nightmare trying to dig out that vital nugget of information if it's buried deep in a series of step-by-step instructions. So, wherever possible, I've split each chapter into clearly identifiable sections so that you can come back much later and use it as a reference book. The projects are intended to be challenging, rather than the lightweight examples you find in a lot of beginners' books. By the end of Chapter 12, you will have built the following applications in Flash and PHP:

- An online feedback form
- A tool that converts 24 different types of weights and measures
- An RSS feed aggregator
- A word game with a vocabulary of more than 21,000 words
- A scoring system that remembers a player's score on returning to a site
- An online registration system
- An intelligent Flash component to format and display dates (intelligent enough to know how many days there are in each month, even in a leap year)
- A multitable relational database

Along the way, you'll also learn how to protect sensitive parts of your website using PHP sessions, as well as cover the basics of database management, and you'll take some first steps in OOP with PHP. The focus throughout is on learning how to work with PHP and MySQL, so I've deliberately kept the graphical aspects of design simple, but—I hope—elegant.

Mac-friendly, too

I have a confession to make. For many years, I worked with a Mac enthusiast who loathed Windows so much that he rarely began a conversation without cursing Bill Gates and all his works. (I know some Windows users like that, too, but that's beside the point.) As a result, he turned me into a Mac-hater (sorry). Then, one day, I read lots of good things about Mac OS X and decided to try it out. I liked what I saw, but it's difficult to change the habits of two decades of working with DOS and Windows. Still, I've tested everything on a PowerBook G4 running OS X 10.3, and I've given separate instructions for the Mac wherever appropriate. Fortunately, PHP and MySQL are almost entirely operating system–neutral, so if I don't give specific instructions for the Mac, it's not because I have forgotten or am ignoring you.

> *Support for PHP 5 on versions of Mac OS X prior to 10.3 appears to be very thin on the ground. If you are running Jaguar or earlier, you will probably be restricted to using PHP 4. Most of the code in this book will run on PHP 4, but the only Mac testing has been done on Panther.*

Layout conventions used in this book

I've tried to keep this book as clear and easy to follow as possible, so I've used the following text conventions throughout.

When you first come across an important word, it will be in **bold** type, then in normal type thereafter.

I've used a fixed-width font for code, `file names`, and any other text you need to type in for yourself.

Sections of code that need to be added to an existing script or that deserve special attention are additionally highlighted **`like this`**.

You'll see menu commands written in the form Menu ➤ Submenu ➤ Submenu.

When there's some information I think is really important, I'll highlight it like this:

> *This is very important stuff—don't skip it!*

When I ask you to enter code that spills onto two lines **without** using a carriage return, I'll use a code continuation character, like this: ➥

Getting help when you're stuck

We all make mistakes (although I hope there aren't any in this book!), so it's useful to know where to go for help when things don't turn out as expected. Throughout the text, I've identified the most common pitfalls, but if the answer isn't there, the first place to look for it is this book's page on the friends of ED website (`www.friendsofed.com/books/1590594665/index.html`). Check to see if any errata or updates have been posted. The download files are also provided to help you troubleshoot problems. If the download file works, but not yours, it's a clear sign that there's a mistake in your code. Finding it is just a matter of searching patiently.

If you still draw a blank, go through the troubleshooting steps outlined in Appendix A, and make sure that your system is using versions no earlier than the ones used by me and the friends of ED technical team during testing. All the code in the book has been tested on Windows 2000, Windows XP Pro, and Mac OS X Panther, using the following versions:

- **PHP**: 4.3.4, and all versions from 5.0.0 through 5.0.3
- **MySQL**: 3.23.38, 4.0.20, 4.0.21, and all versions from 4.1.5 through 4.1.9
- **Apache**: 1.3.33, 2.0.40, and 2.0.46
- **phpMyAdmin**: 2.5.5 and 2.6.0

Even if you have the most up-to-date versions on your local computer, your applications could fail when uploaded to a remote server that uses an older configuration. The PHP `Database` classes in Chapter 7 are designed to get around these incompatibilities, by enabling the same code to work regardless of server configuration, so make sure you upload the correct one.

If the answer still eludes you, then post a question in the friends of ED support forums at `www.friendsofed.com/forums`. Try to give a brief description of the problem; indicate which version of Flash, PHP, and MySQL you are using; and note any remedies that you have tried, but failed. Someone, maybe even me, should soon be along to share the misery—and hopefully provide an answer that puts a smile back on your face.

Stop the presses: Changes to MySQL 4.1.9

The development team at MySQL, never slouches at any time, were particularly hyperactive during the last few months of this book being written. I managed to incorporate all the relevant changes into the main text, but two more were announced in January 2005, after Chapters 1 and 6 had already been typeset.

New filename for the Windows Essentials installer

The name of the installation file for MySQL Windows Essentials has been changed. Instead of `mysql-4.1.`*x*`-essential-win.msi`, it is now `mysql-essential-4.1.`*x*`-win32.msi`. (The value of *x* will depend on the number of the latest release.) The installation instructions in Chapter 6 are otherwise unaffected.

New MySQL startup method for Mac OS X 10.3

The changes affect steps 3 and 4 of the instructions in the section titled "Installing MySQL on Mac OS X" in Chapter 1, but they do *not* apply to Mac OS X 10.2 (Jaguar).

When the DMG file is mounted on your desktop, you should see something similar to the image shown here. It includes an extra icon labeled MySQL.prefPane. As of late January 2005, the ReadMe.txt file had not been updated to reflect the changes, so it's not clear whether MySQLStartupItem.pkg will continue to be included in later versions, as it no longer seems to be necessary.

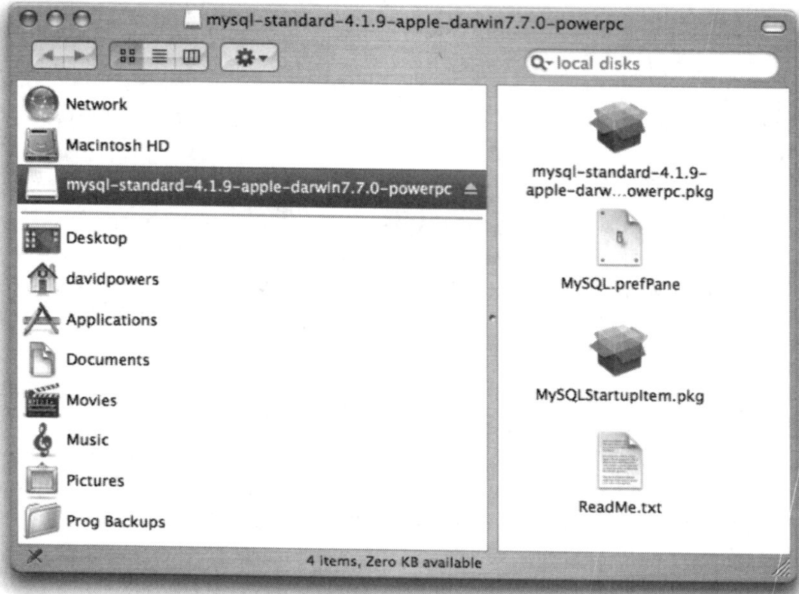

Double-click the icon of the PKG file that begins with mysql-standard-4.1.*x* and follow the onscreen instructions to install MySQL. When installation is complete, drag the MySQL.prefPane icon onto System Preferences, either in your Dock or in Finder ➤ Applications. This will open a dialog box asking if you want to install it (see image below). Select whether you want to install it just for yourself or for all users, and then click Install.

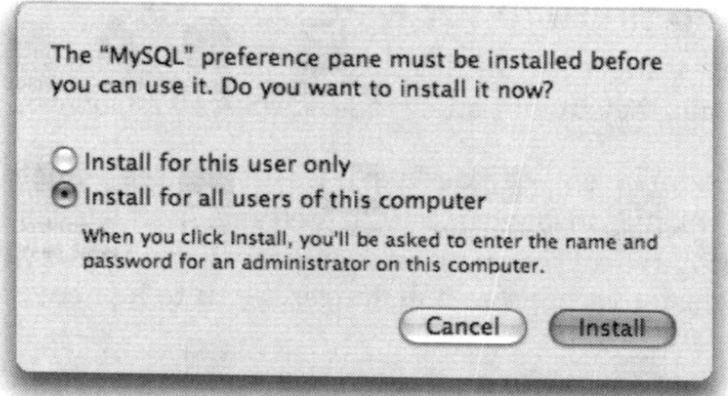

When the MySQL preference pane has been installed, it will open and should show you that MySQL server is running. The preference pane (as shown in the following image) is self-explanatory. It not only provides a convenient Mac-friendly way of starting and stopping MySQL, but also gives you the option to start MySQL automatically whenever your computer starts up.

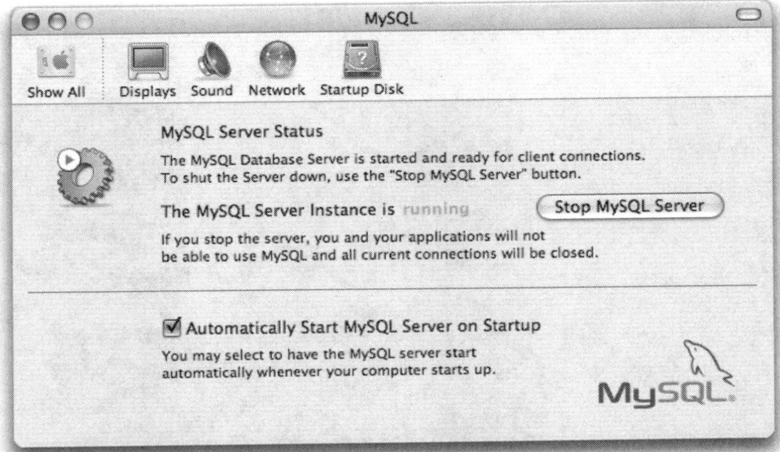

Close the preference pane in the normal manner by clicking the close button at the top left of the pane. To access it again, open System Preferences. The MySQL icon will be at the bottom of the System Preferences window in the Other section.

Continue with the installation instructions from step 5.

If you have installed the MySQL preference pane, always use this method to start and stop MySQL instead of the instructions in the main text of the book. This applies to Mac OS X only. The Windows instructions are not affected.

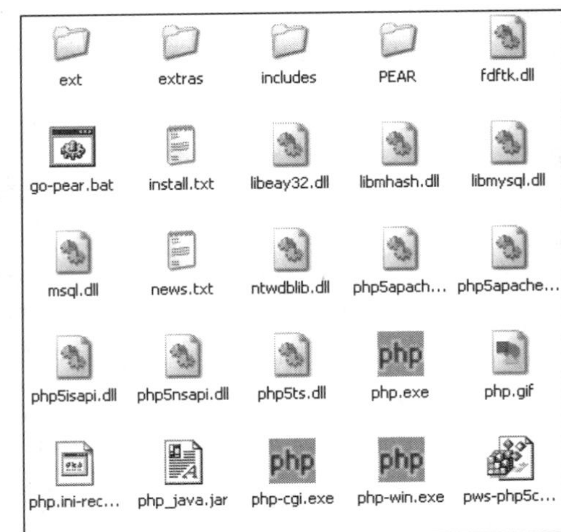

Chapter 1

GETTING READY TO WORK WITH PHP

What this chapter covers:

- Expanding Flash's horizons by linking to external data sources
- Choosing the appropriate server-side technology
- Examining similarities and differences between PHP and ActionScript
- Installing Apache and PHP
- Testing the installation
- Setting up your work environment

Flash is fun. It's also extremely powerful. Its power lies not only in its incredible animation capabilities, but also in ActionScript. With the release of Flash MX 2004, ActionScript was upgraded to version 2.0 and became a fully object-oriented programming (OOP) language with support for classes, inheritance, interfaces, and other common OOP concepts. Whether you're making your first personal website, creating immersive online games, or building a serious business site, Flash offers a rich development environment.

Yet, in spite of its power, Flash *on its own* has a severe limitation: the need to embed virtually all content and processing logic within the same medium as the user interface. Even the most minor change means republishing and uploading a new version of the Flash movie. Sensitive content is easily extracted by anyone with a decompiler, several of which are freely available. Most important of all, even with the rapid spread of broadband, download times restrict the optimum size of a movie and therefore the amount of information it can contain. Fortunately, all these limitations are easily overcome by linking your SWF movie to an external data source such as a database or RSS feed. That's what this book is all about, using the latest version of the most popular open source server-side technology, PHP. By the end of this chapter, you should understand how PHP interacts with ActionScript, and you will have installed PHP and the Apache web server on your development computer. (By the way, if you're not sure what an RSS feed is, it's one of those online news feeds that seem to be popping up all over the place these days. Take a quick peek at "What an RSS feed does" in Chapter 5, where you'll be working with two of them.)

Accessing external data with Flash

A Flash movie—the SWF file—is frequently its own self-contained world. Everything is there within the one file: graphics, timeline animations, and ActionScript functions to control the movie and respond to events initiated by the user. The more you have going on within the movie, the bigger the file gets. To get around this problem, you can load other SWF or JPG files into the main movie only if and when required. Although this can be regarded as accessing external data, it's extremely limiting. Everything has to be fixed in advance and scripted inside the main movie. Real flexibility comes only once you connect to an external database, news feed, or similar source of independent data. This makes possible such things as online reservation systems, news sites, or online forums, all built in Flash. And it's not just a one-way process. Once you've tied up with a server-side technology, you can capture user input, inserting it into a database or sending it across the Internet through email. By tying up Flash with PHP, you open up a whole new range of possibilities and rich Internet applications—not just fixed sources of information or entertainment, but ones that offer real interactivity with the user.

Choosing the right technology

There are three ways of communicating between a Flash movie and an external data source:

- Flash Remoting
- Web services
- Direct interaction with a server-side technology, such as ASP, ASP.NET, ColdFusion, or PHP

Flash Remoting is a proprietary technology developed by Macromedia, the makers of Flash. Its major advantages are speed and the ability of Flash to handle external data as native ActionScript objects. Its major disadvantage is that it requires the installation of a Flash Remoting Server at a cost of approximately $1,000 per CPU.

Flash MX 2004 Professional introduced the concept of connecting to web services using Simple Object Access Protocol (SOAP) or XML through specialized data components. This led many developers to believe the curtain was coming down on Flash Remoting. However, the Flash web services approach is often slower than Flash Remoting, and it's far from clear whether these technologies will continue to exist side by side, or whether one will prevail. For an in-depth analysis of the advantages and disadvantages of the two methods, see `www.macromedia.com/devnet/mx/flash/articles/ria_dataservices.html`.

The third method—direct interaction with Flash using a server-side technology—should not be regarded as "second best" or inferior in any way. The Ujiko search engine at `www.ujiko.com/flash.php` is built entirely in Flash, and it displayed the results shown in Figure 1-1 just as quickly on a broadband connection as the same search on Google or Yahoo did using ordinary HTML pages. Flash is used not simply to give the search engine a "pretty face," but also to add extra functionality through using the Flash `SharedObject` to enable you to refine your searches and set individual preferences. As you hover your mouse pointer over each result, a trash can and a heart appear on either side. Choosing the trash can or the heart removes the result from the list or adds it to your favorites, respectively, helping to refine further searches. A context-sensitive list on the right side of the page presents further keywords to help burrow further down and filter the results until you find what you want. Creating such a rich user experience with a standard HTML interface would be very difficult, if not impossible.

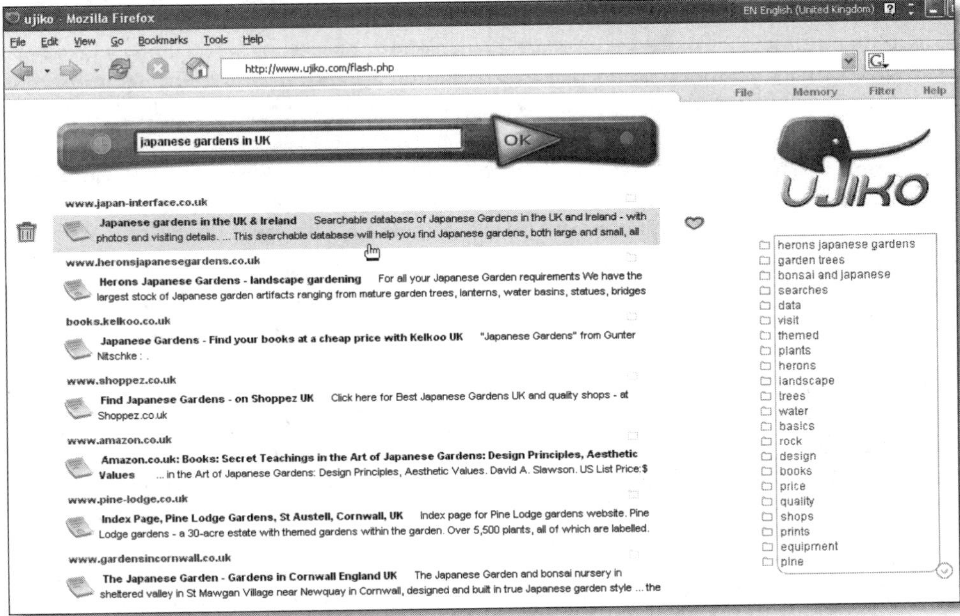

Figure 1-1. Ujiko combines the power of Flash and PHP to create a search engine that, like an elephant, never forgets.

> *The Flash `SharedObject` offers functionality very similar to cookies by storing information on the user's local hard drive. However, the `SharedObject` is much more powerful and can store up to 100KB of information. Like cookies, though, the `SharedObject` can be disabled by the user. You'll use the `SharedObject` to store a player's score in Chapter 7.*

Arguments of almost religious intensity rage over whether one server-side technology is superior to the rest, but I'm not going to be drawn down that path. Each has its merits and drawbacks, and all do just about the same with equal efficiency. You have to choose one, and the choice for this book is PHP in conjunction with the Apache web server and the MySQL relational database system.

What PHP, Apache, and MySQL have to offer

Several factors stand behind the decision to choose this particular combination:

- **Cost**: They're free. While this is an obvious attraction to individuals on a limited budget, don't be put off by the thought that "you get what you pay for." The release of PHP 5 in mid-2004 brought full object-oriented capability to the language, as well as greatly improved methods of handling XML. MySQL is used by many leading organizations, including NASA, the U.S. Census Bureau, Yahoo!, and the New York Stock Exchange. The fact that more than two out of every three web servers run on Apache speaks for itself.
- **Open source**: As open source technologies, all three benefit from a rapid upgrade policy based on need rather than commercial pressures. If a bug or security risk is identified, the input of many volunteers helps the core development teams solve any problems rapidly. Future versions are available for beta testing by anybody who wants to take part, and they aren't declared stable until they really are. The same thriving community offers assistance and advice to newcomers and experienced programmers alike.
- **Cross-platform capability**: PHP, Apache, and MySQL all work on Windows, Linux, and Mac OS X. You can develop on your personal computer and deploy exactly the same code on the production server, even if it's running on a different operating system.
- **Security**: Although it is impossible to predict future developments, Apache servers are rarely targeted by virus attacks. Sensitive content can also be stored more securely in a database, with access restricted through PHP session control (this is the subject of Chapter 9).
- **Widespread use**: Both PHP and Apache are the most widely used technologies in their respective spheres. A regular survey by Netcraft (`http://news.netcraft.com/archives/web_server_survey.html`) shows that Apache has consistently maintained a market share in excess of 60% of all web servers. In November 2004, it stood at more than 67%—more than three times that of Windows-based servers. PHP availability seems to march on ever upward; in late 2004, it was in use on nearly 17 million domains. And according to the MySQL website (`www.mysql.com`), MySQL is the world's most popular open source database, with more than 5 million active installations in late 2004.

One thing missing from that list is "ease of learning." That's not because they're difficult—far from it. All are relatively easy to pick up, but they do require a bit of effort on your part. If you have experience with other programming languages, your progress is likely to be much faster than a complete beginner. This book is designed to ease your progress, whatever your level of expertise.

One final point in favor of PHP: although Macromedia does not support Flash Remoting with PHP, a project called AMFPHP (`www.amfphp.org`) is developing an open source alternative that enables objects in PHP to be recognized as objects by ActionScript. At the time of this writing, the project was at an advanced stage, but still subject to considerable change. Although this book touches only briefly on PHP objects, the fundamental knowledge contained in these pages will be essential to anyone contemplating exploring AMFPHP in the future. The ***AMF*** *in the project's name, by the way, refers to* ***Action Message Format****, the Macromedia protocol used in Flash Remoting.*

How everything fits together

To understand how to work with PHP, Apache, and MySQL, it helps to know how they interact with each other and the role they play in bringing greater data-processing power to Flash movies. As noted before, Flash movies are frequently self-contained. A single request from a web browser is sent to the remote **server**, resulting in the SWF movie being downloaded to the **client** computer. Thereafter, all interaction between the user and the Flash movie is conducted locally on the user's computer, as illustrated in Figure 1-2. Normally, the only times further requests are made to the remote server are when other movies, images, or predetermined assets are loaded into the main movie.

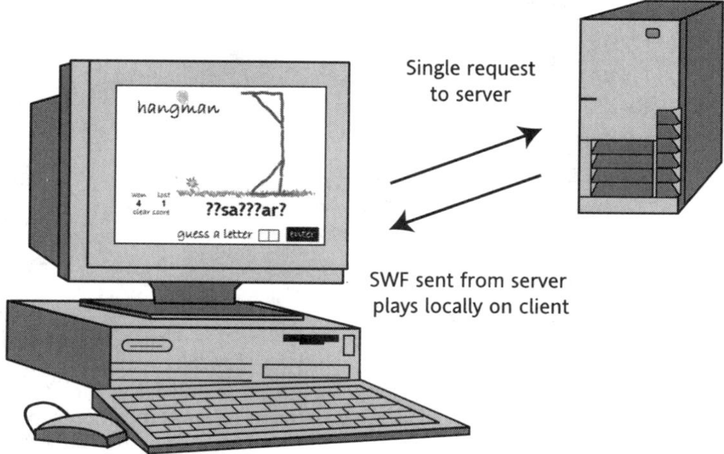

Figure 1-2. Once a Flash movie has been downloaded, all interaction with it is normally conducted entirely on the client computer.

*The words **client** and **server** tend to get bandied around a lot when talking about databases and technologies like PHP. A server can mean either a computer or a program on a computer that responds to requests from clients (or users). For instance, your website is more than likely hosted on a remote computer known as a server. Running on that computer will be a web server—a program, such as Apache, that sends web files to any client computer that requests them. To be able to work with databases, you also need a database server, which is another program that responds to requests to either store or retrieve information from the database. For development purposes, it's normal to install both a web server and database server on your local computer. These are simply programs that you install like any other—and they do not involve the need to buy any extra hardware.*

When you add PHP to the equation, what happens depends on what you want to do. In many cases, the Flash movie will be downloaded in exactly the same way as illustrated in Figure 1-2. There is no interaction with PHP until the user triggers an event that calls a PHP script. This is the case with the application you'll build in the next chapter—a feedback form that uses PHP to format user input and email it to your mailbox. If the user decides not to use the form, the PHP script will never be called. In other cases, the Flash movie calls a PHP script as soon as it loads into the client computer, and what appears on the screen is determined by the result of that script. For instance, the headlines on a news site are likely to be drawn from a database and will be different each time someone visits the site. At other times, the changing content depends on user input, as with the Ujiko search engine shown in Figure 1-1. The sequence of events is depicted in Figure 1-3.

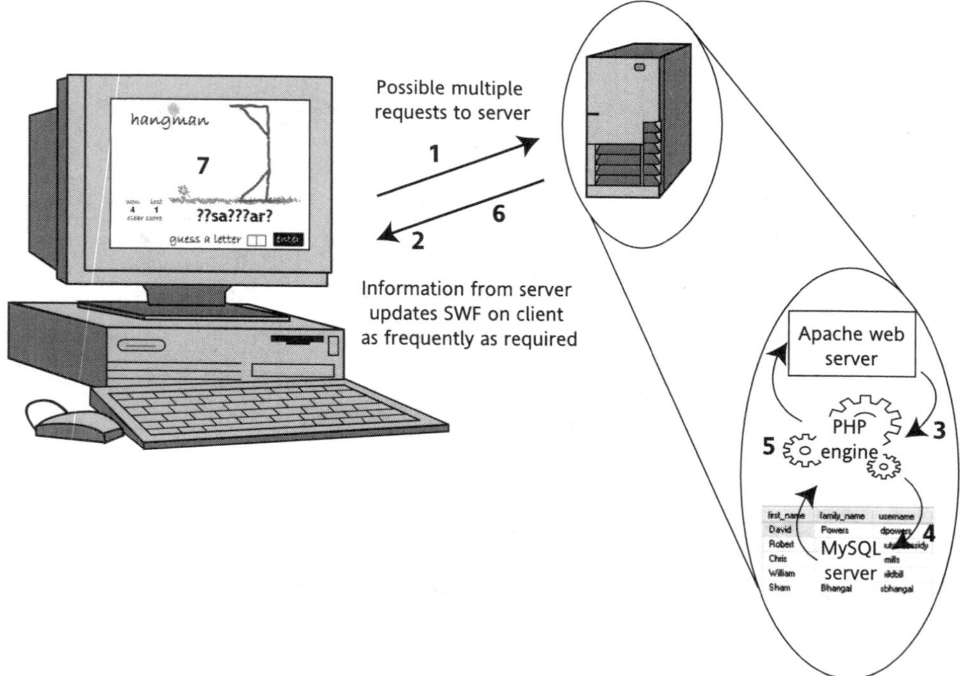

Figure 1-3. A diagrammatic representation of what happens when a Flash movie makes a request to PHP

1. The client computer sends a request to the web server (normally Apache).
2. The server delivers the Flash movie.
3. If the Flash movie sends a request to a PHP script (either automatically through ActionScript when initially loading or in response to user interaction), the web server passes the script to the PHP engine for parsing.
4. If the PHP script initiates a database query, a request is sent to the MySQL server.
5. The results of the database query are sent back to the PHP engine for processing.
6. The web server sends the processed data back to the client.
7. The Flash movie reacts in accordance with the data received.

There's a lot going on, and this process can be repeated many times as the user interacts with the movie. Sometimes all seven stages of this process are required. At other times, PHP may simply do all the processing itself without having to query the database. Although it sounds complicated, PHP, MySQL, and Apache can search through many thousands of records in a fraction of a second, so the user may be totally unaware of anything going on in the background. The biggest delay is often caused by a slow Internet connection or network bottlenecks.

As Figure 1-3 shows, Apache, PHP, and MySQL are frequently located on the same computer (although in large operations, they may be distributed across several). Apache and MySQL are **daemons** (what Windows calls **services**) that run unobtrusively in the background, consuming very few resources, and that are ready to spring into action whenever a request comes in. The most efficient way of running the PHP engine is as an Apache module, and that's the way you'll install it later in the chapter. First, though, let's take a look at the similarities and differences between PHP and ActionScript.

PHP and ActionScript: Distant cousins

PHP and ActionScript both trace their roots back to the mid-1990s. The first version of PHP appeared in 1995, and JavaScript (on which ActionScript is closely based) followed a year later. ActionScript didn't actually emerge until the release of Flash 4 in 1999, and it underwent significant changes with each subsequent version of Flash, culminating with a major version upgrade to ActionScript 2.0 in September 2003. PHP underwent fundamental changes with the release of version 4 in 2000, followed by a major, evolutionary upgrade to version 5 in July 2004.

One of the main driving forces behind the great upheavals in the way ActionScript has evolved has been Macromedia's commitment to compliance with ECMAScript. In spite of its name sounding like a rather unpleasant skin disease, ECMAScript is a universally recognized standard set by ECMA International (`www.ecma-international.org`). (The organization was originally called the European Computer Manufacturers Association [ECMA], but since 1994 it has been known as ECMA International, the European association for standardizing information and communication systems.) ECMAScript is the standard behind JavaScript, making it easier for programmers to migrate their skills from one language to another. PHP follows no internationally recognized standard (other than itself), but both PHP and ActionScript can now be considered mature programming languages. They will continue to evolve, but the highly disruptive changes of the previous few years are likely to be a thing of the past. That means the methods taught in this book should continue to be of relevance even when a new version of Flash is released.

The common heritage shared by PHP and ActionScript is that both have been strongly influenced by the classic C programming language. As a result, they share a lot of structures in common. The syntax of conditional statements using `if`, `else`, and `switch` is almost identical. They also share the same methods of looping through repetitive processes using `while` and `for`. Virtually all the arithmetic and conditional operators are the same, too. Don't worry if you're not familiar with these; everything will be explained as the book progresses.

Another feature they used to have in common was **loose typing**. This will be explained in more detail in Chapter 2, but it basically relieves the developer of the need to decide in advance whether to use a number or a string (text) in a particular situation, because the language automatically chooses what it thinks is most appropriate. That has changed with the introduction of ActionScript 2.0; although you can still create scripts that use loose typing, it's no longer recommended, and this book adheres to strict typing throughout. PHP 5, on the other hand, remains a loose-typed language, with one exception: the new OOP model in PHP allows developers to enforce strict typing in classes.

ActionScript 2.0 is supported by Flash Player 6, so there is no reason to avoid adhering to strict typing, unless you need to support older versions. If you are using Flash MX, though, you will need to adapt the scripts by removing the datatype declarations (see Appendix B for details). The download files for this book also contain versions compatible with Flash MX, so you can always check your code against them if you get stuck.

Although these many similarities speed up the learning process, PHP and ActionScript are very different, and it takes a bit of adjustment to get used to the differences. Throughout the book, I'll highlight those differences most likely to catch you out. The thing most likely to trip you up is the need to prefix all variables in PHP with a dollar sign ($). When moving back and forth between ActionScript and PHP, it's easy to leave it out, but doing so will bring your PHP scripts to a grinding halt.

Table 1-1 highlights some of the main things to keep in mind when working with the two languages.

Table 1-1. Important differences and similarities between ActionScript and PHP

Feature	ActionScript	PHP
Variables	Declared with `var` keyword No distinguishing prefix	No keyword, except in classes Always prefixed with $
Variable typing	Strict (ActionScript 1.0 was loose typed)	Loose, except in classes
Case sensitivity	Yes (ActionScript 1.0 was not case sensitive)	Yes

(Continued)

Feature	ActionScript	PHP
Concatenation operator	Plus sign (+)	Dot or period (`.`).
OOP	Fully object-oriented	Not object-oriented, but has extensive OOP capabilities.
Built-in functions	Applied as object methods through dot notation (e.g., `myVar.toUpperCase()`)	Applied directly by passing variable as argument (e.g., `strtoupper($myVar)`).
User-defined functions	Yes	Yes
Callback functions	Yes	Anonymous functions can be created but are rarely used.

Don't worry if you're not familiar with some of this terminology. All will be explained in good time. Things will become a lot clearer (I hope!) once you have Apache and PHP installed.

Installing the necessary software

As I mentioned earlier, it's normal for development purposes to install a web server and database server on your local computer. This avoids the need to constantly upload files to your website for testing. In effect, what you're doing is re-creating the setup shown in Figure 1-3 on a single computer. This involves no extra hardware, and it doesn't require a particularly high-spec computer, although the more processor power and memory you have, the better.

The instructions for Windows and Mac OS X are completely different, so this is a parting of the ways. I'll deal with Windows first. Mac OS X users should skip ahead to the section titled "Setting up on Mac OS X."

Setting up on Windows

Some people are so terrified of installing programs not originally designed for Windows that they freeze at the thought of having to do any manual configuration and will desperately seek a precompiled package that bundles Apache, PHP, and MySQL together. If you have the skill to work with ActionScript, installing and configuring this trio should present few, if any, difficulties. A precompiled package robs you of a great amount of control. You may not get the most up-to-date version of each program, and many people have reported problems uninstalling some packages when things go wrong. I strongly recommend using only the individual programs directly from their source, and I'm here to guide you through the process.

If you're using Windows 2000 or later, make sure you're logged on as an Administrator.

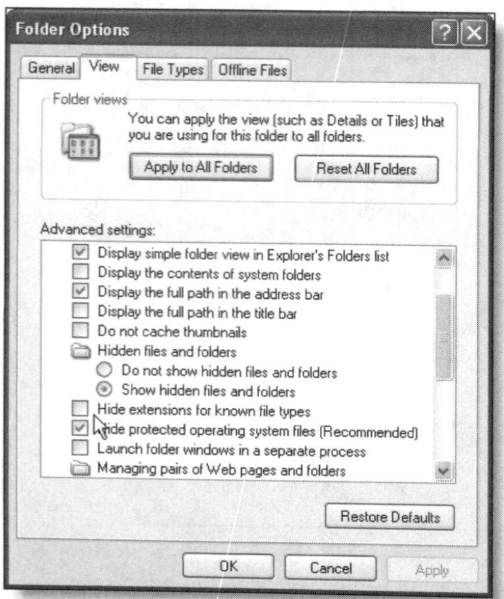

Figure 1-4. Setting Windows so that it automatically displays the extension on all filenames

Getting Windows to display filename extensions

By default, most Windows computers hide the three- or four-letter filename extension, such as `.doc` or `.html`, so all you see in dialog boxes and Windows Explorer is thisfile, instead of `thisfile.doc` or `thisfile.html`. The ability to see these filename extensions is essential for installing the necessary software for this book.

If you haven't already enabled filename extensions on your computer, open My Computer (it's on the Start menu on some systems and on the desktop as an icon on others). Then from the menu at the top of the window, choose Tools ➤ Folder Options ➤ View. Uncheck the box marked Hide extensions for known file types, as shown in Figure 1-4. Click OK.

I recommend you leave your computer permanently at this setting, as it is more secure— you can tell if a virus writer has attached an EXE or SCR executable file to an innocent-looking document. It will also make changing HTML files to PHP ones a lot easier when you come to do so later in the book.

Which version of Apache?

Apache is currently available in two versions: the 1.3 series and the more recent 2 series (first released in 2002). When you visit the Apache site, you will notice it describes the 2 series as "the best available version" while the 1.3 series is simply "also available."

You naturally want the best—we all do. The more important question is, which version is better for the job? As of late 2004, the PHP documentation still contains a warning against using PHP on Apache 2 in a *production* environment. A full explanation can be found at `www.php.net/manual/en/faq.installation.php#faq.installation.apache2`, but it basically boils down to the fact that some of the code libraries that PHP relies on cause unpredictable bugs in Apache 2's threaded environment. What makes the choice for Windows users more difficult is that Apache 2 performs much better on Windows.

Technically, the 1.3 series is the safer option; is recommended by Rasmus Lerdorf, the creator of PHP; and is still being updated by the Apache development team. However, I have been running PHP on both Apache 1.3 and 2 on Windows computers for a long time without any problems. My advice, therefore, is to find out which version of Apache is being used by your hosting company or remote server, and to install that on your local computer. It makes sense to replicate the setup on your website as closely as possible on your local testing computer. That way, you get a much better idea of what to expect when you finally deploy your PHP-driven applications on the Internet.

The instructions here are based on Apache 1.3, but note any important differences if you decide to opt for Apache 2.

Installing Apache

1. Go to `http://httpd.apache.org/download.cgi`. Scroll down to the section for Apache 1.3.*xx*, as shown in Figure 1-5, and select the file marked Win32 Binary. The download for Apache 1.3 is approximately 5MB; for Apache 2, it is 6.4MB. Save the file to a temporary folder on your hard disk.

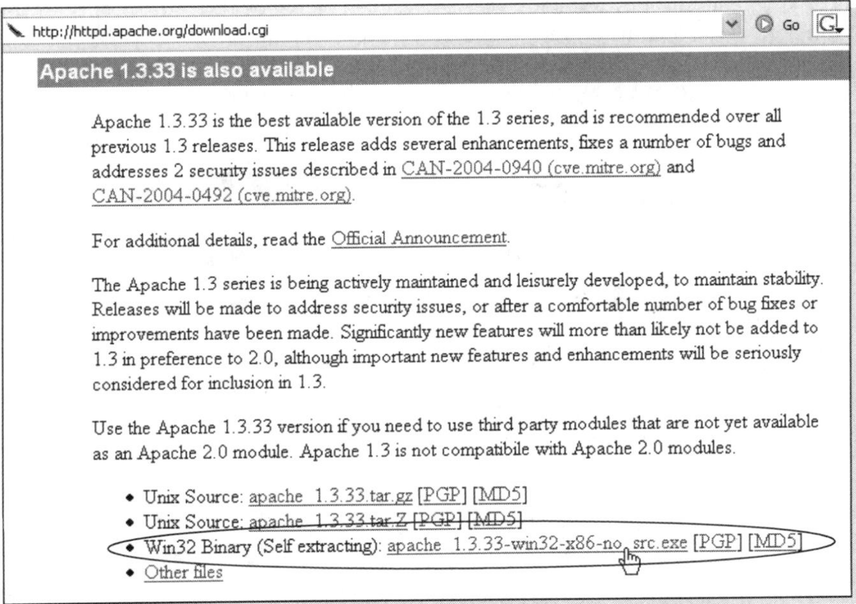

Figure 1-5. Selecting the Windows download for Apache 1.3.*xx*

2. Open the folder where you downloaded the Apache installer. Double-click the icon. A wizard will appear to take you through the installation process.

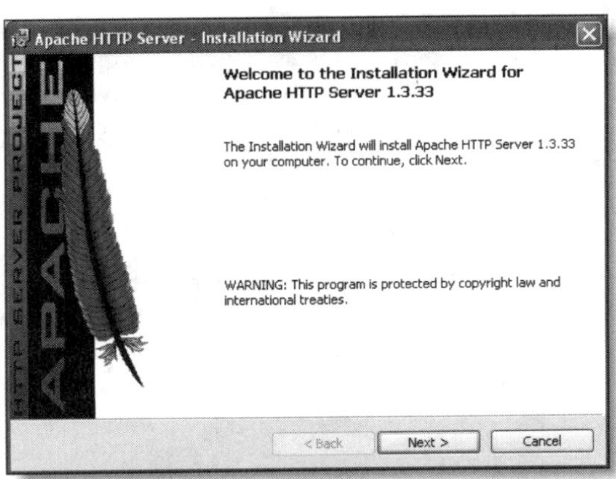

3. Click Next to continue the installation. The first thing to appear is the Apache License agreement. Read the conditions and terms of use, select the Accept terms radio button, and click Next.
4. The following screen contains useful information about Apache. Read it. If you're using Windows XP, don't worry if XP isn't listed as being supported by Apache 1.3—it works just fine. Click Next.
5. Next is the Server Information screen, as shown in Figure 1-6. This is where you enter the default settings for your web server. In the Network Domain and Server Name fields, enter localhost, and in the last field, enter an email address. The `localhost` address tells Apache you will be using it on your own computer. The email address does not need to be a genuine one. It has no bearing on the way the program runs and is normally of relevance only on a live production server.

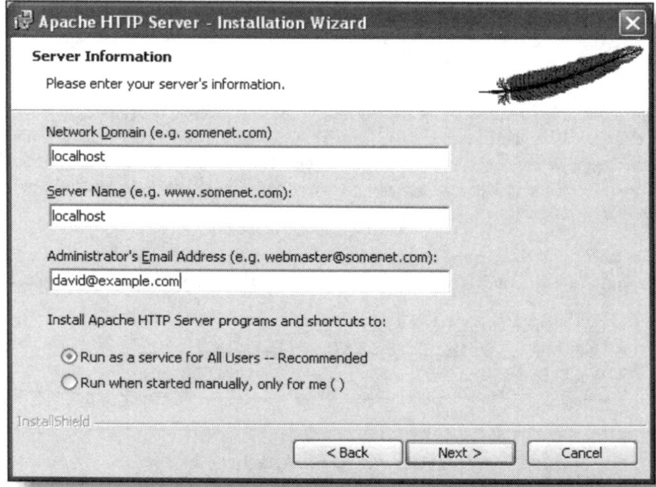

Figure 1-6. This is the most important dialog box in the Apache installation process.

6. If you are running Windows NT, 2000, or XP Professional, select the Run as a service for All Users option. That way, Apache runs as a service in the background and you don't need to worry about starting it. If you are running Windows 98, ME, or XP Home, select the Run when started manually option because you will be unable to run Apache as a service and must manually start it each time. Click Next.
7. Select the Complete option (as shown in Figure 1-7). This also installs the Apache documentation on your local computer. Click Next to continue.
8. Specify the location where Apache will be installed. The default location, `C:\Program Files\Apache Group`, is fine. Click Next and Install to finish the Apache installation.

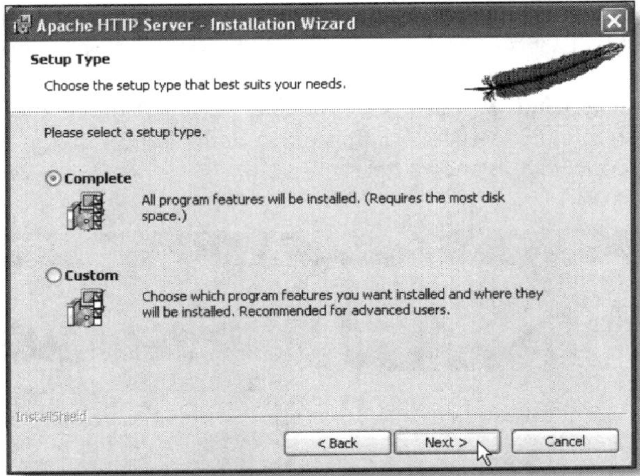

Figure 1-7. Choose the complete installation.

9. That completes the first part of Apache installation process. Check that Apache is running by opening your browser and entering http://localhost/ in the address bar. If all went well you should see the default Apache test page in your browser, as shown in Figure 1-8.

   If you are running a version of Windows that requires Apache to be started manually, choose Start ➤ Programs ➤ Apache HTTP Server ➤ Start Apache in Console. This will open a Command Prompt (DOS) window, which must be kept open the entire time you are using Apache. Click the icon in the top-right corner to minimize the window to your taskbar.

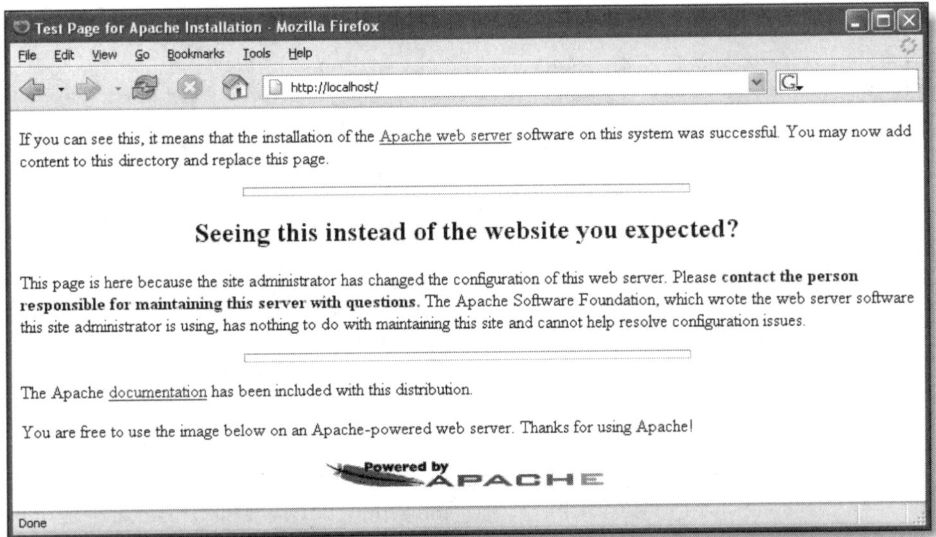

Figure 1-8. Congratulations! Apache is up and running.

10. If you get an error message, check that the server is running. You can do this by selecting Apache HTTP Server ➤ Control Apache Server from your program menu and selecting Start. If you don't have the Control Apache Server option on your menu, and you are running Windows 2000, XP Professional, or NT, open the Windows Control Panel, and then double-click Administrative Tools followed by Services. Highlight Apache and click Start, as shown here:

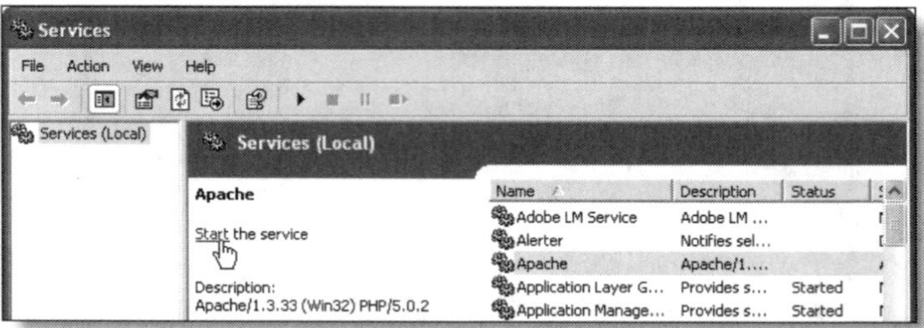

You need to make some manual changes to the Apache configuration file, but before you do so, you must install PHP.

Downloading and installing PHP

Forgoing the luxury of a Windows installer means you have to roll up your sleeves a bit, and do some manual configuration, but the process is very straightforward. It also means you know exactly what is happening to your system files, because you are in charge—not an anonymous installer program. There are quite a few steps involved, so give yourself plenty of time, and you should have no problems.

These instructions are for a completely new installation of PHP. The recommended method of installing PHP on Windows changed in August 2004, and it no longer involves copying DLL files and the configuration file `php.ini` *to the Windows system folders. If PHP has never been installed on your computer, simply follow the instructions.*

If you are upgrading an earlier version of PHP, you need to remove any PHP related files from your main Windows folder (`C:\WINDOWS` *or* `C:\WINNT`*, depending on your system) and the* `system32` *subfolder. Changing the contents of the Windows system folders is not to be undertaken lightly, so I suggest that, rather than just deleting them, you cut and paste them to a temporary folder. Then, if anything goes wrong, you can easily restore them. The PHP files you need to remove are* `php.ini` *(in the main Windows folder) and* `php4ts.dll` *or* `php5ts.dll` *in the* `system32` *subfolder. You should also remove any other PHP-related DLL files from the* `system32` *subfolder. They are easy to recognize because they all begin with* `php`.

1. Go to `www.php.net/downloads.php` and select the Windows binaries ZIP file for the latest stable version of PHP. At the time of this writing, it was PHP 5.0.3. Make sure you choose the right file. The version you need should be marked PHP 5.*x.x* zip package, and it's about 7.5MB. You do *not* want the PHP Windows installer. This runs PHP in a very restricted way and is not suitable for the projects in this book.

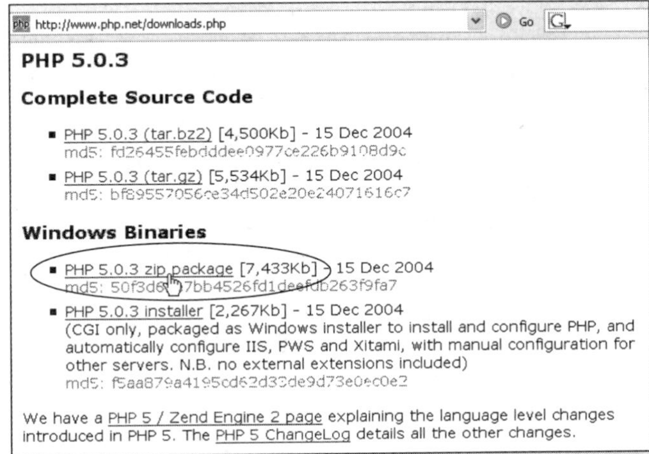

When you click the download link, you will be presented with a list of mirror sites. Choose the one closest to your location, and download the ZIP file to a temporary folder on your hard disk.

2. Unzip the contents of the ZIP file to a new folder called `C:\php5`. You can choose a different location, but this is where PHP will be run from, so you will need to substitute the name of your new folder in later steps. The instructions given here should be sufficient, but if you run into difficulties, there are more details in the text file called `install.txt` in the new folder you have just created.

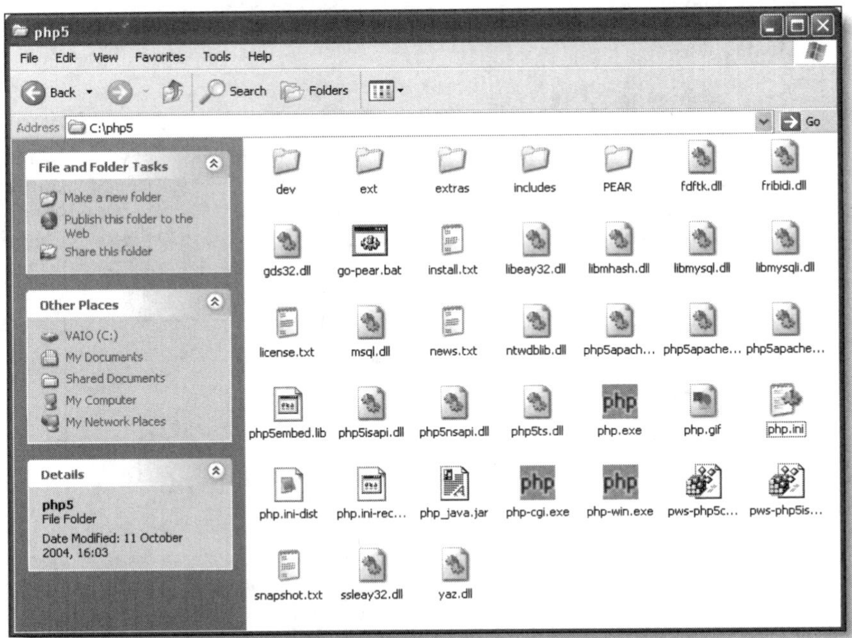

3. Locate the file `php.ini-dist` in the same folder, copy it, and rename the copy `php.ini`. This is the main configuration file for PHP, which you need to edit slightly to get everything running correctly. You should now be able to open `php.ini` by double-clicking its icon. It will open as a plain text file in Notepad.

   You may find it easier to open `php.ini` in a dedicated script editor such as TextPad or SciTEFlash instead, because the file contains more than 1,000 lines. Most script editors have a feature that allows you to display line numbers, which will make finding the relevant sections much easier. (PHP is under constant development, so the line numbers given in the following steps should be taken only as a rough guide. Also note that the line numbers shown in the following screenshots are *not* part of `php.ini`; they have been generated by a script editor.)

   All lines that begin with a semicolon (;) are treated as comments, so make sure all the changes you make in the following steps are to actual configuration settings and not to comments.

> *PHP comes with two files that can be used as the basis for* `php.ini`*:* `php.ini-dist` *and* `php.ini-recommended`*. If you're wondering why I didn't tell you to use the "recommended" version, it's because it contains much stricter settings and is designed for production servers. The settings in* `php.ini-dist` *are better suited to a development environment.*

4. Scroll down (or use a search facility—*Ctrl+F* in Notepad and SciTEFlash or *F5* in TextPad) until you find the following line (around line 288):

   ```
   error_reporting  =  E_ALL & ~E_NOTICE & ~E_STRICT
   ```

   Change it to

   ```
   error_reporting  =  E_ALL
   ```

   This sets error reporting to the highest level, and it will help you debug your PHP scripts so they don't cause problems for your Flash movies. As the following screenshot shows, this is one of the cases where there is an identical line in a comment about 12 lines above. Make sure you edit the second one (marked here with an arrow), which does not begin with a semicolon.

```
272 ; Examples:
273 ;
274 ;   - Show all errors, except for notices and coding standards warnings
275 ;
276 ;error_reporting = E_ALL & ~E_NOTICE & ~E_STRICT
277 ;
278 ;   - Show all errors, except for notices
279 ;
280 ;error_reporting = E_ALL & ~E_NOTICE
281 ;
282 ;   - Show only errors
283 ;
284 ;error_reporting = E_COMPILE_ERROR|E_ERROR|E_CORE_ERROR
285 ;
286 ;   - Show all errors except for notices and coding standards warnings
287 ;
288 ▶error_reporting  =  E_ALL & ~E_NOTICE & ~E_STRICT
289
```

5. About seven lines further down, there should be a setting for `display_errors`. Make sure it looks like this:

```
display_errors = On
```

This should be the default setting. If it's set to `Off`, check that you didn't use `php.ini-recommended` by mistake. It's important to be able to see the output of any error messages during development, although their display should be turned off when you deploy PHP pages live on the Internet.

6. As you scroll down, you will notice a setting called `register_globals` in the Data Handling section (around line 385):

```
register_globals = Off
```

This is the default setting, and under no circumstances should you be tempted to alter it. Even though turning register_globals on makes PHP scripts easier to run, it also gives crackers an open invitation to your site. A lot of scripts you will find online and in older books were written on the assumption that `register_globals` was On, so they no longer work. I will show you later how to adapt such scripts and keep your site more secure.

7. A few lines further down (around line 404), you will see this line:

```
magic_quotes_gpc = On
```

Opinions are divided as to whether this setting should be On or `Off`. When On, it automatically inserts backslashes in front of quotes to prevent them from terminating user input prematurely. Some developers dislike this and prefer to control everything themselves. The best advice I can offer is to leave the setting On for the time being, and check the setting on the production server to which you'll eventually be deploying your scripts. You can always come back and change the setting later.

8. In the Paths and Directories section, locate the final line in the following screenshot:

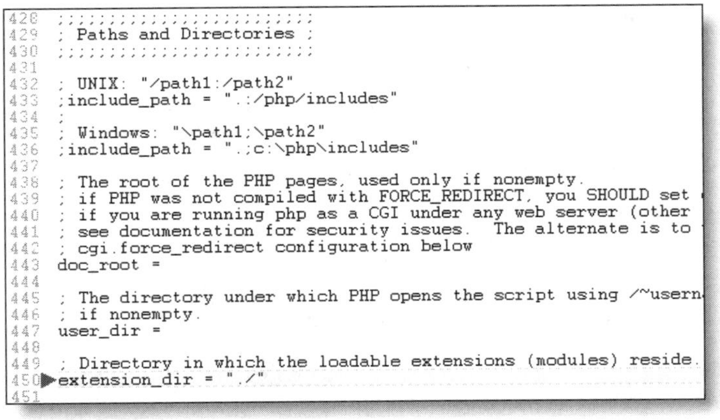

```
;;;;;;;;;;;;;;;;;;;;;;;;;
; Paths and Directories ;
;;;;;;;;;;;;;;;;;;;;;;;;;

; UNIX: "/path1:/path2"
;include_path = ".:/php/includes"
;
; Windows: "\path1;\path2"
;include_path = ".;c:\php\includes"

; The root of the PHP pages, used only if nonempty.
; if PHP was not compiled with FORCE_REDIRECT, you SHOULD set
; if you are running php as a CGI under any web server (other
; see documentation for security issues. The alternate is to
; cgi.force_redirect configuration below
doc_root =

; The directory under which PHP opens the script using /~usern
; if nonempty.
user_dir =

; Directory in which the loadable extensions (modules) reside.
extension_dir = "./"
```

Change it to

```
extension_dir = "C:\php5\ext\"
```

This is the name of the folder where PHP will look for any extensions. This assumes you extracted the PHP files to the recommended location. If you chose a different location, you will need to change the path from `C:\php5\`.

9. Scroll further down until you come to Dynamic Extensions. You will see a long alphabetically ordered list titled Windows Extensions (around line 549), all of them commented out.

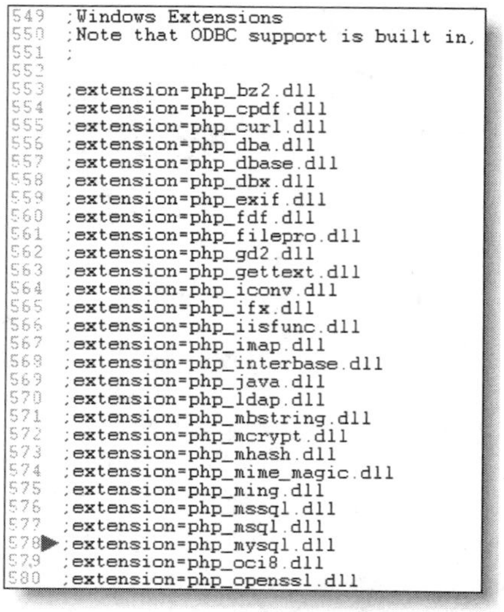

```
549 ;Windows Extensions
550 ;Note that ODBC support is built in,
551 ;
552
553 ;extension=php_bz2.dll
554 ;extension=php_cpdf.dll
555 ;extension=php_curl.dll
556 ;extension=php_dba.dll
557 ;extension=php_dbase.dll
558 ;extension=php_dbx.dll
559 ;extension=php_exif.dll
560 ;extension=php_fdf.dll
561 ;extension=php_filepro.dll
562 ;extension=php_gd2.dll
563 ;extension=php_gettext.dll
564 ;extension=php_iconv.dll
565 ;extension=php_ifx.dll
566 ;extension=php_iisfunc.dll
567 ;extension=php_imap.dll
568 ;extension=php_interbase.dll
569 ;extension=php_java.dll
570 ;extension=php_ldap.dll
571 ;extension=php_mbstring.dll
572 ;extension=php_mcrypt.dll
573 ;extension=php_mhash.dll
574 ;extension=php_mime_magic.dll
575 ;extension=php_ming.dll
576 ;extension=php_mssql.dll
577 ;extension=php_msql.dll
578 ;extension=php_mysql.dll
579 ;extension=php_oci8.dll
580 ;extension=php_openssl.dll
```

These extensions add extra features to the core functionality of PHP. You can enable any of them at any time simply by removing the semicolon from the beginning of the line for the extension you want, saving `php.ini`, and restarting Apache. This is a lot easier, incidentally, than on Mac OS X or Linux, where enabling a new extension usually means completely reinstalling PHP.

Although you won't install MySQL until Chapter 6, it's worthwhile enabling the relevant extension now. Locate the following line (around line 578):

```
;extension=php_mysql.dll
```

> *It is quite possible that, by the time you read this, the line will have changed to*
>
> ```
> ;extension=php_mysqli.dll
> ```
>
> *There are two separate PHP extensions for working with MySQL:* `php_mysql.dll` *and* `php_mysqli.dll`*. The first one works with older versions of MySQL; the second works only with MySQL 4.1 and above. For maximum flexibility, I suggest you install both.*

Remove the semicolon at the beginning of the line. Highlight the whole line, and then copy (*Ctrl+C/⌘+C*) and paste (*Ctrl+V/⌘+V*) it on the line immediately below. Amend the two lines so they look like this:

```
extension=php_mysql.dll
extension=php_mysqli.dll
```

10. In the Module Settings section immediately following the list of extensions, look for the code shown alongside:

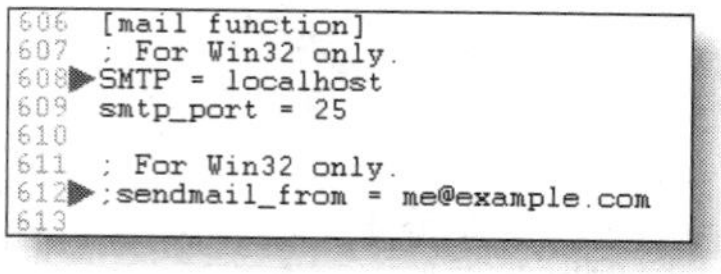

```
[mail function]
; For Win32 only.
SMTP = localhost
smtp_port = 25

; For Win32 only.
;sendmail_from = me@example.com
```

Unless you have already installed and configured SMTP on your computer (and if you don't know what I'm talking about, you almost certainly haven't), change the line shown in the screenshot as line 608 to the name of the SMTP server you normally use for sending email. This is the name your ISP will have given you for outgoing mail. If your email address is, for instance, david@example.com, your outgoing address is most probably smtp.example.com. In that case, you would change the line indicated to this:

```
SMTP = smtp.example.com
```

If you can't immediately identify the correct outgoing mail address, don't worry. It's not vital for getting PHP to work, although it means you won't be able to test the application in the next chapter on your local computer, but will have to upload it to your remote server instead.

11. Remove the semicolon from the beginning of line 612, and put your own email address in place of me@example.com:

```
sendmail_from = your email address
```

This puts your correct email address in the From: field of emails sent through PHP.

12. The final change you need to make to php.ini is considerably further down (around line 879). Locate the line at the bottom of this screenshot:

```
872  ; The file storage module creates files using mode 600 by default.
873  ; You can change that by using
874  ;
875  ;     session.save_path = "N;MODE;/path"
876  ;
877  ; where MODE is the octal representation of the mode. Note that this
878  ; does not overwrite the process's umask.
879 ;session.save_path = "/tmp"
880
```

Remove the semicolon from the beginning of the line, and change the setting in quotes to your computer's Temp folder. On most Windows computers, this will be C:\WINDOWS\Temp or C:\WINNT\Temp. Use either of the following, depending on your system setup:

```
session.save_path = "C:\WINDOWS\Temp"
session.save_path = "C:\WINNT\Temp"
```

13. Save php.ini. In the past, it used to be necessary to copy this file to your main Windows folder. **This should no longer be done, and any PHP-related files from previous installations should be removed as described at the beginning of this section**.

Adding PHP to your Windows startup procedure

The installation of PHP is complete, but it still needs to be added to your Windows startup procedure. The method differs depending on your Windows system.

Adding PHP to Windows NT, 2000, XP, and 2003

1. Open the Windows Control Panel (Start ➤ Settings ➤ Control Panel or Start ➤ Control Panel). Double-click the System icon. Select the Advanced tab, and click Environment Variables, as shown in the following screenshot.

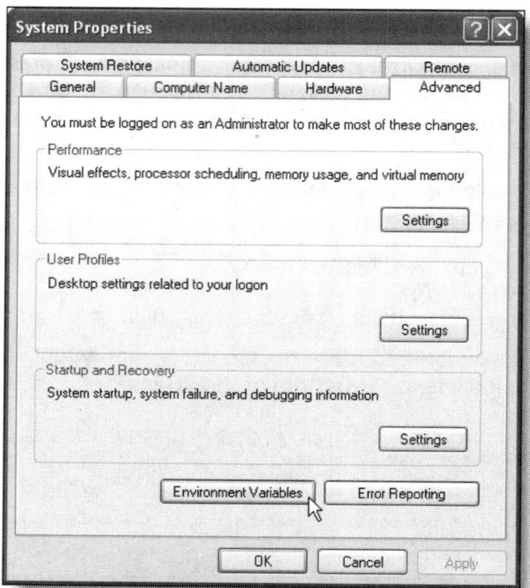

2. In the System variables pane at the bottom of the dialog box that opens, highlight Path and click Edit. This will open a smaller dialog box, as shown here. Click inside the Variable value field, and move your cursor to the end of the existing value. Type a semicolon followed by the name of the PHP folder you created in step 2 of the previous section (;C:\php5). As shown in the screenshot, there should be no spaces between the existing value or in the new path name.

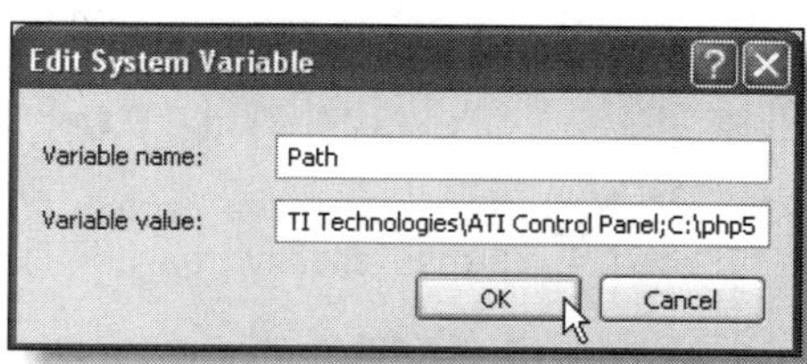

3. Click OK. With the Environment Variables dialog box still open, click New in the System variables pane. This will open another small dialog box for you to enter the details of the new system variable. In the Variable name field, type PHPRC. In the Variable value field, enter the path of the PHP folder (C:\php5).

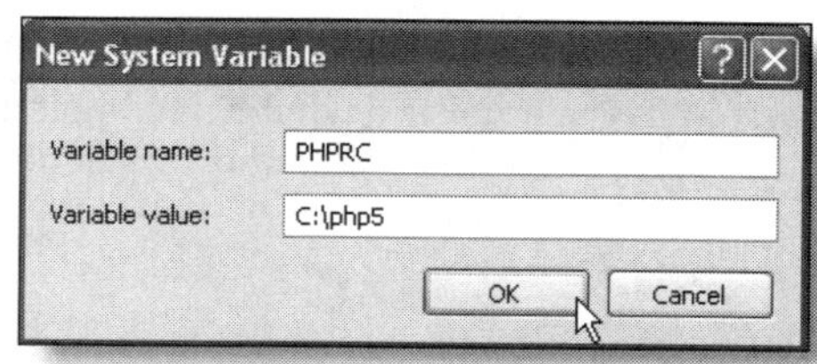

4. Click OK to close all the dialog boxes. The changes will take place the next time you restart your computer.

Adding PHP to Windows 98 and ME

1. Open C:\autoexec.bat in Notepad and locate the line that begins PATH=C:\WINDOWS.
2. At the end of the line, add a semicolon and the name of the PHP folder created in step 2 of the previous section (;C:\php5).
3. On a new line at the end of the file, add the following:

```
set PHPRC C:\php5
```

4. Save autoexec.bat. The changes will take effect the next time you start your computer.

Configuring Apache to work with PHP

Now that all the configuration settings have been made for PHP, you need to make some adjustments to the main configuration file for Apache.

> *Note that all the path names in the Apache configuration file use* **forward** *slashes, instead of the Windows convention of backward slashes. So,* c:\php5 *becomes* c:/php5.

1. The Apache configuration file, httpd.conf, is located in C:\Program Files\Apache Group\Apache\conf. You can either use Windows Explorer to locate the file directly and open it in a script editor or select Start ➤ All Programs ➤ Apache HTTP Server ➤ Configure Apache Server ➤ Edit the Apache httpd.conf Configuration File. Like php.ini, httpd.conf is a very long file composed mainly of comments, which in this case can be distinguished by a pound or hash sign (#) at the beginning of the line.
2. Scroll down until you find a long list of items that begin with LoadModule (all of them will be commented out). At the end of the list, add the following on a new line, as shown:

```
LoadModule php5_module c:/php5/php5apache.dll
```

```
# Example:
# LoadModule foo_module modules/mod_foo.so
#
#LoadModule vhost_alias_module modules/mod_vhost_alias.so
#LoadModule mime_magic_module modules/mod_mime_magic.so
#LoadModule status_module modules/mod_status.so
#LoadModule info_module modules/mod_info.so
#LoadModule speling_module modules/mod_speling.so
#LoadModule rewrite_module modules/mod_rewrite.so
#LoadModule anon_auth_module modules/mod_auth_anon.so
#LoadModule dbm_auth_module modules/mod_auth_dbm.so
#LoadModule digest_auth_module modules/mod_auth_digest.so
#LoadModule digest_module modules/mod_digest.so
#LoadModule proxy_module modules/mod_proxy.so
#LoadModule cern_meta_module modules/mod_cern_meta.so
#LoadModule expires_module modules/mod_expires.so
#LoadModule headers_module modules/mod_headers.so
#LoadModule usertrack_module modules/mod_usertrack.so
#LoadModule unique_id_module modules/mod_unique_id.so

LoadModule php5_module c:/php5/php5apache.dll
```

You want this and all following settings to work, so do *not* put a # at the beginning of the line. The path name assumes you've installed PHP in `c:\php5`. Change it accordingly, if you used a different installation folder, and don't forget to use forward slashes in the path name. (If you're using Apache 2, the name of the DLL file should be changed to `php5apache2.dll`.)

3. About a dozen lines further down, you will find a list of items that begin with `AddModule`. At the end of the list, add the following on a new line:

```
AddModule mod_php5.c
```

(Apache 2 does not require the `AddModule` setting.)

4. Scroll down again until you find the next line (around line 303):

```
DocumentRoot "C:/Program Files/Apache Group/Apache/htdocs"
```

This is the name of the folder that Apache uses to serve all web pages from. It's not a good idea to keep all your web pages and SWF movies in the same place as your vital program files, so change this line to

```
DocumentRoot "C:/htdocs"
```

5. About 25 lines further down, you will find

```
<Directory "C:/Program Files/Apache Group/Apache/htdocs">
```

This needs to be changed to the same path name as in step 4:

```
<Directory "C:/htdocs">
```

6. Scroll down a bit further until you come to the following section:

```
# DirectoryIndex: Name of the file or files to use as a pre-written HTML
# directory index.  Separate multiple entries with spaces.
#
<IfModule mod_dir.c>
    DirectoryIndex index.html
</IfModule>
```

This is the setting that tells web servers what to display by default if a URL doesn't end with a filename, but contains only a folder name or the domain name (for instance, `www.friendsofed.com`). Apache will choose the first available page from a space-delimited list. So, if you normally create pages using just an `.htm` extension, you should add index.htm and, since the whole purpose of this book is to work with PHP, index.php, as follows:

```
DirectoryIndex index.html index.htm index.php
```

In Apache 2, the `DirectoryIndex` configuration command stands alone (around line 321). It is not enclosed in `<IfModule mod_dir.c>` tags. The change you make to the command is identical: add index.htm index.php to the end of the list.

7. Close to the end of `httpd.conf`, you will find the Document types section. Add the following line in that section on a line of its own, as shown:

```
AddType application/x-httpd-php .php
```

```
#
# Document types.
#
<IfModule mod_mime.c>

    #
    # AddType allows you to tweak mime.types without actually editing
    # make certain files to be certain types.
    #
    AddType application/x-tar .tgz

    AddType application/x-httpd-php .php

```

The layout is slightly different in Apache 2. Find the following line (around line 772):

```
AddType application/x-gzip .gz .tgz
```

Add the PHP command on the following line, like this:

```
AddType application/x-gzip .gz .tgz
AddType application/x-httpd-php .php
```

8. Save and close `httpd.conf`.

9. You now need to create the new web server root folder `C:\htdocs` and a test file before you can check whether your efforts have been successful. Open Notepad or the text editor of your choice, and type the following code:

```
<?php
phpinfo();
?>
```

Save the file as `index.php` in the new `htdocs` folder, making sure that your text editor doesn't add a `.txt` extension to the filename.

10. One final thing before you can test your PHP installation—you need to restart Apache. From your program menu, choose Apache HTTP Server ➤ Control Apache Server ➤ Restart. A Command Prompt window may open briefly, displaying the message The Apache service is restarting.

> *One of the difficulties of writing about open source software is that frequent updates can lead to minor changes that experienced users take in stride, but that may confuse newcomers. If the* Control Apache Server *option is not available, refer back to step 10 of the "Installing Apache" section and use the Windows Services panel to restart Apache.*

If you have made any mistakes in `httpd.conf`, Apache will refuse to start. Depending on the version you have installed, you may get a helpful message in a Command Prompt window that tells you what the problem is and which line of `httpd.conf` it occurred on. Reopen `httpd.conf` and correct the error (probably a typo). On the other hand, Windows may simply display this very unhelpful message:

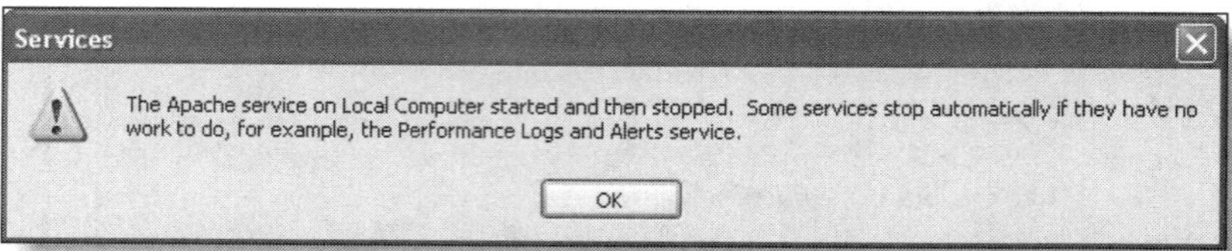

The answer is to open a Command Prompt window yourself (select Start ➤ Run, and then type cmd in the Open field and click OK). Inside the Command Prompt window, change to the Apache folder by typing the following command (assuming you accepted the default location when installing) and pressing *Enter*:

```
cd \program files\apache group\apache
```

Then type this (followed by *Enter*):

```
apache
```

The reason for the failure should appear onscreen, usually with a line number pinpointing the problem in `httpd.conf`. The following screenshot shows what happened when I mistyped the location of `php5apache.dll`.

After you correct any problems in `httpd.conf`, resave the file and restart Apache.

11. Once Apache has restarted, open your browser and type http://localhost/ into the address bar. You should see a page similar to the one shown in Figure 1-9. Welcome to the world of PHP!
12. In the unfortunate event that anything goes wrong, retrace your steps, and make sure you have followed the instructions precisely. Check the short piece of code in step 9, and make sure there is no gap in the opening <?php tag. Try an ordinary HTML page in the same `C:\htdocs` folder. If it displays correctly, there's something wrong with the PHP part of your installation. If it doesn't display, then the problem lies in the way you configured Apache.

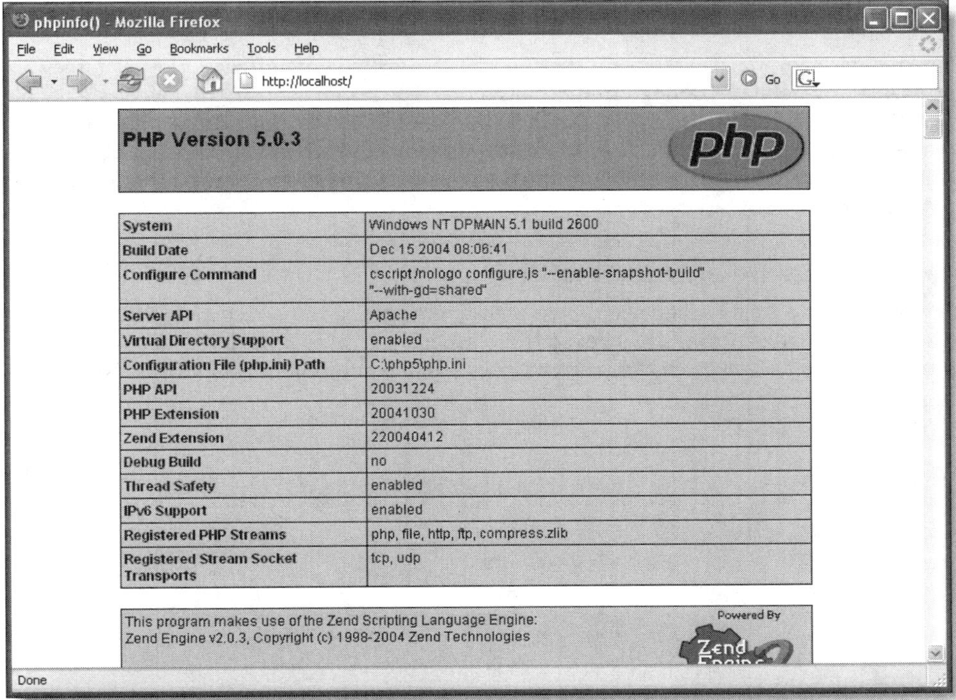

Figure 1-9. The `phpinfo()` command displays copious data showing your PHP configuration.

The screen full of information produced by `phpinfo()` is a useful way of checking your configuration, and it provides a lot more detail than you would get by studying `php.ini`. At this stage, most of the information will mean little to you, but it's a useful command to remember.

> *The Apache and PHP configuration files are read only when Apache first starts up, so any changes to* `php.ini` *or* `httpd.conf` *always require Apache to be restarted for them to take effect.*

Now it's time to get the Mac folks up and running with the necessary software. Windows users should join me again at the end of the chapter in the "Setting up your environment" section. As you flip through the pages, you'll probably notice that Mac users are being told to set up MySQL. Don't worry, they need to do it now because the Mac version of PHP doesn't include the necessary code libraries for MySQL. Full instructions for installing MySQL on Windows will be given in Chapter 6.

Setting up on Mac OS X

The good news for Mac OS X users is that Apache and PHP are preinstalled. However, they are not enabled by default. Starting up Apache is a piece of cake. Enabling PHP involves a couple of minor amendments to a configuration file—something most Mac users will never have dreamed of doing, but it's not at all difficult. Depending on when your installation was created, you may need to upgrade PHP to the latest version. The easiest way to check is to start up Apache and view a test page.

Starting Apache and testing PHP

You need to use a utility called sudo when making changes to the Apache and PHP configuration files. This utility can be invoked only when you're logged into Mac OS X with Administrative privileges, so make sure you are logged in appropriately before starting.

1. Open System Preferences and double-click Sharing in Internet & Network.

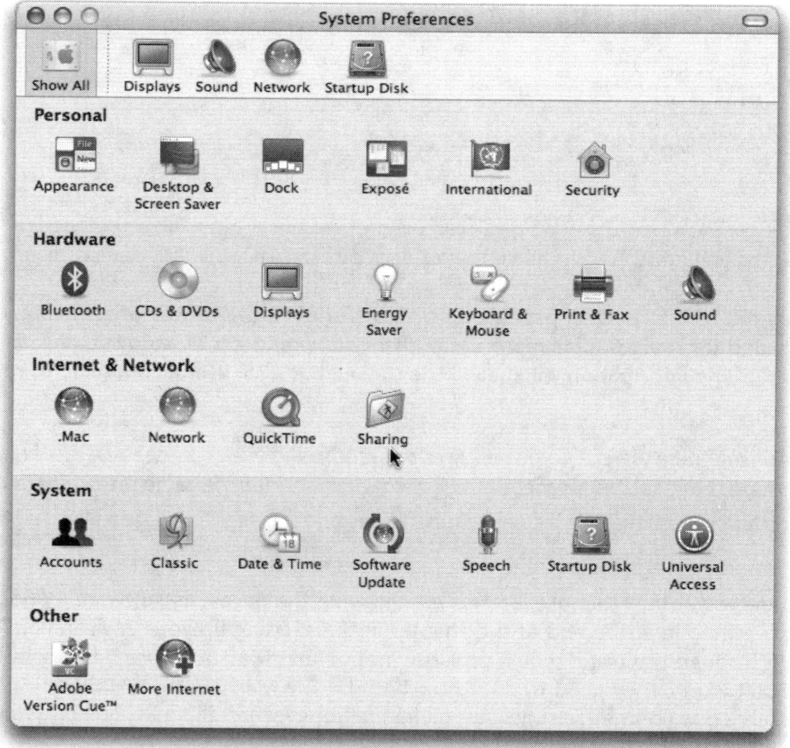

2. In the dialog box that opens, highlight Personal Web Sharing on the Services tab, as shown in Figure 1-10, and then click the Start button on the right. A message will appear informing you that personal web sharing is starting up. Once it's running, the label on the button changes to Stop. Use this button to stop and restart Apache whenever you install a new version of PHP or make any changes to the configuration files.

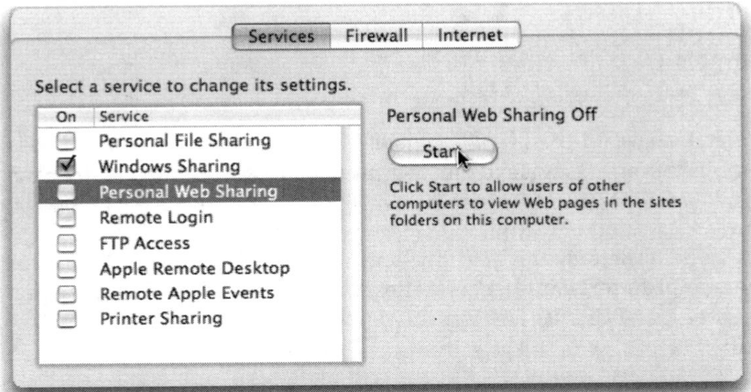

Figure 1-10. The Apache web server on a Mac is switched on and off in the Sharing section of System Preferences.

3. Open your favorite browser and type http://localhost/~*username*/ into the address bar, substituting your own Mac username for *username*. You should see a page like that shown in Figure 1-11, confirming that Apache is running.

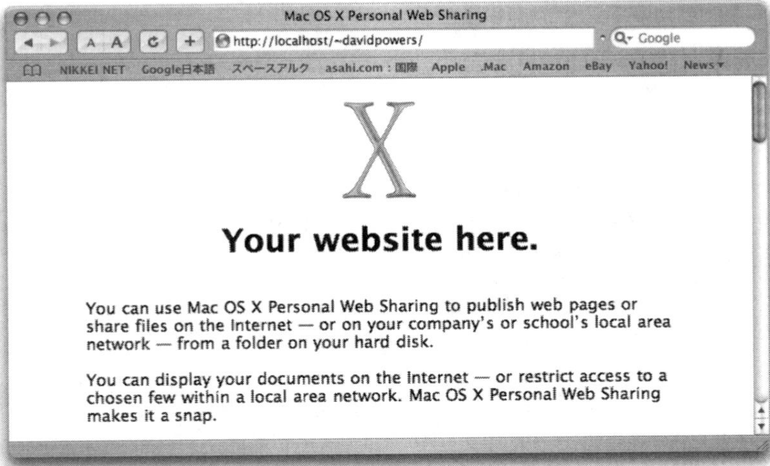

Figure 1-11. Confirmation that Apache is running successfully on Mac OS X

4. Next, you need to find out which version of PHP has been installed on your computer, and whether it has been enabled (it normally hasn't, but you never know your luck). To do this, you need to create your first PHP page. Open a text editor. TextEdit is fine, but it's better if you have a dedicated editor for scripting, such as BBEdit or its budget-price equivalent, TextWrangler (both from Bare Bones Software; `www.barebones.com`). Enter the following code in a new document:

   ```
   <?php
   phpinfo();
   ?>
   ```

5. Save the document as `index.php` in your `Sites` folder (`Macintosh HD:Users:Username:Sites`). If you are using TextEdit, you must first convert the file to plain text before saving. In TextEdit, select Format ➤ Make Plain Text (*Shift*+⌘+*T*). When you click Save, choose Don't Append from the dialog box that appears, as shown in Figure 1-12. This needs to be done only the first time you save a PHP file. TextEdit saves all subsequent changes as plain text with the correct extension, but you do have to repeat this process with every new PHP file. Life is a lot simpler with a dedicated script editor—you just save the file in the normal way.

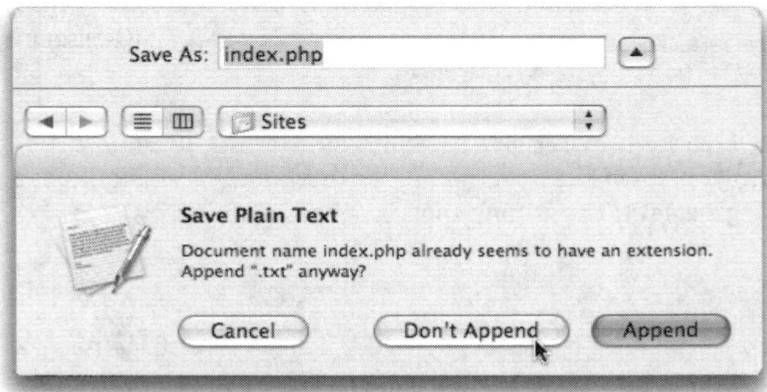

Figure 1-12. TextEdit tries to add a `.txt` extension to your PHP file when first saving it.

6. Reopen your browser and change the URL in step 3 to http://localhost/~*username*/index.php. If you see a PHP configuration page similar to Figure 1-13, then bingo—you're in business. If, on the other hand, you see the same raw code that you entered in step 4, you need to enable PHP, as described shortly. In either case, you need to get to know Terminal to work with the Unix operating system that lies underneath Mac OS X.

Sharp-eyed readers will notice that the version number shown in Figure 1-13 is different from the Windows version in Figure 1-9. It's a fact of life that Mac users have to get used to. Unless you have the technical skills to compile PHP and other programs from source code, you will have to wait for Mac versions to be created. The delay is normally only a matter of days, but it can sometimes take several weeks.

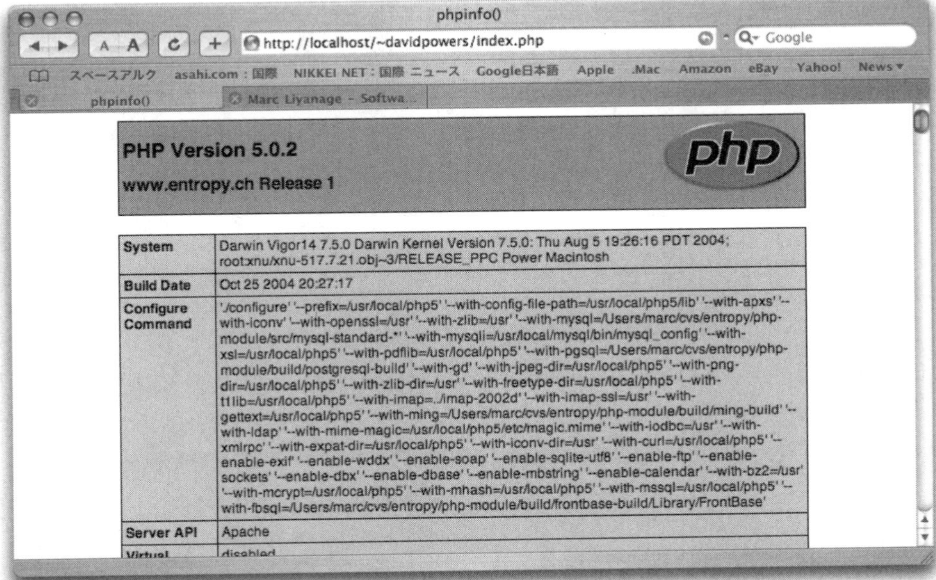

Figure 1-13. Displaying the PHP test page on Mac OS X

Introducing Terminal

Apache and PHP are configured using ordinary text files, but you cannot open them the normal way in a text editor, because they are protected from unauthorized or accidental changes. Using Terminal may seem unfamiliar if all your computer experience has been with a graphical interface, but if you follow these instructions carefully, it should hold no unpleasant surprises.

1. Open Applications ➤ Utilities and locate Terminal. This is the gateway to the Unix underworld. Since you need to access configuration files several times during the course of this book, you may find it useful to drag Terminal to your Dock. Open Terminal by double-clicking the icon (or single-click it if it's in your Dock).

2. A window like that in Figure 1-14 will open.

   It doesn't look very impressive, but if you've ever worked on a Windows or DOS computer, it should be familiar as the Command Prompt, and it performs the same function. All instructions to the computer are inserted as written commands at what's known as the **shell prompt**. This is the final line in Figure 1-14, and it looks something like this:

   ```
   Vigor14:~davidpowers$
   ```

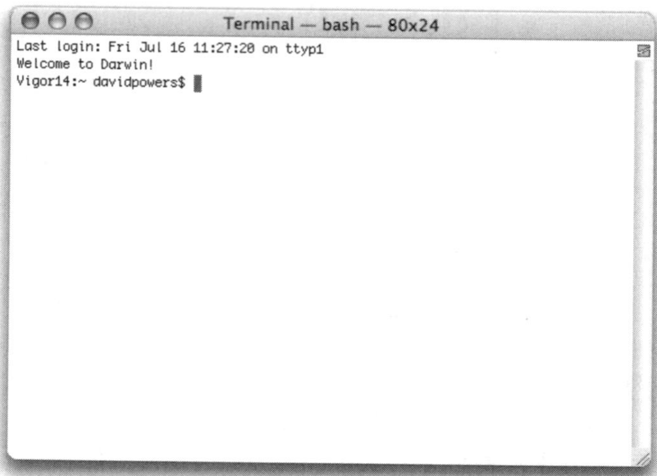

Figure 1-14. The Terminal window is the gateway to the Unix system that underlies Mac OS X.

The first part is the name of your Macintosh hard disk. The tilde (~) is the Unix shorthand for your home directory (or folder). This should be followed by your username and a dollar sign. As you navigate around the hard disk, your location is indicated in place of ~, but the prompt where you write commands should always be your username followed by a dollar sign. If the dollar sign is replaced by a hash sign (#), that means you have been logged in as the superuser known as root. The **root user** has unrestricted power to alter any file, including system files. Unless you know exactly what you are doing, you should log out immediately from the root account, and log back in using your personal account.

3. Before making any changes to configuration files, it's wise to back them up first. To copy a file, type cp followed by a space and the old filename, and then another space and the new filename. Since you are working in your home folder, you need to add the full path name to both files. Type the following command at the shell prompt:

```
cp /etc/httpd/httpd.conf /etc/httpd/httpd.conf.original
```

4. Check you have spelled everything correctly (use your left and right arrow keys to move along the line to correct any mistakes). Then press *Return*. (All commands at the shell prompt are invoked by pressing *Return*, so I won't repeat this instruction every time.)

5. You should see the following message:

```
cp: /etc/httpd/httpd.conf.original: Permission denied
```

This is the Unix system protecting important files from accidental or unauthorized changes. To override this, you need sudo. No, it doesn't mean you have to become a pretentious fraud; sudo stands for *superuser do*. Use it every time you need to carry out a command that requires superuser status (e.g., changes to configuration files or anything that results in a "permission denied" message).

To use sudo, simply put it in front of the normal command. When you press *Return*, you will be prompted for your password to make sure you have administrative privileges. If you use sudo again within five minutes, you won't need to give your password, but as soon as the five-minute window elapses, the extra security kicks back in.

If you have experience with Linux or Unix, you may find sudo's *nannylike attitude annoying. You can enable the root user on your Mac through the NetInfo Manager in* `Applications:Utilities`*. Although a lot of commands are exactly the same as on Linux and Unix, you need to familiarize yourself with the special features of the Mac OS X version of Unix. A good place to start is* Foundation Mac OS X Web Development *by Phil Sherry (friends of ED, ISBN: 1-59059-336-7). For the purposes of this book, though, sudo is more than adequate—and definitely much safer than enabling the root user.*

Enabling PHP on Mac OS X

If your test PHP page displayed something similar to Figure 1-13, PHP is already enabled. Read the following tip and then move on to the next section. Otherwise, get ready to dive into the Unix underworld.

To avoid retyping everything at the shell prompt, you can press the up arrow on your keyboard to reveal previous commands. Then use the left and right arrow keys to move the cursor along the line to make any changes. It doesn't matter if your cursor is not at the end of the line when you press Return; the whole command will be executed. Pressing the up arrow repeatedly will cycle through previous commands. Pressing the down arrow recalls more recent ones. If you decide not to execute a recalled command, cancel it by pressing Ctrl+C.

1. If Terminal is not still open, open a Terminal window as described in the previous section.
2. Enter the following command at the shell prompt (use the arrow keys to edit the command you entered in the previous section):

   ```
   sudo cp /etc/httpd/httpd.conf /etc/httpd/httpd.conf.original
   ```

3. If it's the first time you've used sudo, you'll probably get a dire warning about the consequences of using it. Read the message and enter your password when prompted.
4. Terminal will simply display the shell prompt again. To make sure your backup has been saved, use the `ls` command to list the files in the target directory. Enter the following command (you don't need sudo this time):

   ```
   ls /etc/httpd
   ```

5. You should see your backup file listed along with about eight other files. If you make a mistake later on, you can always restore the Apache configuration file to its original state by reversing the order of the filenames in step 2:

   ```
   sudo cp /etc/httpd/httpd.conf.original /etc/httpd/httpd.conf
   ```

6. Next, open the configuration file in the pico text editor by typing the following command:

```
sudo pico /etc/httpd/httpd.conf
```

7. This opens the Apache configuration file `httpd.conf` in the pico editor directly inside the Terminal window, hiding the shell prompt until you exit. As you can see from the following screenshot, the file is more than 1,000 lines long. Most of it consists of comments (lines that begin with #).

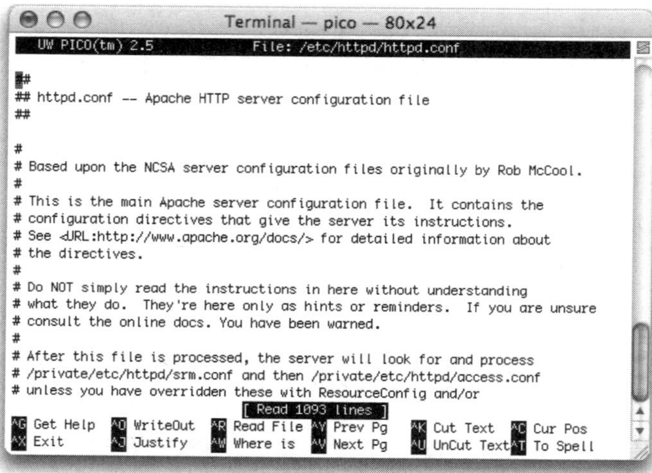

8. You are interested in just two lines at the moment. To find them, use pico's search feature by pressing *CTRL+W*. Use loadmodule php as your search term, and press *RETURN*. The cursor should jump to a line that begins

```
#LoadModule php4_module
```

If you bought or upgraded your Mac recently, you may be lucky enough to see `php5_module` instead of `php4_module`. Whichever it is, press *BACKSPACE* once to delete the #. This uncomments the line and makes the configuration command active.

9. Do another search by pressing *CTRL+W* and entering addmodule mod_php. The cursor should jump to a line that reads

```
#AddModule mod_php4.c
```

Again, a more recent version of Mac OS X may have `mod_php5.c`.

10. Delete the # at the beginning of the line. PHP is now enabled.

11. Exit pico by pressing *CTRL+X*. When prompted to Save modified buffer, press *Y* (as long as you're happy with the changes). Pico will ask for the File name to write and automatically fill in the existing name. All you need do is press *RETURN* to confirm the name, and you will be returned to the shell prompt.

12. For the changes to take effect, you need to restart Apache. You can do this from the shell prompt with the following command:

```
sudo apachectl restart
```

13. Reload the `index.php` page in your browser. You should now see a page similar to that shown in Figure 1-13. PHP here we come! At the time of this writing, Mac OS X normally ships with PHP 5. If you have an older installation (like I did!), you need to upgrade it to be able to take full advantage of all the applications in this book. Before that, however, you need to install MySQL.

Installing MySQL on Mac OS X

Although you won't be using MySQL until Chapter 6, changes in the way PHP accesses MySQL code libraries mean that it is advisable to install MySQL before upgrading to PHP 5.

The following instructions assume that you're installing MySQL for the first time. MySQL is available as a Mac PKG file, so installation is a breeze.

> *If you have an existing installation of MySQL and plan to upgrade, read the important notes in Appendix E before going any further.*

1. Go to `www.mysql.com/downloads`.
2. Select the link for the recommended Generally Available release of MySQL database server and standard clients (MySQL 4.1.7 at the time of this writing). Scroll down to the Mac OS X downloads section and choose the standard installer package. Make sure you get the right one for your version of Mac OS X. (This book was written before the release of Tiger, but there were separate versions for Jaguar and Panther.) The size of the download file is approximately 23MB.
3. When the download is complete, the DMG file will automatically mount the contents on your desktop. If this doesn't happen automatically, double-click the icon. There should be three files, as shown here: `ReadMe.txt` and two PKG files.

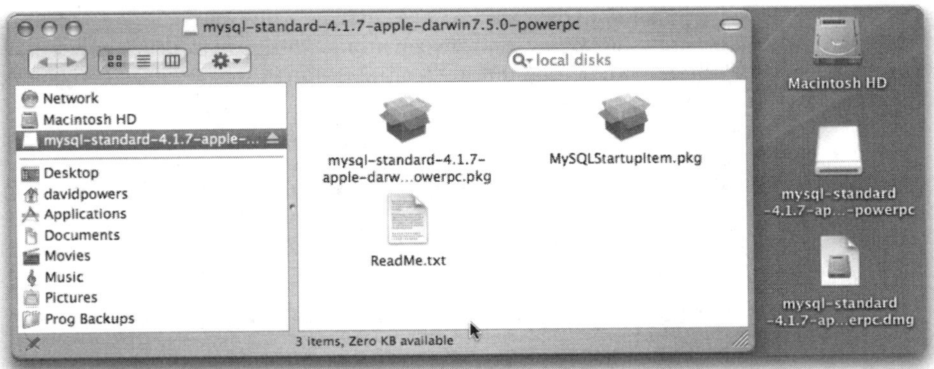

Double-click the mysql-standard-4.1.x.pkg icon to start the installation process (the precise name of the file will depend on the version downloaded). This opens the Mac OS X installer. Follow the instructions on the screen.

4. Double-click MySQLStartupItem.pkg and follow the installation instructions onscreen. This is a one-time-only operation. You won't need to reinstall it when upgrading to a later version of MySQL.

5. You can now discard the PKG and DMG files, although it's a good idea to keep the `ReadMe.txt` in case of problems.

6. Most of the time, you will access MySQL through a graphical interface called phpMyAdmin (see Chapter 6 for details), but there will be times you'll want to use Terminal. To avoid having to type out the full path to the `mysql/bin` directory every time, you can add it to the PATH in your environmental variables. Open Terminal and check the title bar. If it says Terminal — bash, as in Figure 1-14, you need to edit your profile file. Type the following to open the file in pico (it's your own file, so you don't need to use sudo):

   ```
   pico ~/.profile
   ```

   Then move your cursor to a new line following any content (although it may be empty), and enter the following line of code:

   ```
   export PATH="$PATH:/usr/local/mysql/bin"
   ```

   Save the file by pressing *Ctrl+X*, and then press *Y* and *Return*.

7. If the title bar of Terminal says Terminal — tcsh, enter the following command at the shell prompt and press *Return*:

   ```
   echo 'setenv PATH /usr/local/mysql/bin:$PATH' >> ~/.tcshrc
   ```

MySQL will start up automatically the next time you reboot.

Upgrading PHP on Mac OS X

There are two ways of upgrading: using a precompiled PKG file or compiling PHP from source code. The latter route should be taken only by people who have a good working knowledge of the Unix operating system that underlies Mac OS X. Compiling from source is not particularly difficult, but it can turn into a nightmare if things go wrong. I propose to cover only installation from a precompiled PKG, but if you want to try compilation from source, a good place to start is with the tutorials at `www.phpmac.com`.

PHP 5 relies heavily on the availability of external code libraries. Whichever upgrade route you take, it is essential that you have installed all the latest Apple system software updates before proceeding. The following instructions have been tested on a fully up-to-date version of Mac OS X 10.3.5.

Support for PHP 5 on OS X 10.2 or earlier appears to be nonexistent. If you are running Jaguar and cannot upgrade to the latest version of OS X, I suggest you install the PHP 4.3.4 PKG from Marc Liyanage (as described in the next section). Most of the applications in this book should work on PHP 4, although some use features available only in PHP 5.

Using a PKG file to upgrade PHP

A software engineer by the name of Marc Liyanage is highly respected in the Mac PHP community for the packages he creates for all major upgrades of PHP. Not only are Marc's packages very easy to install, but also he takes the trouble to configure them to support a wide range of extra features. The only possible drawback is that they involve a much bigger download (nearly 22MB, as opposed to 4.4MB for the source code direct from `www.php.net`).

Even if you have a slow Internet connection, the large download is worth it. You get a full-featured version of PHP that works "straight out of the box" without the need to sort out all the code library dependencies that can be a major headache in compiling programs from source code. I successfully compiled an early version of PHP 5 from source, but ran into problems trying to upgrade to version 5.0.2. So I tried Marc's PKG instead. Once downloaded, it was installed and running without a hitch in approximately two minutes. No heartache, no fuss. If you do run into problems, there's a searchable support forum on Marc's website, where answers tend to be fast and accurate. It should be your first port of call in case of installation problems.

1. Go to `www.entropy.ch/software/macosx/php/` and select the version of PHP you want to install. At the time of this writing, Marc offered four PKG files for the latest version of PHP (5.0.2). Choose the version that doesn't require a commercial license for `PDFLib` (unless you have a license key) and that also matches the version of Apache running on your computer. As of late 2004, this was still Apache 1.3, although this may change in future. If you aren't sure which version of Apache you're running, type the command httpd -v in Terminal, and the version number will be displayed as shown here:

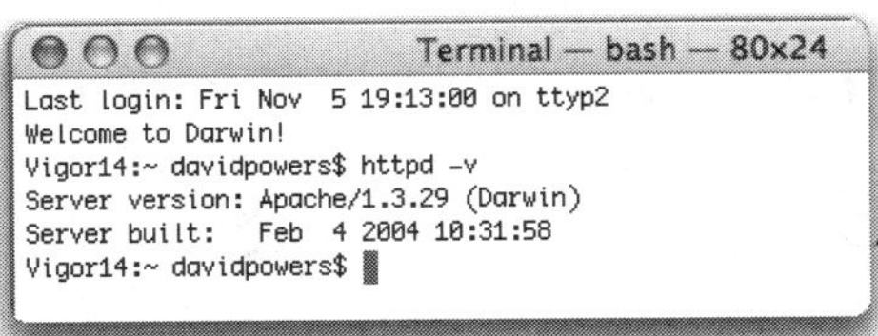

   Read any installation instructions on the site, as they'll contain the most up-to-date information about special requirements or restrictions. If you're using Jaguar, you'll probably be limited to downloading PHP 4.3.4 for Apache 1.3. It's extremely good, but it doesn't, of course, support the new features of PHP 5.

2. When the download is complete, the DMG file will automatically mount the contents on your desktop, as shown in Figure 1-15. (If it doesn't, just double-click it.) The `Extras` folder contains either the commercial or the noncommercial version of the `PDFLib` library, neither of which is required for this book. Copy the `Extras` folder to your hard disk, and read the documentation if you want to explore it at a later date. All you are interested in at the moment is the PKG file (`php-5.0.2.pkg` in Figure 1-15). Double-click it and follow the instructions onscreen.

3. Your upgraded version of PHP will become available as soon as you restart Apache, but before you do that, it's wise to make a minor change to the PHP configuration file, `php.ini`.

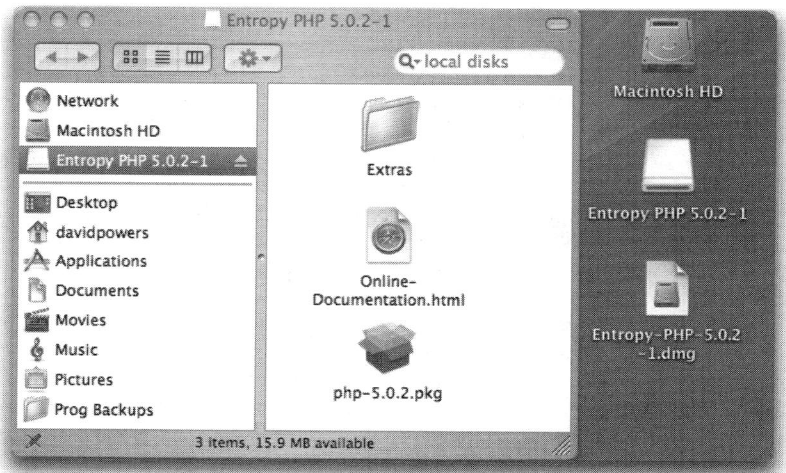

Figure 1-15. The PHP installation package automatically mounts on your desktop when the download is complete.

Configuring PHP to display errors on Mac OS X

Nearly there! When developing applications with PHP, it's important to know when things go wrong. Depending on where your installation of PHP came from, it may have been configured not to display any error messages or to hide some of them. Scroll down the test page shown in Figure 1-13, and look for the display_errors directive (it's in PHP Core, close to the top of the page). If the value is On, that's exactly what you want. Also check the setting for error_reporting. It should read 2047. If display_errors is set to Off, or if error_reporting is anything other than 2047, use the following instructions to change them.

1. Open Terminal, and open `php.ini` in the pico editor. If you have used one of Marc Liyanage's PKG files for PHP 5, or you have a preinstalled version of PHP 5, the command should be

   ```
   sudo pico /usr/local/php5/lib/php.ini
   ```

   If you have used his PHP 4 package, or if you are using an older Mac installation of PHP, the command should be

   ```
   sudo pico /usr/local/php/lib/php.ini
   ```

   In the unlikely event that neither of these commands works, check the Configuration File (php.ini) Path value on the test page shown in Figure 1-13. (It's approximately the sixth item from the top.)

2. Press *Ctrl+W*. Type display_errors = and press *Return*. This will take you to the first instance, which is not on a line of its own. Press *Ctrl+W* again. Your previous search term will still be there, so just press *Return*. This time, you should find `display_errors = Off` (or On) on a line of its own. If necessary, change it to `display_errors =` **On**, as shown in Figure 1-16.

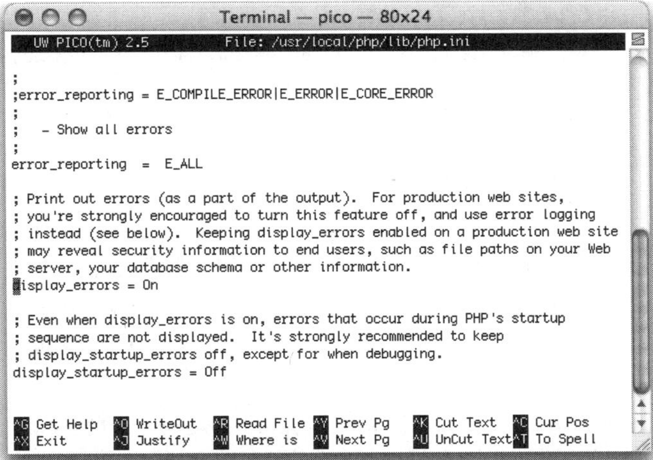

Figure 1-16. Turning on display_errors in `php.ini` makes debugging your scripts a lot easier.

3. Check just a few lines further up, and make sure that the previous uncommented line reads

   ```
   error_reporting = E_ALL
   ```

4. Exit pico by pressing *Ctrl*+*X*, and save the change to `php.ini` by pressing *Y* and *Return*.

Automatic starting of Apache on a multiuser Mac

If you're the only person using the computer, Apache will start up automatically whenever you reboot your Mac. If you have more than one user account, though, and you want Apache to start automatically on bootup for all users, you need to make a minor adjustment to the `hostconfig` file.

1. In Terminal, type the following command to make a backup copy:

   ```
   sudo cp /etc/hostconfig etc/hostconfig.orig
   ```

2. Open `hostconfig` in the pico editor by typing the following:

   ```
   sudo pico /etc/hostconfig
   ```

3. Look for the following line:

   ```
   WEBSERVER=-NO-
   ```

   and change it to

   ```
   WEBSERVER=-YES-
   ```

4. Exit pico by pressing *Ctrl* + *X*, and save the changes to `hostconfig` by pressing *Y* and *Return*.

Restarting Apache from Terminal

In addition to using System Preferences to restart Apache after making any changes to the php.ini or httpd.conf configuration files, you can restart Apache from the shell prompt by typing

```
sudo apachectl restart
```

Setting up your work environment

After all that, you're no doubt raring to go and want to see how PHP works. Before doing so, let's just pause to review what all this hard work has been for. You have now created a setup that emulates Figure 1-3 at the beginning of the chapter (although Windows users won't be adding MySQL to the mix until Chapter 6). Instead of being spread across the Internet, everything is now on your own computer. This will speed up development considerably, because it avoids the need to upload files to a website for every minor change. For your setup to work properly, it's important to realize that you're now running a full-fledged web server, albeit for your own exclusive use.

When designing standard web pages with XHTML or Flash, it doesn't matter where you store the files on your computer. You can double-click them in Explorer or Finder, and they will automatically display in your default browser and look the same as if they were coming from a live website. Now that you have added PHP to the equation, you can no longer do that. PHP needs to be **parsed** by the PHP engine before you can display the results of its output. What this means is that PHP has to convert all your code into meaningful information that will either be displayed in a browser or sent to your Flash movie. This is very similar to the way you get Flash to compile an FLA file into a SWF, only the PHP script stays in its original form and is compiled by the server each time it is accessed. For the server to be able to do this, PHP scripts must be located within what's known as the **server root** and they must be served through a web server. Figure 1-17 shows a diagrammatic representation of this on your computer.

- **Locating the server root**: For Windows users, this is `C:\htdocs` or whatever you chose as the value for `DocumentRoot` in steps 4 and 5 of the "Configuring Apache to work with PHP" section. On the Mac, it is `Macintosh HD:Users:`*`username`*`:Sites`, where *username* is your actual username.
- **Viewing PHP files in a browser**: PHP files must always be accessed through a URL in the browser address bar. On Windows, the address of the server is `http://localhost/`. On the Mac, it is `http://localhost/~`*`username`*`/` (don't forget the tilde before your username). Any subfolders are added to the URL in the same way as on a live website. All of the files for this book should be stored in `C:\htdocs\phpflash` (`Macintosh HD:Users:username:Sites:phpflash`) and there should be separate subfolders for each chapter. So `today.php`, which you will create shortly, will be located in `C:\htdocs\phpflash\ch01\today.php` or the Mac equivalent. To view the page, the URL becomes `http://localhost/phpflash/ch01/today.php` (Mac users should always add *~username* as indicated earlier). If you try to use Open File from your browser's File menu, the browser will either display the raw PHP code or prompt you to save the file, even if the file is located in the server root. **So it's not just the location of files that's important—you must access them with the `localhost` URL as well.**

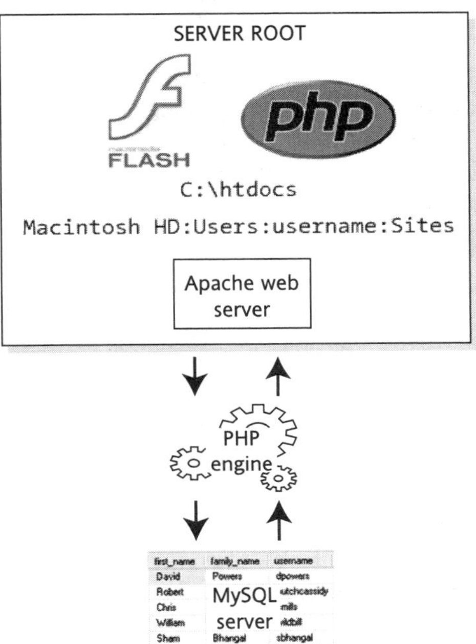

Figure 1-17. All published files related to your Flash movies, together with PHP scripts, must be located in the Apache server root to interact with the PHP engine and the database server.

Strictly speaking, it's not absolutely necessary for a PHP script to be stored inside the server root. By definition, any file inside a server root must be publicly accessible through a browser (although it may be password protected). So, for security reasons, it's sometimes a good idea to store files outside the server root (for example, if they contain passwords or other sensitive information). As long as the server knows where to find the files (usually with a path name in an include directive), the file can be anywhere. You can even include files from a different server, although this is probably less secure than leaving sensitive files in the server root unless both servers are under your direct control (even so, if the other server is down, your script won't run). For the purposes of this book, all PHP files should be stored within the server root, both on your local computer and when deploying them to a remote server. With the proper coding techniques you'll learn in this book, PHP scripts stored in the server root should be perfectly secure anyway.

Throughout this book, you'll be working in a subfolder of the server root called `phpflash`. To keep things tidy, you'll create a further subfolder for each chapter, and this is where you'll need to publish all your SWF movies and associated HTML files, as well as create your PHP files. Whether you decide to store your FLA files within the server root is a matter of personal choice. Although keeping everything together is convenient, you never normally deploy FLA files on a web server that's live on the Internet, so there's a strong argument for keeping them out of the server root on your development computer. I suggest you also keep your downloaded source code in a separate folder so you can easily find it if you need to compare it against your own files. If you're using Flash MX 2004 Professional, the Projects panel offers a convenient way of keeping track of related files in different folders.

The final consideration in setting up your work environment lies in the choice of program for creating your PHP files. Up to now, I have suggested using a text editor such as Notepad, SciTEFlash, TextEdit, or BBEdit. Since PHP files are written in plain text, you don't need anything more sophisticated. However, if you're already using Flash, there's a strong likelihood that you may also have Dreamweaver at your disposal, either as a stand-alone program or as part of Studio MX. As long as your version of Dreamweaver is MX or later, it offers the following advantages:

- Close integration with Flash
- Site management
- Color syntax coding for PHP
- Line numbering
- PHP code hints and auto-completion

Other dedicated script editors offer similar features, so all the code in this book is designed to work regardless of your choice of PHP editor. If you do decide to use Dreamweaver, before going any further, you need to define a PHP site.

Defining a PHP site in Dreamweaver

These instructions apply to Dreamweaver MX 2004. Other versions may differ slightly.

1. Choose Manage Sites from the Dreamweaver Site menu.
2. In the dialog box that opens, choose New ➤ Site.

3. When the Site Definition dialog box opens, select the Advanced tab, and make sure Local Info is highlighted in the Category column on the left. Fill in the details as shown in Figure 1-18, depending on your operating system. Mac users should, of course, use their own username in the Local root folder and HTTP address fields.

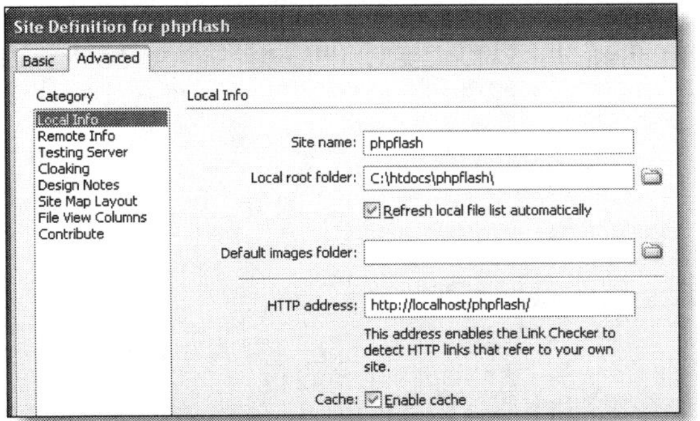

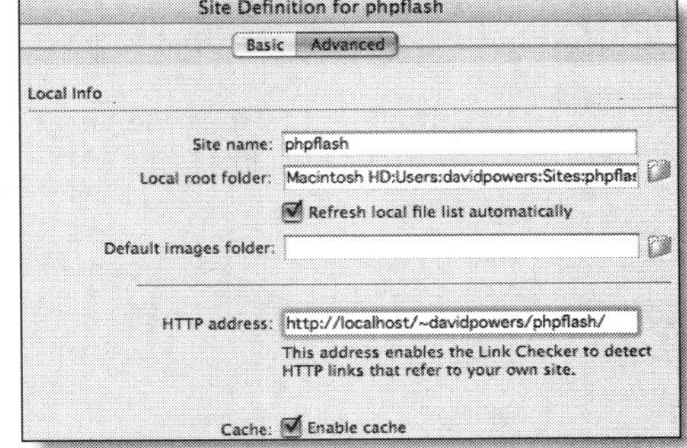

Figure 1-18. Local Info details for Windows (left) and Mac OS X (right)

4. Select Remote Info from the Category list. If you plan to use Dreamweaver to upload your files to a remote server, use the drop-down menu marked Access to select the method you plan to use (such as FTP), and fill in the necessary fields. Otherwise, check that it's set to None.

5. Select Testing Server from the Category list. Set the drop-down menu for Server Model to PHP MySQL. From the Access drop-down menu, select Local/Network. Three extra fields will appear, as shown in Figure 1-19. Dreamweaver should automatically insert the correct address for Testing server folder. However, you need to amend the URL prefix field. On Windows, it should be http://localhost/phpflash/. On Mac OS X, it should be http://localhost/~*username*/phpflash/. Make sure not to omit the trailing slash on the URL prefix.

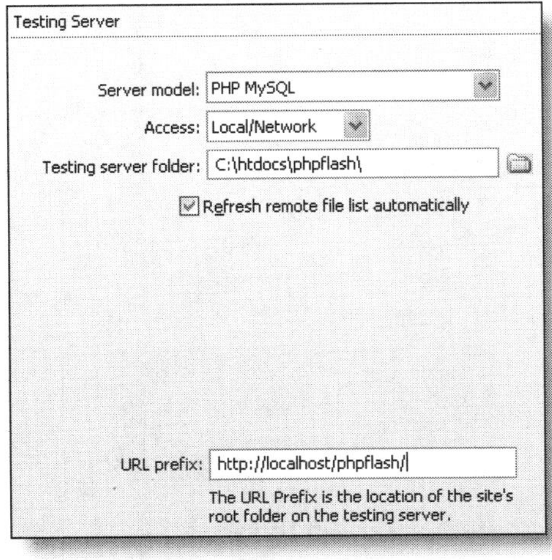

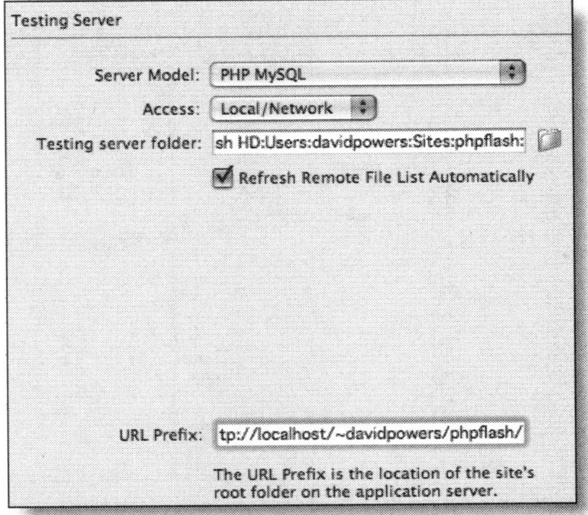

Figure 1-19. Testing server details for Windows (left) and Mac OS X (right)

6. If you plan to store your FLA files in the same folder as your site, and do not need to share them with others, select Cloaking from the Category list. Select the check box marked Cloak files ending with, and make sure the field contains .fla (with a leading period), as shown in the image.

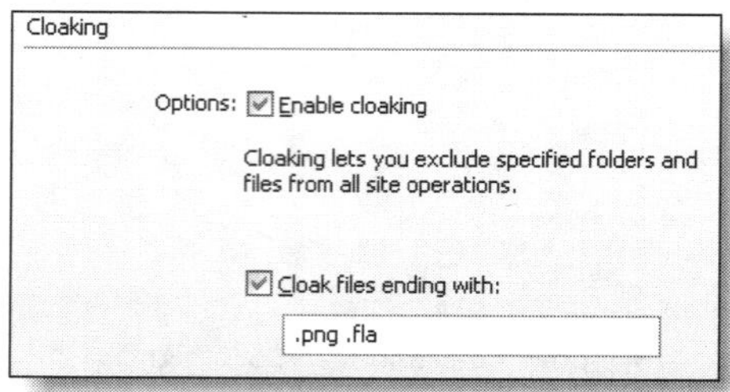

7. The Site Definition dialog box has other optional settings, but these are all you normally need. Click OK, and then click Done.

You should always select the `phpflash` site from the Files panel (Window ➤ Files or *F8*) when working on PHP pages for the exercises this book, and save your pages within the site's folder or subfolders. One advantage of doing so is that you can launch any page within the site just by pressing *F12*. This saves you the effort of typing the full URL in your browser every time.

To create a new PHP page, choose File ➤ New. Then from the General tab, select Dynamic Page ➤ PHP, and click Create.

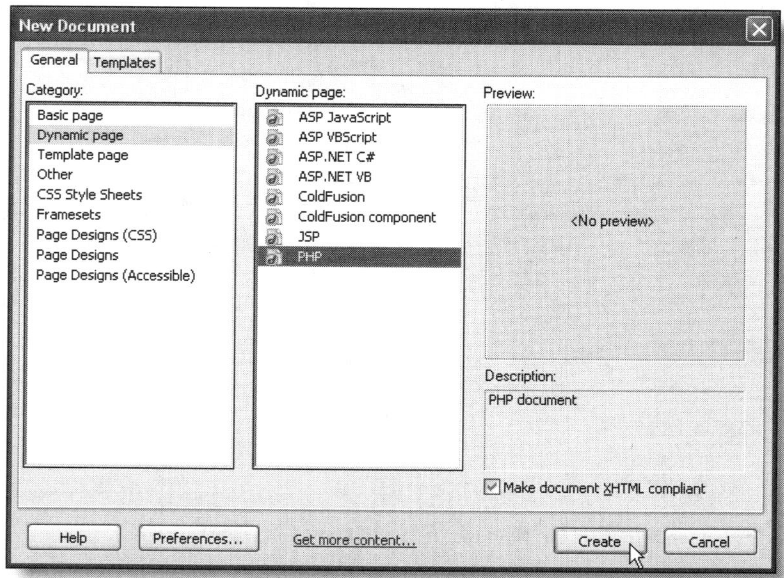

For the vast majority of PHP pages in this book, you will need to switch to Code view and strip out all the XHTML code Dreamweaver inserts by default. While this may seem annoying, the most common way of using PHP is embedded in normal web pages. On the occasions you need the XHTML code, you'll quickly appreciate that it's a lot easier to strip it out when you don't need it than to have to re-create it when you do.

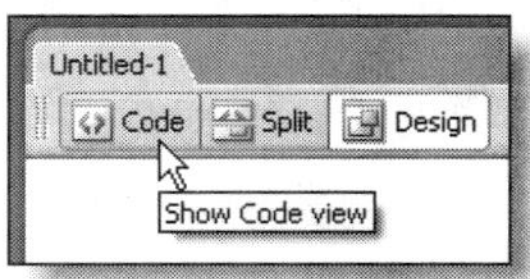

To benefit from all the visual aids Dreamweaver offers in Code view, click the View options icon at the top right of the Code view workspace. Make sure the options shown here are selected (you toggle them on an off by clicking them—a check mark means a particular option is turned on).

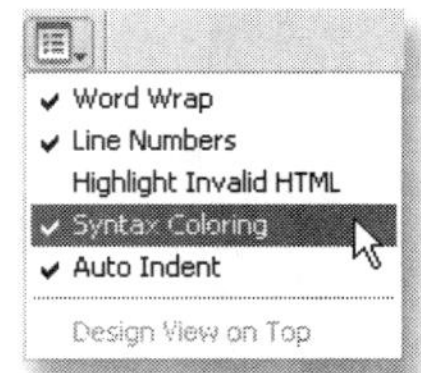

Also select Edit ➤ Preferences (Dreamweaver ➤ Preferences on a Mac). Then choose Code Hints. Enable auto tag completion and Enable code hints should be on by default. Make any adjustments to suit your own style of working.

Getting a first taste of the power of PHP

Actually, you've already done that: the `phpinfo()` command used to verify that everything is running, together with the surrounding tags, is a perfectly valid PHP page. But after all the hard work of installing and configuring your web server and PHP, perhaps you were hoping for something a bit more interesting. That's really what the rest of this book is about, but to whet your appetite, type the following code into a new PHP document:

```
<?php
echo date('l, F jS, Y');
?>
```

Save the file as `today.php` in `C:\htdocs\phpflash\ch01` (or the Mac equivalent), and then view it in a browser (Dreamweaver users press *F12*). The result should be something like this:

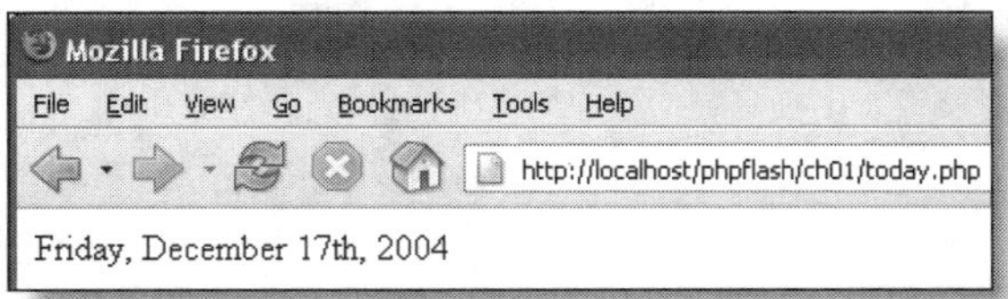

Not the most exciting of first pages, admittedly, but just think if you had tried to do the same thing with ActionScript. You would need to assign a `Date` object to a variable; use four separate methods to extract the day of the week, month, date, and year; create and query arrays to get the names of the weekday and month; and design a function to append the ordinal suffix to the date (1st, 2nd, and so on). PHP does it all in one short line of code.

That's one of the attractions of PHP: it's often extremely compact. It's also usually very fast. Over the next 11 chapters, I'll show you how to team up the agility of PHP and the MySQL database with the power of ActionScript 2.0 and the graphical brilliance of Flash.

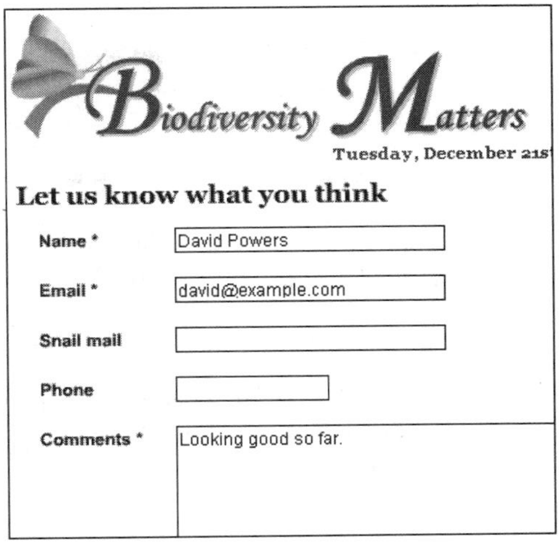

Chapter 2

FLASH BREAKS FREE

What this chapter covers:

- Using LoadVars to communicate with external data sources
- Taking a first look at PHP syntax
- Making sure Flash variables are being received by PHP
- Checking PHP output before sending the results back to Flash
- Validating user input
- Using PHP to send Flash form output by email

Stand-alone Flash movies are a tightly self-enclosed world. Although they can load JPGs, sound files, and video, the only outward communication is normally to load another web page in your browser. Once you tie up Flash with a server-side language like PHP, you open up whole new possibilities, such as interaction with a database. Before you can do that, you need to learn some of the basic grammar of PHP.

You also need to learn how to get data in and out of your Flash movies. It's vital to check that what's going in and out is what you expect it to be. Once you start working with external data, it's not always possible to use `trace` to check the value of variables. I will show you strategies to overcome this problem.

By the end of the chapter, you will have put your newfound knowledge to good use by using PHP to send feedback from an online form in a Flash movie to your mailbox. So, without further ado . . .

Communicating with external sources

There are a variety of ways of communicating between a Flash movie and external data sources. Among the most important are

- **`LoadVars`**: Provides an easy way to export and import variables. Requires Flash Player 6 or above.
- **`XML`**: A powerful class for manipulating the content of XML documents, and sending XML-formatted data to and from Flash. Requires Flash Player 5 or above.
- **`FlashVars`**: Provides one-way communication only, passing variables from a web page to a SWF file when first instantiated. Requires Flash Player 6 or above.
- **`loadVariables()`**: This global function was the original means of providing two-way communication. It's now superseded by the more versatile `LoadVars` class. Introduced in Flash Player 4, and still supported in Flash Player 7.

Throughout this book, I plan to concentrate on the first of these methods, `LoadVars`, mainly because it's extremely efficient and easy to handle. Unlike like the older `loadVariables()` and the closely related `loadVariablesNum()` global functions, `LoadVars` allows you to select precisely which variables are sent to the server, thereby cutting down on transfer time and bandwidth. `LoadVars` also has a fuller set of events associated with it, making the handling of data transfer in both directions much easier. Although the older functions are still supported in Flash Player 7, there's no guarantee they'll always be part of ActionScript. If you're an old Flash hand, you'll be delighted with the improvements offered by `LoadVars`. If you're a newcomer, you can regard `loadVariables()` and `loadVariablesNum()` as historical curiosities.

The `XML` class is of great importance for advanced developers dealing with XML documents, but it requires considerable familiarity with the XML Document Object Model. Its great disadvantage is the abstract way in which it handles documents. Fortunately, PHP 5 makes handling simple XML documents much less complicated. So, I'll show you how to convert XML documents into Flash variables before transferring them—a solution that is often faster than manipulating a raw XML document with ActionScript.

FlashVars is mainly of interest to developers using HTML pages only, because it's designed to import variables when a Flash movie is first loaded in a browser. It's not covered in this book.

So let's take a quick look at the tool you'll be using—LoadVars—in action.

Using LoadVars to load data in Flash

In spite of its name, LoadVars facilitates two-way communication: it can both send and load. To start off with, you're going to use the class in its literal sense—to load variables, or one variable, to be precise.

> *You should create all the work for each chapter in a new folder inside* phpflash, *the subfolder of your server root that you created at the end of Chapter 1. For Windows users, that means* C:\htdocs\phpflash; *for Mac OS X users, that means* Macintosh HD:***username***:Sites:phpflash.

1. Create a new folder inside phpflash called ch02. Make a copy of today.php (from the previous chapter), and save it in the ch02 folder as today2.php.
2. Open today2.php and change the PHP script like this (the additional code is in bold type):

   ```
   <?php
   echo 'theDate='.urlencode(date('l, F jS, Y'));
   ?>
   ```

   Although this is quite a short line of PHP code, there is quite a lot going on here. Rather than explain everything at this stage, I want to concentrate on showing you how to get data from PHP into Flash (handling dates in PHP is covered in Chapter 11). There is one thing I would like to draw your attention to, though. It's the command right at the beginning of the second line: **echo**. This is one of the main PHP methods of displaying output in a browser, and you will be using it a lot throughout this book. It's described in detail in Chapter 4.

   Make sure there is nothing else in your file other than the code shown here. **The PHP scripts in this book should not be embedded in HTML or XHTML tags unless specifically stated otherwise. Nor should they include any Doctype. You are using PHP strictly as a server-side programming language—not to create web pages.**
3. Load today2.php into a browser—remember to use http://localhost/ (http://localhost/~*username*/ on a Mac) instead of the path to the phpflash folder, so you will have a URL in your browser address bar like that shown in the following image. (Dreamweaver users can just press *F12*.) You should see something like this:

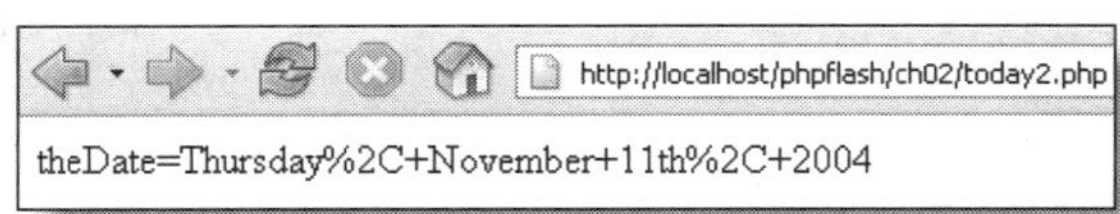

If you got a blank screen, two things are almost certainly true: you made a mistake in copying the script, and `display_errors` *is set to* `Off` *in your PHP configuration. Go back to the previous chapter and follow the instructions for configuring PHP to ensure* `display_errors` *is set to On.*

If you got an error message, good! At least they're displaying correctly. Don't try figuring out what it means (PHP error messages and how to handle them are covered in detail in Appendix A). Just check the code carefully again, paying particular attention to missing quotes, brackets, or the period (full stop) in the middle of the second line. Alternatively, use the version in the download files for this book at `www.friendsofed.com`.

4. You're probably thinking this is even less impressive than the first time. The date is now barely intelligible. Certainly, that's the case for human readers, but the `%2C` toward the end gives you a clue that this isn't intended for humans, but for a computer. The date has been reformatted according to the rules of URL encoding (as you would use for a query string on the end of a URL). Variables loaded into Flash must be in this format, and by displaying the output in a browser, you have performed an essential test of the PHP script. There's no point trying to load variables from an external source if they're not correctly formatted. Even if you run `trace` in ActionScript, all you will get is `undefined` and no clue as to what the problem is. So always test in this manner if you encounter problems loading variables from PHP.

   Once you have confirmed `today2.php` is displaying the date as shown in the illustration (spaces replaced by + and the comma replaced by %2C), and that there are no spaces surrounding the equal sign (=), you can load the output of the PHP script into a Flash movie.

5. Open `biodiverse01.fla` from the download files for this chapter and save it as `biodiverse.fla`. The file contains a movie clip butterfly logo and a banner heading. I used Monotype Corsiva for the text, but converted it to a graphic because it's not a font likely to be on everyone's computer. If you prefer, you can create a new Flash document of your own, and add a banner heading suitable for a website.

6. Create two new layers above the title layer: name one date and the other actions. Lock the actions layer to avoid placing any graphics on it inadvertently.

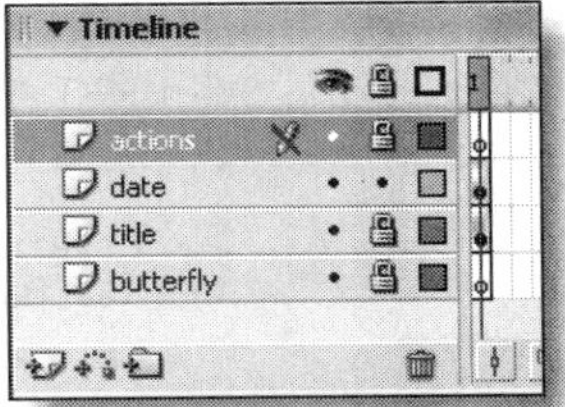

If you learned ActionScript from one of Sham Bhangal's many friends of ED books (you did, didn't you?), you'll know that ActionScript should always be placed on a keyframe on a layer of its own, and that layer should always be at the top of your timeline. The convention is to call the layer actions *(although some people prefer* scripts*). If you accidentally place graphics on the* actions *layer, they may load in the wrong order and confuse Flash. Locking the layer prevents this from happening, but you can still highlight the* actions *layer and attach scripts to it in the Actions panel.*

7. On the date layer, insert a dynamic text field, and use the Properties panel to give it the instance name theDate_txt. Where you put it is a matter of taste. The following screenshot shows the settings I used to align the date just below the M of Matters. I also set the font to size 12, bold, _serif, and set the color to #730F73 to match the title. One of the problems I always find with dynamic text fields is getting the width right, so I'll fix that with ActionScript.

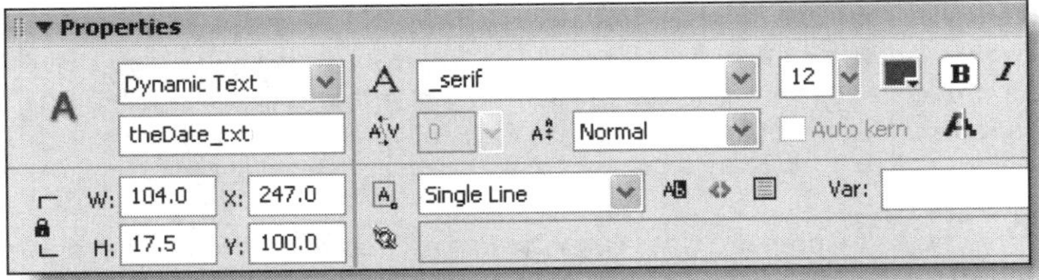

8. Highlight the actions layer, and open the Actions panel (*F9*). Enter the following code:

```
// create and apply text format for date
var dateDisplay:TextFormat = new TextFormat();
dateDisplay.font = "Georgia,Times,_serif";
theDate_txt.setNewTextFormat(dateDisplay);
theDate_txt.autoSize = "left";
```

This creates a `TextFormat` object and applies it to theDate_txt dynamic text field. Most of the necessary formatting was applied through the Properties panel, but it's nice to use a smarter font than the default Flash _serif. By setting the `font` property like this, the movie will choose the first available specified font on the user's computer, and fall back on _serif only if neither is available.

Also, by setting the `autoSize` property of theDate_txt to `left`, the dynamic text field will automatically resize to display the full date aligned to the left. Obviously, if you use this setting, you need to make sure there's going to be plenty of room to accommodate the longest dynamic text likely to be generated. With dates, it's fairly easy to predict how much space you'll need.

9. Now comes the important part of the ActionScript: the code that creates the LoadVars instance and loads the data from the PHP script. Insert this immediately beneath the code in the previous step:

```
// create LoadVars instance to retrieve date from PHP script
var getDate:LoadVars = new LoadVars();
// load date from PHP
getDate.load("http://localhost/phpflash/ch02/today2.php");
// assign theDate property of the LoadVars instance to text field
getDate.onLoad = function() {
  theDate_txt.text = this.theDate;
};
```

Note that I've used the localhost URL to refer to today2.php. **This is for local testing purposes only**. When deploying your movie on a live server, you need to replace the reference to localhost with the correct path (absolute or relative) to the PHP file.

If you are working on a Mac, the URL in the second line of the preceding code will be http://localhost/~username/phpflash/ch02/today2.php. To avoid repeating this every time, from now on I will usually give only the Windows version. Mac users should remember to insert their own username in the appropriate place.

While it is possible to test Flash movies without using this technique, it involves publishing the SWF file and loading it into a browser after every change. This not only is more time consuming, but also deprives you of the opportunity to use trace to check the value of your variables in Flash.

10. Test the movie by pressing *CTRL+ENTER/⌘+RETURN*. You may have to wait a few seconds while Flash establishes contact with Apache, but eventually you should see something like this:

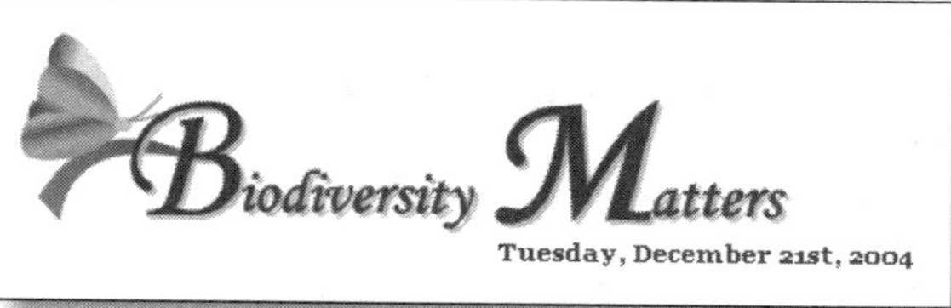

If you run into problems, check your code against biodiverse02.fla and today2.php in the download files for this chapter. The most likely cause of failure is if you have any XHTML code in your PHP file. Remember, you are using PHP as a scripting language, not to produce stand-alone web pages.

Adding a date to a movie is, admittedly, not the most stunning achievement in the world, but this simple script achieves a great deal more in fewer lines of code than would be possible in

ActionScript. The PHP date() function (which will be explained in detail in Chapter 11) uses just five characters to format the current date. To do the same thing in ActionScript, you would need to create arrays of both weekdays and months, not to mention the complexity of creating a custom function to add the correct ordinal suffix (st, nd, rd, or th) to the date. There is also an important difference in that the date is generated not by the user's computer clock, but by the server. Of course, that means you have to ensure your server's clock is always correct, but that's a lot easier than guaranteeing that all your website's visitors will be just as careful about getting the time and date correct. (If you are working in a non-English environment, the strftime() function described in Chapter 11 will format the date and time in your own language. The display generated by date() is always in English.)

Most important of all, you've created a dynamic link to an external data source and seen how easy it is to import external data with the LoadVars class. Exporting data is just as simple. I'll come to that later in the chapter, when I explain how the class works.

First, though, it's time to introduce you to the basics of PHP.

Taking first steps in PHP

One of the first things most people ask about PHP is what the initials mean. For the first three years of its existence, PHP stood for **Personal Home Page**. With the release of version 3 in 1998, it was felt this name promoted the wrong image, and it was changed. PHP now stands for **PHP: Hypertext Pre-processor**. It's a recursive abbreviation of the type beloved by open source developers (GNU, for example, stands for **GNU's Not Unix**). So now you know.

With the release of PHP 5, it has become a sophisticated programming language with extensive object-oriented capabilities (some advanced aspects, such as namespace support and overloading are not implemented). What makes it easy to learn is that OOP is an optional part of the language. You can begin using PHP very quickly and progress to object creation later, once you're more comfortable with the basic aspects.

How PHP fits into web design

The most common use for PHP is to provide dynamic content for standard web pages. It can be embedded directly in HTML or XHTML, and as long as the page is parsed by the PHP engine before being sent to the browser, the output of any PHP script will be rendered as a normal part of the web page.

To take a simple example, many websites include a copyright notice at the foot of each page. Instead of you needing to change the year manually every January, it can be done automatically by embedding the date() function you have been using in the examples so far. Simply insert it at the appropriate place in the page's XHTML like this:

```
<div id="footer">&copy; 1999-<?php echo date('Y'); ?>
David Powers</div>
```

Assuming the page has a suitable stylesheet attached, the result onscreen might look something like this (the full code and stylesheet can be found in `copyright.php` in the download files for this chapter):

© 1999-2004 David Powers

As long as the clock is set accurately on the server, the second date will always display the current year, changing it automatically at midnight on December 31. If you look at the web page's source code in the browser, you will see all the PHP code has disappeared:

```
<div id="footer">&copy; 1999-2004 David Powers</div>
```

The PHP engine parses everything and sends back only the dynamically generated XHTML output. When publishing movies, Flash automatically creates an HTML page (or XHTML since MX 2004) to display your SWF on the Web. You could easily incorporate this line of code just before the closing </body> tag (attributing the copyright to the creator of the site, rather than me, of course). All you need to do for it to work is change the filename extension from `.html` to `.php`.

Most of the time, you'll use the PHP output to generate variables for use within Flash, but it's useful to know that the PHP techniques discussed in this book are equally applicable to XHTML web pages, doubling your skills base at a stroke. Since version 4.3.0, PHP can also be used as a command-line language. This book doesn't cover that aspect, but if you want to learn more about PHP as a command-line language, take a look at the PHP online documentation at `www.php.net/manual/en/features.commandline.php`.

The basic grammar of PHP

Like human languages, computer languages have a set of basic rules—a grammar, or more formally, a **syntax**—that you need to follow if your meaning is to be understood. When listening to a three-year-old talk, we make mental adjustments for bad pronunciation, incorrect word usage, and even missing words. Computers, however, are not so forgiving. They expect you to be word-perfect from day one. Fortunately, PHP syntax is not too difficult. It shares a great deal in common with ActionScript, but you need to be aware of the differences.

By its very nature, much of this section may seem rather dry, but it is necessary reading. I promise that by the time you emerge at the end of the chapter, you will have not only absorbed a great deal of vital information, but also created something of immediate practical use—an online feedback form in Flash and PHP.

Giving pages the correct extension

Any page containing PHP must be saved with the `.php` extension in the filename (for example, `index.php`). Unless you do so, the server has no idea that it's meant to **parse** (or process) the PHP script it contains. Without this simple bit of information, a browser will normally display your code as plain text. This not only looks bad, but also may reveal sensitive information such as your database password.

It *is* possible to reconfigure Apache to treat pages with other filename extensions as PHP, but it's not recommended. It's a waste of resources unless all pages contain code that needs to be processed.

Using PHP tags

Even if you use the correct filename extension, all PHP code must be enclosed in PHP tags. As you have probably already gathered from the examples so far, PHP code begins with `<?php` and ends with `?>`. The PHP engine is interested only in code that lies between these tags. Everything else is ignored.

Nonstandard PHP tags There are several other methods of embedding PHP code. I don't recommend any of them, but I'll mention them here in case you come across them elsewhere.

- **Short tags**: The original method of indicating PHP code was by using `<?` and `?>`. In spite of its convenience, the opening short tag is easily confused with XML processing instructions, so it's no longer recommended. Short tags are enabled by default in PHP 5, but may be turned off by the system administrator. For complete portability of scripts, it's better to use `<?php`.
- **ASP-style tags**: For compatibility with some HTML editors that can't handle correct PHP tags, PHP can be configured to treat anything between `<%` and `%>` tags as PHP. This isn't enabled by default and should be avoided.
- **Direct display**: When using either short tags or ASP-style tags, PHP offers a shorthand way of displaying the output of a single statement, using `<?=` as the opening tag—for example, `<?= date('Y'); ?>` instead of `<?php echo date('Y'); ?>`. While useful, it has limited application, and it fails if short tags are disabled.
- **Script tags**: This is the most verbose way of indicating the presence of PHP: `<script language="PHP"></script>`. The only reason you might want to use this is if your HTML editor supports no other method.

Commenting code

If you're already experienced with ActionScript, you understand the value of adding **comments** to your code. Comments simply describe in plain language what's happening in the script; they're not part of the program itself. In team development, they help everyone know what the code is for. For individual developers, well-commented code is much easier to debug and modify, particularly if you come back to it several months after it was first created.

PHP offers three methods of adding comments, all drawn from other programming languages. The first two are common to both ActionScript and PHP, and they are used in exactly the same way.

C++ comments Whenever PHP encounters two forward slashes (//), everything on the rest of that line is considered a comment and ignored by the PHP engine.

```
//This is a comment: the next line displays the current year
echo date('Y'); //This is also a comment
```

C (or block) comments PHP ignores all code appearing between /* and */, regardless of how many lines intervene. This serves two important but very different functions. In addition to making multiline comments possible, it offers a quick method of disabling a section of code when testing or debugging.

```
/* This is a comment
   that will stretch
   over many lines.
   It's also a useful
   technique for disabling
   code temporarily. */
```

Shell comments PHP treats the hash sign (#) the same way as two forward slashes. This type of comment is borrowed from Unix shell scripting languages. A row of hash signs stands out clearly, making this character particularly useful for signposting important blocks of code.

```
#This is a comment
echo date('Y'); #This is also a comment
######################
# Database connection
######################
```

Experienced ActionScripters need to be alert to this very different use of the hash sign in PHP, when including external files. In ActionScript, # is taken to mean that the rest of the line is a compiler directive, whereas in PHP it causes the rest of the line to be ignored.

```
#include "myFile.as" // Correct ActionScript
#include "myFile.php" This whole line ignored in PHP
```

You may remember from the previous chapter that the PHP configuration file `php.ini` uses a semicolon to comment out lines. This is the only place PHP uses a semicolon in such a way. As you will see in the next section, the semicolon has a completely different meaning in PHP scripts.

Using braces and semicolons

Like ActionScript, PHP consists of a series of statements normally executed in the sequence they appear in the script (unless the statements are inside a function, in which case both languages wait until the function is called before executing them). **Each statement in PHP must be followed by a semicolon**.

Missing semicolons at the end of statements are probably the biggest cause of beginner mistakes in PHP. Although the ActionScript interpreter will attempt to infer the end of a statement if the semicolon is missing, PHP stops in its tracks and reports a fatal error. The only time a semicolon is optional is after the very last statement before the closing PHP tag, but this is considered bad practice. Get into the habit of ending each statement with a semicolon. It will improve your ActionScript and save your sanity with PHP.

Statements can be grouped together between curly braces ({}), for example when you create a conditional test, loop, or function. Although ActionScript recommends a semicolon after the closing curly brace of an anonymous function, you should **never** use a semicolon after a closing curly brace in PHP.

Spreading yourself out with whitespace

PHP's insistence on terminating each statement with a semicolon means that whitespace is ignored, except inside a string (strings are covered in Chapter 4). Consequently, you can choose to bunch everything up on one line or to spread it out so that the script is easier to read. It doesn't take a genius to figure out which is better.

There are no hard and fast rules, but for ease of maintenance indent your code in logical blocks. The one thing PHP doesn't let you do is insert arbitrary whitespace into variables or function names, but as far as I'm aware, neither does any other programming language.

> *Because of the way PHP has evolved, there is no "official" style concerning how far to indent code or where to place the curly braces that surround blocks of code. ActionScript, on the other hand, has an accepted style that derives from the Auto Format feature of the Actions panel. You will notice that throughout the book I use slightly different styles for PHP and ActionScript. I find this helps me distinguish between the two languages. If you find it more natural to use ActionScript-style indenting, feel free to do so. As long as your syntax is correct, that's all that matters.*

Naming variables

Variables are the lifeblood of every programming language—they store values that may change (hence the name) or that you have no way of knowing in advance. A good example of a variable is the balance in your bank account. The value constantly changes, but you always refer to it by the same name. The rules for naming variables in PHP are almost identical to ActionScript, with one major exception: **PHP variables must begin with the dollar sign ($)**. After the initial dollar sign

- Variables must begin with a letter or underscore, followed by any number of other letters, numbers, or underscores.
- Variables must **not** begin with a number.
- Variables must **not** contain any spaces.

Table 2-1 shows examples of what you can and cannot use as PHP variables.

Table 2-1. Examples of valid and invalid PHP variables

Variable	Validity	Reason
`myVar`	Invalid	Doesn't begin with $
`$myVar`	Valid	Begins with $; all characters legal

(Continued)

Table 2-1. Examples of valid and invalid PHP variables *(Continued)*

Variable	Validity	Reason
`$my Var`	Invalid	Contains a space
`$myVar1`	Valid	All characters legal
`$1myVar`	Invalid	First character after $ is a numeral
`$_1myVar`	Valid	First character after $ is an underscore
`$my_Var`	Valid	All characters legal

Naming functions

Functions are the other essential element of any programming language. To borrow an analogy from human language, if variables are the nouns, functions are the verbs; they get things done. PHP has a huge number of built-in functions (more than 2,700 the last time I counted), but building your own functions is just as important in PHP as it is in ActionScript. The rules for naming your own functions are the same as for variables, except they do not begin with a dollar sign. In other words, **they must begin with a letter or the underscore**.

> *Although the rules say you can begin function or variable names with an underscore, it's not good practice to do so. Quite a few built-in features of PHP use an initial underscore, so that usage is best left to PHP to prevent confusion.*

Avoiding reserved words

PHP does not allow you to override built-in functions. Since there are so many of them, it can be difficult at times to avoid choosing a reserved word. One simple strategy is to prefix function names with `my`, `the`, or your own initials.

It's also not allowed to give a variable, function, class, or constant the same name as any of the reserved keywords listed in Table 2-2.

Table 2-2. PHP keywords you cannot use for naming your own functions or variables

PHP Keywords				
`and`	`array()`	`as`	`break`	`case`
`cfunction`	`class`	`const`	`continue`	`declare`
`default`	`die()`	`do`	`echo()`	`else`
`elseif`	`empty()`	`enddeclare`	`endfor`	`endforeach`

(Continued)

PHP Keywords				
endif	endswitch	endwhile	eval()	exception
exit()	extends	for	foreach	function
global	if	include()	include_once()	isset()
list()	new	old_function	or	php_user_filter
print()	require()	require_once()	return()	static
switch	unset()	use	var	while
xor	__CLASS__	__FILE__	__FUNCTION__	__LINE__
__METHOD__				

Case is a sensitive issue

Life would be a lot simpler if we could say that PHP is 100% case sensitive. Unfortunately, it's not quite so easy:

- Variables are case sensitive.
- Function names are **not** case sensitive.
- Class names are **not** case sensitive.

What this means is that accidentally spelling `$myVar` as `$myvar` will result in the variable not being recognized. On the other hand, the built-in function we have used on several occasions to display output can be written as echo, Echo, or eCHo, and PHP won't notice the difference.

Life is made even more complicated by the fact that ActionScript 1.0 was case insensitive, whereas since the release of version 2.0 with Flash MX 2004, ActionScript now enforces strict case sensitivity.

Play it safe by treating both PHP and ActionScript as case sensitive. Decide on a consistent strategy for naming variables and functions, using either camel case (such as `$myVar`*) or the underscore (*`$my_var`*) for compound words, and stick to it. You're asking for trouble if you deliberately create* `$myVar` *and* `$myvar` *to indicate separate values. Sooner or later, you'll end up using the wrong one. Because of PHP's case insensitivity for function and class names, attempting to create different ones based purely on case is doomed to failure. Since the most prevalent style in Flash is to use camel case, it's probably a good idea to use the same style in PHP.*

Choosing names that make sense

Follow the rules just described, and you can call variables or functions whatever you like. PHP is just as happy with a variable called `$a` as `$supercalifragilisticexpialidotious`. Life is a lot simpler, though, if you choose names that indicate what the variable or function is for. Because PHP is server-side code, no one else will ever see it—unless you show it to them on purpose, or your server and scripts are configured incorrectly. So don't be tempted to use the obfuscation techniques adopted by some JavaScript programmers. The only person they will confuse is you or someone who may have to update your code at a later date.

Short, meaningful names are best. They make it a lot easier to understand what the code is for, and consequently it's much easier to maintain. You're also less likely to misspell them. Single-letter variables, such as `$i`, should normally be used only as counters in loops, or where the same variable is needed repeatedly and its meaning is crystal clear.

Hanging loose with PHP

PHP, like JavaScript and the original version of ActionScript, was designed for ease of use. Instead of imposing the burden on programmers of having to decide in advance whether a variable should hold a string, integer, floating-point number, or whatever, PHP was designed as a loose-typed language. In other words, you can create `$myVar` as a string, and then reassign its value as an integer—something not possible in strict-typed languages such as Java.

That freedom has effectively disappeared in ActionScript 2.0, which now recommends declaring the datatype for every variable and function. Although this **static** (or **strict**) **data typing** can seem an intolerable burden after the flexibility of ActionScript 1.0, it actually ends up saving you time, because the compiler automatically warns you of any datatype mismatches. Not only that, the location and nature of the problem is pinpointed for you, relieving you of often endless hours tracking down a bug in your code. The developers of PHP 5, on the other hand, decided against static datatyping, except for one advanced area of the language. Fortunately, this rarely creates problems, thanks mainly to PHP's use of separate operators for addition and joining strings together (described in the next section).

> *Although static data typing is extremely helpful in avoiding bugs, it's important to realize that the checks are performed only when Flash compiles the ActionScript at the time of publishing a SWF file. Flash is not typed during runtime and will not necessarily fail on any change of type caused by PHP. Since all variables received through LoadVars are strings, you may need to cast the value to the correct datatype if you experience unexpected results.*

PHP has eight datatypes, which share many similarities with their equivalents in ActionScript. The following list highlights the points to note about each type:

- **Integer**: This type is a whole number, such as 1, 25, or 346, that is **not enclosed in quotes**. Integers can be written as decimal, octal, or hexadecimal numbers. **Octal** numbers begin with a leading 0. **Hexadecimal** values begin with 0x. This has important implications for numbers, such as phone numbers or ID numbers that you may wish to store with a leading zero. To avoid problems, store them as string values.

- **Floating-point number (double)**: This type can be written either with a decimal point, such as 2.1 or 98.6, or in scientific notation, such as 0.314E1. Like integers, floating-point numbers are **not enclosed in quotes**. Chapter 3 covers both types of numbers.
- **String**: This type is a sequence of characters **enclosed in either single or double quotes**. Strings are covered in Chapter 4.
- **Boolean**: `true` or `false`. The following are treated as `false` in PHP:
  - The keyword `false`
  - The integer `0`
  - The floating-point value `0.0`
  - An empty string (`''` or `""` with no space in between)
  - Zero as a string (`"0"`)
  - An array with zero elements
  - `NULL`

  Everything else is treated as `true`.
- **Array**: A major difference between PHP and ActionScript is that in PHP associative arrays have a length that can be measured and manipulated (something not possible in ActionScript). This will be covered in detail in Chapter 5.
- **Object**: This type is created by built-in or user-defined classes. You will come across the use of objects in Chapter 5, and then you will examine them in more detail in Chapter 7.
- **Resource**: When PHP accesses an external resource, such as a MySQL database or text file, it needs a reference to the connection. From the programmer's point of view, this is simply stored in a variable and requires no special handling.
- **NULL**: This datatype has one value only: the case-insensitive keyword `NULL`. As in ActionScript, it is used to deliberately set a variable to have no value. Note that `NULL` is a keyword and should not be enclosed in quotes.

Tracking changes in variable type

The implication of PHP loose-typing is that a variable can take on a variety of types in the course of a script. This happens quietly behind the scenes and is of no concern to the programmer most of the time. Occasionally, though, it can have unexpected consequences. Although we don't look at PHP operators and conditional statements until the next chapter, the ones used in this exercise work in exactly the same way as in ActionScript, so they should be perfectly understandable.

1. Create a new PHP document in the `phpflash/ch02` folder and call it `variables.php`.
2. Enter the following code:

```
<?php
$myVar = '12';
$type = gettype($myVar);
echo "Value: $myVar Type: $type ";
?>
```

`gettype()` is the PHP equivalent of the `typeof` operator in ActionScript, which is used to determine the datatype of a variable passed to it as an argument. Here, we store the result in the variable `$type`, and then use echo to display the results onscreen. Note that we're using single quotes in line 2, but double quotes in line 4. There's a method to this madness, and all will be explained in the next section.

3. Save the file and view it in a browser. You have probably already guessed the result, which should look like this:

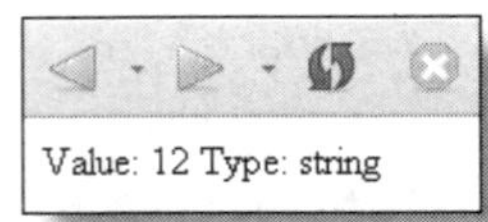
Value: 12 Type: string

4. In `variables.php`, position your cursor between the final e of `gettype` and the opening parenthesis. Insert a couple of spaces, save the file, and load it again. (Use the Refresh button on your browser to reload the page—you'll do this many times throughout this exercise.) There should be no difference. Now insert a few blank lines between `gettype` and `($myVar)`. Save and view the file again. What you see in the browser should remain exactly the same. PHP is ignoring any unnecessary whitespace and looking for the semicolon at the end of the statement. Remove the semicolon after `($myVar)`. Save and view the file again. This time, PHP will tell you in no uncertain terms that it's not happy:

Parse error: parse error, unexpected T_ECHO in **c:\htdocs\phpflash\ch02\variables.php** on line **14**

5. Put the semicolon back in, and amend the second line of the code like this:

```
$myVar = '12' + 1;
```

6. Save and view the file in a browser. PHP has performed a simple addition and changed the variable type.

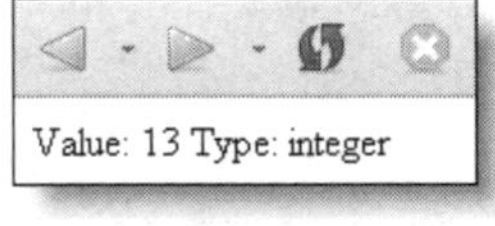
Value: 13 Type: integer

7. This time, change line 2 like this:

```
$myVar = '12' + 0.5;
```

8. Save and view the file. No real surprises. The only difference is that PHP has separate datatypes for integer and double (floating-point numbers), whereas ActionScript treats them all as `Number`.

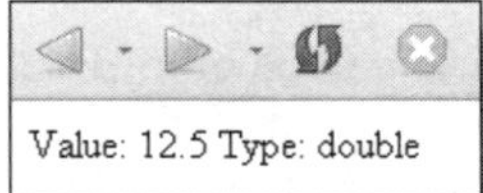
Value: 12.5 Type: double

9. Change line 2 like this:

```
$myVar = '12' + 1.0;
```

10. Save and view the file. This may come as a surprise. The value displayed in the browser is 13, which is an integer, but PHP regards its datatype as a double.

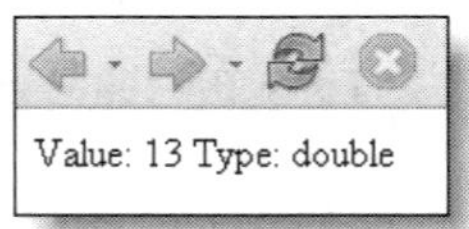
Value: 13 Type: double

This is because the code contains a decimal point. If the value after the decimal point is zero, the decimal fraction is omitted, but the datatype remains a double. The likelihood of this ever causing a problem in your code is extremely small (it would happen only if you were testing for a particular datatype), but it serves as a useful reminder that loose datatyping can hold hidden surprises.

11. This time, you're going to use $myVar as a Boolean. Often, you want to execute a particular block of code only if a calculation produces a result other than zero, or if a variable contains a usable value (in other words, it's not empty). Amend the code so it looks like this (the hash signs in lines 3 and 4 are there to disable part of the code temporarily):

```
<?php
$myVar = '12' + 0.5;
#$type = gettype($myVar);
#echo "Value: $myVar Type: $type";
if ($myVar) echo '<br>Equates to true';
?>
```

12. Save variables.php and view it in a browser. Because $myVar contains a value of 12.5, the Boolean test equates to true.

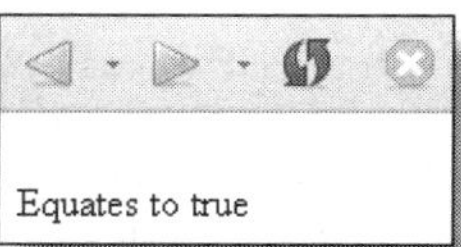

13. Now change line 2 to look like this (make sure you copy it exactly):

```
$myVar = 'false';
```

14. Save variables.php and load it into a browser:

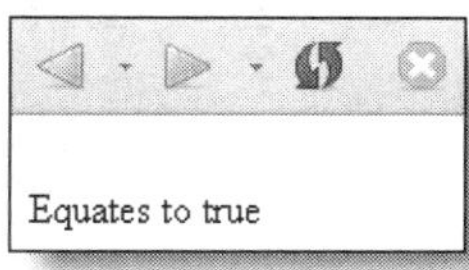

15. No, the printer hasn't made a mistake: you should get exactly the same result as before. Remove the comments in front of lines 3 and 4. When you view the page in a browser again, all should become clear.

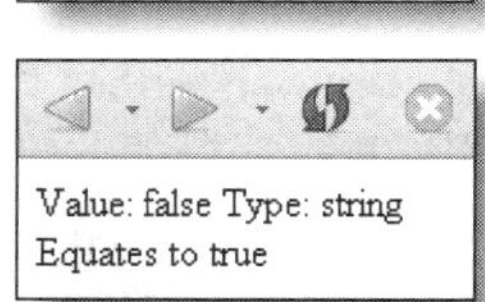

By enclosing false in quotes, it becomes a string. Refer back to the list at the beginning of this exercise: the only strings that equate to false are an empty string (a pair of quotes with nothing between them, not even any space) or 0 as a string. Paradoxical though it may seem, the word "false" **as a string** equates to true.

16. Finally, remove the quotes from around false in line 2. It's now a keyword and works as expected.

Enclosing the Boolean keywords true and false in quotes is a common beginner's mistake in both PHP and ActionScript. Once enclosed in quotes, these keywords lose their special meaning and are treated as strings.

Stringing words and variables together

It's often small things in life that make a difference, and unless you're a microbiologist or physicist, few things come much smaller than the humble period, full stop, or dot—whichever you prefer to call it. In spite of its size, it plays a very important role in PHP and ActionScript, but it's totally different in each language. Whereas the **dot operator** in ActionScript is the primary means of referring to object properties and nested movie clips, in PHP it's used to join strings together. To give it its formal name, it's the **concatenation operator**.

So, to join together two strings:

- **ActionScript style**: `"This is " + "a sentence.";`
- **PHP style**: `'This is ' . 'a sentence.';`

Note that PHP works in the same way as ActionScript by not adding any space between strings when joining them together. The amount of whitespace between the strings and the concatenation operator is ignored, so if a space is required, it needs to be added to one of the strings (or added as a string in its own right).

One of the great advantages of using a separate concatenation operator for strings is that PHP avoids the problem with ActionScript 1.0 when you attempt addition where at least one number is a string. When the plus operator is used, ActionScript accords precedence to strings, but PHP simply converts the strings to their equivalent number types.

```
"12" + "34" // ActionScript returns 1234
'12' + '34' // PHP returns 46
'12' . '34' // PHP returns 1234
```

PHP goes even further. If it can extract a number from the beginning of a string, it will happily perform a calculation with it.

```
'10 green bottles' - 1 // PHP returns 9
'green bottles 10' - 1 // PHP returns -1
```

Note that in the previous example, the text within the string is ignored. The first line returns just the number 9, not "9 green bottles." The 10 is ignored in the second line because it does not come at the beginning of the string, so it equates to zero.

The great disadvantage of the PHP concatenation operator is that it's so small, it's easy to miss, both when you check your scripts onscreen and when you copy code from a book. It's also easy to get confused when working with both ActionScript and PHP. You need to stay alert and make sure you always use the appropriate concatenation operator. Attempting to use the PHP operator in ActionScript will generate a compilation error, but PHP won't complain if you use the ActionScript operator. Instead, it may produce some strange results that are difficult to track down.

Double or single quotes? You will have noticed that most of the PHP examples in this chapter so far have used single quotes, but line 4 of the preceding exercise used double quotes. There are important reasons for this, although PHP programmers do not always adhere to them:

- Anything contained between single quotes is treated as a string literal.
- Double quotes signal to the PHP engine that they contain material to be processed.

A simple example should demonstrate what that means. If you want to test any of the following examples in a browser yourself, don't forget that all PHP must be enclosed in opening and closing PHP tags (<?php and ?>):

```
$name = 'David';
echo 'Hi, $name'; // Displays 'Hi, $name'
echo "Hi, $name"; // Displays 'Hi, David'
```

When using single quotes, $name is displayed literally without being processed. When enclosed in double quotes, the variable is interpreted and its value is displayed.

Another advantage of double quotes is that they enable you to include an apostrophe in a string.

```
echo "It's fine"; // Displays correctly
echo 'It's fine'; // Generates an error
```

The reason the second line generates an error is because the PHP interpreter sees the apostrophe (between the t and s) and treats it as the matching closing quote. You can get around this with an **escape sequence**, which tells PHP to treat the character in a special way. PHP escape sequences all begin with a backslash (\). By preceding the apostrophe with a backslash, PHP no longer treats it as a closing quote, and the string displays as intended.

```
echo 'It\'s fine'; // Displays correctly
```

Double quotes are so handy that many PHP programmers use them all the time, but the official recommendation is to use the method that requires the least processing power. If your strings contain variables that require processing, it makes sense to use double quotes. If they contain only literal characters, the PHP engine traverses the entire string looking for variables to process, finds none, and then backtracks before treating the string as plain text. On short scripts, it all happens in a fraction of a second, but the longer and more complex your scripts become, the more time is wasted. If that doesn't convince you, just consider that, on most keyboards, the double quote requires pressing two keys (*Shift+"*), whereas the single quote is a single keystroke.

While we're on the subject of escape sequences, Table 2-3 lists the main ones used within double quotes, because you'll use some of them in the PHP script for the Flash application you're about to build.

Table 2-3. The main escape sequences used in PHP strings

Escape sequence	Character represented in double-quoted string
\"	Double quote
\n	New line
\r	Carriage return
\t	Tab
\\	Backslash
\$	Dollar sign
\{	Opening curly brace
\}	Closing curly brace
\[	Opening square bracket
\]	Closing square bracket

It may seem that quotes are a simple subject to spend such a long time on, but when you come to work with database queries later in the book, you will realize just how important building strings with the right combination of quotes can be.

Sending feedback from Flash by email

Still with me? I certainly hope so, because it's time to put some of the knowledge you've gained thus far to good use. Don't worry if everything didn't sink in the first time around. One of the aims of this book is to provide you with a useful reference that you can come back to in the future.

You're going to build a Flash form for visitors to your site to send comments, orders, subscription details, or whatever you like. The form can have any number of fields, but to keep things simple, I decided on just five. The finished form is shown in Figure 2-1.

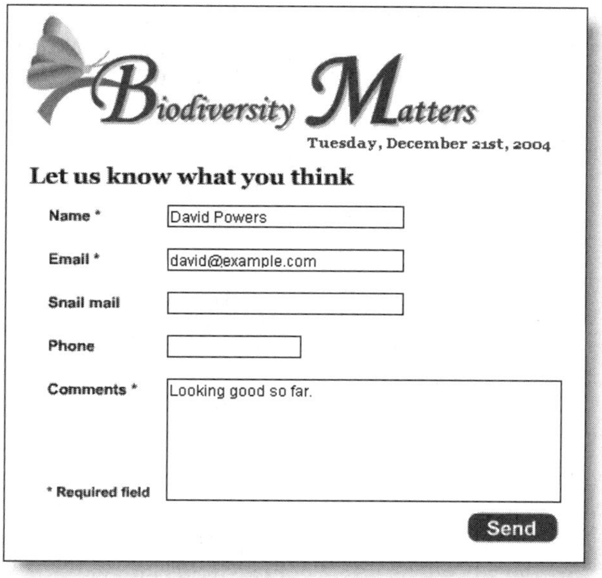

Figure 2-1. The completed feedback form

Building the Flash feedback form

You can build the form yourself following these instructions, or if you just want to concentrate on the PHP and ActionScript, the final version is `biodiverse05.fla` in the download files for this chapter.

Creating this type of feedback form is the ideal situation in which to use the version 2 `TextInput` and `TextArea` components introduced in Flash MX 2004. I have decided against using them, though, because I know that some readers may still be using Flash MX. More important, Macromedia has announced that fundamental changes will be made to component architecture in the next full release of Flash (expected sometime during 2005). Consequently, I have stuck with the basics: using static and dynamic text fields. Once you have the basic PHP/Flash functionality working, you can adapt this application to use either version 2 components or whatever eventually replaces them.

> *Where you keep your FLA files is a matter of preference. I prefer to keep them in a separate folder outside the server root. If you do this, you need to open* File ➤ Publish Settings *(Ctrl+Shift+F12/Opt+Shift+F12) and set the file location for your SWF and HTML files to the relevant folder in your server root. In this case, it would be* `C:\htdocs\phpflash\ch02` *on Windows or the equivalent folder in* `Sites` *on a Mac.*
>
> *If you are using the download files, save each one as* `biodiverse.fla` *before working in it. That way, you can always go back to a file that you know is correct if anything goes wrong.*

1. Continue with the Flash document you created at the beginning of this chapter to display the date from PHP, or use `biodiverse02.fla` from the download files. Insert three new layers between the date and actions layers. Your timeline should now look like the one shown here:

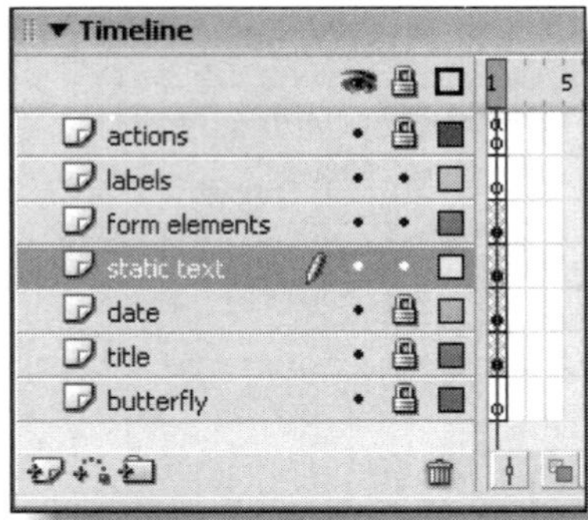

2. Lay out the form on the static text and form elements layers. For the static text labels, I used Arial 12pt bold and left 35 pixels vertical space between each one. This is to leave room for error messages that will be added later above the three required fields if the user leaves any of them blank.

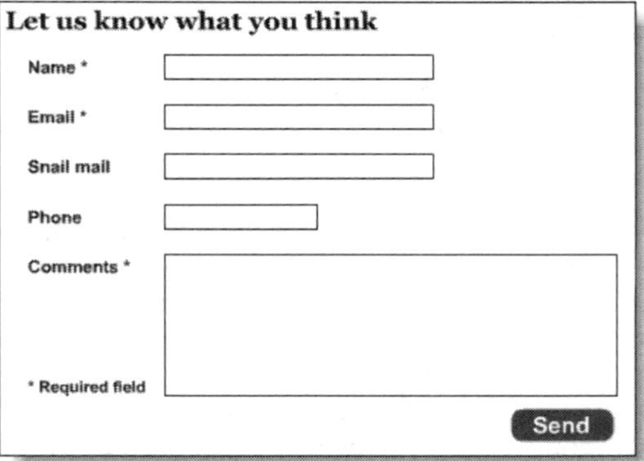

3. Alongside each of the static text labels, insert an input text field for the user to enter the necessary details. Give each one an instance name, naming them as follows from top to bottom: name_txt, email_txt, snail_txt, phone_txt, and comments_txt. The following screenshot shows the settings I used for the first one.

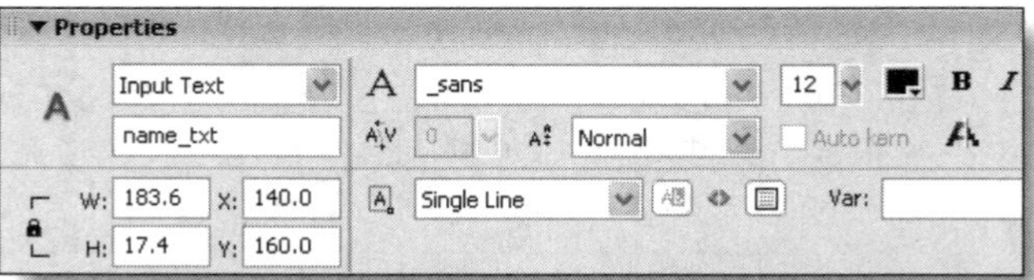

4. The final input text field is where the user will wax lyrical (you hope!) about your site, so give it plenty of room and make it a multiline field. Since this is an example application, I have used only a single-line input field for the user's address. In a real application, you would probably want to add one or more extra fields for city, zip code, and so on.

5. Create a button symbol for the user to submit the form, and place it at the bottom with an instance name of submit_btn. If you are using `biodiverse02.fla`, you will find one already made in the Library panel (*Ctrl+L/⌘+L*).

6. Test your movie (*Ctrl+Enter/⌘+Return*). It should look like Figure 2-1.

7. There's nothing more frustrating with online forms than receiving incomplete information, so let's take a few simple steps to try to make sure users fill in the required fields. Just above the name_txt input text field, insert a dynamic text field and give it an instance name of error1_txt. To make the text stand out, set the text color to red (#FF0000). The following image shows the settings I used:

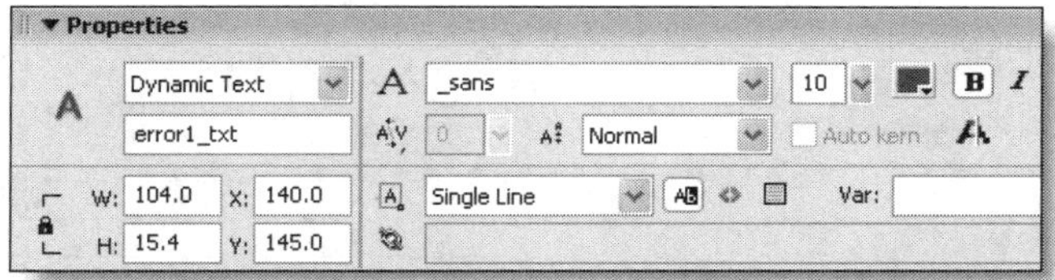

8. Create two more dynamic text fields, with instance names of error2_txt and error3_txt, and place them above the input text fields for email and comments. Figure 2-2 shows where the dynamic text fields should go. The instance names have been displayed inside each field purely as a guide to their location. When building the form yourself, leave the fields blank. Again, I will use ActionScript to make sure the dynamic fields are wide enough to contain the text to be displayed. If you test your movie now, it should still look exactly the same as Figure 2-1. If you need to check your code, compare it with `biodiverse03.fla`.

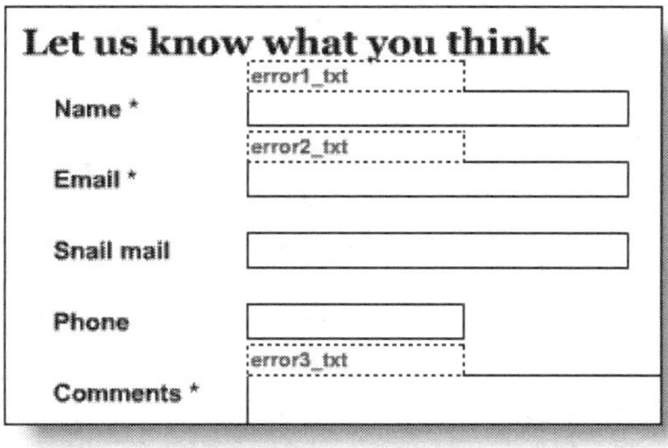

Figure 2-2. Where to locate the three dynamic text fields that will display error messages

Coding the back-end of the interface

When the user clicks the Send button, you need to check whether the required fields have been filled in and display an appropriate error message if there's a problem. Equally, if everything's OK, you need to keep users informed of their progress.

1. Continue working with the same file, or open `biodiverse03.fla` from the download files for this chapter. In the timeline, highlight frame 40 on all layers and enter a blank frame (*F5*) to extend them to the same length. If you just want to inspect the movie without typing all the code yourself, open `biodiverse04.fla`.
2. On the labels layer, enter keyframes (*F6*) on frames 5, 15, 25, and 35, and label them as follows in the Properties panel: theForm, sending, acknowledge, and failure. When you've finished, your timeline should look like this:

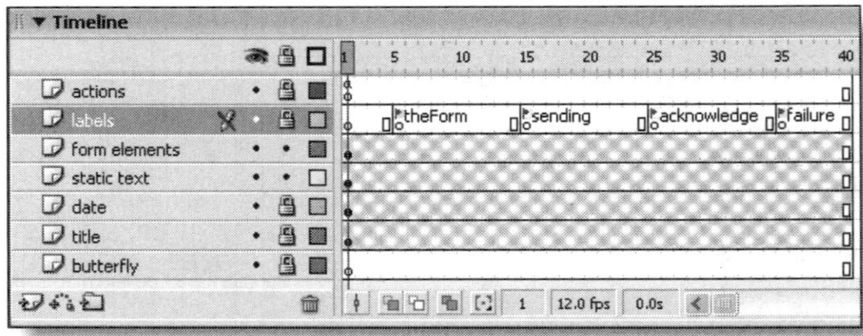

3. Enter keyframes on frames 5 and 15 of the form elements and static text layers. This will ensure the form labels and text fields are copied across to both frames. You want to keep everything on frame 5, but frame 15 needs to be cleared of all form elements. Delete the entire content of both layers on frame 15 so the only things that remain are the butterfly logo, the main title, and the dynamic text field for the date.
4. Create a static text field to inform the user that the message is being sent.

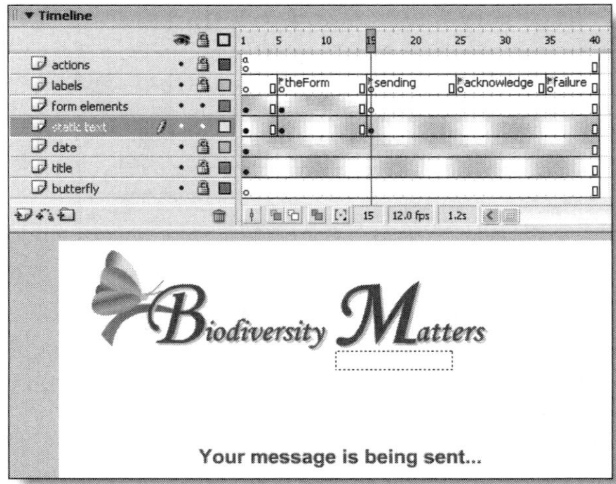

5. If you test your movie now, it will constantly loop between displaying the form and the message on frame 15. To prevent that from happening, you need to stop the playhead. Highlight frame 1 on the actions layer and open the Actions panel. If you are using the download files, the script from the beginning of the chapter will be there. Immediately below the existing script, type

```
gotoAndStop("theForm");
```

You put the form on a separate keyframe because the existing script will attempt to load the date from `today2.php` every time the playhead returns to frame 1—a small but totally unnecessary waste of bandwidth for information that changes only once every 24 hours.

6. Scroll to the top of the Actions panel and enter the following script:

```
function checkForm():Boolean {
  // this checks whether required fields have been filled in
  // initialize missing flag on assumption everything OK
  var missing:Boolean = false;
  // clear all error text fields
  error1_txt.text = error2_txt.text = error3_txt.text = "";
  // check each field
  // if problem is encountered, display message
  // and set missing flag to true
  if (name_txt.text == "") {
    error1_txt.text = "Please enter your name";
    missing = true;
  }
  if (email_txt.text.indexOf("@") == -1) {
    error2_txt.text = "Please enter a valid email address";
    missing = true;
  }
  if (comments_txt.text == “”) {
    error3_txt.text = “You have not entered any comments”;
    missing = true;
  }
  // if missing is true, return false
  // otherwise return true
  return missing ? false : true;
}
```

The ActionScript in this book uses static (strict) data typing, employing the new post-colon syntax introduced in ActionScript 2.0. If you are using Flash MX or simply prefer doing things the old way, leave the datatype declarations out. See also Appendix B for advice on converting the scripts in this book to work with Flash MX.

For more information on data typing, see Foundation ActionScript for Flash MX 2004 *by Sham Bhangal (friends of ED, ISBN: 1-59059-305-7).*

The purpose of this function is to check that the form has been correctly filled in. Unfortunately, ActionScript is not very well adapted to this type of thing. It can be done much more efficiently in PHP. The downside is that using PHP to validate user input involves a round-trip to the server if any errors are discovered. So it's a good idea to do some rough and ready checks first with ActionScript to catch any obvious errors before you do more thorough checks with PHP.

The function begins by declaring a Boolean variable called `missing` and setting it to `false`, on the assumption that the user would not normally click the Submit button unless the form was complete. All the error messages are then set to an empty string. This is necessary to clear any error messages triggered by previous problems. Then follow three conditional statements that run very simple tests on the name, email and comments fields. If the name or comments fields are empty, or if the submitted email address doesn't contain the @ character, an appropriate error message is displayed, and the `missing` variable is set to `true`. Finally, the function uses the **conditional operator** to check whether `missing` is `true` or `false`, and it returns the appropriate value.

> *If you're not familiar with the conditional operator (`?:`), sometimes known as the **ternary operator**, it's a useful shorthand found in ActionScript, PHP, and many other programming languages that performs the same function as an `if...` else statement. Its use is described in the next chapter.*

7. Immediately after the `checkForm()` function, insert the following code (on about line 26):

```
function sendMessage():Void {
  // check whether form has been correctly filled in
  var formOK:Boolean = checkForm();
  // if no problems, process the form and send variables to PHP script
  if (formOK) {
    // Form processing goes here
    // display message informing user that email is being sent
    gotoAndStop("sending");
  }
};
```

When it's completed, this is the main function that will send the message when the user clicks the Send button. It starts by calling `checkForm()` and assigns the result to a Boolean variable called `formOK`. If `checkForm()` returns `true`, the form will be processed, and the email will be sent. This is where `LoadVars` will eventually do much of the hard work. At the moment, there's just a placeholder comment to indicate where the code will go. Finally, the playhead is sent to the frame labeled sending, which displays the message set in step 4.

8. You now need to assign the function to the `submit_btn.onRelease` event handler on frame 5. A lot of Flash developers attach button events directly to buttons, but I prefer to keep all the main ActionScript functionality on the main timeline, where it's easier to access and maintain. Close the Actions panel, select frame 5 on the actions layer, and insert a keyframe. With the keyframe still selected, open the Actions panel again and insert the following line of code:

```
submit_btn.onRelease = sendMessage;
```

This simply assigns the `sendMessage()` function to the Send button's `onRelease` event. Note that you should **not** add parentheses to the end of `sendMessage`. This is because you are assigning the function to an event handler, not running it.

9. Test the movie, and click the Send button without entering anything in any of the fields. The error messages should appear over the three required fields, like this:

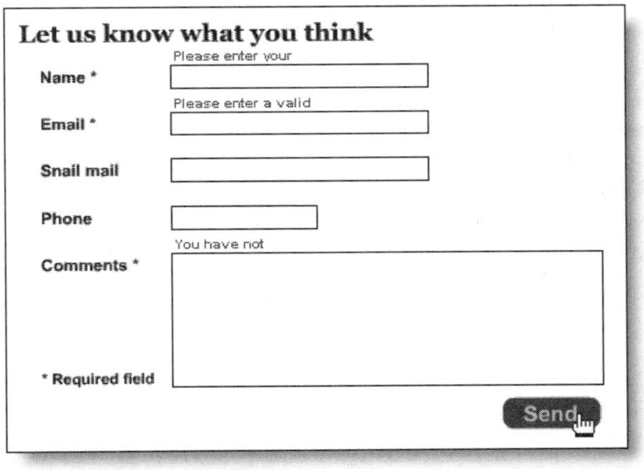

If nothing happens, make sure all the input and dynamic text fields and the Send button have the correct instance names on both frames 1 and 5. If you named them correctly before inserting the keyframes on frame 5, the instance names should have been copied automatically.

All the error messages are truncated, so you need to set them to expand automatically.

10. Open the Actions panel on frame 5 of the actions layer, and add the following code beneath the function assignment you added in step 8:

```
error1_txt.autoSize = true;
error2_txt.autoSize = true;
error3_txt.autoSize = true;
```

11. Test the movie again. Type something into the name field and click Send. The error message over the name field should disappear, but the other two error messages should now display at their full width. Do the same with the other fields, and when all required fields are filled, you should be taken to the sending page created in step 4.

The design side of the Flash movie is almost complete. You just need to add two simple frames and a little ActionScript before moving on to the heart of the matter: making it all work with `LoadVars` and PHP.

12. Highlight frame 25 on the static text layer and insert a keyframe. This is the frame that will display when the message has been sent successfully. I have simply edited the previous text to say Thank you, but in a real application, you would probably want to take the user to some other content or navigation.

13. To make the application a little more user-friendly for testing, insert keyframes on frame 25 of the form elements and actions layers. Put a button labeled Back on the form elements layer and give it an instance name of back_btn. (There's a ready-made button in the Library of `biodiverse03.fla`.) Select the keyframe on frame 25 of the actions layer, and insert the following line of code in the Actions panel:

```
back_btn.onRelease = backToForm;
```

The `backToForm()` function will be created soon.

14. Highlight frame 35 (the one that you labeled failure in step 2) on the static text and form elements layers, and enter keyframes on both layers. Lay the frame out as shown in the following image. The Back button should already be there from frame 25, although you may need to reposition it to make room for the rest of the content. On the static text layer, insert a message informing the user there has been a problem, and on the form elements layer, insert a multiline dynamic text area with an instance name of failure_txt.

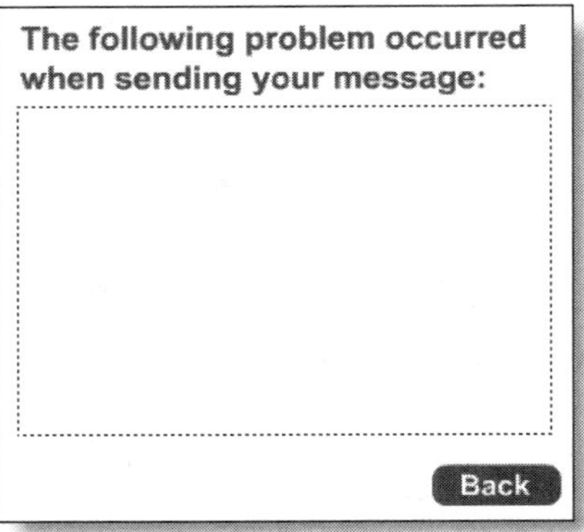

15. Highlight frame 35 on the actions layer, and insert a keyframe. Open the Actions panel, and assign the same function to the Back button as in step 13:

```
back_btn.onRelease = backToForm;
```

16. You now need to create the `backToForm()` function. It goes with the main ActionScript on frame 1 of the actions layer. Place it immediately after the `sendMessage()` function (around line 36). It simply sends the playhead back to the frame labeled theForm.

```
function backToForm():Void {
  // send playhead back to the main form
  gotoAndStop("theForm");
} .
```

You can compare your code and layout of the movie with biodiverse04.fla in the download files. The next stage tackles the important business of sending and receiving data from PHP with LoadVars.

Using LoadVars to gather and send variables

As I mentioned before, what makes LoadVars far more efficient than its predecessor, the loadVariables() global function, is that LoadVars doesn't simply gather every variable on your main timeline and shoot them off at your target external source. You choose which variables you want to send. If there are many of them, this means a lot more work at scripting time, but it makes the transfer much faster. You can also create different instances of LoadVars to respond to different events, and it's very easy to handle large amounts of incoming data—as you'll see later, when you start working with databases. So the advantages of using LoadVars greatly outweigh any extra work involved.

You need to create a new LoadVars instance before you can access the methods of this class. It's also considered good practice to create separate instances for sending and receiving data. This makes it easier to keep tabs on what's coming and going.

1. Continue working with the same Flash document or open biodiverse04.fla from the download files. (If you prefer to look at the completed code, it's in biodiverse05.fla.) Select frame 1 of the actions layer. Open the Actions panel, and insert the following code close to the bottom of the existing script. If you are using the date script from the beginning of the chapter, it should go just after the code to initialize the getDate instance of LoadVars (around line 47).

   ```
   // initialize LoadVars to send form data
   // and receive response from the PHP script
   var message:LoadVars = new LoadVars();
   var messageSent:LoadVars = new LoadVars();
   ```

   This creates two instances of LoadVars: message will be used to send the form contents to the PHP script, and messageSent will be used to check the response from the PHP script, informing you whether the email was sent successfully.

   The LoadVars class works by treating all external data as properties of a LoadVars instance. So outgoing variables will need to be assigned to properties of message, and incoming variables will be accessible inside Flash as properties of messageSent. Don't worry if you don't understand what I mean by "properties"—you soon will.

2. At the beginning of this chapter, you used LoadVars to receive the date from a PHP script. So let's look at this aspect in more detail first. When using LoadVars to receive external data, you use the LoadVars.onLoad event handler to determine when all the data has been received. The PHP script (which you'll create shortly) will send back a variable called sent. If there's a problem, it will also send back a variable called reason. The values held in these variables automatically become properties of messageSent. So, inside Flash you can access the values of the PHP variables as messageSent.sent, and—if it's been set—as messageSent.reason.

Insert the following function immediately before the last line of the existing code (gotoAndStop("theForm");) in the Actions panel (around line 57):

```
messageSent.onLoad = function() {
  if (this.sent == "OK") {
    gotoAndStop("acknowledge");
  } else {
    gotoAndStop("failure");
    failure_txt.text = this.reason;
  }
};
```

Because the function is assigned to the messageSent.onLoad handler, the variables received from the PHP script can be referred to using the this keyword. So this.sent is the same as messageSent.sent; it just involves less typing. If the PHP script is successful in sending the email, it sends the following name/value pair to messageSent:

```
sent=OK
```

Inside the Flash movie, this becomes messageSent.sent with a value of OK. In that event, the function sends the playhead to the frame labeled acknowledge.

If the operation fails, what will be sent back to the Flash movie will begin like this:

```
sent=failed&reason=there...
```

Inside the Flash movie this is treated as the equivalent of the following:

```
messageSent.sent = "failed";
messageSent.reason = "there...";
```

If the value of sent is not OK, the movie displays the frame labeled failure and sets the content of failure_txt to whatever value is returned in the reason variable.

3. That deals with the result, but you still need to send the message in the first place. This works the same way as receiving data, but in reverse. Anything you want to send as a variable to PHP needs first to be assigned to a property of the LoadVars instance being used to send the data—in this case, message.

Scroll back to the sendMessage() function, and find the Form processing goes here placeholder (around line 31). There are five input text fields in the form, so you need to assign their text values to five new properties of the message instance of LoadVars. Immediately after the placeholder, insert this code:

```
message.from = name_txt.text;
message.email = email_txt.text;
message.snail = snail_txt.text;
message.phone = phone_txt.text;
message.comments = comments_txt.text;
```

LoadVars sends each property to the PHP script using the HTTP POST method, so once received by PHP, message.from is treated as a PHP variable called $_POST['from'], message.email becomes $_POST['email'], and so on. What these five lines of code do, in effect, is assign the value of each text field to variables that can be accessed easily inside PHP.

Note that when creating the new properties of message, you don't use the var keyword, because you are simply adding new properties to an existing object. The names of the properties can be anything, as long as they are valid as variable names in both PHP and ActionScript.

4. All that's left to do now is send your new variables to the PHP script. That's easily done by using the sendAndLoad() method of LoadVars. This method requires two arguments: a string containing the address of the external script and a reference to the object that will receive the server's response. A third argument is optional. This is a string specifying the HTTP method (GET or POST) used to send the data. If omitted, the default is POST.

The principal difference between GET and POST is that GET sends variables as part of the URL, whereas POST sends them separately. GET also imposes certain limitations on the length of information that can be transferred. Most applications involving LoadVars are better suited to POST, so its availability as the default is particularly convenient. Use the third, optional argument to LoadVars only when there's a specific reason for wanting to use GET.

Enter the following line of code immediately after the five lines inserted in the previous step:

```
message.sendAndLoad("http://localhost/phpflash/ch02/feedback.php?ck="
➥+ new Date().getTime(), messageSent);
```

"What on earth is that ?ck=" + new Date().getTime() doing at the end of the address of the PHP file?" you may well ask. It's to get around a little problem with browsers caching data from external sources. Most of the time, the browser will think, "Oh, we've seen that lot before," and it will send Flash the old data. To force a fresh reload of data, you have to add a query string that's likely to be unique. It can be anything, such as a randomly generated number. I've chosen ck (for cache killer) and the current time (you can't get more unique than that!). You can check your code against biodiverse05.fla in the download files.

Everything is now ready on the Flash side. At long last, it's time to bring on the PHP!

Testing that PHP is receiving the right variables

At the beginning of the chapter, you tested the output of a PHP page to make sure it was sending the correct information to Flash. It's a good idea to do the same test in reverse. Once you're familiar with the way Flash and PHP interact with each other, you probably won't have to do this every time, but the technique is very simple. It's worth learning now, so you can use it for any project, big or small.

1. Open whichever script editor you plan to use for PHP, and enter the following code:

```
<?php
foreach ($_POST as $key=>$value) {
  $received .= "$key = $value\r\n";
  }

$printout = fopen('variables.txt', 'w');
fwrite($printout, $received);
fclose($printout);
?>
```

   In Mac OS X, this script requires that read/write permissions be applied to the `phpflash/ch02` folder. Highlight the `ch02` folder in Finder and set the same permissions as described on pages 335 and 336.

2. Save the page in phpflash/ch02 as `feedback.php`.
3. In Flash, test your movie by pressing *Ctrl+Enter/⌘+Return*. Fill in each of the fields with some test data, and click the Submit button.

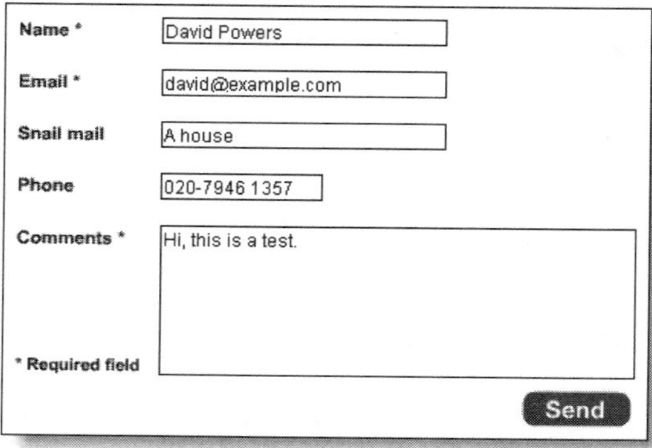

4. If all goes well, you should see this friendly message:

   Your message is being sent...

   followed by this:

   The following problem occurred when sending your message:
   undefined

To borrow a little advice from the cover of the most remarkable book ever to come out of the great publishing corporations of Ursa Minor, *DON'T PANIC*. Rather than indicating a problem, it tells you that everything is probably working.

5. Use Windows Explorer (or Finder on the Mac) to browse to the phpflash/ch02 folder (it will be in the C:\htdocs folder on Windows or in the Sites folder for your *username* on a Mac). You should now find a text file called variables.txt. Double-click the icon to open it, and you should see something like this:

   They may not be in the order you expected, but all your variables are there. If they're not, you need to go back and check both your PHP file and the ActionScript in your FLA file. If you can't work out what the problem is, check them both carefully against the files from this book's download site.

6. The script uses a simple loop to gather the values of all the variables, and then it uses some PHP file-manipulation functions to write the output to a text file. It will work with any Flash application where you need to check the value of variables being sent by LoadVars. This can be very useful if you are using ActionScript to manipulate data before transmitting it to PHP. Remember the programmer's motto: Garbage In, Garbage Out (GIGO). Unexpected output from PHP may be the result of unexpected input, so it's always worth checking. Rename feedback.php and save it as variable_checker.php.

Loops will be covered in detail in Chapter 5. To learn more about PHP file-manipulation functions, consult Beginning PHP 5 and MySQL: From Novice to Professional *by W. Jason Gilmore (Apress, ISBN 1-893115-51-8), or see the PHP online documentation at* www.php.net/manual/en/ref.filesystem.php.

Processing the data and sending the email with PHP

Finally, the pièce de résistance—the bit you've been waiting for: sending the form output by email. PHP has a very nifty function called mail(), appropriately enough. It takes up to four arguments, three of them required and one optional:

- The address the email is being sent to
- The subject (which appears in the email subject line)
- The content of the message
- Any additional headers recognized by the email protocol (optional)

All you have to do is gather the information and pass it to the mail() function. So, let's do it!

1. In theory, you can just put all the details between the parentheses of the mail() function, but it's far simpler to gather everything into variables first. Reopen feedback.php and remove all the code you entered in the previous section. (It should now be safely backed up in variable_checker.php for future use.) All you should leave are the opening and closing PHP tags.

2. Decide where you want to send the email to and what the subject line will be. Assign both to variables, like this:

```
$to = 'david@example.com';
$subject = 'Feedback from Flash site';
```

3. The next stage is to build the message. Flash is sending the form input as five separate variables, but PHP needs the message passed to it as a single string. Enter the following line of code between what you have just typed and the closing PHP tag:

```
$message = 'From: '.$_POST['from']."\n\n";
```

The first part, `$message = 'From: '`, is simple enough. It assigns to the variable `$message` a string containing the word "From" followed by a colon and space. Then comes a period—the concatenation operator. This means that whatever value the following variable contains will be added to the string. All the data sent by `LoadVars` was transmitted using the HTTP `POST` method. PHP gathers this in a special `POST` array, which you access by putting the variable name—**without** a leading dollar sign—in quotes between the square brackets of `$_POST[]`. So `$_POST['from']` contains whatever was sent from Flash as `message.from`. (Arrays are covered in detail in Chapter 5.)

Then comes another concatenation operator followed by `"\n\n"`. Note that this time I've used double quotes, so this part of the string will be processed. If you refer back to Table 2-3, you'll see this will be interpreted as two new-line characters. This ensures that the email arrives in a human-friendly format, with two lines between each item.

Quite a bit going on there! Fortunately, the next few lines are very similar.

> *You may wonder why I didn't put the whole line in double quotes, because it contains a variable that also needs processing. Like all languages, PHP has its strange quirks, and putting `$_POST['from']` in a double-quoted string would generate an error. All will be revealed in Chapter 5.*

4. Before typing in the next line, take a really close look at it:

```
$message .= 'Email: '.$_POST['email']."\n\n";
```

See anything unusual about the way the value is assigned to the variable? Look again. There's a period immediately to the left of the equal sign. This has the same effect as += in ActionScript (at least where strings are concerned). It adds the value on the right to the existing value of the variable, in this case `$message`.

> *Because the PHP concatenation operator is so tiny, it's easy to miss. Flash developers have a reputation for loving tiny text, but when working with PHP, you may find increasing the default font size of your text editor saves both your eyes and any hair you may still have left.*

5. The next three lines are straightforward. They add the contents of the three remaining input fields to the variable containing the message.

```
$message .= 'Address: '.$_POST['snail']."\n\n";
$message .= 'Phone: '.$_POST['phone']."\n\n";
$message .= 'Comments: '.$_POST['comments'];
```

6. The script has already gathered the information needed for the three required arguments, so you could just pass them to `mail()` and be done with it. By using the fourth, optional argument, though, you can add a really special touch to the way your feedback form works. There's a full list of valid email headers at `www.ietf.org/rfc/rfc2076.txt`. There are a lot of them, but you're going to use just two. Add the following lines to the existing code:

```
$additionalHeaders = "From: Flash feedback<feedback@example.com>\n";
$additionalHeaders .= 'Reply-To: '.$_POST['email'];
```

The first line adds the address the email has come from. When using the `mail()` function, it's Apache that sends the message, so you end up with a rather unfriendly-looking nobody (or whatever name the server is running as) in the `From:` line of the email. Put the name you want displayed after the `From:` and the actual address you want to use inside the angle brackets. Notice that the entire string is in double quotes and ends with `\n`. This places a new-line character at the end of the string, because the email protocol requires each header to be on a separate line.

The second line assigns the user's email address to the `Reply-To:` header. You'll see what a smart move this is when you come to test everything later.

7. Now you're ready to send the email. Again, you could just put all four variables between the parentheses of `mail()` and be done with it, but it would be nice to let the visitor know the message has been sent successfully. You also need to send the appropriate data back to Flash to avoid the `undefined` variable you got when testing everything during the previous exercise. The `mail()` function returns `true` if the message was sent successfully, so you need to capture that value in a variable and use it to send the appropriate data back to Flash. I cover the use of conditional statements in the next chapter, but if you're familiar with ActionScript, the structure will come as no surprise.

Enter the final section of the PHP script as follows:

```
$OK = mail($to, $subject, $message, $additionalHeaders);
if ($OK) {
  echo 'sent=OK';
  }
  else {
  echo 'sent=failed&reason='. urlencode('There seems to be a
➥problem with the server. Please try later.');
  }
```

As you can see, arguments to a PHP function are separated by commas, in the same way as in ActionScript. They must also be in the order the function expects them to be. The Boolean value returned by `mail()` is captured in the variable called `$OK`, which is then used to control the script's output. If the message is sent successfully, the PHP script sends the string sent=OK to the browser. If you were creating an ordinary web page, that is what you would see onscreen. In this case, though, the script is only being called by your Flash movie. When it receives this output, it triggers the messageSent.onLoad event handler in your ActionScript.

LoadVars expects data as a string of name/value pairs. Each variable name is separated from its value by an equal sign (=), with no spaces on either side. Multiple name/value pairs are separated by an ampersand (&), again with no spaces on either side. Variables that contain anything other than unaccented alphanumeric characters must be URL encoded. Fortunately, PHP has a handy function called urlencode() to do just that. You can pass urlencode() a string literal or a variable containing a string. On this occasion, it's simpler to pass the value of the reason variable as a string literal, but in future chapters you'll see when it's more convenient to use variables. Although you need to URL encode the PHP output, Flash does the decoding automatically. So, depending on the result it receives, your movie will display either a thank-you message or a failure message and reason. Here's the messageSent.onLoad handler from the ActionScript to remind you of how it works:

```
messageSent.onLoad = function() {
  if (this.sent == "OK") {
    gotoAndStop("acknowledge");
  } else {
    gotoAndStop("failure");
    failure_txt.text = this.reason;
  }
};
```

If you're wondering why the reason is sent back and displayed as dynamic text, it's because I plan to come back to this application in Chapter 4 and add some server-side validation, so the reason for failure won't always be the same.

8. Save feedback.php and check your PHP script for accuracy. The full listing follows with inline comments added (substitute your own email details in the $to and $additionalHeaders variables).

```
<?php
// initialize variables for To and Subject fields
$to = 'david@example.com';
$subject = 'Feedback from Flash site';

// build message body from variables received in the POST array
$message = 'From: '.$_POST['from']."\n\n";
$message .= 'Email: '.$_POST['email']."\n\n";
$message .= 'Address: '.$_POST['snail']."\n\n";
$message .= 'Phone: '.$_POST['phone']."\n\n";
$message .= 'Comments: '.$_POST['comments'];

// add additional email headers for more user-friendly reply
$additionalHeaders = "From: Flash feedback<feedback@example.com>\n";
$additionalHeaders .= "Reply-To: $_POST[email]";
```

```
// send email message
$OK = mail($to, $subject, $message, $additionalHeaders);
// let Flash know what the result was
if ($OK) {
  echo 'sent=OK';
  }
  else {
  echo 'sent=failed&reason='. urlencode('There seems to be a
➥problem with the server. Please try later.');
  }
?>
```

9. Now for the moment of truth. Test the Flash movie, either within Flash or by publishing the SWF file and loading `biodiverse.html` in your browser, which you can do by pressing *F12*. Enter some details in the form, and click Send. If you have built everything correctly, the sending message will display, and after a few seconds . . .

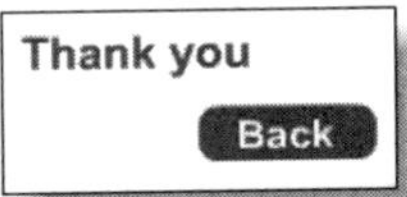

10. Didn't work? Assuming you've already tested that the variables are being received by PHP as described in the previous section, check your script against the full listing in step 8 or the download files for this chapter. Also check that Apache is running on your computer, that you are connected to the Internet, and that your mail settings are correct. (Windows users need to set SMTP in `php.ini`, as described in Chapter 1. Mac OS X should automatically use the computer's default outgoing mail setting.) If you still can't get it to work, publish the movie and upload `today2.php`, `feedback.php`, `biodiverse.html`, and `biodiverse.swf` to your hosting server, and test it there.

> *Remember that before uploading your SWF files to a remote server, you must change the address of the PHP file in all LoadVars routines. The* `localhost` *address is for testing purposes within Flash only.*

11. Before uploading your SWF file to a remote server, remove the testing address like this. Find the following line in the ActionScript attached to frame 1 of the actions layer:

```
message.sendAndLoad("http://localhost/phpflash/ch02/feedback.php?ck="
➥+ new Date().getTime(), messageSent);
```

Change it to this:

```
message.sendAndLoad("feedback.php?ck="
➥+ new Date().getTime(), messageSent);
```

This assumes the SWF and the PHP file will be in the same folder on the remote server. Adjust the address accordingly with the right path if you want to keep your PHP scripts in a dedicated folder.

12. After sending a test message, check your email. Your inbox should contain a nicely formatted feedback message something like the one shown in Figure 2-3. Perfect. Well, almost. Take a look at the apostrophes. They're preceded by backslashes, as though

escaped in a PHP double-quoted string. It's because of a `php.ini` setting called `magic_quotes_gpc`. In the previous chapter, I drew the attention of Windows users to this setting and suggested they leave it on for the time being. Mac users who installed the PHP package from Marc Liyanage won't have any backslashes, because the version of `php.ini` included with his PKG file has `magic_quotes_gpc` turned off. The reality of the situation is that some servers use this setting, while others don't. I'll come back to this issue in Chapter 4, and show you how to deal with apostrophes and quotes if this happens.

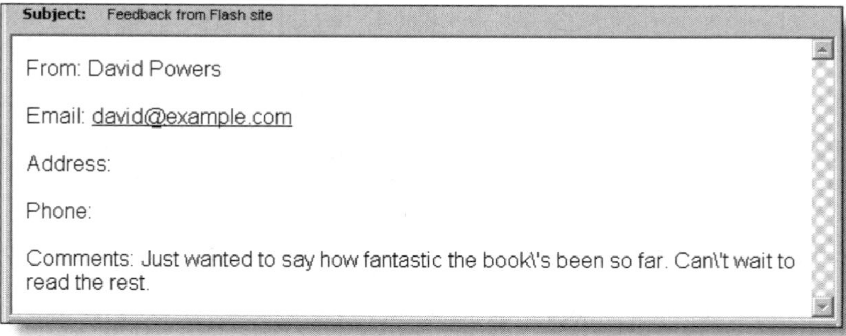

Figure 2-3. The email is nicely formatted, but some configurations of PHP automatically insert backslashes in front of the apostrophes.

13. Click the Reply button in your email program and you'll see why I suggested you use the `Reply-To:` additional header. Although the email has come from `feedback@example.com`, the reply will go automatically to the person who sent the feedback (assuming, of course, that a genuine address was given in the first place).

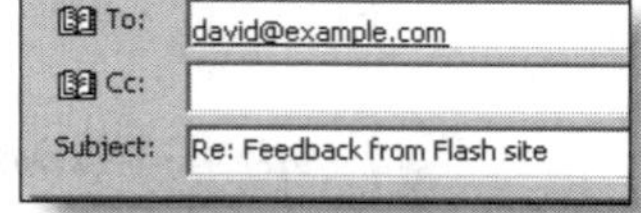

Experienced PHP scripters spend a lot of their time consulting the PHP online documentation. It's a good habit to get into. The descriptions are often short and include useful examples. You can read more about the `mail()` function at `www.php.net/manual/en/ref.mail.php`.

Progress so far

Phew! It's been quite a journey. Most introductory books on PHP start off by doing things that are of little practical use, but not only have you learned the basic grammar of PHP, you've also created a useful application that brings together the power of Flash and PHP. Along the way, you've learned how to use `LoadVars` to send and receive data, and how to check the right data is being transmitted.

Let's just pause a moment and recap some of this chapter's most important points:

- All pages containing PHP scripts should have a PHP extension, and they should be served through Apache.
- PHP scripts must be enclosed between PHP tags (`<?php` and `?>` are the preferred style).
- PHP variables are case sensitive and must be prefixed with a dollar sign—`$myVar`, `$myvar`, and `$MYvaR` are all different.
- PHP names must begin with a letter or an underscore, and they can contain only alphanumeric characters and the underscore.
- All statements must end with a semicolon.
- Whitespace is ignored, except within strings.
- PHP uses a period or full stop (`.`)—not the plus sign (+)—to join strings together.
- PHP uses the hash sign (#) as a third method of commenting. The two other methods (// and /* */) are identical to ActionScript.
- Variables sent from Flash by `LoadVars` are retrieved by putting the variable name in quotes between the square brackets of `$_POST[]` (for example, `$_POST['from']`).
- Variables returned to `LoadVars` must be in name/value pairs with an equal sign (=) separating each name and value, and an ampersand (&) separating each pair. Any non-alphanumeric characters must be URL encoded with the PHP `urlencode()` function.

Although you've come far, there's still a long way to go. Next, you'll learn about arithmetic operators, math functions, and conditional statements in PHP. You'll be relieved to hear that most of them work in an identical way to ActionScript.

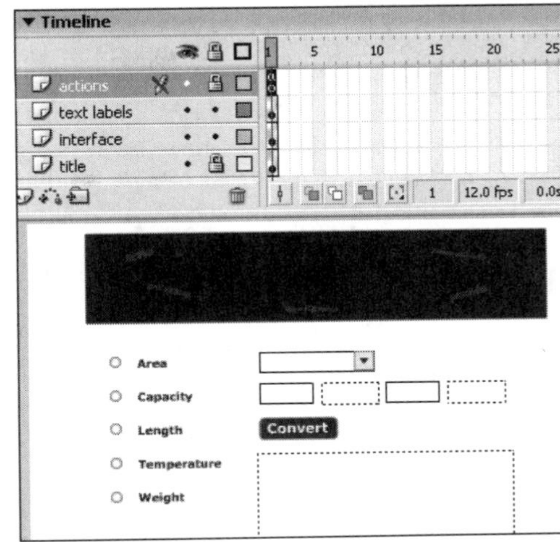

Chapter 3

CALCULATIONS AND DECISIONS

What this chapter covers:

- Working with arithmetic operators
- Formatting and rounding numbers
- Using helpful math functions
- Combining calculations and assignment
- Using comparison and logical operators
- Making decisions with conditional statements
- Building a multiconverter Flash application

One of the great advantages of learning programming or scripting languages is that many of them share a lot in common. They all provide some method of performing calculations and making decisions. As far as calculations are concerned, the basic rules of addition, subtraction, and multiplication have been laid down since ancient times. Decision making is also a logical process that follows a fairly standard pattern—although whether the resulting decision is logical is often quite a different matter!

If you have learned how to do calculations and make programmatic decisions in ActionScript, all the PHP constructs will be very familiar to you. Beware, though: there are many subtle differences that might catch you out. The first half of this chapter discusses the differences. Then, in the second half, you'll put your newfound knowledge to practical use by constructing the first half of a Flash application—a multiconverter that will convert pounds to kilograms, gallons (both U.S. and Imperial) to liters, Fahrenheit to Celsius, and much, much more.

Performing calculations with PHP

PHP can perform a full range of arithmetic and complex mathematical calculations. In fact, PHP not only matches every method and property of the ActionScript `Math` object, but considerably more.

> *If you're already familiar with ActionScript, you already know that the equal sign (=) is used to assign a value to a variable, not to signify the result of a calculation. The same is true in PHP, and in both languages it is known as the* ***assignment operator****. No matter what you learned in elementary school, think of = as meaning "is set to" and forget thinking about it as the equal sign.*

Both languages allow you to work with the same range of numbers, 1.7E-308 to 1.7E+308 with 15 digits of accuracy. If your reaction to that statement is, "What on earth does that mean?" (and, I'll be honest, that's exactly what I first thought), you probably don't need to worry. The "E" in the figure indicates what's called **scientific notation**, and the number following it tells you how many numbers come after the decimal point (or if the number is negative, how many numbers come before the decimal point). So the biggest number supported by both PHP and ActionScript is approximately 17 followed by 307 zeros—more than enough for all except the most specialized needs.

PHP and ActionScript also use the same notation for decimal, octal, and hexadecimal numbers, so there is no problem passing such numbers back and forth between the two languages. Decimal numbers are the same as regular numbers, octal numbers begin with a leading zero and a sequence of digits from 0 to 7, and hexadecimal numbers begin with 0x followed by digits from 0 to 9 or letters from A to F (either uppercase or lowercase).

```
255  // decimal
0377 // 255 expressed as an octal number
0xFF // 255 expressed as a hexadecimal number
```

A nice feature of PHP is that it has functions to convert numbers from decimal to octal or hexadecimal and back. It also has functions to convert binary numbers to decimal or hexadecimal and back. There's even a function that will perform a base conversion for any base between 2 and 36. Most of these functions are quite esoteric, but they're there if you need them (for details, see `www.php.net/manual/en/ref.math.php`). The most useful functions from the Flash or website design point of view are `dechex()` and `hexdec()`, which convert between decimal and hexadecimal—ideal if you need to convert colors to or from RGB.

Because there are so many similarities between PHP and ActionScript, the big question becomes when to use one language over another. It's not an easy question to answer, but if you're working mainly with Flash, you should entrust your mathematical calculations to PHP only if PHP offers a superior way of arriving at the result you need. The reason is simple: any calculation entrusted to PHP involves a round-trip to the server. The speed at which it will be calculated depends not only on the server's capability, but also on any delays in network communication between the user's computer and the web server.

At the same time, if you find yourself in a situation where you need to do calculations *after* data has already been sent from your Flash movie to the PHP server, it makes no sense to send everything back to the user's computer without first doing the calculation. The decision of where to perform calculations needs to be made on a case-by-case basis. Most, if not all, the calculations in this and the following chapter could be done entirely within Flash without the intervention of PHP, although many of them would involve considerably more steps to arrive at the same answer. By seeing how calculations work within PHP, and how they differ from ActionScript, you can choose the most suitable for your purpose.

Working with arithmetic operators

The standard arithmetic operators all work exactly as you would expect, and are the same in both PHP and ActionScript. Table 3-1 shows them all in action. To demonstrate their effect, the following variables have been set:

```
$a = 20;
$b = 10;
$c = 4.5;
```

Table 3-1. Arithmetic operators used in PHP

Operation	Operator	Example	Result
Addition	+	`$a + $b`	30
Subtraction	-	`$a - $b`	10
Multiplication	*	`$a * $b`	200
Division	/	`$a / $b`	2
Modulo division	%	`$b % $c`	1
Increment	++	`$b++`	See text
Decrement	--	`$b--`	See text

The **increment** and **decrement** operators can come either before or after the variable, and the effect is the same in both languages. When they come before the variable, 1 is added or subtracted from the value before any further calculation is carried out. When they come after the variable, the main calculation is done first, and then 1 is either added or subtracted. If you're wondering where the operators go when used in front of the variable, the answer is *before* the dollar sign, which is regarded as an integral part of a PHP variable name:

```
++$b;
--$b;
```

The **modulo** operator often strikes newcomers to programming as being rather weird, because it returns the remainder of a division, like this:

```
$a = 26 % 5;  // $a is 1
$a = 26 % 27; // $a is 26
$a = 26 % 2;  // $a is 0
```

It can have a lot of uses, though. One of them is demonstrated by the final example above: modulo division by 2 is a quick way of finding whether a number is odd or even.

Experimenting with numbers

Later in the chapter, you'll build a multiconverter for weights, temperatures, area, and so on. Many of the calculations involve straightforward multiplication or division, but others are a bit more complicated. Even on straightforward calculations, figures often need rounding to the nearest whole number or to a set number of decimal places. Let's take a look at some ways of handling such situations.

Apologies to readers who live in countries that have embraced the metric system wholeheartedly, but for the United States (and many people in Britain, which can't make up its mind) pounds, ounces, gallons, pints, and so on are still the measurements of choice. Even if this type of conversion isn't part of your everyday needs, the methods of calculation and dealing with awkward figures are of universal relevance.

1. Create a new PHP page in the folder for this chapter, `phpflash/ch03`, and call it `conversion.php`.
2. There are 454 grams in a pound, so the conversion formula for converting kilograms to pounds is *`kilos divided by .454`*. Enter the following code:

```
<?php
$value = 6;
$unit1 = ' kg';
$unit2 = ' lb ';
$pounds = $value / .454;
echo $value.$unit1.' equals '.$pounds.$unit2;
?>
```

3. View the page in a browser. You should get the following result:

6 kg equals 13.2158590308 lb

4. Hmm. Even if you're happy with a decimal conversion of kilograms to pounds, it's rather untidy. Fortunately, PHP has a very handy function to sort that out. Change the line before the closing PHP tag as follows:

```
echo $value.$unit1.' equals '.number_format($pounds,2).$unit2;
```

5. Save the file and view the page in the browser again (you can simply click Refresh in the browser to do this).

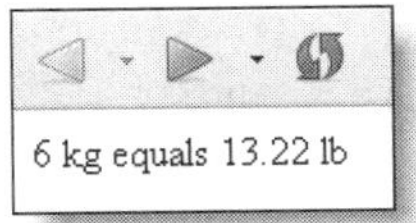

Much better! number_format() is a built-in PHP function that does exactly what its name suggests. It takes one, two, or four arguments:

- The first argument should be a literal number (or a variable containing one) that you want to format.
- The second (optional) argument is an integer specifying the number of decimal places. (If you omit this argument, the number is rounded to the nearest integer.)
- The third and fourth arguments (also optional) are both strings that specify the decimal-place character and the thousand separator. You must use either both these arguments or neither. If the arguments are omitted, PHP will use the default decimal-place character (a period) and thousand separator (a comma).

Most programmers in the English-speaking world will never need to use the last two arguments, but not all languages follow the convention of a period for the decimal-place character and a comma for the thousand separator. In France, for instance, the decimal-place character is normally a comma, and a space is used to separate thousands. To format a number like that with number_format()

```
number_format(1234.5678, 2, ',', ' '); // 1 234,56
```

The provision of an alternative reflects PHP's dedication to internationalization. Note that if you set the third argument, the fourth argument ceases to be optional, even if you want the default value.

6. Undo the change you made to the final line in step 4. Also, alter the fifth line like this:

```
$pounds = number_format($value / .454, 2);
```

7. View the page again. It should look exactly the same. PHP is quite happy for you to pass calculations as an argument to a function. Arguments are separated by commas, exactly as in ActionScript, so the function knows to treat the 2 separately from the calculation. And as long as the calculation produces the type of data the function is expecting, it will handle it all in stride.

8. Now remove the comma and the number 2, so the line reads

```
$pounds = number_format($value / .454);
```

9. If you view the page again, you will see the value has been rounded to the nearest whole number.

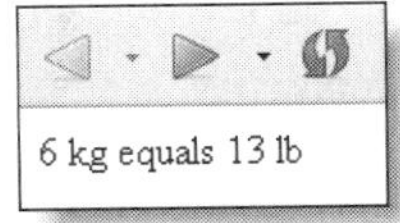

10. In fact, you could have done the same with a different PHP function called, logically enough, round(). So, what's the difference? The best way to find out is to try it in a browser. Change the script back to the way it was in step 3, and add an extra line, so it looks like this:

```
<?
$value = 6;
$unit1 = ' kg';
$unit2 = ' lb ';
$pounds = $value / .454;
echo $value.$unit1.' equals '.number_format($pounds,2).$unit2;
echo '<br />Using round():'.round($pounds,2);
?>
```

11. When you view the result in a browser, both figures will be 13.22. Now add five zeros to the first variable so it reads

```
$value = 600000;
```

12. Look at the page in a browser again.

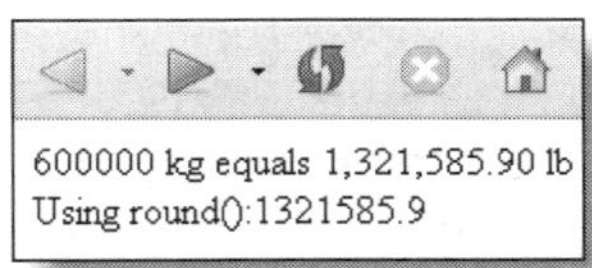
600000 kg equals 1,321,585.90 lb
Using round():1321585.9

The first figure is formatted in a human-friendly way and is now *a string that cannot be used for further calculations* without removing the thousand separator character. The second is less easy to read, but it's *still a number that can be processed further*. Also note that, even though you specified precision to two decimal places, round() has omitted the final figure because it's a zero. The implication of this is that you shouldn't format figures that you're likely to need in future calculations. The safest way to handle this is to assign the number to be formatted to a new variable, like this:

```
$pounds = $value / .454;
$poundsFormatted = number_format($pounds,2);
echo $value.$unit1.' equals '.$poundsFormatted.$unit2;
```

It means a little more code, but $pounds remains a number that can be used safely in further calculations.

> *If you experience unexpected results with* number_format() *or* round()*, check your version of PHP. A bug with inconsistent handling of rounding up and down was corrected in version 4.3.5. These functions now work in the exactly the same way as ActionScript's* Math.round()*: positive numbers with a fractional portion less than .5 and negative numbers with a fractional portion greater than .5 are rounded down. All other numbers are rounded up.*

13. As you will have noticed, there are two major differences between the way `round()` works in PHP and ActionScript. **PHP offers the useful option of rounding to a number of decimal places**. This is a major improvement over the cumbersome way of achieving the same thing in ActionScript. The other thing is that you don't prefix `round()` with `Math`—the function works on its own and isn't treated as a method of an in-built object. There's another surprise in store. Replace the second argument with a negative number in the last line of the script, like this:

```
echo '<br />Using round():'.round($pounds,-3);
```

14. View the page in a browser again. If you used `-3`, the figure has been rounded to the nearest 1,000.

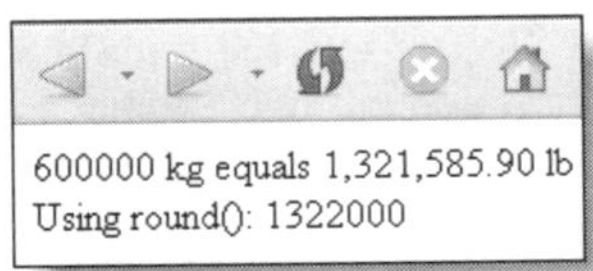
600000 kg equals 1,321,585.90 lb
Using round(): 1322000

    A curiosity, maybe, but if you ever need to round a figure to the nearest ten, hundred, and so on, PHP provides a quick and elegant method of doing so. Note that this works with `round()` only—it doesn't work with `number_format()`.

15. All this rounding is fine, but it still hasn't solved the problem of converting a decimal fraction of a pound to the unit users would expect: ounces. You could extract the decimal part of the result using string manipulation and then calculate the number of ounces, but there's a much simpler way.

    First convert kilograms to ounces. Rather than hunting for a new conversion formula, the current one will do quite nicely. Just multiply it by the number of ounces in a pound (16). Divide the result by 16, and round down to get the number of pounds. Finally, use modulo division by 16 to find the remainder, which gives you the number of ounces. It all fits together like this:

```
<?php
$value = 6;
$unit1 = ' kg';
$unit2 = ' lb ';
$unit3 = ' oz';
$oz = $value / .454 * 16;
$pounds = floor($oz / 16);
$oz = $oz % 16;
echo $value.$unit1.' equals '.$pounds.$unit2.$oz.$unit3;
?>
```

    Who said modulo was useless? This, by the way, is one of the key calculations for the multiconverter application that you'll start building later in the chapter.

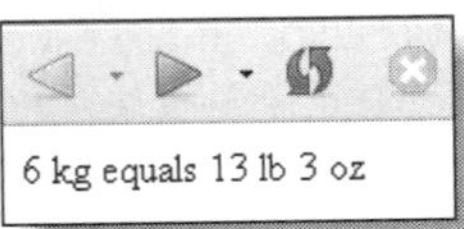
6 kg equals 13 lb 3 oz

Useful math functions

The preceding exercise introduced you to `round()`, one of more than 30 math functions in PHP. Apart from the fact that you don't prefix these functions with `Math`, most of them work in exactly the same way as they do in ActionScript, so now is a good time to list the most common ones in PHP (see Table 3-2).

Table 3-2. Most frequently used PHP math functions

Function	Example	Result	Use
`abs()`	`$a = abs(-3);`	3	Returns the absolute value of a number. Useful for converting a negative value to the equivalent positive number.
`ceil()`	`$a = ceil(12.1);`	13	Rounds positive numbers up and negative numbers down to the next integer. Leaves the number unchanged if it's already an integer.
`dechex()`	`$a = dechex(255);`	ff	Converts base-10 (decimal) numbers to base-16 (hexadecimal). Useful if you need to calculate colors from RGB to hex.
`floor()`	`$a = floor(12.1);`	12	Rounds positive numbers down and negative numbers up to the next integer. Leaves the number unchanged if it's already an integer.
`hexdec()`	`$a = hexdec('2f');`	47	Converts base-16 (hexadecimal) numbers to base-10 (decimal). Useful if you need to calculate RGB colors from hexadecimal. Note that if the hexadecimal number includes any letters from A to F, the entire number must be in quotes. Letters can be uppercase or lowercase.
`max()`	`$a = max(2,34,-20);`	34	Returns the largest number from a comma-delimited list. Also accepts a single array as an argument, and returns the largest number from the array.
`min()`	`$a = max(2,34,-20);`	-20	Returns the smallest number from a comma-delimited list. Also accepts a single array as an argument, and returns the smallest number from the array.
`pow()`	`$a = pow(4,3);`	64	Takes two arguments. Returns the first number raised to the power of the second.

(Continued)

Table 3-2. Most frequently used PHP math functions *(Continued)*

Function	Example	Result	Use
`rand()`	`$a = rand(1,6)`		Takes two arguments and returns a random number from the first to the second inclusive. If no arguments are supplied, it returns a random number between zero and the result of `getrandmax()`. The maximum random value is system dependent: on Windows, it's 32767, whereas on Mac OS X and my remote Linux server, it's 217483647.
`round()`	`$a = round(12.1);`	`12`	Rounds down to the next integer all positive numbers with a fractional portion less than .5 and all negative numbers with a fractional portion of .5 or more. All other numbers are rounded up. Takes an optional second argument to determine the number of decimal places (see "Experimenting with numbers" in the previous section).
`sqrt()`	`$a = sqrt(6.25);`	`2.5`	Returns the square root of a number.

As you can see, the PHP method of generating a random number between two values is much simpler than in ActionScript.

PHP also has a full range of trigonometric functions, plus frequently used math constants such as pi (`M_PI`). For details, see `www.php.net/manual/en/ref.math.php`.

Performing calculations in the right order

In the "Experimenting with numbers" exercise, you divided the number of kilograms by .454 and multiplied it by 16 all in the same operation. PHP handled the calculation without difficulty, because mathematically it makes no difference whether the division or the multiplication is performed first. The result is always the same.

Some calculations, though, are potentially ambiguous. For example, to convert a temperature from Celsius to Fahrenheit, you divide by 5, multiply by 9, and then add 32. To convert in the opposite direction, the formula is subtract 32, divide by 9, and multiply by 5. So, let's test it by converting normal body temperature, which is 98.6°F or 37°C.

Testing operator precedence

1. Enter the following code in a new PHP page called `temperature.php`:

```
<?php
$c = 37;
$f = 98.6;
$cToF = $c / 5 * 9 + 32;
echo $cToF.' fahrenheit<br />';
$fToC = $f - 32 / 9 * 5;
echo $fToC.' celsius';
?>
```

2. Load the page into a browser, and if you were paying attention in math class at school, the totally inaccurate second result will come as no surprise to you.

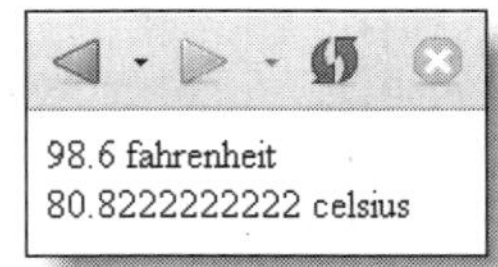

3. Anybody with a body temperature of 80.8°C has more than a heavy sweat coming on. He would be seriously dead. What's interesting about these two calculations, though, is that the conversion from Celsius to Fahrenheit is spot on, whereas the one in the opposite direction is disastrously wrong. The answer lies in operator precedence. The same rules apply in PHP and ActionScript as in ordinary mathematics: **multiplication and division take precedence over addition and subtraction**. So, in the case of converting Celsius to Fahrenheit, the division and multiplication take place before the addition—which is exactly what you want. In the second calculation, though, the subtraction must take place first; otherwise, the result is wildly inaccurate. The way to ensure that precedence is to surround the subtraction in parentheses. Amend the sixth line like this:

```
$fToC = ($f - 32) / 9 * 5;
```

4. View the page again in a browser, and you can see the patient has been restored to health:

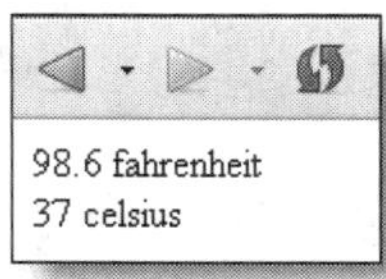

While this exercise demonstrates a principle of elementary arithmetic that you're probably already aware of, it's amazing how working with variables, as opposed to real numbers, can make you forget such simple things. Because the calculation worked without parentheses in one direction, you cannot assume that it would be safe to omit them in the reverse calculation. *Always test your code thoroughly before deploying it in a critical situation.*

Table 3-3 summarizes the precedence of arithmetic operators.

Table 3-3. Rules of precedence for arithmetic operators

Precedence	Group	Operators	Rule
Highest	Parentheses	`()`	Operations contained within parentheses are evaluated first. If these expressions are nested, the innermost is evaluated first.
Next	Multiplication and division	`* / %`	These operators are evaluated after any expressions in parentheses. If an expression contains two or more operators of equal precedence, they are evaluated left to right.
Lowest	Addition and subtraction	`+ -`	These are the last operators to be evaluated in any expression. If the expression contains two or more of equal precedence, they are evaluated left to right.

Combining calculations and assignment

You will often want to perform a calculation on a variable and assign the result back to the same variable. PHP offers the same convenient shorthand as ActionScript. Table 3-4 shows the main combined assignment operators and their use.

Table 3-4. Combined arithmetic assignment operators used in PHP

Operator	Example	Equivalent to
+=	`$a += $b`	`$a = $a + $b`
-=	`$a -= $b`	`$a = $a - $b`
*=	`$a *= $b`	`$a = $a * $b`
/=	`$a /= $b`	`$a = $a / $b`
%=	`$a %= $b`	`$a = $a % $b`

You met the other important combined assignment operator in the previous chapter (`.=`), which adds another string on the end of the existing one held in the variable. Don't forget that **the plus sign is used in PHP only as an arithmetic operator**, and not to concatenate strings, which is done with the dot (`.`) operator instead.

Making decisions with PHP

Branching code on the basis of decision making is fundamental to all programming languages. Usually, decisions are made by using comparison or logical operators to test whether a condition is true. These will be described shortly, but it's easier to do so if you have a context within which to use them.

PHP offers three methods of running code, depending on whether a condition is true:

- `if... else` conditional statements
- `switch` statements
- The conditional or ternary operator

They work in an identical way to ActionScript, but with a few minor differences that might catch you out.

Using if... else conditional statements

The general pattern is exactly the same as in ActionScript:

```
if (condition is true) {
  // Execute this code
  }
else {
  // Do this instead
  }
```

PHP also has the `else if` construction in common with ActionScript. However, `elseif` is normally written as one word in PHP:

```
if (condition is true) {
  // Execute this code
  }
elseif (alternative condition is true) {
  // Do this instead
  }
else {
  // Do this as a last resort
  }
```

Curly braces are optional when there is only one statement to be executed:

```
if ($morning) echo 'Good morning';
elseif ($afternoon) echo 'Good afternoon';
else echo 'Good evening';
```

More than one statement, however, requires the use of curly braces:

```
if ($morning) {
  echo 'Good morning';
  displayNews();
  }
elseif ($afternoon) {
  echo 'Good afternoon';
  displayWeather();
  }
else {
  echo 'Good evening';
  displayTVSched();
  }
```

These examples contain variables that are being tested to see if they evaluate to `true`. PHP has a very liberal interpretation of what equates to `true`—or, to be more precise, a very narrow interpretation of what it regards as being `false` (the full list was given in the last chapter when the Boolean datatype was first introduced). Frequently, though, you will want to base your decisions on more precise criteria. For that purpose, you need to build conditional statements using PHP's comparison operators.

Using comparison operators

Comparison operators are used to compare two values (known as **operands** because they appear on either side of an operator). If both values meet the criterion being tested for, the expression evaluates to `true`; otherwise, it evaluates to `false`. Computers want to know yes or no. They make decisions on the basis of whether two values are equal, whether one is greater than the other, and so on. "Well, maybe" doesn't cut any ice.

Table 3-5 lists the comparison operators used in PHP. With one exception, they are the same as in ActionScript.

Table 3-5. PHP comparison operators used for decision making

Symbol	Name	Use
`==`	Equality	Returns `true` if both operands have the same value; otherwise, returns `false`.
`!=`	Inequality	Returns `true` if both operands have different values; otherwise, returns `false`.
`<>`	Inequality	In PHP, this has the same meaning as `!=`. It's no longer used in ActionScript.

(Continued)

Table 3-5. PHP comparison operators used for decision making *(Continued)*

Symbol	Name	Use
===	Identical	Determines whether both operands are identical. To be considered identical, they must not only have the same value, but also be of the same datatype (for example, both floating-point numbers).
!==	Not identical	Determines whether both operands are not identical (according to the same criteria as the previous operator).
>	Greater than	Determines whether the operand on the left is greater in value than the one on the right.
>=	Greater than or equal to	Determines whether the operand on the left is greater in value than or equal to the one on the right.
<	Less than	Determines whether the operand on the left is less in value than the one on the right.
<=	Less than or equal to	Determines whether the operand on the left is less in value than or equal to the one on the right.

Seasoned hands will recognize <> from Flash 4, but it's no longer used in ActionScript as the inequality operator. Since the alternative != is common to both languages, it's recommended you use it exclusively to avoid confusion. <> is included here purely for the sake of completeness, in case you come across it in PHP scripts from other sources.

> *While I'm on the subject of comparison operators, don't forget that a single equal sign assigns a value. To make a comparison, you must use the equality operator (two equal signs). The conditional statement* `if ($a = 5)` *will always evaluate to* `true`*, because it sets the value of* `$a` *to* `5`*, rather than testing it.*

Thinking back to the earlier example about converting temperatures, you could now use an `if... else` statement in combination with the equality operator to decide whether a temperature is to be converted from Celsius to Fahrenheit or vice versa. One way you could do it is like this (the code is in `temperature2.php` in the download files for this chapter):

```
<?php
$value = 37;
$conversionType = 'cToF'; // Celsius to Fahrenheit
if ($conversionType == 'cToF') {
```

```
  $result = $value / 5 * 9 + 32;
  $resultUnit = ' degrees F';
  }
else {
  $result = ($value - 32) / 9 * 5;
  $resultUnit = ' degrees C';
  }
echo $result.$resultUnit;
?>
```

If you view the output of the preceding code in a browser, this is what you'll see:

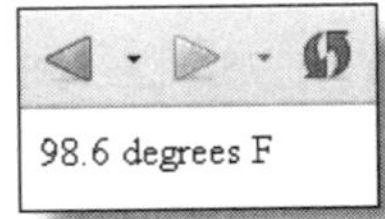

Change the value of `$conversionType` in line 4, and the result is 2.77777777778 degrees C. Don't worry about rounding the result. You'll use this formula in the multiconverter application a little later and take a slightly different approach to formatting the result of each calculation. In this particular example, PHP doesn't care what value you set `$conversionType` to. If it's not an exact match for `cToF` (with the same mixture of uppercase and lowercase), it skips the first block of code and executes the code in the `else` part of the conditional statement.

Testing more than one condition

Frequently, comparing two values is not enough. PHP and ActionScript both allow you to set a series of conditions, using **logical operators** to specify whether all, or just some, need to be fulfilled.

All the logical operators in PHP are listed in Table 3-6. They include some that are not found in ActionScript. **Negation**—testing that the opposite of something is true—is also considered a logical operator, although it applies to individual conditions rather than a series.

Table 3-6. Logical operators used for decision making in PHP

Symbol	Name	Use
&&	Logical AND	Evaluates to `true` if both operands are `true`. If the left-hand operand evaluates to `false`, the right-hand operand is never tested.
and	Logical AND	Exactly the same as &&, but it takes lower precedence. (PHP only.)
||	Logical OR	Evaluates to `true` if either operand is `true`; otherwise, returns `false`. If the left-hand operand returns `true`, the right-hand operand is never tested.

(Continued)

Table 3-6. Logical operators used for decision making in PHP *(Continued)*

Symbol	Name	Use
or	Logical OR	Exactly the same as ||, but it takes lower precedence. (PHP only.)
xor	Exclusive OR	Evaluates to true if only one of the two operands returns true. If both are true or both are false, it evaluates to false. (PHP only.)
!	Negation	Tests whether something is not true.

Technically speaking, there is no limit to the number of conditions that can be tested. Each condition is considered in turn from left to right, and as soon as a defining point is reached, no further testing is carried out. When using && or and, every condition must be fulfilled, so testing stops as soon as one turns out to be false. Similarly, when using || or or, only one condition needs to be fulfilled, so testing stops as soon as one turns out to be true.

```
$a = 10;
$b = 25;
if ($a > 5 && $b > 20) // returns true
if ($a > 5 || $b > 30) // returns true, $b never tested
```

The implication of this is that you should always design your tests with the condition most likely to return false as the first to be evaluated. If any of your conditions involve complex calculation, place them so they are the last to be evaluated. Doing so will speed up execution.

If you want a particular set of conditions considered as a group, enclose them in parentheses.

```
if (($a > 5 && $a < 8) || ($b > 20 && $b < 40))
```

Operator precedence is a tricky subject. Stick with && and ||, rather than and *and* or, *and use parentheses to group expressions to which you want to give priority.*

Using exclusive OR

Exclusive OR (xor) is a concept you won't come across in ActionScript unless you delve into the advanced territory of bitwise operators (which work on the binary representation of operands—see, I told you it was advanced). In PHP, though, it's also available as a logical operator. Usually, you want all conditions to be met or you're happy with at least one. Exclusive OR is unusual in that it returns true *only* if one condition is false. Paradoxically, this can be of use when you need either *both conditions* to be true or *both of them* to be false.

Say, for example, you have a form that stores articles in a database for a news site. Some articles will be accompanied by pictures, but some won't. If there's a picture in an article, it must have a caption; but if there's *no* picture, neither must there be a caption. The PHP function `empty()` checks whether a variable contains any data:

```
if (empty($picture) xor empty($caption)) {
  echo 'You must set both or neither';
  }
```

The logic of this is more easily understood by looking at Table 3-7.

Table 3-7. How exclusive OR works

Picture	Caption	xor Result
Not set (empty is `true`)	Not set (empty is `true`)	`false`
Set (empty is `false`)	Set (empty is `false`)	`false`
Not set (empty is `true`)	Set (empty is `false`)	`true`
Set (empty is `false`)	Not set (empty is `true`)	`true`

So, if both are `true` or both are `false`, the warning is not triggered. Yet, if one is `true`, but not the other, the warning is triggered.

Using negation to test for opposites

The previous example using `xor` could be rephrased as follows:

```
if ($picture is empty and $caption is not empty) {
  // issue a warning
  }
if ($picture is not empty and $caption is empty) {
  // issue a warning
  }
```

By placing an exclamation mark (!) in front of an expression, PHP (like ActionScript) tests for the opposite of that condition. So, in real code the previous example becomes

```
if (empty($picture) && !empty($caption)) {
  // issue a warning
  }
if (!empty($picture) && empty($caption)) {
  // issue a warning
  }
```

In ActionScript, this test would involve comparing each variable with the `undefined` *datatype. This serves the dual function of checking not only whether a variable contains a value, but also whether the variable actually exists. PHP draws a distinction between these two states and provides two separate tests:* `empty()`*, which tests whether a variable contains any value, and* `isset()`*, which checks whether a variable has been set. This is important to remember when transferring data between Flash and PHP. Variables passed by* `LoadVars` *to a PHP script will always return* `true` *if tested with* `isset()`*, even if they contain no value. You also need to be alert to a curious aspect of* `empty()`*: it treats zero (either as a string or as a number) as having no value. If it's important to establish the presence of zero, test for it specifically with the equality operator like this:* `if ($var == 0)`.

Using switch for long decision chains

Although there is no limit to the number of `if... else` decisions you can chain together, both PHP and ActionScript offer an alternative approach through the use of **`switch` statements**. This method is more efficient when a large number of alternatives are involved, because the condition is tested only once, whereas it's tested each time in an `elseif` statement. `switch` statements are also often easier to read. The PHP script for the multiconverter you'll build in this chapter (yes, you're nearly there) handles more than 20 choices, so it's an ideal candidate for `switch`.

The structure of a `switch` statement is identical in both languages:

```
switch(variable being tested) {
  case value1:
  statements to be executed
  break;
  case value2:
  statements to be executed
  break;
  default:
  statements to be executed
  }
```

Although the syntax and use of `switch` *is identical in PHP and ActionScript, there is one major difference. ActionScript imposes strict datatyping when testing the condition; PHP does not. For example, PHP will match a string containing a number with the equivalent number (*`'5'` *and* `5` *are treated as equal), whereas ActionScript will treat them as different values.*

Using `switch`, you can rewrite the temperature-conversion code from earlier in the chapter as follows (the code is in `temperature3.php` in the download files for this chapter):

```
<?php
$value = 37;
$conversionType = 'cToF'; // Celsius to Fahrenheit
// uncomment the next line to convert Fahrenheit to Celsius
// $conversionType = 'fToC'; // Fahrenheit to Celsius
switch($conversionType) {
  case 'cToF':
    $result = $value / 5 * 9 + 32;
    $resultUnit = ' degrees F';
    break;
  case 'fToC':
    $result = ($value - 32) / 9 * 5;
    $resultUnit = ' degrees C';
    break;
  }
echo $result.$resultUnit;
?>
```

Normally, there is no need to use the break keyword on the final option, but this section of code will eventually be incorporated in a much bigger switch statement in the multiconverter application.

Here are other points to note about switch:

- The expression following the case keyword must be a simple datatype. You cannot use arrays, objects, or comparison operators.
- When a match is made, the switch statement will execute every line of code until it reaches the next break keyword. Each block of statements should normally end with break, unless you specifically want to continue executing code within the switch statement.
- You can group several instances of the case keyword together to apply the same block of code to them (you will see this technique demonstrated when completing the multiconverter application in the next chapter).
- If no match is made, any statements following the default keyword will be executed. If no default has been set, the switch statement will exit silently and continue with the next block of code.

Using the conditional operator

The **conditional operator** (?:) is a shorthand method of representing a simple conditional statement, and it's something you either love or hate. Beginners usually hate it because it's not as intuitive as if... else, which follows the patterns of human language. Once you get to know it, though, you'll wonder how you ever did without it—and it's available in both PHP and ActionScript. This is how it works:

```
condition ? value if true : value if false;
```

Here is a simple example:

```
$var = 10;
echo $var > 20 ? 'big' : 'small'; // Displays "small"
```

The equivalent code using `if... else` looks like this:

```
if ($var > 20) {
  echo 'big';
  }
else {
  echo 'small';
  }
```

The same construction can be used to assign a value to a variable:

```
$size = $var > 20 ? 'big' : 'small';
```

The conditional operator is normally confined to a simple `if... else` choice between two alternatives. If you're the sort of person who likes to live dangerously, you can nest expressions using the conditional operator inside each other using parentheses:

```
$size = $var > 20 ? 'big' : ($var > 10 ? 'medium' : 'small');
```

I don't recommend this type of ultra-coding, because it can be very difficult to understand the logic when you come to amend it several months later, unless you write a detailed inline comment (which probably defeats the purpose of the shorthand code anyway). Single-level use of the conditional operator, though, is extremely useful shorthand. Even if you don't feel comfortable using it in your own scripts yet, it's something you should learn to recognize.

Flash application: A multiconverter

It's time to put all that theory to use. The multiconverter application was inspired by the mess the United States and Britain have created through their slowness to adopt the metric system. Both countries are gradually going metric, but at a snail's pace. The British parliament, believe it or not, voted as long ago as 1863 for the compulsory adoption of the metric system but backpedaled eight years later. Apparently, one argument that swayed the decision was that it would "be letting down America and our colonies," who had harmonized their systems with the ones in use in Britain. Yet an American pint is much smaller than one served in a British pub. And gas-guzzling vehicles aren't the only reason American drivers get so few miles to the gallon—the gallon's smaller, too.

This is quite a complex project, so it will be spread over two chapters, pulling together every strand of PHP theory in each chapter. Definitely nothing lightweight about this exercise—it's designed to stretch your skills. Let's get to work.

Planning the conversion script

Before diving into writing the PHP script, let's consider what will be needed and how the multiconverter will work. The multiconverter will handle measurements of area, capacity, length, temperature, and volume. Table 3-8 shows the conversion formulas and input units that will be needed.

Table 3-8. Categories and conversion formulas used by the multiconverter

Category	Conversion	Formula	Input units
Area	Acres to hectares	Acres × .405	Acres
	Hectares to acres	Hectares × 2.471	Hectares
	Square feet to square meters	Square feet × .0929	Square feet
	Square yards to square meters	Square yards × .836	Square yards
	Square meters to square feet	Square meters ÷ .0929	Square meters
	Square meters to square yards	Square yards ÷ .836	Square meters
Capacity	Pints to liters	U.S. pints × .473 or Imperial pints × .568	Pints
	Liters to pints	U.S. pints ÷ .473 or Imperial pints ÷ .568	Liters
	Gallons to liters	U.S. gallon × 3.785 or Imperial gallons × 4.546	Gallons
	Liters to gallons	U.S. gallon ÷ 3.785 or Imperial gallons ÷ 4.546	Gallons
	U.S. to Imperial	U.S. pints ÷ 1.201	Gallons and pints
	Imperial to U.S.	Imperial pints × 1.201	Gallons and pints
Length	Inches to centimeters	Inches × 2.54	Inches
	Centimeters to inches	Centimeter ÷ 2.54	Centimeters
	Feet to meters	Feet × .305	Feet
	Meters to feet	Meters ÷ .305	Meters

(Continued)

Table 3-8. Categories and conversion formulas used by the multiconverter *(Continued)*

Category	Conversion	Formula	Input units
Length	Yards to meters	Yards × .914	Yards
	Meters to yards	Meters ÷ .914	Meters
Temperature	Celsius to Fahrenheit	C ÷ 5 × 9 + 32	Degrees
	Fahrenheit to Celsius	(F – 32) ÷ 9 × 5	Degrees
Weight	Pounds to kilograms	Ounces ÷ 16 × .454	Pounds and ounces
	Kilograms to pounds	Complex calculation	Kilograms
	Pounds to stones	Complex calculation	Pounds
	Stones to pounds	Stone × 14 + pounds	Stone and pounds

The reason for choosing this extensive array of conversion formulas is that most of them require a slightly different method of calculation. If the idea of typing everything out fills you with horror, you can either choose just a handful of examples or use the download files for this chapter. They show the project at various stages of development, allowing you to skip a stage or simply to examine the files alongside the text in the book. The choice is yours.

One of the great advantages of the metric system is that every measurement can be expressed in decimal terms—or, to put it in terms of PHP datatypes, as a floating-point number. If you study the right-hand column of Table 3-8, though, it soon becomes clear that some of the calculations involve working with two different types of input units, such as pounds and ounces, which cannot be represented as decimal figures. At first sight, this is a problem, but it is easily overcome.

Earlier in the chapter, I showed you how to convert kilograms to pounds and ounces by doing the initial calculation in the smaller unit, ounces. The same principle applies when you convert from pounds and ounces to kilograms: multiply the pounds by 16, and add the result to the ounces, then do the calculation in ounces. All of the conversion formulas can be simplified by working with just one input unit (even though two weight calculations are described as complex, they follow the same pattern).

The other thing that should become clear is that each calculation has a unique identity. What this means is that the PHP script is not really interested in pounds and ounces, kilograms, or centimeters, but in *values*. It's also interested in the *conversion type*.

Consequently, in spite of this complex-looking table, all you need from the Flash movie is a maximum of five variables:

- `value1` for larger units, such as pounds or gallons
- `value2` for smaller units, such as ounces or pints

- **unit1**, representing the name of the larger unit
- **unit2**, representing the name of the smaller unit
- **conversionType**

Depending on the conversion type, each calculation will result in the output either of a single value and unit (such as kilograms or liters), or of two values and units (such as pounds and ounces). So the output variables can be reduced to a maximum of four:

- **$r**, representing the sole output value or the value of the larger unit
- **$r2**, representing the value of the smaller unit, if any
- **$unitsR**, representing the name of the sole unit or larger unit
- **$unitsR2**, representing the name of the smaller unit, if any

Since all that's required in Flash is to display the result, these output values will be compiled into a string by the PHP script and sent back as a single variable. Each conversion calculation has to be treated separately, but breaking the results into two or four variables means the process of compiling the output string can be modularized.

Handling the basic calculations

Some of the calculations require more complex data manipulation than others. Let's start with the straightforward ones.

1. Create a new PHP page in phpflash/ch03 and call it converter.php. If you are using a script editor, such as Dreamweaver, that inserts XHTML code, remember to strip everything out. The only things the page should contain are the opening and closing PHP tags; all the following code goes between them. You can find the completed code for this first section in converter01.php in the download files for this chapter.
2. The five variables from Flash will be sent by LoadVars by the POST method. To avoid the need to type out the full POST array variable reference every time, assign the incoming variables to more succinct ones:

```
// assign data incoming from Flash to simpler variables
$a = $_POST['value1'];
$b = $_POST['value2'];
$type = $_POST['conversionType'];
$units1 = $_POST['units1'];
$units2 = $_POST['units2'];
```

   There are two things to note about this code. First, I am ignoring my own advice by naming two of the variables with a single letter, rather than a more meaningful name. This is because $a and $b will be used only in the conversion formula for each type of calculation, and it will save a lot of repetitive typing. Another programmer reading the script later will be able to see their meaning immediately from this block of code right at the top of the page. Second, you should normally verify the existence of variables received by the POST method with isset() before using them in a script. If a variable is missing, it will generate a warning and could result in your script failing to run.

However, the Flash movie is designed to send all five variables, whether they contain a value or not. So, even if a value is missing, Flash will simply assign an empty string to the appropriate variable. That's why you can safely avoid this check on this occasion.

3. Although the multiconverter handles 24 different types of conversion, only one is required each time the script is run. Determining the right formula to use is handled by a switch statement, which checks the value of $type and then searches for the appropriate case. Insert the following code beneath the previous block:

```
// select the appropriate conversion formula
switch($type) {
  // Area conversion
  case 'acreToHa':
    $r = $a * .405;
    $unitsR = 'hectares';
    break;
  case 'haToAcre':
    $r = $a * 2.471;
    $unitsR = 'acres';
    break;
  case 'sqftToM2':
    $r = $a * .0929;
    $unitsR = 'm?';
    break;
  case 'sqydToM2':
    $r = $a * .836;
    $unitsR = 'm?';
    break;
  case 'M2toSqft':
    $r = $a / .0929;
    $unitsR = 'sq ft';
    break;
  case 'M2toSqyd':
    $r = $a / .836;
    $unitsR = 'sq yd';
    break;
  }
```

This handles all the area conversion calculations. The name following each case keyword is designed to indicate the purpose of the conversion. The meanings should be fairly obvious—for example, sqftToM2 indicates "square feet to square meters." In the next line, the input value, $a, is either multiplied or divided by the appropriate amount to produce the output value, which is assigned to $r. The next line fixes the name of the output unit, and the break keyword brings the switch statement to an end. Use your operating system's insert symbol method to create the superscript 2 for m^2. It should survive the journey back to Flash intact.

4. Create a few blank lines beneath the switch statement, and insert the following code:

```
// format the result for transfer to Flash
switch($type) {
  default:
```

```
    $output = "$a $units1 = ";
    $output .= "$r $unitsR";
    }
// send the data back to Flash
echo $output;
```

5. Test the script by temporarily commenting out parts of the code inserted in step 2 and hard-coding some test values, like this:

```
/*
$a = $_POST['value1'];
$b = $_POST['value2'];
$type = $_POST['conversionType'];
$units1 = $_POST['units1'];
$units2 = $_POST['units2'];
*/
$a = 50;
$type = 'sqftToM2';
$units1 = 'sq ft';
```

6. When you view the page in a browser, it should display the results shown here:

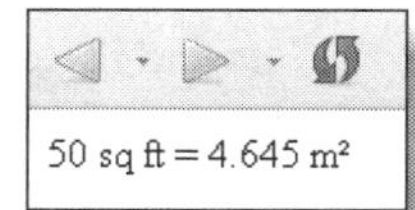

Try it with several other measurements to make sure your page is working as expected.

7. Add the following six conversion formulas to the first `switch` statement, which you created in step 3. Make sure they go *inside* the final curly brace of the original statement.

```
// Length conversion
case 'inToCm':
  $r = $a * 2.54;
  $unitsR = 'cm';
  break;
case 'cmToIn':
  $r = $a / 2.54;
  $unitsR = 'in';
  break;
case 'ftToM':
  $r = $a * .305;
  $unitsR = 'm';
  break;
case 'ydToM':
  $r = $a * .914;
  $unitsR = 'm';
  break;

// Temperature conversion
case 'cToF':
  $r = ($a / 5) * 9 + 32;
  $unitsR = '°F';
  break;
```

```
case 'fToC':
  $r = ($a - 32) / 9 * 5;
  $unitsR = '°C';
  break;
```

8. Amend the final line of the page from this:

```
echo $output;
```

to this:

```
echo 'output='.urlencode($output);
```

9. Test the page again. If your test variables are the same as in step 5, the output in the browser will look like this:

Pretty hideous, eh? But that's the way Flash loves it. All the spaces and nonalphanumeric characters (including the superscript 2 of m^2) have been URL encoded by PHP, ready for transmission back to Flash.

10. Remove the test variables you inserted in step 5, and also remove the comments from around the original block of code. The first five lines of the page should be restored to the way they were in step 2. Compare your code with `converter01.php` in the download files.

The PHP page isn't finished yet, but it's a nuisance to keep hard-coding test variables. Let's build the Flash movie to interact with the PHP script.

Building the Flash interface

This sort of application lends itself greatly to all sorts of Flash wizardry, using graphics and animations to depict the results of conversions. For instance, you could build a scalable thermometer to show the results of temperature conversions, or you could use familiar objects, like milk bottles, to show conversions from liters to pints, like this:

While such things are fun to build—and give Flash the leading edge over XHTML-based dynamic websites—they get in the way of the main objective, which is to learn how to integrate Flash and PHP. So I've made a deliberate decision to keep the visual side of this application to the minimum. Once you have the data flowing back and forth between Flash and PHP without problems, you can let your visual imagination rip.

Designing the front-end

1. Open a new Flash document and save it as `converter.fla`. If you aren't keeping the FLA files in your server root, open File ➤ Publish Settings and change the file locations of the SWF and HTML files so they'll be created in `phpflash/ch03`. By doing so, you can then test them in a browser and see exactly how they would look on a live website. If you would like to use the same graphic elements as I have, use `converter01.fla` from the download files for this chapter. All the graphics are in the Library panel. The completed interface is in `converter02.fla`.

2. In the timeline, add three extra layers, and name them (from top to bottom) actions, text labels, interface, and title. Lock the actions layer to avoid accidentally attaching any graphics to it. Your eventual layout will look like Figure 3-1.

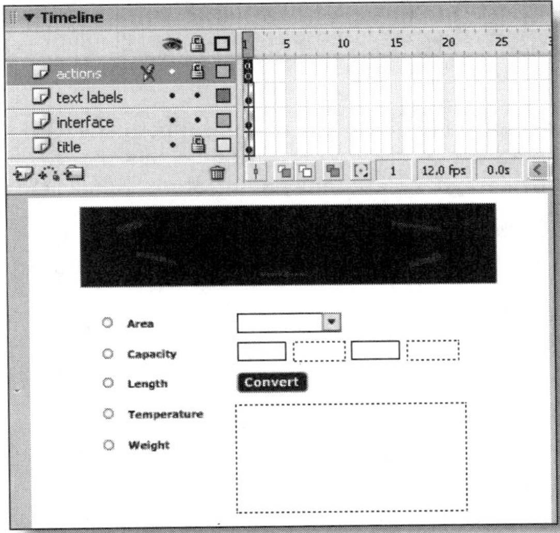

Figure 3-1. The basic layout of the multiconverter interface in Flash

3. For the title, I created a movie clip that uses both timeline and ActionScript effects to give a sense of the confusion caused by the need to work in different units. All the lettering was created using a font called Ravie, but it has been converted to graphic symbols in case you don't have it on your computer. All the ActionScript is inside the movie clip, so you simply need to drag it onto the title layer and give it an instance name of title_mc. It's important to use this exact instance name, because the final sequence relies on the `setInterval()` global function, which requires a precise reference to each of the movie clips inside the title to fade them and trigger the final animation. Take a look at the fully commented code on the final frame of the actions layer inside the title movie clip if you want to know how it works.

4. Open the Components panel (Window ➤ Development Panels ➤ Components or *CTRL+F7/⌘+F7*). Drag onto the interface layer a `ComboBox` and five `RadioButton` components. Rearrange the components so they are laid out as shown in Figure 3-1. At this stage, each of the radio buttons will be labeled Radio button.

> *As in the previous chapter, I've opted to use the Flash MX UI components (which you can download free of charge from Macromedia Exchange at* `www.macromedia.com/exchange`*), because they're lighter and slightly easier to code than the version 2 components in Flash MX 2004. The most important difference lies in how you attach functions to respond to user interaction. The MX UI components use what is known as a* ***change handler****, while version 2 components use* ***event listeners****. Since it's highly probable that the component architecture in the version of Flash planned for release in 2005 will also use event listeners, I'll describe the differences at the appropriate points, so you'll be able to adapt the script that follows.*

5. Highlight the topmost radio button. In the Properties panel (Window ➤ Properties or *CTRL+F3/⌘+F3*), make sure the Parameters tab is selected. Give the radio button an instance name of area_rb, delete the content of the Label field, and fill in the other parameters as shown here.

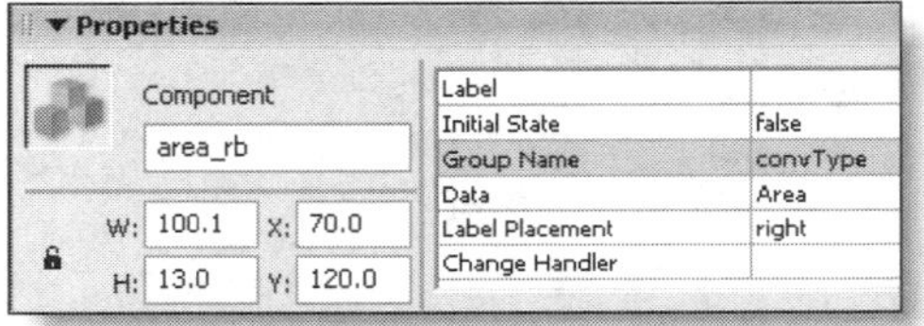

You can use the Label field to insert a text label alongside the radio button, but I think it looks nicer to use static text that you can style yourself. The Initial State parameter determines whether the radio button is selected when the movie loads. You don't want any radio buttons to be selected initially, so leave it at the default false. The next parameter, Group Name, identifies which group of radio buttons it belongs to (the equivalent of name in HTML). All the radio buttons will be used to determine the conversion type, so I have chosen convType as the group name. The Data parameter identifies what the radio button is for (it's the equivalent of the `value` attribute in an HTML radio button). This first radio button will be used to select area conversion, so I have named it Area.

You don't need to do anything with the final two settings—the label has been removed, and the change handler will be set later in ActionScript for the whole group.

6. Highlight each of the remaining radio buttons, and use the settings shown in Table 3-9.

Table 3-9. Settings for the radio button parameters

Instance name	Label	Initial state	Group name	Data
area_rb	Leave blank	false	convType	Area
capacity_rb	Leave blank	false	convType	Cap
length_rb	Leave blank	false	convType	Len
temperature_rb	Leave blank	false	convType	Temp
weight_rb	Leave blank	false	convType	Weight

This gives all the radio buttons the same Group Name, convType, and all of them will be deselected when the movie first loads. Make sure you use an initial uppercase letter for the Data parameter in each case, because ActionScript 2.0 is case sensitive, and the script you will create shortly will fail if there is a mismatch of cases.

7. Highlight the ComboBox component and give it an instance name of dropDown_cb. The combo box will be populated entirely by ActionScript, so don't change any of the default settings in the Properties panel.

8. Beneath the combo box, you need to create two input text fields with instance names of input1_txt and input2_txt. This is where the user will enter the amount to be converted. Two fields are required, because some conversions use a combination of units (for instance, gallons and pints). In the Property inspector, give the input fields a border. Alongside each of the input text fields, you also need a dynamic text field, which will display the names of the units to be entered. These two fields should be given instance names of measure1_txt and measure2_txt. They don't require a border, because the text will appear only when needed. Lay them out as shown in the image here:

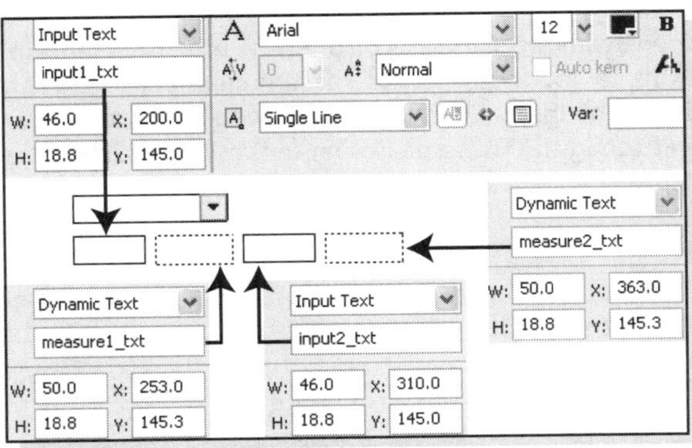

9. Place a button labeled Convert beneath the input and dynamic text fields, and give it an instance name of convert_btn. There is a suitable button in the Library panel of `converter01.fla`.

10. Another dynamic text field is required beneath the button. Its location is indicated by the dotted lines in Figure 3-1. This dynamic text field will be used to display the results returned from PHP. It needs to be a multiline field, and you can make it selectable so that the result can be copied and pasted into another document. Give it an instance name of output_txt. These are the settings I used:

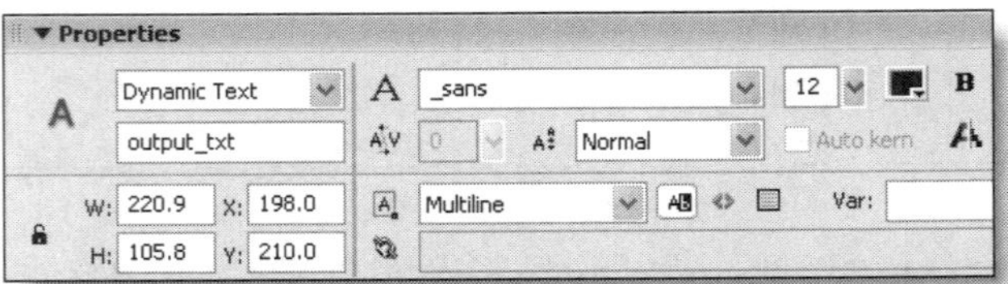

11. Finally, on the text labels layer, label each of the radio buttons (from top to bottom) Area, Capacity, Length, Temperature, and Weight. For the font, I chose Verdana 10pt bold in the same color as the title background (#000033). To check your progress, compare your file with `converter02.fla` from the download files for this chapter.

That completes the graphical interface. Everything else is driven by ActionScript, so get your scripting hat on.

Initializing the interface with ActionScript

When the SWF first loads, apart from the title, the static text fields and radio buttons will be the only things visible. The rest of the interface is initialized when the user selects one of the radio buttons.

1. Continue working with the same FLA or use `converter02.fla` from the download files. If you just want to follow the script for this next section, open `converter03.fla`. Highlight frame 1 of the actions layer, and open the Actions panel (*F9*). The entire script will be attached to this frame, so pin the script by clicking the pushpin button at the bottom left of the panel.

2. Hide the combo box, text input components, and button by setting their visibility to `false`.

```
// initialize interface by hiding combo box, button and input fields
dropDown_cb._visible = false;
dropDown_cb.setSize(200);
input1_txt._visible = false;
input2_txt._visible = false;
convert_btn._visible = false;
```

This is straightforward—just setting the `_visible` property of four elements to `false`, and setting the width of the combo box to 200 pixels, using the `setSize()` method.

> *When setting the visibility of Flash version 2 components, omit the underscore at the beginning of the* `visible` *property.*

The reason for hiding the main part of the interface is because a combo box with 24 options is unwieldy. It's better to get the user to select a category and then fill the combo box with only the relevant options. The choice of category will also affect how many input boxes are displayed, as well as the labels alongside them.

3. The first step in this process is to find out which radio button has been selected. This is done by creating a change handler function that can be assigned to the convType radio button group. Insert the following above the code inserted in the previous step:

```
function radioSelect():Void {
  // this function changes the contents of the combo box
  // whenever a radio button is selected
  // reset interface

  // get the value of the selected radio button
  selVal = "conv" + convType.getValue();
  trace("Chosen category " + selVal);
  // populate combo box

  // set input fields and labels
}
```

At the moment, this function contains only two lines of code, apart from comments. This is the important line:

```
selVal = "conv" + convType.getValue();
```

It uses the radio button's `getValue()` method to find out which radio button has been selected, and it concatenates the value with the string conv. The resulting string is assigned to `selVal`, which will be used to identify the selected category in both this and the change handler function for the combo box. Because it's needed in two functions, `selVal` must not be declared as a local variable, but it will be added on the main timeline in the next step.

4. For all the radio buttons to be able to respond to the `radioSelect()` function, it needs to be assigned as the change handler for the convType radio button group. The following code does that and declares `selVal` on the main timeline (insert it immediately after the code in step 3):

```
// set change handlers
convType.setChangeHandler("radioSelect");

// initialize variables
var selVal:String;
```

5. Test the movie, and click each of the radio buttons in turn. You should get the output shown here:

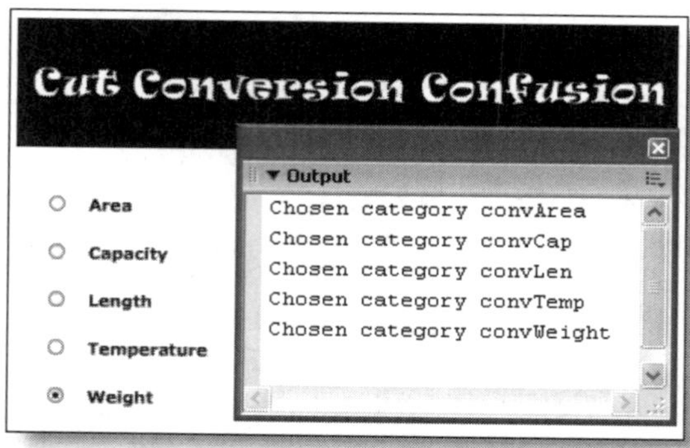

As noted earlier, the main difference between Flash MX components and their successors is in the way you assign functions to respond to events. The limitation of Flash MX change handlers is that you can attach only one event to a component, whereas the event listeners used by version 2 components (and probably their successors) allow you to program components to respond in different ways to different events. This involves a three-stage process. First, create an object to act as the event listener. Second, assign a callback function to the appropriate event property (such as `change` *or* `click`*) of the event listener. Finally, attach the event listener to the target component with the* `addEventListener()` *method, which takes two arguments: a string representing the event and a reference to the event listener object.*

It sounds complicated, but it's fairly simple in practice. This is how you would do it with the `convType` *radio button group and the* `radioSelect()` *function:*

```
var radioButtonListener:Object = new Object();
radioButtonListener.click = radioSelect;
convType.addEventListener("click", radioButtonListener);
```

The content of the `radioSelect()` *function remains exactly the same. It's just the method of attaching it to the radio button group that's different. You can learn more about event listeners in Chapter 13 of* Foundation ActionScript for Flash MX 2004 *by Sham Bhangal (friends of ED, ISBN: 1-59059-305-7).*

Populating the combo box

The normal way to populate a combo box dynamically through ActionScript is by using the `dataProvider` property. Unfortunately, this won't work because the values in the combo box will be changed each time the user selects a different radio button. The values display correctly the first time, but once you switch to another selection, the data is destroyed.

The solution is to store the details in a series of multidimensional arrays and to use a loop to populate the combo box with the relevant data.

If you're using this book to try to learn PHP and ActionScript simultaneously, you may find it useful to skip ahead to Chapter 5 and read about arrays and loops before going any further.

If the concept of multidimensional arrays sends shivers down your spine, fear not. It's not as bad as it sounds. Hopefully, a couple of screenshots will clarify matters. When the combo box is opened, it will display a series of options, as shown here:

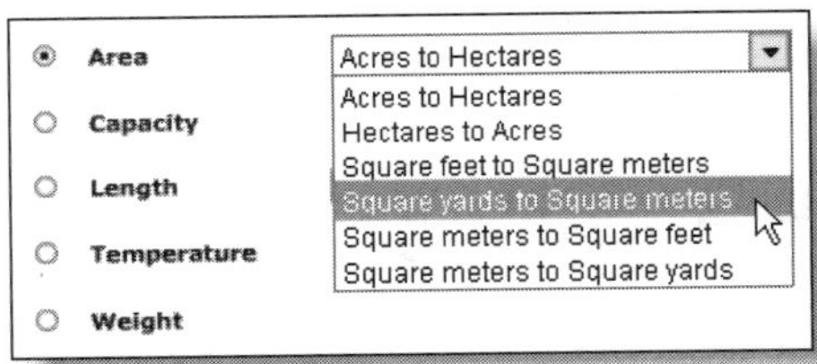

The content of the combo box is determined by whichever radio button has been selected. As you saw in the final step of the previous section, clicking a radio button concatenates the button's value (such as `Area`) with a string to create one of the five following values:

- `convArea`
- `convCap`
- `convLen`
- `convTemp`
- `convWeight`

These are the names of top-level arrays assigned as properties of the combo box. By assigning the selected value to the variable called `selVal` on the main timeline, the correct array can be identified as `dropDown_cb[selVal]`. Each of the top-level arrays contains a series of subarrays with details of each conversion type. The subarrays contain either three or four items, which can be accessed by their numeric index keys:

- **`[0]`**: A string containing the `label` to be displayed in the combo box.
- **`[1]`**: A string that identifies which item has been selected (Flash components refer to this as the `data` property). This will also be used as the value for the `conversionType` variable sent to the PHP script.
- **`[2]`**: A string that will be displayed in `measure1_txt`. This is a dynamic label for the left-hand text input field.
- **`[3]`**: A string that will be displayed in `measure2_txt`. Not all conversion types require a smaller unit. By checking the length of the array, you can determine whether the second input field needs to be displayed or hidden.

Figure 3-2 demonstrates the relationship between the arrays and the data they contain.

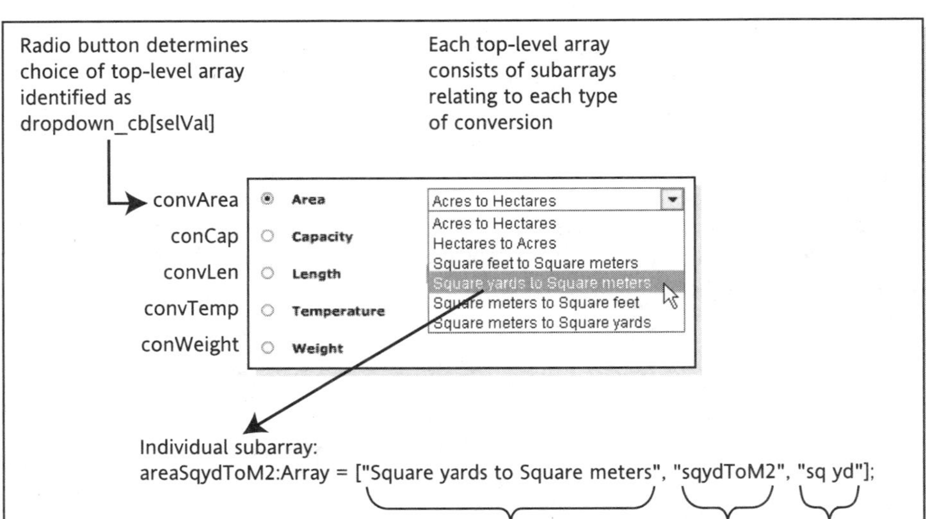

Figure 3-2. The relationship between the two levels of the multidimensional arrays used to populate the combo box

1. The arrays for the five top-level categories and all 24 subcategories involve 40 lines of typing—quite a chore, and it's easy to make a mistake. (I know—I had to type them all in the first place!) To save yourself the effort, use `convTypes.as` in the download files for this chapter. You can either copy and paste them into your Actions panel or use an #include command like this:

```
// include conversion type arrays
#include "convTypes.as"
```

Whichever you decide to do, the code should go immediately after the `selVal` declaration that you entered in step 4 of the previous section.

> *When you use an #include command, the external file should be in the same directory (folder) as the FLA. Otherwise, you need to give the full file path. The filename or path should be enclosed in quotes, but without a semicolon at the end of the command. All code included this way is compiled into the SWF at the time of compilation, so there is no need to upload the external file to the web server.*

Do, however, study the arrays to see how they work. First, a subarray is created for each conversion type, and then a series of top-level arrays is created as properties of `dropdown_cb.convArea`, `convCap`, `convLen`, `convTemp`, and `convWeight`.

In the area- and temperature-conversion subarrays, you will come across \u00b2 and \u00ba. These are Unicode escape sequences to represent the superscript 2 in m^2 and the degree sign, respectively. Flash 6 and above supports UTF-8 Unicode encoding, which enables you to incorporate nonstandard characters, as well as most of the world's writing systems, by using \u followed by the character's Unicode code point in hexadecimal. You can find the code points at www.unicode.org/charts.

```
// Sub-arrays for area conversion
var areaAcreToHa:Array = ["Acres to Hectares","acreToHa","acres"];
var areaHaToAcre:Array = ["Hectares to Acres","haToAcre","hectares"];
var areaSqftToM2:Array = ["Square feet to Square meters","sqftToM2",
➥ "sq ft"];
var areaSqydToM2:Array = ["Square yards to Square meters","sqydToM2",
➥ "sq yd"];
var areaM2toSqft:Array = ["Square meters to Square feet","M2toSqft",
➥ "m\u00b2"];
var areaM2toSqyd:Array = ["Square meters to Square yards","M2toSqyd",
➥ "m\u00b2"];

// Sub-arrays for capacity conversion
var capPtToLtr:Array = ["Pints to Liters","ptToLtr","pints"];
var capLtrToPt:Array = ["Liters to Pints","ltrToPt","liters"];
var capGalToLtr:Array = ["Gallons to Liters","galToLtr","gallons"];
var capLtrToGal:Array = ["Liters to Gallons","ltrToGal","liters"];
var capUStoImp:Array = ["US Gallons/Pints to Imperial","UStoImp",
➥ "gallons","pints"];
var capImpToUS:Array = ["Imperial Gallons/Pints to US","ImpToUS",
➥ "gallons","pints"];

// Sub-arrays for length conversion
var lenInToCm:Array = ["Inches to Centimeters","inToCm","in"];
var lenCmToIn:Array = ["Centimeters to Inches","cmToIn","cm"];
var lenFtToM:Array = ["Feet to Meters","ftToM","ft"];
var lenMtoFt:Array = ["Meters to Feet","mToFt","m"];
var lenYdToM:Array = ["Yards to Meters","ydToM","yd"];
var lenMtoYd:Array = ["Meters to Yards","mToYd","m"];

// Sub-arrays for temperature conversion
var tempCtoF:Array = ["Celsius to Fahrenheit","cToF","\u00baC"];
var tempFtoC:Array = ["Fahrenheit to Celsius","fToC","\u00baF"];

// Sub-arrays for weight conversion
var weightLbToKg:Array = ["Pounds to Kilos","lbToKg","lb","oz"];
var weightKgToLb:Array = ["Kilos to Pounds","kgToLb","kg"];
var weightLbtoSt:Array = ["Pounds to Stones","lbToSt","lb"];
var weightStToLb:Array = ["Stones to Pounds","stToLb","st","lb"];

// Top-level arrays to populate combo box
dropDown_cb.convArea = [areaAcreToHa,areaHaToAcre,areaSqftToM2,
➥ areaSqydToM2,areaM2toSqft,areaM2toSqyd];
```

```
dropDown_cb.convCap = [capPtToLtr,capLtrToPt,capGalToLtr,capLtrToGal,
➥ capUStoImp, capImpToUS];
dropDown_cb.convLen = [lenInToCm,lenCmToIn,lenFtToM,lenMtoFt,
➥ lenYdToM,lenMtoYd];
dropDown_cb.convTemp = [tempCtoF,tempFtoC];
dropDown_cb.convWeight = [weightLbToKg,weightKgToLb,
➥ weightLbtoSt, weightStToLb];
```

2. With all the data in place, you can now finish the rest of `radioSelect()`, the change handler function, that you created in step 3 of the previous section. Begin by inserting the following code under the `reset interface` comment:

```
input2_txt._visible = false;
measure2_txt._visible = false;
clearAll();
dropDown_cb._visible = true;
dropDown_cb.removeAll();
```

The first two lines hide the right-hand input text field and label. Although hidden when the movie is initialized, they will be displayed whenever you select a conversion type that requires both input fields, so you need to make sure they're not left out when they're no longer required. `clearAll()` is a custom-built function that clears any text in the input and output fields. It will be built later. The final two lines make the combo box visible and remove all existing items from it.

There will be nothing to remove the first time, but you need to do it on subsequent occasions. Otherwise, previous values from a longer array may be left at the bottom of the list when you choose a shorter one. For example, `convTemp` contains only two values, so the last four items of `convArea` would remain visible when switching from temperature to area.

3. Now that you've cleared everything out the way, it's time to populate the combo box. The next line, which records the selected radio button's value in the main timeline variable `selVal`, was already there. Remove the following line:

```
trace("Chosen category " + selVal);
```

Insert this code beneath the `populate combo box` comment:

```
for (var i:Number = 0; i < dropDown_cb[selVal].length; i++) {
  dropDown_cb.addItemAt(i, dropDown_cb[selVal][i][0],
➥ dropDown_cb[selVal][i][1]);
}
```

This loops through the selected array and uses the `addItemAt()` combo box method to add the `label` and `data` properties for each subarray. The method takes three arguments: `index`, `label`, and `data`. The loop variable `i` keeps count of the `index`, and the first and second items of each subarray are used as the `label` and `data`, as shown in Figure 3-2.

4. Immediately below the preceding code, add this line to set the drop-down depth of the combo box so that all items are visible:

```
dropDown_cb.rowCount = dropDown_cb[selVal].length;
```

5. The final section of the `radioSelect()` function should be inserted under the `set input fields and labels` comment:

```
input1_txt._visible = true;
measure1_txt.text = dropDown_cb[selVal][0][2];
if (dropDown_cb[selVal][0][3]) {
  input2_txt._visible = true;
  measure2_txt._visible = true;
  measure2_txt.text = dropDown_cb[selVal][0][3];
}
convert_btn._visible = true;
focusManager.setFocus(input1_txt);
focusManager.defaultPushButton = convert_btn;
```

   This block of code needs little comment, apart from the `if` clause, which tests for the existence of a fourth element in the subarray. If a fourth element has been set, the right-hand input text field and label are displayed. Otherwise, they remain hidden.

6. Test the movie. You'll see that the combo box now fills with the right categories, but when you change from the default category at the top of the list, the label to the right of the input text field doesn't change. In the following image, for example, it displays inches instead of meters. This calls for another change handler function, this time for the combo box. If you would like to check your code so far, compare it with `converter03.fla` in the download files for this chapter.

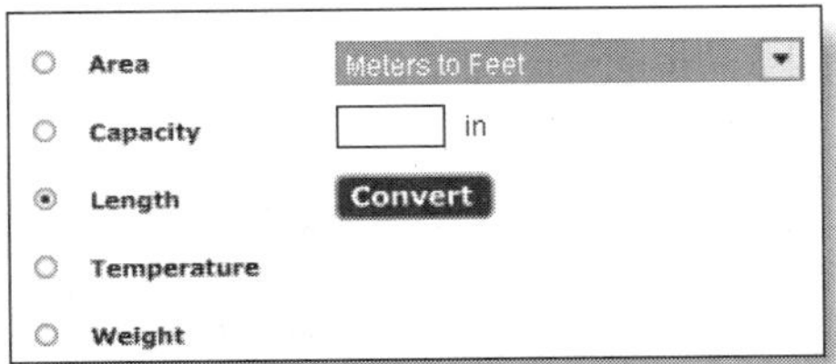

Reacting to changes in the combo box

Changing the interface in response to whatever is selected in the combo box requires a very similar function to `radioSelect()`. First, you need to establish which item has been selected in the drop-down list. Then a simple loop uses the `selVal` variable to choose the correct options from the appropriate array.

1. Continue working with the same FLA or use `converter03.fla` from the download files. If you just want to follow the code, use `converter04.fla`. Insert the following code immediately after the `radioSelect()` function (around line 30):

```
function comboChange():Void {
  // This function acts in response to changes in the combo box,
  // and displays the appropriate input and dynamic text fields
  // depending on the conversion type selected.
```

```
  // It begins by clearing any existing display.
  clearAll();
  // get value of selected item in combo box
  var newSelection:String = dropDown_cb.getValue();
  // loop through the appropriate array
  for (var i:Number = 0; i < dropDown_cb[selVal].length; i++) {
    // set the unit for the left-hand input text field
    if (dropDown_cb[selVal][i][1] == newSelection) {
      measure1_txt.text = dropDown_cb[selVal][i][2];
      if (dropDown_cb[selVal][i][3]) {
        // if the sub-array contains a fourth item,
        // display the right-hand input field and unit
        input2_txt._visible = true;
        measure2_txt._visible = true;
        measure2_txt.text = dropDown_cb[selVal][i][3];
      } else {
        // if no fourth item, ensure right-hand field
        // and unit are hidden
        input2_txt._visible = false;
        measure2_txt._visible = false;
      }
      break;
    }
  }
  focusManager.setFocus(input1_txt);
  focusManager.defaultPushButton = convert_btn;
}
```

The inline comments explain most of what is going on inside the comboChange() function. After clearing any existing display, the function uses the combo box's getValue() method to identify which item has been selected. This returns the data property of the selected item, which is assigned to the variable newSelection.

Flash version 2 components use inconsistent ways of identifying selected items. Although the version 2 radio button component uses the getValue() *method, in the same way as its MX counterpart, the version 2 combo box stores it as the* value *property. So, instead of* dropdown_cb.getValue()*, you need to use* dropdown_cb.value*. Hopefully, this sort of inconsistency will be removed in the planned new component architecture.*

If you take the example shown in Figure 3-2, this is sqydToM2. The data property is the second element of each conversion type subarray, so the loop iterates through the selected array (identified by selVal) until it finds a match for newSelection. So, in Figure 3-2, the match is made like this:

```
dropDown_cb[convArea][3][1] == "sqydToM2";
```

The third item in the subarray (identified by index number 2) is then used to display the appropriate unit in measure1_txt (in this example, sq yd).

A second conditional statement checks for a fourth item in the subarray, and displays input2_txt and measure2_txt with the appropriate unit. If no fourth item exists (as in the case of this example), any existing display of these two text fields is removed.

2. The comboChange() function won't work until it is assigned as the combo box change handler. Before doing that, insert the following function immediately after comboChange() (around line 61):

```
function clearAll():Void {
  // this clears both input text fields and any existing result
  input1_txt.text = "";
  input2_txt.text = "";
  output_txt.text = "";
}
```

   The inline comment says it all. This function is called by both radioSelect() and comboChange().

3. Now assign the change handler for the combo box. Put this line after the radioSelect() change handler (around line 69):

```
dropDown_cb.setChangeHandler("comboChange");
```

4. Test the movie again, and this time the labels and input fields should work properly, displaying two where appropriate. If you encounter any problems, compare your code with converter04.fla.

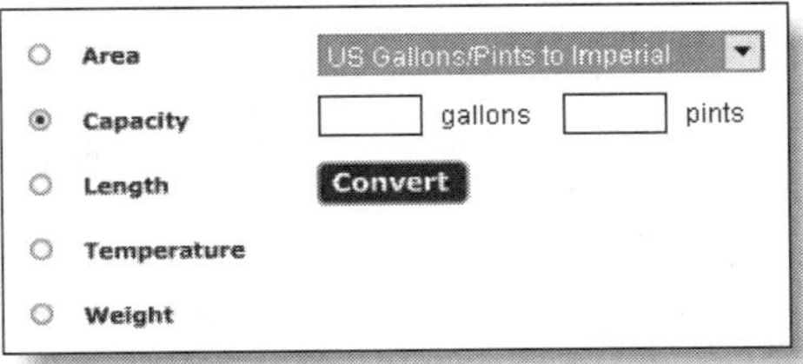

Sending the data to the PHP script and receiving the result

You're now on the homestretch—at least as far as the Flash movie is concerned. All that remains is to be done is set up the process for sending and receiving the data. This requires the creation of two simple functions—doConvert() and displayResult()—plus two instances of LoadVars.

1. Continue working with the same file, or use converter04.fla from the download files. The completed code is in converter05.fla.

   To communicate with the PHP script, create two instances of LoadVars: one for sending the data to be processed and the other for receiving the result. As I mentioned in the previous chapter, it's not essential to use separate instances, but it's a good habit to get into. When you get to the content management system in Chapter 10, you'll use one instance to send the data, but half a dozen to receive the results, depending on the action required. Declare the instances toward the bottom of your ActionScript, along with the other variables being initialized (around line 74):

```
var sendData:LoadVars = new LoadVars();
var receiveData:LoadVars = new LoadVars();
```

2. While working in the same part of the script, assign the two new functions to their appropriate event handlers. Insert this code immediately after the code in the previous step:

```
// assign functions to button and LoadVars instance
convert_btn.onRelease = doConvert;
receiveData.onLoad = displayResult;
```

You could use anonymous functions directly on these event handlers, but code maintenance becomes a lot easier if you follow the ActionScript best practice of declaring functions first.

> *It's important to create the instance of* `LoadVars` *that will receive the data from PHP before assigning a function to its* `onLoad()` *event handler. If you reverse the order of steps 1 and 2, the application won't work.*

3. Scroll back up to just beneath the `clearAll()` function (around line 67) and insert the `doConvert()` function as follows:

```
function doConvert():Void {
  // this gathers the input data and values of the units,
  // assigns them as properties of the sendData instance of
  // LoadVars, and sends them to the PHP script for processing
  sendData.conversionType = dropDown_cb.getValue();
  sendData.value1 = input1_txt.text;
  sendData.value2 = input2_txt.text;
  // display error message if no values input
  if (sendData.value1 == "" && sendData.value2 == "") {
    output_txt.text = "You have not entered any units to convert";
  } else {
    // get units to be converted, and send everything to PHP
    sendData.units1 = measure1_txt.text;
    sendData.units2 = measure2_txt.text;
    sendData.sendAndLoad("http://localhost/phpflash/ch03/converter.php?
➥ ck"+ new Date().getTime(), receiveData);
  }
}
```

The names of any properties created on a LoadVars instance are used as variables once they are passed to the PHP script, and they contain the same value. If you check the first few lines of converter.php, you will see it expects a total of five variables in the POST array:

```
$a = $_POST['value1'];
$b = $_POST['value2'];
$type = $_POST['conversionType'];
$units1 = $_POST['units1'];
$units2 = $_POST['units2'];
```

The value of the selected item in the combo box is assigned to the conversionType property of sendData. So, if the value is sqydToM2, the same value is made available to PHP as $_POST['conversionType']. The same happens with value1 and value2, which are taken from the input text fields. Even if the second input field isn't displayed, its text property is set by the clearAll() function to an empty string, so it won't cause any problems for the PHP script (because even though it's empty, it's not undefined).

What happens if the user clicks the button without entering anything in the input fields? Not a lot, apart from a wasted journey to the PHP server and back. To prevent that from happening, a conditional statement checks for empty fields and displays a warning message. Otherwise, the final two variables are assigned as properties of sendData, and the data is sent to converter.php. As in the previous chapter, I've used the current time as a cache killer to ensure that Flash always loads the new result. The receiveData instance of LoadVars is set as the target to receive the incoming data.

4. The displayResult() function is simplicity itself. Insert this immediately after the code in the previous step:

```
function displayResult():Void {
  // display the result in the multiline dynamic text field
  output_txt.text = this.output;
}
```

output is the name of the sole variable returned by the PHP script. It's assigned to the text property of the output_txt dynamic text field. You can refer to it using the this keyword because the function is assigned to the receiveData.onLoad event, so this is treated as receiveData.

5. Test the movie, but don't forget that not all formulas have been created in the PHP script yet. Any of the area and temperature conversions should be fine.

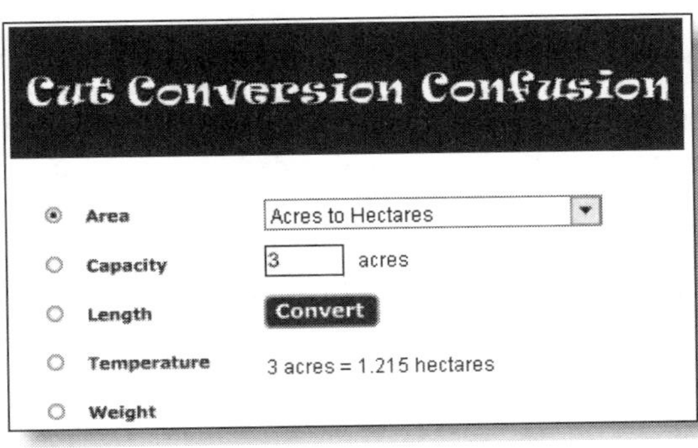

6. It would be nice to think all users will act sensibly and enter only numbers. What happens if they don't?

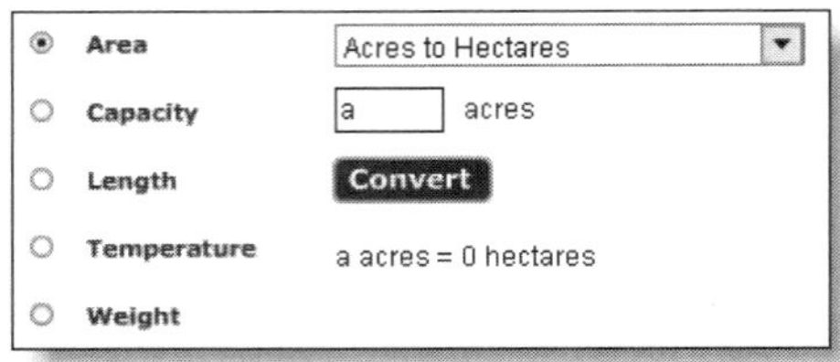

7. There are two ways to prevent this from happening. One is to highlight each input text field on the interface layer, and click the Character button at the bottom right of the Property inspector. This will open the Character Options dialog box, as shown here:

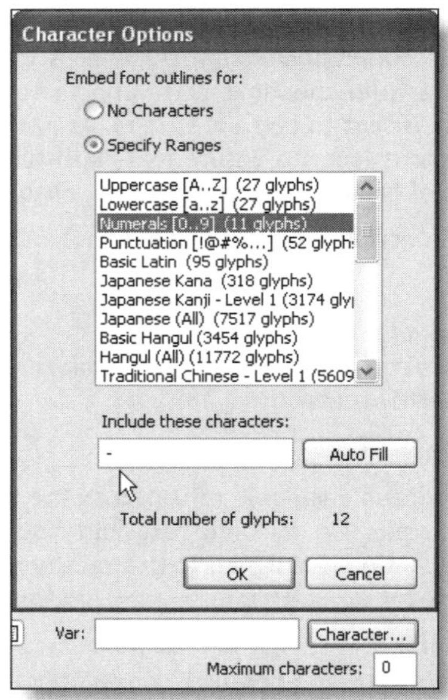

Select the Specify Ranges radio button and highlight Numerals. You will notice it says 11 glyphs alongside. A **glyph** is a technical term for a character or symbol. Although there are only ten numerals from 0 to 9, the mysterious eleventh glyph is the decimal point. To allow users to enter negative numbers, put your cursor in the Include these characters field at the bottom of the dialog box, and enter a hyphen (which doubles as a minus sign). Click OK. I suggest you include a hyphen only for input1_txt. For input2_txt, just select Specify Ranges and Numerals. If negative numbers are entered into the minor units field, you will get strange results from the PHP script.

The alternative way to restrict characters is to use ActionScript. Add the following two lines just before the #include command for the long list of arrays used to populate the combo box:

```
input1_txt.restrict = "0-9.\\-";
input2_txt.restrict = "0-9";
```

The hyphen between 0 and 9 indicates a range of characters (so you get all ten numerals). To permit a hyphen to be used as the minus sign, you need to escape it with *two* backslashes. The advantage of using ActionScript for input2_txt is that you can prevent decimal numbers from being inserted by omitting the period from the range of permitted characters.

8. Things are looking pretty good now, but some calculations show that a bit of number formatting would be welcome.

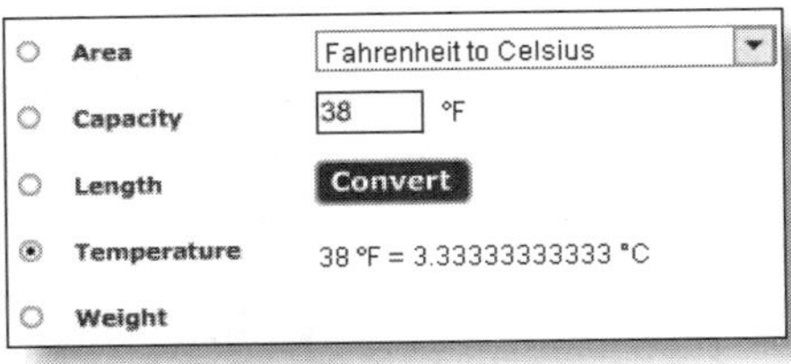

You'll be able to sort that out after studying in more detail the way PHP formats strings in the next chapter.

Summing up

You may be thinking that everything you've done in this application so far could have been achieved just as well in Flash alone. That's perfectly true, but the techniques for gathering data from a Flash interface and transferring them to a server-side script are essential for the more complex tasks you'll tackle later in the book when working with databases. Also, once you've designed the Flash interface, you can change the PHP back-end very simply, without any need to upload a new version of your SWF for every minor change. The formulas and conversion type arrays could be stored in a database, opening up the possibility of an infinitely expandable converter application.

The deeper you get into PHP, the more you'll realize how similar to ActionScript many of the concepts and methods are. It certainly speeds the learning process, but there are also subtle differences that can catch you out. You'll encounter more similarities and differences in the next chapter, in the way both languages handle strings and functions. PHP's background as a language designed to display dynamic content on web pages means it has many powerful string-manipulation features, so formatting the results can be achieved in far fewer lines of script than would be possible if everything were done in Flash alone. See you there.

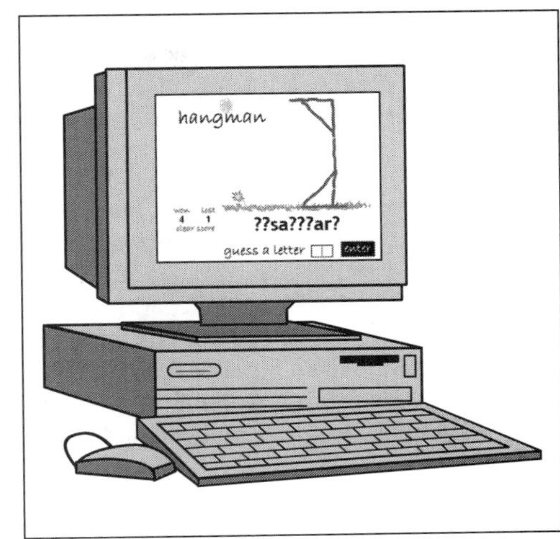

Chapter 4

OF STRINGS AND THINGS

What this chapter covers:

- Working with strings and formatting text
- Extracting information from strings
- Building your own PHP functions
- Understanding how variable scope differs between ActionScript and PHP
- Completing the multiconverter application
- Handling user input
- Using regular expressions to match text patterns
- Improving the feedback application

In view of the close integration between PHP and (X)HTML, it's little wonder that PHP boasts more than 80 string-related functions designed to make word processing easier. Flash, by contrast, has just 12. I've no intention of dragging you through all 80 or so, but I will highlight some of the most important ones likely to make your life easier when integrating PHP and Flash.

Although PHP has a vast number of built-in functions, each project is different, and you'll soon find yourself looking for ways to perform specialized tasks. When the same tasks crop up again and again throughout a project, it's time to combine them into a custom-built function of your own. Function creation in PHP is almost identical to function creation in ActionScript. The main difference lies in how the functions remain in computer memory. ActionScript functions on the main timeline can be called at any time, whereas PHP functions remain in memory only while a script is being run—often only a matter of microseconds. ActionScript and PHP also treat variable scope in exactly the opposite way, so you need to be alert to the differences.

After reviewing these issues, you'll put your new knowledge to work and complete the multiconverter Flash application from the last chapter, and you'll also improve the feedback form from Chapter 2.

Manipulating strings with PHP

Even after working with programming languages for years, I still find the expression "string" faintly ridiculous. In most circumstances, it refers to words or sentences that make sense to humans (at least that's the intention), but computers know nothing of words—human language is treated as a string of continuous data. Let's begin this overview of strings in PHP by looking at how to output them.

How PHP outputs strings

You've already used echo on many occasions to send the results of a PHP script back to Flash. Now's the time to make a more formal introduction to echo and related PHP constructs.

echo

This is one of those strange terms that dates back to almost prehistoric times, at least as far as computing is concerned. In the bad old days of DOS, the computer would tell you everything it was doing by displaying a constant stream of messages known as an **echo**.

So much for ancient history. What you need to know about echo in PHP is that it outputs strings (or the value of string variables) to the browser. As was mentioned in Chapter 2, literal strings in double quotes are processed, and any variables are replaced with their value before being output. Because of PHP's loose datatyping, integers and floating-point numbers (or variables holding such values) can be passed directly to echo, and are automatically converted to strings. When used with a single argument, echo can be used with or without parentheses:

```
echo 'Display me';
echo 5;
$name = 'David';
echo $name;         // David
echo "Hi, $name";   // Hi, David
```

```
echo ('Display me');
echo (5);
echo ("Hi, $name"); // Hi, David
```

There is no particular advantage in using parentheses. When used *without* parentheses, echo also accepts a comma-delimited list of arguments:

```
echo 'Hi, ', $name; // Hi, David
```

A PHP string can contain just about anything, including HTML tags and any of the escape characters (such as \n for new line) listed in Table 2-3. HTML tags can be in either single or double quotes, but escape characters and variables that you want to be processed must always be in double quotes:

```
echo "<b>$name</b>\n"; // <b>David</b> followed by a new line character
```

This means you can use PHP to apply HTML formatting to database content before sending it to Flash for display in a text field or area that has HTMLtext enabled. You can also add custom classes or any other tags required to work with the improved CSS capabilities introduced in Flash MX 2004.

print

This does the same as echo, but it can accept only one value.

```
print 'Display me';
print 5;
$name = 'David';
print $name;          // David
print "Hi, $name";    // Hi, David
print ('Display me');
print (5);
print ("Hi, $name"); // Hi, David
print 'Hi, ', $name; // Generates an error
```

It does *not* send output to a printer.

When working with Flash, the output of echo *or* print *does not normally appear directly onscreen, but is used to transmit data to the Flash movie. For speed freaks,* echo *is marginally faster. It's also one less letter to type. Otherwise, the choice between* echo *and* print *is mainly a matter of personal preference.*

Both echo *and* print *output exactly what you tell them to. They add no extra formatting, such as spacing or a new line at the end. If you were to run the preceding example code, everything would appear in a continuous string on one line. If you want a new line (or several), you must explicitly add* \n *in a double-quoted string or*
. Flash does not understand the XHTML form
.

Neither echo *nor* print *can be used to display the contents of an array. If you attempt to do so, PHP simply outputs the word "Array". (Arrays are covered in detail in Chapter 5.)*

urlencode()

This function is your constant friend in sending data to Flash from PHP. It needs to be applied to all data that contains spaces or any other characters that would be illegal in a URL—and since your output is generated dynamically, that means you should take the precaution of applying it to just about everything.

> *Do not be tempted to apply* `urlencode()` *to the entire output string being sent to Flash. It needs to be applied separately to the value of each variable. If you pass the entire output string to* `urlencode()`, *it converts the equal sign separating the name/value pair of each variable to* `%3D` *and the ampersand (&) separating individual pairs to* `%26`. *When this happens, Flash is unable to interpret any data from PHP.*

The multiconverter you built in the last chapter demonstrates the importance of applying `urlencode()` only to the value of each variable. The data returned from `converter.php` consists of only one name/value pair, but it includes two equal signs. The first separates the variable name (output) from its value, while the second is intended to be displayed in the Flash movie. As Figure 4-1 shows, passing the entire output string to `urlencode()` results in both equal signs being encoded, and Flash fails to recognize the incoming data. Figure 4-2 shows the correct way—passing only the value of the variable to `urlencode()`, thus enabling Flash to recognize the name/value pair.

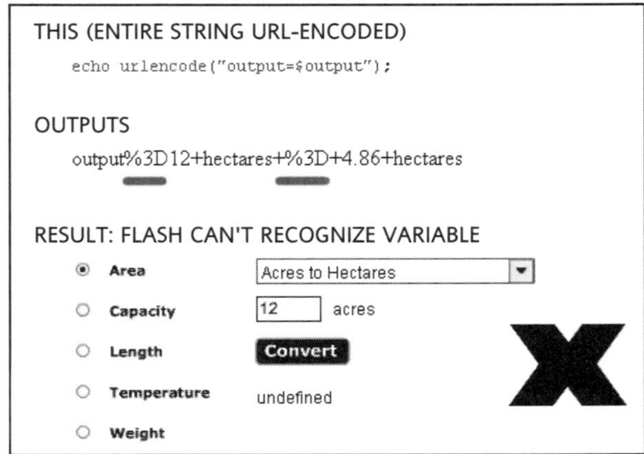

Figure 4-1. Don't try to cut corners by passing the entire output of a PHP script to `urlencode()`. It won't work.

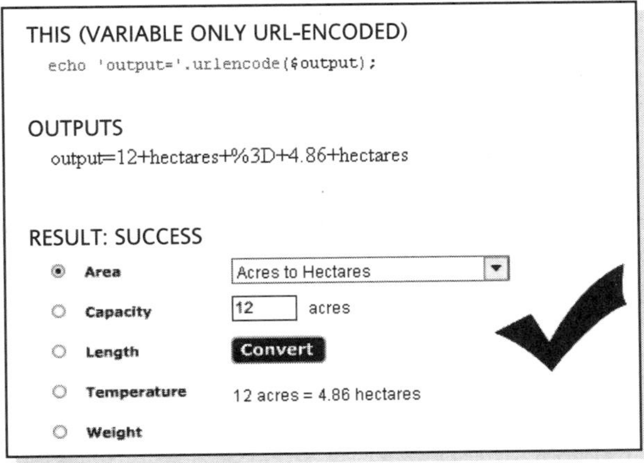

Figure 4-2. By passing only the value of each variable to `urlencode()`, Flash can identify name/value pairs correctly.

printf() and sprintf()

These closely related functions are used to format output according to set patterns. They are modeled on identical functions in the C programming language and can be a nightmare to get your head around. Nevertheless, they can be extremely useful, so they need to be part of your PHP toolbox.

The difference between the two is that `printf()` sends output straight to the browser, whereas `sprintf()` returns a string value that can be stored in a variable. Otherwise, they are identical. Because of the ability to store the result in a variable, `sprintf()` is more useful when working with Flash. Both functions take a minimum of two arguments:

- A string with any elements you want formatting replaced by **conversion specifications** (see Figure 4-3). The conversion specifications and their meanings are described in detail on the next page.
- A comma-delimited list of the elements to be formatted. The list must contain the same number of elements as the conversion specifications and be in the same order.

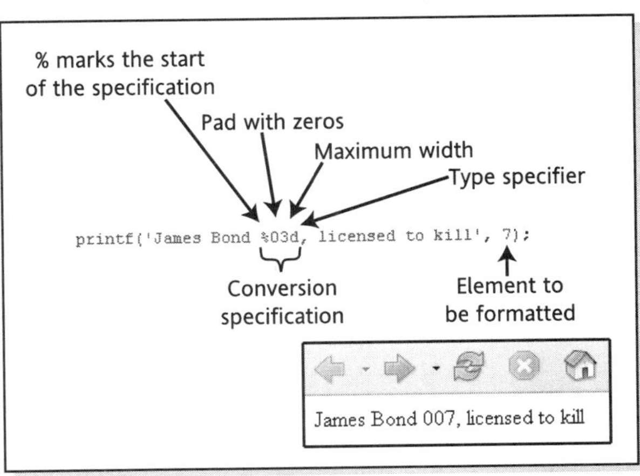

Figure 4-3. An example of `printf()` at work: an innocent-looking 7 turned into a license to kill

As you can see from Figure 4-3, the conversion specification is not exactly what you might call intuitive, but it does follow a regular pattern. This is how you build a conversion specification. Each conversion specification begins with %, followed by a series of specifiers that must be in the following order:

- **An optional padding specifier**: This can be a zero, a space, or any character preceded by a single quote. If the string used as the first argument to `printf()` or `sprintf()` is already in single quotes, you must escape the single quote in the conversion specification. For instance, to use x instead of zeros in the example shown in Figure 4-3, you must use either a double-quoted string or a backslash to escape the single quote like this:

```
printf("James Bond %'x3d, licensed to kill", 7);
printf('James Bond %\'x3d, licensed to kill', 7);
```

- **An optional alignment specifier**: The output is right-justified by default. To make it left-justified, insert a dash (-). Using this in the previous example would result in 7xx instead of xx7.
- **An optional width specifier**: This indicates the minimum number of characters to be output. If the result would be fewer than this number, PHP pads the result in accordance with the two preceding settings. If no padding specifier has been set, PHP uses spaces.
- **An optional precision specifier for floating-point numbers**: This is a period followed by a number specifying the number of digits to follow the decimal point (for example, `.2`). This has no effect unless the type specifier (which comes next) is set to floating-point.
- **A type specifier (required)**: The most useful ones are as follows:
  - d: Treats the element to be formatted as an integer
  - f: Treats the element to be formatted as a floating-point number
  - s: Treats the element to be formatted as a string

Because `printf()` and `sprintf()` treat % as the start of a conversion specification, to include a literal percentage sign in a string, use %%.

These functions are often used to format currencies, for example:

```
$total = .4;
// Displays "Total price: $0.40"
printf('Total price: $%0.2f’, $total);
// Displays "Total price: €0.40"
printf('Total price: &euro;%0.2f', $total);
```

The main difference between this method and number_format() is that printf() and sprintf() take the entire string as the first argument, which can contain an unlimited number of conversion specifications. A useful example is formatting a date, as shown in the following image:

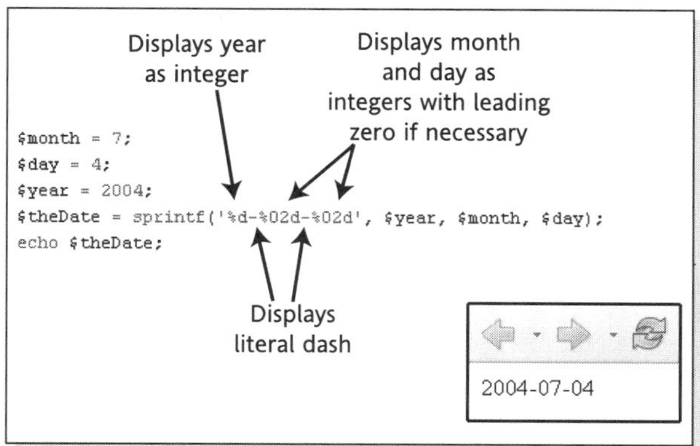

In this example, %d is used to format the year, and %02d is used to format the month and day with a leading zero if they are single figures. The dashes between each of the conversion specifications are treated as string literals. Why put the year first? Because the MySQL database likes it that way. In fact, it not only likes it, it insists on it.

If your brain is now beginning to suffer excruciating pain, don't worry. There are normally other, much more user-friendly ways of formatting output in PHP, and in Chapter 11 you will build a simple Flash component that automatically formats any date ready for MySQL. The reason for introducing you to the delights of printf() and sprintf() is that they're found in a lot of existing scripts, so it's useful to know what they're for. sprintf() can be useful for building SQL queries (if you ever use Dreamweaver's PHP server behaviors, you'll see it used all the time). You'll see sprintf() in action later in this chapter when you complete the PHP script for the multiconverter.

> *A full list of type specifiers used in* printf() *and* sprintf() *can be found in the PHP documentation at* www.php.net/manual/en/function.sprintf.php.

Changing case

After the rigors of printf() and sprintf(), now it's time for something much less taxing on the brain. Computers normally treat uppercase and lowercase characters as having completely different meanings, so it's often useful to change the case of a string, either when comparing two values or when you want user input to be formatted in a uniform way. Both ActionScript and PHP have simple methods of converting a string to uppercase or lowercase. ActionScript uses dot notation to apply the method to a string variable, while PHP requires the string to be passed to a function as an argument, as shown in Figures 4-4 and 4-5.

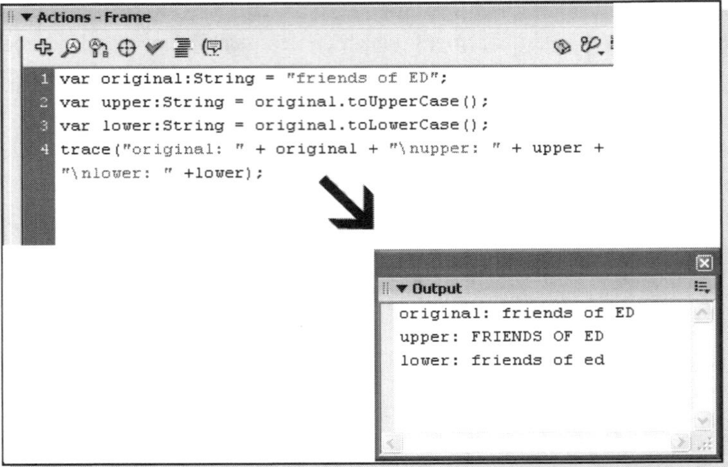

Figure 4-4. ActionScript uses dot notation to convert strings to uppercase or lowercase.

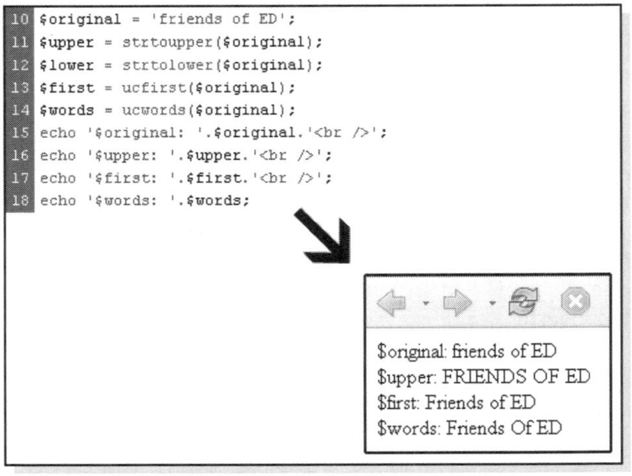

```
$original = 'friends of ED';
$upper = strtoupper($original);
$lower = strtolower($original);
$first = ucfirst($original);
$words = ucwords($original);
echo '$original: '.$original.'<br />';
echo '$upper: '.$upper.'<br />';
echo '$first: '.$first.'<br />';
echo '$words: '.$words;
```

$original: friends of ED
$upper: FRIENDS OF ED
$first: Friends of ED
$words: Friends Of ED

Figure 4-5. PHP offers four ways of changing case by passing a string to a function.

As Figure 4-5 shows, in addition to converting between uppercase and lowercase, PHP has two other case-conversion functions that have no equivalent in ActionScript. Table 4-1 describes them all.

Table 4-1. Case conversion in PHP and ActionScript

PHP function	ActionScript equivalent	Description	Result
`strtoupper()`	`toUpperCase()`	Converts entire string to uppercase.	FRIENDS OF ED
`strtolower()`	`toLowerCase()`	Converts entire string to lowercase.	friends of ed
`ucfirst()`	No equivalent	Capitalizes first character of string if alphabetic. Leaves other characters unchanged.	Friends of ED
`ucwords()`	No equivalent	Capitalizes first character of each word if alphabetic. Leaves other characters unchanged.	Friends Of ED

It's important to note that PHP has no idea what constitutes a word. `ucwords()` simply capitalizes the first character after any space.

A combination of these functions can ensure that people's names gathered from an online form are formatted uniformly.

```
$name = 'oLiveR twiST';
$name = strtolower($name);
$name = ucwords($name);
echo $name;  // Oliver Twist
```

This example shows the way most beginners would code the transformation, first to lowercase, then to initial capitals, followed by echo *to display the result. PHP, however, is quite happy to nest functions within one another—as long as the logic is preserved. A much shorter way of achieving the same result would be to combine the last three lines of code into one, like this:*

```
echo ucwords(strtolower($name));
```

PHP can be a very compact programming language when functions are combined like this, but you should always test the results thoroughly to ensure that PHP agrees with your view of logic!

Working with substrings

Both ActionScript and PHP offer methods of identifying the position of a character or group of characters in a larger string, and of extracting a substring. They work in similar ways, but with some important differences. Table 4-2 lists the equivalent functions and methods in each language.

Table 4-2. PHP functions for working with substrings and their ActionScript equivalents

PHP function	ActionScript equivalent	Description
`strpos()`	`indexOf()`	Returns the position of the first instance of a character or substring within a string. Both languages count the first letter as zero.
`stripos()`	No equivalent	Case-insensitive version of `strpos()`. New to PHP 5.
`strrpos()`	`lastIndexOf()`	Returns the position of the last instance of a character or substring within a string. Both languages count from the beginning of the string. If a substring is passed as an argument, versions prior to PHP 5 use only the first character of the substring in the search. PHP 5 searches for the full substring.
`strripos()`	No equivalent	Case-insensitive version of `strrpos()`. New to PHP 5.
`$stringVariable{}`	`charAt()`	Returns the character at the indicated position within a string. This is not a function in PHP, but a direct reference to the string variable. The syntax differs between PHP 4 and PHP 5.
`strlen()`	`length`	Returns the length of a string.
`substr()`	`substr()`	Extracts a substring.
`substr_replace()`	No equivalent	Modifies a substring within a larger string.
`str_replace()`	No equivalent	Replaces all instances of a substring within a larger string. It can also be used with arrays.
`explode()`	`split()`	Converts a string into an array by splitting it on a specified character or substring.
`implode()`	`join()`	Converts an array into a string. PHP also uses `join()` as a synonym for `implode()`.

If you are familiar with the ActionScript equivalents, you will find using the PHP functions quite straightforward. PHP does not use dot notation. So, instead of applying a method by adding it to the end of a variable with a period, the variable goes inside the parentheses as an argument of the appropriate PHP function. Most of the time, the variable is used as the first argument, but `str_replace()`, `explode()`, and `implode()` place it later in the list of arguments. The following illustration should make things clearer.

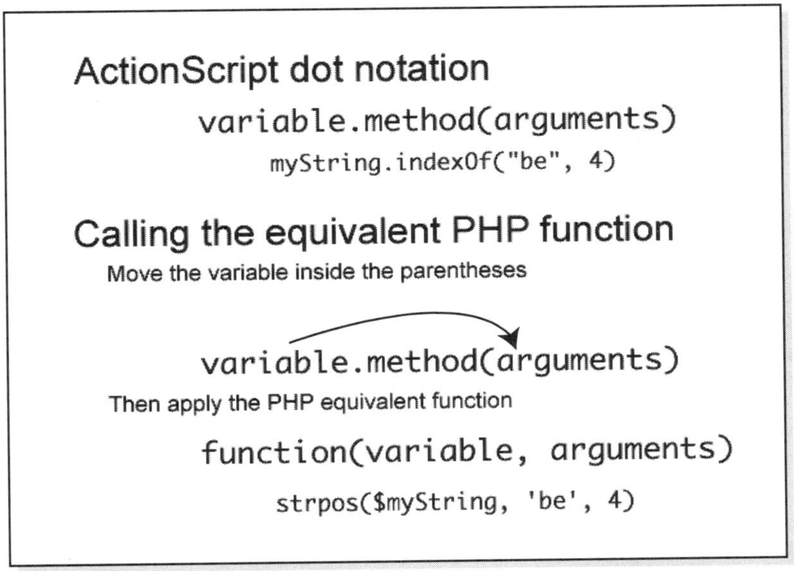

ActionScript dot notation

```
variable.method(arguments)
    myString.indexOf("be", 4)
```

Calling the equivalent PHP function

Move the variable inside the parentheses

```
variable.method(arguments)
```

Then apply the PHP equivalent function

```
function(variable, arguments)
    strpos($myString, 'be', 4)
```

> *Most of the examples in the following sections assign results to variables, as you would do in a normal program. To see the results in a browser yourself, use* echo *or* print *to display the value held by the variable. For the sake of brevity, I have not added a new line character in those examples where I have used* echo*. You will also find a lot of the examples in the download files for this chapter—all the filenames begin with* string_examples.

Getting the position of a character or substring

To find the position of the first instance of a character or substring, `strpos()` takes two arguments:

```
strpos($haystack, $needle)
```

For example:

```
$myString = 'To be or not to be';
$pos = strpos($myString, 't');  // $pos is 11
$pos = strpos($myString, 'be'); // $pos is 3
```

The count starts from zero, representing the position of the first character in the string, and spaces are counted as characters. The search is case sensitive. To find the first instance of "t" regardless of case, use stripos().

```
$pos = stripos($myString, 't'); // $pos is 0
```

To find the last instance of a character or substring, use strrpos(), which is case sensitive, or its case-insensitive equivalent strripos(). These search from the opposite end of the string. The position, however, is still counted from the *beginning* of the string.

```
$pos = strrpos($myString, 'T');   // $pos is 0
$pos = strripos($myString, 'T');  // $pos is 13
$pos = strrpos($myString, 'be');  // $pos is 16
```

The case-insensitive versions, stripos() and strripos(), are not available in versions prior to PHP 5. If your server still uses PHP 4, first convert the string to lowercase using strtolower().

Another important difference between PHP 4 and PHP 5 is that in PHP 4 strrpos() is not capable of searching for a string of characters. Instead, it searches only for the first character. So, a search for "or" with strrpos() looks only for "o" in PHP 4 and produces a result of 14 (the "o" in the final instance of "to"). PHP 5, on the other hand, searches for "or" and produces the correct result (6). If you want to use these functions, make sure you know which version of PHP your hosting server is running. Code designed for PHP 5 will give the wrong result on a PHP 4 server, and code designed for PHP 4 will cease to give the right result as soon as the server is upgraded. It's because of issues like this that hosting companies are often slow to upgrade. Even if they run PHP 5 on new servers, they may not automatically offer it to you unless you specifically request it. Fortunately, this sort of compatibility problem is easier to handle than with coding for different versions of the Flash Player. It's easy to find out which version of PHP your server is running, but you have no control over the version of Flash Player on each visitor's computer.

In the same way as indexOf() and lastIndexOf(), the PHP equivalents take an optional argument indicating the start position of a search. A negative number counts the starting position from the end of the string.

```
$pos = strpos($myString, 'be', 4);  // $pos is 16
$pos = strrpos($myString, 'be', -3); // $pos is 3
```

Take care not to mix up strpos() *and* strrpos()*, or their case-insensitive equivalents,* stripos() *and* strripos()*. That extra "r" makes all the difference. As you may have already gathered, most PHP function names are abbreviations of what they're used for. Think of this pair as* ***str****ing* ***pos****ition and* ***str****ing* ***r****everse* ***pos****ition. The* ***i*** *stands for* ***i****nsensitive, which is a shame, because PHP code warriors can really be quite caring (honest, we can).*

When testing the result of these four functions, always use the identical operator (===). This is because PHP treats zero as false. Consequently, if the character being sought is the first in the string, even a positive result will be treated as a failure.

Getting the character at a known position

PHP does not use a function to identify a character at a known position within a string. Instead, it uses curly braces to identify the position (as always, starting from zero). This is the equivalent of using the `charAt()` method in ActionScript.

ActionScript style:

```
var myString:String = "To be or not to be";
var char:String = myString.charAt(1);
```

PHP 5 style:

```
$myString = 'To be or not to be';
$char = $myString{1};
```

In both cases, the result is "o" (the second character).

> *Prior to PHP 5, square brackets were used, like this:* `$myString[1]`. *In effect, this treats the individual characters in a string as elements of an array. This syntax still works in PHP 5 but has been deprecated. You should always use curly braces to identify a character at a particular position, unless your server does not support PHP 5.*

Getting the length of a string

Finally, an answer to the ancient riddle about the length of a piece of string!

ActionScript style:

```
var ultimateQuestion:String = "of Life, the Universe and Everything";
var len:Number = ultimateQuestion.length;
```

PHP style:

```
$ultimateQuestion = 'of Life, the Universe and Everything';
$len = strlen($ultimateQuestion);
```

Neither Flash nor PHP has been around long enough to work out the answer to the Ultimate Question, but at least both agree that its length is 36. Give them another 7.5 million years, and they'll probably work out the answer, too:

```
$ultimateAnswer = 'Flash is Life, the Universe and Everything';
$len = strlen($ultimateAnswer);
echo $len;    // Try string_examples2.php for the result
```

(Apologies to the late Douglas Adams.)

Although the position of characters in a string is counted from zero, the length is always the actual number of characters (including spaces). Therefore, to find the final character in a string, subtract 1 from the length:

```
$finalChar = $ultimateAnswer{$len-1}; // g
```

Extracting a substring

Whereas ActionScript offers three methods for extracting a substring (substr(), substring(), and slice()), PHP offers just one: substr(), which works mainly like its ActionScript namesake but also incorporates some elements of slice().

The PHP version of substr() takes two required arguments and one optional argument:

- The string from which the substring is to be extracted.
- The position of the first character in the substring.
- The length of the substring (optional). If this is not specified, the substring contains all characters to the end of the string.

When the second argument and the third one (if specified) are positive, substr() works exactly the same in PHP as in ActionScript.

```
$myString = 'To be or not to be';
$sub = substr($myString, 9);     // $sub is "not to be"
$sub = substr($myString, 9, 3); // $sub is "not"
```

The operation is also identical when the start position is given as a negative number. The position is measured from the end of the string, with -1 representing the last character, -2 the second to the last character, and so on.

```
$sub = substr($myString, -5);     // $sub is "to be"
$sub = substr($myString, -5, 2); // $sub is "to"
```

The difference between ActionScript and PHP lies in the ability to specify a negative number as the final argument in PHP. When you do this, the substring ends that number of characters from the end of the string.

```
$sub = substr($myString, 9, -3);  // $sub is "not to"
$sub = substr($myString, -5, -1); // $sub is "to b"
```

You can experiment with substr() by using string_examples3.php in the download files. It contains an interactive form that displays the results of using any combination of arguments.

Replacing a substring

Closely related to substr() is the substr_replace() function, which makes possible a variety of string modifications. This PHP function, which has no counterpart in ActionScript, takes three or four arguments:

- The string to be modified.
- The new substring to be inserted.

- The starting point at which insertion is to begin.
- The length of the section to be replaced in the original string. If this is not specified, everything is replaced from the starting point to the end of the original string.

This is an example of how it works:

```
$original = 'Now is the time';
$modified = substr_replace($original, 'a good', 7, 3);
echo $modified; // "Now is a good time"
```

To insert without deleting, set the length to zero:

```
$modified = substr_replace($original, 'not ', 7, 0);
echo $modified; // "Now is not the time"
```

To replace all instances of a substring, use `str_replace()`. This takes three or four arguments:

- The substring to be replaced.
- The replacement text.
- The string to be searched.
- An optional variable to record the number of replacements made. (This was not available prior to PHP 5.)

The following example shows how it works:

```
$original = 'I want money, money, money';
$modified = str_replace('money','love',$original);
echo $modified; // "I want love, love, love"
```

Do not forget that PHP has no idea what a word is. The following is just as valid:

```
$modified = str_replace('m','h',$original);
echo $modified; // "I want honey, honey, honey"
```

As of PHP 5, `str_replace()` accepts a fourth, optional variable, which records the number of replacements made:

```
$modified = str_replace('m','h',$original,$count);
echo $count; // displays "3"
```

Converting strings into arrays and back

Although arrays aren't covered until the next chapter, this is a convenient point to explain the rather alarmingly named `explode()` function in PHP. It works the same way as `split()` in ActionScript, creating an array of substrings from a longer string. It takes two arguments:

- A string indicating where the original string is to be split
- The string to be converted into an array

This function is particularly useful for splitting up a comma-delimited list or for extracting the component parts of a date. The separator string is not retained in the array substrings. The following example shows how explode() works:

```
$list = 'dog, cat, horse';
$animals = explode(', ', $list);
echo $animals[0]; displays "dog"
echo $animals[1]; displays "cat"
echo $animals[2]; displays "horse"
```

Note that in this example the separator string includes a space after the comma. If you don't do this, the second and subsequent array elements will all begin with a blank space. If you are uncertain as to whether a comma-delimited list contains spaces, PHP does have functions to trim leading and trailing whitespace from strings. These functions will be covered later in the chapter when you deal with user input.

Also note that you must explicitly assign the result of explode() to a variable. There is no need to create an empty array beforehand. The function does that automatically.

The converse of explode() is implode(), which joins the elements of an array as a string. It takes as its first argument a string to be inserted between each element. To reconstitute the comma-delimited list, use implode() or its synonym join() like this:

```
$listCopy = implode(', ', $animals);
$listCopy = join(', ', $animals);
```

There is no difference between implode() and join(). They are fully interchangeable.

> *Even though the* Array.join() *method in ActionScript does the same as* join() *in PHP, beware of treating all functions with similar names as direct equivalents. PHP has a function called* split()*, which can also be used to split a string into an array. However,* split() *is designed to work with regular expressions and is much slower than* explode()*.*

Armed with all this knowledge about manipulating strings, you are now almost ready to complete the PHP script for the multiconverter from the previous chapter. Before doing so, let's take a quick look at creating custom-built functions in PHP.

Modularizing code with functions

If you've been working with ActionScript for any length of time, you should be very much at home with creating your own **custom-built functions**. Functions do things, and as the language's name suggests, that's what ActionScript is all about—doing things. You can't get very far unless you start building your own functions.

Understanding where PHP functions run

Custom-built functions are also important in PHP, but unlike ActionScript functions, they don't reside in the client computer's memory. So, before getting down to the details of creating functions in PHP, it's worth pausing for a moment to consider the wider implications of this difference. If you recall the discussion in Chapter 1 of how Flash, PHP, Apache, and MySQL fit together, a Flash movie is downloaded to the user's computer and runs locally, so an ActionScript function remains in *local* memory until needed (see Figure 4-6). PHP, on the other hand, is a server-side language. Everything is processed on the remote server, and all that's sent to the client computer is the result. Once it has completed its task, PHP frees the server's memory for other things. If you think about it, this makes a lot of sense. Busy web servers may handle thousands of requests a second. If every PHP function remained in memory until needed again, the server would slow to a crawl or simply grind to a halt.

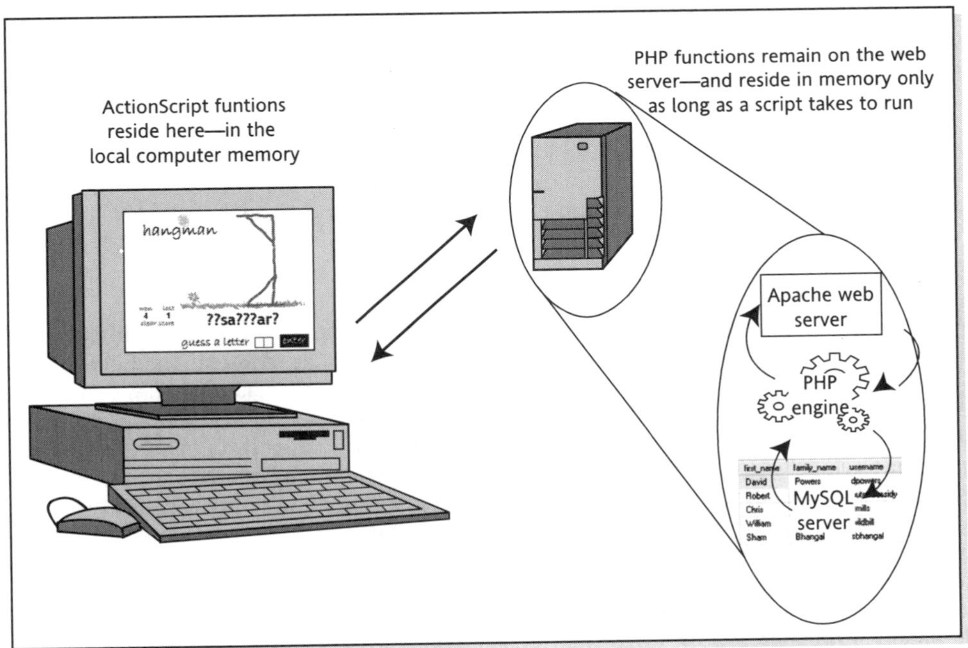

Figure 4-6. Every call to PHP involves a round-trip to the server, so it's important to design applications that do so efficiently.

This has important implications for how you design PHP applications. If your ActionScript background makes you think in terms of events, consider the request to the server as the event that drives a PHP script. The request may involve a very simple task, such as getting the date (as in Chapter 2), or it may be much more complex, such as searching through a database according to user-specified criteria (you'll do this in Chapter 10). No matter how simple or complicated, such requests involve a round-trip to the server, usually across an Internet connection. The only time this won't happen is when you're using an intranet or testing locally.

Because you're currently developing everything on your local computer, it's easy to forget that the response to a PHP-driven event won't always be instantaneous. A well-designed PHP script will normally be processed in microseconds. What you can't predict is the speed of the user's Internet connection or how busy the remote server may be at the time.

When you build a Flash application that uses PHP, both the SWF and PHP files will probably be located in the same folder on your web server, so they're logically connected in your head, but that's as far as it goes. The only connection between them is through an HTTP request, and each request is treated completely separately. Connecting to the Internet to refresh the date every time your Flash movie loads a particular frame is obviously wasteful, so a suitable strategy was devised in Chapter 2 to avoid that situation. For similar reasons, the word game in Chapter 7 will simultaneously load 250 words to be stored in an ActionScript array, rather than each time the player starts a new game. On the other hand, it's impossible to anticipate the criteria for a database search, so you need to devise a script that will do it as quickly and as efficiently as possible. By default, PHP servers are configured to terminate a script if it runs for more than 30 seconds. Although you can override this restriction, it's usually better to rethink your application if you find yourself running afoul of this limitation. Unless you're performing a complex search in a huge database, it normally indicates overly complex looping.

Well-designed PHP code is very fast and light on its feet—even more so since the release of PHP 5. As long as you plan your applications so they don't make unnecessary calls to the remote server, you'll find that Flash and PHP make perfect partners.

Why roll your own?

With more than 2,700 built-in functions in PHP, you may wonder why anyone would ever need to custom-build their own. The answer is that every application is different. The built-in functions are invaluable, but sooner or later you will need to create specialist routines that can be used over and over again while the script is running—often to perform calculations or format text in a specific way. For instance, in the multiconverter application, you need to determine whether the units displayed should be singular or plural. Without a custom function, the same conditional statement would need to be repeated more than 20 times throughout the script. Not only does a custom function save a lot of typing, but also it makes maintenance easier. If you discover a problem with the code, only the function needs updating, not the same code scattered in dozens of places.

You build a function in PHP the same way you create a basic function in ActionScript—by declaring the `function` keyword, followed by the name of the function and parentheses containing arguments (if any). The code to be executed is enclosed in curly braces.

```
function functionName(arguments) {
  // code to be executed
  }
```

> *PHP does have the equivalent of an ActionScript anonymous function, but it's rarely used. If you're curious, you can find the details in the PHP documentation at* `www.php.net/manual/en/function.create-function.php`.

Understanding how PHP and ActionScript functions handle variables

Although the structure of functions is identical in both languages, a major difference lies in the concept of **variable scope**. The best way to demonstrate how they differ is with an example.

Testing variable scope

1. Open a new Flash document. With the first frame of Layer 1 highlighted, open the Actions panel and insert the following code:

```
function doubleIt() {
  myNum *= 2;
}
var myNum:Number = 3;
trace("Before: " + myNum);
doubleIt();
trace("After :" + myNum);
```

2. Test the movie by pressing *CTRL+ENTER/⌘+RETURN*. You should see the result shown in Figure 4-7. ActionScript doubles the value of `myNum`.

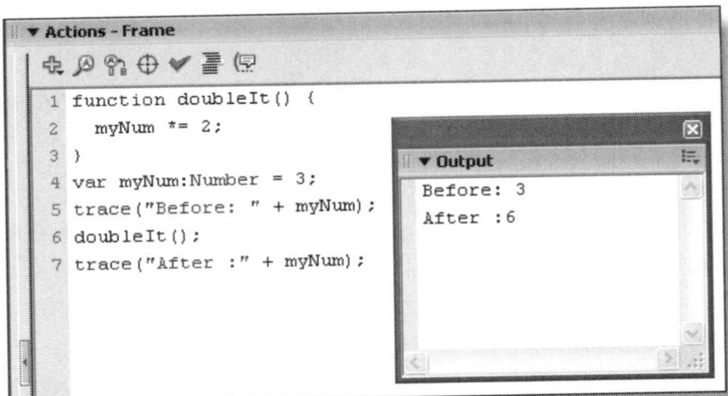

Figure 4-7. Variables inside ActionScript functions are automatically accessible to the rest of the script unless explicitly declared local in scope.

3. Now create a new PHP page called `scope.php`, and enter the following code:

```
<?php
function doubleIt() {
  $myNum *= 2;
  }
$myNum = 3;
echo 'Before: '.$myNum.'<br />';
doubleIt();
echo 'After :'.$myNum;
?>
```

On the face of it, this is simply the same code adapted for PHP by prefixing the variables with dollar signs, substituting echo for `trace`, and using the appropriate concatenation operator.

4. Test `scope.php` in a browser. You should see something like this:

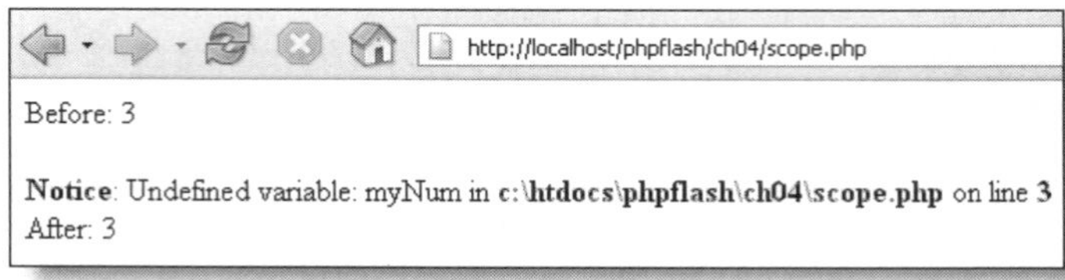

Not only is the value of `$myNum` unchanged, but also PHP has reported an undefined variable. The line number may differ on your page, but it's clear from the position of the error message that it's coming from inside the function.

> *If you don't get the notice about the undefined variable, that means you have not set up the* `error_reporting` *configuration command in* `php.ini` *as recommended in Chapter 1. Many PHP developers prefer to work with notices turned off, because they are not fatal errors. I think notices help you develop more robust, future-proof code.*

What is the reason for this behavior? It's because **variables inside PHP functions are visible only to code inside the same function**. To use the technical expression, they have only **local scope**. Even though `$myNum` has already been declared earlier in the script, it is not accessible inside the function. The fact that both variables have the same name is irrelevant. As far as PHP is concerned, they are completely separate. In fact, you get the same result in ActionScript if you use the `var` keyword in front of a variable inside a function, as shown in Figure 4-8.

```
function doubleIt() {
  var myNum:Number;
  myNum *= 2;
}
var myNum:Number = 3;
trace("Before: " + myNum);
doubleIt();
trace("After :" + myNum);
```

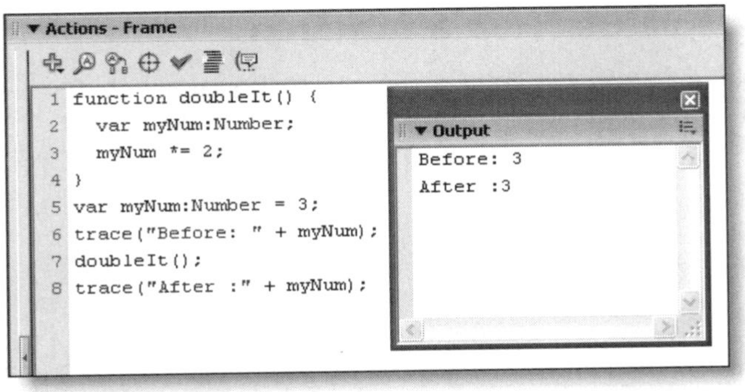

▼ Actions - Frame

```
function doubleIt() {
  var myNum:Number;
  myNum *= 2;
}
var myNum:Number = 3;
trace("Before: " + myNum);
doubleIt();
trace("After :" + myNum);
```

▼ Output

```
Before: 3
After :3
```

Figure 4-8. Using the var keyword inside an ActionScript function keeps the variable local in scope.

PHP does not have the equivalent of the `var` keyword; variables inside functions are automatically treated as having local scope. The only exceptions are variables that belong to the **superglobal arrays** or variables that are explicitly declared as global. The superglobal arrays (of which `$_POST[]` is an example) are listed in Table 5-1 and will be described in the next chapter. To give an ordinary variable global scope in PHP, prefix it with the `global` keyword inside the function, like this:

```
function doubleIt() {
  global $myNum;
  $myNum *= 2;
  }
```

If you run the script in `scope.php` again (it's `scope2.php` in the download files), the warning about the undefined variable will disappear, and the result of the function will be the same as in the original ActionScript (see Figure 4-7).

> *A simple rule is as follows: inside a PHP function, local scope is automatic; in ActionScript, local scope applies only when a variable is declared inside the function with* `var`.

Now that you know how to give a variable global scope in PHP, try to forget all about it. Restricting variable scope inside functions makes it easier to keep track of what's happening. Instead of declaring variables as global, it's normally preferable to pass a variable as an argument to a function and capture the new value in a variable, which is what the next section is all about.

Returning a value from a function

Because the value of a variable inside a function isn't accessible outside, it's necessary to **return** the result using the `return` keyword. So, the `doubleIt()` function needs to be rewritten in PHP like this:

```
function doubleIt($myNum) {
  $myNum *= 2;
  return $myNum;
  }
```

In the first line of the redefined function, `$myNum` is placed between the parentheses after the function name. This has the effect of turning it into an argument or **parameter** being passed to the function. PHP uses the value stored in that variable to perform data manipulation inside the function, and the resulting value is then returned using the `return` keyword. The important thing to remember is that when the variable's datatype holds only a single value (in other words, a string, integer, or floating-point number), the function works on a *copy* of the variable being passed to it. You can see this in action by altering the code in `scope.php` as follows (the code is in `return.php` in the download files for this chapter):

```
<?php
// function takes $myNum as an argument (parameter)
function doubleIt($myNum) {
  // inside the function, $myNum has no relationship
  // to the variable of the same name outside
  $myNum *= 2;
  // after multiplying the argument by 2
  // the result is returned as a new value
  return $myNum;
  }
// the version of $myNum outside the function
// has the same name, but the scope is different
$myNum = 3;
// the value of $myNum is 3
echo 'Before: '.$myNum.'<br />';
$doubled = doubleIt($myNum);
// the value of $myNum is still 3
echo 'After: '.$myNum.'<br />';
// the value of $doubled is the result of passing $myNum (3)
// to the doubleIt() function - 3 * 2 = 6
echo 'Doubled: '.$doubled;
?>
```

If you view the page in a browser, the result you now get is

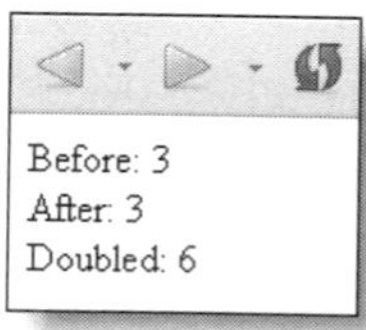
Before: 3
After: 3
Doubled: 6

So, the $myNum variable being used in the function is a totally separate entity from the one outside, and the new value has been captured in a new variable called $doubled. Of course, there is nothing to stop you from reassigning the result of a function to the variable you're working on—in fact, it's very common.

```
$myNum = doubleIt($myNum);
```

Although this is commonly done, the disadvantage should be obvious: $myNum no longer holds the original value. Using a new variable to store the value returned by a function means the original can be preserved and a range of different actions performed on it. This applies equally to ActionScript and PHP.

In this example, I deliberately used a variable with the same name to demonstrate the principle of local scope within a function. Your code will be far easier to understand if you adopt the practice of using different names for variables inside functions. As with all variable names, it's sensible to use short names that convey the variable's purpose. A good choice in this case would be $num or $number.

Functions don't always have to return a value. You can use a function to output text directly to the browser. Since this book is mainly concerned with using PHP to process data to return to Flash, a return value will normally be required. Forgetting to return a value or to capture it in a variable are common beginner's mistakes, so take care!

Deciding where to put functions

PHP parses the entire script before doing anything, so the location of functions isn't as critical as in ActionScript. Functions can be gathered together at the top (as is good practice in ActionScript) or at the bottom, or they can be simply left where they're first used. In spite of this seemingly devil-may-care attitude, it's definitely a good idea keep functions all together for ease of maintenance. I normally put my PHP functions at the bottom, but that's purely a matter of personal preference. If your ActionScript background makes you want to put all your functions at the top of the script, PHP won't object—nor will I.

As your projects become larger and more ambitious, you may want to keep your custom-built functions in external files. That's when location *does* matter—an external file must be included *before* you can call any functions it contains. (Including external files is covered in Chapter 5, when you build an application that uses a third-party script to parse RSS feeds.)

Completing the multiconverter script

At the end of the previous chapter, the multiconverter was functional, but only for half the conversion types. The other half remain to be completed because they all require special handling. The string manipulation functions presented in the first half of this chapter now come into their own. First of all, you need to create a custom-built function to display the correct version of the measurement units, dependent on whether they need to be singular or plural.

Formatting the main measurement units

Life would be a lot simpler if all that was necessary to make a word plural was to add "s". What about "feet"? What about "inches"? Sure, you can use abbreviations, such as "ft" and "in"—they don't need pluralizing—but you still need a way of knowing when to add the final "s" to other words. One solution is to add the "s" by default, and remove it only if the unit is less than or equal to one.

> *All the necessary files for the multiconverter project can be found in the download files for this chapter. Because the application is a continuation of the previous chapter, the first FLA is named* `converter05.fla`*, and the PHP file is named* `converter01.php`*. Both contain the application as it was left at the end of Chapter 3. You will also need to include* `convTypes.as` *in the same folder. Either use your own files from the previous chapter and copy them to* `phpflash/ch04`*, or use the download files.*
>
> *If you're using your own files, change the URL for* `sendData.sendAndLoad` *(around line 81) from* `phpflash/ch03` *to* `phpflash/ch04`*. When using the download files, always rename them omitting the version number (so* `converter05.fla` *becomes* `converter.fla`*, and so on).*

1. Open `converter.php` and insert the following code just before the closing PHP tag (the finished code for this section is in `converter02.php`):

```
// remove final "s" from measurement unit if number 1 or less
function plural($number, $unit) {
  // if 0 or 1, and unit ends in "s"
  if (abs($number) <= 1 && strrpos($unit, 's') ==
➥ (strlen($unit) - 1)) {
    // concatenate and remove final "s"
    return $number.' '.substr_replace($unit, '', -1);
    }
  else { // concatenate without changing
    return $number.' '.$unit;
    }
  }
```

This creates a function called `plural()`, which takes two arguments: a number (the result of the conversion calculation) and a measurement unit. The function opens with a conditional statement, which checks whether the number is less than or equal to 1, and if the last letter of the measurement unit is "s". If both these conditions are met, the "s" is removed. Otherwise, the number and measurement unit are returned unchanged. So, if the arguments passed to `plural()` are `1` and `pints`, the return value will be `1 pint`. If, on the other hand, the arguments are `1` and `ft`, the return value will be `1 ft`. Values in excess of `1` would return, for example, `5 pints` or `5 in`.

Let's break the function down to see how it works. The first part of the conditional statement is quite straightforward:

```
abs($number) <= 1
```

abs() is one of the useful math functions introduced in the previous chapter (see Table 3-2). It returns the absolute value of a number or—to put it more simply—turns negative numbers into positive ones. Any number smaller than –1 requires a plural measurement unit. By checking the absolute value, we can be sure the number is no greater than ±1. Note that you're only checking the absolute value of the variable, not assigning it. A negative number will still be negative after the check. If the result is true, the conditional statement goes on to check the next part:

```
strrpos($unit, 's') == (strlen($unit) - 1)
```

This uses two of the string manipulation functions presented earlier in this chapter. strrpos() returns the position of the last instance of "s" in the measurement unit, while strlen() finds out how many characters it contains. Since character positions are counted from zero, the length of the string minus 1 represents the final character. If the two numbers are the same, the final letter must be an "s". If both parts of the conditional statement are true, the next block of code is executed:

```
return $number.' '.substr_replace($unit, '', -1);
```

The second argument of substr_replace() is an empty string, which has the effect of deleting from the starting point specified in the third argument. Because the starting point is a negative number, you count from the end of the string. The final letter is –1, which we already know must be an "s". So, the "s" is removed, and the (now singular) unit is concatenated with the number and a space in between. The return keyword ensures the result is returned from the function.

If the conditional statement fails, the number and unchanged measurement unit are concatenated with a space between them, and returned.

2. Now that you have a way of formatting the result of calculations, you can apply the plural() function to the default return value in the second switch statement in converter.php. Find this code near the bottom of the page:

```
switch($type) {
  default:
    $output = "$a $units1 = ";
    $output .= "$r $unitsR";
    }
```

3. Change the code as follows:

```
switch($type) {
  default:
    // format first unit for singular and plural values
    $output = plural($a, $units1).' = ';
    $output .= "$r $unitsR";
    }
```

4. Now test the Flash movie. Try one of the active conversion types with a variety of positive and negative numbers. (Don't forget that not all conversion formulas have been added to the PHP script yet, so Area and Temperature are the only ones fully active.) You should get results like this:

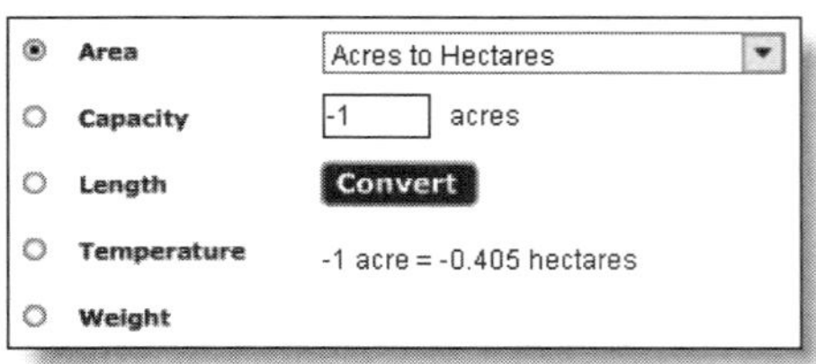

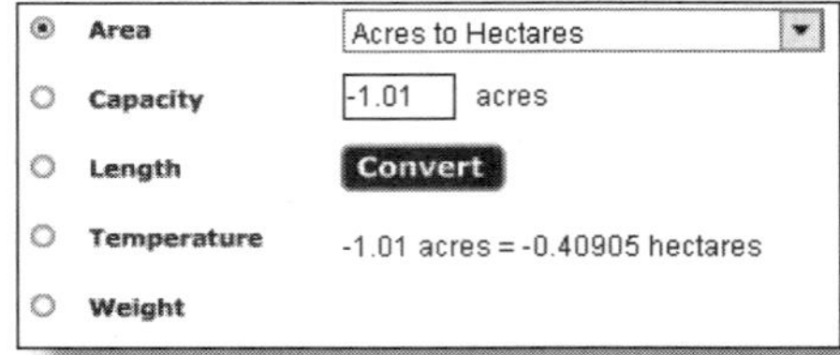

At –1, the unit is displayed as acre, but at –1.01, it becomes acres. Admittedly, negative figures make little sense, except for temperatures, but it has demonstrated a useful application of abs() that will come in handy in other projects.

5. As you can see from the preceding screenshots, the conversion results can sometimes be rather long, so some rounding is in order. One way would be to use number_format(), but since you have just gone through the trauma of studying sprintf(), let's use that. The result of each calculation is held in the variable $r. So, to format $r to two decimal places and a leading zero, the code is sprintf('%0.2f',$r). That takes care of the number format, but you also need to format the measurement unit with the plural() custom-built function, which takes two arguments: the number and the unit. You could format the number, and then apply plural() like this:

```
switch($type) {
  default:
    // format first unit for singular and plural values
    $output = plural($a, $units1).' = ';
    $r = sprintf('%0.2f',$r);
    $output .= plural($r, $unitsR);
    }
```

Let's be a bit more ambitious, though. PHP allows you to nest a function call inside the arguments of another. So the last two lines can be combined like this:

```
$output .= plural(sprintf('%0.2f',$r), $unitsR);
```

6. If you test your movie now, you'll see that both input and output are properly formatted. Still, it feels rather strange to display temperatures to two decimal places. One decimal place looks much nicer. Since you're using the degree sign followed by F or C for the measurement units, there's no need to use the plural() function. The following code is sufficient:

```
sprintf('%0.1f', $r).$unitsR
```

The way to identify a temperature result is by examining $unitsR. The first character is the degree sign, so strpos() is perfect for the job. Remember, though, that the first character in a string is at position 0, and PHP regards 0 as `false`. To make sure you have an exact match, you need to use the identical operator, like this:

```
strpos($unitsR, '°') === 0
```

7. Let's put everything together. You could use an `if... else` conditional statement, but this is an ideal place to deploy the conditional operator (?:). The condition being tested for goes to the left of the question mark. If the degree sign is found, the code to the right of the question mark is executed, and the single decimal place format is used. If the degree sign is not found, the code to the right of the semicolon is used, and the output is formatted to two decimal places. The entire code block looks like this:

```
switch($type) {
  default:
    // format first unit for singular and plural values
    $output = plural($a, $units1).' = ';
    // format second unit, adjust temperatures to one decimal place
    $output .= strpos($unitsR, '°') === 0 ? sprintf('%0.1f',
➥ $r).$unitsR : plural(sprintf('%0.2f',$r), $unitsR);
    }
```

8. Test the movie now, and make sure the temperature and area measurements are being formatted correctly. You can compare your code against `converter02.php` in the download files for this chapter.

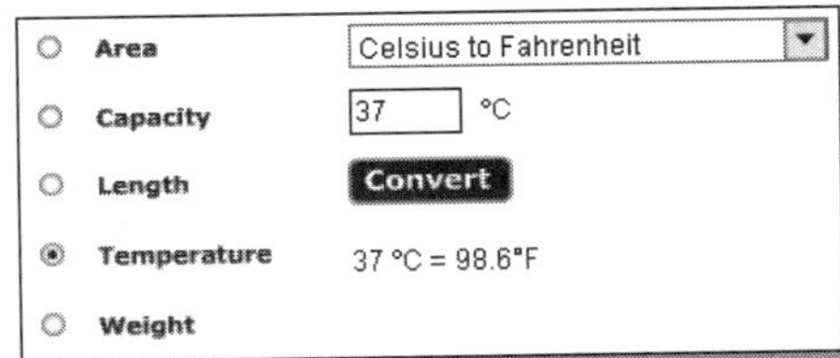

That takes care of all the main conversion formatting. Now it's a question of going through the remaining conversion types and handling the specific problems they pose.

Handling gallons, pints, and liters

In addition to working with gallons and pints, the difference between U.S. and British (Imperial) measurements requires some logical thought, but nothing beyond the skills of the code warrior that you're in the process of becoming.

1. Continue working with the same PHP file or use `converter02.php`. Like the list of conversion type arrays in the previous chapter, this section involves quite a lot of typing, so you may prefer just to follow the finished code in `converter03.php`. If you're typing along, insert the following code just before the closing bracket of the *first* `switch` statement (the one that contains the area, length, and temperature conversion formulas):

```
// Capacity conversion
case 'ptToLtr':
  $r = $a * .473;
  $r2 = $a * .568;
  $unitsUS = 'US pints';
  $unitsImp = 'Imperial pints';
```

```
    $unitsR = 'liters';
    break;
  case 'galToLtr':
    $r = $a * 3.785;
    $r2 = $a * 4.546;
    $unitsUS = 'US gallons';
    $unitsImp = 'Imperial gallons';
    $unitsR = 'liters';
    break;
```

In each case, `$r` uses the formula to convert from U.S. pints or gallons, while `$r2` uses the formula for Imperial measures. The `$unitsUS` and `$unitsImp` variables are labels for use in the output, and they should be self-explanatory.

2. The default output format you've been using up to now won't work with these new formulas, so you need to create a specific one for these two. Insert the following code in the *second* switch statement immediately above the default case you were working on in the previous section:

```
case 'ptToLtr':
case 'galToLtr':
  // format the result for US pints/gallons to liters
  $output = plural($a, $unitsUS).' = '.plural(sprintf('%0.2f', $r),
➥ $unitsR)."\n";
  // format the result for Imperial pints/gallons to liters
  $output .= plural($a, $unitsImp).' = '.plural(sprintf('%0.2f', $r2),
➥ $unitsR);
  break;
```

Although the code may look confusing, all it does is use the `plural()` and `sprintf()` functions to format the result. The meaning should become a lot clearer when you look at the following image.

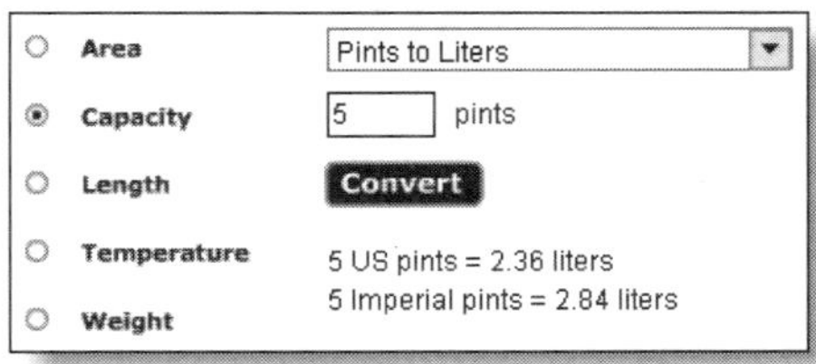

The first line takes `$a` (the original input value) and displays it with the value of `$unitsUS` (either US pints or US gallons). It then displays an equal sign followed by the result of the calculation and a new line character. The second line does the same with the Imperial units, using `$r2` as the result of the conversion.

Note that this is an example of grouping several instances of the case keyword together and applying the same block of code to them. You can do the same with the other conversion formulas, applying the same display pattern to several, rather than creating a separate one for each of them.

3. The conversion back to pints and gallons works in a similar way. Add the following conversion formulas to the first switch statement, after those you inserted in step 1:

```
case 'ltrToPt':
  $r = $a / .473;
  $r2 = $a / .568;
  $unitsR = 'US pints';
  $unitsR2 = 'Imperial pints';
  break;
case 'ltrToGal':
  $r = $a / 3.785;
  $r2 = $a / 4.546;
  $unitsR = 'US gallons';
  $unitsR2 = 'Imperial gallons';
  break;
```

4. The output code for these two conversion formulas follows. Put it in the second switch statement after the code entered in step 2.

```
case 'ltrToPt':
case 'ltrToGal':
  // format result of liters to US pints/gallons
  $output = plural($a, $units1).' = '.plural(sprintf('%0.2f', $r),
➥ $unitsR)."\n";
// format result of Imperial equivalent
  $output .= 'or '.plural(sprintf('%0.2f', $r2), $unitsR2);
  break;
```

The code's purpose is made clearer by seeing an example of its output.

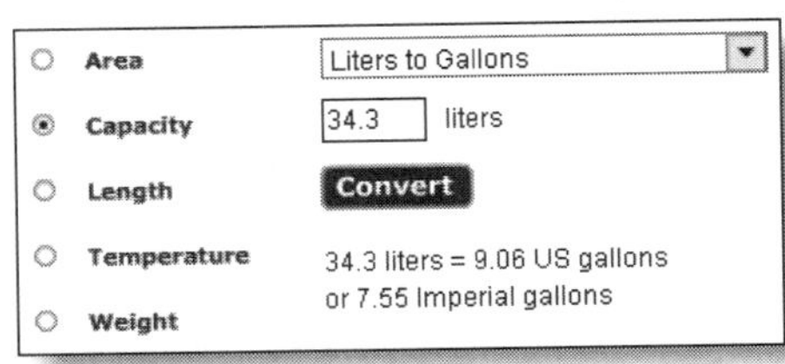

As you can see, I decided not to convert fractions of a gallon. There are more important things in life, such as the rest of this book! In any case, the multiconverter already has an option to convert liters to pints.

5. The final set of formulas needed for the capacity category deals with conversion between U.S. and Imperial measures. This requires slightly more complex code. Insert the following block at the end of the formulas in the first switch statement:

```
case 'UStoImp':
  $pints = $a * 8 + $b;
  $pints /= 1.201;
  $units1 = 'US gallons';
  $units2 = empty($a) ? 'US pints' : 'pints';
  $unitsR = 'Imperial gallons';
  $r = floor($pints / 8);
  $unitsR2 = $r ? 'pints' : 'Imperial pints';
  $r2 = $pints - ($r * 8);
  break;
```

```
case 'ImpToUS':
  $pints = $a * 8 + $b;
  $pints *= 1.201;
  $units1 = 'Imperial gallons';
  $units2 = empty($a) ? 'Imperial pints' : 'pints';
  $unitsR = 'US gallons';
  $r = floor($pints / 8);
  $unitsR2 = $r ? 'pints' : 'US pints';
  $r2 = $pints - ($r * 8);
  break;
```

It's easier to understand what's going on here by first taking a look at the input the multiconverter expects when you select one of these categories. The interface for converting U.S. gallons and pints to their Imperial equivalents looks like this:

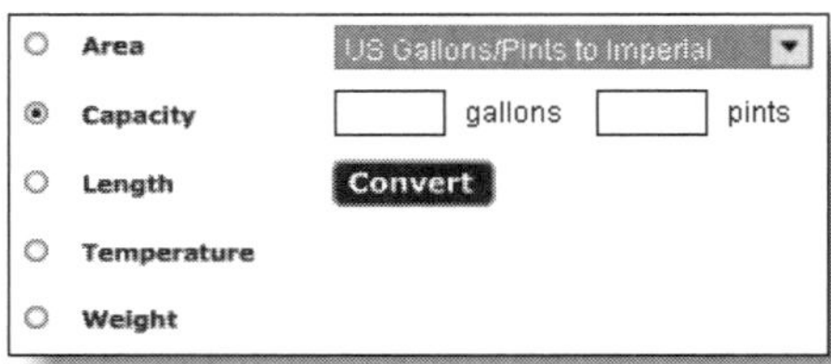

This is the first time you have encountered two input fields. The value from the left-hand one (gallons) will be stored in $a, and the value from the right-hand one (pints) will be stored in $b. First, it's necessary to convert everything to pints, so the following line multiplies $a by 8 and adds $b:

```
$pints = $a * 8 + $b;
```

The pints are then converted to the equivalent number of pints in the other system. For example, there are 1.201 U.S. pints in a British pint.

`$units1` and `$units2` assign labels to show the amount being converted. In the first case, a simple assignment is sufficient, but the following line needs explanation:

```
$units2 = empty($a) ? 'Imperial pints' : 'pints';
```

It uses the conditional operator to check whether $a is empty. If it is, `$units2` is set to Imperial pints. Otherwise, the label is set to pints. The following images show the effect (this won't work until the code in step 6 has been inserted).

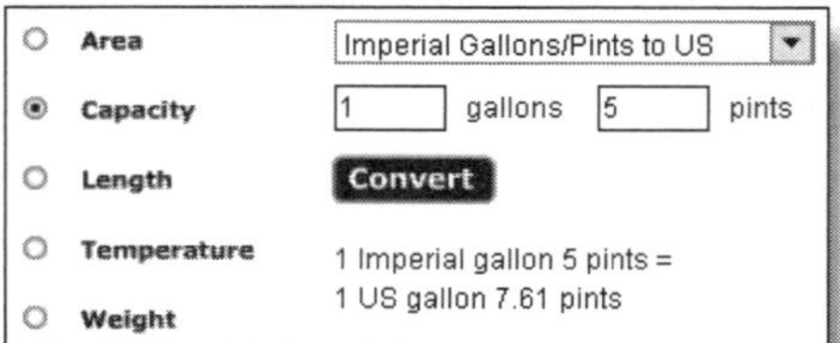

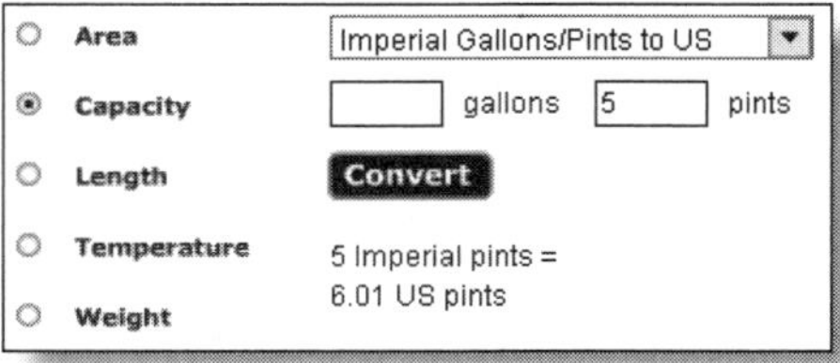

The result of the conversion then needs to be converted back to gallons and pints. Getting the gallons is easy: divide by 8 and round down, using `floor()`. This figure is assigned to `$r`, but if there are fewer than 8 pints, `$r` will be zero. Since zero equates to `false`, and any other number to `true`, `$r` on its own can be used as a Boolean. So the following line uses another conditional operator to set the labels for the result:

```
$unitsR2 = $r ? 'pints' : 'US pints';
```

This is a very terse but convenient way of writing the following:

```
if ($r != 0) {
  $unitsR2 = 'pints';
  }
else {
  $unitsR2 = 'US pints';
  }
```

Finally, you need to calculate the number of pints in the result. The simplest way of doing this is `$r2 = $pints % 8`. Unfortunately, modulo returns only whole numbers. So, converting 1 U.S. pint to British pints produces a result of `0`. The following formula gives a more accurate result:

```
$r2 = $pints - ($r * 8);
```

This subtracts from the total number of pints the number of gallons multiplied by 8.

6. All that's left now is to display the result. The following code goes in the second switch statement immediately below the code inserted in step 4:

```
case 'UStoImp':
case 'ImpToUS':
  // check left and right input fields; if not empty, format result
  // if no input, return empty string for relevant field
  $output = (!empty($a)) ? plural($a, $units1).' ' : '';
  $output .= (!empty($b)) ? plural($b, $units2) : '';
  // output equal sign followed by new line character
  $output .= " =\n";
  // if $r (gallons) is not zero, format result
  $output .= $r ? plural($r, $unitsR).' ' : '';
  // format $r2 (pints)
  $output .= plural(sprintf('%0.2f',$r2), $unitsR2);
  break;
```

This code uses a series of conditional operator statements that determine whether to display the gallons and pints labels for the input and output. The first two statements use `empty()` with the negation operator to check whether `$a` and `$b` contain a value. If they do, the result is formatted with `plural()` and added to `$output`. If they are empty, an empty string (nothing) is added to `$output`. The easy way to think of `(!empty($a))` is *`if $a is not empty`*. Everything else follows the same pattern as before. Compare your file with the finished code so far in `converter03.php`.

Dealing with kilograms, pounds, and stones

Fortunately, handling weight conversion is much simpler. Rather than go into a tortuous explanation of each one, I'll give you the code to examine at your leisure, and then I'll briefly describe how the results are displayed.

1. If you are bravely typing along, continue working in your existing PHP file or use `converter03.php`. The finished code for this section can be found in `converter04.php`.

   The following code goes in the first switch statement just before the closing curly brace. The formulas make use of simple arithmetic and show good examples of the modulo operator, dividing by 16 to get the number of ounces when converting from kilograms to pounds, and dividing by 14 to convert pounds to stones (the traditional British measure for body weight).

```
// Weight conversion
case 'lbToKg':
  $oz = $a * 16 + $b;
  $r = $oz / 16 * .454;
  $unitsR = 'kg';
  break;
case 'kgToLb':
  $oz = $a / .454 * 16;
  $r = floor($oz / 16);
  $r2 = $oz % 16;
  $unitsR = 'lb';
  $unitsR2 = 'oz';
  break;
case 'lbToSt':
  $r = floor($a / 14);
  $r2 = $a % 14;
  $unitsR = 'st';
  $unitsR2 = 'lb';
  break;
case 'stToLb':
  $r = $a * 14 + $b;
  $unitsR = 'lb';
  break;
```

2. The code to display the results goes in the second switch statement, immediately below the code in step 6 of the previous section. Note that the second block of case keywords includes the display method for two length measurements for which conversion formulas haven't yet been created. I'll deal with them in the next section.

```
case 'lbToKg':
case 'stToLb':
  $output = (!empty($a)) ? plural($a, $units1).' ' : '';
  $output .= (!empty($b)) ? plural($b, $units2) : '';
  $output .= ' = ';
  $output .= $unitsR == 'lb' ? $r : sprintf('%0.3f', $r);
  $output .= ' '.$unitsR;
  break;
```

```
case 'mToFt':
case 'mToYd':
case 'kgToLb':
case 'lbToSt':
  $output = "$a $units1 = $r $unitsR $r2 $unitsR2";
break;
```

The display pattern for pounds to kilograms and stones to pounds is similar to the one used in step 6 of the previous section. The only line that probably needs explanation is this:

```
$output .= $unitsR == 'lb' ? $r : sprintf('%0.3f', $r);
```

You should be quite used to the conditional operator by now. The condition to the left of the question mark checks whether the output unit is "lb" (pounds). If it is, the value of the conversion is added to `$output` without formatting, because it should always be an integer. If the output unit isn't pounds, it must be kilograms, so the value of the conversion is formatted to three decimal places to give a result accurate to the nearest gram. There's no need to use `plural()`, because neither "lb" nor "kg" ends in "s". If you're building this yourself, check your code so far against converter04.php.

Handling meters to feet and yards

The final two conversion formulas make use of PHP's weak typing to convert a number to a string, break it into two substrings, and then use an arithmetic operator to perform a calculation on one of them, something ActionScript 2.0 won't permit if strict typing is enforced (unless you explicitly cast the strings to numbers).

1. Continue with the same PHP file, or use converter04.php. The final code is in converter05.php. Insert the following code at the end of the length conversion section in the first `switch` statement.

```
case 'mToFt':
  $ft = sprintf('%0.2f', $a / .305);
  $ft = explode('.', $ft);
  $r = $ft[0];
  $r2 = $ft[1]/100 * 12;
  $unitsR = 'ft';
  $unitsR2 = 'in';
  break;
case 'mToYd';
  $yd = sprintf('%0.2f', $a / .914);
  $yd = explode('.', $yd);
  $r = $yd[0];
  $r2 = $yd[1]/100 * 3;
  $unitsR = 'yd';
  $unitsR2 = 'ft';
  break;
```

Both formulas work exactly the same way. The only difference lies in the numbers and units used. So, I'll just explain the first, which converts meters to feet.

The second line of the code performs two operations in one. It divides $a (the number of meters) by .305 to obtain the number of feet. At the same time, it uses `sprintf()` to format the result. You could write the same thing this way:

```
$ft = $a / .305;
$ft = sprintf('%0.2f', $ft);
```

Combining the calculation with the formatting simply makes the script more compact.

If $a is 12, the result of the calculation so far would be 39.34 ft. The problem is how to convert the .34 fraction of a foot into inches. The next line uses `explode()` to split the result into two parts, using the decimal point as the separator. Arrays are covered in the next chapter; all you need to know at the moment is that `$ft` is transformed into an array, with the whole number held in the first element and the decimal fraction in the second. In this case, `$ft[0]` is 39, and `$ft[1]` is 34.

The whole number of feet can be displayed as it is, so it is assigned to `$r`. The decimal fraction is now a string with a value of 34. PHP's loose typing means you can treat it as an integer. First, you divide it by 100 to restore the decimal fraction, and then you multiply by 12 to get the number of inches.

You've already created the display pattern for these conversion formulas, so that's all there is to it. The multiconverter is now complete.

2. If you've been using the download files, don't forget to change the name of `converter05.php` to `converter.php`, and to make the same change in the URL called by `sendData.sendAndLoad` (around line 81) in `converter.fla`. The completed files for both the Flash interface and the PHP script are available in the download files as `converter.fla` and `converter.php`.

Reviewing the multiconverter project

This has been quite a complex project, and you may wonder whether it has been worthwhile spending so much time on so many small calculations. Indeed, you may wonder whether the same thing could not have been achieved entirely in ActionScript. The answer to the second question is, yes, it could. *So what was the point of using PHP?*

The conversion formulas for weights and measures are fixed in stone for all time, but what about currency rates? Tax rates? Hotel or flight availability? High and low scores for an online game? All of these are values you can't predict even a minute in advance, never mind over the months or years you intend your Flash application to remain online. The purpose of working with fixed information has been to lay the foundation for working with dynamic information that may be changing all the time, something you'll tackle in the next chapter, when you build an RSS aggregator that draws in constantly updated information from two independent sources.

By working with static figures, you can test the accuracy of the result much more easily, giving you the confidence to move on to working with dynamic data. The other main objective of this application has been to bring together every single aspect of PHP that you've covered so far:

- Arithmetic operators
- Comparison operators
- Logic operators
- Conditional statements and the conditional operator
- `switch` statements
- Math functions
- String manipulation
- Custom-built functions

I could have opted for a much simpler application, picking just a handful of the easiest conversion formulas, but I deliberately chose not to, so as to give you a better understanding of the thought processes that go into the development of any complex project. If you look back over the past two chapters, you'll see that I began with the most straightforward calculations—12 of the 24 formulas were completed in Chapter 3, and they could all be formatted using the same default pattern at the foot of the second `switch` statement. I developed the remaining 12 over a period of time, looking for common patterns and then working out how to format them.

Surprising though it may seem, particularly if you're a graphic design–centered person, I enjoyed sitting down and playing with the code, honing it until I got it just right. It's no different from working with a tween, making sure the timing, lighting, and angles of the graphic elements all work in harmony. The more you experiment with code, both PHP and ActionScript, the more comfortable you will become with it, and soon you will come to regard it with a familiarity equal with any of the graphic design tools in Flash.

Taking the project further

This is primarily a book about incorporating PHP and MySQL into Flash applications, rather than building super-cool visual effects with Flash. Consequently, I have concentrated on the technical side of working with PHP and transferring data between Flash and the web server. Once you have that working smoothly, why not add some Flash wizardry of your own? Here are a couple of ideas to get you going:

- Create small icons to represent various units, and create a movie clip to display the appropriate number. You could use `parseInt()` or `parseFloat()` in ActionScript to extract the number, and `split()` to separate different results by a new line character. It may be simpler, however, to send the numbers and units back from the PHP script as separate variables. You saw how to do that in Chapter 2, so it should not be difficult to adapt the PHP script.

- Create two thermometers for the temperature display—one for temperatures above freezing and the other for minus temperatures. Because there's no upper or lower limit to the temperatures that can be input, you could animate the thermometer to burst into flames or shatter into pieces when it gets particularly hot or cold.

> *If you're looking for visual inspiration, grab hold of a copy of* New Masters of Flash, Vol. 3 *(friends of ED, ISBN: 1-59059-314-6), and be prepared to have your socks knocked off.*

Dealing with user input

Before moving on from strings, it's important to consider how to handle user input. Many PHP-based Flash applications involve users entering data of some sort that could affect the integrity of files on your server. Three aspects need to be taken into account:

- Genuine user mistakes
- Malicious intent
- PHP-related issues

Even with the best will in the world, we all make mistakes, so it's a good idea to devise strategies to trap them. You implemented such a strategy in the feedback form in Chapter 2 by doing some simple checks on three input fields. Because of its large range of string-related functions, PHP can do a lot more than ActionScript in this regard. And by performing some simple checks on input, you can cut down on the damage caused by anyone with malicious intent. You also need to be alert to the effect of a PHP configuration setting called `magic_quotes_gpc`. If you refer back to Figure 2-3, you will see that, if this setting is on, an email sent by the feedback application will have backslashes in front of every quote or apostrophe.

Trimming leading and trailing whitespace

The simple validation implemented in the feedback application in Flash in Chapter 2 only checks the name field for an empty string. So anyone could easily fool it by entering a blank space. PHP has three functions to remove leading and trailing whitespace:

- **`trim()`** removes whitespace from both ends of a string.
- **`ltrim()`** removes whitespace from the beginning (left side) of a string.
- **`rtrim()`** removes whitespace from the end (right side) of a string.

You may also come across `chop()`, which is a synonym for `ltrim()`. Table 4-3 lists all the characters removed by these functions.

For example:

```
$string = "\tfriends of ED   \n";
$trimmed1 = trim($string);  // "friends of ED"
$trimmed2 = ltrim($string); // "friends of ED   \n"
$trimmed3 = rtrim($string); // "\tfriends of ED"
```

Table 4-3. Whitespace characters removed by `trim()` and related functions

Character	Name
`" "`	Space
`"\t"`	Tab
`"\n"`	New line
`"\r"`	Carriage return
`"\0"`	NUL-byte
`"\x0B"`	Vertical tab

Stripping HTML tags

This is particularly important if user input is going to be displayed in an HTML environment, because it is quite easy for a malicious user to link to another site or to include a pornographic image. The function to do this is, appropriately enough, `strip_tags()`. Its use is equally simple:

```
$string = 'Enjoy! <img src="nastyimage.jpg" />';
$string = strip_tags($string); // $string is now "Enjoy! "
```

`strip_tags()` removes all (X)HTML tags from a string. No argument—whoosh, they're gone. It does take an optional argument to allow specified tags to be preserved, but when handling user input, it's normally safer to strip them all out.

Removing backslashes

The PHP configuration setting `magic_quotes_gpc` is designed to make life simpler by automatically inserting a backslash to escape all instances of single or double quotes passed from one page to another by the `POST` and `GET` methods. Quotes or apostrophes in strings need to be escaped before they are entered into a database, so this setting can be very useful. However, opinions differ on whether this automatic insertion of backslashes is a good thing. As a result, some configurations have `magic_quotes_gpc` turned on, while others have it turned off. I'll return to this issue later when working with database input, but what you need to know at the moment is how to get rid of backslashes if they appear in variables received from your Flash movies. The answer is to use the function `stripslashes()`, which works like this:

```
$string = 'It\'s a \"good idea\"';
$stripped = stripslashes($string) // $string is "It's a "good idea""
```

Using regular expressions to identify patterns

One of the great disappointments in ActionScript is that it has no support for **regular expressions**, a powerful programming tool for recognizing patterns in textual data. Thanks to its background in text processing, though, PHP has superb support for regular expressions (regexes). In fact, PHP supports two different flavors: POSIX and Perl-compatible regular expressions (PCRE). That's the good news. The bad news is that regexes are not easy. The following example shows why:

```
/^\w[-.\w]*@([-a-z0-9]+\.)+[a-z]{2,4}$/i
```

That, believe it or not, is how you identify a genuine email address using a PCRE. Once you understand how a regex is put together, it's nowhere near as horrendous as it first looks. Rather than attempt to teach you all there is to know about regexes, the following section gives a brief outline of their structure and then concentrates on showing you how to use a handful of particularly useful regexes.

> *Many PHP books use POSIX regexes because they're thought to be easier to understand. I disagree. They're longer, less powerful, and usually slower than PCRE. What's more, PCRE are used in a wide variety of languages, including Perl, Python, Ruby, JavaScript, .NET, Java, and C/C++. If you have experience with any of those languages, you'll have a head start. Even if you don't, using PCRE with PHP will give you a more portable skill. To learn about regexes in detail, see* Regular Expression Recipes: A Problem-Solution Approach *by Nathan A. Good (Apress, ISBN: 1-59059-441-X).*
>
> *PHP uses a completely different set of functions for POSIX and PCRE. POSIX functions all begin with* `ereg` *or* `split`*. PCRE functions all begin with* `preg`*. They cannot be mixed.*

Understanding regex basics

A regex can be used to look for literal text, text patterns, or a combination of both. To find a match with a PCRE, use the PHP function `preg_match()`, which normally takes two arguments: a string containing the pattern being searched for and the string to be searched. Although you can pass the pattern directly to the function, it's often more convenient to store it first in a variable.

PCREs are always enclosed in a pair of delimiters. Traditionally, forward slashes are used (for example, */pattern/*), but you can use any nonalphanumeric character other than a backslash. You can also use a pair of curly braces ({}), square brackets ([]), or angle brackets (<>) as delimiters. This can be useful when the pattern includes slashes—for example, when you're searching for a path name or URL.

Placing an `i` after the final delimiter, as in the previous email example, makes the search case insensitive.

This is how you use the regex to check whether an email address is likely to be genuine (note that the pattern is enclosed in quotes, as it must be a string):

```
$email = 'david@example.com';
$pattern = '/^\w[-.\w]*@([-a-z0-9]+\.)+[a-z]{2,4}$/i';
$ok = preg_match($pattern, $email);
if (!$ok) {
  // code to handle spurious address
  }
```

Setting the limits of the pattern If you look at the email regex, you will notice that the first character after the opening delimiter is ^, and the final character before the closing delimiter is $. These are known as **anchors**:

- ^ as the *first* character in a regex indicates the following pattern must come at the beginning of the line or string.
- $ as the *final* character in a regex indicates the preceding pattern must come at the end of the line or string.

Since a regex can be used to match literal text, the following examples demonstrate the effect of using anchors:

```
$pattern = '/^ment/';              // must come at start
preg_match($pattern, 'mentor')     // match
preg_match($pattern, 'mentality') // match
preg_match($pattern, 'cement')     // no match

$pattern = '/ment$/';              // now must come at end
preg_match($pattern, 'mentor')     // no match
preg_match($pattern, 'cement')     // match
```

By using both anchors in the email regex, you are specifying that there must be an exact match. Consequently, the regex will match an email on its own, as you would expect it to be entered in a form. It will not match the same email in the middle of a sentence. This degree of precision is often very important when validating user input.

There are two other important anchors:

- **\b** indicates a word boundary (the beginning or end of a word).
- **\B** indicates a nonword boundary (in other words, the pattern must come inside a word).

The following examples show how they work:

```
$string = 'A host of golden daffodils';
$pattern = '/old/';      // matches golden
$pattern = '/\bold\b/'; // no match
$pattern = '/\Bold\B/'; // matches golden
$pattern = '\bgold\b/'; // no match
$pattern = '/\bgold/'   // matches golden
```

These examples show why regexes can be difficult to understand, even when they search for literal text. Any character preceded by a backslash has special meaning in a regex. `\bold` is not looking for "bold," but for "old" at the beginning of a word. Similarly, \Bold is not looking for "Bold" with a capital "B," but for "old" in the middle of a word.

Looking for patterns, rather than literal text The email regex contains only one literal character: the @ mark that divides the name from the domain. Everything else is represented by what are known as **character classes** or **metacharacters**.

The simplest of these is a period (.), which represents any single character, except for a new line character. To represent a literal period, escape it with a backslash (\.). Some examples follow:

```
$pattern = '/c.t\./';
preg_match($pattern, 'cat.')      // match
preg_match($pattern, 'cot.')      // match
preg_match($pattern, 'Scotch')    // no match
preg_match($pattern, 'coat.')     // no match
```

You can also specify a range of specific characters by enclosing them in square brackets, like this:

```
$pattern = '/c[au]t/';
preg_match($pattern, 'cat')       // match
preg_match($pattern, 'cot')       // no match
preg_match($pattern, 'cut')       // match
preg_match($pattern, 'cauterize') // no match
```

The reason the last example doesn't match is that the character class within the square brackets represents a single character. It's looking for a or u, but not both. For the pattern to match, you need to add a **quantifier** after the brackets. Quantifiers determine how many instances of a character class to match. We'll come to them a little later.

Character classes within square brackets can specify a range of characters. For instance, the email regex contains [-a-z0-9]. This means it will match a hyphen, any letter from a to z, or any number from 0 to 9. Character classes are case sensitive, unless you use the i flag after the final delimiter. In a case-sensitive search, you would need to change the character class to [-a-z**A-Z**0-9].

If the first character inside the square brackets is ^, it means you will accept a match of anything except the following characters. This confuses a lot of people to start off with. It's important to remember that ^ at the beginning of a regex is an anchor, but as the first character within square brackets, it negates the entire character class. So, [a-z] matches any lowercase letter from a to z, while [^a-z] looks for anything other than lowercase a to z.

```
$pattern = '/cat[^a-z]/';
preg_match($pattern, 'catapult') // no match
preg_match($pattern, 'catBox')   // match
preg_match($pattern, 'cat12')    // match
```

In addition to creating your own character classes with square brackets, you can use a number of convenient shorthand metacharacters. The most important ones and their meanings are shown in Table 4-4.

Table 4-4. Some of the most important metacharacters used in regexes

Metacharacter	Equivalent	Meaning
`.`	`[^\n]`	Any single character, except a new line
`\s`	`[\n\r \t]`	Whitespace (new line, carriage return, space, and tab)
`\S`	`[^\n\r \t]`	Nonwhitespace (anything other than a new line, carriage return, space, or tab)
`\w`	`[A-Za-z0-9_]`	Word character (defined as A to Z, a to z, 0 to 9, and the underscore)
`\W`	`[^A-Za-z0-9_]`	Nonword character (defined as anything other than the characters included in the preceding definition of a word character)
`\d`	`[0-9]`	Digit (0 to 9)
`\D`	`[^0-9]`	Nondigit (anything other than 0 to 9)

Matching repeating sequences If you have any experience with DOS or working at the command line in any major computing system, you will be familiar with the concept of ? and * as wildcard characters, representing a single character or many characters, respectively. They have a similar, but more precisely defined meaning in regexes. They are known as quantifiers that determine the number of matches to be made of the preceding pattern, metacharacter, or character class. Table 4-5 shows the main quantifiers available in PCRE.

Table 4-5. Principal quantifiers used in PCRE

Quantifier	Meaning
`?`	Match one or zero times.
`??`	Match zero or one time, but as few times as possible.
`*`	Match zero or more times.
`*?`	Match zero or more times, but as few times as possible.
`+`	Match one or more times.
`+?`	Match one or more times, but as few times as possible.
`{n}`	Match exactly n times.

(Continued)

Table 4-5. Principal quantifiers used in PCRE *(Continued)*

Quantifier	Meaning
{n,}	Match at least n times.
{n,}?	Match at least n times, but as few times as possible.
{x,y}	Match at least x times, but no more than y times.
{x,y}?	Match at least x times, no more than y times, and as few times as possible.

Creating alternatives and subpatterns To search for alternatives of literal strings or character classes, separate them with a vertical pipe (|), for example:

```
$pattern = '/cat|mouse/';
preg_match($pattern, 'The cat smiled broadly')   // match
preg_match($pattern, 'The mouse sat on the mat') // match
```

To create a subpattern, surround it with parentheses:

```
$pattern = '/(really )+/';
preg_match($pattern, 'really really confusing') // match
```

Building some useful regular expressions

Unless you have previous experience with regexes, your head is probably ready to burst, but now you have the knowledge to create some really useful patterns. First of all, let's analyze the email regex introduced a few pages ago:

```
/^\w[-.\w]*@([-a-z0-9]+\.)+[a-z]{2,4}$/i
```

It begins with /^. This tells you it's the beginning of a PCRE, and that it's seeking a match at the beginning of a line or string.

The next part is \w. This matches a single word character (an alphanumeric character or the underscore).

[-.\w]* matches zero or more hyphens, periods, and word characters until it reaches a literal @.

Following the @ is a subpattern ([-a-z0-9]+\.)+. If you look inside the subpattern, it contains a character class [-a-z0-9], which must be repeated one or more times, followed by a literal period. The + outside the closing parenthesis of the subpattern indicates that the pattern inside the parentheses must be appear at least once.

[a-z]{2,4}$ looks for no fewer than two but no more than four letters in sequence at the end of the string (something like com, uk, gov, edu).

`/i` closes the regular expression and makes it case insensitive.

Admittedly, this is a rather advanced regex, but even if you don't fully understand it, it's extremely useful to know how to use it to validate user input.

Though we only scratched the surface of regexes, the information in this section is sufficient to start you on your way to building other useful validation patterns.

Checking North American telephone numbers The following regex will match standard phone numbers in the United States, Canada, and much of the Caribbean:

```
/^(?[2-9]\d{2})?[ -]?[2-9]\d{2}-\d{4}$/
```

It matches

```
(555)-222-2222
(555)222-2222
555-222-2222
555 222-2222
```

Checking U.S. zip codes U.S. zip codes consist of five numbers, followed by an optional additional four digits after a hyphen (zip+4). The following regex will validate both types:

```
/^\d{5}(-\d{4})?$/
```

Don't expect to start creating complex regexes of your own overnight. It's a fascinating but time-consuming subject. There's an excellent online repository of regexes at `http://regexlib.com` *with more than 700 regexes contributed by programmers all over the world. It's searchable, and each regex is explained and rated by users. The site also contains patterns for phone and postcode validation for many countries.*

Fine-tuning the feedback application

Armed with the knowledge you gained in the previous section, you can now make some important improvements to the feedback application from Chapter 2. You will now strip any backslashes from user input, check that the name contains at least two letters, and confirm that the email address is in a valid format.

You can either work with your original files from Chapter 2 or use the download files for this chapter. If you're using the download files, copy `feedback01.php`, `today2.php`, *and* `biodiverse.fla` *into your* `phpflash/ch04` *folder. If you just want to look at the completed PHP script, it's in* `feedback02.php`. *When you use either* `feedback01.php` *or* `feedback02.php`, *remove the version number from the filename so that it matches the URL on line 37 of the ActionScript in the FLA file.*

1. Open feedback.php and insert several new lines immediately after the opening PHP tag. This is where you will add all of the new code, except for a closing curly brace in the final step.

2. Add the following code in the space you have just created:

```
// if magic quotes turned on, remove slashes from escaped characters
if (get_magic_quotes_gpc()) {
  $_POST['from'] = stripslashes($_POST['from']);
  $_POST['snail'] = stripslashes($_POST['snail']);
  $_POST['comments'] = stripslashes($_POST['comments']);
  }
```

Although the comment makes it sound like an extract from a bizarre jailbreak movie, this code block performs the important task of removing backslashes from quotes and apostrophes. Not all servers use magic quotes, so the if statement uses get_magic_quotes_gpc() to check. If the setting is on, the function returns true and the code block strips out the unwanted characters. Otherwise, it leaves them untouched. This test makes your code completely portable, regardless of server configuration.

3. Next, you need to validate the name. The test presented here won't stop anyone from saying they're Mickey Mouse or the Wizard of Oz, but at least it ensures you get something resembling a name. Insert the following immediately after the block you've just entered:

```
// initialize variables for validating input
$valid = true;
$reason1 = '';
$reason2 = '';
// strip whitespace from both sides of sender's name
$_POST['from'] = trim($_POST['from']);
// create regex to make sure name contains at least two letters
$namePattern = '/[a-z]{2,}/i';
if (!preg_match($namePattern,$_POST['from'])) {
  // if name fails the test, reset $valid flag and set $reason1
  $valid = false;
  $reason1 = 'Please enter a valid name.';
  }
```

The first line sets a Boolean value that will be used later to determine whether to send the feedback. The next two lines set $reason1 and $reason2 to empty strings. There's normally no need to initialize variables like this in PHP, but doing so prevents the generation of warning notices if you later try to refer to a nonexistent variable. The reason for this will become clearer in step 5. Then, in the following line, trim() is used to remove whitespace from both ends of the input.

The fifth line creates a simple regex, /[a-z]{2,}/i. This uses a to z as a character class, followed by a quantifier that looks for a minimum of two matches. The i after the closing delimiter makes the pattern case insensitive. So, someone signing herself as "Jo" would be accepted, but "K9" and "J" on their own would be rejected. Obviously, it's up to you to make the regex as restrictive or permissive as you like (or use none at all).

The conditional clause then tests the name submitted against the regex. If it fails, `$valid` is set to `false`, and an error message is stored in `$reason1`.

4. A similar test is applied to the email address. The following code should go immediately after the block in the preceding step:

```
// create regex to validate email address
$emailPattern = '/^\w[-.\w]*@([-a-z0-9]+\.)+[a-z]{2,4}$/i';
if (!preg_match($emailPattern,$_POST['email'])) {
  // if address fails the test, reset $valid flag and set $reason2
  $valid = false;
  $reason2 = 'The email address you submitted does not conform to
  the recognized standard for email addresses.';
  }
```

The logic is exactly the same as in step 3. The reason for setting `$valid` again is that the name could be valid, but not the email.

> *Although the email regex is very robust, it can only tell you whether the user has entered what **looks** like a valid address—in other words, one that has all the correct elements. It cannot tell you whether the address is genuine or whether the user has typed it correctly. Although DNS lookup can establish the existence of a domain used in an email address, the only way of verifying that an email comes from a particular person is to send a reply requesting confirmation. The problem of mistyped addresses can be overcome by getting a user to enter the same details twice. This technique is used for password registration in Chapter 8.*

5. If either or both of the tests fail, you need to tell the user why, and prevent the email from being sent. This is where the Boolean `$valid` does its job. Enter the following code immediately after the previous block:

```
// if any test has failed, $valid will be false, so send failure msg
if (!$valid) {
  // if only one test has failed, either $reason1 or $reason2
  // will be an empty string, you can concatenate them
  // and only the right one will be output
  if (empty($reason1) xor empty($reason2)) {
    echo 'sent=failed&reason='.urlencode($reason1.$reason2);
  }
  else {
  // otherwise send both reasons separated by a new line character
    echo 'sent=failed&reason='.urlencode("$reason1\n$reason2");
  }
  }
else {
```

If $valid is false, there are three possibilities:

- The name test failed, but not the email test ($reason1 is no longer empty, but $reason2 is).
- The email test failed, but not the name test ($reason2 is no longer empty, but $reason1 is).
- Both tests failed ($reason1 and $reason2 both have values).

If both tests failed, you need to add a new line between the two error messages. Rather than use three conditions, this is a good opportunity to use the exclusive OR operator xor (see the section "Testing more than one condition" in Chapter 3). If only one of the tests failed, one of the variables holding the reason will still be an empty string, so you can concatenate them like this: $reason1.$reason2. If $reason1 is empty, $reason2 will be displayed on its own. If you don't initialize both variables and then try to concatenate them like this, PHP will generate a warning notice, which could prevent LoadVars in your Flash movie from receiving the intended response.

If the xor condition fails, both reasons need to be displayed with a new line character between them like this: "$reason1\n$reason2" (note the use of double quotes so the new line character is correctly interpreted).

In both cases, the value of the reason being sent back to the Flash movie needs to be URL-encoded with urlencode().

The else { in the last line controls the execution of all the original script in feedback.php—in other words, the compilation and sending of the email message. So, if $valid remains true, the message is sent.

6. The last change to the code is adding a closing curly brace just before the closing PHP tag right at the bottom of the page. This encloses the original script in the final else clause you created in step 5.

If you copied the code correctly, everything should work smoothly. Should things go wrong, temporarily hard-code some values into the variables at the top of feedback.php, and test the page in a browser. The most likely cause is a mismatch of quotes, or a missing semicolon, parenthesis, or curly brace. You can also consult the troubleshooting section in Appendix A. If you still have problems, compare your code with feedback02.php in the download files for this chapter.

A pause for breath

This has been another long chapter crammed with information for you to absorb. Some of it, like the section on regular expressions, strayed into quite advanced territory. Don't worry if you find it a lot to take in. The important thing is to get a broad overview of what PHP is capable of doing for you. Come back later, and use the relevant sections of each chapter as a reference.

The examples in this chapter have concentrated on working with short snippets of text, but the wealth of string manipulation functions offered by PHP should make life a lot easier if you are working with a text intensive site. ActionScript, like its close relative JavaScript, is particularly weak at handling text, so using PHP to format your content before passing it to Flash will save a lot of effort.

You'll also be pleased to know that, after you study arrays and loops in the next chapter, you'll have covered all the basics of PHP. Then you can team up PHP and Flash with the MySQL database. That's when things get *really* interesting—although I certainly hope you haven't been bored so far!

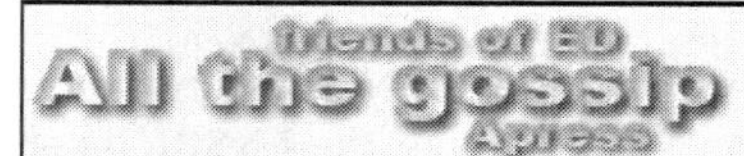

Wed Nov 24

Browser War Update

IE share is falling!The number of friendsofed.com's visitors using IE has fallen almost 15% to around 75% in the past six months! More from friends of ED newsfeed

A Programmer's Introduction to C#, Third Edition - Finally Underway

Nick Wienholt writes: After a few false starts and a fortnight of email tag, I've finally nutted through all those administrative details that need to get completed before you write a book, and I'm underway on the update to Eric's book. We're looking at a "mid 2005" release, but I am aiming to... More from Ablog

Tue Nov 23

Linus Torvalds dubbed most influential executive of 2004

Jason Gilmore writes: From Slashdot: As if the giant leaps

Chapter 5

WORKING SMARTER WITH ARRAYS AND LOOPS

What this chapter covers:

- Organizing related information in arrays
- Handling indexed, associative, and multidimensional arrays
- Making light work of repetitive tasks with loops
- Ensuring security with the $_POST superglobal array
- Manipulating and sorting arrays
- Parsing an RSS feed with MagpieRSS
- Building an RSS feed aggregator

Just two more aspects of the basic grammar of PHP need to be covered before you can move on to integrating the MySQL database with Flash: working with arrays and loops. If you are already an ActionScript wizard, you may be tempted to skip this chapter, thinking there will be nothing in it for you. Think again. Arrays and loops are *very similar* in PHP and ActionScript, but beneath that similarity lurk some surprising differences that could easily catch you out, such as the way PHP calculates an array length and treats all arrays as associative. Although you can skip the first section on the basics of arrays and loops, make sure you read the rest of the chapter, taking particular note of the highlighted points.

Arrays and loops lie at the foundation of working with databases. That presented me with a little problem: how to illustrate their use in a practical way without using a database. I think I've come up with a cool solution that you'll enjoy. It's an RSS feed aggregator that retrieves the latest news and gossip from the friends of ED and Apress websites, organizes it, and displays it in a Flash movie. Much of the hard work is done by a free PHP utility called MagpieRSS, which is simplicity itself to use.

Understanding the basics of arrays and loops

If you're new to programming, you need a little background knowledge about arrays and loops before the rest of the chapter will make sense. When you first see them written down in code, arrays and loops can seem rather off-putting, but if you think of them applied to real-life situations, their mystery rapidly falls away. One problem is that most definitions of arrays begin with something high-sounding or scary, such as "a composite datatype holding numbered values" or "a data structure that can encompass multiple individual data values." I have a much simpler explanation: arrays are lists or ways of grouping things to bring order to your life. And the array's best friend—a loop—is simply a way of doing the same thing over and over again, just as you might do when searching through a pile of old photographs looking for a particular one. In fact, one of the primary uses of loops in PHP is when searching through the records of a database.

Organizing items in arrays

The simplest example of an **array** is a shopping list:

1. *milk*
2. *bread*
3. *cookies*
4. *butter*

Both PHP and ActionScript put the number in square brackets after the variable, and both start counting at zero. So, my shopping list would look like this in PHP:

```
$shoppingList[0] = 'milk';
$shoppingList[1] = 'bread';
$shoppingList[2] = 'cookies';
$shoppingList[3] = 'butter';
```

The same array in ActionScript would simply drop the dollar sign at the beginning of `$shoppingList`. The number in square brackets is called the **array key** or **index**, and it is used to identify individual items within an array. In both languages, you refer to the entire array by the variable on its own and to individual items by the array variable followed by its key, like this:

```
$shoppingList    // the whole array
$shoppingList[2] // my favorite - cookies!
```

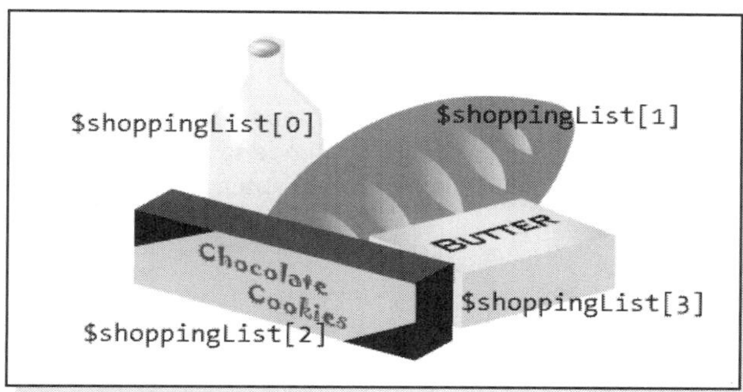

Grouping similar items in multidimensional arrays

Whenever I go shopping, it's the third item that tends to dominate my thoughts. One packet of cookies is never enough for me, so I need another list:

```
$cookies[0] = 'chocolate digestives';
$cookies[1] = 'chocolate chip';
$cookies[2] = 'Jaffa cakes';
$cookies[3] = 'chocolate wafers';
```

Although there are now two arrays, they're both really part of the same shopping list, so in computer terms, you could replace the string `cookies` in the `$shoppingList` array with the `$cookies` array:

```
$shoppingList[2] = $cookies;
```

In other words, you have created an array within an array—or, to use the technical term, a **multidimensional array**.

At the supermarket checkout, everything is bundled into a new multidimensional array—three or four shopping bags. Then, back home, everything gets sorted into the right cupboard, or the fridge, or the freezer—yet more array creation. Or, if you're like me, the stress of shopping is so great that you just need to have a cookie before you can do anything else. With mutterings of "I know they're in here somewhere," I root through each shopping bag until—success. The computer equivalent of rooting through a shopping bag is a **loop** that performs the same action over and over again until told to stop (usually when a certain condition—or a packet of chocolate cookies—is reached).

Using loops for repetitive tasks

In ActionScript, loops are frequently used to attach a large number of identical movie clips at runtime. Loops can also be used in PHP for automating the generation of repetitive code. For instance, in an XHTML page, the structure of a table is uniform, so a loop is an ideal way to output all the <tr> and <td> tags. Even if the table contains hundreds of rows, a loop reduces the necessary code to just a few lines.

When creating Flash applications with PHP, you will have less need for this type of use, at least within your PHP scripts. Where you will find loops invaluable is when it comes to arrays, particularly the results of a database query, which PHP stores as a multidimensional array. So understanding loops and arrays is vital to your progress through the rest of this book. The rest of the first half of this chapter describes arrays and loops in much more detail, but if you're new to all this, just try the following simple piece of code to see a loop in action. You can find it in `simple_loop.php` in the download files for this chapter.

```
<?php
$i = 1;
// displays the numbers 1-10
while ($i <= 10) {
  echo $i.'<br />';
  $i++;
  }
?>
```

Save the file in `phpflash/ch05`, and view it in your browser. As the comment indicates, it will display the numbers from 1 through 10. Not very exciting, maybe, but the only line actually producing any output is the one highlighted in bold. Change the fourth line like this:

```
while ($i <= 10000) {
```

Save the page and hit the Refresh button in your browser. It will now display every number up to 10,000. On my Pentium IV computer, it takes a fraction over one-hundredth of a second to do so! Loops are very powerful, but you also need to be aware of the danger of an **infinite loop**—one that never stops running. I'll come back to that a little later, but with this basic knowledge, you should now be able to delve into the delights of PHP loops and arrays.

Creating arrays in PHP

Both PHP and ActionScript offer two ways of identifying the elements in an array: using a number (an **indexed array**) or a string (an **associative array**). For example:

```
$cookies[1]          // indexed array element
$cookies['chocChip'] // associative array element
```

Just in case you're wondering, my fascination with chocolate cookies won't cause any conflict with computer cookies. PHP refers to them using `$_COOKIE[]`*, one of the superglobal arrays described later in this chapter.*

The method of creating an array in PHP is very similar to ActionScript—you assign the array() construct to a variable:

```
$characters = array();              // PHP style
var characters:Array = new Array(); // ActionScript style
```

Unlike ActionScript, PHP does *not* use the new keyword to create an array. Also, the array() construct is normally written entirely in lowercase in PHP. In ActionScript, you must capitalize the initial "A" because ActionScript always uses initial capitals when referring to classes.

The only time you'll use a declaration like this in PHP is if you deliberately want to create an empty array or clear the entire contents of an existing array. Normally, you populate the array at the same time as you create it.

Indexed arrays: Organizing by number

The simplest way to create an indexed array is to list the elements, separated by commas, between the parentheses of the array() construct.

```
$characters = array('Bilbo', 'Frodo', 'Sam');
```

To add further elements, use empty square brackets after the array variable name, like this:

```
$characters[] = 'Gandalf';
```

PHP automatically assigns each element the next number available. The previous code produces exactly the same array as if you assigned the numbers yourself. Either method is acceptable.

```
$characters[0] = 'Bilbo';
$characters[1] = 'Frodo';
$characters[2] = 'Sam';
$characters[3] = 'Gandalf';
```

The numbers are simply a means of keeping track of each value internally within PHP. You can, for instance, use purely arbitrary numbers—although I strongly advise against doing so. You'll see why shortly.

```
$characters[665] = 'Arathorn';
```

If you add another element using the [] syntax, PHP will simply assign the next available number.

```
$characters[] = 'Saruman';
```

Nothing is gained by doing this, and it can cause your scripts to act in unexpected ways or break. This can be demonstrated by displaying the contents of an array onscreen, and then using PHP built-in functions to determine its length and to sort the elements. You can find the code used in the following exercise in arrays1.php, arrays2.php, and arrays1.fla in the download files for this chapter. Read the inline comments in the files to activate certain parts of the code.

Examining the contents of an array

1. Create a new PHP page called `arrays.php` in `phpflash/ch05`.
2. Enter the first four elements of `$characters` as shown previously, either by using the `array()` construct or by assigning the numbers 0 to 3 as the key of each variable. Then add the last two elements using any large number as the key for the first and the `[]` syntax for the second.
3. The next piece of code introduces you to a useful PHP debugging function, `print_r()`, which displays onscreen the contents of an array. It's the PHP equivalent of `Array.toString()` in ActionScript, only it's more convenient, because it also displays each element's key. The HTML `<pre>` tags make the output easier to read. Insert the following immediately after the array you have built:

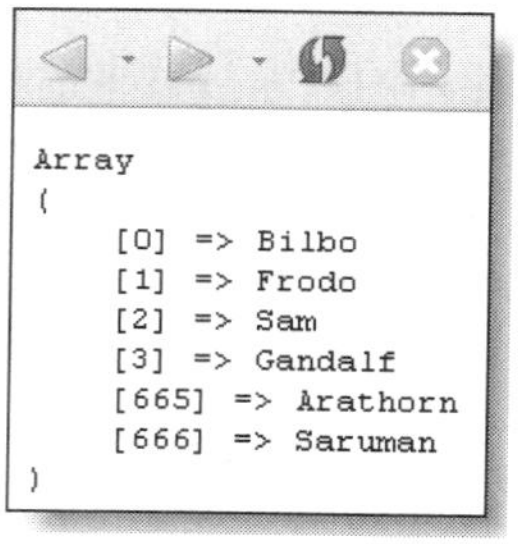

```
echo '<pre>';
print_r($characters);
echo '</pre>';
```

```
Array
(
    [0] => Bilbo
    [1] => Frodo
    [2] => Sam
    [3] => Gandalf
    [665] => Arathorn
    [666] => Saruman
)
```

4. View the page in a browser. You should see the array keys and values displayed onscreen as shown above.
5. The significance of the => will become clearer later, but as you can see, PHP has assigned Saruman the number 666 (spooky).
6. Say you want your array to be in alphabetical order. Even if it's right to start with, adding another element later will almost certainly destroy the alphabetic sequence. PHP provides functions to sort arrays in a variety of ways, and it should come as no surprise that the basic one is called `sort()`. Alter the code you inserted in step 3 so it now reads as follows:

```
sort($characters);
echo '<pre>';
print_r($characters);
echo '</pre>';
```

> *There is no need to assign the result of `sort()` to a variable. If you attempt to do so, the new variable will **not** contain the sorted array, but a value indicating whether the sort was completed successfully (1) or not (0). **All sort functions permanently change the order of the original array**, rather than working on a copy. The other sort functions will be explained later in the chapter.*

7. View the page in a browser again. Not only has the `sort()` function rearranged the array in alphabetical order, but also Saruman has been purged of his devilish number.

```
Array
(
    [0] => Arathorn
    [1] => Bilbo
    [2] => Frodo
    [3] => Gandalf
    [4] => Sam
    [5] => Saruman
)
```

8. This result gives you a pretty good clue as to what PHP regards as the length of the array, but let's check that your instincts are right. The PHP function `count()` returns the equivalent of the `Array.length` property in ActionScript. Type this at the bottom of your existing script:

```
echo 'Array length: '.count($characters);
```

9. When you view the page again, it should confirm that the array length is 6, as shown in the left-hand image of Figure 5-1.

10. Now, comment out `sort($characters);` and view the page again. As the right-hand image in Figure 5-1 demonstrates, the length of the array remains 6 regardless of the highest number used as a key. This is a major difference from the way ActionScript treats arrays, as you'll now see.

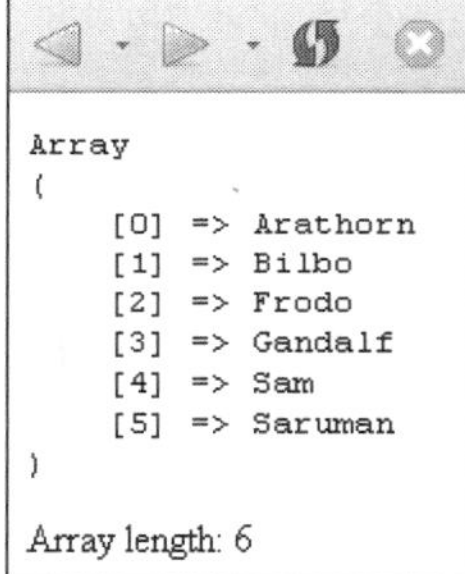

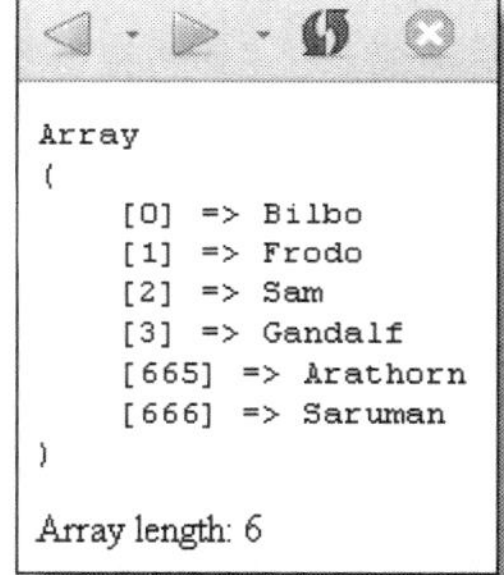

Figure 5-1. The highest key in a PHP indexed array has no effect on the length of the array.

11. Open a new Flash document and type the following code into the Actions panel:

```
var characters:Array = new Array();
characters[666] = 'Saruman';
trace("Array length is " + characters.length);
```

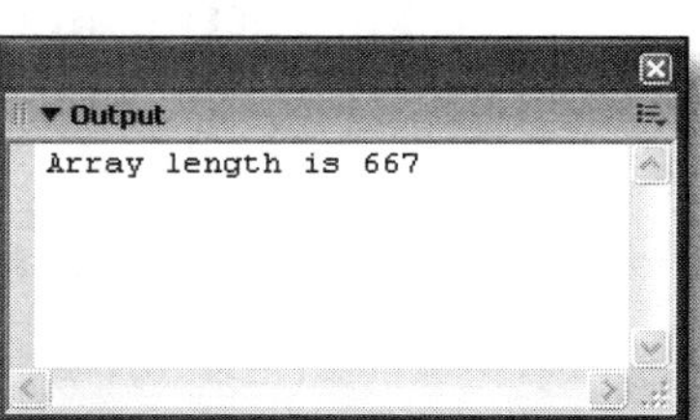

12. Test the movie. The result is very different. Even though you have inserted only one element into the array, ActionScript uses the value of the index to calculate the length, which is always one more than the highest index number, because the first element is numbered 0.

> *PHP is concerned only with the number of elements actually present in an array. It does not share the ActionScript concept of empty elements, unless they have been explicitly declared (for example, with a null value or an empty string).*

13. Add two more elements to $characters in arrays.php, like this:

```
$characters[] = null;  // null is a keyword, so no quotes
$characters[] = '';
```

14. View the page in a browser again, both with sort() enabled and disabled. As you can see in Figure 5-2, **PHP preserves only those empty elements that have been explicitly declared. All others are discarded (in fact, they never existed).**

Figure 5-2. Empty elements in PHP arrays must be explicitly declared.

Associative arrays: Organizing by name

It's often more convenient to categorize things by name. You do this in PHP by assigning the key and the value of each array element at the same time. When you use the array() construct, you use the => operator (equal sign followed by the greater than operator) to assign each value to its respective key.

```
$characters = array('finder'  => 'Bilbo',
                    'bearer'  => 'Frodo',
                    'helper'  => 'Sam',
                    'wizard'  => 'Gandalf',
                    'father'  => 'Arathorn',
                    'thepits' => 'Saruman');
```

Although you don't need to declare each key/value pair on a separate line like this, it makes the code easier to read. PHP ignores whitespace, so it doesn't matter. Make sure you don't put a space between the = and >, because => is an operator and cannot be split.

The elements of the same array can also be declared individually with the standard assignment operator:

```
$characters['finder']  = 'Bilbo';
$characters['bearer']  = 'Frodo';
$characters['helper']  = 'Sam';
$characters['wizard']  = 'Gandalf';
$characters['father']  = 'Arathorn';
$characters['thepits'] = 'Saruman';
```

The key of an associative array is a string, and it should always be quoted; otherwise, it's treated as a constant by PHP. The only exception to this rule is when you're using an array element in a double-quoted string.

```
echo "Aragorn, son of $characters['father']"; // generates an error
echo "Aragorn, son of $characters[father]";   // displays correctly
```

This is one of those quirks common to many programming languages, where apparently correct code generates an error. There's no obvious logic to it; it's just one of those things you have to remember. Also note that `print_r()` *displays named elements without any quotes (as shown in Figure 5-3).*

The key of an indexed array, on the other hand, is a number, so it shouldn't be surrounded by quotes.

I've done something here that you would not normally do in real life: I've used the same variable as an existing indexed array to create an associative one. This illustrates some very important points.

Danger ahead: Mixing indexed and associative arrays

You can find the code for the following example in arrays3.php and arrays4.php in the download files for this chapter.

1. Use the download files, or adapt your file from the previous exercise. First, use the array() construct to build the indexed and associative versions of the $characters array, like this (arrays3.php):

```
<?php
// indexed array (numbers used for keys)
$characters = array('Bilbo', 'Frodo', 'Sam');
$characters[] = 'Gandalf';
$characters[665] = 'Arathorn';
$characters[] = 'Saruman';
// associative array (strings used for keys)
$characters = array('finder'  => 'Bilbo',
                    'bearer'  => 'Frodo',
                    'helper'  => 'Sam',
```

```
                    'wizard'  => 'Gandalf',
                    'father'  => 'Arathorn',
                    'thepits' => 'Saruman');
echo '<pre>';
print_r($characters);
echo '</pre>';
echo 'Array length: '.count($characters);
?>
```

2. Save the file and view it in a browser. You should see the results shown in Figure 5-3. The associative array has completely replaced the indexed array, as you can tell both from the print_r() display and from the array length (a result that might surprise you if you have a sound knowledge of ActionScript—more on that later). The reason the indexed array no longer exists is that **the array() constructor always builds a new array**.

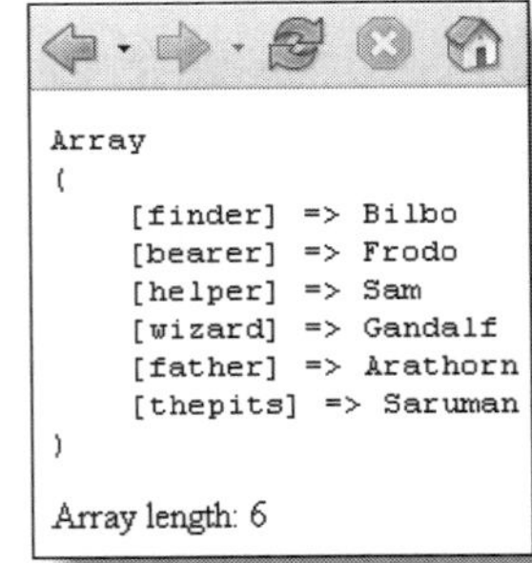
Array
(
[finder] => Bilbo
[bearer] => Frodo
[helper] => Sam
[wizard] => Gandalf
[father] => Arathorn
[thepits] => Saruman
)
Array length: 6

Figure 5-3. Using the array() construct overwrites the original array.

3. You can verify this further by adding the following line immediately above the first echo statement:

```
$characters = array();
echo '<pre>';
```

4. Save the page and refresh the browser. The print_r() statement will show an empty array, and the array length will be displayed as 0.

5. Now create the indexed and associative arrays by assigning the keys directly in the square brackets, like this (arrays4.php):

```
<?php
// indexed array (numbers used for keys)
$characters[0] = 'Bilbo';
$characters[1] = 'Frodo';
$characters[2] = 'Sam';
$characters[3] = 'Gandalf';
$characters[665] = 'Arathorn';
$characters[] = 'Saruman';
// associative array (strings used for keys)
$characters['finder']  = 'Bilbo';
$characters['bearer']  = 'Frodo';
$characters['helper']  = 'Sam';
$characters['wizard']  = 'Gandalf';
$characters['father']  = 'Arathorn';
$characters['thepits'] = 'Saruman';
echo '<pre>';
print_r($characters);
echo '</pre>';
echo 'Array length: '.count($characters);
?>
```

6. Save the file and view it in a browser. You should see the results shown in Figure 5-4. What you have created is quite valid in both PHP and ActionScript, but in PHP it behaves in a way that is difficult to predict. Like Frankenstein, you will end up ruing the day you ever created such a monster.

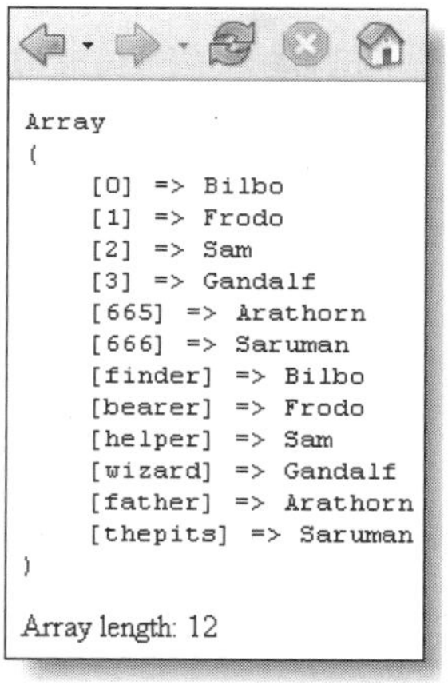

7. The obvious problem with this mixed array is that you now have duplicate values with different keys. Even if you avoid such duplication, it's the way that a mixture of numbered and named elements is treated by PHP that causes the real problems. In the previous exercise, you used `sort()` to rearrange the array alphabetically. Do that again, by adding the function immediately above the first echo command:

```
sort($characters);
echo '<pre>';
```

```
Array
(
    [0] => Bilbo
    [1] => Frodo
    [2] => Sam
    [3] => Gandalf
    [665] => Arathorn
    [666] => Saruman
    [finder] => Bilbo
    [bearer] => Frodo
    [helper] => Sam
    [wizard] => Gandalf
    [father] => Arathorn
    [thepits] => Saruman
)

Array length: 12
```

Figure 5-4. Mixing numbered and named elements is valid, but not recommended.

8. Save the page and refresh your browser. You should get the result shown in Figure 5-5. All the elements are now in alphabetical order, but all the named keys have disappeared! If you attempt to access any of the elements in the associative array by, for instance, adding **`echo $characters['finder'];`** at the foot of the script, you will get either no output or a notice warning you of an undefined index.

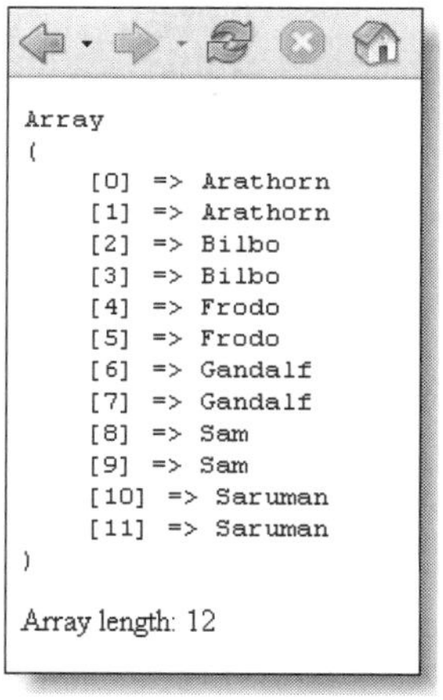

9. PHP experts might object to this example, because `sort()` should be used only on indexed arrays. But, as Figure 5-5 demonstrates, PHP will not object, and all your named elements are gone in a . . . I was going to say "Flash." The point is that they are irretrievably destroyed.

   The correct way to sort associative arrays is by using `asort()` (to sort by value) or `ksort()` (to sort by key). These sort functions will be covered in detail later in the chapter, but Figure 5-6 (on the next page) shows the problems that arise when using them on a mixed array.

   When you sort by value (as shown on the left of Figure 5-6), the key order appears to be random—sometimes a numbered element will come first, other times it's the named element. Sorting by key (as shown on the right) is not random, but the order is counterintuitive. First the named elements that have the same number of letters are sorted, then comes `0`. This is because numerals have a higher code position than letters. `thepits` comes next because its key has one more letter than the other named elements. By now, I hope the message is clear. **In PHP, don't attempt to mix numbered keys and named keys in the same array. It's perfectly valid, but it's a nightmare to control.**

```
Array
(
    [0] => Arathorn
    [1] => Arathorn
    [2] => Bilbo
    [3] => Bilbo
    [4] => Frodo
    [5] => Frodo
    [6] => Gandalf
    [7] => Gandalf
    [8] => Sam
    [9] => Sam
    [10] => Saruman
    [11] => Saruman
)

Array length: 12
```

Figure 5-5. Using `sort()` on a mixed array deletes all associative keys.

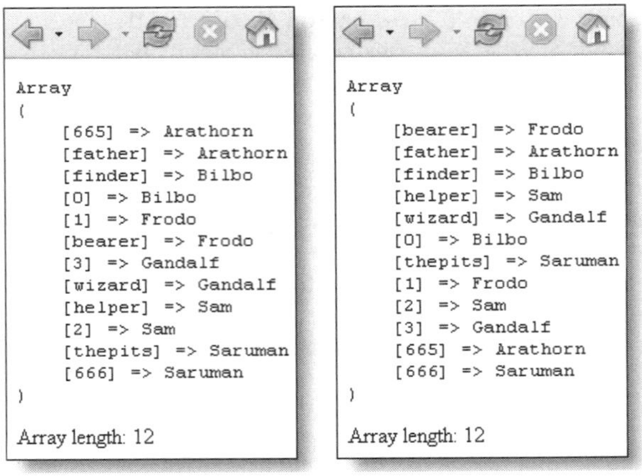

```
Array
(
    [665] => Arathorn
    [father] => Arathorn
    [finder] => Bilbo
    [0] => Bilbo
    [1] => Frodo
    [bearer] => Frodo
    [3] => Gandalf
    [wizard] => Gandalf
    [helper] => Sam
    [2] => Sam
    [thepits] => Saruman
    [666] => Saruman
)

Array length: 12
```

```
Array
(
    [bearer] => Frodo
    [father] => Arathorn
    [finder] => Bilbo
    [helper] => Sam
    [wizard] => Gandalf
    [0] => Bilbo
    [thepits] => Saruman
    [1] => Frodo
    [2] => Sam
    [3] => Gandalf
    [665] => Arathorn
    [666] => Saruman
)

Array length: 12
```

Figure 5-6. A mixed array can be sorted by value (left) or by key (right), but the results are not what you might expect.

Array length: Key to understanding the difference between PHP and ActionScript arrays

You've already seen that PHP and ActionScript treat the length of indexed arrays in very different ways. ActionScript treats the key number as indicative of the number of elements, even if they're undeclared. PHP doesn't; it's interested only in the number of declared elements. As you will have gathered from Figures 5-3 through 5-6, PHP also counts the number of named elements in an associative array, whereas ActionScript doesn't.

> *In ActionScript, the* `length` *property of an array includes numbered elements only; named elements are treated as properties of the* `Array` *object. In PHP, the* `count()` *function returns the length of the entire array, regardless of whether the elements are indexed by numbers or names. This is because all arrays in PHP are, in effect, associative arrays, and the length is always the number of declared elements, regardless of whether they are referenced by a name or a number.*

Figure 5-7 shows the effect of retrieving the size of identical associative arrays in ActionScript and PHP. ActionScript reports a `length` of 0, whereas PHP recognizes there are six elements in the array.

This difference in behavior probably comes as more of a shock to PHP programmers, who are likely to find the inability to retrieve the length of an associative array inconvenient, to say the least. What it means is that PHP has more than one way to loop through the contents of an associative array, as you'll see shortly.

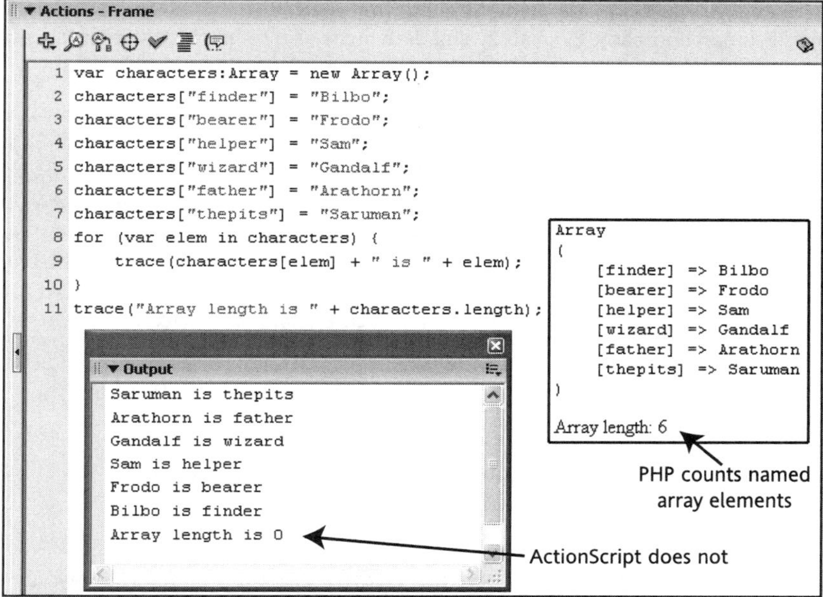

Figure 5-7. Testing the length of an identical associative array produces very different results in ActionScript and PHP.

Multidimensional arrays: Nesting arrays

An array can hold any sort of data. There is nothing to stop you from creating an associative array that contains every datatype: strings, integers, floating-point numbers, objects, whatever. Unless you're careful, this can soon get out of control. It's usually better to keep things of the same category in an array and create separate arrays for different categories of things. You'll see this in practice when it comes to building the RSS feed aggregator later in the chapter, where complex information is broken down into simple categories. At other times, it's equally convenient to create arrays of arrays, which is how the combo boxes for the multiconverter application in Chapter 3 were populated.

PHP multidimensional arrays work in a similar way to those in Flash. You assign the nested array as a normal array element, and retrieve values by using the square bracket notation. For example, you could reorganize the array elements in the examples so far like this (to avoid confusion, I'll give the top-level array a different name this time):

```
// First create individual arrays of related characters
$hobbits = array('finder' => 'Bilbo', 'bearer' => 'Frodo',
  'helper' => 'Sam');
$goodguys = array('wizard' => 'Gandalf', 'father' => 'Arathorn');
$badguys = array('thepits' => 'Saruman');

// Then build an array of arrays
$cast = array('Hobbits' => $hobbits, 'Goodguys' => $goodguys,
  'Badguys' => $badguys);
```

Although $badguys has only one element at the moment, a few Orcs and the Balrog could soon keep Saruman company. Even so, a single-element array is perfectly acceptable, as is an empty array.

> *It's often quite useful to make sure an array is empty before populating it with new data. PHP and ActionScript handle this very differently when an array already exists. As you've already seen, simply assigning* `array()` *to a variable in PHP destroys everything previously held in the same variable. Arrays are much more persistent in ActionScript. Even using the* `delete` *operator on an array element in ActionScript only sets the value to* `undefined`*, but leaves the element intact. To empty an existing array, you need to set the* `length` *property to* `0`*. This is how you empty an existing array in both languages:*
>
> ```
> $myArray = array();  // PHP (same as creating a new array)
> myArray.length = 0;  // ActionScript (array must already exist)
> ```

You access the elements of a multidimensional array through the name keys:

```
echo $cast['Hobbits']['bearer'] // Frodo
```

What you *cannot* do is attempt to access the elements through numbered keys *unless* the array was originally created as an indexed array. This is not a problem, because PHP has a convenient way of accessing associative array elements, as you will see in the next section.

```
echo $cast[0][1]           // undefined
echo $cast[0]['bearer']    // undefined
```

If you find it difficult to grasp the concept of a multidimensional array, you might find it easier to visualize this example as a cast of characters (such as in a theater).

Visualized as a theater program, the entire cast list is the top-level array. Within the cast list are three subarrays: one each for Hobbits, Good Guys, and Bad Guys. Each of the subarrays contains one or more name/value pairs, with the name (or key) on the left, separated by a row of dots from the value on the right. Seen like this, a multidimensional array loses any sense of being intimidating and is just the way a computer handles the type of categorization we do without thinking in everyday life.

CAST OF CHARACTERS

HOBBITS

Finder....................................Bilbo
Bearer...................................Frodo
Helper....................................Sam

GOOD GUYS

Wizard................................Gandalf
Father...............................Arathorn

BAD GUYS

The pits............................Saruman

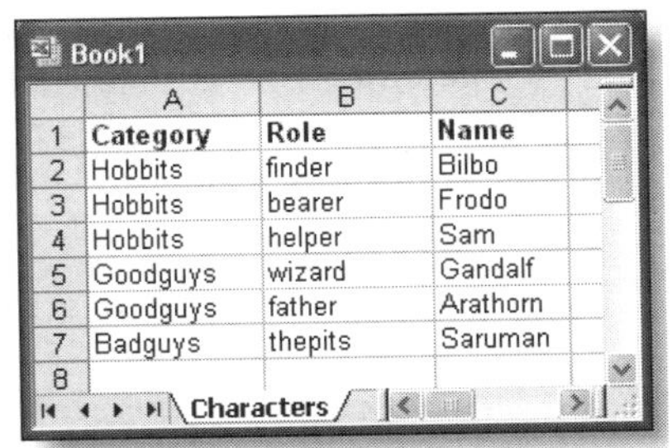

	A	B	C
1	**Category**	**Role**	**Name**
2	Hobbits	finder	Bilbo
3	Hobbits	bearer	Frodo
4	Hobbits	helper	Sam
5	Goodguys	wizard	Gandalf
6	Goodguys	father	Arathorn
7	Badguys	thepits	Saruman
8			

To borrow a familiar computer analogy, another way of looking at this multidimensional array is as a spreadsheet. The spreadsheet itself represents the top-level array. The subarrays are identified by the entry in the `Category` column, and the individual name/value pairs are listed in each row, and identified by making reference to the `Role` and `Name` columns. Looking at arrays in terms of spreadsheets is, in fact, very useful, as you will realize when you start working with the MySQL database from the next chapter. For instance, everything in row 5 in the spreadsheet shown alongside is connected with Gandalf. When you retrieve information from a database, the results are fetched by MySQL as a series of rows, just as illustrated here. PHP then sorts through each row in turn, looking for information that you specify and processing it accordingly.

So, how do you process a series of rows or arrays? Loops are just the thing, but loops aren't only for arrays. They can handle any repetitive task.

Zipping through repetitive tasks with loops

As the name suggests, a **loop** is a programming device that performs a task, then goes back to the beginning and does it all over again, going around and around in a continuous loop until it runs out of data to work on or until it reaches a preset condition.

Earlier, you used `print_r()` to display the contents of an array. This is useful only as a debugging device at development time, because it doesn't let you process the contents of an array. Loops, on the other hand, can contain any number of PHP statements—from the most basic to complex functions—so you can process data however you like.

> *All the examples for this section are in the download files for this chapter. The name of each file begins with loops, and the actual filename is given in the text accompanying each example.*

Looping through arrays with foreach

The `foreach` loop is used exclusively with arrays and is similar to the `for...` in loop in ActionScript. It can be used to loop either through the values of an array or through both the keys and values at the same time. To loop through the values, it takes the following basic pattern:

```
foreach (arrayName as variable) {
  do something with the variable
  }
```

> *Note that `foreach` is written as one word. Attempting to put a space between `for` and `each` will generate an error.*

You can choose any valid name for the variable. PHP uses it exclusively within the loop as a pattern, so it's best to choose something that makes sense in the context of your code. For instance, you can apply a `foreach` loop to the `$characters` array like this to display the names of each character in the order they appear in the array (see `loops1.php`):

```
<?php
$characters = array('finder' => 'Bilbo',
  'bearer' => 'Frodo', 'helper '=> 'Sam',
  'wizard' => 'Gandalf', 'father' => 'Arathorn',
  'thepits' => 'Saruman');
foreach ($characters as $character) {
  echo "$character<br />";
  }
?>
```

To work on both key and value at the same time, the basic `foreach` pattern looks like this:

```
foreach (arrayName as key => value) {
  do something with both key and value
  }
```

This time you provide two variables: one for the key and the other for the value. If you replace the `foreach` loop in the previous example with the following code, it produces the output shown alongside (see `loops2.php`):

```
foreach ($characters as $role => $name) {
  echo "$name is $role<br />";
  }
```

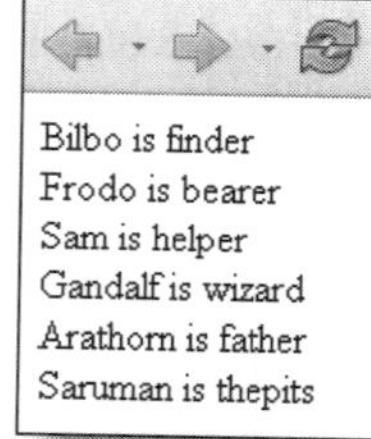

Note that the order of the variables within the parentheses is fixed, but you can use the temporary variables however you like inside the loop. In this example, the order of the key (`$role`) and value (`$name`) of each array element has been reversed.

Using the versatile for loop

The `foreach` loop works only with arrays. More versatile is the `for` loop, which not only works with arrays, but can also be used to perform most repetitive tasks. The syntax is exactly the same as in ActionScript, and takes the following basic pattern:

```
for (initialize counter; test; increment) {
  // code to be executed
  }
```

Note that the expressions within the parentheses are separated by semicolons, *not* commas. For a simple demonstration of how it works, the following code will display all the numbers from 0 to 100 (see `loops3.php`):

```
<?php
for ($i = 0; $i <= 100; $i++) {
  echo $i.'<br />';
  }
?>
```

The three expressions inside the parentheses control the action of the loop:

- The first expression shows the starting point. You can use any variable you like, but $i is the one traditionally favored by PHP coders (just as i is used as the traditional counter in ActionScript and JavaScript). When more than one counter is needed, $j and $k are frequently used, but this is no more than a convention.
- The second expression is a test that determines whether the loop should continue to run. This can be a fixed number, a variable, or an expression that calculates a value (such as the length of an array).
- The third expression shows the method of stepping through the loop. Most of the time, you will want to go through a loop one step at a time, so using the increment (++) or decrement (--) operator is convenient. There is nothing stopping you from using bigger steps. For instance, replacing $i++ with $i+=10 in the previous example would display 0, 10, 20, 30, and so on.

In both PHP and ActionScript, the first and third expressions can take multiple arguments separated by commas. Altering the previous example as follows produces the output shown alongside. The variables $i and $j have separate values, which are changed at different rates until the condition in the second expression is satisfied (see loops4.php).

$i is 0; $j is 100
$i is 20; $j is 98
$i is 40; $j is 96
$i is 60; $j is 94
$i is 80; $j is 92
$i is 100; $j is 90

```
for ($i = 0, $j = 100; $i <= 100; $i += 20, $j -= 2) {
  echo "\$i is $i; \$j is $j<br />";
  }
```

When working with for loops to handle arrays in ActionScript, it's common to use the array length as the second argument, like this:

```
for (var i = 0; i < myArray.length; i++) {
```

Now that you know that count() gives you the length of an array in PHP, you have probably worked out that the PHP equivalent is

```
for ($i = 0; $i < count($myArray); $i++) {
```

You can also test it with the following code (see loops5.php):

```
<?php
$characters = array('Bilbo', 'Frodo', 'Sam', 'Gandalf',
  'Arathorn', 'Saruman');
for ($i = 0; $i < count($characters); $i++) {
  echo $characters[$i].'<br />';
  }
?>
```

It will display the output shown alongside—no surprises yet.

If you try it with the following array, though, you will get either a blank screen or a series of error notices (see `loops6.php`):

```
$characters = array('finder'  => 'Bilbo', 'bearer'  => 'Frodo',
  'helper'  => 'Sam', 'wizard'  => 'Gandalf', 'father'  => 'Arathorn',
  'thepits' => 'Saruman');
```

> *To iterate through an associative array, you must use a* `foreach` *loop. A* `for` *loop works only with indexed arrays.*

Simple loops with while and do

Most books on programming begin their explanation of loops with the simplest loop of all, the `while` loop. The reason I've left it to the last is because simple loops are the easiest to get wrong and end up creating the programmer's nightmare, the infinite loop (that is, one that has no way of coming to a stop).

The basic pattern of the `while` loop is the same in both PHP and ActionScript:

```
while (condition is true) {
  // execute this code
  }
```

The problem with the `while` loop is that it's easy to forget to build in a safeguard to ensure the condition will eventually equate to `false`. (The following code is *not* included in the download files, for obvious reasons.)

```
<?php
$i = 0;
while ($i < 100) {
  echo $i;  // fills your screen with more zeros than you knew existed
  }
?>
```

Fortunately, PHP will normally stop such madness if the loop fails to terminate within the maximum time set for scripts. By default this is 30 seconds, but this can be altered in `php.ini`. In some browsers, though, an infinite loop is likely to induce the browser to crash. So, if your browser hangs or crashes when testing a script with a loop, you know where to start looking for the problem.

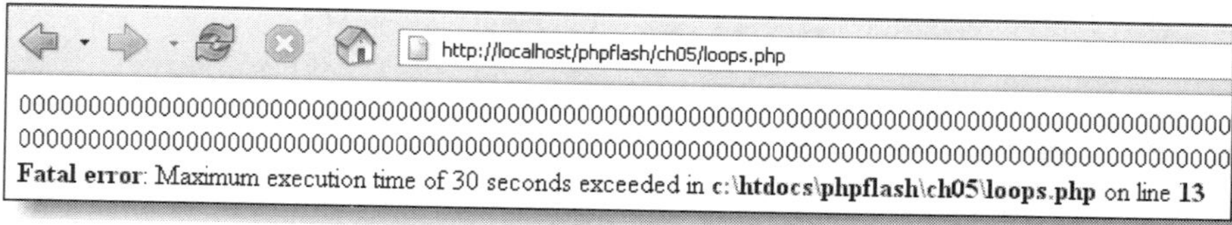

Flash is not so patient. It brings infinite loops in ActionScript to an end in 15 seconds and displays an equally embarrassing error message.

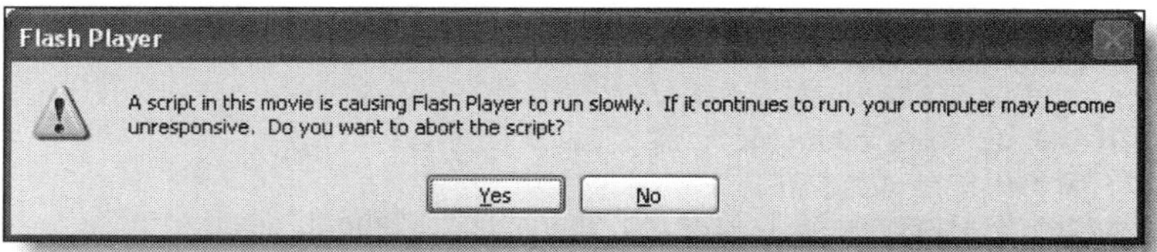

Infinite loops are not a good idea—in fact, they are a downright bad idea. Avoid them at all cost, and remember to ensure all loops will naturally come to an end. The earlier example contains nothing to increase the value of $i. Rewrite the loop as follows, and everything will be all right (a similar example is in simple_loop.php):

```
<?php
$i = 0;
while ($i < 100) {
  echo $i;
  $i++;
  }
?>
```

It doesn't take a genius to realize that lines 2, 3, and 5 of the preceding script contain the same initialize, test, and increment expressions as in a for loop:

```
for ($i = 0; $i < 100; $i++) {
  echo $i;
  }
```

Because the for loop keeps all three expressions together, you may find it a lot easier to work with than a while loop, as you are less prone to create the conditions for an infinite loop.

A variation of the while loop uses the keyword do and follows this basic pattern (which is the same in both languages):

```
do {
  // code to be executed
  } while (condition to be tested);
```

The only difference between a do... while loop and an ordinary while loop is that the code within the do block will always be executed *at least once*, even if the condition is never true. This type of loop is rarely used, but it's there should you ever find a need for it.

Breaking out of loops

You need a way of breaking out of loops or skipping some iterations. PHP uses the same keywords as ActionScript: break and continue.

You encountered break in the switch statement in Chapter 3. It works exactly the same way and brings all further execution of a loop to an end. Say, for example, you have a loop that divides a series of numbers by a figure generated by a previous calculation. Division by zero is impossible, so you need a method of preventing the loop from going ahead. One way is to use break, like this:

```
for ($i = 0; $i < count($items); $++) {
  if ($result == 0) {
    $errorMessage = 'Calculation abandoned. Cannot divide by zero.';
    break;
    }
  else {
    // perform the calculations
    }
  }
```

Frequently, you don't want to bring the whole loop to an end, but just skip execution of the code when a particular condition is met. continue stops execution of the current iteration and returns to the top of the loop to work on the next value. Say you are looping through the results of a database query. You want to add all family names to an array, but skip all entries where the family name is missing. The code would work like this:

```
for ($i = 0; $i < $numRows); $i++) {
  // code to fetch database query results one row at a time
    if (empty($row['familyName'])) {
    continue;
    }
  else {
    // process the data
    }
  }
```

Nesting loops

Repetitive work often involves doing not just one thing over and over again, but making a slight adjustment for each repetition. This is where nested loops can come in handy. Until you get the hang of them, they can seem impenetrably difficult to understand. The classic example of the nested loop is using one to display all the multiplication tables from 1 through 12. It's effective, because the multiplication tables are something just about everyone learns as a child, so it's easier to grasp what's going on inside the code.

Let's start with the basic code (see loops7.php):

```
<?php
$i = 1;
for ($j = 1; $j <= 12; $j++) {
  echo "$i x $j = ".$i*$j.'<br />';
  }
?>
```

What happens here is that $i is initially set to 1 and never changes. The other variable, $j, is set to 1, but it is increased by 1 every time the loop executes. The echo command inside the loop displays a multiplication sign between the values of $i and $j, followed by an equal sign and the result of the calculation. In other words, it displays the 1 times multiplication table:

```
1 x 1 = 1
1 x 2 = 2
1 x 3 = 3 // and so on
```

To reproduce all multiplication tables from 1 through 12, the value of $i also needs to be incremented, but only after $j has gone through the full cycle. Once $j has reached 12, $i needs to be incremented to 2, and it needs to remain at 2 until $j has gone all the way around to 12 again. The way to do this is to nest the current loop inside a loop that increments $i, like this (see loops8.php):

```
<?php
for ($i = 1; $i <= 12; $i++) {
  for ($j = 1; $j <= 12; $j++) {
    echo "$i x $j = ".$i*$j.'<br />';
    }
  }
?>
```

As soon as the inner loop reaches 12, the outer loop moves to the next number, but the inner loop goes back to the beginning of its own cycle, producing

```
1 x 12 = 12
2 x 1 = 2
2 x 2 = 4 // and so on
```

Apologies if you already know this, but it's something that causes a lot of problems for newcomers to programming. Once you understand it, the next leap is a lot easier, because the same pattern is used to handle multidimensional arrays by nesting foreach loops inside each other.

This next example looks very complicated, but it is identical in structure to the multiplication tables. What makes it *look* more difficult is the fact that it's looping through named elements rather than numbers. It uses the $cast multidimensional array from earlier. It also makes use of three of the string functions you studied in the previous chapter.

```
<?php
// First create individual arrays of related characters
$hobbits = array('finder' => 'Bilbo', 'bearer' => 'Frodo',
  'helper' => 'Sam');
$goodguys = array('wizard' => 'Gandalf', 'father' => 'Arathorn');
$badguys = array('thepits' => 'Saruman');

// Then build an array of arrays
$cast = array('Hobbits' => $hobbits, 'Goodguys' => $goodguys,
  'Badguys' => $badguys);
```

```
// loop through the multidimensional array and display the contents
foreach ($cast as $category => $members) {
  echo strtoupper($category).'<br />';
  foreach ($members as $role => $name) {
    echo ucfirst($role).sprintf("%'.40s",$name).'<br />';
    }
  echo '<br />';
  }
?>
```

The result shown below should look somewhat familiar. The top-level array $cast has been separated out into two temporary variables: $category, which holds the key of each array element, and $members, which holds the value. The first $category is Hobbits. Since this is an array key, it holds only a single value, so it can be displayed immediately by using echo. To make it stand out, it is converted to uppercase with strtoupper().

HOBBITS
Finder.................................Bilbo
Bearer.................................Frodo
Helper.................................Sam
GOODGUYS
Wizard.................................Gandalf
Father.................................Arathorn
BADGUYS
Thepits.................................Saruman

The value of $members, however, is an array (containing 'finder' => 'Bilbo', and so on). To extract the contents of this subarray, another foreach loop is created *inside* the first loop. This time, the key of each element in $members is assigned to a temporary variable called $role, and the value to another temporary variable called $name. So, in the first run-through of this inner loop, $role equals finder and $name equals Bilbo. The values are simply formatted using ucfirst() and sprintf().

After the inner loop finishes processing all elements of the Hobbits subarray, it returns to the main loop, where the whole process starts all over again, handling the Goodguys and Badguys arrays until there are no more elements in the top-level array.

Passing information securely with $_POST

The discussion of arrays so far has omitted arguably the most important category of all: what PHP calls **superglobal arrays**. As their name suggests, these arrays are automatically global in scope, so they can be used anywhere inside a script. PHP superglobals pass external information to your scripts, such as when transferring data from a Flash movie to PHP. LoadVars uses the HTTP POST method to do this, and a PHP script retrieves the information from the superglobal $_POST array, which you have been using since Chapter 2.

From a structural point of view, this and all the other superglobal arrays (listed in Table 5-1) are simply associative arrays; the name of each variable becomes the key used to identify the value being passed from an external source. So, a Flash variable called action that is sent to a PHP script through LoadVars is received as $_POST['action']. You use superglobal variables in exactly the same way as any other variable, but the fact that most of them contain data from external sources means you often have no control over their content, and malicious users may attempt to crack your system by exploiting poorly written scripts.

The good news is that the introduction of the superglobal arrays in PHP 4.2.0 in April 2002 helped make PHP much more secure. The bad news is that some hosting companies didn't implement the security measures that the superglobals rely on. For you to understand the problem, it's necessary to make a brief detour into PHP history.

Why register_globals is so important

PHP was designed to make life as easy as possible for web developers. When information was passed from an online form using the POST or GET method, all you had to do was prefix the name of the form field with a dollar sign, and voilà, it was immediately available as a variable in your PHP script. PHP automatically registered such variables as global in scope. This was very useful, but it also left gaping security holes in many scripts. To solve the problem, PHP turned off a setting called `register_globals` in php.ini. As the name suggests, this setting controls automatic registration of global variables. Turning it off by default closes an important security loophole. Instead of developers around the world jumping for joy at the improved security, many were up in arms. Scripts that once worked smoothly were broken overnight. Hosting companies in search of a quiet life switched `register_globals` back on, and the scripts worked again. Peace was restored, but security was done immeasurable damage.

Hopefully, sufficient time has now passed for this practice to have been abandoned by all reputable hosts. The reason for this digression is to warn you against any "advice" you may find that suggests your life will be made easier by turning `register_globals` on. If you are reliant on a hosting company that still uses that setting, you may one day find that the policy changes and all your scripts break. If you run your own server and fall afoul of the temptation to turn `register_globals` on, be prepared for crackers to wreak havoc on your data.

The reason it's so dangerous to turn on `register_globals` is that all a malicious user has to do is to guess the names of vital variables (which is very easy, since a lot of beginners simply copy scripts from books or online resources without any changes). A new value for those variables can then be created by adding a name/value pair to the URL like this: `http://insecure.example.com/admin/login.php?admin=yes`.

If login.php has a variable called `$admin`, the cracker has now probably broken into the system with full administrative privileges or will do pretty quickly after a few more guesses at the right combination. The superglobal arrays use a simple, yet effective device to improve security. With `register_globals` off, the only variables that accept data from external sources must belong to a specific superglobal array. So, if you specify your `admin` variable as `$_POST['admin']`, it will accept a value supplied only through the POST method. Any attempt to change it through a URL (which uses the GET method) will fail. Also, if the `admin` variable is registered as a session variable (`$_SESSION['admin']`), it can't be changed by either POST or GET. It's not 100% secure (nothing online is), but it's much more difficult for a malicious user to circumvent.

You may come across online resources or books that refer to the predecessors of the superglobal arrays, so Table 5-1 shows the main superglobal arrays, along with their deprecated equivalents.

Table 5-1. The most important PHP superglobal arrays and their equivalents

Superglobal array	Deprecated equivalent	Description
`$_POST`	`$HTTP_POST_VARS`	Contains variables sent through the `POST` method, the default way of receiving data from Flash movies through `LoadVars`. Transmitted information is hidden from the user.
`$_GET`	`$HTTP_GET_VARS`	Contains variables sent through the `GET` method, mainly used for online search functions. Data is transmitted through the browser address bar. This makes it easy to bookmark pages and retrace steps through the browser's Back button, but data can easily be altered by the user.
`$_COOKIE`	`$HTTP_COOKIE_VARS`	Contains cookie variables, which are stored on the user's hard disk to perpetuate information about user preferences and so on.
`$_SESSION`	`$HTTP_SESSION_VARS`	Contains session variables, which are normally used for user authentication. This is covered in detail in Chapter 9.
`$_FILES`	`$HTTP_POST_FILES`	Contains variables related to files uploaded to a server using the `POST` method.
`$_SERVER`	`$HTTP_SERVER_VARS`	Contains variables that identify a wide range of information about the local and remote web servers, as well as the browser being used.

To convert between the deprecated version and the superglobal, simply substitute the appropriate array name, like this:

```
$HTTP_POST_VARS['action']      // becomes $_POST['action']
$HTTP_SESSION_VARS['password'] // becomes $_SESSION['password']
```

For more details, see `www.php.net/manual/en/language.variables.predefined.php` and `www.php.net/manual/en/security.globals.php`.

Manipulating arrays

Because of its wide use in creating XHTML pages, PHP has more than 60 functions that do just about everything imaginable with arrays. Most are of limited interest when working with databases, as they duplicate actions that are much more efficiently dealt with by extracting the right information from a database in the first place.

Still, it is useful to know how PHP handles the equivalent ActionScript methods. Most are identical in operation, but there are some important differences. Table 5-2 lists the PHP equivalents and describes how they are used. Arguments are given only for the PHP equivalents (those in square brackets are optional). For details of the ActionScript methods, consult the Flash ActionScript Dictionary (Window ➤ ActionScript Dictionary).

Table 5-2. PHP equivalents of ActionScript array methods and properties

ActionScript	PHP equivalent	Description
`concat()`	`array_merge(`*`arr1, arr2 [,arrN]`*`)`	Returns a new array, consisting of the elements of the arrays passed to it. If associative arrays are used, elements with the same key are overwritten with the most recent value. Indexed arrays preserve all values, including duplicates.
`join()`	`implode(`*`delimiter, array`*`)`	Described fully in Chapter 4. It takes two arguments: a string delimiter and the array. It returns a string containing each element of the array separated by the delimiter.
`length`	`count(`*`array`*`)`	Described earlier in this chapter. It returns the number of elements in an array. The major difference between PHP and ActionScript is that PHP counts *both* numbered and named elements. ActionScript counts *numbered* elements only.
`pop()`	`array_pop(`*`array`*`)`	Removes the last element of an array and returns the value of the element deleted.
`push()`	`array_push(`*`value1 [,valueN]`*`)`	Adds one or more elements to the end of an existing array. Both languages return the length of the amended array. If you are adding just one element to an array, it is more efficient to use the [] syntax in PHP.

(Continued)

Table 5-2. PHP equivalents of ActionScript array methods and properties *(Continued)*

ActionScript	PHP equivalent	Description
`reverse()`	`array_reverse(`*`array`*`)`	Reverses the order of an array. This works on the original, not a copy.
`shift()`	`array_shift(`*`array`*`)`	Removes the first element of an array and returns the value of the element deleted.
`slice()`	`array_slice(`*`array, beg [,len]`*`)`	Returns a new array extracted from an existing one. See the "Slicing and splicing arrays" section for details of important differences between PHP and ActionScript.
`sort()`	`sort(`*`array`*`)`	Sorts an array. See the "Sorting arrays" section for full details.
`sortOn()`	`ksort(`*`array`*`)`	Sorts an array by its keys. See the "Sorting arrays" section for full details.
`splice()`	`array_splice(`*`array, beg [,len [,new]]`*`)`	Removes elements from an array and substitutes new ones. See the "Slicing and splicing arrays" section for details.
`toString()`	`implode(',', `*`array`*`)`	PHP does not have a direct equivalent, but `implode` with a comma as the delimiter serves the same purpose.
`unshift()`	`array_unshift(array, value1 [,valueN])`	Adds one or more elements to the beginning of an array. Both languages return the length of the amended array.

Slicing and splicing arrays

Not only are their names easily confused, but also `slice` and `splice` in both PHP and ActionScript perform similar operations. An easy way to remember the difference is that `slice` is like every child's dream: it lets you have your cake and eat it too. It slices something *out* of an array, but even when you remove the slice, the whole cake (the original array) is left intact! On the other hand, `splice` is more like real life: anything removed from the cake is gone forever. And just as splice in real life means to merge two things, using `splice` with an array is also used for adding *in* extra elements.

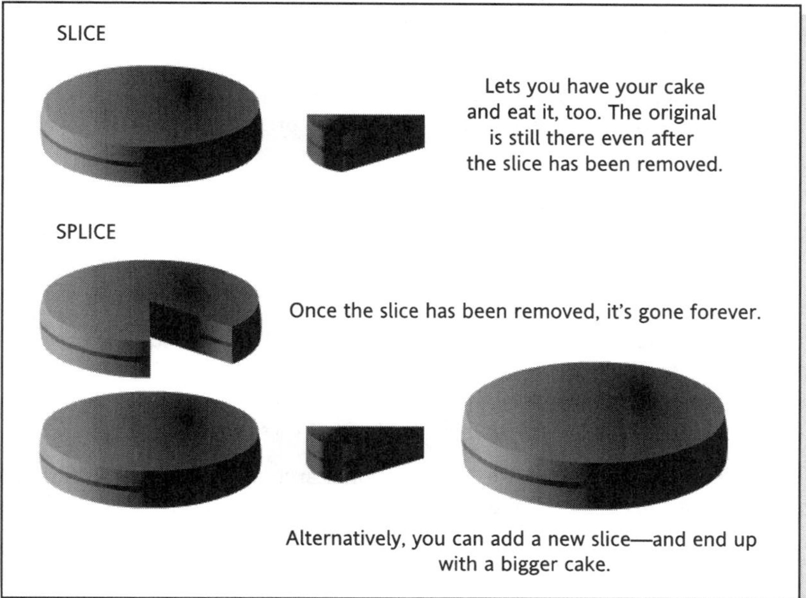

SLICE
Lets you have your cake and eat it, too. The original is still there even after the slice has been removed.
SPLICE
Once the slice has been removed, it's gone forever.
Alternatively, you can add a new slice—and end up with a bigger cake.

As if that weren't confusing enough, PHP and ActionScript use different criteria to identify the elements to be extracted by `slice`. Hopefully, the next two sections will make the situation crystal clear.

Using array_slice() to extract part of an array

The standard pattern for `array_slice()` is as follows:

```
array_slice(array, startIndex [, length])
```

The second argument (*startIndex*) indicates the position of the first element you want to extract to the new array. If the value of *startIndex* is negative, the position is counted from the end of the original array. If the third argument (*length*) is omitted, everything to the end of the original array is included in the new one. So far, both PHP and ActionScript act in exactly the same way, as the following examples show:

```
<?php
$characters = array('Bilbo', 'Frodo', 'Sam', 'Gandalf', 'Arathorn');
$goodguys = array_slice($characters, 3);
$goodguys2 = array_slice($characters, -2);
echo '<pre>';
print_r($goodguys);
print_r($goodguys2);
print_r($characters);
echo '<pre>';
?>
```

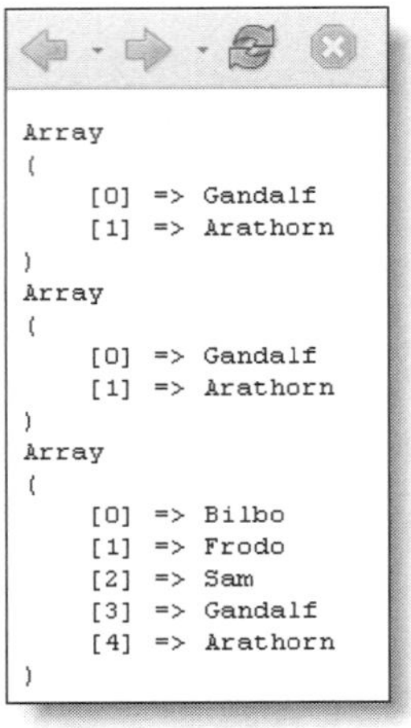

```
Array
(
    [0] => Gandalf
    [1] => Arathorn
)
Array
(
    [0] => Gandalf
    [1] => Arathorn
)
Array
(
    [0] => Bilbo
    [1] => Frodo
    [2] => Sam
    [3] => Gandalf
    [4] => Arathorn
)
```

If you test that code in a browser (it's in `array_slice1.php` in the download files for this chapter), you will get the output shown at the right. The two new arrays ($goodguys and $goodguys2) produce exactly the same result, although the first counts from the beginning of the array, and the second counts from the end of the array. As you can see, the original array (`$characters`) remains intact.

The following code produces a similar result in ActionScript (the code to display the result has been omitted, although it's included in `array_slice1.fla`, or you can use the debugger to view the three arrays if you're creating your own version):

```
var characters:Array = new Array("Bilbo", "Frodo", "Sam",
➥"Gandalf", "Arathorn");
var goodguys:Array = characters.slice(3);
var goodguys2:Array = characters.slice(-2);
```

The two languages still agree when the final, optional argument is negative: that number of elements is excluded from the end of the new array. For example, both the following pieces of code (in `array_slice2.php` and `array_slice2.fla`) produce a single-element array containing the value "Frodo":

```
$theOne = array_slice($characters, 1, -3);  // PHP
var theOne:Array = characters.slice(1, -3); // ActionScript
```

PHP and ActionScript part company when the final argument is *positive*. In PHP, life is very simple—the final argument specifies the length of the new array to be extracted, like this:

```
$thePositiveOne = array_slice($characters, 1, 1);
```

But look what happens if you use the same final argument in ActionScript:

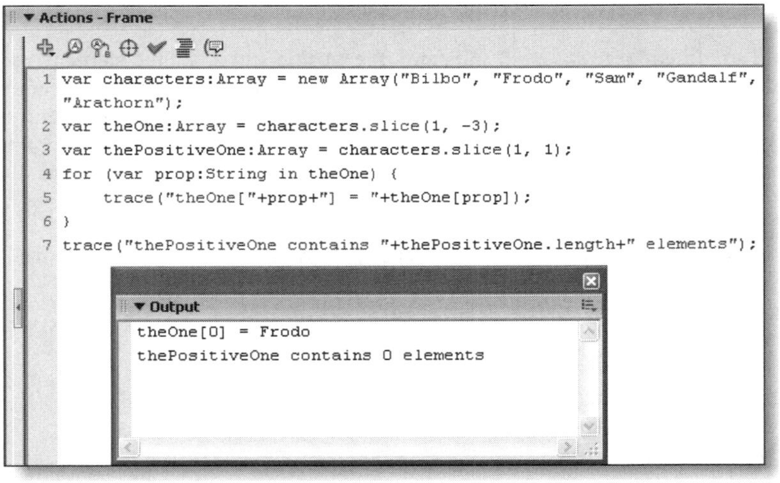

▼ Actions - Frame

```
var characters:Array = new Array("Bilbo", "Frodo", "Sam", "Gandalf",
"Arathorn");
var theOne:Array = characters.slice(1, -3);
var thePositiveOne:Array = characters.slice(1, 1);
for (var prop:String in theOne) {
    trace("theOne["+prop+"] = "+theOne[prop]);
}
trace("thePositiveOne contains "+thePositiveOne.length+" elements");
```

▼ Output

```
theOne[0] = Frodo
thePositiveOne contains 0 elements
```

ActionScript expects the final argument, when positive, to be an end index. In other words, you must give the index of the element *after* the last one you want to include in the new array. So, to select "Frodo," you need to use the following code:

```
var theMorePositiveOne:Array = characters.slice(1,2);
```

Crazy, but that's the way it is. Fortunately, such lunacy doesn't creep into splice—well, not quite so much.

Using array_splice() to amend an array

The general pattern for array_splice() is as follows:

```
array_splice(array, start [, length [, replacement]])
```

In its simplest form, array_splice() takes just two arguments: the array you want to amend and an integer specifying where the changes start. When the final two arguments are omitted, this has the effect of removing everything from the start point to the end of the array. Unlike array_slice(), the elements are gone permanently. However, array_splice() returns the deleted elements, so you can capture them in a variable, like this (see array_splice1.php):

```
<?php
$characters = array('Bilbo', 'Frodo', 'Sam', 'Gandalf', 'Arathorn');
$goodguys = array_splice($characters, 3);
echo '<pre>';
print_r($goodguys);
print_r($characters);
echo '</pre>';
?>
```

The results (shown at the right) are very different from array_slice(). Although the new $goodguys array is the same, $characters has been permanently changed by the removal of all elements from the start position specified as the second argument.

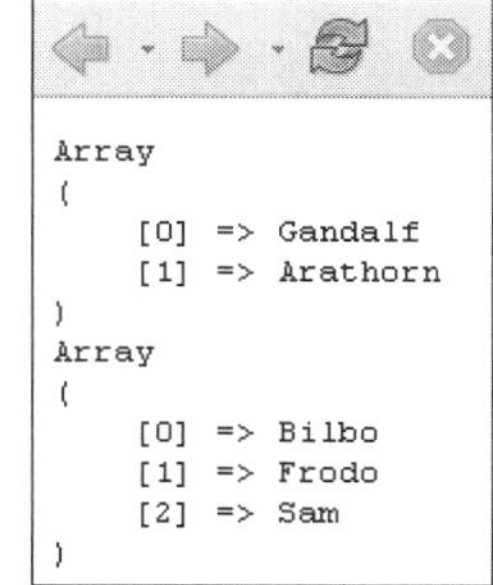

The third argument (*length*) specifies how many elements to delete, so you can make Gandalf disappear (but preserve his identity elsewhere) like this (see array_splice2.php):

```
$characters = array('Bilbo', 'Frodo', 'Sam', 'Gandalf',
➥'Arathorn');
$whiteWizard = array_splice($characters, 3, 1);
```

By using the final argument (*replacement*) you can bring him back exactly where he was:

```
array_splice($characters, 3, 0, $whiteWizard);
```

What this does is start from index number 3, delete no elements, and insert the contents of $whiteWizard at that point.

So far, so good. Up to now, PHP and ActionScript agree on how to splice arrays, but something has to come along to spoil the party. **In PHP, the final argument must be an array unless it consists of just one element. ActionScript expects a comma-delimited list of replacement values.**

ActionScript will accept an array as the final argument, but it treats that array differently, as the following examples demonstrate (see `array_splice3.php`).

```
$characters = array('Bilbo', 'Frodo', 'Sam', 'Gandalf', 'Arathorn');
// removes Frodo, Sam, and Gandalf
$removed = array_splice($characters, 1,3);
// restores array to its original form
array_splice($characters, 1, 0, $removed);
```

Look what happens if you try to do the same thing in ActionScript (see `array_splice.fla`):

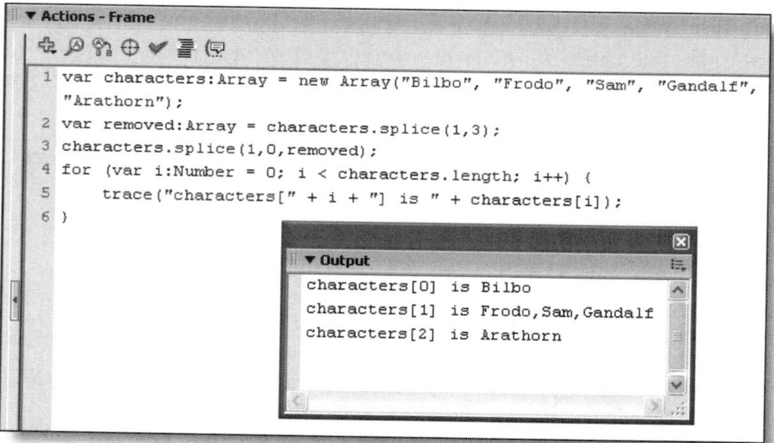

ActionScript preserves the replacement array, rather than flattening it and integrating the individual elements back into the target array. Consequently, you end up with a multidimensional array—something you may not have expected.

> *Don't worry if the intricacies of slicing and splicing arrays have your head spinning. It's not easy, but it's useful to know these differences exist. Just make a mental note of where to find this information in the book. One day, you'll be glad you did.*

Sorting arrays

PHP has a much more versatile arsenal of sort functions than the two offered by ActionScript. The basic pattern is to pass the array to the function as an argument. Table 5-3 lists the main PHP sort functions.

Table 5-3. PHP functions for sorting arrays

Function	Description
`sort()`	Sorts array by values and reassigns keys starting with 0. Use on indexed arrays.
`rsort()`	Sorts array by values in descending (reverse) order and reassigns keys starting with 0. Use on indexed arrays.
`usort()`	Same as `sort()`, but iterates through an array sorting values according to the criteria of a user-defined function passed to `usort()` as a second argument. The function must take two arguments and return a negative integer, zero, or a positive integer depending on whether the first argument is less than, equal to, or greater than the second argument. Use on indexed arrays.
`asort()`	Sorts array by values, but preserves the key/value relationship. Use on associative arrays.
`arsort()`	Sorts array by values in reverse order and preserves the key/value relationship. Use on associative arrays.
`uasort()`	Same as `usort()`, but preserves the key/value relationship. Use on associative arrays.
`ksort()`	Sorts array by keys, while preserving the key/value relationship. Use on associative arrays.
`krsort()`	Sorts array by keys in reverse order and preserves the key/value relationship. Use on associative arrays.
`uksort()`	Same as `uasort()`, but the user-defined sort function is applied to the key of each element, not the value. Use on associative arrays.
`natsort()`	Sorts array by values in a "natural" human order. It differs from `sort()` by treating strings that contain numbers in a way that seems more logical to humans. For example, `sort()` produces the following order: `pic10.jpg, pic1.jpg, pic20.jpg, pic2.jpg`; `natsort()` produces `pic1.jpg, pic2.jpg, pic10.jpg, pic20.jpg`. It preserves the key/value relationship. Use on both indexed and associative arrays.
`natcasesort()`	Case-insensitive version of `natsort()`.
`array_multisort()`	Sorts a multidimensional array or several single-dimensional arrays at once, preserving the key/value relationship of each element.

You've already seen sort() in action. There's little to say about the other PHP sort functions that isn't explained in Table 5-3. They all act on the original array, and they don't require you to capture the result in a variable. Most return a Boolean value indicating whether the sort was successful. The two exceptions, natsort() and natcasesort(), don't produce any return value.

The best way to understand how the sort functions work is to experiment with them and see the result in a browser in exactly the same way as you did earlier in the exercise "Examining the contents of an array" (you did do it, didn't you?). The illustrations show the effects of ksort(), krsort(), asort(), and arsort() on the following associative array:

```
$cast = array('finder' => 'Bilbo', 'bearer' => 'Frodo',
  'helper' => 'Sam', 'wizard' => 'Gandalf',
  'father' => 'Arathorn', 'thepits' => 'Saruman');
```

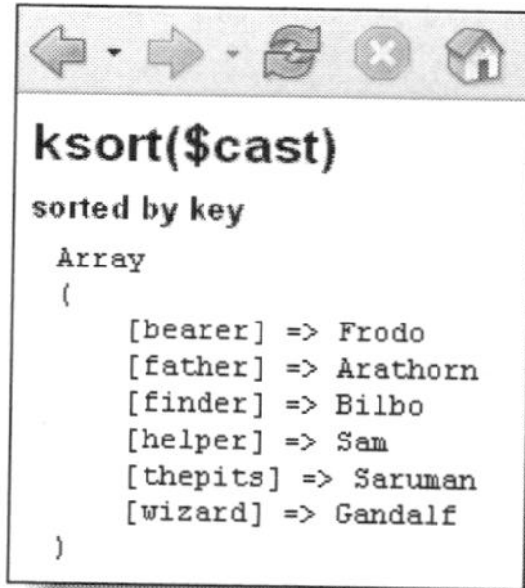

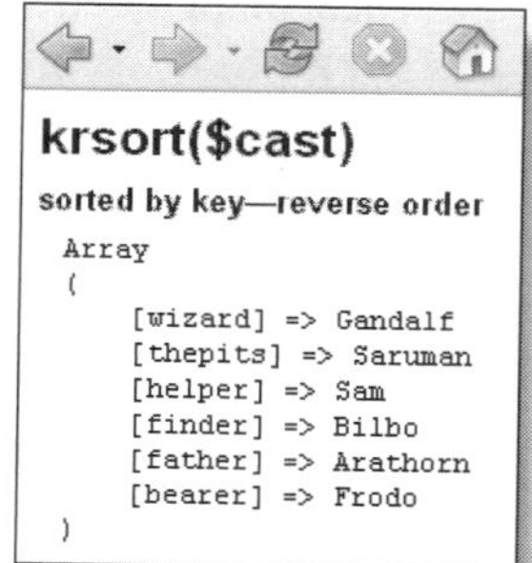

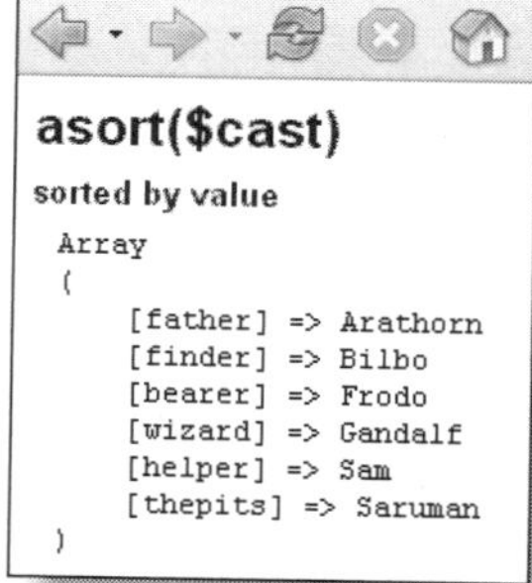

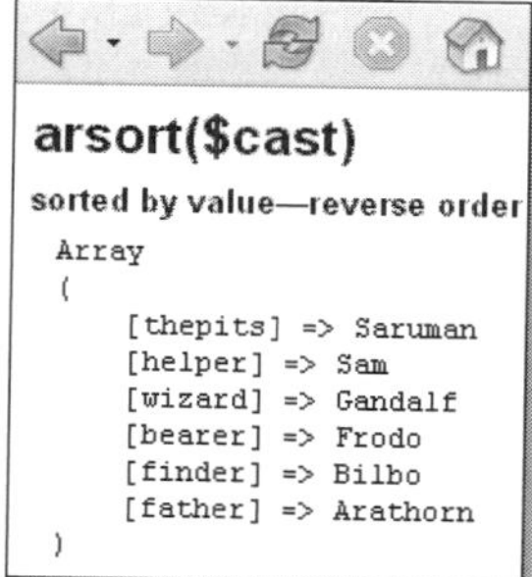

Although natsort() and natcasesort() maintain the relationship between key and value, you should note that they only sort by value. There is no "natural" sort equivalent that uses array keys as the sort criterion.

Perhaps the most interesting of all the PHP sort functions is array_multisort(). Rather than apply it to the fantasy world, let's put it to *real* use in the Flash application for this chapter, in an RSS feed aggregator.

Building an RSS feed aggregator

"What's RSS?" I was afraid you would ask.

According to some people, **RSS** stands for Really Simple Syndication. Others will tell you, "No, it's Rich Site Summary." Yet others say it's RDF Site Summary, and that RDF stands for Resource Description Framework. It's one of those "I say tom-ay-to, you say tom-ah-to" arguments. All explanations are reasonably plausible, and they all give a fair idea of what RSS is about. I like Really Simple Syndication, because it describes RSS perfectly. It's really simple, as this Flash/PHP application will demonstrate.

What an RSS feed does

As you surf around the Web these days, you're sure to have noticed little icons that mysteriously say either XML or RSS. There's one on the friends of ED site at `www.friendsofed.com`. Being a friendly sort of guy, Pete the webmaster has put a little question mark to the side of the icon to help out the uninitiated. Click the question mark, and after some blarney about "releasing millions of tiny joy particles from the upper-funk zone of your hypothalamus," you'll find an explanation that RSS enables you to get a brief summary of the latest news on your favorite sites. The normal way to use RSS is to get a feed aggregator such as FeedDemon (`www.bradsoft.com/feeddemon/index.asp`) or SharpReader (`www.sharpreader.net`) for Windows. If you're a Mac user on OS X, Shrook (`www.fondantfancies.com/shrook`) offers similar capabilities. Once you have a feed aggregator installed, just click the XML or RSS icon on your favorite sites, and the RSS feed will be added to the list of site information it gathers for you to read at leisure.

FeedDemon, SharpReader, and Shrook are great for reading RSS feeds on your own computer, but wouldn't it be cool if you could gather news from selected sites and share the information with others on your own site? That's exactly what you're going to do now. You can see what the finished feed aggregator looks like in Figure 5-11 at the end of the chapter.

> *Like all information on the Web, the content of an RSS feed is normally the copyright of the originating website. Before incorporating someone else's content into your site, make sure the conditions of use allow you to do so, and* ***never*** *pass off other people's material as your own. At the very least, it could earn you a reputation as a cheat. At worst, it could land you a copyright infringement lawsuit.*

The two RSS feeds you'll use in this application come from friends of ED and Apress, friends of ED's parent company. The friends of ED RSS feed carries brief snippets of news and gossip of interest to the web designer community, while the Apress feed keeps you up to date with the latest entries in Ablog, the musings of Apress and friends of ED editors and authors about life, the universe, and everything.

Taking a look inside an RSS feed

As the XML icon suggests, an RSS feed is an XML document. The address of the friends of ED RSS feed is `http://friendsofed.com/news.php`. If you open that page in Internet Explorer or Firefox on Windows, it will display the raw XML. If you're using Safari on a Mac, the browser attempts to display the feed as though it were a normal web page (as shown in Figure 5-8). Use View Source to reveal the underlying XML.

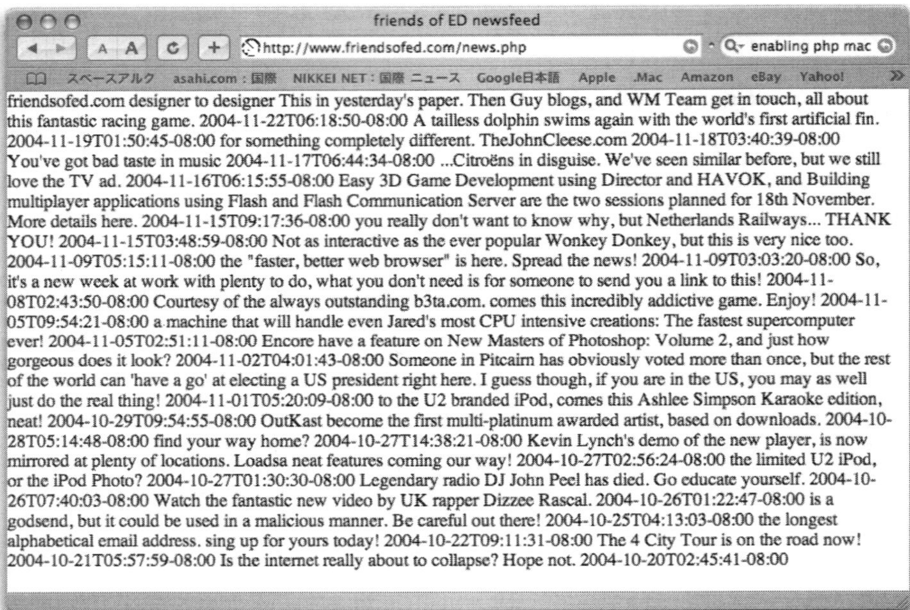

Figure 5-8. Safari attempts to treat the friends of ED RSS feed as a normal page with confusing results.

If you look at the feed in Internet Explorer 6 or Safari Source view, the first thing you will see are details of the XML version, default character set, and namespace. Firefox cuts these out and just displays the RSS content, which is what you are interested in. It will look something like this (only the first two `item` elements are shown for space reasons):

```
<rdf:RDF>
  <channel rdf:about="http://www.friendsofed.com">
    <title>friends of ED newsfeed</title>
    <description> friendsofed.com designer to designer</description>
    <link>http://www.friendsofed.com</link>
    <items/>
  </channel>
  <item rdf:about="http://www.friendsofed.com">
    <title>Coincidences</title>
```

```
      <description>
        This in yesterday's paper. Then Guy blogs, and WM Team get in
        touch, all about this fantastic racing game.
      </description>
      <link>http://www.friendsofed.com/updatED.php?613</link>
      <dc:date>2004-11-22T06:18:50-08:00</dc:date>
    </item>
    <item rdf:about="http://www.friendsofed.com">
      <title>Prosthetics. For dolphins!</title>
      <description>
        A tailless dolphin swims again with the world's first
        artificial fin.
      </description>
      <link>http://www.friendsofed.com/updatED.php?612</link>
      <dc:date>2004-11-19T01:50:45-08:00</dc:date>
    </item>
  </rdf:RDF>
```

Even if you're not familiar with XML documents, this shouldn't be too difficult to understand. XML uses tags very similar to those used in HTML and XHTML web pages. The meaning of most tags used in an RSS feed is obvious. The opening and closing `<rdf:RDF>` tags indicate that this is a document written according to the **Resource Description Framework** (**RDF**), one of the standards used by RSS. The `<channel>` tag identifies the source of the feed, and each `<item>` tag contains a feed item. The dc in the date tags stands for **Dublin Core**, a standardized set of data categories used in RSS feeds. To learn more about Dublin Core and the way an RSS feed is built, a good place to start is an online tutorial created by Mark Nottingham at `www.mnot.net/rss/tutorial`.

The friends of ED RSS feed uses a standard called RSS 1.0. The propeller heads at Apress, perhaps wanting to show off their technical expertise, offer more than one feed, most of them using a newer standard called RSS 2.0. The feed I propose using for this application is available in both RSS 2.0 (`http://blogs.apress.com/index.xml`) and RSS 1.0 (`http://blogs.apress.com/index.rdf`). The format is almost identical, but the RSS 1.0 feed contains a useful snippet of information not available in the other one for some reason: the name of the blog entry's author. So that's the one I propose to use. You can take a look at the raw feeds yourself by using the URLs, although your browser will probably prompt you to save the Apress RSS 1.0 feed to your hard disk. Once you have downloaded it, open it with your favorite text editor.

If you haven't already realized it, these feeds are actually multidimensional arrays. The top-level `<rdf:RDF>` tag is the equivalent of the top-level array, and the `<channel>` and `<item>` tags are subarrays. The challenge is to get the information they contain into arrays that PHP can understand, and then transfer the content to Flash in a way that ActionScript can handle. The first part of that process is made easy thanks to a free PHP utility called MagpieRSS.

Rather than just present you with instructions for how to build the feed aggregator, the following sections spend some time examining the structure of arrays in a practical situation, to give you greater confidence in working with them on your own.

an RSS feed with MagpieRSS

Magpie, as it's usually called) is a PHP parser for RSS that was created by Kellan It is freely available under the **General Public License** (**GPL**, see www.gnu.org/ html). At the time of this writing, Magpie was compatible with RSS 0.9 and RSS o supported most of RSS 2.0 and a similar feed protocol known as Atom led.org).

All you need to do to use Magpie is download the files (approximately 34KB in a compressed file) and place them in a folder that your PHP script can access.

Installing Magpie

1. Download the source files from http://magpierss.sourceforge.net. At the time of this writing, the latest version was MagpieRSS 0.71. Like a lot of open source projects, experimental versions (alphas or betas) will be released from time to time. Read the information on the site and check any release notes to make sure you pick a stable version.
2. Extract the contents to a temporary folder. The download file comes in TAR.GZ format. Mac OS X users need only double-click the icon of the downloaded file. Windows users may need a decompression utility such as WinZip (www.winzip.com).
3. The unzipped contents should contain a folder called magpierss-x.x, where x is the number of the latest release. At the time of this writing, it was mapgpierss-0.71. Rename the folder magpie.
4. Cut and paste the renamed magpie folder so that it is inside a folder that can be accessed by PHP. The simplest way to do this is to paste the magpie folder inside your phpflash/ch05 folder. That's it. Magpie is ready to use.

Now that you've installed the files, you need to test that everything is working OK.

Testing Magpie

Magpie uses an aspect of PHP not yet covered in this book: classes. At the time of this writing, it still made use of PHP 4 coding. This is likely to generate error notices if you have set error reporting to a high level, as recommended in Chapter 1. This is not a problem, as error notices do not indicate anything likely to break your application and can be easily turned off for individual scripts.

1. Create a new PHP page in phpflash/ch05, and call it rssfeed.php. The code for this first section is in rssfeed01.php in the download files.
2. Enter the following code:

```
<?php
// reset error reporting to eliminate advisory notices
error_reporting(E_ALL & ~E_NOTICE & ~E_STRICT);
require_once('magpie/rss_fetch.inc');
// set output encoding to Unicode
define('MAGPIE_OUTPUT_ENCODING', 'UTF-8');
```

The first line of code after the opening PHP tag resets the error reporting level for this particular script to suppress all advisory notices. The arguments inside the parentheses are PHP constants, so they must be in uppercase and *not* enclosed in quotes.

The next line includes the code from Magpie, using the `require_once()` construct. PHP has four different commands for including external files: `include`, `require`, `include_once`, and `require_once`. They can all be used with or without parentheses, but the filename and path should always be enclosed in quotes. The difference between each command is rather subtle. In my experience, using `require_once()`—as shown here with parentheses—is the most reliable.

After including the Magpie file, one of the Magpie constants is set to `UTF-8`. This ensures that the output of the RSS feeds is converted to UTF-8 (Unicode), the default encoding used by the Flash Player. As in ActionScript, the PHP convention is to use uppercase for the names of constants. You declare a PHP constant with the `define()` function, which takes two arguments: the name of the constant and its value, both presented as strings.

Strictly speaking, there should be no need to convert the encoding for feeds that are in English, but it's essential for any language that uses accented characters, such as French or Spanish. Although ISO-8859-1 encoding includes all the accented characters used in Western European languages, their code position in UTF-8 is completely different. Unless you convert them before sending them to Flash, all accented characters (and usually the following one, too) will turn into little boxes.

3. That's all you need to do to use Magpie with any of your scripts. The next step is to retrieve an RSS feed. This application will eventually use two feeds, but for testing purposes, let's start with just one. Enter the following code immediately after the code in the previous step:

```
// Store feed addresses in array of URLs
$urls[0] = 'http://friendsofed.com/news.php';

// Loop through each address and retrieve RSS feed as object
for ($i=0;$i<count($urls);$i++) {
  $rss = fetch_rss($urls[$i]);
  }
```

This assigns the address of the friends of ED RSS feed as the first element of an array called `$urls`. Next follows a `for` loop. The counter (`$i`) is initialized to `0`. The number of times the loop will run is set by calculating the length of the `$urls` array with `count()`. Since there is only one item in the array at the moment, the loop will run just once, but the second feed will be added shortly. Inside the loop is the code that does all the work:

```
$rss = fetch_rss($urls[$i]);
```

`fetch_rss()` is the main method of Magpie. Its name is self-explanatory. It fetches the feed specified in `$urls[$i]` and stores the result in `$rss`.

4. The final section uses `print_r()` to display the contents of `$rss`. This code follows immediately after that in the previous step, and it includes the closing PHP tag for the script:

```
// Display content of object
echo '<pre>';
print_r($rss);
echo '</pre>';
?>
```

5. Make sure you are connected to the Internet, and load `rssfeed.php` into a browser. Assuming the friends of ED server is not down for some reason, you should see something like Figure 5-9.

   The first line of the output tells you that `$rss` is a MagpieRSS Object. Everything else is displayed in the same way as the arrays you have been working with throughout this chapter. The only difference is that there is a lot more information.

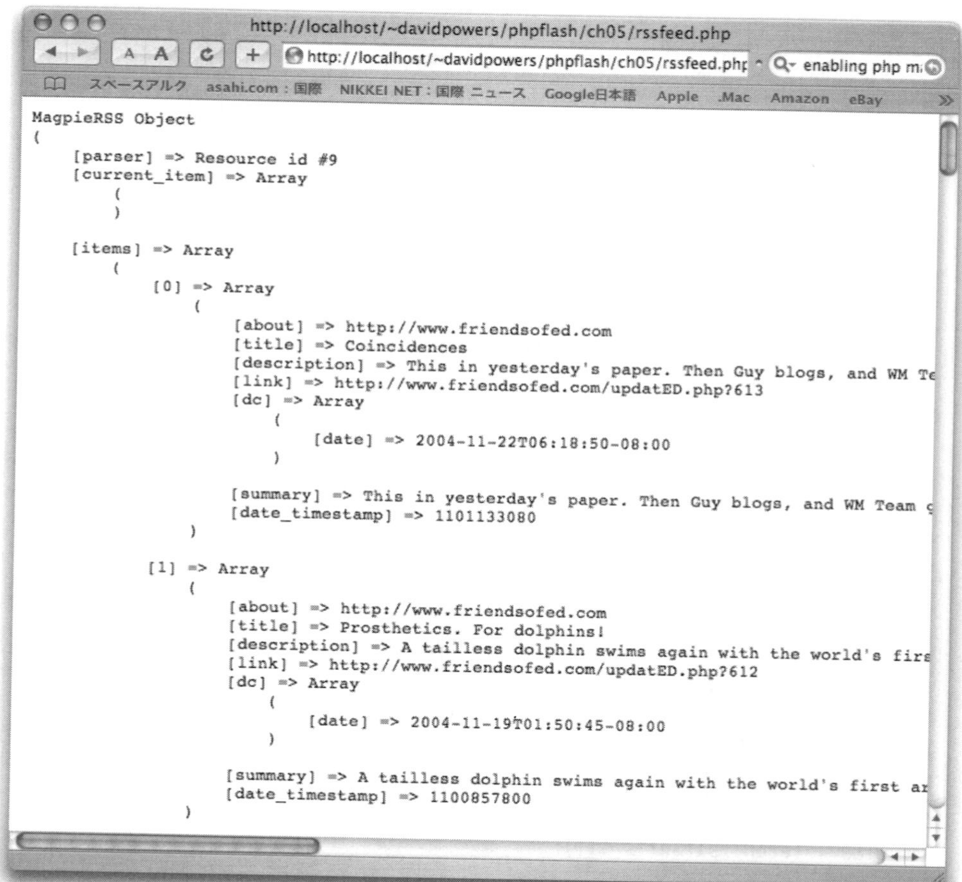

Figure 5-9. Using `print_r()` to examine the contents of the data retrieved by MagpieRSS

If anything went wrong, make sure the `magpie` folder is in the correct path for your PHP script to find. Also take a look at the file named `TROUBLESHOOTING` in the `magpie` folder (it's a plain text file that will open in Notepad or TextEdit). Check the URL of the RSS feed, and try a different one. If all else fails, yell for help in the friends of ED online forums at `www.friendsofed.com/forums`.

6. Take a look at the items array. It's an indexed array (elements 0 and 1 can be seen in Figure 5-9). Each element contains a nested associative array with the following keys: about, title, description, link, dc, summary, and date_timestamp. The dc element is also an associative array containing just one element: date. That's some multidimensional array.

> *By the time you read this, there may be a slightly different number of elements in each item of the RSS feeds, but the underlying principles of creating the feed aggregator will remain the same. You can find a description of the elements at* `http://blogs.law.harvard.edu/tech/rss#hrelementsOfLtitemgt`.

The date of each item is nested three levels deep. Sorting everything out is a lot easier than it first looks. All it requires is a little looping magic.

Parsing the friends of ED and Ablog RSS feeds

Although you have not yet covered classes and objects in PHP (that's a treat in store for you in Chapter 7), retrieving the information from the MagpieRSS object is very simple. The object contains four fields (or properties): `channel`, `items`, `image`, and `textinput`. For this application, you need just the first two, and as you saw in Figure 5-9, they consist of indexed and associative arrays. So, once you have captured `channel` and `items` in variables, you can manipulate them using the techniques described earlier in this chapter.

1. With the output of `rssfeed.php` still in your browser from the previous section, scroll down until you find the output of the `channel` field. It will probably be close to the bottom of the page, and it should look something like this:

```
    [channel] => Array
        (
            [title] => friends of ED newsfeed
            [description] =>  friendsofed.com designer to designer
            [link] =>
http://www.friendsofed.com

            [tagline] =>  friendsofed.com designer to designer
        )
```

As you can see, it's a simple associative array with four elements. The way to refer to an object's field or property is to use the **-> operator** (a hyphen followed by the greater than sign, with no space in between). So, the `channel` field of `$rss` is referred to as `$rss->channel`. Because `channel` is an array, the `title` element is referred to using square bracket notation, like this: `$rss->channel['title']`.

2. Amend the loop in rssfeed.php so it looks like this (the completed code for this section is in rssfeed02.php):

```
// Loop through each address and retrieve RSS feed as object
for ($i=0;$i<count($urls);$i++) {
  $rss = fetch_rss($urls[$i]);

  // Get channel title and display
  $feed[$i]['title'] = $rss->channel['title'];
  echo '<h1>'.$feed[$i]['title'].'</h1>';
  }
```

The new code (shown in bold type) creates a new multidimensional array called $feed. The top level will be an indexed array, which takes its number from the counter $i. Because you have only one URL at the moment, there will be just one element in the top-level array ($feed[0]), and the associative subarray will also have just one element (title).

Comment out the code from step 4 of the previous section (apart from the closing PHP tag) to prevent print_r() from displaying the whole contents of the MagpieRSS object.

3. Reload rssfeed.php in your browser, and you should see the title of the channel display onscreen as shown alongside.

4. Getting the items from the MagpieRSS object also involves the -> operator. Insert the following line immediately after the code you entered in step 2 (make sure you insert it *before* the closing bracket of the for loop):

```
$feed[$i]['items'] = $rss->items;
```

5. Because the items are held in an indexed array, you need a nested loop to extract them. The nested loop requires a different counter, because $i is still needed to keep track of which feed you are processing. Since time immemorial, coders have turned to $j when $i is already in use. So, why break with tradition? Insert the following code immediately after the line you entered in the previous step:

```
// Loop through array of items in each feed
for ($j = 0 ; $j < count($feed[$i]['items']); $j++) {
    echo $feed[$i]['items'][$j]['title'].'<br />';
    }
```

Although that looks horrendous at first sight, it's quite straightforward. The new counter $j is initialized to 0; count() calculates the length of the items array, so the loop knows how many times to run; and $j is increased by 1 each time. Because the loop is nested, $i doesn't change value, so each element in the $feed[0]['items'] array is referred to in turn like this:

```
$feed[0]['items'][0]['title']
$feed[0]['items'][1]['title']
$feed[0]['items'][2]['title']
```

6. Save rssfeed.php and refresh your browser. You should get a screen full of short titles similar to that shown here.

7. The friends of ED feed normally contains about 25 items, so it's a good idea to restrict your selection to the most recent half-dozen or so. Because the most recent items are always first, this is a simple matter of using array_splice() to select a specific number from the beginning of the array and discarding the rest. Amending the code in step 4 as follows selects just the first five items:

```
// select first five items of each feed
$feed[$i]['items'] = array_splice($rss->items,0,5);
```

8. Let's put that outer loop to some practical use. Immediately below the URL for the friends of ED RSS feed, add the following line to retrieve the Ablog RSS 1.0 feed:

```
$urls[1] = 'http://blogs.apress.com/index.rdf';
```

9. Save rssfeed.php, make sure you are connected to the Internet, and refresh your browser. As long as the Ablog server is not down, after a short wait, you should see output similar to that shown here. If you encounter any problems, compare your code with rssfeed02.php.

   By adding the new element to the $urls array, the for loop now runs twice. The first time, the MagpieRSS object stored in $rss contains the friends of ED feed; the second time, it contains the Ablog feed. When you refresh your browser to run the revised PHP file, the time delay is not because PHP is slow at running through such a trivial pair of nested loops—it's because Magpie has to retrieve the information over the Internet. If you refresh your page again, the display should be instantaneous because Magpie caches the result on your local hard drive.

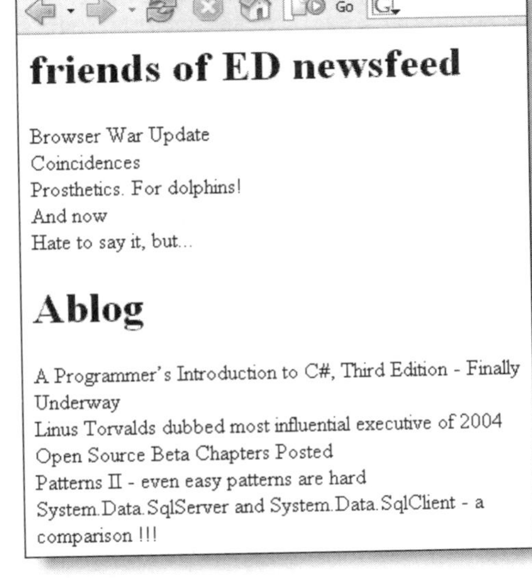

10. Now that you have established how to extract the material from the two feeds, you can build a string of variables to send to Flash in the same way as you have done in the preceding chapters. But the data from both feeds still remains in separate arrays. Wouldn't it be cool to merge them? Fasten your seat belts, because that's what you're going to do next.

Merging the two feeds

As you saw in the last section, it's perfectly possible to refer to deeply nested array items by using square bracket notation. Possible, yes, but is it convenient? Referring to the date of the fourth item in the Ablog results requires this horrendous variable:

```
$feed[1]['items'][3]['dc']['date']
```

Although it looks awful, it's easy to understand if you break it down into more digestible chunks: `$feed[1]` is the Ablog feed, `['items'][3]` represents the fourth item in that feed, and `['dc']['date']` is the date element of that item. Fortunately, there is a remarkably simple way around this cumbersome notation. Filter each type of data into a new indexed array, like this (the name of each new array is in parentheses):

- The channel the item belongs to (`$channel`)
- The title of the item (`$title`)
- The description of the item (`$description`)
- The link to the item (`$link`)
- The date the item was created (`$date`)
- The time the item was created (`$time`)
- The name of the item's creator, if any (`$creator`)

By processing each item inside the nested loop created in step 5 of the previous section, the key of each array will be identical for related items. For instance, `$title[2]` and `$description[2]` both refer to properties of the same news item (just the same as in a database or spreadsheet). Things get even better when you realize that `array_multisort()` enables you to sort these related arrays *without destroying the original relationship*. Even though `$title[2]` may move from the third position in its array, it will still refer to `$description[2]` and all other array elements with the same key, because all arrays are moved in unison. The meaning should become clear once you see the results.

1. Continue working with the same PHP file as before and rewrite `rssfeed.php` as follows (the changes are in bold type). Alternatively, use `rssfeed03.php` from the download files for this chapter.

```
<?php
// reset error reporting to eliminate advisory notices
error_reporting(E_ALL & ~E_NOTICE & ~E_STRICT);
require_once('magpie/rss_fetch.inc');
// set output encoding to Unicode
define('MAGPIE_OUTPUT_ENCODING', 'UTF-8');

// Store feed addresses in array of URLs
$urls[0] = 'http://friendsofed.com/news.php';
$urls[1] = 'http://blogs.apress.com/index.rdf';

$k=0;
```

```
// Loop through each address and retrieve RSS feed as object
for ($i = 0; $i < count($urls); $i++) {
  $rss = fetch_rss($urls[$i]);

  // Get channel title and display
  $feed[$i]['title'] = $rss->channel['title'];
  // select first five items of each feed
  $feed[$i]['items'] = array_splice($rss->items,0,5);

  // Nested loop to filter items in each feed into new arrays
  for ($j = 0; $j < count($feed[$i]['items']); $j++, $k++) {
    $channel[$k] = $feed[$i]['title'];
    $title[$k] = $feed[$i]['items'][$j]['title'];
    $description[$k] = $feed[$i]['items'][$j]['description'];
    $link[$k] = $feed[$i]['items'][$j]['link'];
    $date[$k] = substr($feed[$i]['items'][$j]['dc']['date'],0,10);
    $time[$k] = substr($feed[$i]['items'][$j]['dc']['date'],11,8);
    $creator[$k] = isset($feed[$i]['items'][$j]['dc']['creator']) ?
➥ $feed[$i]['items'][$j]['dc']['creator'] : '';
    }
  }

// Display contents of filtered arrays
echo '<pre>';
print_r($channel);
print_r($title);
print_r($description);
print_r($link);
print_r($date);
print_r($time);
print_r($creator);
echo '</pre>';
?>
```

2. So far, $i has been used to keep track of the feeds, and $j has been used to keep track of the item numbers. This time, a third counter is needed to generate the correct keys for the new filtered arrays. I decided to be incredibly original and use $k. This new counter needs to be initialized *outside* both loops. It's also important to make sure it's not reset to zero by either loop. That's why $k = 0; sits in splendid isolation on a line of its own.

3. $k needs to increase by 1 after each item is processed. This is done by adding $k++ to the third expression in the nested for loop, as described in "Using the versatile for loop" section earlier in the chapter. Even though $k was declared outside the loop, it's perfectly valid to increment it this way. Putting it here also makes the purpose of the loop much clearer.

```
for ($j = 0; $j<count($feed[$i]['items']); $j++, $k++) {
```

4. Each line inside the nested loop assigns the appropriate value to the filter arrays. The value stored in $channel comes directly from the channel field, so no reference is required to the items array:

```
$channel[$k] = $feed[$i]['title'];
```

5. In all the other lines, $i keeps track of the feed, and $j keeps track of the elements in the items array. The code for handling the date and time deserves special attention:

```
$date[$k] = substr($feed[$i]['items'][$j]['dc']['date'],0,10);
$time[$k] = substr($feed[$i]['items'][$j]['dc']['date'],11,8);
```

RSS feeds sometimes use slightly different formats for the date the item originated:

```
YYYY-MM-DD HH:MM:SS
YYYY-MM-DDTHH:MM:SS UTC offset
```

Fortunately, they have a common pattern. By using substr() (see Chapter 4), it's possible to assign the date and time to separate arrays by extracting the first ten characters (date) and the next eight characters beginning from position 11 (time).

6. Ablog has a creator element in the dc array, but friends of ED does not. The following line uses the conditional operator (?:) and isset() (both covered in Chapter 3) to check whether the creator element exists. If it does exist, the conditional operator assigns the value to the filter array; if it doesn't exist, an empty string is assigned instead. (Note that the code right at the end of the line just before the semicolon is two single quotation marks with no space in between.)

```
$creator[$k] = isset($feed[$i]['items'][$j]['dc']['creator']) ?
➥ $feed[$i]['items'][$j]['dc']['creator'] : '';
```

7. Finally, for testing purposes, each filtered array is displayed using print_r(). Reload rssfeed.php into your browser, and your screen should fill with the results of the filter process. Shown here is just the final array, $creator. As you can see, the first five elements are empty. This is important, because when using array_multisort(), each array must be the same length, even if it means creating empty elements. Otherwise, it becomes impossible to keep track of them when sorting. If you have problems, compare your code with rssfeed03.php.

```
Array
(
    [0] =>
    [1] =>
    [2] =>
    [3] =>
    [4] =>
    [5] => Matt Stephens
    [6] => Jason Gilmore
    [7] => Sahil Malik
    [8] => Jason Gilmore
    [9] => Steve Anglin
)
```

8. Now for a nifty bit of PHP magic. array_multisort() will take all the filtered arrays and re-sort them according to the priorities you determine. It is a rather unusual function in that each array passed to it as an argument can take up to two optional sorting flags: one to specify the sorting order and the other to specify the type of sort operation. If either or both flags are omitted after an array, the default method is invoked. The flags are described in Table 5-4.

Table 5-4. Sorting flags for array_multisort()

Flag	Sorting method	Description
SORT_ASC	Order	Default; sorts in ascending order.
SORT_DESC	Order	Sorts in descending order.
SORT_REGULAR	Type	Default; compares items according to ASCII order, so all uppercase letters come before lowercase ones. For instance, Z comes before a.
SORT_STRING	Type	Compares items as strings. Uses a more natural sort order, so lowercase a comes before Z.
SORT_NUMERIC	Type	Compares items numerically.

9. To sort all the filtered arrays with the most recent first, insert this code after the closing brace of the outer for loop and just before the final block that displays the contents of each array (if you're in any doubt, check the location in rssfeed04.php):

```
// Sort the new arrays according to date and time, latest first
array_multisort($date,SORT_DESC,$time,SORT_DESC,$channel,$title,
➥ $description,$link,$creator);
// Display contents of filtered arrays
```

10. Save rssfeed.php. Before reloading it in your browser, make a note of the position of several items (it's probably easiest to do it with people's names and the title of articles they've written). Now reload the page. Has anything changed? If yes, even though the key of a particular name is different, the title should also have the same key. As luck would have it, when I was writing this chapter, nothing changed. It wasn't a problem with the code. It was simply a case of those gossipy types at friends of ED being in overdrive, while the eggheads at Apress were taking it easy—everything from friends of ED had been uploaded more recently than Ablog. If that happens to you, move $creator to the beginning of the arguments. The sort order is determined not only by the flags, but also by the order arrays are used as arguments to the function. (Don't expect $creator to be sorted by family name—the sort sequence starts with the first character and works through each one in order. To sort by family name, you would have to create separate arrays for first name and family name, as you've done for date and time.) Play around with the order and experiment with the various flags, and then put the code back in the same order as in step 9.

11. Finally, you're ready to build the output string for Flash. Replace the block of code used to display the contents of the filtered arrays (in other words, all the code under the comment line // Display contents of filtered arrays) with the following:

```
$output = 'records='.$k;
for ($i=0;$i<count($date);$i++) {
  // Convert date to timestamp and format
```

```
    $temp = strtotime($date[$i]);
    $date[$i] = date('D M j', $temp);

    // Create ActionScript variables as nameNumber and URL encode value
    $output .= "&date{$i}=".urlencode($date[$i]);
    $output .= "&channel{$i}=".urlencode($channel[$i]);
    $output .= "&title{$i}=".urlencode($title[$i]);
    $output .= "&description{$i}=".urlencode($description[$i]);
    $output .= "&link{$i}=".urlencode($link[$i]);
    $output .= "&creator{$i}=".urlencode($creator[$i]);
    }

echo $output;
```

When sending the data to Flash, it's useful to know how many records are being sent, so the first line creates a Flash variable called `records` and sets its value to `$k`. If you have chosen to display just five items from each feed, as in the code shown earlier, `$k` will equal 10.

> *You may be scratching your head as to why `$k` is set to 10, when the final key in each filtered array is only 9. The reason is that a `for` loop increments the third expression within the parentheses at the **end** of each pass through the loop. Consequently, `$k` is incremented to 10 after creating items with an array key of one less. Yes, computers **are** fun, aren't they?*

`$i` is no longer needed to keep track of the feeds, so it can be safely reset to 0 and reused here to loop through all the filtered arrays. The first line inside the loop uses a PHP function called `strtotime()` to convert the date to a timestamp that PHP can use to format the date in a more human-friendly manner. Because functions always work on a copy of array values, the result needs to be assigned to a temporary variable before the new value can be reassigned to the same array variable in the following line. The `date()` function formats the date as a three-letter abbreviation of the weekday, followed by a three-letter abbreviation of the month and the date (for instance, Wed Aug 11). The way PHP works with dates will be covered in detail in Chapter 11.

The other important thing to note about the loop is the way `$i` is enclosed in curly braces, as in this line:

```
$output .= "&date{$i}=".urlencode($date[$i]);
```

Because `&date{$i}=` is enclosed in double quotes, the curly braces ensure that PHP substitutes the value of `$i`, rather than treating it literally. So, if `$i` is 2, this line would produce `&date2=` followed by the URL-encoded value of `$date[2]`. Adding the number to the end of each variable ensures you can still match up the elements of each item once you get them into your Flash application.

12. Test `rssfeed.php` in your browser to make sure it produces no errors. You should see a long string like that shown in the following image, ready to send to your Flash movie. The final code for the PHP file is in `rssfeed04.php`.

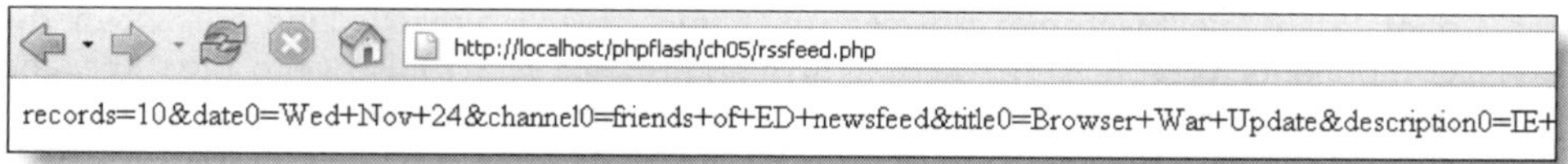

Displaying the merged RSS feed in Flash

Finally, the moment of truth has arrived! Displaying the merged feed in Flash is relatively simple. You retrieve the data with `LoadVars`, and then you use your Flash skills to manipulate it however you want. This solution relies almost exclusively on ActionScript and the new CSS capabilities of Flash Player 7.

Creating the Flash movie

1. Open a new Flash document, and save it as `rssfeed.fla`. If you want to use the same graphics as I did, you can find them in `rssfeed01.fla`. Alternatively, if you just want to study the code and test the application, the final version is in `rssfeed02.fla`.
2. The document has just two layers: background and actions. As always, lock the actions layer to stop you from placing any graphical elements on it by accident. At the top of the background layer is an imported JPG file with a suitable heading, as shown here. I set the stage background color to #FEFEBE and resized it to 450×450 pixels. (You can make these changes by clicking the stage and setting the relevant properties in the Property inspector, or you can use the more traditional method of selecting Modify ➤ Document.)

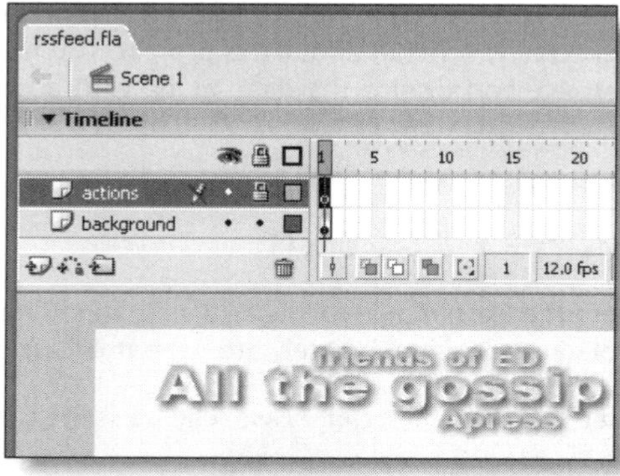

3. The data from the RSS feeds will be displayed in a dynamic text field. Insert one just below the title JPG to cover most of the rest of the stage. Set it to display multiline with selectable text, and give it an instance name of feedDisplay_txt.

4. Once all the data from the RSS feeds is displayed, it's almost certain to be too much to fit in this space, so a scrollbar will be needed. I'm going to be lazy and use a ready-built component scrollbar. A version 2 component scrollbar was included in the Flash 7.2 updater, but the MX UI component is much lighter (download the Flash MX UI components from the Macromedia Exchange if you haven't already done so). Open the Components panel (*Ctrl+F7/⌘+F7*), drag an instance of ScrollBar onto the stage, and drop it so that it snaps onto the right-hand side of the dynamic text field. If you can't get it to snap to the text field, enable Snap to Objects (View ➤ Snapping ➤ Snap to Objects or toggle the magnet icon in the toolbar). Give the scrollbar an instance name of vertSB.

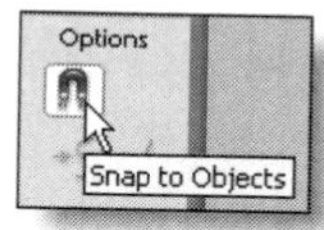

5. You also need to store a preloader movie clip in the Library to display something while the RSS feed is being retrieved. I used the simple timeline animation shown here, which loops to reveal an extra dot every six frames until all three can be seen, and then hides them again. It's in the Library of `rssfeed01.fla` if you don't want to make your own.

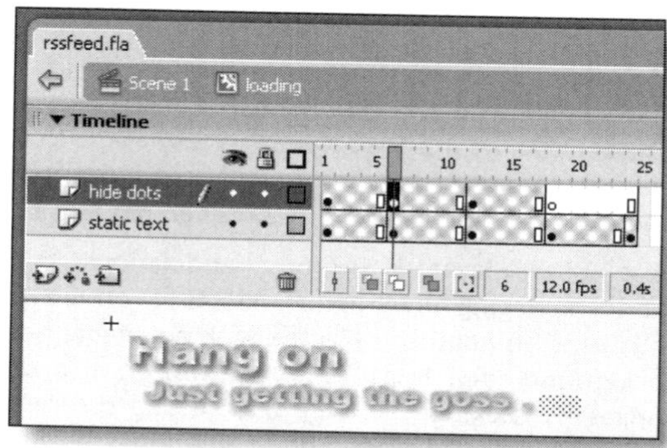

6. Select the actions layer, open the Actions panel (*F9*), and get ready to flex your ActionScript muscles. After all that PHP, it takes a little mental change of gear, but there's nothing particularly difficult about this project. You need to create an instance of `LoadVars` to retrieve and display the data, along with a few styling flourishes, and that's about it.

7. Start by creating a `LoadVars` object:

```
var getFeed:LoadVars = new LoadVars();
```

8. No data is sent from the Flash movie to `rssfeed.php`, so calling the `load` method is sufficient. Add the following line immediately after the previous one:

```
getFeed.load("http://localhost/phpflash/ch05/rssfeed.php?ck=" +
➥ new Date().getTime());
```

As before, the `localhost` address is needed only while testing locally, and the `Date` object ensures each call to `rssfeed.php` is handled directly and not served from the browser's cache. (This is separate from the Magpie cache.)

9. Create a callback function to display the data once it has been loaded successfully. Before diving into a full-blown script, it's a good idea to check first that the data is being received successfully. Enter the following code:

```
getFeed.onLoad = function(success) {
  if (!success) {
    trace("Can't load rss feed data");
  } else {
    var records:Number = this["records"];
    trace("Total records: " + records);
    for (var i:Number = 0; i < records; i++) {
      trace("date" + i + ": " + this["date"+i]);
      trace("title" + i + ": " + this["title"+i]);
    }
  }
};
```

10. Test the movie. You should see something like this:

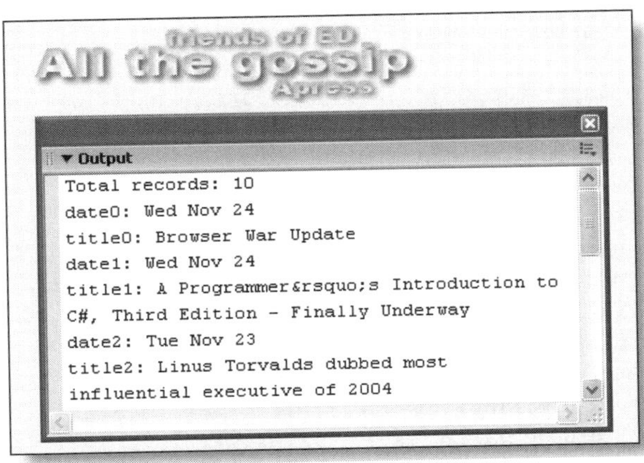

If you get `undefined`, go back to `rssfeed.php` and make sure there is no whitespace in the output string, particularly around the equal signs. (Yes, I found out the hard way!) Also make sure you did not pass the entire string to `urlencode()`, just the value of each variable.

> *If you look closely at the previous image, you will notice that* title1 *contains* `’`. *This is an HTML entity for a right single curly quote or apostrophe, which Flash* `HTMLText` *cannot display correctly. This means a small adjustment is needed to the PHP script, which will be dealt with later.*

11. Now that you know that proper communication exists between Flash and PHP, all you have to do is display the information in whatever format you like. PHP has already sorted the items and assigned each element a variable name that ends in a number. So, `date3` goes with `title3`, `creator3`, and so on. You can refer to these inside the callback function by using the loop and square bracket notation, such as `this["date" + i]`, `this["title" + i]`, and so on.

12. Rather than give you blow-by-blow instructions on how to display the results from the RSS feeds, I have reproduced the entire ActionScript listing, liberally commented so you can see what's happening. It's not the only solution, just a suggested one. If you don't want the hassle of typing it all out yourself, copy and paste it from `rssfeed02.fla`. (This is a complete listing, so it replaces any existing code you may have in the Actions panel.)

```
// Create LoadVars instance to retrieve data from rssfeed.php
var getFeed:LoadVars = new LoadVars();
getFeed.load("http://localhost/phpflash/ch05/rssfeed.php?ck="+new
➥ Date().getTime());
// display the results from the PHP script when loaded
getFeed.onLoad = function(success) {
  // Display error message if load fails
  if (!success) {
    feedDisplay_txt.text = "<headline>Sorry, can't load rss feed
➥ data</headline>";
  } else {
    // remove the loading movie clip
    loading_mc.removeMovieClip();
    // Get number of records returned by PHP script
    var records:Number = this["records"];
    // Initialize display text
    var displayText:String = "<body>";
    // Create variable to hold current date
    var prevDate:String;
    // Loop through variables and build HTML text
    for (var i = 0; i<records; i++) {
      // Display date only if it has been displayed before
      if (i == 0 || this["date"+i] != prevDate) {
        displayText += "<date>"+this["date"+i]+"</date>";
      }
      // Store date for comparison on next loop
      prevDate = this["date"+i];
      displayText += "<headline>"+this["title"+i]+"</headline><p>";
      if (this["creator"+i] != '') {
        displayText += "<b>"+this["creator"+i]+" writes:</b> ";
      }
      displayText += this["description"+i]+" <a href='";
      displayText += this["link"+i]+"'>More from ";
      displayText += this["channel"+i]+"</a></p>";
    }
    // Add closing body tag and display HTML output
```

```
      displayText += "</body>";
      feedDisplay_txt.text = displayText;
      // make scrollbar visible
      vertSB._visible = true;
    }
};
// Create CSS styles for RSS feed display
var styles = new TextField.StyleSheet();
styles.setStyle("body", {fontFamily:'Arial, Helvetica, sans-serif',
➥ marginRight:'15px', color:'#000000'});
styles.setStyle("p", {fontSize:'12px', marginLeft:'30px'});
styles.setStyle("headline", {fontSize:'16px', display:'block',
➥ fontWeight:'bold', marginLeft:'15px', color:'#000066'});
styles.setStyle("date", {fontSize:'14px', display:'block',
➥ color:'#000066', fontWeight:'bold'});
styles.setStyle("a:link", {textDecoration:'underline',
➥ color:'#1C0DCB'});
styles.setStyle("a:hover", {textDecoration:'underline',
➥ color:'#F5020C'});
// scrollbar styles
var scrollBarFormat = new FStyleFormat();
scrollBarFormat.arrow = 0x535A64;
scrollBarFormat.darkshadow = 0x727679;
scrollBarFormat.face = 0xD9E0E7;
scrollBarFormat.highlight3D = 0xE7EBF0;
scrollBarFormat.scrollTrack = 0xE9EDF1;
// apply styles to scrollbar and display text
scrollBarFormat.addListener(vertSB);
feedDisplay_txt.styleSheet = styles;
feedDisplay_txt.html = true;
// hide scrollbar until feed results are displayed
vertSB._visible = false;
// Display loading movie clip while waiting for data retrieval
_root.attachMovie("loading", "loading_mc", 1);
loading_mc._x = 30;
loading_mc._y = 160;
```

The main point to note about this script is the use of the improved CSS features that are new to Flash Player 7. Flash supports only a limited number of HTML tags and CSS properties, but you can style content with your own tags, rather like working with XML. For instance, this script defines two custom tags, headline and date, which are used within the loop that builds the HTML text for the feedDisplay text field. To learn more about CSS in Flash, use the online help files (*F1*) and search for CSS (this is not available in Flash MX).

The scrollbar is hidden and the preloader is displayed dynamically when the movie first loads. Once the data has been received from PHP, the preloader is removed, and the scrollbar is made visible.

You probably won't see your preloader when testing locally. Apache has no equivalent of Flash's feature to simulate a slow download. Instead, you can delay the output from the PHP script by using a function called, appropriately enough, `sleep()`. It takes one argument: an integer representing the number of seconds you want a script to pause. Place it just before the line that outputs the results from your script. In `rssfeed.php`, this is the last line before the closing PHP tag:

```
// delay output for 10 seconds
sleep(10);
echo $output;
?>
```

Don't forget to remove the delay after you've finished local testing!

The finished RSS feed aggregator is shown in Figure 5-10. As you can see, the date is displayed only when it differs from the previous one, and items from friends of ED and Ablog have been integrated in chronological order. But there's a problem—right in the middle of the second headline is `’`, an HTML entity that Flash doesn't understand. PHP to the rescue . . .

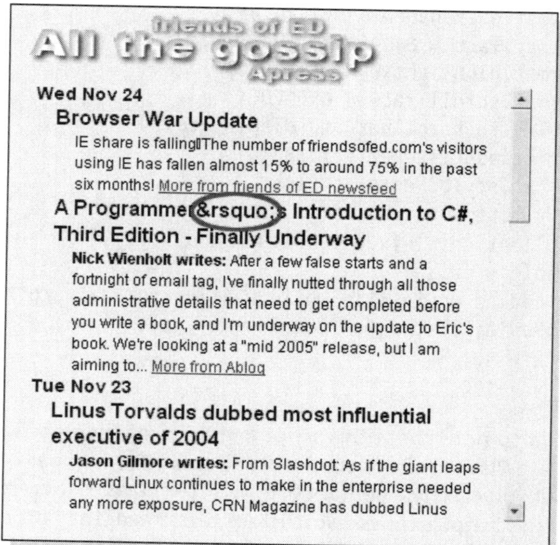

Figure 5-10. Flash is not capable of displaying most HTML entities, but PHP can solve the problem.

Eliminating HTML entities that Flash cannot handle

One of the problems with the Ablog feed is that the blogging software allows the many contributors to use curly quotes, which Flash can't display correctly. The answer is to substitute them with straight quotes just before sending the data to Flash. Working out how to do this involved a little detective work, but it's quite simple. The conversion needs to be done after the output has been URL encoded, because the curly quotes are easier to identify since they will have been converted to HTML entities.

Flash requires data received through LoadVars to be URL encoded. This means that ’ is converted to %26rsquo%3B. (The numbers and letters following the percentage sign are the code points of the encoded characters expressed as hexadecimal numbers.) Table 5-5 lists the four types of curly quotes that need to be replaced by straight quotes, together with their encoded equivalents.

Table 5-5. Curly quotes and their encoded equivalents that need to be replaced for Flash

Description	Symbol	HTML entity	URL encoded	Replace with
Left single quote	‘	‘	%26lsquo%3B	%27
Right single quote	’	’	%26rsquo%3B	%27
Left double quote	“	“	%26ldquo%3B	%22
Right double quote	”	”	%26rdquo%3B	%22

The best way to do this is with preg_replace(), which you met in the previous chapter. This function has the great advantage that it will accept arrays as arguments for both search patterns and their replacements. Although the search patterns don't use regular expressions, preg_replace() requires them to be enclosed in delimiters like PCREs. The array of replacements requires no delimiters, so the two arrays look like this:

```
$curly=array('/%26lsquo%3B/','/%26rsquo%3B/','/%26ldquo%3B/',
➥ '/%26rdquo%3B/');
$straight=array('%27','%27','%22','%22');
```

To make the code neater, I've wrapped up everything in a custom-built function and amended the last few lines of rssfeed.php as follows (you can find the complete script in rssfeed05.php):

```
echo removeCurlyQuotes($output);
function removeCurlyQuotes($string) {
  $curly = array('/%26lsquo%3B/','/%26rsquo%3B/','/%26ldquo%3B/',
➥ '/%26rdquo%3B/');
  $straight = array('%27','%27','%22','%22');
  $amended = preg_replace($curly,$straight,$string);
  return $amended;
  }
?>
```

After making this change, the quote now displays correctly, as shown in Figure 5-11.

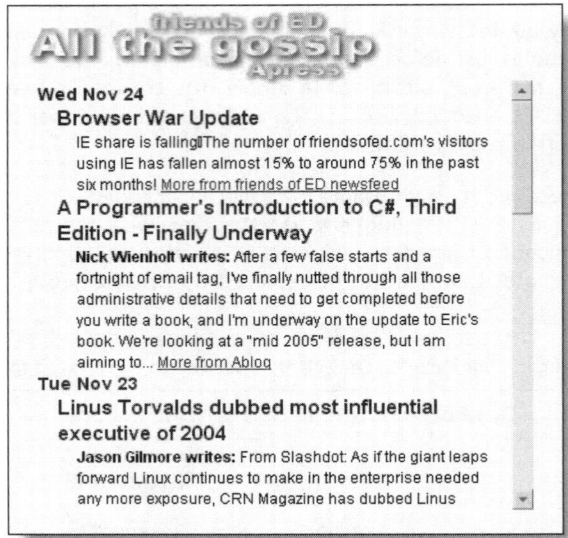

Figure 5-11. The completed RSS aggregator now displays the quote correctly.

Deploying the feed aggregator on the Internet

Putting the feed aggregator online is easy. Before publishing the SWF, make sure you remove the localhost address from the getFeed.load method (around line 3 of the ActionScript). Assuming rssfeed.php will be in the same folder on your remote server, change the line to this:

```
getFeed.load("rssfeed.php?ck="+new Date().getTime());
```

You also need to upload the MagpieRSS files. As long as you maintain the same folder structure as now, the files will all work together smoothly. Simply create a subfolder called magpie, and upload the following files: rss_cache.inc, rss_fetch.inc, rss_parse.inc, and rss_utils.inc, as well as the extlib subfolder and its contents. Magpie will automatically create a cache folder on your remote server, but this occasionally fails, so you may have to create the cache folder yourself. See the TROUBLESHOOTING text file in the magpie folder or the Magpie website at http://magpierss.sourceforge.net for the most up-to-date information. The creator of MagpieRSS also posts details of updates in the Magpie Blog at http://laughingmeme.org/magpie_blog, so it's worth checking there, too.

Progress report

This has been another long chapter, but I hope you think it's been worth it. Arrays and loops are so fundamental to programming languages, it's important to understand how to work with them efficiently. PHP and ActionScript have a great deal in common when it comes to arrays, but they also have important differences. Refer back to the reference material in the first half of this chapter when you encounter unexpected behavior.

As with the multiconverter application, you could probably build a similar RSS feed aggregator entirely in Flash, although converting the encoding of incoming feeds to UTF-8 could present a problem. Magpie looks after the conversion, and makes retrieval and parsing of multiple RSS feeds extremely simple. In addition, PHP's `array_multisort()` makes light work of merging and sorting deeply nested information. The finished PHP script is just over 30 lines long (excluding comments). It's fast and efficient, speeded along by the automatic caching of feed data by MagpieRSS, and it almost certainly requires far less coding than if you tried building the same thing entirely in Flash. If it helped you understand PHP loops and arrays, it has more than served its purpose.

When it comes to sorting large volumes of data, you really need the power of a database. Talking of which, that's exactly what the next chapter is all about.

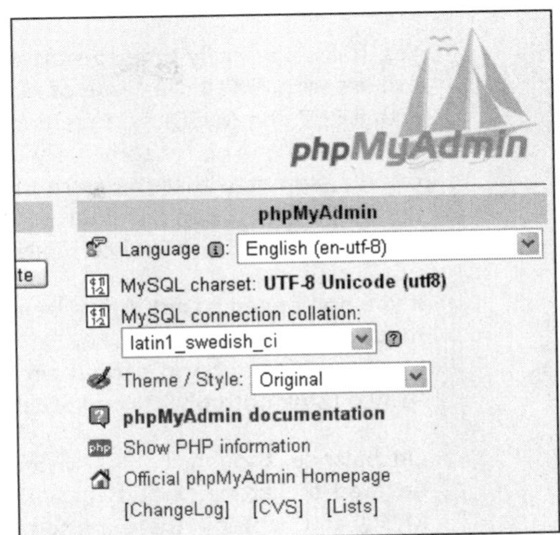

Chapter 6

PHP AND DATABASES: PACKING REAL POWER BEHIND YOUR APPLICATIONS

What this chapter covers:

- Introducing MySQL, the most popular open source database
- Assessing MySQL's strengths and weaknesses
- Considering SQLite as an alternative database system
- Installing and configuring MySQL on Windows
- Configuring MySQL on Mac OS X
- Working at the command line with MySQL
- Building a first database
- Exploring graphical interfaces to MySQL

Yes, folks, it's finally time to start working with databases. MySQL isn't the *only* database you can use with PHP. It's just one of many, but the reason I chose to concentrate on it in this book is that PHP and MySQL go together particularly well. As mentioned in Chapter 1, MySQL is the database of choice for some very large organizations that regard speed and reliability as critical. It's estimated that there are more than 5 million active installations of MySQL, making it the world's most popular open source database. What's good enough for the likes of Yahoo!, Google, and NASA should certainly do your Flash applications proud.

If you don't need an industrial-strength database system, PHP 5 offers an alternative that doesn't require any installation: SQLite. In spite of its name, SQLite is very powerful and is definitely worth consideration in certain circumstances. The application in the next chapter is demonstrated using both MySQL and SQLite, so you can see both systems in operation for yourself.

On balance, though, I think MySQL is the better choice, so a large part of this chapter is devoted to getting MySQL up and running. Although Mac OS X users should have installed MySQL in Chapter 1, there are some important configuration changes to make before using it. And Windows users need to do both the installation and configuration. Once MySQL is running, the operation is the same on both systems, but the setup procedure is different for Windows and Mac OS X, so make sure you are reading the right part of the chapter before banging your head too hard on the keyboard.

The traditional way of working with MySQL is at the command line, so I'll give you a flavor of that before taking a look at some graphical user interfaces that make working with MySQL easier. By the end of the chapter, you will have built your first database, ready for use in the fiendish word game that's the subject of Chapter 7.

First, though, a few words about MySQL, what it can and cannot do, and choosing the right version—issues of interest and importance to Windows and Mac OS X users alike.

Why MySQL?

There are many reasons for choosing MySQL not only for this book, but also as the database management system for just about any project, large or small. It's fast, it's light, and it's extremely powerful. What's more, it's inexpensive. In fact, for many—perhaps most—people, it's completely free.

MySQL's shortcomings

Like all successful ventures, MySQL has its critics. At the time of this writing, MySQL doesn't support some of the more advanced features offered by commercial databases, such as Microsoft SQL Server. For instance, it doesn't yet have full support for **foreign keys** (a means of identifying related records in different tables to help maintain consistency of data), and it can't perform stored procedures. All of these features are planned to be incorporated into MySQL, and some of them may already have been implemented by the time you read this. The list of most requested features and the version scheduled to include them can be found at `http://dev.mysql.com/doc/mysql/en/Roadmap.html`.

The absence of these advanced features in no way detracts from the value of using MySQL. Most of these features *are* advanced and of interest only to high-end developers. Moreover, the same effects can normally be achieved by coding the necessary routines in PHP. What is impressive about MySQL is the speed at which development has taken place and the robustness of the program once it is released. This is due in a large part to the open source nature of the development process. As soon as a new feature is added and considered stable enough for testing by a wider body of users, it is made freely available in an alpha, beta, or gamma release. Literally thousands of members of the hyperactive MySQL community put the software through its paces, feeding back bug reports and suggestions to the core development team. Consequently, when a full version is released, it is extremely rare for it not to work exactly as it should.

Perhaps the biggest shortcoming for some users is the fact that MySQL doesn't come with a glossy graphical user interface (GUI). If you are used to working with commercial databases, such as Access or FileMaker Pro, the main interface of MySQL might come as a rude shock, harking back to the days of DOS (if your computer experience goes back that far). When working directly with MySQL, everything is done at the command line by opening a Command Prompt in Windows or Terminal in Mac OS X, as shown in Figure 6-1.

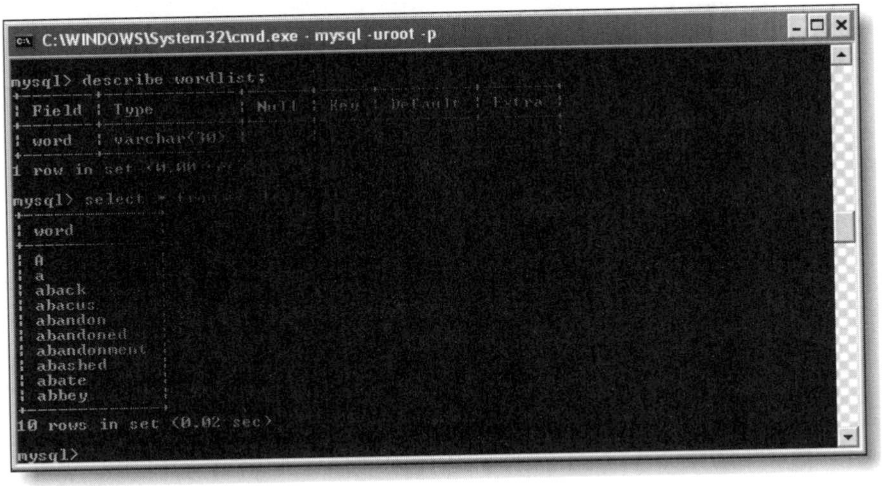

Figure 6-1. The unadorned interface of MySQL as seen in a Windows Command Prompt

There's no denying—it's not a pretty sight. Its beauty lies, however, in its simplicity. Most of the time when working with databases, particularly for online applications, the only people who will ever see the glossy interface of a commercial database system are those in the back-end office. Rather than spending time learning a proprietary system of menus and dialog boxes, you work directly with the database.

Nevertheless, it can be helpful to use a graphical interface, and some excellent ones are available, such as phpMyAdmin, which comes at a very attractive price (it's free). Later in the chapter, I'll show you how to install phpMyAdmin, and you'll take a look at two other free offerings from the company behind MySQL, MySQL AB.

MySQL's strengths

I have already mentioned the main ones:

- **Speed**: One of the main objectives of the MySQL development team has been to produce a database system that's nimble. As you can see in Figure 6-1, the time it takes to perform a query is displayed onscreen. The queries performed there were rather trivial, so it's perhaps unsurprising they took a fraction of a second. Figure 6-2 shows the results of a search of a database containing more than 10,000 news items. It took one-twentieth of a second to retrieve the titles and dates of all items containing both the words "Iraq" and "Sadr." Even more complex searches can usually be performed at very high speed. To speed up things further, MySQL caches query results and compares them with new queries.

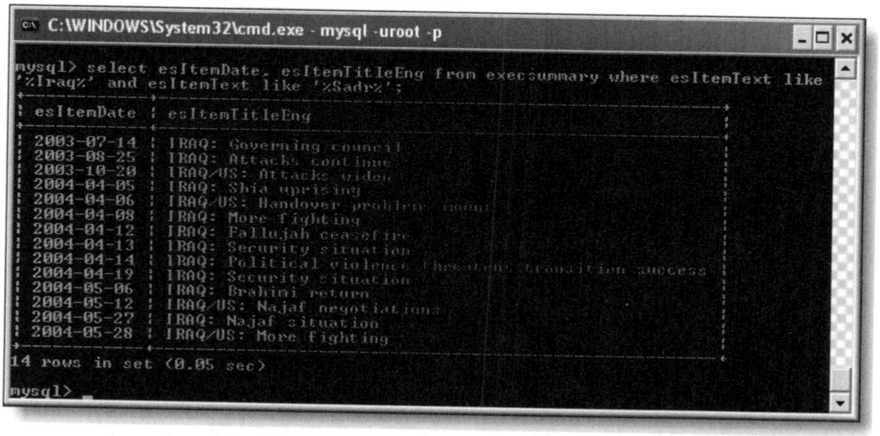

```
C:\WINDOWS\System32\cmd.exe - mysql -uroot -p

mysql> select esItemDate, esItemTitleEng from execsummary where esItemText like
'%Iraq%' and esItemText like '%Sadr%';
+------------+------------------------------------------------------+
| esItemDate | esItemTitleEng                                       |
+------------+------------------------------------------------------+
| 2003-07-14 | IRAQ: Governing council                              |
| 2003-08-25 | IRAQ: Attacks continue                               |
| 2003-10-20 | IRAQ/US: Attacks widen                               |
| 2004-04-05 | IRAQ: Shia uprising                                  |
| 2004-04-06 | IRAQ/US: Handover problems mount                     |
| 2004-04-08 | IRAQ: More fighting                                  |
| 2004-04-12 | IRAQ: Fallujah ceasefire                             |
| 2004-04-13 | IRAQ: Security situation                             |
| 2004-04-14 | IRAQ: Political violence threatens transition success |
| 2004-04-19 | IRAQ: Security situation                             |
| 2004-05-06 | IRAQ: Brahimi return                                 |
| 2004-05-12 | IRAQ/US: Najaf negotiations                          |
| 2004-05-27 | IRAQ: Najaf situation                                |
| 2004-05-28 | IRAQ/US: More fighting                               |
+------------+------------------------------------------------------+
14 rows in set (0.05 sec)

mysql>
```

Figure 6-2. MySQL can search the text of thousands of news items in a fraction of a second.

- **Lightness**: Database files are typically much smaller than those created by Access. The database of news items shown in Figure 6-2 was originally built in Access and had grown to 0.5MB with just 300 articles. When ported to MySQL, it contained well over 1,000 articles before it reached that size.
- **Power**: MySQL is capable of handling many simultaneous requests. According to Jeremy Zawodny of Yahoo! Finance, Yahoo!'s MySQL installation was handling an average of 120 queries *per second* in early 2004. Access is likely to seize up with fewer than a dozen simultaneous connections.
- **Cost**: For most users, MySQL is free. Even if you buy a commercial license (see the section "Choosing the right license and cost" later in this chapter), the cost is much less than most commercial equivalents, and at the time of this writing, there is no constant demand for extra cash each time an upgrade comes along.

Although several negative comparisons have been made with Access, the intention isn't to knock Microsoft. Because of familiarity and its graphical interface, Access is the choice of many web designers when they make their first database-driven web application. Unfortunately, in spite of its many advanced features, Access was never designed for the Web. It's primarily for small office or home use, and it's excellent in that environment. For the Web, you need something more robust, like Microsoft SQL Server, Oracle, PostgreSQL, or MySQL. The first two both have a steep learning curve and high costs. PostgreSQL is MySQL's main rival in the open source field. It is extremely powerful, but less widely available than MySQL. All four use **Structured Query Language (SQL)**, the international standard behind all major relational databases, so the basic skills you learn with MySQL will be portable if you eventually decide to move to a different database system.

Since I'm singing MySQL's praises, though, let's list a few more of its strengths:

- **Full SQL92 compliance planned**: The MySQL development team plans to implement the whole of the international standard for SQL jointly laid down by the American National Standards Institute (ANSI) and the International Organization for Standardization (ISO). It's not there yet, but with the exception of support for foreign key constraints, the missing features are primarily of interest to advanced users.
- **Powerful MySQL extensions to standard SQL**: MySQL offers a wide range of functions that can be combined with SQL to refine and improve search results.
- **Multilingual capability**: MySQL supports many languages and character sets. With support for Unicode (UTF-8) since the release of version 4.1, MySQL now supports almost every writing system on the planet (including some dead ones, such as Etruscan, Linear B, and Runes), and it also allows you to use different character sets in the same table.
- **Platform neutrality**: MySQL provides optimized binary files for a dozen different operating systems, including Windows, Mac OS X, and Linux. That means you can develop on your local computer, regardless of the operating system your site will eventually be deployed on. (Although it's possible to build a database on your local computer and transfer the data, I strongly recommend that you *design* your database locally, but populate the operational one with fresh data. See Appendix E for details of backups and methods of copying database files from one server to another.)

Choosing the right version of MySQL

One of the songs that dominated my teenage years was Bob Dylan's classic "The Times They Are A-Changing." It inspired my generation, and it became an anthem of the 1960s. The issues he was singing about still have a great relevance today, but one line in the last verse has taken on a completely new meaning for me: "As the present now will later be past."

Because of its open source background, new versions of MySQL are being released all the time. Most of the time, the new versions add minor enhancements and fix bugs that have been discovered, but the development team is also pressing ahead to eliminate the gaps in its implementation of the full SQL standard. These involve major upgrades, and it's important to understand the differences, because features available in the latest release may not yet be available in the version your hosting company is running. The way to tell the difference is by looking at the version number, which always consists of three numbers separated by periods—for example, 4.1.4.

- Changes to the first number indicate a major upgrade. MySQL 5.0, which went into alpha development at the end of 2003, will add stored procedures, updateable views, and rudimentary triggers—advanced features that many corporate users have been demanding.
- Changes in the middle number indicate a new series, which adds important new features to MySQL. For instance, it has already been announced that MySQL 5.1 will add more sophisticated triggers, as well as full support for foreign keys.
- Changes in the final number indicate a minor upgrade or bug fix.

The first two numbers are the most important. Data created with a particular series is normally compatible with any version of the same series. So, data created on MySQL 4.1.2 is compatible with MySQL 4.1.7, for instance, but *not* with MySQL 4.0.20. You can normally convert data from an older version to work with a newer one, but not always the other way around. You must be running the MySQL 4.1 series or higher to convert data to run on either MySQL 3.23 or MySQL 4.0 (see "Using `mysqldump` to copy to older versions of MySQL" in Appendix E).

You can always find out what the most recent version is by going to the MySQL Developer Zone at `http://dev.mysql.com` and looking for MySQL Database Server in the Downloads section. MySQL has been changing the terminology, but the latest stable release is normally referred to as Generally Available (GA) or Production. Versions not yet regarded as suitable for a production environment are labeled Snapshot, Alpha, Beta, or Gamma. Snapshot and Alpha versions are early releases of interest only to experts. Beta and Gamma releases are much more stable, Gamma being the final testing stage to catch any bugs that may still be lurking.

Which version of MySQL should you choose to develop Flash applications on your local computer? My advice is to install the one referred to as Generally Available (GA). Unless you have your own dedicated server, your hosting company won't offer anything that isn't recognized as stable. So, even if the next version has *the* feature you're dying to use in your application, it will work only on your local computer, and you won't be able to show off your brilliant skills until the hosting company catches up. Alternatively, install whichever version is currently offered by your hosting company—assuming, of course, that it's still available for download from the MySQL site.

Unfortunately, as of late 2004, some hosting companies were still offering only MySQL 3.23, the version that should have been retired by mid-2003. If you discover your hosting company is still offering something as outdated as 3.23, complain loudly. Most of the files in this book should still work with MySQL 3.23, but some parts of Chapter 11 require MySQL 4.1 as a minimum.

Another potential problem is that PHP 5 has completely overhauled the way it interacts with MySQL, but the new methods work only with MySQL 4.1.2 and above. To overcome all these difficulties, I have created three versions of PHP classes that provide the same interface when working with any of the following configurations:

- PHP 4 and all versions of MySQL from 3.23.*x*
- PHP 5 and MySQL 3.23.*x* and 4.0.*x*
- PHP 5 and versions of MySQL from 4.1.2

By including the appropriate external file in all your scripts, all you will have to do is replace one page when upgrading from one version to another.

Choosing the right license and cost

MySQL is open source software, but it's also available under a commercial license. This confuses a lot of people. It needn't. MySQL is distributed under the GNU General Public License (GPL). If you use MySQL to develop open source programs and adhere to the GPL, MySQL is completely free of charge. Under the terms of the GPL, the complete source code for any application you redistribute must be available and freely redistributable under reasonable conditions. The licensing section of the MySQL website at `www.mysql.com/products/licensing/opensource-license.html` states clearly, "Our software is 100% GPL (General Public License); if yours is 100% GPL compliant, then *you have no obligation to pay us for the licenses*" (italics added). In other words, it's free.

If you don't want to release your source code, you must purchase a commercial license. At the time of this writing, pricing information varied depending on your location. Accessing the MySQL online store from the United States, the cost of a "Classic" license was $295, and a "Pro" license was $595. The Pro license includes use of the InnoDB storage engine, which is capable of more-sophisticated operations. The equivalent prices in Europe were €250 and €500, approximately 15% higher, given the exchange rate at the time. Since the dollar/euro exchange rate changes rapidly, these prices should be regarded only as a guideline. For more information, visit the MySQL website at `www.mysql.com/products/licensing`, and also study the frequently asked questions about the GPL at `www.fsf.org/licenses/gpl-faq.html`.

Considering SQLite as an alternative

Although I intend to concentrate on MySQL as the database of choice in this book, you should be aware of an interesting alternative that has become available with the release of PHP 5. It's called SQLite, and one of its main attractions is that it requires no installation. SQLite is enabled by default in PHP 5 (although system administrators do have the option to turn it off). This makes it particularly attractive to anyone on a slow Internet connection, because the Windows download of MySQL 4.1.*x* is more than 13MB. The Mac OS X binaries for MySQL 4.1.*x* weigh in at more than 22MB.

In spite of its name, SQLite is a powerful database system. It is also completely free. For the technically minded, it's a small C library that implements an embeddable database engine that is totally self-contained and requires no configuration. It was developed by Dr. Richard Hipp of a small software company called Hwaci (pronounced "wha-chee") in North Carolina. He has dedicated the code to the public domain, and anyone contributing improvements is also required to do the same (`www.sqlite.org/copyright.html`).

SQLite's strengths

In addition to being free and requiring no initial setup, SQLite has many attractive features:

- It implements most of SQL92, the international standard, including some features not yet available in MySQL. Perhaps the most important of these is **transactions**—the ability to group a series of queries to ensure that no changes are made to any data unless the entire series is successful. (MySQL has partial support for transactions, but not on the default table type.)

- It is extremely fast for most operations.
- Each database is stored in a single file, making backup and transfer of data very easy.
- Virtually no administration is required, making it easy to learn.
- It is highly configurable through the use of user-defined functions in SQL queries.

SQLite's shortcomings

In spite of its benefits, SQLite does have some important drawbacks:

- Among the SQL92 features SQLite does not support are foreign key constraints, so it has no advantage over MySQL in this regard.
- Once a table has been created, you cannot alter its structure except by transferring all the data to a temporary table, dropping the old table, creating a new one, and transferring all the data again.
- Access to a database is controlled by setting the file's permissions. Although this makes administration a lot simpler, it makes it more difficult to control who has the right to update or delete data.
- SQLite has a much smaller set of built-in functions than other databases, particularly in comparison with MySQL. The need to create user-defined functions leads to more complex code and longer development time.
- SQLite is not suited to applications that receive a high volume of traffic or concurrent connections.

Choosing the right database system

SQLite is relatively new and has a tiny user base in comparison with MySQL. The online documentation is also much less extensive. It's too early to predict which way things will go. PHP began from similarly modest beginnings to become the most widely used server-side language. SQLite certainly has the power to make it worthwhile keeping an eye on, and it's worth considering for personal websites that need some form of database functionality.

The major drawback with SQLite is that it isn't suited to heavy-duty use. You may start off with modest ambitions, but if your project suddenly takes off, you don't want the hassle of having to rebuild everything from scratch. MySQL may seem like overkill for a small project, such as the single-table database used in the word game in the next chapter. Its overwhelming advantage lies in its flexibility. Tables can be easily restructured and small projects scaled up. Its wide range of built-in functions also makes writing SQL a lot easier—although, of course, there's a lot more to learn before you can use them all. Perhaps the most important argument in favor of learning MySQL is that it adds a valuable marketable skill to you as a web developer. MySQL is not particularly difficult, and if you are competent in MySQL, you will find it easy to transfer your skills to most other relational databases. You will certainly pick up SQLite in no time. Making the transition from SQLite to MySQL would require a lot more effort. For that reason, I propose to concentrate on working with PHP and MySQL in the rest of this book, although the next chapter will also show you how to use SQLite so that you can compare the two systems for yourself.

The rest of this chapter is devoted to the installation and configuration of MySQL, followed by the creation of a simple database that will be used as the back-end of a word game in the next chapter. If you're tempted to try SQLite first, you should be able to do so by building the Flash movie as described in the next chapter and using the SQLite database instructions at the end of the chapter. However, **I strongly recommend working through the next chapter in the order presented**. This is because the custom-built MySQL classes in Chapter 7 are used to teach the fundamentals of **object-oriented programming (OOP)** in PHP 5. Even if you decide SQLite is the database system you eventually want to adopt, understanding the principles of OOP in PHP 5 is essential for anyone who wants to use PHP to its fullest potential. The next chapter explains OOP in more detail, but the main aspect of interest to anyone already familiar with ActionScript is that it gives PHP the ability to create classes, objects, and methods.

> *Throughout the rest of the chapter, there are frequent references to MySQL,* `mysql`*, and* `mysqld`*, and it's important to understand the difference between them.* ***MySQL*** *refers to the entire database system. It's always spelled in uppercase, except for the "y." It's not just a single program, but a client/server system with a number of related programs that perform various administrative tasks. The two main components of the client/server system are* **`mysql`** *and* **`mysqld`**, *with both terms entirely in lowercase.* `mysqld` *is the server (or, to give it its proper technical name,* ***daemon****) that runs in the background listening for requests made to the database. Once it has been started, you can ignore it.* `mysql` *is the client program used to feed those requests to the database itself. Although you will use the* `mysql` *client at the command line later in this chapter, you will do most of your interaction through PHP or a graphic interface called phpMyAdmin (described later in this chapter). Finally,* `mysql` *is also the name of the main administrative database that controls user accounts, and on Windows it is the name of the Windows service that starts and stops the database server. Once you start working with them, differentiating between them is not as confusing as it first sounds.*

But first, Windows users need to get sorted out with the installation of MySQL. Mac OS X users should skip ahead to the section "Configuring MySQL on Mac OS X."

Installing MySQL on Windows

Installing MySQL on Windows got a whole lot easier with the release of MySQL 4.1. What used to be a 40MB download was reduced to a little more than 13MB (still a lot if you're on a dialup connection, but a massive slimming operation nonetheless), thanks to the release of **Windows Essentials**. As the name suggests, it contains all the important stuff, and certainly everything you need for this book. The problem—for some people, at least—is that a lot of the default settings, including the location of data files, have changed. If you have definitely never installed MySQL before on your current computer, you can go straight to the section titled "Installing the Windows Essentials version of MySQL." Otherwise, first follow the instructions in the next section. If you are in any doubt as to whether MySQL has ever been installed on your computer, perform steps 1 and 2 of the "Upgrading to Windows Essentials from an earlier version" section. If step 2 reports that The MySQL service was stopped successfully, you must remove it as described in step 3 before continuing. This restriction does *not* apply if your existing version of MySQL is 4.1.5 or later. An upgrade from one version of Windows Essentials to a more recent one in the same series (for instance, from 4.1.5 to 4.1.8) can be done without uninstalling.

- Most of the installation process is done through Windows dialog boxes, but it's occasionally necessary to work in a Windows Command Prompt window (just like in the old days of DOS). Although I have used a mixture of uppercase and lowercase for filenames and path names, Windows is case insensitive and will happily accept everything in lowercase.
- **If you want to install a version of MySQL prior to 4.1.8, refer to Appendix C.**

Upgrading to Windows Essentials from an earlier version

Because of the changes introduced by the new Windows Essentials version of MySQL, you must uninstall any version of MySQL earlier than MySQL 4.1.5, the first public release of Windows Essentials. Otherwise MySQL will fail to set up correctly.

1. Open a Windows Command Prompt by choosing Start ➤ Run. Enter cmd in the Open box and click OK.
2. Close down the MySQL server by entering the following command and pressing *Enter*:

   ```
   net stop mysql
   ```

3. If you get a message saying The specified service does not exist as an installed service, skip to step 4. Otherwise, remove MySQL as a service by typing the following commands, each followed by *Enter*:

   ```
   cd c:\mysql\bin
   mysqld --remove
   ```

4. Make a backup copy of your database files. They will normally be located in `C:\mysql\data`. (The uninstall process in the next step normally leaves your data files untouched, but this is a wise precaution.)
5. Open the Windows Control Panel from the Start menu and double-click Add or Remove Programs. Locate your existing installation of MySQL and click Remove.

If you have previously installed new versions of MySQL on top of existing ones, you may see more than one version of MySQL listed in the Control Panel. Unless the versions were installed in different folders, removing any one of them removes MySQL completely from your system. However, the other versions will remain listed in the Control Panel. This appears to have been a bug with the original MySQL installation process for Windows. The only way of getting rid of them from the list appears to be to install them again, and then go through the uninstall process for each individual version. You can, however, leave the old ones listed without causing any problems. Because the Windows Essentials version of MySQL has a new default installation folder, there should be no danger of uninstalling your new version by mistake in future.

Installing the Windows Essentials version of MySQL

These instructions are based on MySQL 4.1.8, which was released in December 2004. MySQL made minor adjustments to the installation process in each new release following the initial launch of Windows Essentials, so it is possible that you may encounter some variation from the steps outlined here, although the basic process should be the same. The 4.1 series of Windows Essentials is installed by default in `C:\Program Files\MySQL\MySQL Server 4.1`. When MySQL 5.0 becomes the Generally Available (recommended) version, all references to the `MySQL Server 4.1` folder should be replaced by `MySQL Server 5.0`.

Installation isn't at all difficult, but as you'll see by glancing through the following pages, there are a lot of dialog boxes. In most cases, you just accept the default setting, but I've described them all so you know what it is you're choosing.

1. Go to the MySQL downloads page at `http://dev.mysql.com/downloads`. Select the link for the Generally Available (recommended) release of MySQL database server & standard clients, as shown here:

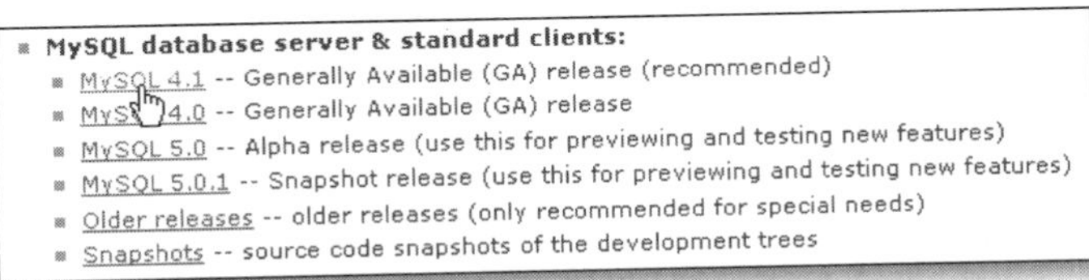

2. In the page that opens, scroll down to find the section marked Windows downloads. Choose Windows Essentials (x86), and click the download link. (It may say Download or Pick a mirror—either will do.)

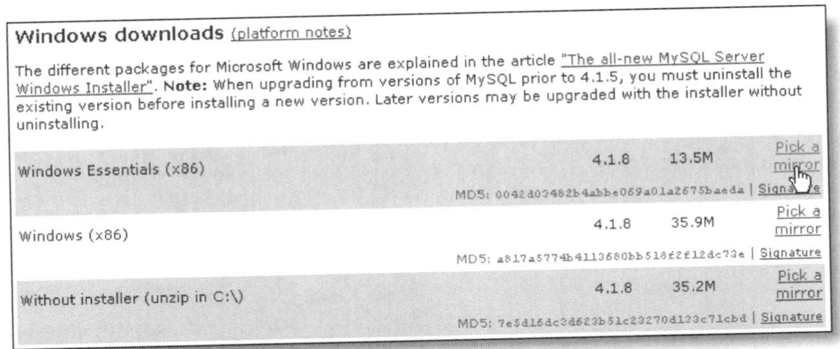

3. You may be taken to a further screen to fill in a survey or choose a suitable mirror site. The survey is optional. Follow the instructions onscreen, and download the file to a suitable location on your hard disk. It will have a name like `mysql-4.1.x-essential-win.msi`, where `x` represents the version number.

4. Exit all other Windows programs, and double-click the icon of the file you have just downloaded. This is a self-extracting Windows Installer package that will immediately begin the installation process.

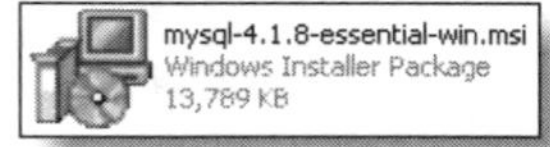

5. Windows Installer will begin the installation process and open a welcome dialog box, as shown. If you're upgrading an existing version of Windows Essentials to a more recent one, the dialog box will inform you that it has detected your current installation. You may also see extra dialog boxes connected with the upgrade process. Normally, they require no user input; they're there to inform you what's happening. Click Next to continue.

6. The next dialog box gives you the opportunity to change the installation destination. Accept the default (C:\Program Files\MySQL\MySQL Server 4.1\) and click Next.

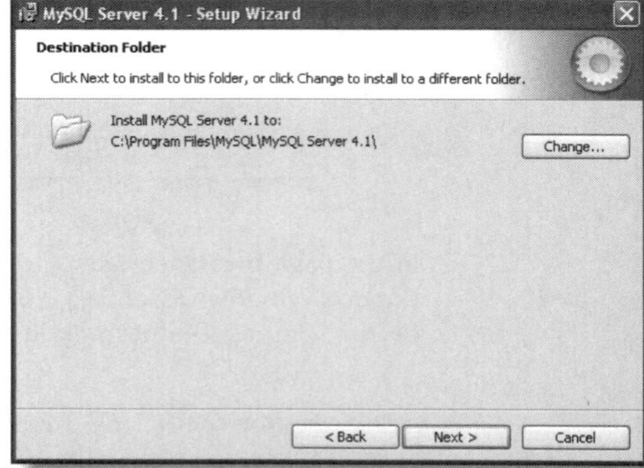

7. The next dialog box offers various options for installation. Accept the default (Typical) and click Next.

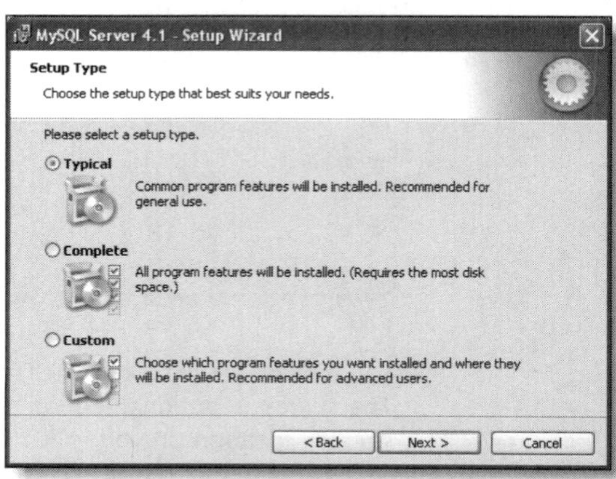

8. The next dialog box gives you an opportunity to check the details of your installation. If you're happy, click Install to proceed with the installation. Otherwise, click Back and make any necessary changes.

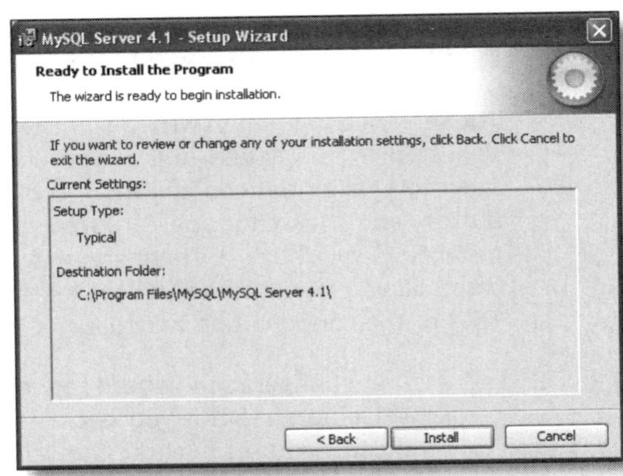

9. Before launching into the actual installation, MySQL invites you to become a member of its (I hope) happy family of developers by signing up for a free MySQL.com account. If you're like me, you run a mile (or 1.6 kilometers) when suddenly confronted by this type of "offer," particularly as the dialog box gives no details of what's involved. As it turns out, I've had a MySQL.com account for ages, and have found it both useful and unobtrusive. For me, the main benefit has been regular news updates by email. If you would like to sign up at this point, you need to be connected to the Internet. I suggest, however, that you select Skip Sign-Up and click Next. After you've finished setting everything up, visit `www.mysql.com/register.php` to see if you're interested in the benefits offered. Signing up is quick and hassle-free.

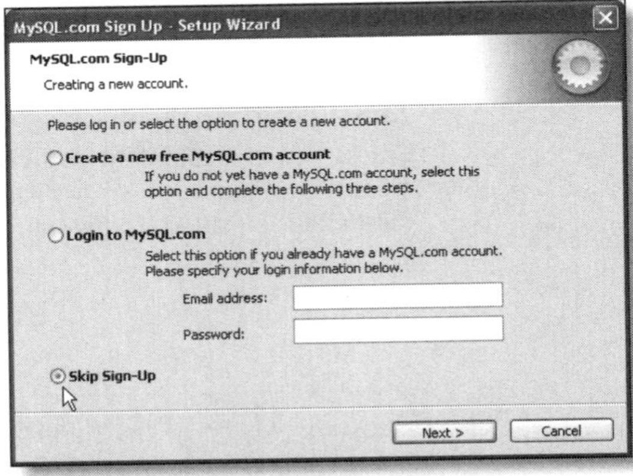

10. The actual installation now takes place and is normally very quick—although this will depend on the speed of your processor. When everything's finished, you're presented with a final dialog box, as shown. Although MySQL is now installed on your Windows system, you need to configure the server. In theory, you can do this later, but there's little point leaving the job only half done. The installation wizard automatically checks the option to start the configuration process immediately, so just click Finish.

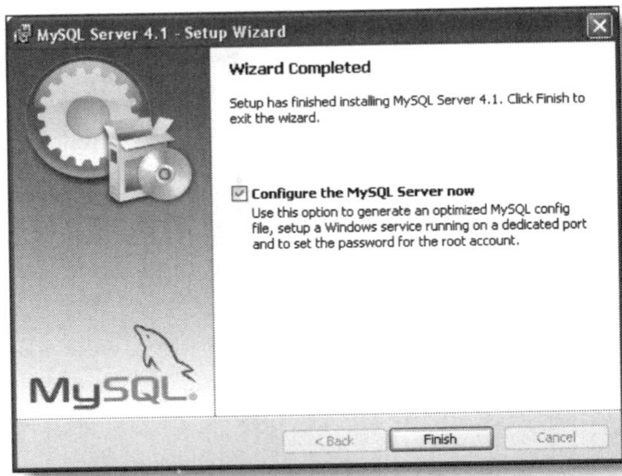

Configuring the MySQL server on Windows

The server configuration wizard launches automatically when you click the Finish button in the final step of installation (unless you uncheck the option). If it fails to launch, or if you ever need to change the configuration, you can access it any time by clicking the Windows Start button, and then choosing All Programs ➤ MySQL ➤ MySQL Server 4.1 ➤ MySQL Server Instance Config Wizard. There are quite a lot of dialog boxes to go through, although in most cases, all you need to do is accept the default setting. These instructions are based on version 1.0.3 of the configuration wizard. Later versions may differ slightly.

1. The configuration wizard opens with a welcome screen. If you decide not to go ahead, you can click Cancel on any screen, and no changes will be made. To proceed with the configuration, click Next.

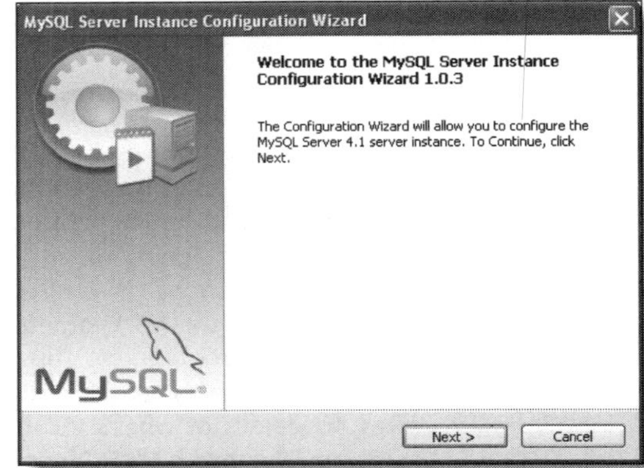

2. The first dialog box asks whether you want a detailed or standard configuration. Unless you are confident you can handle manual configuration of MySQL, choose the default Detailed Configuration option and click Next.

You should choose the Standard Configuration *option if you wish to configure MySQL yourself manually. You should use this option only on machines that do not already have MySQL server installed, because it will configure the server to use port 3306, which might cause conflicts with existing installations. No further instructions will be given for this option.*

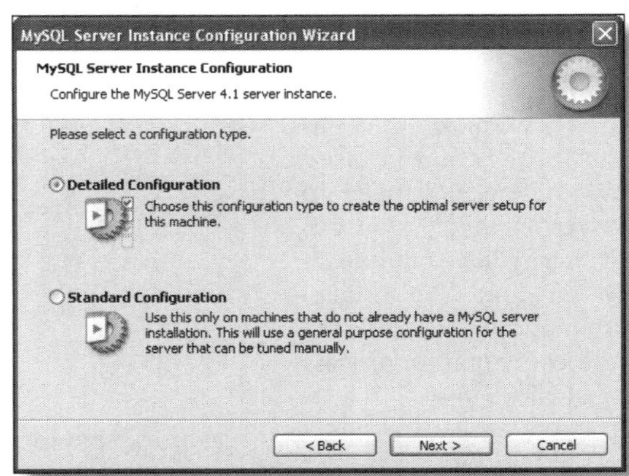

3. The three options on the next screen affect the amount of computer resources devoted to MySQL. The default Developer Machine allocates 12% of the available memory to MySQL, which is perfectly adequate. The two other options, Server Machine and Dedicated MySQL Server Machine allocate 50% and up to 95%, respectively, so use them only if the computer is going to be used as a live server. Otherwise, be prepared for all your other programs to slow down to a crawl. After making your choice, click Next.

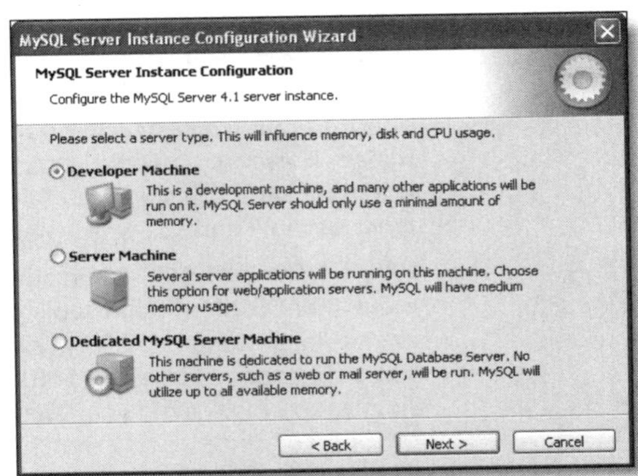

4. The next dialog box asks you to select the type of database you want. This needs a little explanation before you make your choice, mainly because MySQL has made what seems an odd decision regarding the default. All the data in a database is stored in tables, which organize records rather like a spreadsheet in neat rows and columns. The default table structure in MySQL is called MyISAM, but you can also choose several alternatives, the most important of which is called InnoDB, developed by a Finnish company, Innobase Oy, not MySQL AB. It has several advantages over the MyISAM format, in that it has full support for advanced features such as transactions and foreign key constraints. However, MyISAM has the edge when it comes to compact file sizes and speed (although InnoDB is also very fast).

   This dialog box asks you to choose from the following:

   - Multifunctional Database: Allows you to use both InnoDB and MyISAM tables.
   - Transactional Database Only: InnoDB tables only. MyISAM is disabled.
   - Non-Transactional Database Only: MyISAM tables only. InnoDB is disabled.

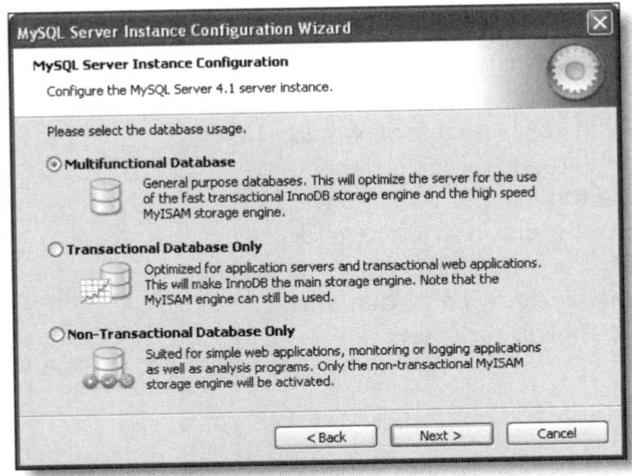

So, which should you choose? All the examples in this book will be built using MyISAM tables, the MySQL default, so Non-Transactional Database Only seems a sensible choice. If space is at a premium, it may be your only choice because both the other options require an extra 30MB of hard disk space, normally within your `Program Files` folder. However, I would strongly encourage you to consider the Multifunctional Database option instead, as this gives you the opportunity to experiment with both types of table and see which suits your purposes best.

Where I think MySQL has made a strange decision is that choosing this option will make InnoDB the default table type, whereas MyISAM is almost certainly the storage engine likely to be used by your hosting company. InnoDB support is normally an optional, chargeable extra. Still, this is only a minor irritation; changing table types is simple, and I will show you later how to make MyISAM the default. That way, you can set up your computer to match the storage engine used on your Internet server, but still have the freedom to experiment.

Unless you cannot afford the disk space, choose Multifunctional Database and click Next. If you select Non-Transactional Database Only, the next dialog box will either not appear or will be grayed out.

5. The next dialog box allows you to specify the location of the InnoDB tablespace. It will be grayed out if you are upgrading or if you chose Non-Transactional Database Only in the preceding step.

   The InnoDB engine stores database files in a completely different way from MyISAM. Everything is kept in a single "tablespace" that acts as a sort of virtual file system. You need to specify where this should be created on your hard disk. Two disadvantages of the InnoDB storage engine are that, once created, files cannot be made smaller, and they require up to twice as much space as equivalent MyISAM tables. As long as you have sufficient space on your `C` drive, leave the settings in this dialog box unchanged. This will put the tablespace in `C:\Program Files\MySQL\MySQL Server 4.1\data`. This is the default location for all database files, regardless of the format used. There is no danger of them getting mixed up, because MyISAM tables automatically create a subfolder for each new database.

   If you want to locate your InnoDB tablespace elsewhere, the drop-down menu offers some suggested alternatives. The example shown in this screenshot would create a new folder called `MySQL InnoDB Datafiles` at the top level of your `C` drive. If you want to use a different drive, click the button with the three dots on it to select an alternative location. When you have made your choice, click Next.

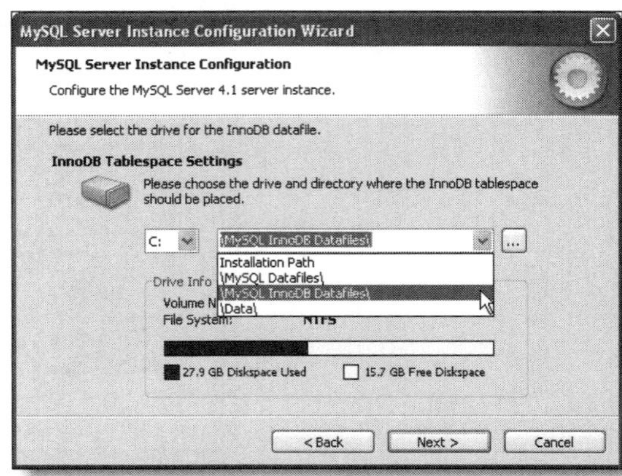

6. Unless you are configuring a live server that will encounter very heavy traffic, leave the next dialog box at its default setting of Decision Support (DSS)/OLAP and click Next.

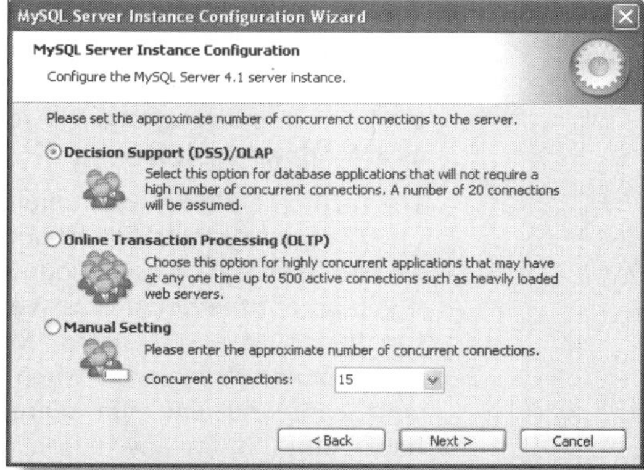

7. The MySQL server needs to communicate with Apache and your PHP scripts. By default, it does this through port 3306. Accept the default, and make sure Enable TCP/IP Networking is checked. Click Next.

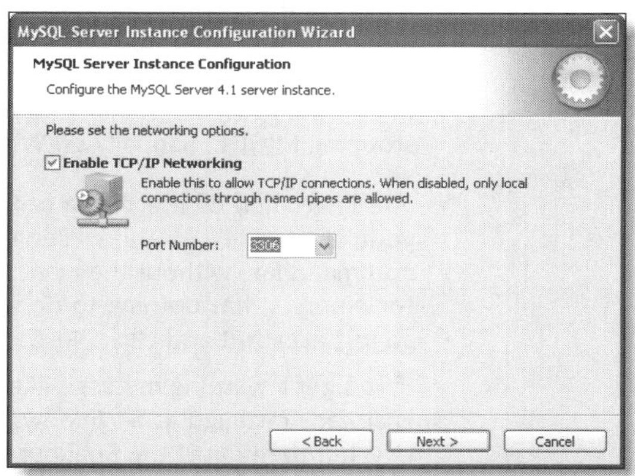

8. As mentioned earlier, MySQL has impressive support for most of the world's languages. The next dialog box invites you to choose a default character set. In spite of what you might think, this has no bearing on the range of languages supported—all are supported by default. The character set mainly determines the order in which data is sorted. This is a complex issue that affects only developers with specialized needs, and it is covered in detail in Appendix D. Unless you have a specific reason for choosing anything other than the default Standard Character Set, I suggest you accept it without making any changes. You can always change it later. Click Next.

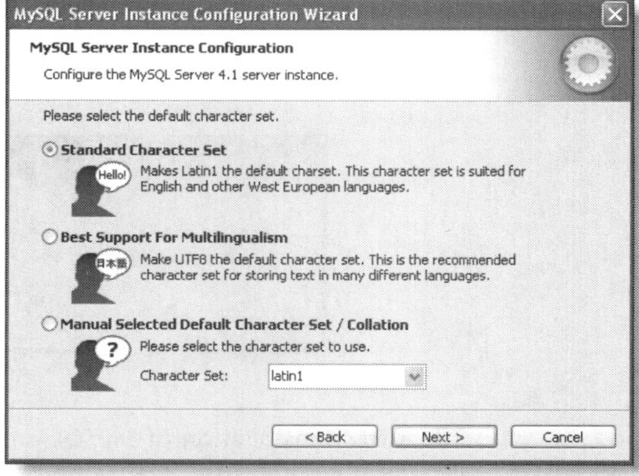

9. The top section of this next dialog box either will not appear on older versions of Windows, such as 98 or ME, or will be grayed out. If you are using such a system, make sure you read "Starting and stopping MySQL manually on Windows" later in the chapter. It will also be grayed out if you are upgrading and MySQL has already been installed as a Windows service.

   The recommended way of running MySQL on NT-based systems like Windows 2000, XP, or Server 2003 is as a Windows service. If you accept the defaults as shown in the top half of this screenshot, MySQL will always start automatically when you boot your computer and run silently in the background. If, for any reason, you don't want MySQL to start automatically, uncheck the Launch the MySQL Server automatically option. You can easily change this option if you change your mind later (see the section "Starting and stopping MySQL manually on Windows").

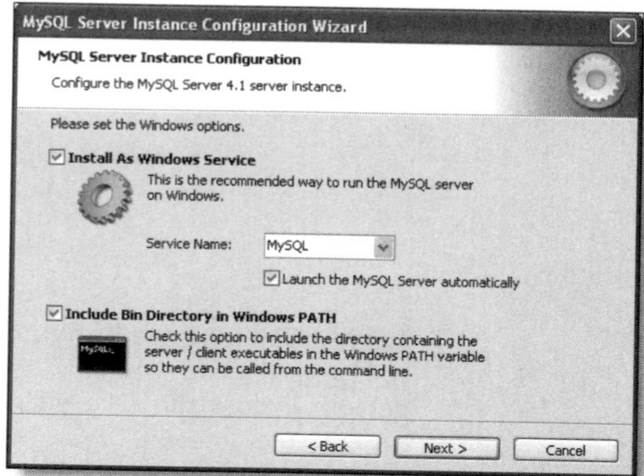

   The lower half of the dialog box gives you the option to include the bin directory in your Windows PATH. This will enable you to interact directly with MySQL Monitor at the command line without the need to change directory every time. By the way, bin stands for *binary*; it has nothing to do with the Windows Recycle Bin. It's checked by default, so just accept it and click Next.

   If you get a warning message like the one below after clicking Next, that means MySQL is already installed as a Windows service. If you click Yes, the wizard will continue happily, but then fail at the final hurdle (I know—I found out the hard way). You must click No, and either choose a different name or click Cancel to abandon the configuration wizard. Then go back to "Upgrading to MySQL 4.1 from a previous version" and remove MySQL as a Windows service. (This shouldn't be necessary if you heeded my earlier warning.)

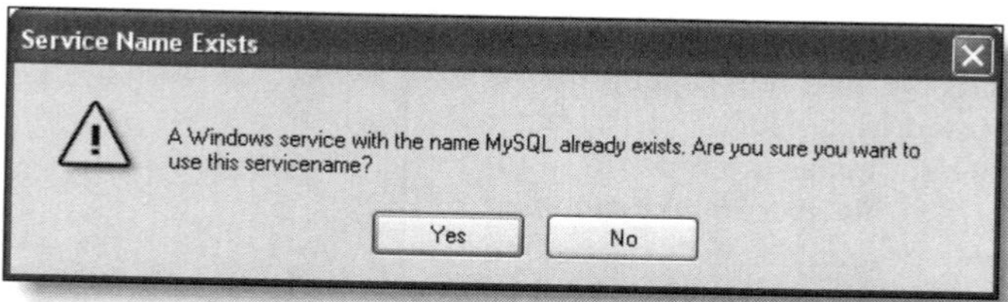

10. A fresh installation of MySQL has no security settings, so anyone can tamper with your data. MySQL uses the name "root" to signify the main database administrator with unrestricted control over all aspects of the database. Choose a password that you can remember, and enter it in both boxes. Unless you need to connect to the database over a network from a different computer, check the Root may only connect from localhost check box. This option will be grayed out if you are upgrading an existing version of Windows Essentials.

Do *not* check Create An Anonymous Account. It will make your database very insecure. I'll have more to say about user accounts later in the chapter. Click Next.

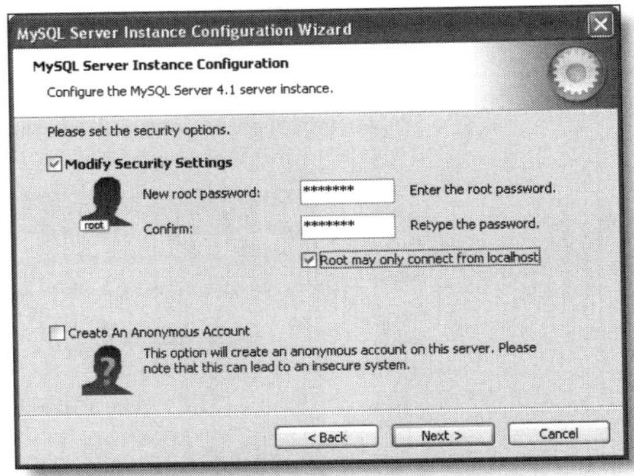

11. At long last, everything is ready. Click Execute.

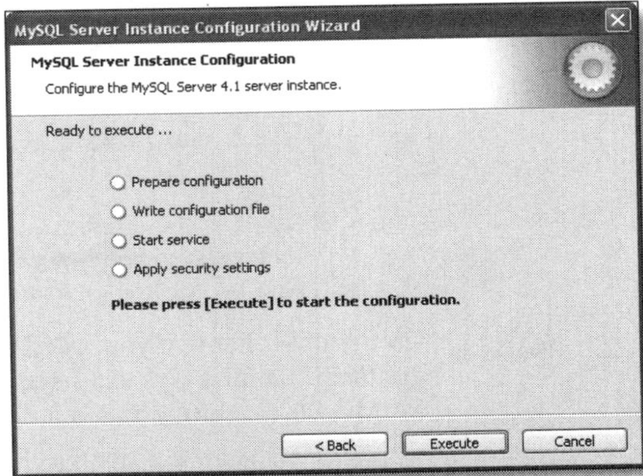

If you have installed a software firewall, such as Norton Internet Security, it will probably warn you that MySQL is trying to connect to a DNS server and suggest that you always block it. You must allow the connection; otherwise, MySQL will never work. Configure your firewall to allow inward and outward connections on port 3306, or take the less paranoid view and allow MySQL to connect using all ports. Since MySQL is configured to work on port 3306 only, the less paranoid option is probably fine, but the choice is up to you.

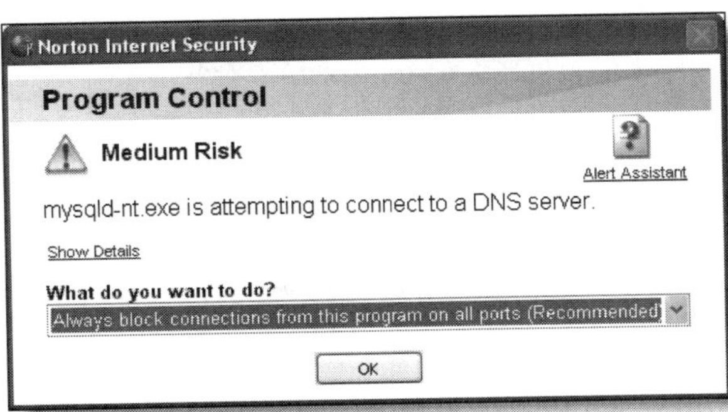

12. Assuming all was OK, you should see the following screen, which confirms that everything is up and running. Unless you are using an older version of Windows, MySQL should now be running—even if you selected the option not to start automatically (the option applies only to automatic start on bootup).

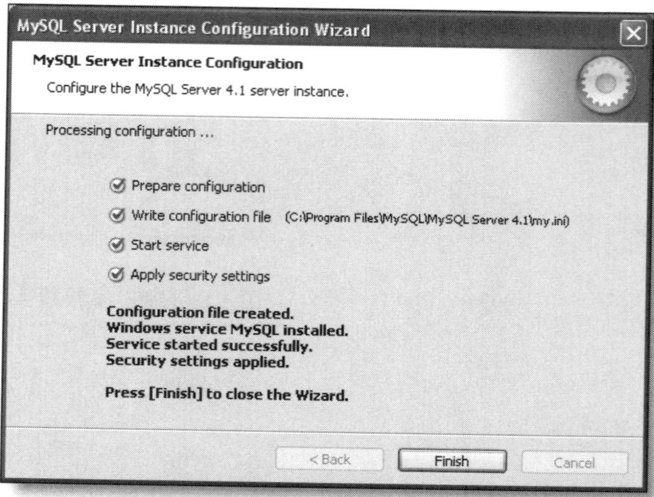

On the other hand, if you failed to heed my earlier warnings, everything will come to a grinding halt, and you will need to sort out why Windows refused to create a service for MySQL. Hopefully, this is a dialog box you will never see.

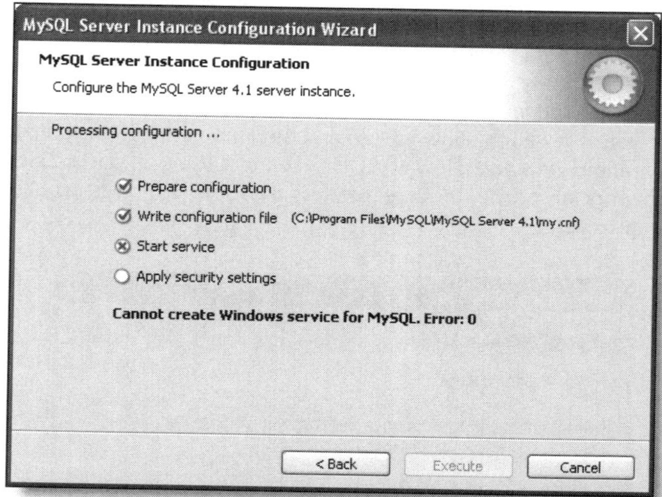

13. If you want to change the configuration at a later date or to remove MySQL as a Windows service, launch the configuration wizard from the Windows Start button by choosing All Programs ➤ MySQL ➤ MySQL Server 4.1 ➤ MySQL Server Instance Config Wizard. You will be presented with the following dialog box:

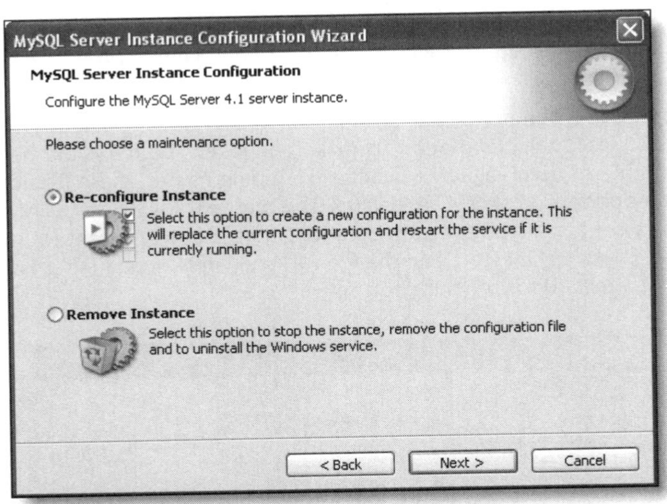

This dialog box gives you the option to change the various settings by going through all the dialog boxes again or to remove the server instance. This second option does not remove MySQL from your system, but it is intended for use if you no longer want Windows to start MySQL automatically each time you boot your computer. Unfortunately, it removes not only the automatic startup, but also the configuration file. The section “Starting and stopping MySQL manually on Windows” offers a far less radical solution.

The version of the wizard included with MySQL 4.1.5 caused a conflict with existing InnoDB log files and prevented the MySQL server from restarting, either manually or as a Windows service. The solution was to delete two files from `C:\Program Files\MySQL\MySQL Server 4.1\data`: `ib_logfile0` and `ib_logfile1`. The problem was resolved in a later release, but there were some reports that it had reoccurred. If you encounter similar difficulties, it may be worth moving the files temporarily to a different location to see if it helps. MySQL automatically rebuilds the two files if it can’t find them. They’re separate from InnoDB data files, so your data should remain intact. If it solves the problem, you can then delete the old files from their temporary location.

Changing the default table type on Windows Essentials

As I mentioned earlier, using the Windows configuration wizard sets InnoDB as the default table storage engine. According to the MySQL development team, this was a deliberate decision because they say inexperienced users found it very confusing not to be able to use transactions unless they specified InnoDB. Personally, I think it’s even more confusing for the standard installation of MySQL to default to one thing and for the Windows wizard to default to something different. Still, it's easy to change table types; even better, it's easy to reset the default. All you need to do is make a simple change to one of the MySQL configuration commands.

All the configuration commands are stored in a file called `my.ini`. This is a simple text file that can be opened and edited in any text editor.

1. Use Windows Explorer to navigate to the folder where MySQL was installed. The default is `C:\Program Files\MySQL\MySQL Server 4.1`.
2. You should see a number of files with names like `my.ini`, `my-huge.ini`, `my-small.ini`, and so on. Resist the temptation to make any jokes about `my.ini` being bigger than yours. In spite of their vaguely ridiculous-sounding names, these files contain the configuration options for MySQL at startup. The one that MySQL actually reads is `my.ini`. The others contain suggested configurations that you might want to use in the future. Double-click the my.ini icon, and the file will open in Notepad (alternatively, right-click and select a text editor of your choice).

3. Approximately 80 lines from the top you should find a line that reads

   ```
   default-storage-engine=INNODB
   ```

   Change it to

   ```
   default-storage-engine=MyISAM
   ```

4. Save the file and close it. To make the change effective, restart MySQL. Unless you are using Windows 98 or ME (in which case, refer to the section "Manual control on older versions of Windows"), do this by opening a Windows Command Prompt (Start ➤ Run ➤ cmd) and typing the following commands, each followed by *Enter*:

   ```
   net stop mysql
   net start mysql
   ```

MySQL will now create all new tables in the default MyISAM format. You can still use InnoDB tables, and you can change the table type any time you want. Details of how to do that are in Appendix E.

Starting and stopping MySQL manually on Windows

Most of the time, MySQL will be configured to start up automatically, and you can just forget about it entirely. There are times, though, when you need to know how to start or stop MySQL manually—whether for maintenance, to conserve resources, or because you're paranoid about security (a physical firewall is probably a much better solution). Of course, if you're running an older version of Windows, you have no choice but to do things manually. It's particularly important to know how to stop MySQL correctly; using Task Manager or some similar method to halt the server could cause irreparable damage to your data files.

Manual control on Windows NT 4, 2000, XP, and later

If you chose to install MySQL as a Windows service (see step 9 in the section "Configuring the MySQL server on Windows"), you can start and stop the server by opening a Windows Command Prompt (Start ➤ Run ➤ cmd) and typing net start mysql or net stop mysql. Windows should recognize these commands and report whether the command was successful.

An alternative is to use the Windows Services panel, which is where you can also change the option to start automatically on bootup.

1. Select Control Panel from the Windows Start menu. Double-click the Administrative Tools icon, and then double-click the Services icon in the window that opens.

2. In the Services panel, scroll down to find MySQL, and highlight it by clicking once. You can now use the video recorder–type icons at the top of the panel to stop or start the server as shown. The text links on the left of the panel do the same.

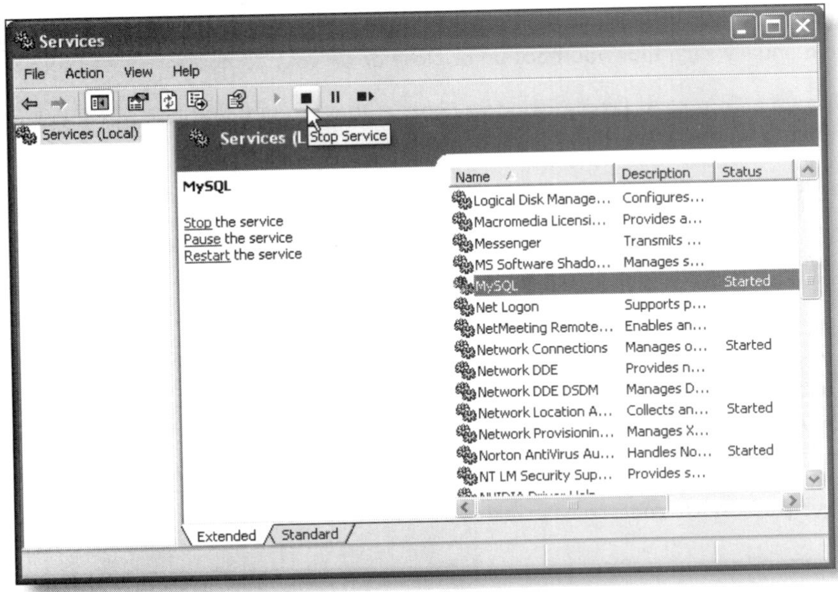

3. To change the automatic startup option, highlight MySQL in the Services panel, right-click to reveal a contextual menu, and choose Properties.
4. In the dialog box that opens, activate the Startup type drop-down menu, and choose Automatic, Manual, or Disabled. Click OK. That's all there is to it.

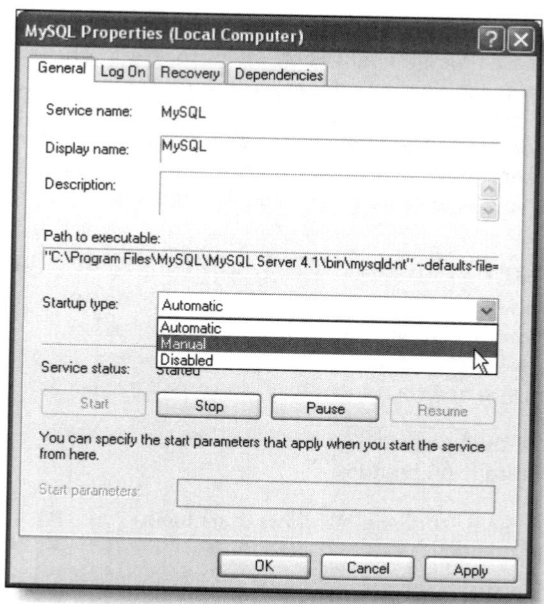

Manual control on older versions of Windows

Windows 98 and ME do not support services, so you have to start the MySQL server and shut it down manually each time you boot up or close down your computer.

1. Open a Command Prompt window (Start ➤ Run ➤ cmd) and type the following command, followed by *Enter*:

   ```
   mysqld
   ```

   This assumes that the MySQL `bin` directory was added to your Windows `PATH` by the Windows Essentials configuration wizard. Otherwise you need to change directory first to `C:\Program Files\MySQL\MySQL Server 4.1\bin`. Amend this path accordingly if your MySQL installation folder is different.
2. When the MySQL server has started, Windows will look as though it's waiting for another DOS command. Do *not* close this window; just minimize it.
3. Before you close down your computer, or when you have finished working with MySQL, restore the Command Prompt window and enter the following command:

   ```
   mysqladmin -u root -p shutdown
   ```

When prompted, enter the root password you set in step 10 of the section "Configuring the MySQL server on Windows."

4. When the server has shut down, you can safely close the Command Prompt window and close down your computer.

Launching MySQL Monitor on Windows

Although most of your interaction with MySQL will be through a graphic interface called phpMyAdmin (which is described later in this chapter) or through PHP scripts, you need to know how to access MySQL the traditional way through MySQL Monitor. The method of launching MySQL Monitor differs slightly depending on the version you have installed.

MySQL 4.1.8 or later

The Windows Essentials version of MySQL adds MySQL to the Programs menu accessed from the Start button. Select MySQL ➤ MySQL Server 4.1 ➤ MySQL Command Line Client. (At this stage, your menu will not have all the options shown in the screenshot alongside.) This will open a Windows Command Prompt window and ask you for your password. Type in the root password you chose in step 10 of the section "Configuring the MySQL server on Windows" and press *Enter*. As long as the server is running—and you typed your password correctly—you will see a welcome message similar to the one shown in Figure 6-3.

If you get your password wrong, your computer will beep and close the window. If you get Error 2003 instead, see the section "Error 2003: Beginner's curse."

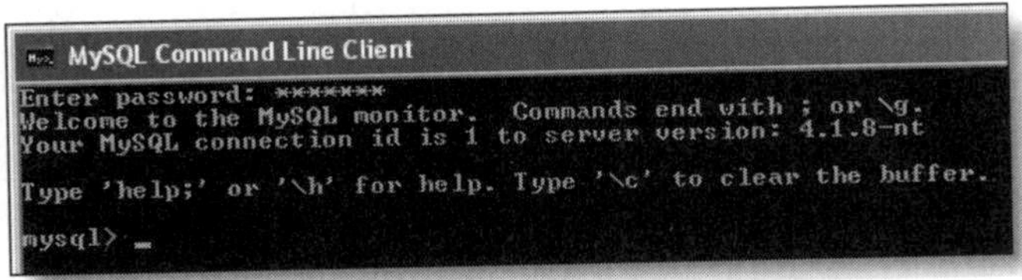

Figure 6-3. MySQL Monitor runs in a Command Prompt window, and provides a direct means of creating and querying databases.

All other installations

If your Programs menu does not have an option for MySQL Command Line Client, you need to open a Windows Command Prompt window and access MySQL Monitor from there.

1. Open a Command Prompt window (Start ➤ Run ➤ cmd). If the MySQL `bin` directory has been added to your Windows PATH, skip to step 2. Otherwise, change directory by typing cd followed by a space and the path to the MySQL server program, and then press *Enter*. Depending on your installation, this is likely to be either of the following:

```
cd C:\Program Files\MySQL\MySQL Server 4.1\bin
cd C:\mysql\bin
```

2. Type the following command, followed by *Enter*:

```
mysql -u root -p
```

   This tells MySQL that you want to enter as the root user and that you will be using a password.

3. When prompted, type in the root password you chose in step 10 of the section "Configuring the MySQL server on Windows" and press *Enter*. As long as the server is running—and you typed your password correctly—you will see a welcome message similar to that shown in Figure 6-3.

4. If you get your password wrong, go back to step 2 and repeat. If you get Error 2003 instead, see the next section.

Error 2003: Beginner's curse

This is probably the most common error encountered by beginners, and it's the cause of frequent cries of help to online forums. "I did everything according to the instructions and typed in my root password, but it won't let me in . . ."

Why not? Because MySQL isn't running, that's why! Here's the proof—and the solution (restart MySQL):

```
C:\WINDOWS\system32\cmd.exe - mysql -u root -p
Microsoft Windows XP [Version 5.1.2600]
(C) Copyright 1985-2001 Microsoft Corp.

C:\Documents and Settings\David>mysql -u root -p
Enter password: *******
ERROR 2003 (HY000): Can't connect to MySQL server on 'localhost' (10061)

C:\Documents and Settings\David>net start mysql

The MySQL service was started successfully.

C:\Documents and Settings\David>mysql -u root -p
Enter password: *******
Welcome to the MySQL monitor.  Commands end with ; or \g.
Your MySQL connection id is 1 to server version: 4.1.8-nt

Type 'help;' or '\h' for help. Type '\c' to clear the buffer.

mysql>
```

If the instructions earlier in this chapter fail to get MySQL running again, that suggests something more fundamentally wrong. You may need to reinstall MySQL, or ask for help in the friends of ED forums at `www.friendsofed.com/forums`.

Ending your session

When you have finished working with MySQL Monitor, type exit at the mysql> prompt, followed by *Enter*. If you used the Windows Essentials MySQL Command Line Shell, it will automatically close the window. Otherwise, the operating system will return you to the Windows Command Prompt but leave the window open. Either way, it's important to realize that what you are closing down is simply a session with MySQL Monitor; **the MySQL server keeps running in the background**.

Now take a well-earned rest while I get the good Mac folks sorted out. Skip ahead a couple of pages to the section "Working with MySQL Monitor (Windows and Mac)."

Configuring MySQL on Mac OS X

After flicking through all those Windows-centric pages to get here, you'll be pleased to know that there's very little to do to configure your installation of MySQL. Most of it was done in Chapter 1. All you need do now is set up an administrative password and remove anonymous access to MySQL—simple, but important security procedures. As in Chapter 1, you need to launch a Terminal window (Applications ➤ Utilities ➤ Terminal). All commands in Terminal and MySQL Monitor are followed by *RETURN*.

1. Open Terminal and type the command to start MySQL Monitor:

   ```
   mysql -u root
   ```

   The command contains three elements:

   - **mysql**: The name of the program
   - **-u**: Tells the program that you want to log in as a specified user
   - **root**: The name of user

   > *The MySQL root user is the main database administrator with unlimited powers over database files. Mac OS X is Unix-based, and it has a totally unrelated root user of its own, which has equally unlimited powers over the operating system and can do irreparable damage in inexperienced hands. Because of this, the Mac OS X root user is disabled by default. Enabling root for MySQL has* ***no*** *effect on the OS X root user, so you can do this without fear.*

2. You should see a welcome message like this:

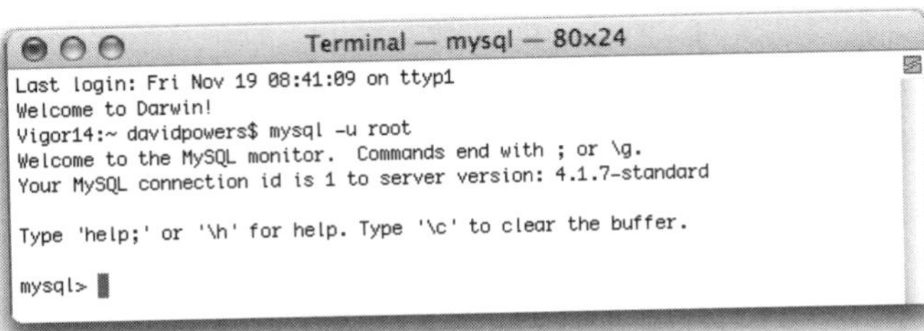

3. The most common problem is to instead get an error message like the following one:

```
Terminal — bash — 80x24
Last login: Thu Nov 25 21:46:56 on ttyp1
Welcome to Darwin!
Vigor14:~ davidpowers$ mysql -u root
ERROR 2002 (HY000): Can't connect to local MySQL server through socket '/tmp/mys
ql.sock' (2)
Vigor14:~ davidpowers$
```

It means that mysqld, the MySQL server, is not running. If you installed the MySQL Startup Item as recommended in Chapter 1, this should not normally happen. As long as the MySQL Startup Item has been installed, the command to restart the MySQL server is

```
sudo /Library/StartupItems/MySQLCOM/MySQLCOM start
```

This uses the sudo superuser command, so you need to enter your Mac Administrator password when prompted.

If you are working on a computer that had an older version of the MySQL Startup Item installed, the command is slightly different:

```
sudo /Library/StartupItems/MySQL/MySQL start
```

4. As explained earlier, the root user has unlimited powers over database files, but you have just logged in without a password! That means anyone can get in and wreak havoc with your files—a situation that needs rectifying immediately. Assuming you have logged in successfully as described in step 2, type the following command at the mysql> prompt:

```
use mysql
```

5. This tells MySQL you want to use the database called mysql. This contains all the details of authorized users and the privileges they have to work on database files. You should see the message Database changed, which means MySQL is ready for you to work on the files controlling administrative privileges. Now enter the command to set a password for the root user. Substitute *myPassword* with the actual password you want to use. Also make sure you use quotes where indicated and finish the command with a semicolon.

```
UPDATE user SET password = PASSWORD('myPassword') WHERE user = 'root';
```

6. Next, remove anonymous access to MySQL:

```
DELETE FROM user WHERE user = '';
```

The quotes before the semicolon are two single quotes with no space in between.

7. Tell MySQL to update the privileges table:

```
FLUSH PRIVILEGES;
```

The sequence of commands should produce a series of results like this:

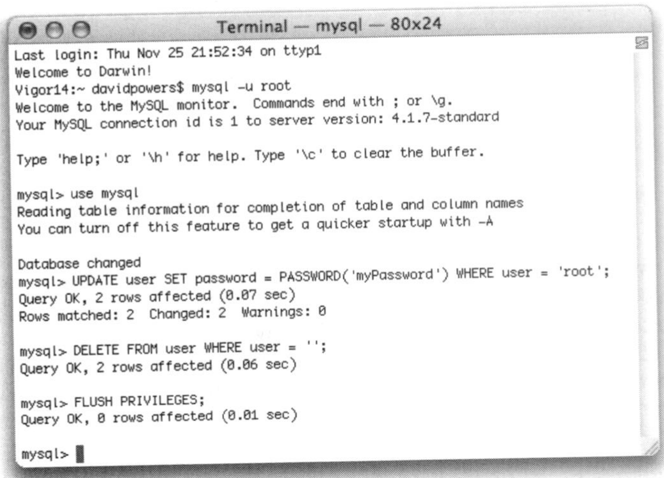

8. To exit MySQL Monitor, type exit, followed by *Return*. This simply ends your session with MySQL Monitor. **It does not shut down the MySQL server.**

9. Now try to log back in, using the same command as in step 2. MySQL won't let you in. Anonymous and password-free access have been removed. To get in this time, you need to tell MySQL that you want to use a password:

```
mysql -u root -p
```

10. When you press *Return*, you will be prompted for your password. Nothing will appear onscreen as you type, but, as long as you enter the correct password, MySQL will let you back in. Congratulations, you now have a secure installation of MySQL.

Working with MySQL Monitor (Windows and Mac)

From this point on, 99.9% of everything you do is identical on both Windows and Mac OS X. If you are used to working exclusively with a GUI like Windows or Mac OS, it can be unsettling to work at the command line with MySQL Monitor. It's not difficult, and you should get used to it quite quickly. Here are a few pointers to make you feel more at home:

- When you work inside MySQL Monitor, most commands need to end with a semicolon (;). The only exceptions are use *databaseName* and exit. MySQL Monitor is quite happy if you use a semicolon after these two commands, so the simple rule is this: **if in doubt, put a semicolon on the end of each command**.

- If you forget to put a semicolon at the end of a command that needs one, MySQL Monitor will patiently wait for you to do so, like this:

```
mysql> use mysql
Reading table information for completion of table and column names
You can turn off this feature to get a quicker startup with -A

Database changed
mysql> UPDATE user SET password = PASSWORD('myPassword') WHERE user = 'root'
    ->
```

  This behavior enables you to spread long queries over a number of lines. Not only is this easier to read onscreen, but also it's useful if you make an error (as you'll find happens quite often, both in the early days and when you start experimenting with more ambitious queries). MySQL Monitor remembers previous commands line by line, and you can retrieve them by pressing the up and down arrow keys on your keyboard. Once a previous command has been redisplayed, you can use your left and right arrow keys to move along the line and edit it in the normal way. This will save your sanity many times, especially with a 15-line command that fails because of a single typing error. Once you have completed the command, just type a semicolon and press *ENTER/RETURN*. MySQL Monitor will then process it.

- If you spot a mistake before pressing *ENTER/RETURN*, use your left and right arrow keys to edit the current line. If the mistake is on a previous line, there is no way to go back. Abandon the command by typing \c. MySQL Monitor will ignore everything you have entered and present you with the mysql> prompt.

- By convention, SQL queries are written with SQL commands in uppercase. This is nothing more than a convention to make them easier to read. **SQL is case insensitive**. The following commands have exactly the same meaning and effect:

```
UPDATE user SET password = PASSWORD('myPassword') WHERE user = 'root';
update user set password = password('myPassword') where user = 'root';
```

  When not writing books, I tend to use lowercase for otherwise case-insensitive code all the time, but putting SQL keywords in uppercase does make it easier to distinguish keywords from the names of tables, columns, and other data. So, although switching back and forth between uppercase and lowercase can be a nuisance, it can save a lot of time later when troubleshooting or reading code that you wrote a long time ago. (This last point applies only to SQL in your PHP scripts.)

- Although SQL keywords can be written in any combination of uppercase or lowercase, **database names and table names are case sensitive in MySQL on all systems except Windows**. The Windows version of MySQL now automatically creates all database and table names in lowercase. Since most hosting companies offering PHP and MySQL use Linux servers, Windows users should stick to lowercase names on both systems to avoid problems. Confusingly, the names of columns within database tables are case insensitive. If in doubt, treat all names in a database as case sensitive.

Creating your first database in MySQL

So, now you're the proud owner of a fully working MySQL database system—at least, I assume you are, if you're reading this without having already thrown the book or your computer (or both) out of the window. It's not much fun—or use—without any real data in it. Actually, there is real data: the new root password you created in the previous section. Still, it doesn't do anything other than let you rattle around inside an empty data store.

The news database shown in Figure 6-2 at the beginning of the chapter comprises 17 interconnected tables, one of which contains more than 10,000 records. That's a tad overambitious for your first effort with MySQL. I intend to start you off more gently with a single table that contains just a single column. Then, in the next chapter, I'll show you how to link this database to a fiendish word game, which will be familiar to readers of *Foundation ActionScript for Flash MX 2004* by Sham Bhangal (friends of ED, ISBN: 1-59059-305-7). If all this talk of tables and columns is meaningless to you, bear with me. By the time you have finished this book, you should have a solid understanding of the basics of database design.

The game is a Flash-based adaptation of a word-guessing game that has been popular among schoolchildren for many, many years and goes by the rather gruesome name of "Hangman." I played it a lot as a child in Britain and recently discovered that it's just as well known on the other side of the Atlantic. For those of you who may not be familiar with the game, the idea is to guess the letters of a word. For every wrong guess, a line is drawn on a piece of paper, building the outline of a gallows and then a condemned man. The idea is to guess the word before you come to a grisly end. The Flash version looks like the image above.

You'll be pleased to know that I was always good at spelling bees and managed to work out in time that the word was "deflate." As a result, the gallows were swept away, and . . . well, the picture tells the story.

If you've already created the Hangman game from Sham's book, you may be wondering why I'm bothering with it again. The answer is that with a database behind it, this game becomes much more powerful, and you'll also add a scoring system that remembers your score every time you come back. If you're new to this game, don't worry. Full instructions on how to build it are in the next chapter.

What makes the database version of this game so much more powerful is that you can really keep players guessing by drawing on a huge vocabulary. The original version relies on an array of 20 words hard-coded into the Flash movie. Although the words are picked at random, it doesn't take long before you know them by heart, and the game loses all appeal. You're going to beef it up by creating a database with more than 21,000 entries. What's more, creating that database won't take much longer than hard-coding the array of just 20 words. Even if the idea of creating a word game doesn't appeal, you can apply the method of creating the database and extracting data from it to a wide range of more serious projects.

Typing all 21,000 or so entries into the database would be a mammoth undertaking. Fortunately, there are many ready-made word lists freely available on the Internet. The one you're going to use was compiled by Adam Beale, and it has been released to the public domain. It's part of a package known as `12dicts`, a project intended to create a list of words approximating the common core of the vocabulary of American English (if you prefer British English, `12dicts` contains a list to suit this as well). You can find this and many other downloadable word lists at `http://wordlist.sourceforge.net`, a site maintained by Kevin Atkinson.

Up until now, you've worked with MySQL as the root user. If you're the only person using the database, you may be tempted to continue working as root, but it's not a good idea. When you deploy your MySQL applications on a live Internet server, you should always connect to the database as a user with the least number of privileges necessary. That way, even if the password is revealed, a malicious user wouldn't have the unrestrained root privileges to destroy all your valuable data. So it's a good idea to create two users for your Flash applications: an administrator and a user capable only of viewing records.

First of all, though, you need to create a database to work in. A fresh installation of MySQL contains only two databases:

- **`mysql`**: This database contains the names of all authorized users and details of the privileges they have been granted. It should **not** be used for anything else.
- **`test`**: This database is completely empty. It contains no data or tables, and is about as much use as the wings on an ostrich.

> *On Windows, database files are normally stored in* `C:\Program Files\MySQL\MySQL Server 4.1\data`. *On Mac OS X, they are hidden away from the prying eyes of Finder in* `/usr/local/mysql/data`. *Rather than copying the actual files, the way to back them up safely is to use a utility called* `mysqldump`*, which is described in Appendix E.*

Creating a database and named users

1. On Windows, open MySQL Monitor as described in the section "Launching MySQL Monitor on Windows." On the Mac, open Terminal, and log on to MySQL Monitor as root:

```
mysql -u root -p
```

2. On both systems, enter your root password, and then select the `test` database:

```
use test
```

Note that I didn't use a semicolon at the end of that command. As mentioned earlier, `use` *`databasename`* and `exit` are the only commands that don't end with a semicolon, but there's no harm in using one anyway.

3. The way to find out what tables exist in a database is simple. Type the following command:

```
show tables;
```

4. If you have never used the `test` database, you should see the following result:

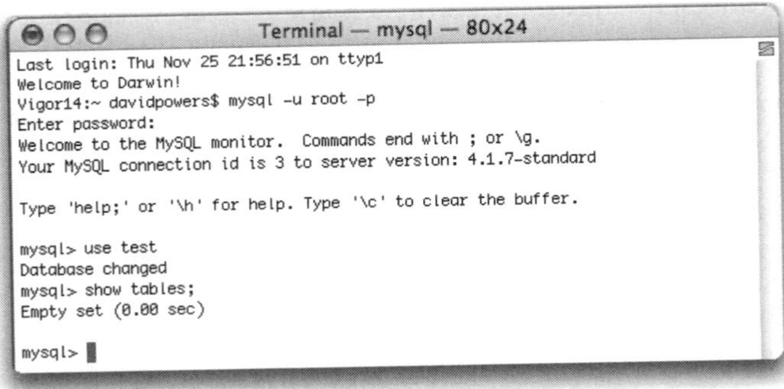

`Empty set` means there is nothing there, so it's safe to delete.

> *One of the dangers of writing books about open source software that is frequently updated, like MySQL and PHP, is that what was true at the time of this writing may have changed by the time you come to read the book. If there is no* `test` *database, or if the* `show tables` *command produces a different result, skip this section and just note its contents. Deleting the* `test` *database isn't the object of this exercise. Demonstrating the awesome power of the root user is what's important here.*

5. As long as you got the empty set result, type the following command, and watch carefully what happens onscreen when you press *ENTER/RETURN*.

```
DROP DATABASE test;
```

`DROP DATABASE` is a SQL command. As explained before, SQL is case insensitive, so feel free to use all lowercase.

6. You should have gotten a result like this:

```
mysql> use test
Database changed
mysql> show tables;
Empty set (0.00 sec)

mysql> DROP DATABASE test;
Query OK, 0 rows affected (0.29 sec)

mysql>
```

7. Type the following command, and you will see: `test` is no longer there.

   ```
   show databases;
   ```

   Unlike a commercial program, no reassuring (or annoying, depending on your viewpoint) message popped up asking whether you really want to delete the database. One of MySQL's great strengths is its speed, and it takes the view that, if you ask it to do something, you mean what you say (or type). The `test` database has gone—and there's no way to get it back. No Recycle Bin or Trash to retrieve your mistakes from. `DROP DATABASE` means exactly that.

   That's why it's sensible to create users with limited privileges. Even experienced people make mistakes and, although you can—and should—back up your data, it's preferable to avoid the need for using a backup, which may not be fully up to date. (See Appendix E for details of how to back up.)

8. After that moment of destruction, let's be more creative. Type the following:

   ```
   CREATE DATABASE phpflash;
   ```

   MySQL Monitor should respond with Query OK, 1 row affected followed by how long it took to execute the query (probably 0.00 sec).

9. You now have a database to work in, but no users. These need to be set up by the root user in the `mysql` database. Before working in a database, you need to select it:

   ```
   use mysql
   ```

10. Deciding what privileges to give the user restricted to retrieving data is easy. All that is needed is the ability to `SELECT`, the SQL command for, well, selecting data from a database. (SQL is thankfully written in almost plain English, making it easy for anyone with a good knowledge of English to pick up.) For the sake of simplicity, let's call this user flashuser. The command to create this user with the appropriate privileges is

    ```
    GRANT SELECT ON phpflash.* TO flashuser@localhost
    IDENTIFIED BY 'deepthought';
    ```

    Notice that I spread this command over two lines. As long as you don't put a semicolon at the end of the first line, MySQL Monitor will treat both lines as a single command. `GRANT` is the SQL command for granting privileges and creating new users. It is followed by the names of the privileges to be granted, in this case `SELECT`. Then you identify which databases the user can access. You want the user to access all tables in `phpflash`, so type ON and follow the database name with .* (a period and an asterisk). If you wanted the user to have access to all databases, you would type ON *.*. Next, comes TO and the name of the user. By adding `@localhost`, you restrict the user to accessing the database only from the same computer on which the database is located, which makes everything much more secure. Finally, `IDENTIFIED BY` assigns the user's password. Although the password is entered here in plain text, it's stored by MySQL in encrypted form. If you ever forget a username's password, it's simpler to assign a new one.

11. The choice of privileges for the administrator is a little more difficult. Ideally, an administrator should have the ability to create and drop databases, but you've already seen how easy it is to destroy a database with no way of getting it back. In all probability, you'll need to use the administrative account in applications you deploy on the Internet—for instance, to allow users (including yourself) to enter new records into a database. The best compromise is to restrict the creation and dropping of databases to the root user, and give the administrative user only those privileges needed to insert and update records. Let's call the administrative user account flashadmin. The SQL command is similar to the one for flashuser.

```
GRANT SELECT, INSERT, UPDATE, DELETE ON phpflash.*
TO flashadmin@localhost IDENTIFIED BY 'fortytwo';
```

Apart from the username and password, the only difference between this GRANT command and the previous one is that the privileges are presented as a comma-delimited list. In addition to SELECT (retrieving records), the administrative user will be allowed to INSERT, UPDATE, and DELETE—privileges that say exactly what they mean. DELETE works only on records, not an entire database, but as you will see later, it can have devastating results if used incorrectly.

12. The instructions so far have assumed you haven't made a single mistake. What happens, though, if you're not supertypist? You may get something like this:

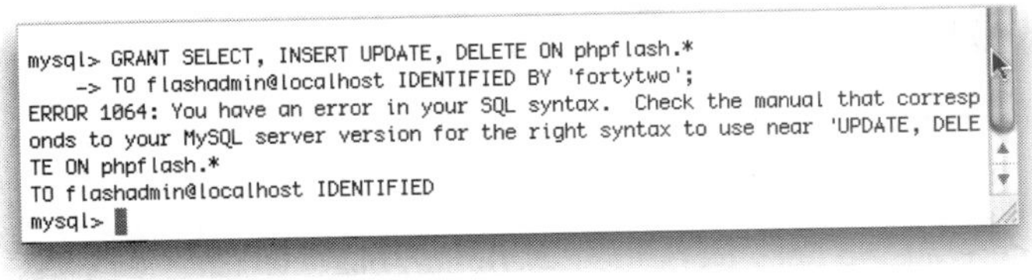

```
mysql> GRANT SELECT, INSERT UPDATE, DELETE ON phpflash.*
    -> TO flashadmin@localhost IDENTIFIED BY 'fortytwo';
ERROR 1064: You have an error in your SQL syntax.  Check the manual that corresp
onds to your MySQL server version for the right syntax to use near 'UPDATE, DELE
TE ON phpflash.*
TO flashadmin@localhost IDENTIFIED
mysql> 
```

The error message is helpful—after a fashion—but not very. It tells you there is an error in your SQL syntax near 'UPDATE, DELETE ON phpflash.*, and so on. Normally this means that there is a problem immediately before the section identified by near. If you look at the illustration, you'll see there's a comma missing between INSERT and UPDATE. If this happens to you, rather than retype everything, press the up arrow on your keyboard twice. This will bring back the first line of the command. Use your left arrow key to move the cursor to the right of INSERT (or wherever your mistake lies), and edit the line as you normally would by using the character keys, the *Delete* key, and the spacebar. Press *Enter/Return*. MySQL Monitor will accept the corrected line and wait for you to complete the command. Press the up arrow again until you get the second line of the command. When you're happy that the command is OK, execute it by pressing *Enter/Return*.

Experiment with the up and down arrows, and you'll soon come to appreciate this quick way of bringing back previous commands. It's particularly useful when testing a variety of SQL statements. Instead of typing everything each time, you can call up a previous, successful statement and simply amend a small part of it to see how the result differs.

13. Check that you have set up the two users correctly by executing the following two commands:

```
SHOW GRANTS FOR flashuser@localhost;
SHOW GRANTS FOR flashadmin@localhost;
```

The second command should give you a result similar to this:

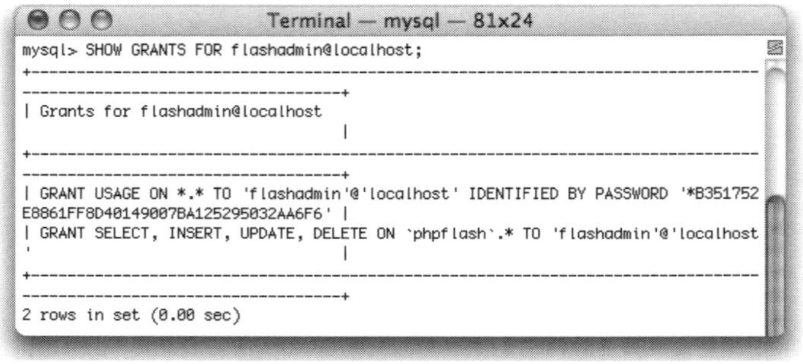

```
Terminal — mysql — 81x24
mysql> SHOW GRANTS FOR flashadmin@localhost;
+--------------------------------------------------------------------------------
----------------------------------+
| Grants for flashadmin@localhost
                                  |
+--------------------------------------------------------------------------------
----------------------------------+
| GRANT USAGE ON *.* TO 'flashadmin'@'localhost' IDENTIFIED BY PASSWORD '*B351752
E8861FF8D40149007BA125295032AA6F6' |
| GRANT SELECT, INSERT, UPDATE, DELETE ON `phpflash`.* TO 'flashadmin'@'localhost
'                                 |
+--------------------------------------------------------------------------------
----------------------------------+
2 rows in set (0.00 sec)
```

As you can see, the password is displayed in encrypted form, and flashadmin has SELECT, INSERT, UPDATE, and DELETE privileges. You're getting ready to roll.

Downloading and installing the word list

1. Go to Kevin's Word List Page at `http://wordlist.sourceforge.net`. Scroll down to the section marked Official 12Dicts Package, where you will find links to a page describing the package and to the download page for the ZIP file containing the word lists. (There are no links from the description page, which is why I suggest using this route. Sourceforge.net is the largest online depository of open source code and applications, so it's unlikely the page will have disappeared by the time you read this. If it has, use a search engine like Google to find `12Dicts` or any similar word list.)
2. Download the ZIP file (`12dicts-4.0.zip` was the most recent at the time of this writing), and extract the contents to a suitable location on your hard disk.
3. The ZIP file contains eight text files and a copy of `readme.html`, which describes in detail what each word list contains. One of the text files is a text version of `readme.html`; the remaining seven are different word lists. The one I suggest you use is `3esl.txt`. The reason for choosing this one is that it is compiled from dictionaries for learners of English as a second language. In other words, it's less likely to contain the sort of mind-boggling, obscure, or specialist words beloved of Scrabble fans.

Open `3esl.txt` in any text-editing program. You will see that every word is on a separate line. If you are using a program that is capable of displaying line numbers, turn that feature on (in TextPad for Windows, choose View ➤ Line Numbers, or in BBEdit for the Mac, choose Edit ➤ Text Options ➤ Display ➤ Line Numbers). You will see there are nearly 22,000 entries. If you don't have a program that displays line numbers, open the file in a word processor and do a word count. The figure will probably come to more than 22,000, because some entries are hyphenated or comprised of two words that form a phrase, such as "youth hostel."

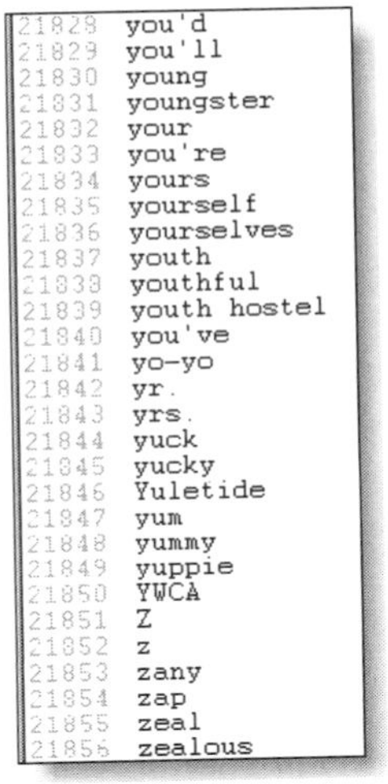

```
you'd
you'll
young
youngster
your
you're
yours
yourself
yourselves
youth
youthful
youth hostel
you've
yo-yo
yr.
yrs.
yuck
yucky
Yuletide
yum
yummy
yuppie
YWCA
Z
z
zany
zap
zeal
zealous
```

4. Scroll down to the bottom of the list. As you can see in the image on the right, some entries have apostrophes (such as you'd), others are abbreviations with or without a period (such as yr. and YWCA), some are even single letters (z). If I suggested going through all 21,000 or more entries by hand, removing the ones you don't want, you would no doubt be wishing me a grisly end—and not just in the make-believe terms of the Hangman game. Weeding out abbreviations like YWCA does present a problem, but a combination of the PHP skills you picked up in the previous chapters, together with MySQL, will strip out all other unwanted entries. First, though, you need to get the words from the list into the database.

5. Close `3esl.txt` and copy it to a temporary location. On Windows, paste it in the top level of your `C` drive. On a Mac, put it in the top level of your `Documents` folder.

6. If you have not already logged into MySQL Monitor as the root user, do so now. Select the `phpflash` database:

```
use phpflash
```

7. To store information in a database, you need to create tables designed to hold the data in a logical manner. The Hangman game uses the simplest of all possible tables: a single column with one entry on each line (or row). You need to tell MySQL what to call the column and what type of data you plan to store in it. Type the following command in MySQL Monitor:

```
CREATE TABLE wordlist (
word VARCHAR(30)
);
```

`CREATE TABLE` is the SQL command that does exactly what you would expect: create a new table. It's followed by the name of the new table (in this case, `wordlist`) and a series of column definitions inside parentheses. There's just one column here, called `word`. `VARCHAR` defines the column as text with a variable number of characters. The 30 in parentheses sets the maximum number of characters that can be contained in any single row. There are many different column types you can use in a database table—I'll come back to the others in Chapter 8.

If you installed the Windows Essentials version of MySQL and selected the Multifunctional Database *option, this table will use the InnoDB storage engine unless you changed the default as described in the section "Changing the default table type in Windows Essentials." Chapter 8 explains table types, and you can find out how to change them in Appendix E.*

8. Check that you have created the table correctly with the following command:

```
DESCRIBE wordlist;
```

The entire sequence of commands should produce output similar to the following:

```
mysql> use phpflash
Database changed
mysql> CREATE TABLE wordlist (
    -> word VARCHAR(30)
    -> );
Query OK, 0 rows affected (0.07 sec)

mysql> DESCRIBE wordlist;
+-------+-------------+------+-----+---------+-------+
| Field | Type        | Null | Key | Default | Extra |
+-------+-------------+------+-----+---------+-------+
| word  | varchar(30) | YES  |     | NULL    |       |
+-------+-------------+------+-----+---------+-------+
1 row in set (0.00 sec)

mysql>
```

This shows you that the field name is word; that its type is a variable-length text, with a maximum of 30 characters; and that it permits NULL values, which are also the default. A NULL value is when nothing is entered into a field. Having empty fields is unimportant in this table, but there are often cases where you need to prevent that from happening. For instance, an address book with empty fields in the family name column would be of little practical value. To prevent that type of thing from happening, you would declare a field to be NOT NULL, as you will see in later chapters. I will explain the significance of Key and Extra in Chapter 8, as well as defining precisely what is meant by "field" and "column." These last two terms are frequently used interchangeably in a way that can be confusing until you understand the close relationship between them.

9. To get the contents of the word list into the database, you need to use a command called LOAD DATA INFILE. The command needed for Mac OS X is slightly different from Windows, so let's look at Windows first. Note that a *double* backslash is needed in the filename to indicate the top level of the C drive.

```
LOAD DATA INFILE 'c:\\3esl.txt'
INTO TABLE wordlist
FIELDS TERMINATED BY '\r\n'
LINES TERMINATED BY '\r\n';
```

Now, here's the command for Mac OS X (replace *username* in the first line with the long version of your Mac username):

```
LOAD DATA LOCAL INFILE '/Users/username/Documents/3esl.txt'
INTO TABLE wordlist
FIELDS TERMINATED BY '\r\n'
LINES TERMINATED BY '\r\n';
```

Apart from the location of the file, the difference in the command for Mac OS X is the need to include the keyword LOCAL. This is because of the way file permissions are set on a Mac.

10. You should see a result similar to this:

```
mysql> LOAD DATA LOCAL INFILE '/Users/davidpowers/Documents/3esl.txt'
    -> INTO TABLE wordlist
    -> FIELDS TERMINATED BY '\r\n'
    -> LINES TERMINATED BY '\r\n';
Query OK, 21877 rows affected (0.17 sec)
Records: 21877  Deleted: 0  Skipped: 0  Warnings: 0

mysql>
```

Take a look at the number of records and how fast the query was executed—21,877 records in less than one-fifth of a second. Pretty slick work!

11. Check that everything's OK by typing the following command:

```
SELECT * FROM wordlist LIMIT 10;
```

The asterisk says you want to select all columns (there's only one in this case, but it's a convenient bit of shorthand). As you might expect, LIMIT prevents the entire list from being displayed, and it retrieves just the first ten records. Make sure the output looks similar to the image alongside:

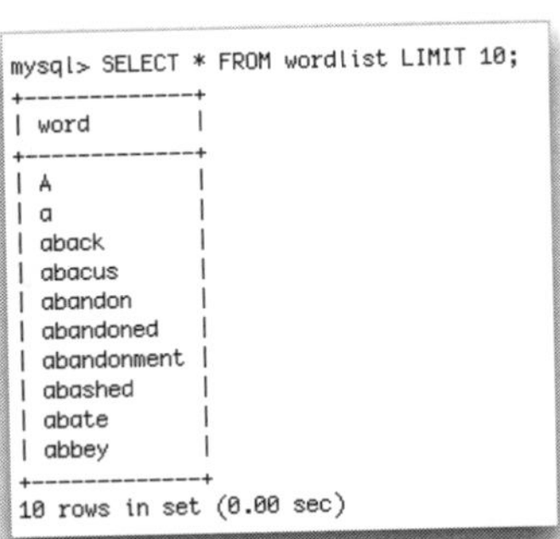

12. The most likely thing to go wrong is if the format of the word list is different from that included in `12dicts-4.0.zip`. The last two lines of the command in step 9 tell MySQL that each field and each line is terminated by a carriage return and new line, which is standard for Windows text files. Unix text files do not use a carriage return, so if you find your table has lots of blank lines in it, delete the contents and repeat the command in step 9 without `\r`. To delete the contents of the table without destroying the table structure itself, use the following command:

```
DELETE FROM wordlist;
```

This removes every single record in a table. Like the DROP DATABASE command, it doesn't question the wisdom of your request. It just deletes everything, with no way of getting it back. This is very useful when you really mean it, but not if you intend to get rid of just one record. I'll show you how to do selective deletes in Chapter 10.

Loading data from an external file

The ability to load data directly from a file is extremely useful. In addition to working from a simple text file, as you just did in the last exercise, you can export data from other databases or spreadsheets and load them rapidly into MySQL. Here is the general syntax for `LOAD DATA INFILE`:

```
LOAD DATA [LOW_PRIORITY | CONCURRENT] [LOCAL] INFILE 'file_name.txt'
[REPLACE | IGNORE]
INTO TABLE tbl_name
[FIELDS
  [TERMINATED BY '\t']
  [[OPTIONALLY] ENCLOSED BY '']
  [ESCAPED BY '\\' ]
  ]
[LINES
  [STARTING BY '']
  [TERMINATED BY '\n']
  ]
[IGNORE number LINES]
[(col_name,...)]
```

If you have never used SQL before, that will probably make very little sense to you. Reading SQL syntax takes a little getting used to, so let's start by explaining the conventions.

Reading SQL syntax

To make it easier to look up anything you're unsure about, the conventions used in this book are the same as in the MySQL online documentation at `http://dev.mysql.com/doc/mysql/en/index.html`.

- Everything in uppercase represents a SQL command. When building commands, you can use either uppercase or lowercase. The uppercase convention simply makes it easier to recognize keywords.
- Anything in square brackets ([ ]) is optional.
- Items separated by a single upright bar or pipe (|) are alternatives. When they are enclosed in square brackets, you may choose one or none. When they are enclosed in curly braces ({ }), you *must* choose one.
- Text in constant-width font surrounded by quotes (for instance, `'.txt'`) is used for filenames and path names. Substitute the appropriate name, and enclose it in quotes.
- Text in constant-width italics (for instance, *`file_name`*) indicates variable input for which you need to substitute a value of your own choosing.
- An ellipsis (`...`) can mean either that a longer piece of code has been omitted for readability or that the preceding element can be repeated.

See `http://dev.mysql.com/doc/mysql/en/Manual_conventions.html` for the full list of typographic conventions used in describing MySQL syntax.

The MySQL online documentation is superb, and you should develop a habit of exploring it. Perhaps its only real drawback is that it is so vast, but it is fully searchable and annotated with user comments. What's more, if English isn't your best language, there are links on every page of the documentation to versions in French, German, Japanese, Portuguese, and Russian, although some of these are not as extensive as the English one. There is also a copy of the MySQL documentation in the `docs` *subfolder of the main* `mysql` *folder on your hard drive (*`/usr/local/mysql` *on a Mac), but it's contained in a single HTML page nearly 4MB in size (there's a text version, but it's not much smaller). Unless you are on a slow Internet connection, the online documentation is easier to use and likely to be more up to date.*

Using LOAD DATA INFILE

Now that you know the syntax conventions, let's go through LOAD DATA INFILE section by section to see how it works.

```
LOAD DATA [LOW_PRIORITY | CONCURRENT] [LOCAL] INFILE 'file_name.txt'
```

LOAD DATA is the first part of the SQL command. It's not in square brackets, so it is required. The next part is in square brackets, so it is optional. It offers a choice of LOW_PRIORITY and CONCURRENT. These SQL commands determine the priority to be given to LOAD DATA INFILE. As you might expect, the first option waits until no one else is using the table before loading the new data.

LOCAL is also in square brackets, so it is an optional condition that tells MySQL how to treat the file. Its use can be difficult to grasp, but the simple rule is to try LOAD DATA INFILE without LOCAL. If that doesn't work, edit the command to include LOCAL. (The details of LOCAL are complex, but you can find a full description at the URL given at the end of this section.)

The final part of the first line is straightforward: the keyword INFILE is followed by the name of the file in quotes. The file *must* be a text file.

The next line sets another optional condition:

```
[REPLACE | IGNORE]
```

REPLACE tells MySQL to replace existing records that have the same unique identifier or primary key as data in the input file. IGNORE skips such duplicates. You will cover primary keys in Chapter 8.

The third line specifies which table the data is to be loaded into. The table must exist before the command is executed.

```
INTO TABLE tbl_name
```

The next few lines are optional, but contain some of the most important information in the command:

```
[FIELDS
  [TERMINATED BY '\t']
  [[OPTIONALLY] ENCLOSED BY '']
  [ESCAPED BY '\\' ]
  ]
```

These commands tell MySQL how to recognize the fields in the text file. If you don't specify any of these options, the defaults are fields terminated by a tab character, with no enclosing characters (such as quotes), and using a backslash to escape any special characters. When loading the data from `3esl.txt`, you used `FIELDS TERMINATED BY '\r\n'` to indicate that each field ended with a carriage return and new line (the standard way a Windows text file treats a new line). The value of each option must be a string, enclosed in quotes, and it can include any of the special characters in Table 6-1.

Table 6-1. Special characters to specify field and line options in `LOAD DATA INFILE`

Character	Meaning
\0	ASCII 0 (not a zero-valued byte)
\b	Backspace
\n	New line (linefeed)
\r	Carriage return
\s	Space (blank character)
\t	Tab
\'	Single quote
\"	Double quote
\\	Backslash

`OPTIONALLY ENCLOSED BY` is a particularly useful option. You can specify fields as being optionally enclosed in double quotes, and MySQL will strip any quotes as it loads the data into your table. If you omit the keyword `OPTIONALLY`, each field *must* be enclosed in the characters specified.

The next section specifies how each line of the text file is formatted.

```
[LINES
  [STARTING BY '']
  [TERMINATED BY '\n']
  ]
```

The `STARTING BY` option allows you to specify a string sequence that you want removed from the beginning of each line. It must be a constant sequence. You cannot, for example, specify that any date be cut off (although you could handle that by inserting the date into the table and then dropping the date column—as long as the date is in a separate field of its own).

The penultimate option, `[IGNORE` *`number`* `LINES]`, can be used to skip a specified number of lines at the beginning of the file. You might need to do this if the first lines contain header material or anything else that you don't want inserted into the table.

The final option, `[(`*`col_name,...`*`)]`, allows you to specify the names of the columns that each field should be entered into. This should be presented as a comma-delimited list in parentheses. In the case of the word list, you could add `(word)` at the end of the SQL command, but this is unnecessary because there is only one column and only one field per line. You would need to use this option, however, if your file contained fewer fields than the number of columns in the table. You would also need it if the fields and table columns were in a different order from the text file.

This is only a brief outline of `LOAD DATA INFILE`. It's not the only method of inserting data into MySQL from an external file, but it's a very versatile command, and it's used mainly with data sources that haven't been formatted specifically for MySQL. A much fuller description with examples can be found in the MySQL documentation at `http://dev.mysql.com/doc/mysql/en/LOAD_DATA.html`.

Using MySQL with a graphical interface

Although working with MySQL Monitor at the command line gives you a really solid grasp of SQL commands, it's rather like a cold bath on a frosty morning—good for the soul, maybe, but not exactly a bundle of laughs. There are several graphical interfaces available for MySQL, which can help speed up the construction and design of databases and database tables. Before moving on to the next chapter and integrating the word list with the Hangman game, let's take a look at three of the best available graphical interfaces. The first two, phpMyAdmin and MySQL Administrator, run on both Windows and Mac OS X. MySQL Query Browser isn't currently available for the Mac.

phpMyAdmin: A golden oldie

As the name suggests, phpMyAdmin is a PHP-based administrative system for MySQL. It was originally created by Tobias Ratschiller as far back as 1998 (medieval history in Internet terms), and it is still actively maintained and developed by an enthusiastic and talented team of volunteers. It works on Windows, Mac OS X, and Linux, and it supports all versions of MySQL from 3.23.32 to 5.0. At the time of this writing, there is no support for MySQL 5.1, but that will no doubt be added as soon as 5.1 comes closer to maturity. phpMyAdmin is provided by a lot of hosting companies as the preferred means of administering databases, so it is well worth getting to know how to use it. Another point in favor of phpMyAdmin is that it works in 47 languages, from Afrikaans to Ukrainian, with Chinese, French, Japanese, Latvian, Spanish, and Thai in between. Oh yes, and did I mention it works in English, too?

Obtaining and installing phpMyAdmin

phpMyAdmin is distributed under the GNU GPL. It is open source software and is free, although the project also accepts donations to help support development. You will use it in later chapters, so I suggest you go ahead and install it now.

1. Go to the project's website at www.phpmyadmin.net and download the latest stable version (2.6.0-pl3 at the time of this writing). The version number of phpMyAdmin is frequently followed by "pl" and a number. The "pl" stands for **patch level** and indicates a fix for a bug or security problem. Like most open source projects, fixes are issued as soon as possible, rather than waiting for the next version release. The files can be downloaded in three types of compressed file: BZIP2, GZIP, and ZIP. Choose whichever format you have the decompression software for. In the case of Windows users, this is most likely to be ZIP (2.3MB). Mac OS X users should be able to choose any format. BZIP2 is the smallest download (1.3MB).
2. Unzip the downloaded file. It will extract the contents to a folder called `phpMyAdmin-x.x.x`, where `x` represents the version number.
3. Highlight the folder icon and cut it to your computer's clipboard. Paste it inside the document root of your web server. If you are on Windows and followed the instructions in Chapter 1, this will be `C:\htdocs`. On Mac OS X, it will be `Macintosh HD:Users:`*`username`*`:Sites` (where *`username`* is the long version of your Mac username).
4. Rename the folder you have just pasted, and call it `phpMyAdmin`.
5. Open the `phpMyAdmin` folder, and locate the file `config.inc.php`. Open this file in a text editor or whichever program you've been using to create your PHP files. (If you're on Windows and grinding out your scripts the "hard" way with Notepad, opening this file will probably blow your mind, because it doesn't contain Windows carriage returns. Use WordPad instead, and save your sanity for another day. Alternatively, use one of the text editors with line numbers suggested in the book's Introduction.)
6. Scroll down until you find the following line (it should be on or around line 39):

   ```
   $cfg['PmaAbsoluteUri'] = '';
   ```

   Amend this line so that the full URL of your phpMyAdmin folder is assigned to the variable. On Windows, this will be

   ```
   $cfg['PmaAbsoluteUri'] = 'http://localhost/phpMyAdmin/';
   ```

   On Mac OS X, it will be

   ```
   $cfg['PmaAbsoluteUri'] = 'http://localhost/~username/phpMyAdmin/';
   ```

   On both systems, make sure you include the trailing slash at the end of the URL.
7. Next, scroll down until you find the following line (around line 73):

   ```
   $cfg['Servers'][$i]['extension']     = 'mysql';
   ```

By the time you are reading this, the default value for this setting may have changed to `mysqli`. Make sure it has the correct value for the version of MySQL you are running, and change it if necessary:

- **MySQL 3.23.*x* to MySQL 4.1.1**: `mysql`
- **MySQL 4.1.2 and above**: `mysqli`

8. Continue scrolling down until you find the following lines. They should be around line 83 (the PHP comments in the original file have been omitted here for readability).

```
$cfg['Servers'][$i]['auth_type']      = 'config';
$cfg['Servers'][$i]['user']           = 'root';
$cfg['Servers'][$i]['password']       = '';
```

   If you are the only person who uses your computer, type your MySQL root password between the empty quotes on the third of these lines. This will enable anyone with access to a browser on your computer to have full root control over your MySQL databases, so exercise caution before choosing this option.

9. If you prefer to use a more secure method, change the three lines in the previous step as follows:

```
$cfg['Servers'][$i]['auth_type']      = 'http';
$cfg['Servers'][$i]['user']           = '';
$cfg['Servers'][$i]['password']       = '';
```

   This way, you will be prompted for a username and password each time you try to access phpMyAdmin.

10. Save `config.inc.php`. (If you're using WordPad, selecting File ➤ Save will save the file in the correct format as plain text. Do *not* save as a rich text file.) Open a browser, and enter http://localhost/phpMyAdmin in the address bar (on a Mac, use http://localhost/~*username*/phpMyAdmin). Enter your access details, if prompted, and you should see the phpMyAdmin welcome screen, as shown in Figure 6-4.

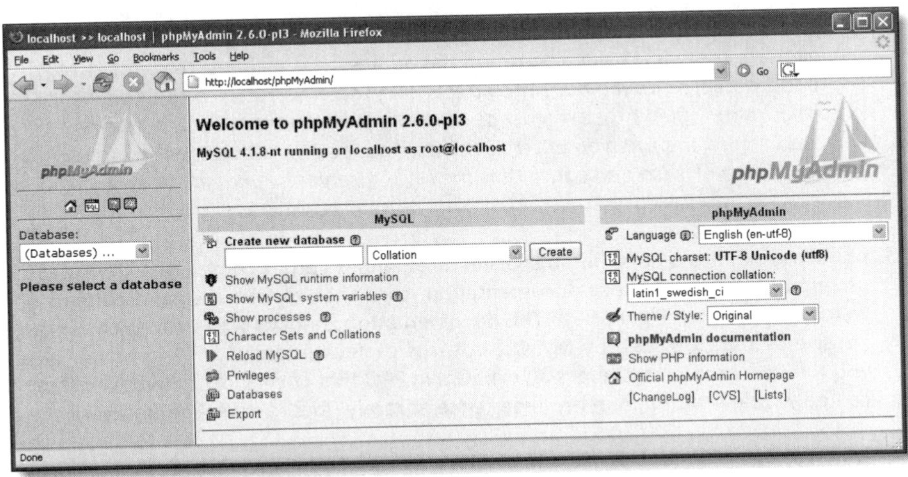

Figure 6-4. phpMyAdmin is a very user-friendly and stable graphical interface to MySQL.

11. If you are using MySQL 4.1.8 or above, a very important setting on this front page is the third item down in the right-hand column: MySQL connection collation. This determines the character encoding of connections to MySQL, which needs to match the character set used in your database tables.

- **Windows users**: If you installed the Windows Essentials version of MySQL and chose Standard Character Set in the configuration wizard, the setting in the drop-down menu should be latin1_swedish_ci, as shown in Figure 6-4. If the setting is different, activate the drop-down menu and reset it as shown.
- **Mac OS X users**: If you installed the standard MySQL PKG, the setting is likely to be utf8_general_ci. Activate the drop-down menu, and reset it to latin1_swedish_ci, as shown in Figure 6-4.

The number of options in the drop-down menu is huge, but it's in alphabetical order, so it shouldn't be difficult to find the right one. Collation is a new feature in MySQL 4.1. It's complex subject that most developers need never bother about except when first setting everything up, but it mainly affects the order in which records are sorted. Surprising though it may seem, the default for English is `latin1_swedish_ci`. (Not so surprising when you realize MySQL is based in Sweden, and that Swedish and English share the same sort order.) This subject is explained briefly in Chapter 8 and in greater detail in Appendix D for anyone working with languages other than English.

12. If you opted for the `http` login method in step 9, you will find two more options listed at the bottom of the MySQL section of the front page, just beneath Export (see the screenshot). These are self-explanatory: they allow you to change your login password and to log out of phpMyAdmin once you have finished. The logout process simply presents you with the login dialog box again. If you click Cancel, you can verify you have been logged out, because you should see a message saying Wrong username/password. Access denied.

If phpMyAdmin fails to load correctly, check that you have entered the correct web address, and not just the file path, in step 6. Because phpMyAdmin runs on PHP, it needs to be correctly parsed through the web server. Also make sure there is a trailing slash on the address. If it still fails to display, it probably means you did not set up `DirectoryIndex` correctly in the Apache configuration file, `httpd.conf`, as described in Chapter 1. Try adding `index.php` to the URL you enter in the browser address bar (but not to the code in step 6). Also make sure that the MySQL server is running.

13. phpMyAdmin has a huge number of features, and it comes complete with its own documentation. To access that documentation, click the link in right-hand column of the welcome page (see Figure 6-4). The documentation is not as well written or as comprehensive as that provided by MySQL, but it is perfectly adequate for most purposes. If you run into problems, there is an exhaustive FAQ that covers just about everything that can go wrong—although in my experience, it rarely does. phpMyAdmin is very stable.

14. I will show you how to use phpMyAdmin in Chapter 8, but just take a quick look at some of its features now. Click the drop-down menu on the left side of the page to reveal the list of databases, as shown in the image to the right. You will probably have only two databases listed: mysql and phpflash. The number alongside each database indicates how many tables it contains. Click phpflash to select it.

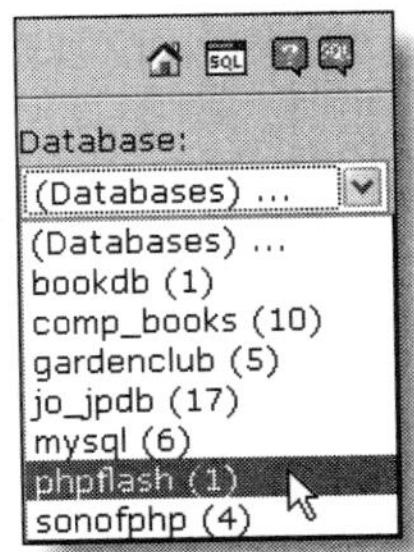

15. A screen containing various details about the phpflash database should display. Do not worry if you get a doom-laden error message like that shown at the bottom of Figure 6-5. It merely tells you that certain advanced features have not been enabled. They are not required for this book, but details of how to enable them can be found in the phpMyAdmin documentation.

    Move your mouse pointer over various parts of the screen, and tooltips will tell you what each icon represents. Find the Browse and Search icons, and explore the pages they bring up. A lot of the screens and menus will probably mean very little to you at this stage, but they will give you a good feel for some of the vocabulary of MySQL and SQL in general.

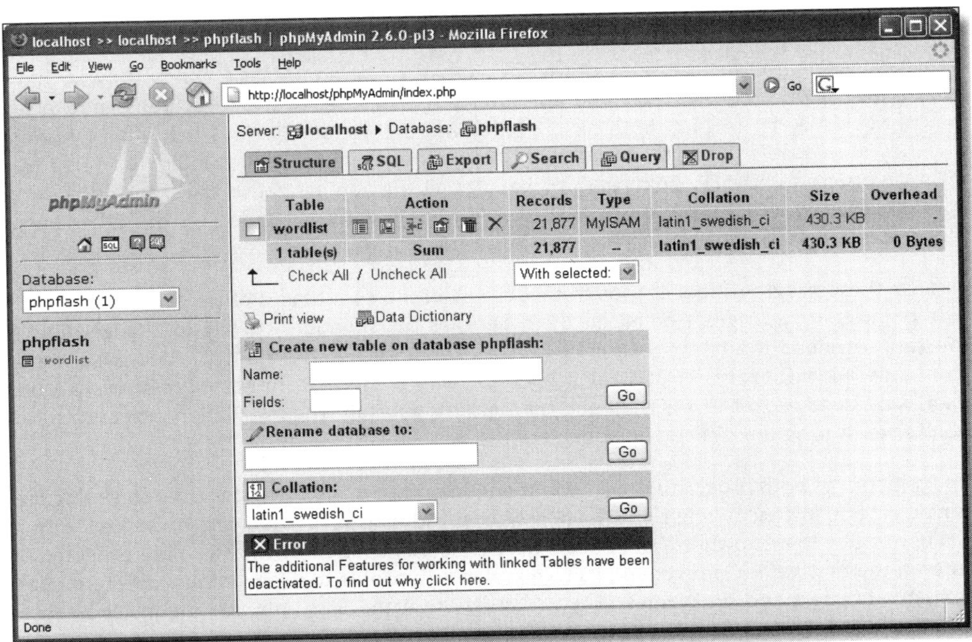

Figure 6-5. phpMyAdmin enables you to interact with databases through a tabbed interface and icons.

16. While you're in the mood for experimentation, click the Drop tab (it's at the top right of Figure 6-5). phpMyAdmin takes a more cautious attitude than MySQL Monitor and warns you of the dire consequences of your action, as this dialog box shows.

17. Don't worry about making a mistake. As you saw earlier in the chapter, it takes less than a second for `LOAD DATA INFILE` to insert the contents of the word list (although one person reported an outrageously slow 3.7 seconds when testing the code for this book!). If you do make a mess of things, open MySQL Monitor again, delete the contents of the table, and rebuild the database.

MySQL Administrator and MySQL Query Browser: Smart new kids on the block

MySQL Administrator first made an appearance as an alpha release in January 2004, and the first production version was released eight months later. A companion program called MySQL Query Browser was also undergoing final testing at the end of 2004. Both come from the same organization as MySQL itself, and they are released under the same combined license—free for anyone working under the GPL open source rules, but a commercial version is available for organizations or individuals who fall outside that category (see `www.mysql.com/products` for the most up-to-date information).

Frankly speaking, the first versions of MySQL Administrator and MySQL Query Browser have more a feel of what's likely to come in the future than of finished products. That's not to say they're not slick—far from it. Both have a much more polished interface than phpMyAdmin, and they are capable of far more, although they suffer from the disadvantage of being two separate programs. MySQL Administrator handles all the administrative tasks, such as setting up new users, granting permissions, and so on. MySQL Query Browser, on the other hand, allows you to test SQL queries and to manipulate data in your databases.

Because these programs feel as though they're still in the early stages of development, there's little point going into great detail on them here, as the situation is likely to change rapidly. You can download the latest version of MySQL Administrator from `http://dev.mysql.com/downloads/administrator` (6.3MB) and MySQL Query Browser from `http://dev.mysql.com/downloads/query-browser` (4.6MB), and try them for yourself. The installation process puts an icon for each program directly on your desktop.

One criticism of both programs is the lack of documentation and the potentially confusing terminology. For instance, when you launch MySQL Administrator, you are presented with a dialog box like that shown in Figure 6-6. There is no explanation of what you are expected to enter in the first field (Connection). Its role is akin to a profile that remembers different combinations of users and hostnames, so you can ignore it the first time you log in (and subsequently, too, unless you need to set up different user profiles). Simply fill in the Username, Password, and Hostname fields (localhost, unless you're connecting to a remote server across a network), and click OK. The Port field defaults to 3306, which is the MySQL default.

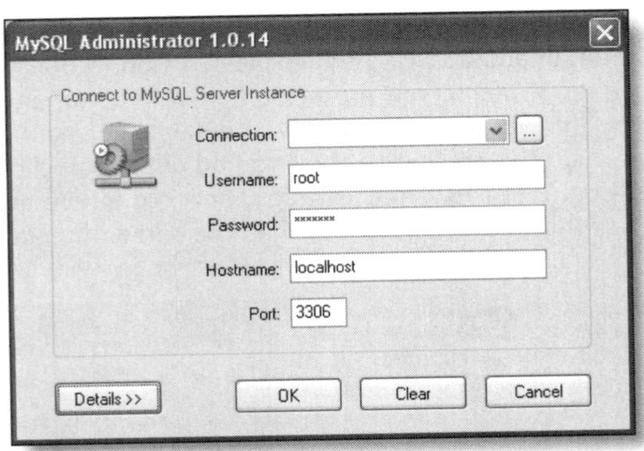

Figure 6-6. Logging on to MySQL Administrator

Once you have logged in, you are presented with all the main administrative areas grouped together in a sidebar on the left side of the screen (as shown in Figure 6-7). Select one of the topics from the sidebar, and the main window changes to show all the various options, usually in a tabbed interface. One of the main problems is that MySQL is so rich in features, the mass of options available is likely to overwhelm a beginner, thereby possibly defeating the purpose of the user-friendly interface. For instance, it probably takes the average user only a few minutes to work out how to get phpMyAdmin to display the contents of a database table. Table definitions in MySQL Administrator are hidden away in the confusingly named Catalogs section, and there is no obvious way to browse the records in a table other than launching MySQL Monitor from within the graphical interface or switching to MySQL Query Browser.

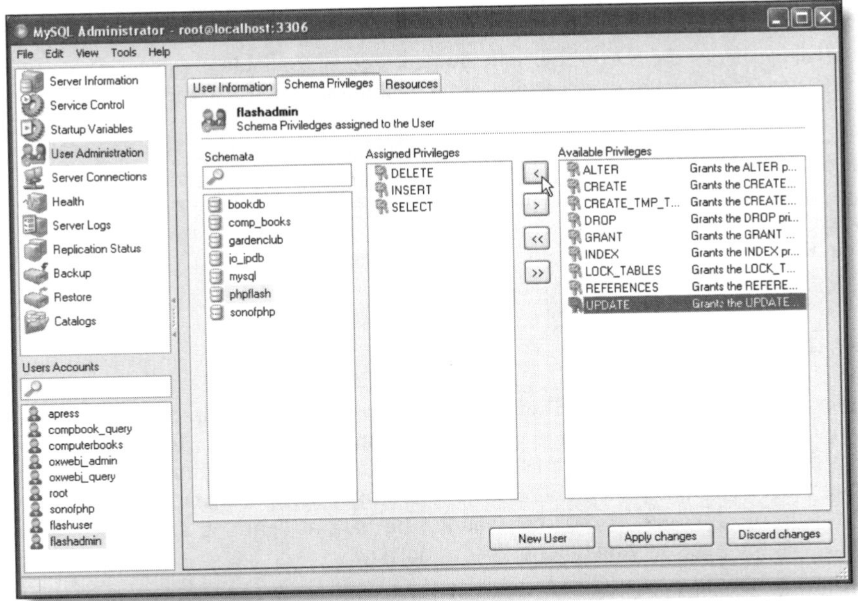

Figure 6-7. MySQL Administrator organizes just about every conceivable task in a clean, easy-to-use interface.

The login process in the gamma release of MySQL Query Browser is even less user-friendly than MySQL Administrator. In addition to the unexplained Connection field, there is another called Schema. If you leave it blank, you are presented with a warning message (shown in Figure 6-8) that tells you that you haven't specified a default schema, but it tells you neither what the expression means in this context nor how to find out. If you click OK, you simply end up back at the login dialog. Eventually, in frustration, I clicked Ignore and was let straight in. Schema, it turns out, is nothing more mysterious than the name of an individual database.

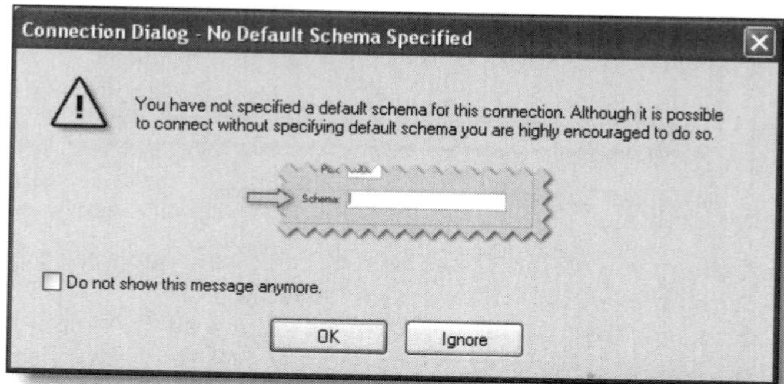

Figure 6-8. Less-than-intuitive terminology makes logging into MySQL Query Browser unnecessarily difficult.

In spite of these criticisms, MySQL Administrator and MySQL Query Browser definitely seem worth keeping an eye on. The developers clearly have the inside track on MySQL's current and future features. Figure 6-7 shows the very intuitive way you set up permissions for a database user in MySQL Administrator. All databases on the server are displayed in the second column. After selecting an individual database, all it takes is a simple point-and-click operation to assign privileges from the list on the right. You can see all available privileges at a glance, and there's no danger of mistyping or leaving out a vital punctuation mark from a SQL query.

MySQL Query Browser also offers some nice features, such as being able to recall previous queries and to display the results in different tabs, rather like those in the Firefox or Safari browser. In fact, the whole idea is to emulate the experience of working with a browser. Once the rough edges are smoothed out, it may be worth switching to these new programs, but at the time of this writing, phpMyAdmin still has the edge.

Looking ahead

By teaming up PHP with MySQL (or indeed any database), you open up completely new possibilities for your Flash movies. Data is no longer confined to the preprogrammed contents of SWF files or simple text files. You can store many thousands of records in a database, use PHP to extract those you want at a particular time, and display them or manipulate them further in your Flash movie. PHP and MySQL can handle the data at lightning speed. If only humans could learn all the necessary techniques just as quickly!

In the coming chapters, I'll show you all the basic SQL commands you need to work with database queries, as well as offer guidance on basic database design. The more you work with databases, the more you'll come to appreciate that learning the SQL commands is very much the easy part. Getting the structure of the database right can be much more difficult and time consuming.

In the next chapter, you'll build the Hangman Flash movie and link it to the word list in the MySQL database. You'll also see how SQLite compares with MySQL. On the PHP side, you'll take an important leap into working with classes: the basis of OOP with PHP. Oh, and by the way, you'll be delighted to know that there's no more downloading or installing. From here on, it's building your knowledge of PHP and MySQL, and hands-on development all the way.

Chapter 7

PLAYING WITH WORDS

What this chapter covers:

- Building the Hangman Flash movie
- Linking the Flash movie to the MySQL database through PHP
- Building and using classes in PHP 5
- Using the Flash `SharedObject` to keep track of scores
- Using `mail()` to alert you automatically to database problems
- Using SQLite as an alternative database

Now for a bit of (semiserious) fun. All the Flash applications in the book so far have been aimed at practical solutions to real problems. So I thought it would make a welcome change to work with a Flash game. Although games are intended to be fun, they're a serious business for a lot of Flash developers. But even if you're not into game development, they teach you a lot of useful techniques that you can apply in other contexts.

As explained in the previous chapter, the game you'll be working with originally appeared in another friends of ED book, *Foundation ActionScript for Flash MX 2004* by Sham Bhangal. I chose an existing game for two reasons: to show you how server-side technology can improve an already high-quality Flash game, and to focus more on PHP and databases, rather than on the intricacies of the Flash movie itself.

For the benefit of those who don't have the other book, I'll briefly outline how to build the game and then get down to the real business: querying the MySQL database, filtering the results, and feeding the results back to the Flash movie. In the process, you'll learn about building classes and using OOP techniques in PHP 5. Then you'll explore the Flash `SharedObject`, a powerful way to store persistent data, so that a movie remembers details about a user even between visits. I'll close out the chapter by showing you SQLite, an alternative database that comes bundled with PHP 5. In spite of its name, SQLite is far from lightweight, and it's certainly worth consideration for some projects.

Building the game's graphical elements

Exactly who came up with the idea of Hangman as a children's game is a mystery. It's been around for a long time—certainly well before the days of computers—and it has been played with glee by generations of schoolchildren, in spite of the gruesome outcome if the player fails to guess the word in time. (Knowing what little monsters children can sometimes be, perhaps that's the reason for its enduring popularity.) Traditionally, it's played on paper, with one player thinking of a word and challenging the other to guess it one letter at a time. The player who issues the challenge marks out on the paper a number of blank spaces, indicating how many letters the word consists of. If the other player guesses a letter correctly, the appropriate blank is filled in (or several, if the same letter occurs more than once in the word). Each wrong guess results in a line being drawn on the paper, first building a gallows, and then a stick man with his head in the noose. After sufficient wrong guesses, the game comes to a grisly end.

It's a children's game, so the graphical elements have a deliberate childlike innocence. If you would like to see it in action before building it yourself, you can try it out online and pit your wits against the database at `http://computerbookshelf.com/php5flash/hangman.html`.

As with all the projects in this book, I have created files showing the graphical elements and code at various stages of development. If you would prefer to concentrate on creating the back-end of the game and linking it to the database, skip to the next section, "Using PHP to communicate with the database," and use `hangman02.fla`*, which contains all the graphical elements ready for you to start scripting the main part of the application. For all the static text, I used a font called Bradley Hand ITC. Since it may not be available on your computer, all the text elements have been converted to graphic symbols in the download files.*

If you have already built the Hangman game, you can use your original file. The ActionScript differs considerably, but the graphical elements are the same. The movie clip to display the score will be created and added later in the chapter.

The hanging man movie clip

I showed you what the game looks like in the previous chapter, so let's get straight down to business. The most complex part brings together the scenery and the gruesome process of stringing up your hapless victim.

1. Create a new Flash document, and call it `hangman.fla`. Alternatively, use `hangman01.fla` from the download files, which already contains many of the graphic symbols in the Library, in addition to all the static text.

2. Press *Ctrl+F8/⌘+F8* and create a movie clip called hanging man. Create four layers inside the movie clip: labels, flower, hangman, and background.

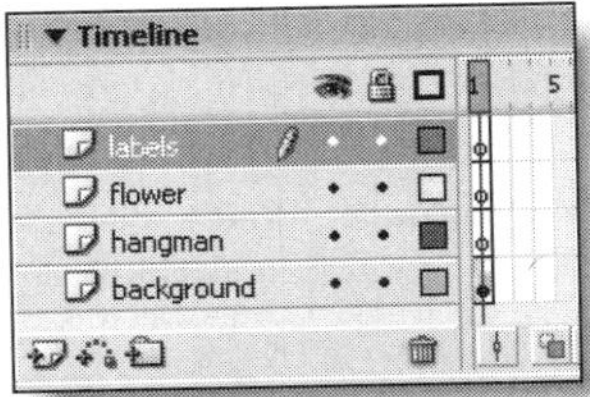

3. Select the background layer and insert two graphic symbols: one for the sun and the other for the grass. (Import the symbols from the Library of download file, if you don't want to go through the tedious process of drawing every blade of grass.) The scenery is needed throughout the movie clip, so select frame 19 of the background layer and press *F5* to insert a frame.

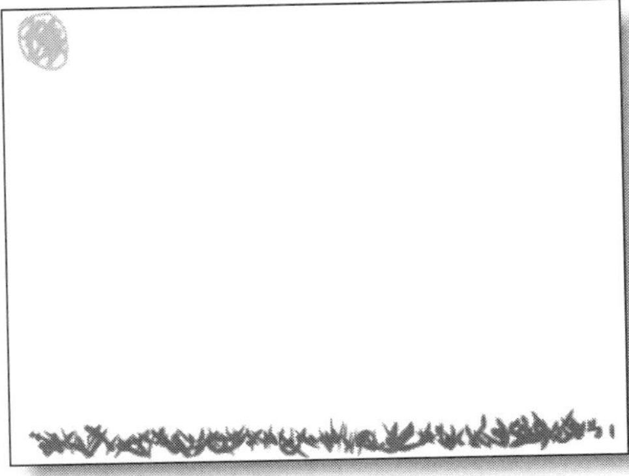

4. Select frame 1 on the labels layer and give it a frame label of play. Insert two keyframes at frames 10 and 15, and an ordinary frame (*F5*) at frame 19. Name the keyframes lose and win, as shown here.

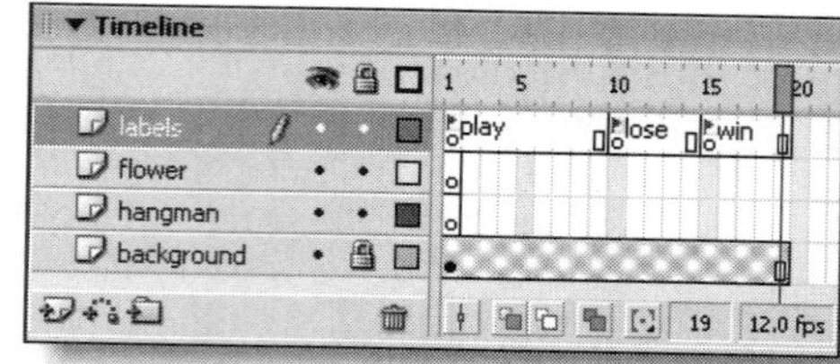

5. Now for the grisly bit. Select frame 19 of the hangman layer and press *F5* to enter a frame. The layer should now be the same length as the background and labels layers. Insert a keyframe (*F6*) on frame 2 of the hangman layer, and draw a thick, brown line on top of the grass. Continue inserting keyframes on every frame up to and including frame 10. On each frame, add another part of the gallows. By frame 7, you should have a gallows complete with a noose.

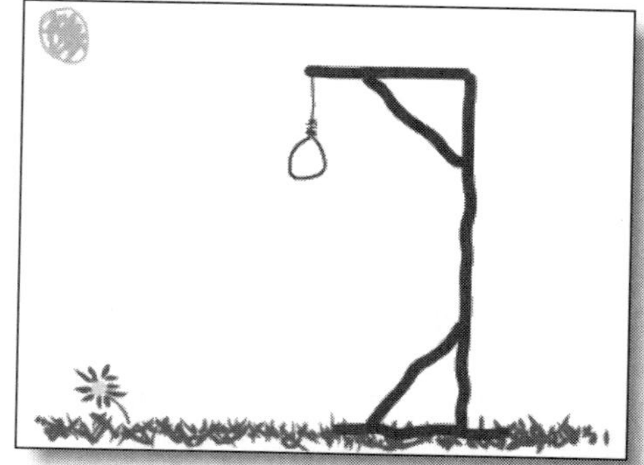

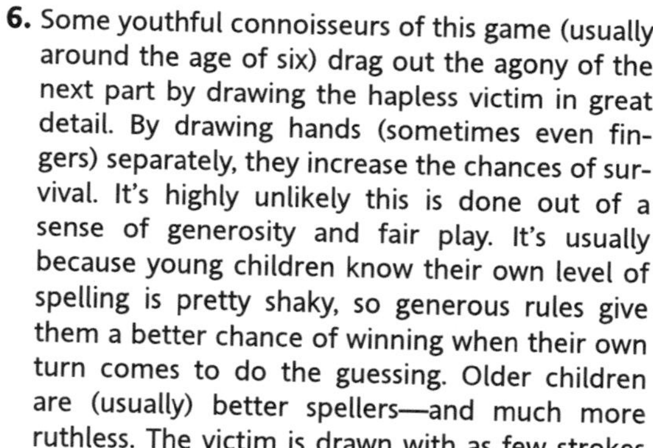

6. Some youthful connoisseurs of this game (usually around the age of six) drag out the agony of the next part by drawing the hapless victim in great detail. By drawing hands (sometimes even fingers) separately, they increase the chances of survival. It's highly unlikely this is done out of a sense of generosity and fair play. It's usually because young children know their own level of spelling is pretty shaky, so generous rules give them a better chance of winning when their own turn comes to do the guessing. Older children are (usually) better spellers—and much more ruthless. The victim is drawn with as few strokes as possible. That's the way I'm going to do it. Draw the head on frame 8 and add the upper part of the body on frame 9, so that by frame 10, it's all over.

7. Of course, the idea of the game is that it should never get that far. Guess all the letters of the word correctly, and there's a much jollier outcome. Insert a keyframe on frame 15 of the hangman layer, sweep away the gallows, and give the victim his well-earned freedom.

8. For a nice little touch to brighten things up, plant a flower in the grass. Select frame 1 of the flower layer, and lock all the other layers. Draw a simple flower as shown. Once you've planted a suitably pretty flower, press *CTRL+A/⌘+A* to select it. Assuming you've correctly locked all other layers, only the flower becomes selected. Then press *F8* to make your flower a graphic symbol called flower. Unlock all the other layers when you've finished. Or if you're feeling lazy, just grab the flower that's already in the Library.

9. Insert a keyframe on frame 15 of the flower layer, and drag the flower so that it looks as though it's in the hand of our champion speller—an artistic, but understated symbol for his regained freedom. (One of those little pieces of information that was lost in the editing of Sham's original book. So now you know.) Finally, insert a blank frame (*F5*) on frame 19 of the flower layer so that it's the same length as the other layers.

10. The final timeline for the hanging man movie clip should look like this.

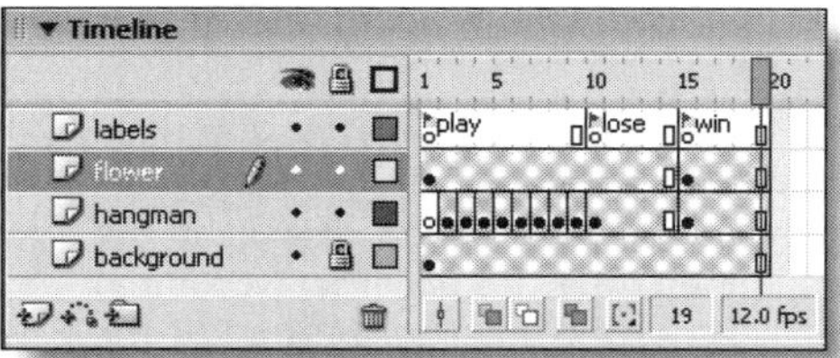

Building the interface movie clip

This is where the mystery word is displayed, first as a series of question marks, and then as individual letters with each correct guess. It's also where you enter each letter you want to try. You'll be pleased to know that it's much simpler to build than the hanging man.

1. Close the hanging man movie clip, and create a new movie clip symbol called interface in `hangman.fla`. Everything in the interface movie clip goes on the first frame of Layer 1.
2. There are just four things on the stage:
   - A dynamic text field with an instance name of display_txt. It should have no border and be just a single line field. I have chosen Trebuchet MS as the font, as it is available on most PCs and Macs. You may want to add alternative font styling in the ActionScript later.
   - A static text field that reads guess a letter.
   - An input text field with an instance name of input_txt. It should have a border (so the player knows where to enter the text) and be single line. Input text does not pick up a font style unless you embed it or use ActionScript for styling. For simplicity's sake, I have used the generic Flash _sans.
   - A button labeled enter with an instance name of enter_btn.

Lay out the items as shown here:

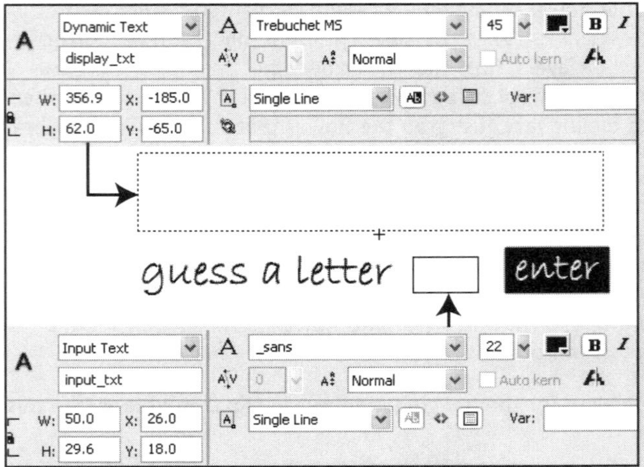

3. Players should be able to enter only one letter at a time, and you want to prevent them from entering invalid characters, such as numbers or punctuation. Highlight the input text field, and in the Properties panel set Maximum characters to 1. Then click the Character button. In the dialog box that opens, select the radio button for Specify Ranges and highlight Lowercase, as shown here. If anyone attempts to enter anything other than lowercase letters, the input text field will remain blank. You don't need to make any allowances for hyphens or other punctuation, because they will be automatically inserted by the script for any words that contain them. (You want the game to be challenging, but not impossible!)

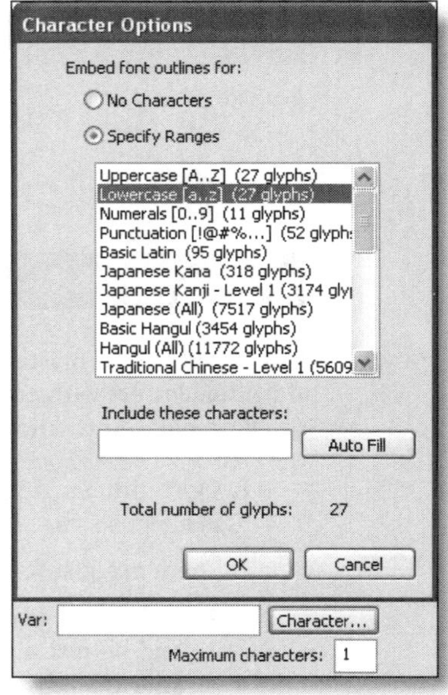

Putting it all together

The main movie timeline contains just one frame and two layers: movie (for the graphical elements) and actions (for the ActionScript).

1. In the main timeline of `hangman.fla`, insert a second layer called actions, and rename Layer 1 as movie. Make sure the actions layer is above the movie layer, and lock it to prevent placing any graphic elements on it by mistake.

2. Select the movie layer and drag instances of the hanging man and interface movie clips onto the stage. Name them hangman_mc and interface_mc, respectively. Lay them out as shown here. As you can see from the image, the word hangman appears just beneath the sun. It is simply a graphic symbol of static text. The play game to the right of the interface movie clip is a button symbol with an instance name of playGame_btn. If you're wondering why there's a gap to the left of the interface movie clip, that's where the score will be displayed when you add that feature later in the chapter. If you need to check that you have everything right, compare your file with `hangman02.fla`.

Using PHP to communicate with the database

In the original Flash version of the Hangman game, the list from which words were selected was hard-coded into the ActionScript. This time, you are going to get the words from the word list table created in the previous chapter. So, you need to put `hangman.fla` to one side while I show you how to make a suitable selection with PHP. Instead of just 20 words, the idea is to pull 250 words at random from the 21,000 or so in the MySQL database.

> *If you have decided that you want to experiment with SQLite first, all the instructions are at the end of this chapter in the section "SQLite: An alternative database system." However, I recommend you come back later and study this part of the chapter to learn about classes and OOP in PHP 5.*

Think back to the last chapter and how you worked with MySQL Monitor to display the first ten entries in the word list. There were four basic steps:

1. Log on to MySQL as a named user.
2. Enter the user's password.
3. Choose the correct database.
4. Execute a SQL query.

When using PHP to communicate with MySQL, you go through the same process, but instead of the results being displayed onscreen, you have to store them in a variable. Once the results have been captured, you can manipulate them with all the PHP functions and techniques you learned in the first half of the book. As mentioned in the last chapter, the way of doing this depends on two factors: which version of PHP you are using and which version of MySQL. In a perfect world, all hosting companies would have switched to PHP 5 and at least MySQL 4.1 by the time you read this, so I could simply show you that method. Unfortunately, many hosting companies are very slow to change over, so I need to provide you with a solution that will work whatever your setup.

A touch of class to emulate mysqli on all setups

Fans of the British TV comedy series *Blackadder* will know that whenever Baldrick says he has "a cunning plan," it's doomed to utter failure. You'll be pleased to know, therefore, that Baldrick had absolutely nothing to do with this cunning plan to make the transition between the different combinations of PHP and MySQL versions as painless as possible.

Earlier versions of PHP communicated with MySQL through a series of built-in functions, and these are still available for the sake of backward compatibility. The Improved MySQL (`mysqli`) extension, which is new to PHP 5, offers a choice: new versions of the old functions or an object-oriented (OO) interface. The first route makes the conversion process easier for anyone used to the traditional procedural functions, but for anyone with an ActionScript background, the concepts of objects, methods, and properties should already be familiar, so the OO interface is a more natural choice. The other main advantage of using the `mysqli` OO interface is that it involves less code. Even if you already have previous experience with PHP's traditional MySQL functions, I suggest you take this opportunity to switch over to the new OO interface. Before I describe how my plan works, you need to check your current setup and understand how the new `mysqli` OO interface works. You also need to know a little about the use of classes and objects.

Understanding classes and objects

Object-oriented programming (**OOP**) is one of the biggest buzzwords in computer programming. The idea is both simple and baffling to beginners. The classic example that's usually given is of a motor car. A car is an object that we're all familiar with, but cars come in many different shapes, sizes, and colors. You can have a red car or a blue car. They're different, but they're both still cars. In OOP terms, they belong to the same **class** of object. The color of a car is a **property** that can be changed without changing the fundamental nature of the object. Cars can also do things, such as start, stop, accelerate—even crash. In OOP terms, an action that an object can perform is known as a **method**. As long as your car is well maintained—and you're a qualified driver—you don't need to know a thing about the workings of the internal combustion engine to get in the driver's seat and take off. In OOP terms, everything is **encapsulated** or hidden from view. It just works, and that's all you need to know, unless, of course, you're a motor mechanic.

That may qualify as one of the shortest lessons ever on OOP, but it's sufficient for the moment. Before covering the custom-built classes, let's first take a look at the `mysqli` OO interface and see it in action.

Using the mysqli object-oriented interface

The following code will work only on systems that are running both PHP 5 and MySQL 4.1.2 or higher. If your setup uses an earlier configuration, just read through this section to familiarize yourself with how the `mysqli` OO interface works.

> *Before trying to use the code in this section, you must make sure that you are running a suitable version of MySQL and that PHP is correctly set up to use* `mysqli`*. If in doubt, perform the simple checks described next.*

Checking your system

The simplest way to check the details of your PHP and MySQL setup is with phpMyAdmin, installation instructions for which were given in the previous chapter:

1. Launch phpMyAdmin in your browser (`http://localhost/phpmyadmin` on Windows or `http://localhost/~username/phpMyAdmin/` on Mac OS X). The MySQL version running on your system is shown directly beneath the Welcome message (see the following image). Any number higher than 4.1.2 will support `mysqli`.

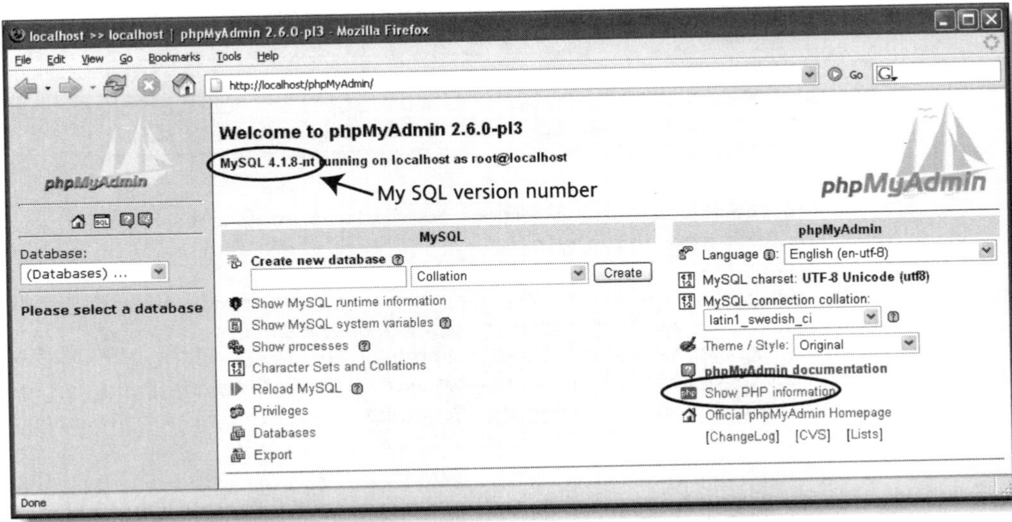

2. To check your PHP configuration, click Show PHP information (circled on the right in the image). This will display all the details of your current PHP configuration in the same way as when you first tested PHP in Chapter 1.
3. Your PHP version number is shown at the top left of the page that appears (see the following image). It needs to be a minimum of 5.0.0 to run `mysqli`.

4. If the PHP version number is 5.0.0 or above, scroll down to find the following section:

mysqli

MysqlI Support	enabled
Client API version	4.1.3-beta
MYSQLI_SOCKET	/tmp/mysql.sock

Directive	Local Value	Master Value
mysqli.default_host	*no value*	*no value*
mysqli.default_port	3306	3306
mysqli.default_pw	*no value*	*no value*
mysqli.default_socket	*no value*	*no value*
mysqli.default_user	*no value*	*no value*
mysqli.max_links	Unlimited	Unlimited
mysqli.reconnect	Off	Off

If you can find this section (all sections are displayed in alphabetical order), your version of PHP is ready to run mysqli.

Although there is a difference of only one letter, do not confuse mysql *and* mysqli*. They both work with the MySQL database, but they are different. It is perfectly OK to configure PHP to support both, so if* mysql *is enabled, you will find the* mysqli *section immediately following.*

5. If you are using Windows and PHP 5, and cannot find the mysqli section, go back to Chapter 1 and follow step 9 of "Downloading and installing PHP." Save php.ini and restart Apache. Refresh the page displaying the PHP configuration. If mysqli still does not appear, check whether you have a duplicate of php.ini in your Windows system folder. If you do, rename it php.ini.old, restart Apache, and refresh the page displaying the configuration. If mysqli shows up this time, and your PHP installation is working correctly, delete php.ini.old. There should be only one php.ini on your computer, so if you need to, consolidate all configuration settings in a single file. If you followed the instructions in Chapter 1, there should be no problem.
6. If you are using a Mac and cannot find the mysqli section, I recommend you install the PHP PKG file from Marc Liyanage, as described in Chapter 1. The only other way is to recompile PHP from source, an advanced subject not covered by this book. If you don't want to install Marc's PKG, just read through the next section, and use the classes designed either for PHP 4 or for PHP 5 and versions of MySQL prior to 4.1.2.

Retrieving records from the word list

1. Create a PHP page called displaywords_oo.php in phpflash/ch07, or use the version in the download files. If you're creating your file from scratch, insert the following

code, and then do the same in each subsequent step through to step 6 (the full listing is given in step 7).

```
<?php
// initialize connection variables
$hostname = 'localhost';
$username = 'flashuser';
$password = 'deepthought';
```

When PHP connects to a database, it needs to know four things: the hostname, the name of the user making the connection, the user's password, and the name of the database. Although it's not necessary to assign the first three to variables, I have done so here because sensitive information like passwords is best stored separately from the main script. In a real-world situation, you would probably include these variables from an external file.

2. The next line of code creates a new instance of the `mysqli` class and assigns it to the variable $db. The method of creating a new instance of a class is exactly the same as in ActionScript: you use the new keyword, followed by the name of the class.

```
$db = new mysqli($hostname, $username, $password, 'phpflash');
```

> *An important difference between PHP and ActionScript is that the* `mysqli` *class in PHP does not begin with an uppercase letter. The normal convention in PHP is to name custom-built classes with an initial uppercase letter, but this has not been done with built-in classes. PHP class names are case insensitive. ActionScript, however, is strictly case sensitive.*

When creating an instance of the `mysqli` class, you can either pass the parameters directly, as just shown, or create an empty object, and then call the `connect()` method. The following is the alternative method of achieving the same result (the following two lines are shown as an example only; there is no need to insert them in the file):

```
$db = new mysqli();
$db->connect($hostname, $username, $password, 'phpflash');
```

As you can see, you call a method on an object with the arrow operator (->), which you came across in Chapter 5 when working with MagpieRSS. Instantiating the object and calling the `connect()` method separately like this offers no particular benefit, so it is simpler to do it all in one operation. Whichever method you choose, you should normally supply four parameters: hostname, username, password, and database name, in that order.

> *The arrow operator is simply a hyphen followed by the greater than sign (->). Don't try to be clever by using your operating system or software to insert a right arrow symbol in your script. It may look more elegant, but it won't work.*

3. Once connected, you can query the database. Not surprisingly, you do this with the query() method. Although you can pass the query directly to the method as a string, many queries can become quite complex, so it makes your code much easier to read if you assign it to a variable first, like this:

```
$sql = 'SELECT * FROM wordlist';
$result = $db->query($sql);
```

To do anything with the result of the database query, you need to capture it in a new variable. In this case, I have used $result, but any valid variable name would do.

4. When using the mysqli OO interface, the query() method returns a new object, to which you can apply methods and properties directly. One of the most useful properties is num_rows, which tells you how many records the result object contains. Like methods, properties are also accessed with the arrow operator. The next two lines get the total number of records, assign it to $total, and then display it as part of browser output as an HTML level one heading:

```
$total = $result->num_rows;
echo "<h1>Total words: $total</h1>";
```

> *Because* num_rows *is a property, and not a method, it is* **not** *followed by parentheses. If you add parentheses by mistake, you will generate a fatal error in your script.*

5. When processing the results of a database query, you need to access each record one row at a time. The mysqli OO interface provides a bewildering variety of methods to do this, but probably the most user-friendly of all is fetch_assoc(). As the name suggests, it fetches an associative array of data. The key (or index) of each array element is the name of the database column, and the value is the contents of the database record for that particular row. By using a while loop, you can assign the contents as an associative array to $row, and then process each element. The word list has only one column, called word, so the following code will display each entry on a separate line in a browser.

```
while ($row = $result->fetch_assoc()) {
  echo $row['word'].'<br />';
  }
```

As the while loop progresses, it keeps track of its position in the $record object, and it comes to a halt when there are no more rows to process. That may sound like a long, drawn-out process, but depending on your processor speed, PHP will loop through nearly 22,000 records in approximately half a second and display the results as shown in Figure 7-1.

6. PHP will automatically close the connection to the database once it has finished processing the data, but it is generally considered good practice to close a connection explicitly when you have no more need for it. The method, as you might expect, is called close(), and it should be called on the original mysqli object, like this (it's the last line of code in this script, so it is followed by the closing PHP tag):

```
$db->close();
?>
```

7. Save `displaywords_oo.php` and test it in a browser. You should see the full contents of the word list displayed one word to a line, as shown in Figure 7-1. (There was a bug in the Windows version of PHP 5.0.1 that caused the script to crash Apache. This was eliminated in PHP 5.0.2.) The full code for the page, with inline comments, follows:

```
<?php
// initialize connection variables
$hostname = 'localhost';
$username = 'flashuser';
$password = 'deepthought';

// create new instance of mysqli class and connect to database
$db = new mysqli($hostname, $username, $password, 'phpflash');

// create SQL, query database, and store result in $result object
$sql = 'SELECT * FROM wordlist';
$result = $db->query($sql);

// use num_rows property to display total number of records
$total = $result->num_rows;
echo "<h1>Total words: $total</h1>";

// loop through $result object one row at a time and display contents
while ($row = $result->fetch_assoc()) {
  echo $row['word'].'<br />';
  }

// close database link
$db->close();
?>
```

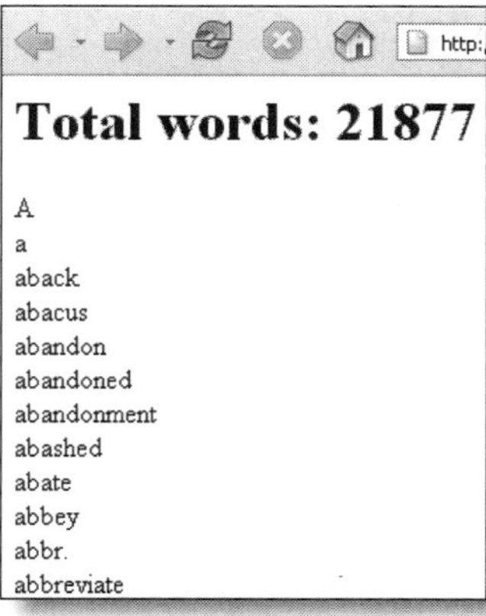

Figure 7-1. The full word list displayed in a browser after being retrieved from the MySQL database

8. Deliberately introduce an error into the arguments supplied to the `mysqli` class by, for instance, misspelling the username. Save `displaywords_oo.php` and view it in a browser again. You should see something similar to Figure 7-2.

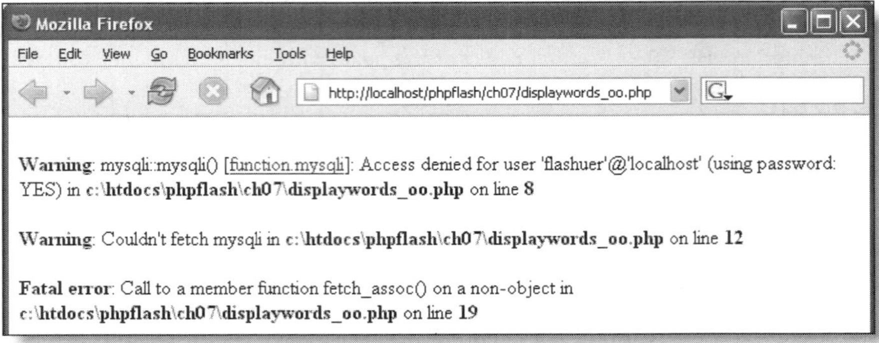

Figure 7-2. Even though the database script is perfect, a wrong username produces a rash of ugly error messages instead of the normal output.

Not only do you not get any output, but also the error messages are ugly and not particularly easy for a beginner to interpret. The errors are *not* the result of mistakes in the PHP code, but in the data supplied to it. A wrong username, password, or database name will stop the script from running correctly, as would an error in a SQL query. Naturally, the ideal is to avoid this type of situation in the first place, but mistakes do happen. The problem with these error messages is that, if you were using this script as the back-end for a Flash application, `LoadVars` would not be able to handle them. Result: a totally unresponsive Flash application.

So, although the `mysqli` OO interface is very simple to use, you need to build in an error-checking routine to handle such eventualities. That's why I have also created custom classes to work with a setup that supports `mysqli`—the error checking is built in. The custom classes are discussed in great detail in the next section.

Creating the database classes

The arrival of PHP 5 and MySQL 4.1 has added a lot of new functionality, and life would be wonderful if someone were to wave a magic wand to make these versions universally available on hosting company servers. Unfortunately, the changeover to new versions is often painfully slow, partly because hosting companies don't want to deploy software that might be incompatible with their clients' existing files. Rather than writing complex instructions that tell you to do one thing if your host offers a particular setup and something else for a different setup, here's my cunning plan. It involves three different versions of PHP classes that enable you to interact with a MySQL database in almost exactly the same way as with the `mysqli` class in the previous exercise—even if your setup doesn't support `mysqli`.

One of the advantages of wrapping everything in classes is that all the internal workings of the code are hidden from view. As a result, you can write a single script, and then just include the appropriate class from an external file. If your setup changes, the only change necessary will be to the filename of the class you require. It also means that you can develop scripts on a PHP

5/MySQL 4.1 setup on your local computer and still use them on your hosting company's server, even if it hasn't yet upgraded.

There are three files:

- `database_mysqli.php`: Written in PHP 5 syntax. Use with setups that support `mysqli` (PHP 5 and MySQL 4.1.2 or higher).
- `database_mysql.php`: Written in PHP 5 syntax. Use with PHP 5 and versions of MySQL prior to 4.1.2.
- `database_php4.php`: Written in PHP 4 syntax. Use with PHP 4 and any version of MySQL.

The full code for each file is given in the following sections. You can also download the classes from the friends of ED website. Simply choose the file(s) to match your setup. If your hosting company offers phpMyAdmin, you can use the same method as shown in the previous section to check your remote server setup. Alternatively, ask your host for the details. You may need to use one class file for your local development and a different one for deployment on your remote server. The best way to handle this is to create master copies with the names indicated in the preceding list and keep them in a special folder. Then change the filename of the version you need to `database.php` when you come to deploy it. For instance, if your hosting company still uses PHP 4, upload `database_php4.php` to your remote server, and then use your FTP program or website control panel to change its name. That way, the name of the external file referred to by all scripts will always be `database.php`, avoiding the need to change the name of the include file in every script that needs it.

The file written in PHP 4 syntax is simply for the benefit of readers who may still need it, and there is no need to study it in detail. You should, however, roll up your sleeves when it comes to the PHP 5 classes. As the programmer, you're not only the user, but in terms of the earlier analogy, you're also the motor mechanic.

The classes do not cover every conceivable aspect of database interaction. Instead, they concentrate on four basic methods and one property, which you can build on later if the need arises. Each file contains two classes: `Database` and `MyResult`.

The `Database` class creates a `Database` object that acts in the same way as a `mysqli` object. It has the following methods:

- **`connect()`**: Establishes a link to a specific database
- **`query()`**: Executes queries
- **`close()`**: Closes the database link

The `query()` method makes a direct call to the `MyResult` class and instantiates (creates) a `MyResult` object, which has access to the following method and property:

- **`fetch_assoc()`**: Gets an array of results
- **`num_rows`**: Gets the number of results

Together, the two classes emulate the equivalent methods and property of the `mysqli` OO interface.

Unlike ActionScript 2.0, PHP does not require you to store each class in a separate file or impose any restrictions on what the file can be called. Also, the location of PHP class files is less of a problem than with ActionScript 2.0. All you need to do is indicate the correct path in the include command. Nevertheless, I recommend naming class files in an unambiguous manner and keeping them in a central location. For the projects in this book, create a new folder called `phpflash/classes`.

The PHP 5/Improved MySQL (mysqli) classes

Use this version if you are running MySQL 4.1.2 or higher and have PHP 5 with the Improved MySQL (`mysqli`) extension enabled. Save it in a file called `database_mysqli.php` in `phpflash/classes`.

```
<?php
class Database {

  protected $host;
  protected $user;
  protected $pwd;
  protected $dbName;
  protected $flash;
  protected $dbLink;
  protected $result;
  protected $resultObj;

  function __construct($host, $user, $pwd, $dbName, $flash=1){
    $this->host = $host;
    $this->user = $user;
    $this->pwd = $pwd;
    $this->dbName = $dbName;
    $this->flash = $flash;
    $this->connect();
    }

  // Connect to the mySQL Server and Select the database
  public function connect() {
    try {
      $this->dbLink = @mysqli_connect($this->host, $this->user,
➥ $this->pwd, $this->dbName);
      if (!$this->dbLink) {
        throw new Exception ("Couldn't connect $this->user to
➥ $this->dbName");
        }
      }
    catch (Exception $e) {
      echo $this->flash ? 'error='.urlencode($e->getMessage()) :
➥ $e->getMessage();
```

```
      exit();
      }
    return $this->dbLink;
    }

  // Execute a SQL query
  public function query($query) {
    try {
      $this->result = mysqli_query($this->dbLink, $query);
      if (!$this->result) {
        throw new Exception ('MySQL Error: ' .
➥ mysqli_error($this->dbLink));
        }
      }
    catch (Exception $e) {
      echo $this->flash ? 'error='.urlencode($e->getMessage()) :
➥ $e->getMessage();
      exit();
      }
    // store result in new object to emulate mysqli OO interface
    $this->resultObj = new MyResult($this->result);
    return $this->resultObj;
    }

  // Close MySQL Connection
  public function close(){
    mysqli_close($this->dbLink);
    }
  }

class MyResult {

  protected $theResult;
  public $num_rows;

  function __construct($r) {
    $this->theResult = $r;
    // get number of records found
    $this->num_rows = mysqli_num_rows($r);
    }

  // fetch associative array of result (works on one row at a time)
  function fetch_assoc() {
    $newRow = mysqli_fetch_assoc($this->theResult);
    return $newRow;
    }
  }
?>
```

If you have been working with ActionScript 2.0 classes or have knowledge of any other OO language, you may be wondering why I did not simply extend the PHP 5 `mysqli` *class. PHP 5 supports inheritance, but the* `mysqli` *class does not (although this may change in future versions of PHP). To get around this problem, I have used procedural functions to create classes that emulate the* `mysqli` *OO interface.*

The PHP 5/MySQL classes

The following code is the same classes rewritten to work with installations that support PHP 5 but still use a version of MySQL that does not understand `mysqli` (any version prior to MySQL 4.1.2). Save it in a file called `database_mysql.php` in `phpflash/classes`.

```
<?php
class Database {

  protected $host;
  protected $user;
  protected $pwd;
  protected $dbName;
  protected $flash;
  protected $dbLink;
  protected $result;
  protected $resultObj;

  function __construct($host, $user, $pwd, $dbName, $flash=1){
    $this->host = $host;
    $this->user = $user;
    $this->pwd = $pwd;
    $this->dbName = $dbName;
    $this->flash = $flash;
    $this->connect();
    }

  // connect to the MySQL server and select the database
  public function connect() {
    try {
      $this->dbLink = @mysql_pconnect($this->host, $this->user,
➥ $this->pwd);
      if (!$this->dbLink) {
        throw new Exception ("Couldn't connect $this->user to mySQL
➥ Server");
        }
      if (!mysql_select_db($this->dbName, $this->dbLink)) {
        throw new Exception ('Couldn\'t open Database: '.
➥ $this->dbName);
        }
      }
```

```
    catch (Exception $e) {
      echo $this->flash ? 'error='.urlencode($e->getMessage()) :
➥ $e->getMessage();
      exit();
      }
    return $this->dbLink;
    }

  // execute a SQL query
  public function query($query) {
    try {
      $this->result = mysql_query($query, $this->dbLink);
      if (!$this->result) {
        throw new Exception ('MySQL Error: ' . mysql_error());
        }
      }
    catch (Exception $e) {
      echo $this->flash ? 'error='.urlencode($e->getMessage()) :
➥ $e->getMessage();
      exit();
      }
    // store result in new object to emulate mysqli OO interface
    $this->resultObj = new MyResult($this->result);
    return $this->resultObj;
    }

  // Close MySQL Connection
  public function close(){
    mysql_close($this->dbLink);
    }
  }

class MyResult {

  protected $theResult;
  public $num_rows;

  function __construct($r) {
    $this->theResult = $r;
    // get number of records found
    $this->num_rows = mysql_num_rows($r);
    }

  // fetch associative array of result (works on one row at a time)
  public function fetch_assoc() {
    $newRow = mysql_fetch_assoc($this->theResult);
    return $newRow;
    }
  }
?>
```

The PHP 4 classes

Use these classes if your server does not yet support PHP 5. Store the following code in a file called `database_php4.php` in `phpflash/classes`.

```
<?php
class Database {

  var $host;
  var $user;
  var $pwd;
  var $dbName;
  var $flash;
  var $dbLink;
  var $result;
  var $resultObj;

  function Database($host, $user, $pwd, $dbName, $flash=1){
    $this->host = $host;
    $this->user = $user;
    $this->pwd = $pwd;
    $this->dbName = $dbName;
    $this->flash = $flash;
    $this->connect();
    }

  // Connect to the MySQL server and select the database
  function connect() {
    $this->dbLink = @mysql_pconnect($this->host, $this->user,
➥ $this->pwd);
    if (!$this->dbLink) {
       $error = 'Couldn\'t connect to mySQL Server';
       echo $this->flash ? 'error='.urlencode($error) : $error;
       exit();
       }
    if (!mysql_select_db($this->dbName, $this->dbLink)) {
      $error = 'Couldn\'t open Database: '. $this->dbName;
      echo $this->flash ? 'error='.urlencode($error) : $error;
      exit();
      }
    return $this->dbLink;
    }

  // Execute a SQL query
  function query($query) {
    $this->result = mysql_query($query, $this->dbLink);
    if (!$this->result) {
      $error = 'MySQL Error: ' . mysql_error();
      echo $this->flash ? 'error='.urlencode($error) : $error;
```

```
      exit();
      }
    // store result in new object to emulate mysqli OO interface
    $this->resultObj = new MyResult($this->result);
    return $this->resultObj;
    }

  function close(){
    // Close MySQL Connection
    mysql_close($this->dbLink);
    }
}

class MyResult {

  var $theResult;
  var $num_rows;

  function MyResult(&$r) {
    $this->theResult = $r;
    // get number of records found
    $this->num_rows = mysql_num_rows($r);
    }

  // fetch associative array of result (works on one row at a time)
  function fetch_assoc() {
    $newRow = mysql_fetch_assoc($this->theResult);
    return $newRow;
    }
  }
?>
```

Using the database classes

Before I launch into an explanation of how to build a class in PHP 5, let's take a look at how to use these classes. The mini-lesson in OOP explained that the idea of a class is to hide the inner workings of the code. Even if you have never created a class of your own in ActionScript, you use built-in classes all the time. Between releases of Flash, Macromedia software engineers may make all sorts of changes to the underlying code of any of the many classes, such as `MovieClip`, but you still access the properties and methods of the class in the same way. The three versions of the `Database` and `MyResult` classes presented here work exactly the same way. They not only wrap (or encapsulate) the underlying PHP code in a common interface, but also automatically perform error testing and display appropriate messages if anything goes wrong.

The advantages of doing this are manifold. Not only do you avoid the need to rewrite large amounts of script if your setup changes, but also you don't need to incorporate the error-checking code in your main script—it's all handled by the class. In Chapter 4, you saw how to build your own PHP functions, to avoid repeating the same code over and over again. A simple way of thinking about classes is as a collection of related functions that make your main script much easier to read and maintain.

Enough theory for the moment. Let's see the classes in action. The next script will form the basis for the PHP back-end of the Hangman game.

Displaying the contents of the word list with a class

Earlier, I showed you how to display the full contents of the word list using the mysqli OO interface. Now try it using the Database and MyResult classes. The code is virtually identical.

1. Make a copy of displaywords_oo.php and save it as displaywords.php in phpflash/ch07. The final script is available in the download files for this chapter.
2. Immediately after the opening PHP tag, insert the following code:

   ```
   require_once('../classes/database.php');
   ```

   This is the same construct you used in Chapter 5 to include the MagpieRSS code. It tells PHP to include the file database.php in the classes folder into your script. You don't have a file with that name at the moment, but you will fix that later.
3. Locate the following line:

   ```
   $db = new mysqli($hostname, $username, $password, 'phpflash');
   ```

   Change it like this (the new code is highlighted in bold type):

   ```
   $db = new Database($hostname, $username, $password, 'phpflash', 0);
   ```

   Instead of creating a mysqli object, this creates a new instance of the custom-built Database class. Each version of the Database class takes up to five parameters. The first four are the same as those used to create a mysqli object and are required; the final one is exclusive to the Database class and is optional. The five parameters are as follows:

   - The hostname where the MySQL server is located.
   - The name of the MySQL user.
   - The user's MySQL password.
   - The name of the database you want to access.
   - An optional parameter indicating whether the results are to be passed to Flash. If omitted, the default is set to Flash. If set to any of the values PHP treats as false (see Chapter 2), error messages are displayed in plain text in a browser.

   In this case, the final parameter has been set to 0, so error messages will not be formatted for Flash. This is because you always need to test PHP scripts in a browser before linking them directly to a Flash movie.
4. Save the page and check your code against this full listing:

   ```
   <?php
   require_once('../classes/database.php');
   // initialize connection variables
   $hostname = 'localhost';
   ```

```
$username = 'flashuser';
$password = 'deepthought';

// create new instance of mysqli class and connect to database
$db = new Database($hostname, $username, $password, 'phpflash', 0);

// create SQL, query database, and store result in $result object
$sql = 'SELECT * FROM wordlist';
$result = $db->query($sql);

// use num_rows property to display total number of records
$total = $result->num_rows;
echo "<h1>Total words: $total</h1>";

// loop through $result object one row at a time and display contents
while ($row = $result->fetch_assoc()) {
  echo $row['word'].'<br />';
  }

// close database link
$db->close();
?>
```

5. Before you test the code in a browser, locate the page containing the Database and MyResult classes appropriate for your setup, open it, and save it as database.php. (That way, you will preserve the master version and have a duplicate that is used as your operational version.) When you view displaywords.php in a browser, you should see exactly the same result as shown earlier in Figure 7-1, when the mysqli OO interface was used. Although the output looks no different, the use of the classes makes a major difference when something goes wrong.

6. Alter either the username or the password, and view displaywords.php in a browser again. Instead of the ugly error messages you got with the mysqli OO interface (see Figure 7-2), you should see something similar to this:

Couldn't connect flashuer to phpflash

7. Correct the mistake, but introduce another deliberate mistake into the SQL query, and view the page in a browser again. You should get another error message similar to this:

http://localhost
MySQL Error: Table 'phpflash.worlist' doesn't exist

8. Leave the mistake uncorrected, but remove the final parameter from the code that creates the instance of the Database class. Change this:

```
$db = new Database($hostname, $username, $password, 'phpflash', 0);
```

to this:

```
$db = new Database($hostname, $username, $password, 'phpflash');
```

9. Now view the page again. The error message will have been URL encoded, ready for sending to a Flash movie, as shown in Figure 7-3. Unlike the morass of error messages generated earlier (see Figure 7-2), this is something your Flash applications will be able to handle gracefully. Even though the application may not work as intended, it will be able to alert the user to the existence of a problem, rather than simply failing to respond.

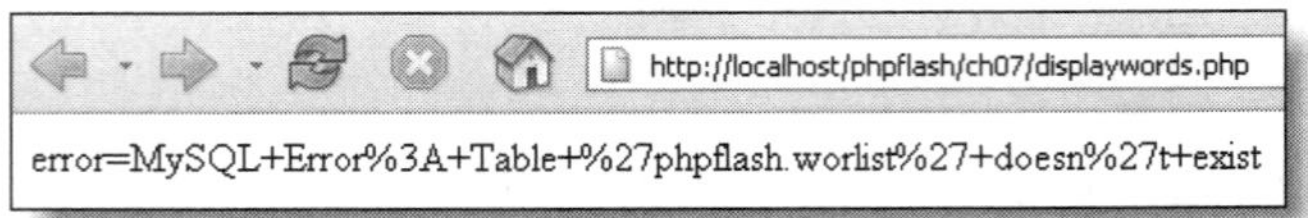

Figure 7-3. The custom-built Database class encodes error messages in a format that Flash can understand.

So, the classes have not just simplified the transition from one PHP/MySQL setup to another, but also incorporated an error reporting system that can toggle between working in a browser and sending properly formatted messages to Flash simply by changing a single parameter. By wrapping everything in custom-built classes, your operational scripts become much simpler to write—and to read. You'll come back to finish this script in the section "Refining the word selection with SQL and PHP" later in the chapter.

Building and using PHP 5 classes

Now that you have seen classes in action, let's pause a while to cover how you create your own custom classes in PHP 5. The mere mention of building custom classes is enough to make many people break out in a cold sweat, but the idea is very simple. In Chapter 4, you saw how to create PHP functions to avoid having to repeat the same code over and over again in your scripts. In essence, a class groups together related functions in a single unit. If you strip down the PHP 5 versions of the Database class to the bare bones, this is what you get:

```
class Database {

  // list of class properties (variables)

  function __construct($host, $user, $pwd, $dbName, $flash=1){
    // variable assignment
    }

  public function connect() {
    // code to connect to database
    }

  public function query($query) {
    // code to execute query
    }
```

```
public function close(){
  // code to close database connection
  }
}
```

Naming and declaring classes

A class is declared using the keyword `class` followed by the name of the class:

- You can use any legal identifier as a class name—in other words, it must not begin with a number, and it can contain only alphanumeric characters and the underscore.
- A class name does not begin with a dollar sign.
- Class names are case insensitive, but the convention is to begin them with an uppercase letter.

The class name is followed by an opening curly brace ({), and all code belonging to the class is enclosed by the matching closing curly brace (}).

Creating class properties

Immediately following the opening curly brace, you should list the class properties. Like ActionScript 2.0, PHP 5 allows you to specify whether individual properties can be accessed and manipulated outside the class. If you have experience with other OO languages, such as Java or C++, this concept will be nothing new, but it is something anyone coming from ActionScript 1.0 or PHP 4 may find hard to grasp initially.

To take the common motor car example of an object or class instance, the color of a car may be blue. If the class imposes no restrictions on access to properties, anyone can come along and change the color of the car to red. In real life, though, however much you want a red car, you can't just declare the color has changed from blue to red. You need to take it to the garage to be repainted. In OOP terms, the color property would be protected from change, except through using the `repaint()` method (which you would have to create as part of the class definition). Although changing properties on the fly is convenient, it goes against the principle of well-designed OOP, which aims to lock away tested routines in (metaphorical) black boxes—just like the car that you get in and drive without understanding the workings of the engine. It also prevents inappropriate values from being assigned to a property. However desirable `RollsRoyce` may be as a car property, it's not a color. By declaring properties as protected in one way or another, you can prevent this type of mistake from happening.

PHP 5 has four different levels of **visibility** for class properties, which also apply to class methods (discussed later in the chapter); ActionScript 2.0 has just two. Table 7-1 lists them and describes their usage.

Table 7-1. Controlling access to class properties and methods in PHP 5 and ActionScript 2.0

Keyword	PHP 5	ActionScript 2.0
`public`	No access restrictions.	No access restrictions.
`private`	Restricts access to within the same class. Properties and methods declared as `private` cannot be accessed by subclasses.	Restricts access to the same class and any of its subclasses.
`protected`	Restricts access to the same class and any of its subclasses.	Not supported.
`final`	Restricts access to within the same class and any of its subclasses, but prevents subclasses from overriding the property or method.	Not supported.

Both PHP 5 and ActionScript 2.0 also have the keyword `static` that can be used to modify class properties and methods. This enables you to access a property or method without creating an instance of the class, in the same way as you work with the `Math` and `Date` objects in ActionScript. You can find more details about `static` in PHP 5 at `www.php.net/manual/en/language.oop5.static.php`.

Unless you have a strong reason for not doing so, it is recommended you declare class properties in PHP 5 as `protected`, as this gives access to both the class itself and any subclasses you may subsequently create.

To declare a class property, precede it with one of the keywords. The property itself is an ordinary PHP variable. Note that you do not use the `var` keyword as in ActionScript 2.0. This is how the first three properties of the `Database` class were declared:

```
protected $host;
protected $user;
protected $pwd;
```

You can initialize a class property with a default value by assigning a value in the normal way with the assignment operator (=), although this is more often done in the **constructor function** (see the next section). If PHP 5 had been around in Henry Ford's day, he might have created a class property for the Model T like this:

```
final $color = 'black';
```

Using the constructor function

When you instantiate a class, it creates a new object for you to work with. Normally, you will want the instance to have some initial properties. These can be either defaults for the class or values passed as arguments. The constructor function has a special reserved name, `__construct()` (beginning with two underscores).

In most other OO languages—including ActionScript 2.0—constructor functions use the same name as the class itself. In fact, PHP 4 followed the same practice, and some developers have criticized PHP for creating confusion by switching to this rather unusual fixed name. It was done for a specific reason: to prevent code in subclasses from breaking if the name of a parent class is changed. For backward compatibility, if PHP 5 cannot find a function called `__construct()`*, it will search for one that has the same name as the class. However, this will make your code less efficient, and it may not always be supported. The safest course of action, as always, is to remember that ActionScript 2.0 and PHP 5 may look similar, but they're different.*

Let's take a look at the constructor function for the `Database` class to see how it works.

```
function __construct($host, $user, $pwd, $dbName, $flash=1){
  $this->host = $host;
  $this->user = $user;
  $this->pwd = $pwd;
  $this->dbName = $dbName;
  $this->flash = $flash;
  }
```

In this case, the function takes five parameters. I'll explain in a moment why the last one (`$flash=1`) differs from all the others, in that it already has a value assigned to it within the parentheses. First, take a look at the code block inside the function. Each line follows the same pattern: the value of each parameter is assigned to one of the class properties. The use of `$this` should be immediately recognizable as performing exactly the same role in PHP 5 as the `this` keyword does in ActionScript: it provides a reference to the current object. Consequently, `$this->host = $host;` sets the `host` property of the object to whatever value is passed when a new instance of the `Database` class is created.

To create a new instance, use the `new` keyword followed by the class name and a pair of parentheses. If the class does not require any parameters, the parentheses are left empty. Frequently, though, you will pass arguments to the constructor function when instantiating an object, as is the case with the `Database` class:

```
$db = new Database($hostname, $username, $password, $dbName, 0);
```

Normally, when you want to set a default value, you do it inside the constructor, without passing an argument. For example, the hypothetical Model T example would almost certainly have looked something like this:

```
function __construct(){
$this->color = 'black';
$this->numWheels = 4;
}
```

Henry Ford would also have made sure there was no `changeColor()` method in the class, either.

The Database class demonstrates another way of setting a default value, but one that can be easily overridden when instantiating an object. It uses an **optional parameter**.

Setting optional function parameters

Although used on a constructor function here, optional parameters can be set when declaring any function. All you need to do to make a parameter optional is assign it a value in the list of arguments between the opening parentheses in a function declaration. In the Database class, declaring the fifth parameter as $flash=1 automatically sets the object's $flash property to 1 (or true). So, you can, in fact, leave it out. Because optional parameters can be omitted when calling a function, **they must always come at the end of the list of arguments**.

> *Unlike ActionScript, PHP does not allow you to supply an arbitrary number of arguments to a function and then retrieve the value of any extra ones from the* arguments *array. PHP expects the same number of arguments as specified when the function is first defined. If you supply more, any extra are ignored. If you supply fewer, PHP will issue a warning message, unless the missing argument(s) already have a default value.*

If, on the other hand, you want to override the default for an optional parameter, simply include a value for it when calling the function, and the new value will take precedence.

Since this book is all about using PHP with Flash, the likelihood of you wanting the Database class to produce Flash-compatible error messages is very high. If, however, you wanted to deploy the class in an XHTML web environment, you would probably want the opposite to happen. In that case, change the first line of the constructor to the following:

```
function __construct($host, $user, $pwd, $dbName, $flash=0){
```

Setting class methods

There is nothing particularly mystical about **class methods**. They are functions just like any other. Like class properties, their visibility (or scope) can be limited by using the keywords in Table 7-1. If you declare a class method without using one of the keywords, it is automatically regarded as being a public method. All the methods in the Database class have been explicitly declared public, but the public keyword could have been omitted without altering the functionality of the class. Explicit declaration of a public method, however, makes your intentions doubly clear.

The reason all methods have been declared public is that you need to be able to use them directly in the body of PHP scripts. The reason for using protected or one of the other keywords on a class method would be to prevent it from being used outside the class itself. For instance, you might want to do some internal formatting of some output, but not expose that function to general use. The plural() function used in Chapter 4 would be an ideal candidate for a protected method if converting the code to a custom-built class.

Accessing public methods

Once an instance of a class has been created, you call any public methods with the arrow operator. So, this is how you call the close() method of the Database class on an instance named $db:

```
$db->close();
```

If the method takes any parameters, you pass them to the method in exactly the same way as you would to an ordinary function, like this:

```
$sql = 'SELECT * FROM wordlist';
$result = $db->query($sql);
```

> *This has been only a brief introduction to the creation and use of PHP 5 classes. The methods in the PHP 5* Database *class use the* try/catch *method of error handling, which is new to PHP 5. For a more thorough discussion of both subjects, see* Beginning PHP 5 and MySQL: From Novice to Professional *by W. Jason Gilmore (Apress, ISBN: 1-893115-51-8).*

Refining the word selection with SQL and PHP

After that detour exploring the mysteries of PHP classes, it's time to get on with building the game. Although you could load all 21,000 or so words into the Hangman movie, choosing about 250 entirely at random should be more than sufficient.

First of all, let's establish the criteria against which the words should be selected. Words should

- Contain at least five characters
- Not contain a period (usually an indication of an abbreviation)
- Not begin with an apostrophe (there are four slang expressions, like 'cause, in the list)
- Not contain any uppercase letters (this may exclude some interesting words, but it gets rid of the problem of abbreviations such as YWCA)

If creating a game for different skill levels, you might also want to set a maximum number of characters. All these criteria can be determined by using the PHP string functions you studied in Chapter 4. Randomization could also be handled by retrieving a large number of records and using the PHP shuffle() function (www.php.net/manual/en/function.shuffle.php). This is possible, yes, but by using a combination of SQL, MySQL functions, and PHP, you can reduce the selection process to a few lines of code.

Selecting appropriate words

The following section assumes that you have already created the Database and MyResult classes, renamed the appropriate version database.php, and stored it in the phpflash/classes folder as described earlier in the chapter.

1. Open displaywords.php, the script you created in the section "Using the database classes" earlier in the chapter, and save it as hangman.php in phpflash/ch07. Load the page in a browser and make sure that any deliberate mistakes you introduced in the previous exercise have been corrected. It should produce the full list of words as shown earlier in Figure 7-1. Also reset the value of the final (optional) argument of the Database class in line 9 to 0. This will ensure any error messages come up in plain language, rather than formatted for Flash. The full code is shown here again for you to check against.

   Alternatively, use the version of displaywords.php in the download files. If you just want to check the final code, that's in hangman.php, also in the download files.

```
<?php
require_once('../classes/database.php');
// initialize connection variables
$hostname = 'localhost';
$username = 'flashuser';
$password = 'deepthought';

// create new instance of mysqli class and connect to database
$db = new Database($hostname, $username, $password, 'phpflash', 0);

// create SQL, query database, and store result in $result object
$sql = 'SELECT * FROM wordlist';
$result = $db->query($sql);

// use num_rows property to display total number of records
$total = $result->num_rows;
echo "<h1>Total words: $total</h1>";

// loop through $result object one row at a time and display contents
while ($row = $result->fetch_assoc()) {
  echo $row['word'].'<br />';
  }

// close database link
$db->close();
?>
```

2. At the moment, the SQL query retrieves everything. You need to limit the results to a maximum of 250 words. One of the other criteria for selection is a minimum number of letters. Both these figures could be hard-coded into the SQL query, but it is better

practice to store them as variables because this makes it easier to change them later. Insert the following code immediately above the comment that begins `// create SQL`:

```
// set limits for words to be retrieved
$numWords = 250;
$min = 5;
```

3. Amend the SQL query like this:

```
$sql = "SELECT word FROM wordlist
        WHERE LENGTH(word) >= $min";
```

The first thing to note is that the query is enclosed in double quotes. This is so that the value of `$min` will be interpreted and correctly inserted into the SQL statement (see Chapter 2 if you need reminding of the difference between the way variables are treated by single and double quotes). The next thing is that I have replaced the * with `word`, so the query begins with `SELECT word FROM wordlist`. This is just more specific than telling MySQL to return all columns. I have also deliberately broken up the SQL query over two lines. Because PHP and MySQL ignore extra whitespace, you can line up the different sections of a SQL query to make it easier to read. This not only helps with understanding what you have written, but also makes it easier to amend the code later.

The new section of the query uses the `WHERE` keyword, which tells the database you want to restrict the results of your search. `LENGTH()` is a MySQL function that performs the same role as `strlen()` in PHP. By passing the name of the column to it, you establish that you want to use the number of characters in each row of the column to determine whether an item should be included in the results. Since `$min` has been set to `5`, only items that contain five characters or more will be chosen.

4. Save `hangman.php` and test it again in a browser. You should get a result similar to the one shown here. By limiting the minimum length of words, you have already eliminated more than 2,000, but as the final word in the screenshot shows, the period at the end of abbr. creeps in. That will be fixed later in PHP with a regular expression (regex), but you can still get MySQL to do a lot of the selection process.

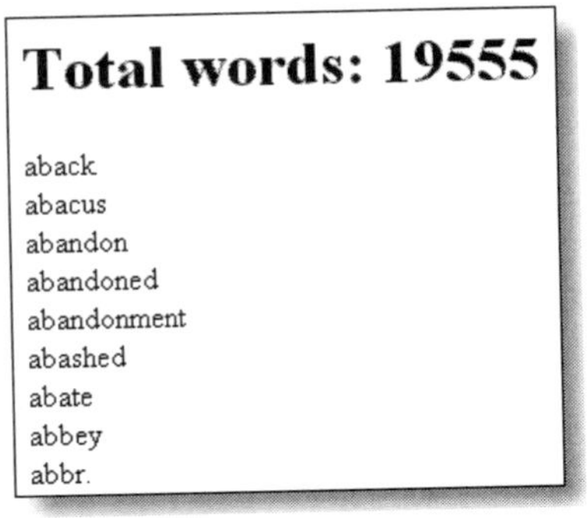

Total words: 19555

aback
abacus
abandon
abandoned
abandonment
abashed
abate
abbey
abbr.

5. You only want 250 words, so you can use `LIMIT` as you did when you first tested MySQL in the previous chapter. Amend the SQL query to look like this:

```
$sql = "SELECT word FROM wordlist
        WHERE LENGTH(word) >= $min
        LIMIT $numWords";
```

This successfully limits the number of words selected, but there's a fatal flaw: they're always the same. You need some way of randomizing the selection. A combination of a SQL command and a MySQL function does the trick.

6. Amend the SQL query again, so it looks like this:

```
$sql = "SELECT word FROM wordlist
        WHERE LENGTH(word) >= $min
        ORDER BY RAND()
        LIMIT $numWords";
```

ORDER BY is a SQL command that determines the order in which the results are returned, and RAND() is a MySQL function that randomizes the order. Note that the ORDER BY command must come before the LIMIT command.

So, in plain English, the SQL query now says:

SELECT records in the word column FROM the wordlist table
WHERE the LENGTH of items in the word column
is greater than or equal to 5
ORDER BY randomizing and LIMIT to a maximum of 250

The formal SQL syntax for SELECT is described in Chapter 10.

7. Save the page and load it into a browser. You should see something like the result shown at the right.

The heading clearly shows that the number of results has been limited to the maximum stipulated. The order of items is also well and truly randomized, but as the image shows, words with uppercase letters are still included. If you scroll down the list, you will probably also find words containing periods. So, to get rid of all proper nouns and abbreviations, you need to call on the services of PHP string functions.

Total words: 250

teddy bear
canned
alley
acrid
campus
imminently
dragon
operational
standpoint
Taurus

8. Change the final section of code so that it looks like this (changes are highlighted in bold):

```
echo "<h1>Total words: $total</h1>";

// initialize counter and regular expression
$count = 0;
$pattern = "/$'|[A-Z\.]/";

// loop through results, but skip any that match the regex
while ($row = $result->fetch_assoc()) {
  if (preg_match($pattern, $row['word']))
    continue;
  echo $row['word'].'<br />';
  $count++;
  }

// display how many words remain after filtering by regex
echo 'Words accepted: '.$count;
$db->close();
```

The changes add a counter ($count) to the while loop and test each word against a regex stored in $pattern. The regex is made up of three parts:

- First it uses the beginning of string anchor ($) to find any words that begin with an apostrophe ($').
- Then a vertical pipe (|) indicates an alternative.
- Finally, square brackets are used to create a character class that matches any uppercase letter or period ([A-Z\.]).

As always, the regex pattern is enclosed in delimiters (I've used the normal convention of forward slashes) and is presented as a string. Because the regex includes an apostrophe (which is the same as a single quote), I've wrapped the regex in double quotes, rather than escape the apostrophe with a backslash. Regexes are hard enough to understand without making life more difficult for yourself than necessary!

What the regex does is match any word that either *begins* with an apostrophe, or contains a capital letter or period *anywhere* in the word. If it finds a match, the continue keyword causes the while loop to skip the current word and move on to the next one. Because the counter is not triggered when this happens, the number of words accepted will normally be fewer than the original 250 selected, as the image alongside shows.

occupancy
bimbo
except
nonfiction
investor
mediate
angelic
ending
pacifism
Words accepted: 243

Look through the selected words. You should no longer see any abbreviations or words with uppercase letters.

9. If your results are satisfactory, it's time to prepare the output to send to the Hangman Flash movie. You can now get rid of the heading that displays the total number of words selected, and change the final block of code to format the output for Flash. The full listing is shown here, with changes highlighted in bold.

```
<?php
require_once('../classes/database.php');
// initialize connection variables
$hostname = 'localhost';
$username = 'flashuser';
$password = 'deepthought';

// create new instance of mysqli class and connect to database
$db = new Database($hostname,$username,$password,$dbName);

// set limits for words to be retrieved
$numWords = 250;
$min = 5;

// create SQL, query database, and store result in $result object
$sql = "SELECT word FROM wordlist
        WHERE LENGTH(word) >= $min
        ORDER BY RAND()
        LIMIT $numWords";
$result = $db->query($sql);
```

```
// initialize results string, counter, and regular expression
$words = '';
$count = 0;
$pattern = "/$'|[A-Z\.]/";

// loop through results, but skip any that match the regex
while ($row = $result->fetch_assoc()) {
  if (preg_match($pattern, $row['word']))
    continue;
  // use counter to create unique variable (word0, etc) and build
  // string of name/value pairs to transmit to Flash
  $words .= '&word'.$count.'='.urlencode($row['word']);
  $count++;
  }

// output string to send data to Flash
// begin with total number of words accepted
// then string of name/value pairs
echo 'total='.$count.$words;
$db->close();
?>
```

Note that the fifth parameter has been removed from the initialization of the Database class. This is so that any error message will now be relayed in a form that Flash can understand. The counter is now used to give each word a unique variable that will be used inside the Flash movie (word0, word1, and so on). Each word is also URL encoded, because some contain apostrophes, hyphens, or spaces (just to make the game more interesting). The penultimate line outputs the results of the search as a single string, ready to be captured by LoadVars. If you test hangman.php in a browser now, the output should look similar to this:

The first variable output by the PHP script (total) contains the value held by the counter. This is needed because the actual number of words will vary each time, depending on how many are eliminated by the regex.

Now that everything's ready on the PHP side, it's time to set up the ActionScript inside the Hangman movie.

Scripting the Flash movie

Because the emphasis here is on improving an existing game, I won't go into great detail about how the main script works. Even if you're not familiar with the game, you should be able to understand the flow of the script from the inline comments. The main part of the explanation will concentrate on the interaction between PHP and Flash.

1. Open hangman.fla and select frame 1 on the actions layer. Alternatively, use hangman02.fla from the download files or hangman03.fla if you just want to follow the completed script for this section. Open the Actions panel and insert the following script:

```
// create LoadVars instance and load data from PHP script
var getWords:LoadVars = new LoadVars();
getWords.load('http://localhost/phpflash/ch07/hangman.php?cache=' +
➥ new Date().getTime());
// when data loaded, loop through variables to create wordList array
getWords.onLoad = function() {
  for (var i:Number = 0;i < this.total; i++) {
    wordList[i] = this["word"+i];
    trace("word"+i+": "+wordList[i]);
  }
};
// initialize variables
var wordList:Array = new Array ();

// hide game interface and stop main timelines
interface_mc._visible = false;
hangman_mc.stop();
stop();
```

   As in all previous projects, a LoadVars object (getWords) is created to access the data output by the PHP script. On this occasion, there is no need to send any data to the script, so calling the load() method on getWords is sufficient to query the MySQL database. The for loop inside the getWords.onLoad callback function uses the value of the first variable (total) to make sure it stops running after assigning all words as elements of the wordList array.

   The final three lines of the script hide the game interface, stop the hanging man movie timeline, and stop the main movie timeline.

2. Press *CTRL+ENTER/⌘+RETURN* to test the movie. The names of all the variables and their values should be displayed in the Output panel, as shown in Figure 7-4. Once you have established that the data is being retrieved successfully, comment out or delete the call to trace() within the loop.

3. Return to the Actions panel and initialize the rest of the variables needed for the script. Insert the following code immediately after the line that initializes the wordList array (around line 13):

```
var lettersNeeded:Array = new Array();
var lettersGuessed:Array = new Array();
var randomNumber:Number = 0;
var selectedWord:String = "";
var lettersLeftToGo:Number = 0;
var foundLetter:Boolean = false;
var notGuessed:Boolean = false;
var wrong:Boolean = false;
```

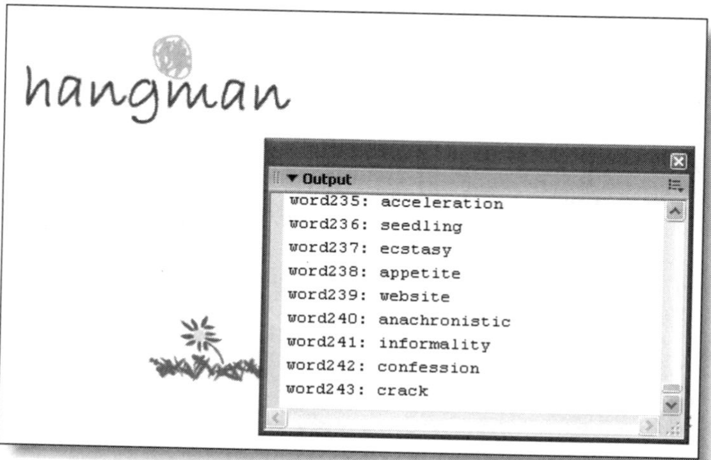

Figure 7-4. Use trace() to make sure that the results of the database query are being received by Flash.

4. The next block of code is the main function that initializes the game when the play game button is clicked. It goes immediately after the getWords.onLoad event handler (around line 11).

```
playGame_btn.onRelease = function() {
  // initialize graphics
  hangman_mc.gotoAndStop("play");
  playGame_btn._visible = false;
  interface_mc._visible = true;
  interface_mc.display_txt.text = "";
  interface_mc.guess_txt._visible = true;
  interface_mc.input_txt._visible = true;
  interface_mc.enter_btn._visible = true;
  Selection.setFocus("interface_mc.input_txt");

  // generate random number to choose word at random
  randomNumber = Math.round(Math.random()*(wordList.length-1));
  selectedWord = wordList[randomNumber];

  // get word length, deduct hyphens, spaces or
  // apostrophes from character count
  lettersLeftToGo = selectedWord.length;
  for (i=0; i<selectedWord.length; i++) {
    if (selectedWord.charAt(i) == "-" || selectedWord.charAt(i) == " "
➥ || selectedWord.charAt(i) == "'") {
      lettersLeftToGo–;
    } else {
      lettersNeeded[i] = selectedWord.charAt(i);
    }
  }
```

```
  // replace everything except hyphens, spaces or
  // apostrophes with question marks
  for (i=0; i<selectedWord.length; i++) {
    if (selectedWord.charAt(i) == "-" || selectedWord.charAt(i) == " "
➥ || selectedWord.charAt(i) == "'") {
      lettersGuessed[i] = selectedWord.charAt(i);
      interface_mc.display_txt.text += selectedWord.charAt(i);
    } else {
      lettersGuessed[i] = "?";
      interface_mc.display_txt.text += "?";
    }
  }
};
```

The comments should explain how the function works. Apart from initializing the interface, the main task of this function is to choose a word at random from the wordList array and replace all the characters with question marks. Because many of the words in the database contain spaces, hyphens, or apostrophes (only apostrophes in the first position have been eliminated by the PHP regex), the function differs slightly from the original Hangman game. Spaces, hyphens, and apostrophes are deducted from the number of characters to be guessed and are displayed in their correct position. The idea, after all, is to make the game sufficiently difficult, but not downright impossible!

5. The next block of code goes immediately after the one entered in step 4 (around line 47). It controls the action of the game each time the player clicks the enter button. The code has been liberally commented, so you should be able to follow what it does. A couple of small refinements have been made to the original code, such as putting the cursor inside the input text field ready for the next guess and relieving some of the misery of losing by displaying the word that brought about the player's undignified and untimely demise.

```
interface_mc.enter_btn.onRelease = function() {
  // assume the guess is wrong until it has been checked
  wrong = true;
  // clear the text in the interface movie clip
  interface_mc.display_txt.text = "";
  // loop through each letter of the word
  // if the guess is one of the letters needed, assign to foundLetter
  // if the letter has not already been found, assign to notGuessed
  for (var i:Number=0; i<selectedWord.length; i++) {
    foundLetter = lettersNeeded[i] == interface_mc.input_txt.text;
    notGuessed = lettersGuessed[i] != interface_mc.input_txt.text;
    if (foundLetter && notGuessed) {
    // guess matches a letter not found before
    // so wrong is no longer true
      wrong = false;
      lettersLeftToGo–;
      lettersGuessed[i] = interface_mc.input_txt.text;
    }
    // rebuild the text for display in the interface movie clip
```

```
    interface_mc.display_txt.text += lettersGuessed[i];
  }
  // clear the input text field
  interface_mc.input_txt.text = "";
  // set the cursor inside the input text field ready for next guess
  Selection.setFocus("interface_mc.input_txt");

  if (wrong) {
    // move the hanging man movie to the next frame
    hangman_mc.nextFrame();
    if (hangman_mc._currentframe == 10) {
      // YOU LOST!
      interface_mc.guess_txt._visible = false;
      interface_mc.input_txt._visible = false;
      interface_mc.enter_btn._visible = false;
      // display the full word you were looking for
      interface_mc.display_txt.text = selectedWord;
      // reset play game button for another try
      playGame_btn._visible = true;
    }
  }
  if (lettersLeftToGo == 0) {
  // all letters have been guessed
    hangman_mc.gotoAndStop("win");
    // reset graphics for next game
    interface_mc._visible = false;
    playGame_btn._visible = true;
  }
};
```

6. Test the movie, and pit your wits against whatever the database throws at you. If you encounter any problems, check your code against `hangman03.fla`. One thing that's missing, though, is a way of keeping score. That's easily fixed.

Building a scoring mechanism that remembers

If you think about it for a minute, keeping score is not all that difficult. The callback function in step 5 of the previous section contains two conditional statements that control the graphical interface when you either run out of chances (in other words, lose) or guess the complete word (win). All that's needed is to include incremental win and lose counters in both `if` statements, and display the results onscreen. The problem is that any score is wiped out as soon as you close the browser. You need a way of preserving information between visits. There are a number of ways around this:

- Store the scores in a database table.
- Create a cookie and store the details on the player's own computer.
- Use the Flash `SharedObject`.

Although you could use PHP to implement the first two solutions, the Flash SharedObject is perfect for this type of situation. So, rather than use PHP just for the sake of it, let's use the most appropriate solution for the job.

> *The Perl programming language has a rather useful slogan:* **TMTOWTDI** *(pronounced "tim-toady"), which stands for "There's more than one way to do it." Even if you never venture as far as learning Perl (some say it can do irreparable damage to your sanity), the slogan is well worth remembering. When working with websites or programming languages, there are often several ways of achieving the same goal. The key is to experiment and decide which is the most appropriate for the job. When experimenting for this chapter, I discovered that the most obvious method of transferring the contents of the word list to the SQLite database took more than 18 minutes. An alternative method took less than one second. Can you guess which one I eventually decided on? Details later in the chapter.*

Introducing the Flash SharedObject

If you have not come across the SharedObject before, it performs a function very similar to cookies by storing information in a special file on the user's hard disk. What makes it preferable to cookies is that the SharedObject allows you to store up to 100KB of information, 25 times as much as a cookie (although the 100KB is shared by all movies on the same domain). Moreover, the information is stored and accessed directly through object properties, rather than as an array of name/value pairs.

Using the SharedObject is simple. Instead of creating an instance, you call the getLocal() method directly on the SharedObject class, passing it the name of the SharedObject you want to create, like this:

```
var score:SharedObject = SharedObject.getLocal("score");
```

If a SharedObject of that name already exists on the user's local computer, the data held in it is retrieved. Otherwise, Flash creates the necessary local file ready to receive data. The files are created in folders unique to each domain, so there is no danger of data from a SharedObject from a different domain getting mixed up, even if it uses the same file name.

To store a value in a SharedObject, you assign it to the data property. So, this is how you store the number of times a player has won in a variable called wins:

```
score.data.wins = timesWon;
```

To retrieve the value already stored in the data property, simply turn the assignment around:

```
timesWon = score.data.wins;
```

To update the values held by the SharedObject, call the flush() method:

```
score.flush();
```

Adding a scoring system to the Hangman game

Although the instructions here are specific to the Hangman game, they can be easily adapted to work with any Flash game.

1. Continue working with the same Flash document as before, or use `hangman03.fla` from the download files. The completed code and graphics for this section are in `hangman04.fla`. Insert a new movie clip symbol called score.
2. Everything in the movie clip goes on frame 1 of Layer 1. There are just five things on the stage:
   - A static text field for won
   - A static text field for lost
   - A dynamic text field called won_txt
   - A dynamic text field called lost_txt
   - A button for clear score called clear_btn

   Lay them out as shown in the image alongside. (The font used for the static text is again Bradley Hand ITC. If you don't have that particular font, use an alternative, or use the graphic symbols in the Library panel of the download file.)

   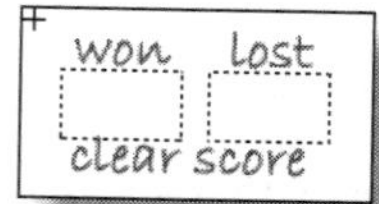

3. When you have finished, click Scene 1 to exit the symbol-editing window and drag an instance of the score movie clip onto the main stage. I placed it alongside the interface movie clip. Give the score movie an instance name of score_mc.

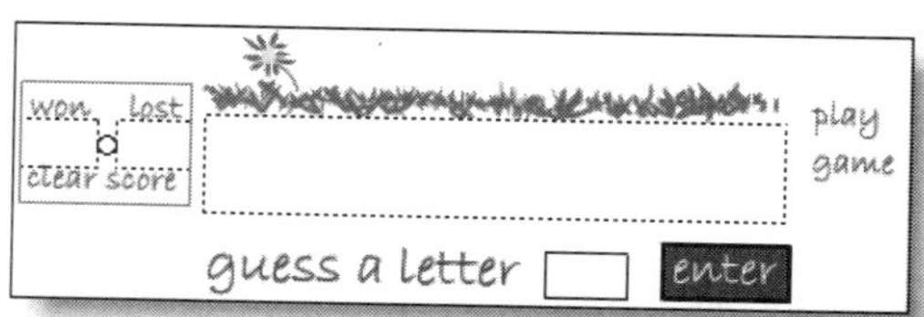

4. Highlight frame 1 of the actions layer, and open the Actions panel. Amend the two conditional statements inside the `onRelease` callback function for enter_btn as follows (the additional code is in bold):

```
if (wrong) {
  // move the hanging man movie to the next frame
  hangman_mc.nextFrame();
  if (hangman_mc._currentframe == 10) {
    // YOU LOST!
    interface_mc.guess_txt._visible = false;
    interface_mc.input_txt._visible = false;
    interface_mc.enter_btn._visible = false;
```

```
      // display the full word you were looking for
      interface_mc.display_txt.text = selectedWord;
      timesLost++;
      score_mc.lost_txt.text = timesLost;
      score.data.lost = timesLost;

      // reset play game button for another try
      playGame_btn._visible = true;
    }
  }
  if (lettersLeftToGo == 0) {
    // all letters have been guessed
    hangman_mc.gotoAndStop("win");
    timesWon++;
    score_mc.won_txt.text = timesWon;
    score.data.won = timesWon;
    // reset graphics for next game
    interface_mc._visible = false;
    playGame_btn._visible = true;
  }
```

The three extra lines of code in each conditional statement increment the timesLost or timesWon variable by 1, and assign the new value to both the dynamic text field and the data property of the score SharedObject.

5. Add the following code close to the end of the script in the Actions panel, just above the final three lines that hide the game interface and stop the main timelines:

```
// initialize score SharedObject and score_mc
var score:SharedObject = SharedObject.getLocal("score");
if (score.data.won == undefined) {
  score.data.won = 0;
}
if (score.data.lost == undefined) {
  score.data.lost = 0;
}
var timesWon:Number = score.data.won;
var timesLost:Number = score.data.lost;
score_mc.won_txt.text = timesWon;
score_mc.lost_txt.text = timesLost;
```

The first time the movie is loaded, there will be no SharedObject file from which to get stored values. Although Flash automatically creates the file, the data property will not contain any defined values. So it is necessary to set won and lost explicitly to zero before assigning them to the timesWon and timesLost variables, and displaying them in the dynamic text fields. On subsequent visits, won and lost will no longer be undefined, so the stored values will be used instead.

6. There's just one final thing to do before the scoring system is complete. Add the following function just above the section where all the main variables are initialized (around line 102):

```
score_mc.clear_btn.onRelease = function() {
  timesWon = 0;
  timesLost = 0;
  score_mc.won_txt.text = score.data.won = timesWon;
  score_mc.lost_txt.text = score.data.lost = timesLost;
  score.flush();
};
```

This will clear the score from score_mc and the score SharedObject by resetting the variables that keep the running score. The new values are then assigned simultaneously to the data property of the SharedObject and the dynamic text fields. Finally, the flush() method is used to write the new values to the SharedObject file. Although Flash should automatically write the values when the browser window is closed, it is more reliable to write them explicitly with flush().

7. Publish the movie and test it in a browser. Not only should the game keep a running score as shown here, but also the score should still be there even after you close down and reboot your computer. If you have any problems, compare your script with hangman04.fla.

Other ways to enhance the game

Once you start adding new features to a game (or any project, for that matter), you will often find your mind beginning to race. What about this? Wouldn't it be cool if . . . ? Here are just a couple of suggestions for you to experiment with. There are no step-by-step instructions, as you should be familiar enough with PHP and ActionScript to implement them yourself by now, with just a little help.

Handling database failures

One of the cool things about the custom-built Database class is that it's capable of sending error messages that Flash can use in some way or another (no, I hadn't forgotten!). In the case of a game like this, you probably don't want to relay the details of the error message to your visitors, but there might be occasions when you want to do so. Consequently, it's useful to have the message in a form that can be used if required. Let's take a quick look at how you might handle database failure.

As Figure 7-3 showed, if an error occurs when using the Database class, it outputs a message that begins with error=, followed by a URL-encoded string. This means you can use the LoadVars.onLoad event handler to check whether the variable error has been set, like this:

```
getWords.onLoad = function() {
  if (this.error !== undefined) {
  // do something with the error message
  } else {
  // handle as normal
  }
};
```

Changing the output of error messages

After testing your PHP script in a browser, you may decide to change the error messages output by the Database class to something you can display in the Flash movie. In that case, change the values of the $error variable in database_php4.php (the version written in PHP 4 syntax) or of the string in parentheses after throw new Exception in the PHP 5 versions. For instance, you might change this line:

```
throw new Exception ("Couldn't connect $this->user to $this->dbName");
```

to this:

```
throw new Exception ('Sorry, game unavailable');
```

However, that makes the Database class less informative than it's intended to be. You don't want visitors to see your mistakes, so it's probably a good idea to get Flash to display the game unavailable message itself (hangman05.fla in the book's download files shows one way this can be achieved).

Then, if only your Flash movie could phone home like ET . . . With the help of PHP, it can.

Getting PHP to phone home

You learned in Chapter 2 how to use the PHP mail() function to send feedback from an online form. Well, you can use the same technique to get a PHP script to alert you silently to any problem that arises, such as a failed database connection. All it requires is a few minor amendments to the Database class. The principle is the same for each version, but the code is different in PHP 4 and PHP 5 syntax. The full code for all these classes is in the download files for this chapter. They all have phonehome in the filename.

Amending the PHP 5 Database classes

The instructions in this section apply to **both** `database_mysql.php` and `database_mysqli.php`.

1. Open the PHP 5 Database class in `phpflash/classes`.
2. Add two more property declarations to the list at the top of the page (the final existing one is shown for clarity, with the additions in bold text), like this:

```
protected $resultObj;
protected $email = 'myaddress@example.com';
protected $subject = 'Database connection problem';
```

   This assigns default values to `$email` and `$subject`. Change the values to the email address and subject line that you want used whenever there is a problem with the database.

3. Locate the following section of code in the `connect()` function:

```
catch (Exception $e) {
  echo $this->flash ? 'error='.urlencode($e->getMessage()) :
➥ $e->getMessage();
  exit();
  }
```

4. If you want to send an email only when Flash is being used, change it to

```
catch (Exception $e) {
  if ($this->flash) {
    mail($this->email, $this->subject, $e->getMessage());
    echo 'error='.urlencode($e->getMessage());
    }
  else {
    echo $e->getMessage();
    }
  exit();
  }
```

   This replaces the existing conditional operator (`?:`) test for Flash with an `if... else` conditional statement. If Flash is being used, the error message is both emailed and sent as data to Flash. If Flash is not being used, the error message is displayed in the browser only.

5. If you want to send the error message by email regardless of whether Flash is being used, change the code in step 3 to this:

```
catch (Exception $e) {
  mail($this->email, $this->subject, $e->getMessage());
  echo $this->flash ? 'error='.urlencode($e->getMessage()) :
➥ $e->getMessage();
  exit();
  }
```

6. Repeat steps 3 to 5 with the `query()` function.

Amending the PHP 4 Database class

1. Open `database_php4.php` in the `phpflash/classes` folder.
2. Add two more property declarations to the list at the top of the page (the final existing one is shown for clarity, with the additions in bold text), like this:

```
var $resultObj;
var $email = 'myaddress@example.com';
var $subject = 'Database connection problem';
```

   This assigns default values to `$email` and `$subject`. Use the email address you want the error message sent to. Also, make any changes you want to `$subject`. This is the text that will appear in the subject line of the email message generated whenever there is a problem with the database.

3. Locate the following section of code in the `connect()` function:

```
if (!mysql_select_db($this->dbName, $this->dbLink)) {
  $error = 'Couldn\'t open Database: '. $this->dbName;
  echo $this->flash ? 'error='.urlencode($error) : $error;
  exit();
  }
```

4. If you want to send an email only when Flash is being used, change it to

```
if (!mysql_select_db($this->dbName, $this->dbLink)) {
  $error = 'Couldn\'t open Database: '. $this->dbName;
  if ($this->flash) {
    mail($this->email, $this->subject, $error);
    echo 'error='.urlencode($error);
    }
  else {
    echo $error;
    }
  exit();
  }
```

   This replaces the existing conditional operator (`?:`) test for Flash with an `if... else` conditional statement. If Flash is being used, the error message is both emailed and sent as data to Flash. If Flash is not being used, the error message is displayed in the browser only.

5. If you want to send the error message by email regardless of whether Flash is being used, change the code in step 3 to this:

```
if (!mysql_select_db($this->dbName, $this->dbLink)) {
  $error = 'Couldn\'t open Database: '. $this->dbName;
  mail($this->email, $this->subject, $error);
  echo $this->flash ? 'error='.urlencode($error) : $error;
  exit();
  }
```

6. You need to make similar changes to the query() function. Locate this section of code:

```
if (!$this->result) {
  $error = 'MySQL Error: ' . mysql_error();
  echo $this->flash ? 'error='.urlencode($error) : $error;
  exit();
  }
```

7. If you're sending email only when Flash is being used, change it to this:

```
if (!$this->result) {
  $error = 'MySQL Error: ' . mysql_error();
  if ($this->flash) {
    mail($this->email, $this->subject, $error);
    echo 'error='.urlencode($error);
    }
  else {
    echo $error;
    }
  exit();
  }
```

8. If you're always sending error messages by email, change the code in step 6 to this:

```
if (!$this->result) {
  $error = 'MySQL Error: ' . mysql_error();
  mail($this->email, $this->subject, $error);
  echo $this->flash ? 'error='.urlencode($error) : $error;
  exit();
  }
```

Getting the Database *class to send automatic emails like this may seem excessive for a game like Hangman, but it is a major improvement for other, more important applications that rely on a database connection. The email silently phones home, alerting you immediately to problems—and reducing to a minimum the likelihood of lost business.*

Setting different skill levels

The word list contains a large number of long words or expressions. If you want to make the game easier for small children, a simple way to do so would be to eliminate all hyphenated words and expressions consisting of more than one word. To do this, change the regex used to filter the results from the database like this:

```
$pattern = "/$'|[-\sA-Z\.]/";
```

By placing the hyphen at the beginning of the custom character class inside the square brackets, the regex treats it as a real hyphen, not as indicating a range of characters. Multiple words are eliminated through a search for any whitespace with the \s metacharacter (see Chapter 4).

Another way of setting skill levels is to impose a maximum length for each word. The code in hangman.php already has a variable for $min. Add one for $max, and change the SQL query like this:

```
// picks between minimum and maximum
$sql = "SELECT word FROM wordlist
        WHERE LENGTH(word) BETWEEN $min AND $max
        ORDER BY RAND()
        LIMIT $numWords";
```

The MySQL comparison operator BETWEEN *min* AND *max* does exactly what you expect—it selects values between *min* and *max*. (The smaller number must come first. It won't work the other way around.) You could hard-code the values into the SQL query, but using PHP variables makes your code far more flexible. For instance, you could create a combo box in your Flash movie to allow players to choose the skill level they want to play at. Using exactly the same techniques as in the multiconverter application that you built in Chapter 3, you could use LoadVars to send the chosen skill level to hangman.php, where a switch statement would set different values for $min and $max.

I could, of course, spoon-feed you the code, but by now you should have built up sufficient confidence to do it on your own. One of the keys to successful web development is cherry-picking techniques from different projects and combining them into something of your own. What's more, I want to devote the remaining pages of this chapter to something new to PHP 5: an alternative database solution called SQLite.

SQLite: An alternative database system

I'll now show you briefly how to add the same database functionality to the Hangman game using SQLite. This section introduces no new PHP techniques, apart from the methods needed to work with SQLite, so feel free to move on to the next chapter and come back later.

SQLite basics

Unlike MySQL, SQLite does not require data to be stored in a particular location. Nor is there any need to set up a root user or, indeed, any other usernames. As long as your PHP script has read and write permissions, you can store your database in any folder. Creating a database is also simplicity itself. The same command is used both to create a new database and to open an existing one. If the database doesn't exist, SQLite creates an empty one for you. Although this can make life easy, it also has a potential danger: if you make a slight mistake in the name of a database or its location, you end up with a new one. Unless you are very careful about file maintenance, you could end up with your data in several different places, and you might insert new records in the wrong file. Also, the lack of strict user privileges makes your data more vulnerable to attack.

SQLite offers both an OO interface and the traditional procedural functions that may be more familiar to PHP old hands. Since I used the OO interface for MySQL, I'll do the same for SQLite.

To open an existing database or create a new one, create a new `SQLiteDatabase` object and pass it the filename as the sole parameter:

```
$db = new SQLiteDatabase('mydatabase.db');
```

This will create or access a database in the same folder as the PHP script. If you want to access a database in a different folder, use either an absolute or a relative path.

One of the things you may have noticed about MySQL is that you never have to provide a path for your database. This is because MySQL keeps all data files in a central location, which depends on your operating system and version of MySQL. Having everything in a single location is generally more secure, and it makes maintenance much easier, although you should normally use a MySQL utility to back up and transfer data files rather than simply attempt to copy them. Refer to Appendix E for details.

Giving the database file a `.db` extension in SQLite is purely convention. You can call the file anything you like—PHP and SQLite don't care, as long as the name doesn't contain any illegal characters (such as ? or /).

To insert or retrieve records from the database, create a SQL query and pass it to the `query()` method, like this:

```
$sql = 'SELECT * FROM wordlist LIMIT 50';
$result = $db->query($sql);
```

SQLite's OO interface takes advantage of new features in PHP 5 that allow you to loop through the results without the need to use the `fetch()` method on each row—it does it for you automatically. The following methods both do the same thing:

```
// using the fetch() method on each row
while ($row = $result->fetch()) {
  echo $row['word'].'<br />';
  }

// using a foreach loop without the fetch() method
foreach ($result as $row) {
  echo $row['word'].'<br />';
  }
```

As you can see, using SQLite is similar in many ways to using the `mysqli` OO interface and the custom-built classes discussed earlier in the chapter. Although there are differences, there are enough similarities to make it easy to switch from one to the other. The biggest difference, though, comes in the range of SQL functions you can use, which can make SQLite much less convenient. The other consideration is the need to set the correct permissions on the database files and the folders you store them in.

Making sure SQLite has the right permissions

When running SQLite with PHP, the web server works directly with the database files and requires at the very least read permission. If you want to be able to insert, update, or delete records, the web server also needs write permission. If both your local computer and web server run on Windows, SQLite should already have the requisite permissions, so you'll simply set up a dedicated folder to store your SQLite databases. For the purposes of this book, create a subfolder called `data` in the `phpflash` folder, and then, if both your servers use Windows, you can skip to the section called "Creating the word list database in SQLite."

If your remote server runs on Linux or Unix (as most PHP domains do), or if you are using Mac OS X, read on.

Operating systems such as Linux, Unix, and Mac OS X work on the basic principle that users should be given the minimum level of access they need to perform their tasks. There are three levels of access, each identified by a letter or number, as listed in Table 7-2.

Table 7-2. Permissions on Linux, Unix, and Mac OS X

Name	Letter	Number	Description
Read	r	4	Allows a user to read a file or the contents of a folder (normally called a **directory** on Linux or Unix).
Write	w	2	Allows a user to create new files and subfolders, and alter existing ones.
Execute	x	1	When applied to a file, this access level allows a user to execute a script or program. When applied to a folder (directory), it gives permission to access the contents, but *only* if the same permission has been granted to the user in all folders higher up the path hierarchy.

In addition to these three levels of access, permissions are set separately for the owner of the file or folder, the group owner, and for everybody else. Normally, the owner has at least read and write permissions, but the group owner may have only read permission, and everyone else may have no permissions at all.

The letters identifying permissions are displayed as a single string when listing the contents of a folder in Mac OS X, Linux, or Unix. Figure 7-5 shows the contents of the `phpflash` folder as seen in Terminal on Mac OS X. You may have seen similar output when using an FTP program with a website or, if you have command-line access, when you type the command `ls -l` (the same command is used on all three systems).

```
Terminal — bash — 80x24
Last login: Sat Sep 18 11:29:05 on ttyp1
Welcome to Darwin!
Vigor14:~ davidpowers$ cd Sites/phpflash
Vigor14:~/Sites/phpflash davidpowers$ ls -l
total 0
drwxr-xr-x  6 davidpow  davidpow  204 19 Jun 13:34 ch02
drwxr-xr-x  3 davidpow  davidpow  102 10 Aug 16:08 ch05
drwxr-xr-x  5 davidpow  davidpow  170 17 Sep 21:52 ch07
Vigor14:~/Sites/phpflash davidpowers$ 
```

Figure 7-5. Displaying the permissions and ownership of a folder in Terminal on Mac OS X

The output in Figure 7-5 shows just three folders, all with the same permissions:

```
drwxr-xr-x
```

The d at the beginning indicates it is a folder (or, to use the correct Unix term, a directory). The next three letters (`rwx`) indicate that the file owner has read, write, and execute permissions. The following three characters (`r-x`) indicate that the group owner has only read and execute permissions. The final three characters (`r-x`) give everyone else the same read and execute permissions. The string always contains ten letters or hyphens. A hyphen indicates a permission that hasn't been granted, or if it's in the first position, a hyphen indicates that the item isn't a directory (in other words, it's a file). So, a file to which only the owner has any access would look like this:

```
-rwx------
```

The number following the permissions indicates the number of items in a folder. That's followed by the usernames of the owner of the file or folder, and of the group owner. As you can see in Figure 7-5, the same user is frequently both the principal owner and group owner.

Although you can use these letters to set permissions, it's much more convenient to use the numbers instead. Simply adding them together gives the appropriate permissions:

- No permissions: 0
- Execute only: 1
- Write only: 2
- Write and execute: 3
- Read only: 4
- Read and execute: 5
- Read and write: 6
- Full permissions: 7

You will recognize these numbers if you have ever been told to `chmod` a file on your web server. The folders shown in Figure 7-5 have all been set to `755`. The example of the file that only the user can access has a setting of `700`.

Most of the time, the appropriate permissions are set automatically by the operating system, depending on the privileges of the user. Unfortunately, the levels set for the web server are usually insufficient to create and modify SQLite databases. A convenient solution to the permissions and security problem is to create a dedicated folder that will be used only for SQLite data, and to give the web server group ownership and full permissions. That way, you retain ownership of the folder and all your normal permissions, while the web server gets the permissions it needs.

Setting up a SQLite folder on Mac OS X

These instructions have been tested on Mac OS X 10.3.5. You may need to adapt them slightly on a different system, but the general principles should still be the same.

1. If you haven't already done so, create a new folder called `data` as a subfolder of `phpflash` (in other words, `phpflash/data`). If using your Mac as a live server on the Internet, you may want to locate the folder at the top level of your server document root, so that all SQLite files are stored in the same place. In that case, I assume you know enough about file paths to be able to adjust the scripts later in the chapter to find your database.
2. Change the permissions on the `data` folder to give Apache full access through group ownership. Although you can do this in Terminal using sudo and chmod, the easier way is through Finder. Highlight the `data` folder, and choose Get Info from the File menu (⌘+I) to bring up a window like that shown in Figure 7-6.
3. In the Ownership & Permissions section at the bottom of the Get Info window, click the triangle next to Details to reveal the names of the file and group owners.
4. Click the lock icon to the right of the Owner's name, as shown in the image below, to unlock the details.

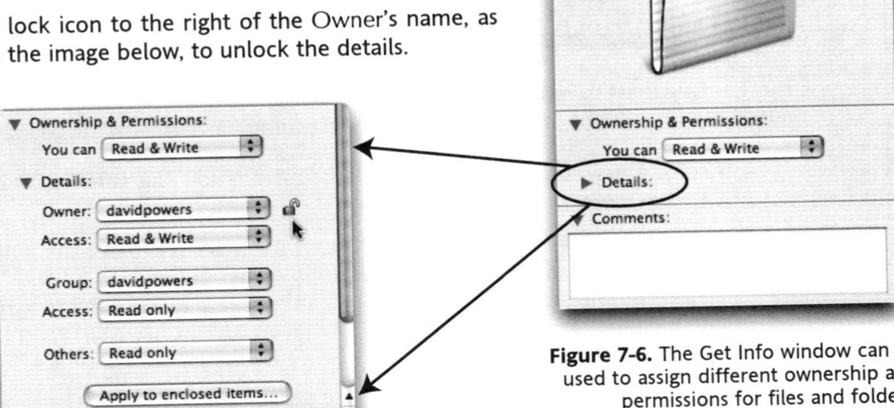

Figure 7-6. The Get Info window can be used to assign different ownership and permissions for files and folders.

5. Click the arrow to the side of the Group drop-down menu, and select www. A dialog box will open that prompts you to authorize this change. Enter your password and click OK. This gives Apache the necessary permissions to work with any SQLite databases you create in this folder. If www is not listed in the Group drop-down menu, skip to step 7.

6. Click the arrow to the side of the Access menu for the Group, and select Read & Write from the drop-down menu. Set the drop-down menu next to Others to No Access. Click the lock icon again to prevent the new settings from being accidentally changed, and close the Get Info window. The settings in the Get Info window should now look like those in Figure 7-7 (obviously, the username for Owner will be your own). You are now ready to use SQLite.

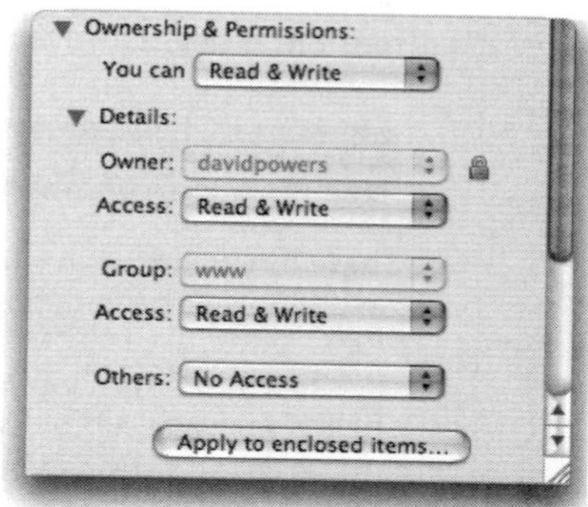

Figure 7-7. The final settings for the data folder on Mac OS X

7. If you could not find www in step 5, or if you cannot access SQLite databases in PHP, activate the drop-down menu next to Others and set it to Read & Write. This is less secure than giving group permission to Apache, but it is unlikely to create problems if you are working only on your local computer.

If you are using your Mac as a server on the Internet, open the Apache configuration file `httpd.conf` as described in Chapter 1. Search for Section 2 in `httpd.conf`, and scroll down about 40 lines to find the username and group name that Apache runs under. When using the default www, the configuration command looks like this:

```
User www
Group www
```

Repeat steps 5 and 6, substituting www with the name shown as User in `httpd.conf`.

Setting up a SQLite folder on a Linux server

These instructions have been tested on Red Hat Enterprise 3. They should work on any Linux server, but restrictions imposed by your hosting company may limit the changes you can make.

1. Create a new folder called `data` in your server root. This is normally called `htdocs`, so the new folder will be `htdocs/data`.

2. If you know the name that Apache runs under, and you have the authority to change group ownership, make Apache the group owner of the `data` folder. If you have access to the command line, change directory to `htdocs` and issue the following command:

```
chgrp apache data
```

This assumes that Apache runs under its own name. On some systems, it runs under the name nobody. Substitute the appropriate name.

3. Change the permissions on the data folder to 770. If you have access to the command line, the command is as follows:

```
chmod 770 data
```

4. If you don't know the name Apache uses, change the permissions on the data folder to 777. This is the least secure setting. Whether you leave it at this setting will depend on whether your hosting company allows you to change group ownership. If it does, create the word list as described in the next section, and then continue with step 5. If you are not allowed to change group ownership, you have no choice but to leave the permissions at 777.
5. Once you have created a database, change directory to the `data` folder, and check the name of the file owner and group owner. You can do this at the command line with the following command:

```
ls -l
```

6. Assign group ownership of the `data` folder to the name that was listed in step 5.
7. Change the permissions on the `data` folder to 770.
8. Delete the database and re-create it using the method described in the next section to make sure everything works as expected.

Creating the word list database in SQLite

Now let's put SQLite to work with the Hangman game. The first thing you need to do is create the database and populate it with data from the word list.

SQLite doesn't have an equivalent of MySQL's `LOAD DATA INFILE` syntax, so there's no way of loading data directly from a text file. Instead, you need to use PHP to extract the data first into an array, and then use an `INSERT` query to load each array element. (If you haven't created the MySQL database, you'll need to download the `12dicts` package from SourceForge and extract the `3esl.txt` file. The instructions are in the section "Downloading and installing the word list" in the previous chapter.)

1. Create a new PHP page called `loadwordlist.php` in `phpflash/ch07`, and insert the following code after the opening PHP tag (the finished code is in the download files for this chapter):

```
$db = new SQLiteDatabase('../data/3esl.db');
```

This will create a new database file called `3esl.db` in the `data` folder. The relative path assumes the `data` folder is a subfolder of `phpflash`. If your `data` folder is elsewhere, amend the path accordingly.

2. Before you can store any data in the file, you need to create a table. You do this with the same SQL query as for MySQL. Add the following lines after the previous code:

```
$createTable = 'CREATE TABLE wordlist (word VARCHAR(30))';
$db->query($createTable);
```

The SQL query is quite short, so you could just as easily have passed it directly to the query() method without first storing it in a variable. The convenience of using a variable becomes more apparent when you're working with more complex queries. (For an explanation of the CREATE TABLE query, refer back to step 7 of "Downloading and installing the word list" in Chapter 6.)

You use SQLite methods in the same way as all PHP OO methods, by following the object name (in this case, $db) with the arrow operator (->) and then the method.

3. You now need to open the text file containing the word list, and read all the words into a temporary array. To make things simple, copy 3esl.txt to the same folder as the script you are currently building. (If you created the word list in MySQL in Chapter 6, your copy of 3esl.txt will be in the top level of the C drive on Windows or in your Documents folder on Mac OS X.) Add the next two lines at the end of your existing code:

```
$words = array();
$fh = fopen('3esl.txt', 'r');
```

This creates an empty array called $words and then uses fopen() to open 3esl.txt in read-only text mode. fopen() takes two strings as arguments: the first is the name of the file to be opened (amend the path accordingly if you saved 3esl.txt in a different location), and the second determines whether the file is to be read, written, or have new material appended to it. Once an external file has been opened, you need to store a reference to it in a variable, in this case $fh.

4. The next block of code uses a while loop to read in the contents of 3esl.txt one line at a time and prepare it for insertion into the database. It uses feof() to test whether the loop has reached the end of the file (which is where the function gets its strange name from: *file, end of*). feof() takes one argument—the reference to the opened file. It returns true only when it reaches the end of the file or encounters an error.

```
while (!feof($fh)) {
  $word = trim(fgets($fh));
  if (!strpos($word, '.') && strlen($word) > 2) {
    $words[] = sqlite_escape_string($word);
    }
  }
```

The second line of this block uses fgets(), which returns the contents of the current line of the open file, and trim(), which is one of the string functions covered in Chapter 4. This removes not only whitespace from a string, but also new line characters. Since each word is on a line of its own, it will have a new line character at the end that needs to be removed. The next line uses two other string functions that you met in Chapter 4. The first (strpos()) is used to make sure the word doesn't contain a period (thereby eliminating abbreviations); the second (strlen()) checks that the word is more than two characters long.

Finally, each word is passed to the SQLite function sqlite_escape_string(). This escapes any quotes that might cause problems with building the SQL query later in the script. PHP, like all computer languages, always tries to match quotes in pairs. An apostrophe is treated the same as a single quote and could unexpectedly terminate a string, as explained in Chapter 2.

SQLite escapes quotes by inserting an extra quote, unlike MySQL, which expects a backslash. When working with SQLite, you should always use the dedicated `sqlite_escape_string()` *function to prepare strings for insertion into a database. The automatic escaping of quotes by the PHP configuration setting* `magic_quotes_gpc` *or manual escaping with* `addslashes()` *will not work.*

5. Now that the contents of the word list have been read into the array, you must close the text file with the following code:

```
fclose($fh);
```

For more detailed coverage of the PHP file manipulation functions, see the PHP online documentation at `www.php.net/manual/en/function.fopen.php`*. Also see* Beginning PHP 5 and MySQL: From Novice to Professional *by W. Jason Gilmore (Apress, ISBN: 1-893115-51-8).*

6. The way to populate the database table is to perform a SQL `INSERT` command for every single element in the `$words` array. Since there are more than 21,000 elements in the array, it's important to choose the most appropriate method of doing so. The SQL query needed for each element is straightforward:

```
$sql = "INSERT INTO wordlist VALUES ('$word');"
```

This tells the database to add the value held in `$word` into the `wordlist` table. (The syntax behind the `INSERT` command is described in more detail in the next chapter.)

The most logical way of inserting all 21,000 or so words would seem to be a `foreach` loop, like this:

```
foreach ($words as $word) {
  $sql = "INSERT INTO wordlist VALUES ('$word');"
  $db->query($sql);
  }
```

It definitely works, but you need to override the default maximum running time for a script (30 seconds), and have a lot of patience. On a Pentium IV 3.20 GHz computer, it takes more than 18 minutes!

Fortunately, SQLite supports **transactions**, which ensure that a series of SQL commands are all executed as a single operation. They either all succeed or all fail. The way you create a transaction in SQLite is by building a massive query surrounded by the keywords `BEGIN` and `COMMIT`. All you need to do is adapt the previous `foreach` loop as follows:

```
$sql = 'BEGIN;';
foreach ($words as $word) {
  $sql .= "INSERT INTO wordlist VALUES ('$word');";
  }
$sql .= 'COMMIT;';
```

Note carefully that the $sql variable is built up using the combined concatenation and assignment operator (.=), with a period in front of the equal sign in the third and fifth lines of the preceding block. Also, there is a semicolon *inside* the closing quote of each string, as well as at the end of each statement. The semicolons are needed in the SQL query to tell SQLite that it's a *series* of commands (nearly 22,000 of them!), not just a single one.

7. Finally, you need to run the transaction and close the database connection. The transaction is performed in exactly the same way as an ordinary query (it's the BEGIN and COMMIT keywords together with the semicolons that make it a transaction):

```
$db->query($sql);
unset($db);
echo 'Done';
```

The unset() function closes down the database connection. The final line is included simply to indicate when the process has finished. Otherwise, the script should produce no output in a browser.

8. Your final code should look like this (inline comments have been added to make it easier to follow):

```
<?php
// create database file and table structure
$db = new SQLiteDatabase('../data/3esl.db');
$createTable = 'CREATE TABLE wordlist (word VARCHAR(30))';
$db->query($createTable);

// initialize array for words and open text file
$words = array();
$fh = fopen('3esl.txt', 'r');
while (!feof($fh)) {
  // remove any whitespace and new line characters from each line
  $word = trim(fgets($fh));
  // eliminate words with periods or less than three characters long
  if (!strpos($word, '.') && strlen($word) > 2) {
    // escape any quotes
    $words[] = sqlite_escape_string($word);
    }
  }
// close text file
fclose($fh);

// create SQL to insert words in a single transaction
$sql = 'BEGIN;';
foreach ($words as $word) {
  $sql .= "INSERT INTO wordlist VALUES ('$word');";
  }
$sql .= 'COMMIT;';

// perform transaction and close database
```

```
$db->query($sql);
unset($db);
echo 'Done';
?>
```

Save the file and run it in a browser. As long as you have not made any typing mistakes, you should see the word Done appear on the screen in next to no time. On the same machine that took more than 18 minutes with just a foreach loop, running the INSERT command as a transaction took fractionally over one second—more than 1,000 times faster! You will test the database in a moment, but a quick way of ensuring that everything went OK is to check the size of the resulting file, 3esl.db. It should be about 617KB. The code will fail if the data folder does not exist or if the right permissions were not set for the folder as described earlier.

You should run this script once only, because it defines the table in the database. Attempting to run it again after the DB file has been created will generate an error. If you need to rerun the script for any reason, first delete any DB file it has created.

Setting appropriate permissions on database files

The following instructions apply only to Mac OS X, Linux, and Unix servers. Windows servers should not require any changes. If you experience difficulty running SQLite databases on a Windows server, contact the server administrator to get the appropriate file permissions changed.

Although the web server needs execute permission on the folder where you store your SQLite databases, the permissions required for individual database files can be more restrictive. If the database will be read-only after it has been created, you can prevent anyone from overwriting it accidentally. Table 7-3 lists the recommended settings for individual SQLite database files.

Table 7-3. Recommended settings for SQLite database files

Purpose	chmod	Mac owner	Mac group	Mac others
Read-only	440	Read only	Read only	No Access
Updateable	660	Read & Write	Read & Write	No Access

If you cannot change group ownership on your remote server, use 444 and 666, respectively, as the chmod settings.

Rewriting the Hangman PHP script for SQLite

Now that you've built the word list database in SQLite format, all that's necessary is to adapt hangman.php. Since the PHP script for MySQL has already been described in detail (see the section "Refining the word selection with SQL and PHP" earlier in the chapter), the rewritten script is shown here with the differences highlighted in bold type. The full code is in hangman_sqlite.php in the download files.

```
<?php
// create instance of SQLiteDatabase
$db = new SQLiteDatabase('../data/3esl.db');

// initialize database query
$numWords = 250;
$min = 5;
$sql = "SELECT word FROM wordlist
        WHERE LENGTH(word) >= $min
        ORDER BY RANDOM(*)
        LIMIT $numWords";

// execute query
$result = $db->query($sql);

// initialize results string, counter, and regular expression
$words = '';
$count = 0;
$pattern = "/$'|[A-Z\.]/";

// loop through results, but skip any that match the regex
foreach ($result as $row) {
  if (preg_match($pattern, $row['word']))
    continue;
  // use counter to create unique variable (word0, etc) and build
  // string of name/value pairs to transmit to Flash
  $words .= '&word'.$count.'='.urlencode($row['word']);
  $count++;
  }
unset($db);

// output string to send data to Flash
// begin with total number of words accepted
// followed by a string of name/value pairs
echo 'total='.$count.$words;
?>
```

The first main difference is the lack of database connection variables—no hostname, username, or password. All that's needed is a new SQLiteDatabase object with the filename of the database as its sole parameter.

The next change is in the SQL query itself. To randomize the order of results in MySQL, you used the MySQL RAND() function. In SQLite, this is called RANDOM(*). SQLite has considerably fewer built-in functions that can be used in SQL commands. Many, but not all, are the same as in MySQL. You can find a full list of them in the SQLite online documentation at www.sqlite.org/lang.html#expr.

The query is executed in exactly the same way as with MySQL, but there is no need to fetch each row individually when looping through the results. The SQLite OO interface does that automatically in a `foreach` loop.

Finally, the database connection is closed by using `unset()` to destroy the instance of the `SQLiteDatabase` object. Apart from that, the script is identical.

To test the SQLite script with the Hangman game, temporarily rename the page containing the MySQL script, and save the preceding code as hangman.php. If you have copied everything correctly and set the right permissions, it should work exactly the same. Note, however, that this script does not do any error checking, nor does it have the ability to phone home when something goes wrong, although you could add both features.

Comparing MySQL and SQLite

Comparisons between the two database systems are difficult, because the systems are intended for different purposes. As its name suggests, SQLite is fast and light, and not really suited to heavy-duty use. It does, however, have some very good features, such as the ability to execute queries as transactions. For small or simple tasks, it's certainly worth considering, but its main drawback is that you could find yourself with an inadequate system if the demands on the database suddenly increase. Setting the right permissions on each file can also be a burden if you are not familiar with such issues.

Ever onward and upward

At the beginning of the chapter, I promised you some semiserious fun. I hope that you enjoy playing the enhanced Flash version of Hangman and that the serious side of this business was not so awful as to have you wishing me the same grisly fate as the victim in the game. This chapter covered a lot of important material. Not only have you seen how to work with two database systems, but also you've taken your first steps with what most people regard as an advanced aspect of PHP: the use of classes and OOP. On top of that, you've also learned how to use the Flash `SharedObject` to save persistent data without the need for a database.

In the next chapter, you'll build a more complex database and use it as the basis for an online registration system.

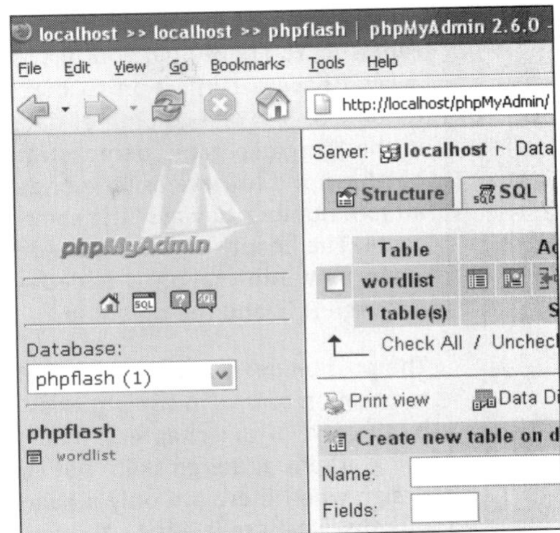

Chapter 8

CREATING A USER REGISTRATION DATABASE

What this chapter covers:

- Understanding the principles of database design
- Understanding MySQL storage formats: MyISAM and InnoDB
- Choosing the right column type
- Using phpMyAdmin to create database tables
- Building a user registration system

Fantastic. You have built your first database-driven Flash movie, but before you get too carried away, I have a confession to make: the word list is the crudest possible form of database. It contains just one column of data, and it has no form of indexing. But even the simple table in the Hangman game demonstrated how you can store a large amount of information in a database and retrieve as little or as much as you want. You can also use that information in an infinite number of ways. The same word list database could be used to drive any word-based game. The beauty of a database-driven site is that there is no need to rebuild the Flash movie when new information is added—your pages are updated automatically by the interaction between PHP and the database.

The possibilities opened up by combining a database with a website are so attractive, there's a temptation to dive in straight away. Building a database isn't difficult—you'll be able to do that by the end of this chapter. What's difficult is *designing* a database, and by that I don't mean using graphical design skills, but creating the right structure. It's easy to make changes to the design when there are only a handful of test records in the database. Once you have several months' worth of live data, though, it can be a nightmare trying to change the structure. Build in haste, and repent at leisure . . .

So, for the first part of this chapter, push the keyboard to one side and settle down for a primer in database design. Not all database designs are complicated, but it's essential to have a broad grasp of the issues involved. A little time spent studying this now will more than repay you in time saved avoiding mistakes later. Then I'll show you how to build a user registration system. It looks very simple, but—as you'll discover—quite a lot goes on in the background of a well-designed online form.

Understanding database types

Database design has undergone considerable changes in the short history of computing. Information in a database needs to be in a logical order for easy retrieval. It sounds simple enough, but when moving house, I have often gone through my possessions and thought, "How on earth did that get in there?" What may have at first seemed a logical place to put something can later strike you as completely bizarre.

The two main types of database are known as flat-file and relational databases.

Keeping things simple with flat-file databases

When personal computers first became popular in the 1980s, one of the main uses for early database software was building a list of personal contacts. The screen was made to resemble an individual card in a card index file, with fields to enter pieces of information such as name, address, and phone number. It's such an intuitive interface that the card index analogy survives even to this day in the Mac OS X Address Book, as shown in Figure 8-1. If you have a Mac and want to launch Address Book to check it out for yourself, just click the icon that looks like a notebook with a big @ on the front (see the image alongside). It's on the default Dock. If you've cleared the Dock and filled it with your own favorites, use Finder ➤ Applications ➤ Address Book.

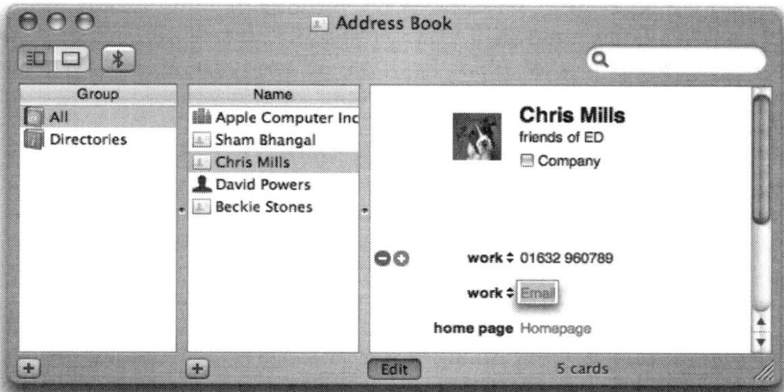

Figure 8-1. Address Book on the Mac gives a modern look to an old concept, using index cards as its interface.

The Mac Address Book is much more customizable than what was available two decades ago, but it uses the same underlying structure, known as a **flat-file database**. The name comes from the way records were stored one record per line in a plain text file, with each field separated by a delimiter, such as a comma or tab space. Although this type of database is normally stored in a different file format these days (the Mac Address Book uses the vCard VCF format), the principle is very similar. The illustration alongside shows the underlying code of the index card in Figure 8-1.

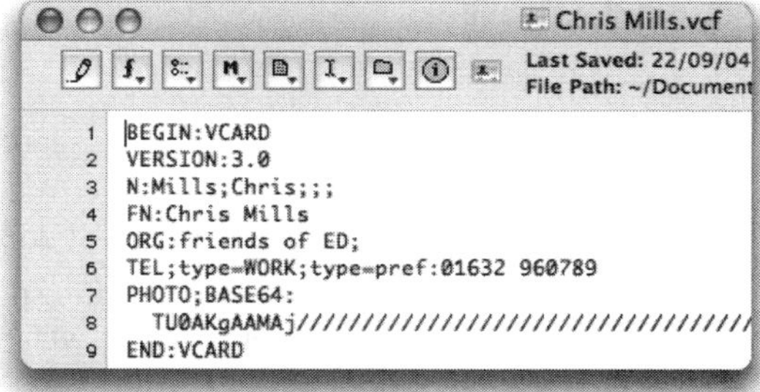


```
BEGIN:VCARD
VERSION:3.0
N:Mills;Chris;;;
FN:Chris Mills
ORG:friends of ED;
TEL;type=WORK;type=pref:01632 960789
PHOTO;BASE64:
  TU0AKgAAMAj/////////////////////////////////
END:VCARD
```

If you have a Windows PC, you can export the contents of the Windows Address Book in the same flat-file format as used by the 1980s databases. Open Address Book, then choose File ➤ Export and, depending on your version of Windows, either Address Book or Other Address Book. The Address Book Export Tool dialog box will open as shown in Figure 8-2.

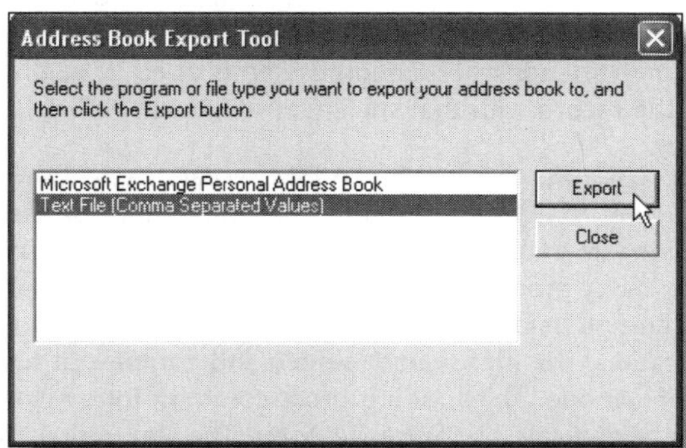

Figure 8-2. Windows Address Book allows you to export your entire contacts list as a CSV text file.

Again, depending on your setup, you will be offered one or more export formats. Text File (Comma Separated Values) should always be available. Select that option and click Export, and you will be offered the choice of which fields to include in the export file. After you have made your choices, follow the onscreen instructions, and the contents of the Address Book will be saved in CSV format. The default program for CSV files is the Excel spreadsheet, but if you open the file in a text editor such as Notepad, you will see something like this:

```
Name,Business Phone,Company,Job Title
David Powers,020-7946 1357,Japan Interface,Senior Partner
Sham Bhangal,0191-498 7654,Futuremedia,Flash Guru Extraordinaire
Chris Mills,01632 960789,friends of ED,Senior Editor
```

Each field is separated by a comma, and the entire contents of the database can be printed out "flat" on paper. Perhaps the most important feature to note is that each record is complete in itself. If the contacts list contained the names of 20 people at the same company, the company name would be repeated 20 times—once for each entry.

The simplicity of a flat-file database makes it easy to understand and maintain. It is ideal for a personal contacts list, but it is limited in terms of flexibility. Among the disadvantages of a flat-file database are the following:

- As the list becomes larger, search speeds slow down much more than with a relational database.
- It can be difficult to control duplicate records.
- There is no control over the spelling or format of important words, such as company names, states, or counties, which may be used as search criteria—resulting in less accurate searches.
- A lot of data is repeated, making searches slower and updating more difficult.

Gaining greater flexibility with relational databases

What makes a flat-file database difficult to work with is that everything is contained in a single table. Let's say you want to use an Address Book as the basis for a more detailed database, containing information about a person's salary, work record, vacation entitlement, and so on. Instead of a handful of fields (or columns), the table would grow and grow. As it grows, it becomes more difficult to maintain, and the likelihood of errors increases. Say, for instance, you misspell a company name—friends of ED becomes fiends of ED. If you're looking for everyone in the same company, the record with that spelling mistake will be left out of any search.

A far more flexible approach was devised by an IBM research scientist Edgar Codd, who published in 1970 a set of rules that was to become the foundation for the **relational database** model, which lies at the heart of all major database systems today, including MySQL, Microsoft SQL Server, Oracle, and many more. It's also the model used by less powerful systems, such as Access and SQLite, so an understanding of relational databases is essential for just about any database-related application. The idea is both simple and complex at the same time. A simple database may consist of just one table, but it is more common for a relational database to consist of several tables, each dedicated to a specific topic. The way you keep track of related data is by assigning each record a unique identifier called a **primary key**. The concept is rather abstract, but if you follow the examples over the next few pages, things should become clearer.

Let's start with something simple: a database to control access to restricted parts of your website. This can be contained in a single table. At the simplest level, all you need is a column for each username and another one for the user's password. It's also useful to know the user's real name. So, you might start off with something like Table 8-1.

Table 8-1. First attempt at creating a table to authorize access to a website

real_name	username	password
David Powers	dpowers	codeslave
Sham Bhangal	sbhangal	flashguru
Chris Mills	cmills	bigboss

On the face of it, there's nothing wrong with this table. In fact, it's identical in structure to the previous flat-file database example—only the column names and content are different. Let's make a couple of small changes, though, as shown in Table 8-2.

Table 8-2. A second attempt at creating the authorization table

user_id	first_name	family_name	username	password
1	David	Powers	dpowers	codeslave
2	Sham	Bhangal	sbhangal	flashguru
3	Chris	Mills	cmills	bigboss

The impact of these small changes can be seen if you put the same data into a spreadsheet like Excel, and use Data ➤ Sort to sort the records alphabetically by name. Figure 8-3 shows the difference in results.

1	real_name	username	password
2	Chris Mills	cmills	bigboss
3	David Powers	dpowers	codeslave
4	Sham Bhangal	sbhangal	flashguru

1	user_id	first_name	family_name	username	password
2	2	Sham	Bhangal	sbhangal	flashguru
3	3	Chris	Mills	cmills	bigboss
4	1	David	Powers	dpowers	codeslave

Figure 8-3. Using a spreadsheet to simulate the difference between sorting a flat-file and a relational database table

There are two important differences. The first one is perhaps not very surprising: because the names in the second table (on the right) have been separated into first name and family name, the sort order is more natural—Bhangal comes first, followed by Mills and Powers. When both first name and family name are in the same column, it's the alphabetical order of first names that wins the day. Far more important, though, is what happens to the `user_id` column. Even though my name is on row 4 of the spreadsheet, my `user_id` (1) has stayed with all my other details. The significance of this becomes apparent if you re-sort the records on the basis of the password. As Figure 8-4 shows, the `user_id` associated with each name remains firmly attached. Chris Mills is always `user_id 3`, wherever he appears in the sort order.

1	user_id	first_name	family_name	username	password
2	3	Chris	Mills	cmills	bigboss
3	1	David	Powers	dpowers	codeslave
4	2	Sham	Bhangal	sbhangal	flashguru

Figure 8-4. No matter how the records are sorted, the `user_id` always remains associated with the same data.

This is what is meant by assigning each record a unique identifier, or primary key. It's a very simple device, but it gives a relational database phenomenal power and flexibility. Let's take a look at the rules for creating tables in a relational database, and then I'll explain why adding the `user_id` to each record even on a single table database is potentially so useful.

Normalizing the data and primary and foreign keys

The basic idea behind a relational database is to remove any redundant duplication of data through a process known as **normalization**. Although there is no duplication in the simple authorization table so far, the type of thing Codd had in mind was the previous example, where the contacts list would have ended up with 20 identical entries for the company name. Such repetition, he reasoned, is not only wasteful, but also results in lost data when mistakes or variations in spelling are introduced. Codd was a mathematician, and his original, very technical language is difficult for non-mathematicians to understand. Fortunately, others have translated Codd's ideas into plain English, so that's the approach taken here. Let's start by defining several terms that will crop up repeatedly from now on.

- **Record**: This is a complete row of related data in a database table. Each row in Figure 8-5 constitutes an individual record and is identified by its primary key (`user_id`).
- **Column**: Each column in a database table stores the same piece of information for each individual record. For instance, the `first_name` column in Figure 8-5 stores the first name of each user, the `family_name` column stores the family name, and so on. In MySQL and most other relational databases, all items in a column will also be of the same type (the selection of column types is covered later in this chapter).
- **Field**: This is the intersection of a record and a column, where each piece of information is stored. It's the equivalent of a spreadsheet cell. In Figure 8-5, the `first_name` field for `user_id 1` contains "David."

> *The terms "column" and "field" are often used interchangeably, which can be a potential source of confusion. A **field** holds one piece of information for a single record, whereas a **column** contains all fields holding the same piece of information for each record. If "field" is used in describing a table, it really means column, not field.*

- **Foreign key**: This is the primary key from one table used as a cross-reference in another.

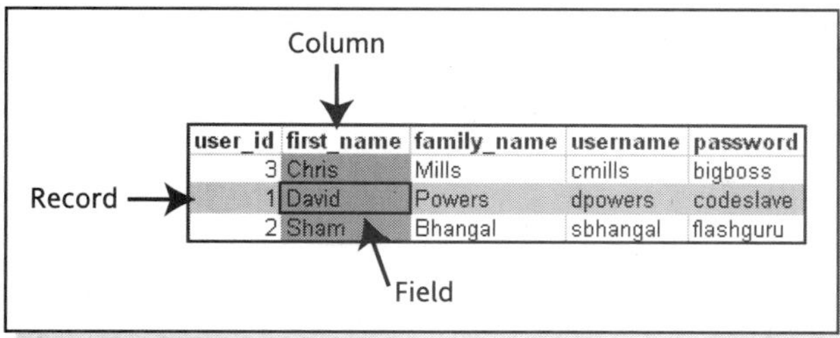

user_id	first_name	family_name	username	password
3	Chris	Mills	cmills	bigboss
1	David	Powers	dpowers	codeslave
2	Sham	Bhangal	sbhangal	flashguru

Figure 8-5. The three main elements that make up each table in a database

"Hang on a moment—you said in Chapter 6 that MySQL and SQLite don't support foreign keys." Well, yes and no. MySQL and SQLite don't have *full* support for foreign keys. They *do* support the use of foreign keys as shown in Figures 8-6 and 8-7, and as described in the following rules.

The rules Codd laid down can be summarized as follows:

- Give each data record a unique means of identification, known as a primary key. This is normally an automatically incremented number, but it can be anything (such as a Social Security number), as long as it is unique.
- Get rid of columns with similar content, and put each group of associated data in a table of its own.
- When columns contain data that is repeated, create a separate table and cross-reference with a unique identifier known as a foreign key. As with a primary key, this can be anything as long as it uniquely identifies the relationship. Most of the time, an automatically incremented number is used.

  So for instance, let's say there are a lot of people in this contacts list who work for friends of ED. Others may work for Apress or for other companies. You could create a new table called `publisher` and link to it from the address book (see Figure 8-6) by storing the publisher's primary key in each user's record. You could now change "friends of ED" to "foED" by changing just one value. If you had the string "friends of ED" duplicated all over your database, you would have to track down and change every single one (and you would lose any misspelled versions).

user_id	first_name	family_name	pub_id
1	David	Powers	1
2	Sham	Bhangal	1
3	Chris	Mills	1

pub_id	publisher
1	friends of ED
2	Apress
3	other

Figure 8-6. Using the primary key of one table as a foreign key in another table

- Store only one item of information in each field. Figure 8-6 shows this in practice on a simple database, but you frequently need to store more than one piece of information. Chris Mills and I, for instance, have written or edited books for both Apress and friends of ED. Sham has displayed his talents further afield. In this type of situation, you maintain the principle of one item of information in each field by using what's known as a **lookup table**. Figure 8-7 shows how this works in practice.

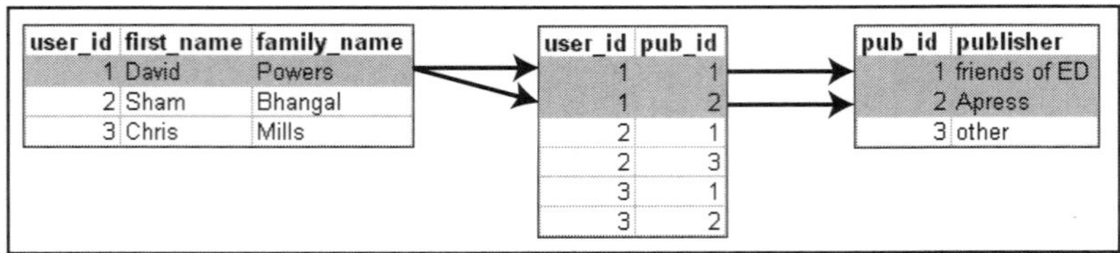

Figure 8-7. You can associate more than one piece of information with a record by using the primary keys from separate tables as the foreign key in a lookup table.

Instead of storing the publisher's primary key in the user's record, a new table stores the primary keys from the two tables you want to link. So, if you follow the arrows in Figure 8-7, you can see that David Powers (`user_id 1`) is linked to `pub_id 1` (friends of ED) and `pub_id 2` (Apress). If you check Sham's links, he has been published by friends of ED (`pub_id 1`) and the mysterious "other" (`pub_id 3`). More important, this linkage works the opposite way. By using the `pub_id` for Apress (`2`), you can find out that Chris (`user_id 3`) and I (`user_id 1`) have been published by Apress, but not Sham. You will see an example of a lookup table in action in Chapter 12.

> *Deciding how far to break down information into discrete elements can be one of the thorniest problems in table design. How far, for instance, should you break down an address or a name? There is no "right" answer—it depends on what your database is for. On balance, though, it's better to err on the side of caution, breaking names into family name and first name, and providing separate columns for city and state, province, or county. That way, searching and sorting become much easier.*

So, what is it that MySQL and SQLite can't do with foreign keys? In addition to the cross-referencing described here, **foreign key constraints** can be used to enforce what's called **referential integrity**. A database with full foreign key support (if set up correctly) would prevent me from removing anyone from the `users` table without first removing all the items cross-referenced to the same `user_id`. Alternatively, it would allow me to perform a **cascading delete**—in other words, removing the record with the primary key would automatically delete all dependent cross-references. However

- The same effect can be achieved by getting PHP to perform the necessary checks before updating or deleting records.
- The convenience of using foreign key constraints is, to some extent, canceled out by the extra steps needed to set them up when first designing the database.
- Full support for foreign keys will be available from MySQL 5.1.
- If you can't wait until then and want support for foreign key constraints now, choose the InnoDB format for your tables (see the next section).

It's not known when or if SQLite will support foreign key constraints.

Understanding MySQL storage formats

In principle, the idea of storing data in tables sounds straightforward enough, but no two databases are ever really alike. Some, like a news archive, just grow bigger and bigger, with items rarely being deleted or updated. Others, like a stock-control system, will have frequent insertions and deletions. In a financial database, you need to make sure that when money is transferred from one account to another, the whole series of operations (a **transaction** in database terminology) is canceled if any single part of it fails.

These different requirements have led to the development of different types of database storage engine. MySQL offers several, the two most important of which are MyISAM and InnoDB. Both are excellent, but they have different benefits and drawbacks. Perhaps the most important difference, as of MySQL 4.1, is that MyISAM does not support either foreign key constraints or transactions, whereas InnoDB does. Put in those terms, InnoDB looks to be the clear winner. Strange though it may seem, I'm going to recommend you use MyISAM. In fact, it's only because of a change to the Windows installation in late 2004 that I'm mentioning storage formats at all.

Since as far back as 2001, MyISAM and InnoDB have been bundled together as part of MySQL, but MyISAM has always been the default. In other words, to create InnoDB tables, you have always had to specify them explicitly. The release of the Windows Essentials version of MySQL muddied the waters: MyISAM is still technically the default, but the Windows configuration wizard switches the default to InnoDB in the vast majority of cases.

Since InnoDB has more features, why not forget about MyISAM? Here's why:

- MyISAM is extremely fast, easy to use, and highly efficient.
- InnoDB tables require up to twice as much disk space as their MyISAM equivalents.
- InnoDB tables never get smaller, even when data is deleted.
- InnoDB does not support full-text indexing. (Text searches are normally very fast, but building a full-text index can be useful in speeding up the process if your database contains a large number of text-intensive records.)
- InnoDB may not be supported by your hosting company, except for an extra charge.
- Both formats can be mixed in the same database, so there is no point creating larger InnoDB files unless you plan to use features not available in MyISAM.
- More features means more to learn; it's a good idea to concentrate on the basics with MyISAM first.
- The basic difference lies in file structure—both use the same SQL commands.
- Changing the storage format type is easy, so you can switch to InnoDB as soon as you're ready or have a specific requirement that can be fulfilled only by InnoDB.

Among the reasons that InnoDB may not be supported by your hosting company are table size, the fact that all data is stored in a common tablespace (creating potential complications for shared hosting), and the higher cost of a commercial license to support InnoDB.

My advice is to stick with MyISAM until you identify a real need for InnoDB. If you are using Mac OS X or any Windows installation other than Windows Essentials, that will be your default anyway. If you installed Windows Essentials, change the configuration file as instructed in Chapter 6. Once you decide you need the features offered by InnoDB, you can convert a table in seconds using the instructions in Appendix E. Converting back from InnoDB to MyISAM is equally simple.

In essence, you need to be aware of the availability of InnoDB, but do not use it unless MyISAM proves too restrictive. By the time you get to the level of expertise that might benefit from InnoDB's advanced features, there's a strong possibility MyISAM will also offer them.

Choosing the right column type

Column types, however, are something you need to get to grips with straight away. These fall into five main categories, although the first two are the most frequently used:

- Text
- Numbers
- Dates and time
- Predefined lists
- Binary

SQLite sidesteps the whole business of column types by treating everything as a text string. The one exception is that SQLite will sort the contents of a column in the correct numerical order if you specify it as numeric (otherwise 100 would appear before 5). At the same time, SQLite will not complain if you enter ten *in a numeric column. Most other databases, including MySQL, will reject such data as invalid. Whether you regard this flexibility as a danger or as a bonus depends on your requirements. Both ActionScript and PHP are moving in the direction of greater precision through strict typing and other rules. Flexibility certainly makes scripting easier, but the gains are frequently outweighed by the extra time it takes to debug unexpected behavior.*

Column types in MySQL

Rather than going into every type, the following sections highlight only those most frequently used. You can find details of all column types at `http://dev.mysql.com/doc/mysql/en/Column_types.html` (the MySQL documentation classifies text, predefined lists, and binary types as strings, but they are presented here separately because it seems a more intuitive way of regarding them). On a first reading, just skim through the column types to familiarize yourself with the basic principles, and then come back and use this section as a reference.

Storing text

The difference between the main text column types boils down to the maximum number of characters that can be stored in an individual field.

- **VARCHAR(n)**: A variable-length character string containing at most n characters. The maximum value of n is 255.
- **CHAR(n)**: A fixed-length character string of n characters. The maximum value of n is 255.
- **TEXT**: Stores text up to a maximum of 65,535 characters (equivalent to the text in about 20 pages of this book).

Although the CHAR column type allocates a fixed length, you can enter text containing fewer characters. The essential difference between CHAR and VARCHAR is that CHAR is marginally faster to search, while VARCHAR takes up less disk space. The space savings offered by VARCHAR normally make it the preferred column type for short text fields, such as names, headlines, book titles, and addresses. Use CHAR only if speed is at an absolute premium or if you have text fields of standard length.

The term "characters" here refers only to characters in the Latin1 (ISO-8859-1) character set—the default encoding for most Western European languages. Since the release of MySQL 4.1, you can specify different character sets for each column in a table. If you use a multibyte character set, such as UTF-8 (Unicode), the figures given here refer to the maximum number of bytes a text column can contain. This has important consequences for anyone using UTF-8 to store French, German, or any language using accented characters. All accented characters require 2 bytes for storage, as do the British pound (£), yen (¥), and cent (¢) symbols. Only the first 128 characters of Latin1 (equivalent to ASCII) can be stored in 1 byte. Languages that use different writing systems, such as Arabic, Chinese, and Japanese, require 3 and sometimes 4 bytes per character in UTF-8.

Storing numbers

Because databases are frequently used for calculations, MySQL offers a wide choice of numeric column types. The most frequently used are as follows:

- **INT**: Any whole number (integer) between –2,147,483,648 and 2,147,483,647. If the column is declared as UNSIGNED, the range is from 0 to 4,294,967,295. Not surprisingly, INTEGER is a synonym for the INT column type.
- **FLOAT**: A floating-point number. If the column is declared as UNSIGNED, negative numbers are not permitted. When creating this type of column, you can optionally add two comma-separated numbers in parentheses. The first number specifies the number of digits before the decimal point, and the second specifies the precision to which the decimal portion should be rounded. For example, FLOAT(10,4) will display up to ten digits before the decimal point and round the decimal to the fourth decimal place. Since PHP will format numbers after calculation (as described in Chapter 3), **it is recommended that you use FLOAT without the optional parameters**.
- **DECIMAL(M,D)**: A floating-point number *stored as a string*. This is a rather strange beast. Its purpose is to store numbers with a fixed number of decimal places in a format that is not subject to the rounding errors that can occur with floating-point numbers on a computer. It takes two parameters: M is the maximum number of digits that can be stored, and D is the number of decimal places. In keeping with its unorthodox behavior,

`DECIMAL(6,2)` can store numbers from –9,999.99 to 99,999.99. The extra digit on the positive side is made possible because space is no longer required for the minus sign. If you omit the parameters (and the parentheses), MySQL treats a `DECIMAL` column as an integer with a maximum of ten digits. **This column type is best avoided**.

`DECIMAL` has been listed here, not so much for its usefulness, but to warn you about its weird behavior. Its main use is intended to be for currencies. However, a far more practical way of storing currencies in a database is to use an `INT` column. For instance, if you are working in dollars or euros, store currencies as cents; if you are working in pounds, use pence. Then use PHP to divide the result by 100, and format the currency as desired. This avoids the problem of rounding errors and speeds up calculations because currencies are stored in numeric form, not strings.

Storing dates and times

Working with dates is a veritable minefield for the unwary, because of the different conventions in use around the world. According to the schedule for this book, the final text for the cover was due on 1/6/2005. To me, as a European, that means the first day of June. Fortunately, I'm used to the strange customs of the Americans (at least as far as dates are concerned), and I knew what it *really* meant was January 6. Otherwise, I would have been five months late. MySQL avoids such ambiguity completely, but it means a change in habits for both Americans and Europeans. Dates must always be formatted according to the ISO style of year-month-date. MySQL has five column types for storing dates and times:

- **`DATE`**: A date displayed in the format `YYYY-MM-DD`. The supported range is 1000-01-01 to 9999-12-31.
- **`TIME`**: A time displayed in the format `HH:MM:SS`. The valid range is –838:59:59 to 838:59:59. This permits you to use a time column for representing elapsed time or a time interval between two events.
- **`DATETIME`**: A combined date and time displayed in the format `YYYY-MM-DD HH:MM:SS`.
- **`TIMESTAMP`**: A timestamp (normally generated automatically by the computer). Legal values range from the beginning of 1970 to partway through 2037. Since version 4.1, MySQL displays a timestamp in the same format as `DATETIME`. Earlier versions display the contents of a `TIMESTAMP` column as `YYYYMMDDHHMMSS` without any spaces or punctuation.
- **`YEAR`**: A year displayed as `YYYY`. The valid range is 1901 to 2155.

The formats shown in this list describe how MySQL displays a value stored in each type of column. It gives you considerable leeway, however, when entering data. The full list of acceptable formats can be found at `http://dev.mysql.com/doc/mysql/en/DATETIME.html`. I strongly recommend that you adhere to the same format as MySQL uses to display dates and times. Adopting a consistent style reduces the likelihood of mistakes.

> *The only check that MySQL performs on dates and times is whether they fall within the valid range for MySQL. It does not check whether a date actually exists. For example, it will accept 2005-04-31, even though April has only 30 days. Fortunately, PHP has a function to verify dates:* `checkdate()`*. Working with dates is such an important subject that the whole of Chapter 11 is devoted to it.*

Storing predefined lists

MySQL lets you store two types of predefined list that could be regarded as the database equivalents of radio button and check box states:

- **ENUM**: This column type stores a single choice from a predefined list, such as "yes, no, don't know" or "male, female." The maximum number of items that can be stored in the predefined list is a mind-boggling 65,535—some radio-button group!
- **SET**: This column type stores zero or more choices from a predefined list. The list can hold a maximum of 64 choices.

While ENUM is quite useful, SET tends to be less so, mainly because it violates the principle of storing only one piece of information in a field. The type of situation where it can be useful is when recording optional extras on a car or multiple choices in a survey. To determine whether a particular option has been chosen, MySQL provides the function `FIND_IN_SET()`. For details, see the online documentation at `http://dev.mysql.com/doc/mysql/en/String_functions.html`.

Storing binary data

Storing binary data in a database is generally not a good idea. Databases are very good at searching text and numbers, but not binary data, such as images or audio files. While that may sound a devastating blow to anyone developing multimedia applications, such as in Flash, it's not at all a limitation. Instead of storing images or audio files inside the database, it's far more efficient to save them outside, and use the database to catalog the details (see Figure 8-8). That way, you can use the search features of the database to identify your visual or audio media quickly, by using either the filename or a written description of what the file contains.

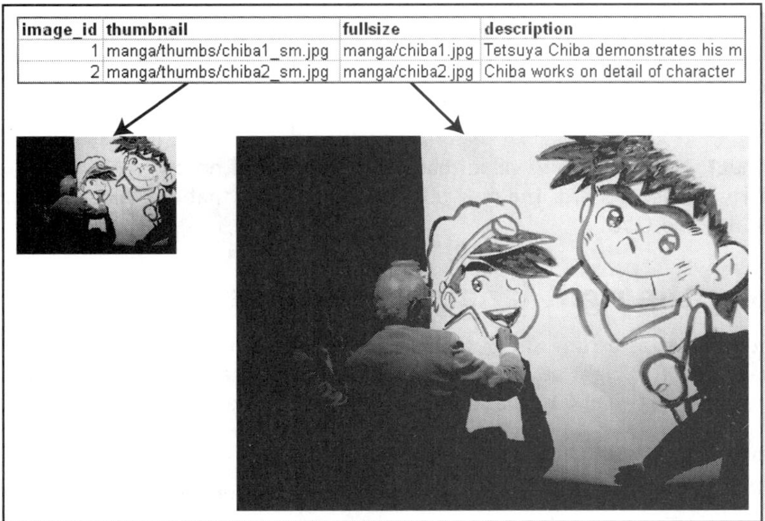

image_id	thumbnail	fullsize	description
1	manga/thumbs/chiba1_sm.jpg	manga/chiba1.jpg	Tetsuya Chiba demonstrates his m
2	manga/thumbs/chiba2_sm.jpg	manga/chiba2.jpg	Chiba works on detail of character

Figure 8-8. Rather than storing images inside the database, it is more efficient to store references to filenames outside the database, together with a textual description.

(Photo shows Tetsuya Chiba, one of Japan's foremost manga artists, at work. Photo © David Powers; original characters © Tetsuya Chiba.)

If you do, for any reason, want to keep everything together—for instance, when you have a small number of images and need to store everything in a single location—binary data should be stored in one of the delightfully named BLOB column types. There are four different sizes:

- **TINYBLOB**: Up to 255 bytes
- **BLOB**: Up to 64KB
- **MEDIUMBLOB**: Up to 16MB
- **LONGBLOB**: Up to 4GB

Although their names are reminiscent of Goldilocks and the three bears, it's a bit of a letdown to discover that BLOB stands for **binary large object**.

Default values and NULL

The whole idea of a database is to save data. Most of the time, you will want to set explicit values for each field in each record. Sometimes, though, there may not be any appropriate data (for instance, a column designed to hold a person's middle name or initial; not everyone has one). At other times, you may want to insert a default value and override it only when necessary. To accommodate these needs, each column can have the following attributes:

- **NOT NULL**: This means an explicit value must be set when entering a new record. The only exceptions are when the column has been assigned a default value or when the column also has the AUTO_INCREMENT attribute. If you fail to set a value for a column that is declared NOT NULL, and it doesn't have a DEFAULT value, MySQL will normally enter 0 or 0000-00-00.
- **AUTO_INCREMENT**: This can be set only on INT (or related column types). It automatically inserts a number 1 greater than the current highest number in the column, and it's used to create the table's primary key. Only one column per table can use this attribute.
- **NULL**: This means the column permits empty values. This is the default setting for columns unless NOT NULL is explicitly specified.
- **DEFAULT**: This is a default value that will be inserted if no other value is entered when inserting a new record. The only text-related columns that can take a default value are VARCHAR and CHAR.

Choosing the right language settings

It frequently comes as a rude shock to many native speakers of English that the Internet is multilingual. MySQL is right at the forefront of supporting a wide range of languages, and since the release of MySQL 4.1 it has added two important new features:

- Support for UTF-8 (Unicode)
- The ability to specify character set and sort order for individual databases, or even individual tables or columns

In other words, a single installation of MySQL can be a miniature United Nations or Tower of Babel, with different languages and writing systems coexisting alongside each other.

Now, before you get carried away with excitement (or overwhelmed with fear), let's put things in perspective. If you work exclusively in English and never use accented characters in your data, this next section is something you'll never have to worry about. It may, however, help satisfy your curiosity about an option called **collation** that you'll come across in phpMyAdmin—and why it's set to Swedish. Simply, collation determines the order in which the results of a query are sorted. Swedish is the default because MySQL AB is based in Sweden, and the Swedish sort order for *unaccented* characters is the same as English. Consequently, if you're working in Swedish or Finnish, the default is just fine for you, too. Feel free to skip to the section "Building a user registration system," although come back here if you experience erratic behavior with the sort order of results.

The only time you need to specify character set and collation is if you want to override the server defaults. The reason I raise the issue here is that creating tables in phpMyAdmin is much less error-prone than working in MySQL Monitor, and since phpMyAdmin displays collation by default, it's important to know what it is—even if you never use it. Don't change it unless you need to.

If you use accented characters in English or any other language, or you are involved in the development of multilingual sites, then you need to know about character sets and collation. Turn to Appendix D for the full story.

That's enough theory for the moment. Let's put some of this new knowledge to work.

Building a user registration system

User registration can be used for a wide variety of purposes: restricting access to various parts of a site, building up the basis of a mailing list, or just finding out who's a regular visitor to your site. The concept is quite simple, but one of the biggest problems with online registration is preventing useless information from cluttering up your database. The following application won't stop Mickey Mouse, Donald Duck, or even xZ qK from registering on your site, but it will definitely reduce the incidence of invalid data. It also forms the basis of the secure login system that you will develop in the next chapter.

Registering users with MySQL

The first step in designing a database is always to decide the table structure. Although I've described how to link multiple tables with foreign keys, I'm going to leave that type of structure until Chapter 12, so you can concentrate first on the basics of working with a database. One of the advantages of a relational database is that you can start with just one table, and as long as it has a primary key, you can add more tables later, as your requirements develop.

user_id	first_name	family_name	username	pwd
1	David	Powers	dpowers	codeslave
2	Sham	Bhangal	sbhangal	flashguru
3	Chis	Mills	cmills	bigboss

The user registration system requires just one table called users, with five columns: `user_id`, `first_name`, `family_name`, `username`, and `pwd`—the structure outlined in Table 8-2 at the beginning of this chapter.

> *I've used lowercase for all column names. As noted in Chapter 6, column names in MySQL are case insensitive, but database and table names aren't. Because the Windows version of MySQL automatically converts all names to lowercase, it's a good idea to use lowercase all the time, and insert an underscore in hybrid names rather than use camel case (`first_name`, not `firstName`). This will prevent your scripts from breaking when transferring to a Linux server, which enforces strict case sensitivity.*
>
> *I've also changed the name of the `password` column to pwd, to avoid any potential conflict with the MySQL `PASSWORD` function. When choosing names for databases, tables, and columns, steer clear of SQL keywords. Avoid anything like `date` or `time`; instead, use a hybrid word like `arrival_date`. Using meaningful names makes a database a lot easier to maintain, too.*

The second step is to decide the type for each column. With the exception of the primary key (`user_id`), each column will hold text. All you need to do is decide how much text you will allow for each column. `VARCHAR` has the advantage of being very flexible. Even if you specify the upper limit of 255 characters, the file space actually used depends on the number of characters entered into each field. If you're feeling lazy, you can set all `VARCHAR` columns to 255, but it's usually advisable to set a more realistic upper limit. For personal names, 30 should be adequate. For the `username` column, 15 is probably more than enough, but for pwd, you should allow 40. This is because the password will be encrypted, requiring 32 or 40 characters, depending on the encryption method.

Creating the users table

These instructions assume you installed phpMyAdmin as described in Chapter 6. If you would prefer to use MySQL Monitor at the command line, use the SQL query given at the end of this section.

1. Open phpMyAdmin in a browser. If you set it up as instructed in Chapter 6, the URL is `http://localhost/phpMyAdmin/` (on a Mac, it's `http://localhost/~username/phpMyAdmin/`).

2. Open the Databases drop-down menu on the left-hand side of the screen and select phpflash, as shown. The list shows all the MySQL databases on your computer. You will probably have only the `mysql` and `phpflash` databases to choose from.

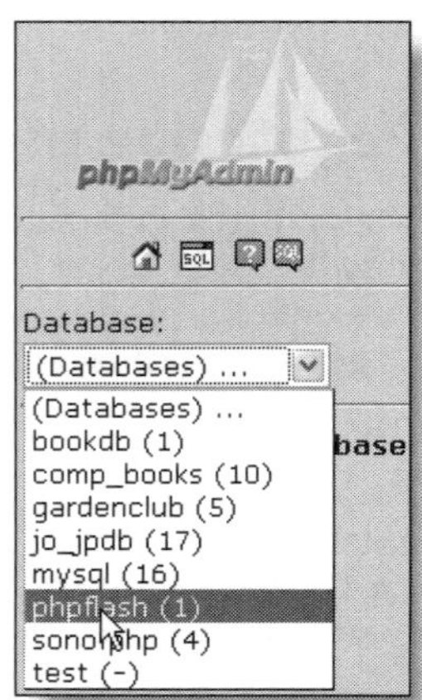

3. You should see a screen similar to Figure 8-9. The top half of the screen displays details of any existing tables in the database, so the `wordlist` table should be listed there. The lower half of the screen offers several options. The one you are interested in is Create new table on database phpflash.

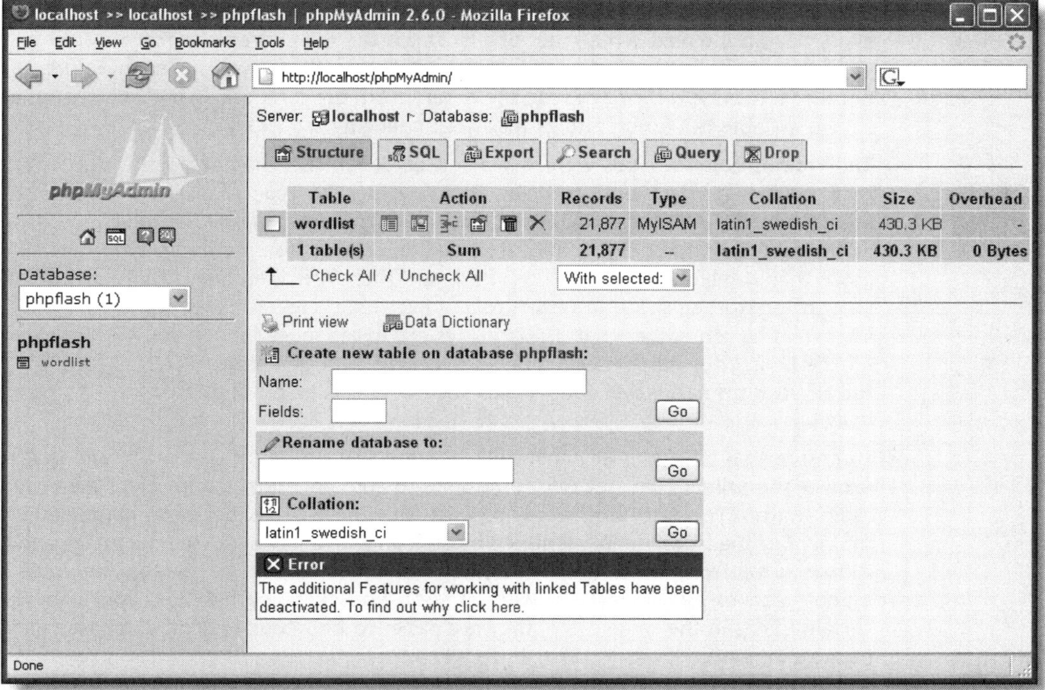

Figure 8-9. After selecting a database in phpMyAdmin, you can see all existing tables and create a new one.

4. In the Name text box, type users, and in the box marked Fields, enter 5. Click the Go button immediately to the right, as shown in Figure 8-10.

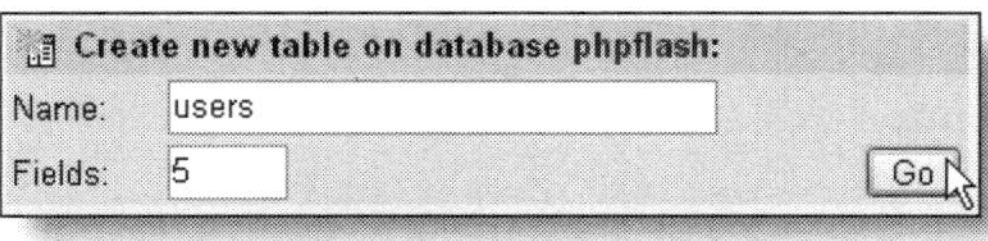

Figure 8-10. Settings for creating the `users` table

> *phpMyAdmin uses "field" as a synonym for "column." Although this is confusing, there's logic to it. Each row of the database contains one record, which usually contains several columns—but only one field per column. Consequently, when looked at from the perspective of a single record, fields and columns are the same. In most cases, I'll refer to a database column by its correct name, but I'll use "field" when referring to onscreen instructions in phpMyAdmin.*

5. Unless you're a designer with a large monitor, you may have to scroll to the right to see everything in the next screen that opens. This is the main screen where you specify the values for each column of a new table. Fill in the details as shown in Figure 8-11. Because it may be difficult to read the details from the screenshot, the settings are also shown in Table 8-3 (only settings that need changing are listed).

   The various column types were explained earlier in the chapter, so the only column that requires special mention is user_id. By setting the Type to INT and the Attributes menu to UNSIGNED, the column will accept only positive, whole numbers, to be used as the table's primary key. It may seem like overkill to use a column type that allows more than 4 billion numbers to be used, and there are alternatives that use a smaller amount of storage space in return for a lower limit. Nevertheless, it's important to remember that primary keys are never reused; once you hit the limit, your numbers start being overwritten. If you stick to INT for all your primary keys, you run no such risk, except on phenomenally busy sites.

   To ensure that user_id is automatically incremented with each new entry, and that it is used as the primary key, set the Extra menu to auto_increment, and select the Primary radio button. This last item is easy to miss—it's the first radio button immediately to the right of the Extra menu, identified by an icon with a key on it (see the image above). It doesn't matter whether the primary key is the first column in the table, although it's a good idea to put it there. As with all good housekeeping habits, if you always put certain things in the same place, they are easier to find later, making database maintenance a lot easier.

   The other thing to note about the settings is that phpMyAdmin overrides the MySQL default for each column by explicitly setting it to not null. In this case, it makes perfect sense—each new record in the `users` table needs a first name, family name, username, and password.

   The settings shown here assume that you are happy with the default language settings in MySQL. If you need to adjust the sort order for a different language, set the Collation drop-down menus as described in Appendix D.

6. Click the Save button (it's at the bottom left of Figure 8-11). That's it—the table has been created.

After creating the table, phpMyAdmin displays a screen with details of the columns and other settings, and at the top of the screen you can see the SQL query that was used to generate it, as shown in Figure 8-12. This happens for every database operation phpMyAdmin carries out, making it a very useful tool for learning SQL. Make it a habit to always study the SQL generated by phpMyAdmin, and you will pick up a lot of SQL in no time.

Table 8-3. Settings for the `users` table

Field	Type	Length/Values	Attributes	Extra	Primary
user_id	INT		UNSIGNED	auto_increment	Selected
first_name	VARCHAR	30			Not selected
family_name	VARCHAR	30			Not selected
username	VARCHAR	15			Not selected
pwd	VARCHAR	40			Not selected

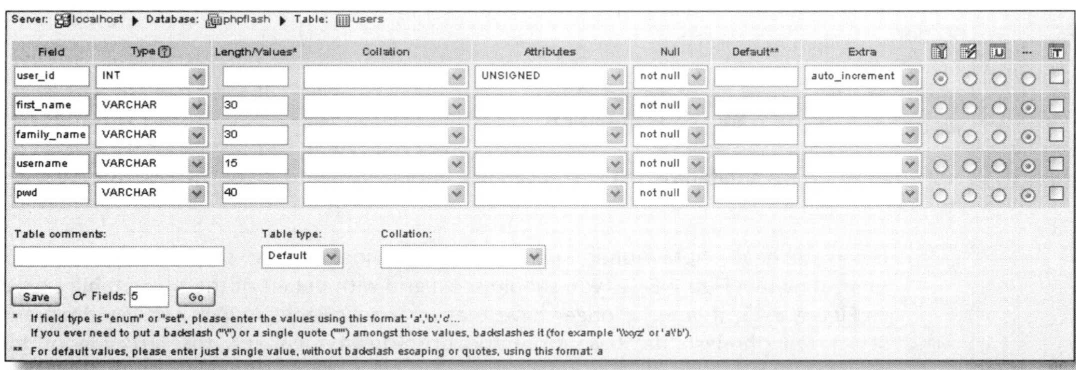

Figure 8-11. Settings in phpMyAdmin for the `users` table

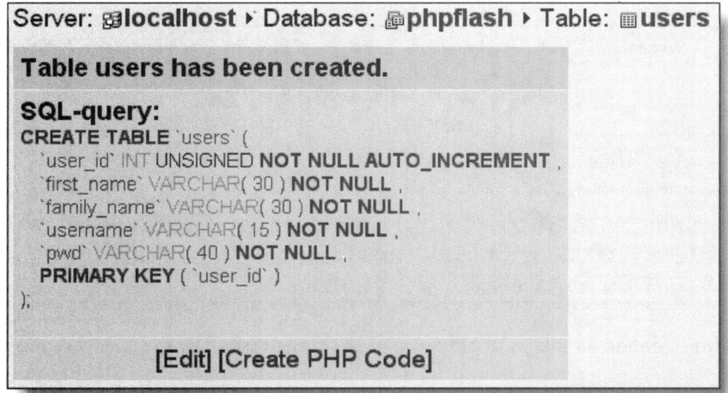

Figure 8-12. After creating the table, phpMyAdmin shows you the SQL query used to perform the operation.

There is just one point to note about the SQL generated by phpMyAdmin: it always places backticks (`) around table and column names. This is a precaution against using reserved or invalid names. Do not confuse the backticks with single quotes. When hand-coding SQL, the backticks are normally omitted, as in the following example, which you would use to create the same table using MySQL Monitor:

```
CREATE TABLE users (
user_id INT UNSIGNED NOT NULL AUTO_INCREMENT,
first_name VARCHAR(30) NOT NULL,
family_name VARCHAR(30) NOT NULL,
username VARCHAR(15) NOT NULL,
pwd VARCHAR(40) NOT NULL,
PRIMARY KEY(user_id)
);
```

I will explain what the Create PHP Code link (at the bottom of Figure 8-12) is for in the next section.

Entering records in the users table

Now that you have a database table, you can use phpMyAdmin to enter the details of authorized users.

1. If you still have phpMyAdmin open after the previous section, beneath the SQL statement shown in Figure 8-12, you should see a grid with details of the users table similar to Figure 8-13. If you no longer have that screen available, launch phpMyAdmin and select the phpflash database from the drop-down menu on the left side of the phpMyAdmin interface. Then select the users table by clicking its name in the list of tables that appears on the left side of the screen. Click the Insert tab as indicated at the top of Figure 8-13.

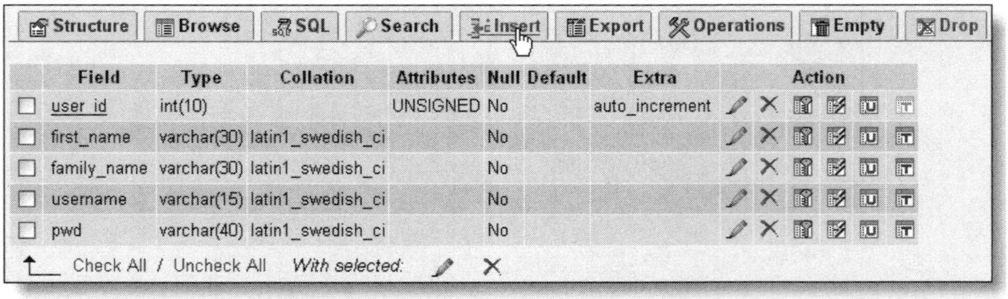

Structure | Browse | SQL | Search | Insert | Export | Operations | Empty | Drop

Field	Type	Collation	Attributes	Null	Default	Extra	Action
user_id	int(10)		UNSIGNED	No		auto_increment	
first_name	varchar(30)	latin1_swedish_ci		No			
family_name	varchar(30)	latin1_swedish_ci		No			
username	varchar(15)	latin1_swedish_ci		No			
pwd	varchar(40)	latin1_swedish_ci		No			

Check All / Uncheck All *With selected:*

Figure 8-13. After creating a table in phpMyAdmin, select the Insert tab to start inserting records.

2. The next screen presents you with a ready-made form to enter a new record in the users table. Figure 8-14 shows how I have filled it in to register my own details.

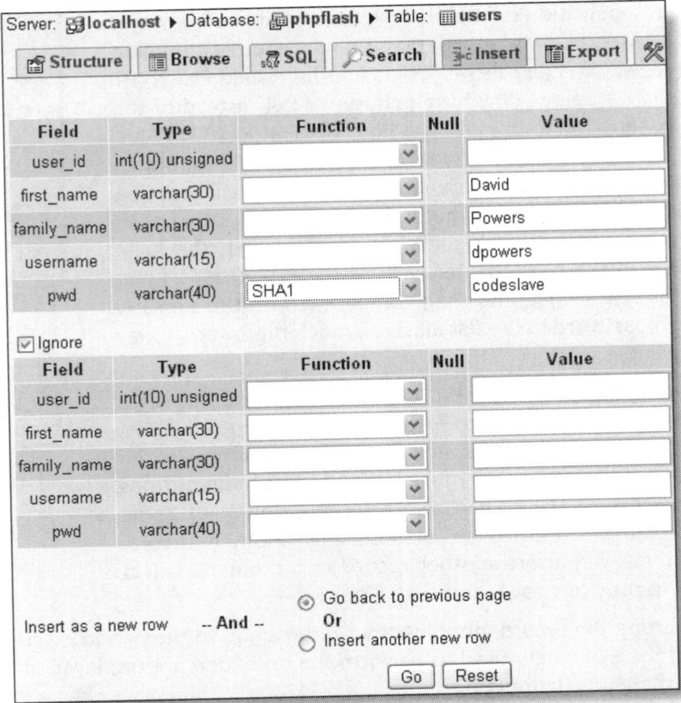

Figure 8-14. Creating the first record in the `users` table with phpMyAdmin

As you can see, I have left blank the Value field for user_id. This is because the `user_id` column was declared with the `auto_increment` attribute. When the record is entered in the table, it will automatically be assigned the next available number. Since this is the first record, the `user_id` will be `1`. The other four values are self-explanatory, but notice that I have selected SHA1 from the Function drop-down menu for the pwd field.

phpMyAdmin uses the information from this form to build the correct SQL query to enter the record in the table. In addition to commands like `SELECT` and `DELETE`, each version of SQL also includes a number of built-in functions that can be used to manipulate data, either as it is entered into a database or when it is retrieved. The Function column in phpMyAdmin lists the available MySQL functions that can be used. `SHA1` is what's known as a **hash function**, which basically performs one-way encryption of a string.

> *Because* `SHA1` *uses one-way encryption, it can't be decrypted. You're not interested in the password itself, but in whether the two encrypted versions match. This means you can't reissue users with the same password if they ever forget their original one, but must create a new one.*
>
> *Both MySQL and PHP offer another, slightly older encryption method called* `MD5`*, which you should use if your version of MySQL is older than 4.0.2.*

When you open the Function drop-down menu (as shown in Figure 8-15), you will notice that there's another function called PASSWORD just above SHA1. Another called ENCRYPT is immediately below. Why have I chosen SHA1 instead of the more obvious-sounding PASSWORD or ENCRYPT? PASSWORD uses the MySQL encryption method, which—although perfectly secure—is not available in PHP. ENCRYPT uses the Linux password encryption method, which is also unsuitable. To avoid storing the user's password in plain text, the login application in the next chapter will use the PHP sha1() function to encrypt it first, and then compare it with the similarly encrypted password in the database—a much more secure way of doing things.

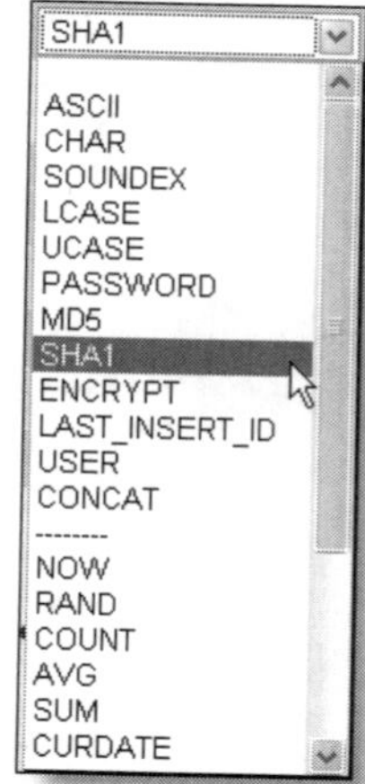

Figure 8-15. The Functions menu offers four methods of encryption.

Since phpMyAdmin 2.6.0, the Insert screen offers a duplicate set of fields to enable you to insert two records at once. The second set remains inactive unless you uncheck the Ignore option (it's at the center left of Figure 8-14). The radio buttons at the bottom of the screen also offer the option of going back to the previous page or inserting another record. Although you will insert another record in a moment, select Go back to previous page, and click Go.

3. After inserting the record, phpMyAdmin returns you to the previous screen. Again, the details of the SQL query used to perform the operation are displayed at the top of the page, as shown in Figure 8-16.

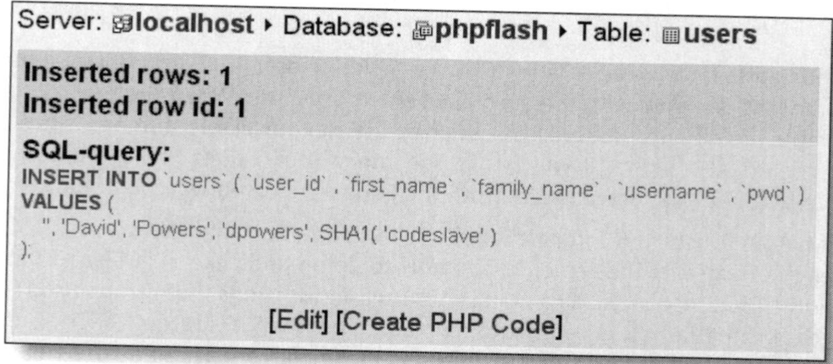

Figure 8-16. After inserting a new record, phpMyAdmin shows you the SQL it generated to perform the operation.

4. Click the Create PHP Code link beneath the query. You should see another screen like that shown in Figure 8-17. The top half of the screen contains a PHP statement that you can highlight and paste directly into a script. As it stands, it's not very useful, because it contains hard-coded values, but you could definitely use it as the starting point for building your own SQL statement with variables. The real value lies in being able to see a SQL statement that you know works. I will explain how this particular statement works in a short while. First, though, a little more exploration . . .

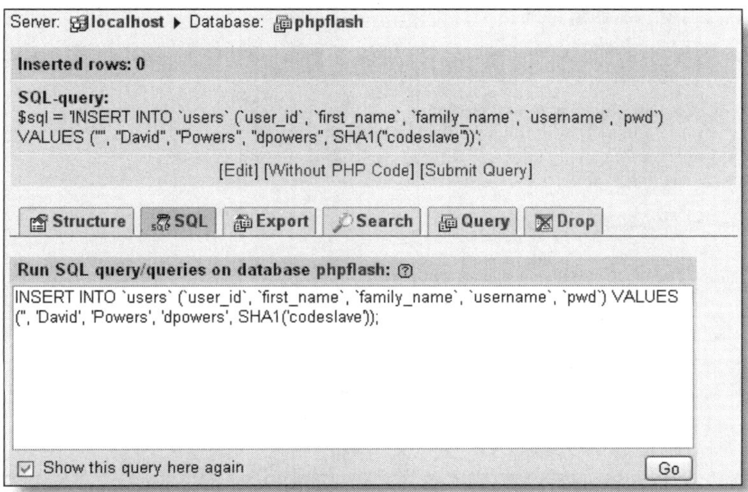

Figure 8-17. phpMyAdmin will generate a PHP variable containing SQL ready to be pasted into a script.

5. The bottom half of the screen shown in Figure 8-17 contains the same SQL query. Now, it may seem excessive to have the SQL query repeated in so many places. The purpose is to accommodate different ways of working—as well as different skill levels. Once you have a sound knowledge of SQL, you'll often find it a lot faster to edit a SQL query in this sort of dialog box than to go through all the drop-down menus again in the normal phpMyAdmin form. Don't edit anything; just click Go.

6. Like greased lightning, phpMyAdmin executes the query and shows you the same page again. To see what's happened to the table, select users from the menu on the left side of the phpMyAdmin screen, and then click the Browse tab. You should see a screen like Figure 8-18.

   As you can see, the nine characters of codeslave have been encrypted and now take the full 40-character width of the column. But there's a major problem—you have a duplicate entry. On this occasion, it doesn't really matter, because the entries are identical and refer to the same person. It could create serious security problems, though, if someone called, say, Diana Powers were to choose the same username. The likelihood of two people both choosing the same password is extremely small, but a security system is only as strong as its weakest point. In the next exercise, you'll overcome this problem by building an online registration form that checks for duplicate entries before allowing a user to register.

   Before moving on, delete the duplicate entry by clicking the large "X" to the left of user_id 2. When phpMyAdmin asks you to confirm the deletion, click OK.

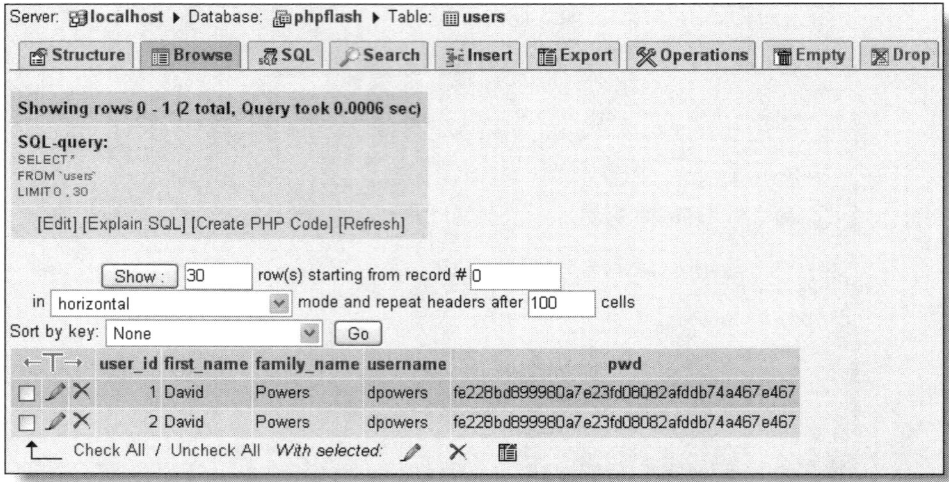

Figure 8-18. A drawback of using phpMyAdmin is that it doesn't prevent duplicate entries.

> *If you're curious about what happens to that* `user_id` *number, it's gone forever. Remember, a primary key must be unique. Once you delete a record, its related primary key is deleted too. You may think it untidy that your primary keys no longer form a consecutive sequence, but that's totally unimportant—what matters is preserving the integrity of your data.*

The next stage involves working with Flash, but you'll come back to phpMyAdmin a bit later, so leave it open for the time being.

Creating an online registration form

The normal method of creating online forms to work with MySQL is to use a mixture of PHP and XHTML. Since this is a book dedicated to PHP and Flash, however, I'm going to use Flash to create the registration form. Even though this particular form is intended only for an administration area, you can apply the same principles to just about any form. And with a nifty combination of PHP, ActionScript, and MySQL, you can do some important checks on user input before committing it to the database.

1. Create a new Flash document named `register_user.fla`, or from the download files open `register_user01.fla`, which has been laid out ready for you to add the ActionScript in the next section. The main timeline should have two layers: actions and interface. Lock the actions layer to avoid placing any graphic elements on it by mistake, and make sure it is the topmost layer. Lay out the form on the interface layer as shown here.

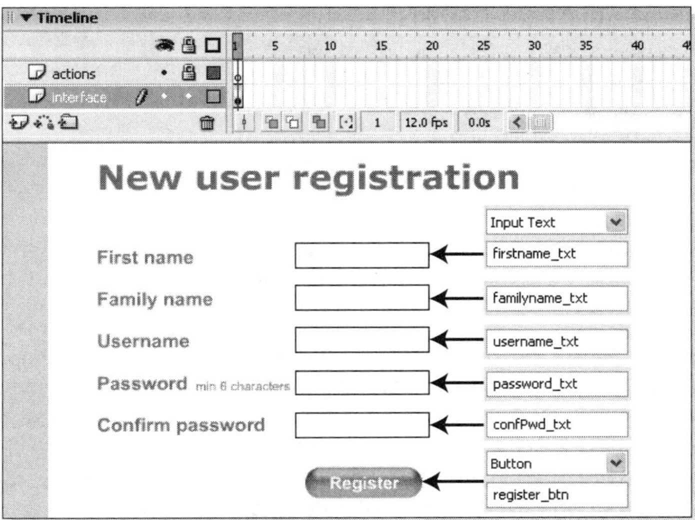

The title and labels are just static text. Each label has a text input field alongside it (five in all). Give the text input fields a border and instance names as shown in the image, from top to bottom: firstname_txt, familyname_txt, username_txt, password_txt, and confPwd_txt.

2. The Register button is made from button - middle and button - side, which can be found in the button assets folder of the Flash Buttons Common Library (Window ➤ Other Panels ➤ Common Libraries ➤ Buttons). If you get the middle and side out of the Common Library yourself, you'll discover they're an uninspiring gray, but all the component parts are movie clips, which means you can apply whatever color you like to them. I gathered all the parts and put them in a folder of their own called `button parts`. If you use the download files, make sure you don't delete this folder; otherwise, your button will vanish into thin air.

   Give the button an instance name of register_btn, as indicated.

3. To prevent users from entering more characters than the equivalent database columns will hold, you need to set a maximum limit. Highlight the firstname_txt text field, and set Maximum characters in the Property inspector to 30, as shown.

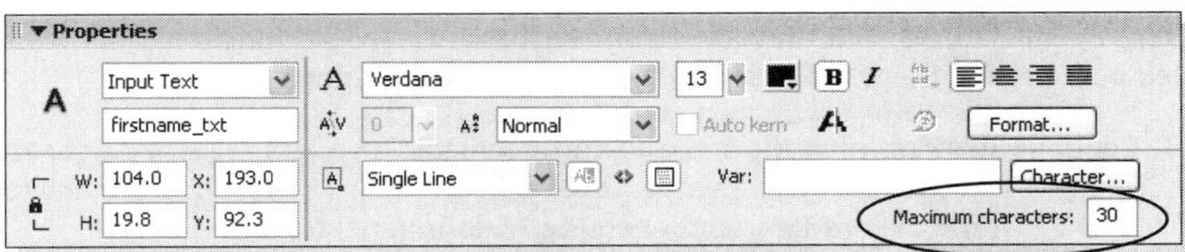

4. Set Maximum characters for familyname_txt to 30, and for username_txt, set Maximum characters to 15.

5. It's also a good idea to restrict the range of characters users can enter. The usual way of specifying a permitted character range for input text fields is through the Character Options dialog box, which you access by clicking the Character button on the Property inspector (it's directly above the Maximum characters field). As you can see from the screenshot, though, both the Uppercase and Lowercase options permit 27 glyphs (a technical name for a character). It took me some time to work it out, but—as far as Flash is concerned—the twenty-seventh letter of the alphabet is a blank space!

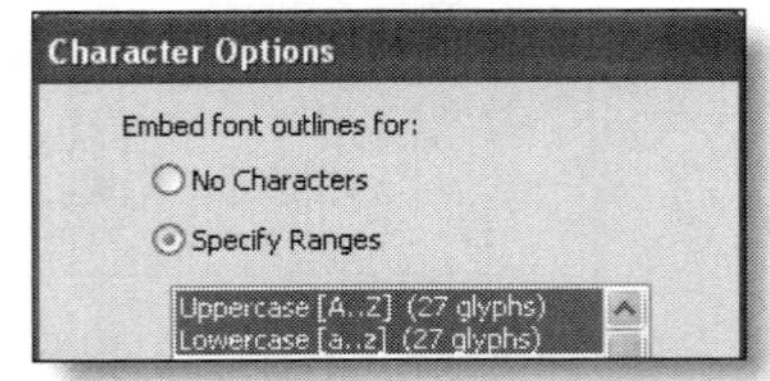

   To avoid problems, I have decided not to permit spaces in any of the input fields. This can be easily accomplished with ActionScript. I'll show you the necessary code in the next section. If you have opened the Character Options dialog box, make sure the No Characters radio button is selected before clicking OK to close it.

6. Both password_txt and confPwd_txt will be used to enter passwords, so they should be configured to prevent any input from being displayed. Set the password option in the Property inspector (it's at the bottom of the drop-down menu that defaults to Single Line).

   In both cases, this will result in a series of dots or stars being displayed when the user enters a password. This does nothing more than hide the display from anyone looking over the user's shoulder. The actual encryption will be done later by the PHP script.

Scripting the registration form

Now that you have the basic registration form, you need to bring it to life with ActionScript. The registration process involves three stages, each handled by custom-built functions:

- Gathering the information from the form and making sure all the fields are filled in correctly will be handled by a function called `registerUser()`.
- Checking that the two versions of the password are the same will be handled by `checkPwd()`.
- Displaying the result from the database and PHP script (indicating success or failure) is the job of `showResult()`.

Breaking up the process like this gives you the basic outline of functions that need to be created in the script. So, without any further ado, let's get scripting.

1. Continue working with the same Flash document, or open `register_user01.fla`. If you just want to check the script, use `register_user02.fla`. In the timeline, select frame 1 of the actions layer and open the Actions panel (*F9*).
2. There's one element missing from the form: a dynamic text field to display any error messages or the response from the PHP script. Although you can create a dynamic text field directly on the stage, my personal preference is to do it with ActionScript because it avoids any problems with distorted text if you accidentally resize the field. So, enter the following code to create the dynamic text field and style any contents it eventually displays:

```
// initialize error message text area
this.createTextField("error_txt", 1, 60, 60, 400, 25);
// set the text format for the error message area and apply it
var errorFormat:TextFormat = new TextFormat();
errorFormat.bold = true;
errorFormat.color = 0xff0000;
errorFormat.font = "Arial,Helvetica,_sans";
errorFormat.size = 18;
error_txt.setNewTextFormat(errorFormat);
```

This creates a text field with an instance name of error_txt that will display any messages in 18pt bold red text and use Arial or Helvetica font if it's available on the user's computer. The x and y coordinates of 60 are correct for the layout in the download files, but you may have to adjust them later to fit your own layout. Of course, if you prefer, you can simply draw a similar dynamic text field on the stage. Just remember to give it the same instance name of error_txt.

3. Immediately above the preceding code, enter the following:

```
function registerUser():Void {
  // this function gathers the input, validates it and
  // transfers it to the PHP script for processing
  // initialize variables
  var validated:Boolean = true;
  var textFields:Array = new Array("firstname", "familyname",
➥ "username");
  error_txt.text = "";
  // check for invalid fields
  // if valid, check password and send to PHP script
}
```

This is the first part of the main function that gathers all the information from the form and eventually sends it to the PHP script if the fields have been filled in correctly. At this stage, the function initializes two local variables: a Boolean called `validated`, which is set to `true`, and an array containing the instance names (without the `_txt` suffix) of the first three text fields that need checking. The text value of the dynamic text field `error_txt` is also set to an empty string. This ensures any previous message is cleared when the form is processed.

4. The next section of code checks that each of the first three fields contains at least two characters. It goes beneath the check `for invalid fields` comment (around line 9):

```
for (var i = 0; i<textFields.length; i++) {
  var theField:TextField = _root[textFields[i]+"_txt"];
  if (theField.text.length < 2) {
    validated = false;
    error_txt.text = "All fields must contain at least 2 characters";
    Selection.setFocus(theField);
    break;
  }
}
```

The checking process is carried out by a for loop, using the textFields array. The first line inside the loop assigns each text input field to a temporary variable, theField, by using bracket notation and adding _txt to the end of each element in the array. So the first one becomes _root["firstname_txt"], and so on. The input text is then tested to see if it contains at least two characters (you can change the number to whatever figure you like, but some people do have genuinely short names). By preventing the use of spaces, you eliminate the risk of empty fields. That's not a guarantee that people will provide a genuine name, but it's a move in the right direction.

If a problem is discovered, validated is set to false; an appropriate error message is displayed; and Selection.setFocus(theField) sets the cursor inside the problem field, ready for the user to amend. One invalid field is enough to make the submission of the form fail, so break is used to bring the loop to an end.

5. If validated is still true, the function proceeds to the final section of registerUser(). This calls a new function, checkPwd(), which you'll create in the next step. If the password fields match, checkPwd() returns true, giving the go-ahead to transmit the form data to the PHP script for further processing. Enter the following code immediately after the final comment (around line 19):

```
if (validated) {
  if (checkPwd()) {
    userDets.first_name = firstname_txt.text;
    userDets.family_name = familyname_txt.text;
    userDets.username = username_txt.text;
    userDets.pwd = password_txt.text;
    for (var prop in userDets) {
      trace("About to send " + prop + " as: " + userDets[prop]);
    }
  } else {
    password_txt.text = confPwd_txt.text = "";
    Selection.setFocus("password_txt");
  }
}
```

The first if statement checks validated. If it's still true, the second if statement makes a call to the checkPwd() function. This returns a Boolean result, which isn't required anywhere else in the script, so there's no need to assign it to a variable. If the passwords match the criteria in checkPwd(), the first code block is executed, assigning the value of each input field to an appropriately named property of userDets. This is the name of the LoadVars instance that will be used to send the form details to your PHP script. It's always a good idea to test that all the variables are being assigned as expected, so the next part of the script uses trace() and a for in loop to verify the properties of userDets. This will be replaced by a LoadVars.sendAndLoad() command once you know everything is working correctly.

If the passwords fail the tests, the else code block is executed, displaying whichever error message was set by checkPwd(), deleting the content of the two password fields, and placing the cursor in the first one.

6. Before you can test registerUser(), you need to create the second of the three functions outlined at the beginning of this section: checkPwd(). Insert the following code immediately after registerUser() (around line 34):

```
function checkPwd():Boolean {
  if (password_txt.length < 6) {
    error_txt.text = "Password must contain at least 6 characters";
    return false;
  }
  if (password_txt.text == confPwd_txt.text) {
    return true;
  } else {
    error_txt.text = "Your passwords don't match";
    return false;
  }
}
```

This function returns a Boolean value, but it also sets the text of the error message field (error_txt.text) if it encounters any problems. It consists of two simple conditional tests. The first checks that the password contains a minimum of six characters. If it doesn't, it sets an appropriate error message and returns false, terminating the function without moving on to the second test. If the minimum number of characters is satisfied, the second test checks whether the passwords match. If they do, the function returns true; otherwise, it sets a different error message and returns false.

7. Two more lines of code and you can test your progress so far. Insert the following immediately after the preceding block (around line 48):

```
register_btn.onRelease = registerUser;
var userDets:LoadVars = new LoadVars();
```

The first line assigns the registerUser() function to the onRelease event of register_btn. Because you are assigning the function to an event handler, rather than calling it, do *not* use parentheses at the end of registerUser. The second line initializes the userDets instance of LoadVars.

8. Test the movie. Try filling in various details and then clicking the Register button. Most of the validation is already in place, so if your passwords don't match, you should get a warning message. Similarly, you'll be warned if you don't fill in all the fields, or if you input too few characters. Make sure all the error messages are working as expected. When you fill in all the fields correctly, you should see the variables that Flash will send to the PHP script in the Output panel, as shown in Figure 8-19.

> *When testing forms in Flash, you normally have to check* Control ➤ Disable Keyboard Shortcuts *to prevent the testing environment from overriding some keyboard strokes. While testing this application, it worked equally well regardless of the setting. If, however, you find some keyboard strokes being ignored, check the setting on the Flash* Control *menu.*

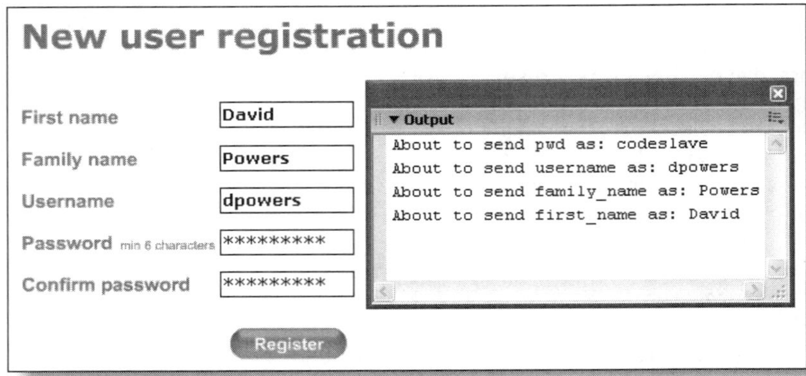

Figure 8-19. Use the Output panel to check that the right variables are about to be sent to the PHP script.

9. If you encounter any problems, check your script against `register_user02.fla`. Once you are happy that everything is as it should be, you can remove the `for in` loop and replace it with the code that will send the variables to the PHP script. Amend the code in step 5 as follows (the new code is highlighted in bold):

```
if (validated) {
  if (checkPwd()) {
    userDets.first_name = firstname_txt.text;
    userDets.family_name = familyname_txt.text;
    userDets.username = username_txt.text;
    userDets.pwd = password_txt.text;
    userDets.sendAndLoad("http://localhost/phpflash/ch08/
➥ register.php?ck=" + new Date().getTime(), userRegistered);
  } else {
    password_txt.text = confPwd_txt.text = "";
    Selection.setFocus("password_txt");
  }
}
```

This uses the LoadVars.sendAndLoad method to send the variables stored in userDets to a PHP script called `register.php`, and it designates userRegistered as the target for the response. Because of printing restrictions, the URL passed to sendAndLoad() has been broken over two lines. Make sure that your code is on the same line and that there is no gap in the URL. (If you are just following the code in the download files, the code from this point onward is in `register_user03.fla`.)

10. userRegistered is a new instance of LoadVars that needs to be instantiated. So do that now by inserting the following line immediately beneath the instantiation of userDets (around line 48):

```
var userRegistered:LoadVars = new LoadVars();
```

11. As I mentioned in the previous section, you need to restrict the acceptable range of characters for each of the text input fields. You do this with the `restrict` property of the ActionScript `TextField` class. Insert the following code immediately after the line in the previous step (around line 49):

```
// set acceptable range of characters for input fields
firstname_txt.restrict = "a-zA-Z\\-'";
familyname_txt.restrict = "a-zA-Z\\-'";
username_txt.restrict = "a-zA-Z0-9";
password_txt.restrict = "\u0021-\u007E";
```

The `restrict` property takes a string containing only those characters or ranges of characters that you want to permit. A range is indicated by a hyphen between the first and last characters in the permitted range. Because hyphens have this special meaning, you need to escape a real hyphen with a double backslash (`\\-`). The first two declarations allow all lowercase letters, as well as all uppercase letters from "a" through "z." They also include `\\-` and a single quotation mark. This permits hyphens (or dashes) and single quotes (or apostrophes). If you wanted to permit spaces as well, you need to include a space in the string, either at the end of or between the indicated ranges. The setting for `username_txt` permits only alphanumeric characters, not spaces or punctuation.

The first three settings are easy to understand, but the setting for `password_txt` looks as though it's already an encrypted password, rather than a range of permitted characters. In addition to characters typed in directly from the keyboard, you can also specify permitted characters and ranges using Unicode escape sequences in the form `\uxxxx`, where `xxxx` represents the hexadecimal code point of the character. The range indicated here includes most characters on an English language keyboard—but not a blank space (that's `\u0020`). This gives your users freedom to choose passwords that are likely to be more secure. You can find the full list of hexadecimal code points at `www.unicode.org/charts/PDF/U0000.pdf`.

> *Although working with Unicode escape sequences is rather cumbersome, it's an important skill for anyone dealing with non-English or multilingual applications. They can be used in conjunction with ordinary characters, so if you are working with French, Spanish, or any other language that uses accented characters, you can enable them by using the following code in place of the settings shown in step 11:*
>
> ```
> // permit accented characters in names
> firstname_txt.restrict = "a-zA-Z\\-'\u00C0-\u00FF";
> familyname_txt.restrict = "a-zA-Z\\-'\u00C0-\u00FF";
> ```
>
> *You can find the Unicode range used here at* `www.unicode.org/charts/PDF/U0080.pdf`*. It includes accented characters used in a wide range of European and other languages. If working with a specific language, you would probably want to select only a few. Although it may seem a nuisance to have to compile a list from Unicode escape sequences, it's a small price to pay for protecting the integrity of data input into your database. You can find all Unicode character ranges at* `www.unicode.org/charts`.

12. Everything is now in place to handle the first two stages of processing the form. The final stage involves getting the result back from the PHP script and displaying it within the Flash movie. Following my principle of test, test, and test again, the showResult() function contains just a loop to capture the response from the PHP script and display it in the Output panel. Insert the following code immediately after the checkPwd() function (on around line 46):

```
function showResult():Void {
  for (var prop in userRegistered) {
    trace(prop + " is: " + userRegistered[prop]);
  }
}
```

13. This function needs to be assigned to the userRegistered.onLoad event handler. This *cannot* be done until the userRegistered instance of LoadVars exists, so place it on the line immediately following the one where you originally declared it. It should be just three or four lines below the code you entered in step 12 (on about line 54):

```
var userRegistered:LoadVars = new LoadVars();
userRegistered.onLoad = showResult;
```

14. Check your code against user_register03.fla.

Using PHP to communicate between Flash and MySQL

Now it's time to start work on the PHP script. PHP acts as the intermediary between your Flash movies and the MySQL database, so it's important to test that the right data is being sent back and forth.

1. Create a new PHP page called register.php and save it in phpflash/ch08.
2. Enter the following code, and save the page:

```
<?php
$output = '';
foreach($_POST as $key=>$value) {
  $output .= "&$key=".urlencode($value);
  }
echo $output;
?>
```

By now, this should be easy for you to understand. It loops through the POST array and stores the key/value pairs in $output. The values are URL encoded for sending back to Flash. (Although there will be no spaces in the values this time, it's a good habit to use urlencode() all the time when transferring data to Flash. It will also be necessary for any accented characters.) After the foreach loop, echo sends the content of $output back to Flash.

3. In Flash, test your movie, fill in all the fields, and click the Register button. If everything goes well, you should see your data returned to you in the Output panel, as shown in Figure 8-20. The output is almost identical to that shown in Figure 8-19. The difference is that, this time, the variables have gone to the web server, been processed by PHP, and then received back by Flash. This is an important confirmation; if anything goes wrong after this point, you'll know the problem lies somewhere on the PHP/MySQL side of things. Half the battle of troubleshooting is knowing where to start looking for likely problems.

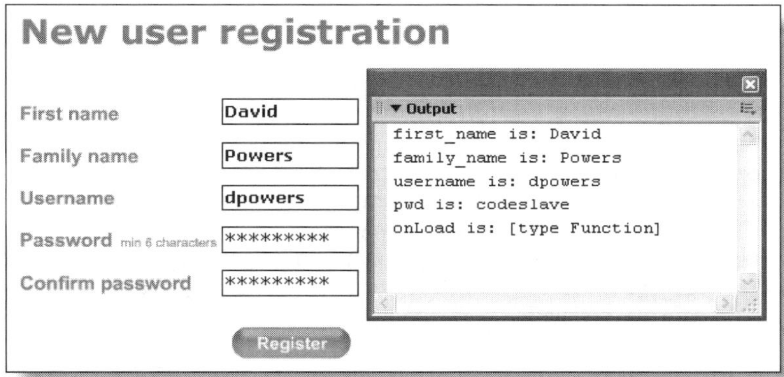

Figure 8-20. The Output panel confirms that the Flash movie is sending the right data to the PHP script and that the response is being correctly loaded.

4. Close the Output panel, and change one of the characters in one of the password fields. You should see an error message, as shown here. Both password fields will have been cleared and the cursor placed in the first one. None of the other fields should have changed, making it easy for the user to change only those fields where there's a problem. Test your movie thoroughly, leaving fields blank or using fewer than two characters. Check that you are getting the right error messages and that the cursor is located correctly for the user to make necessary changes. Make sure everything works as expected before moving on to the next step. Also, make sure your error messages are displaying in the right place. If necessary, adjust the location of the `error_txt` text field.

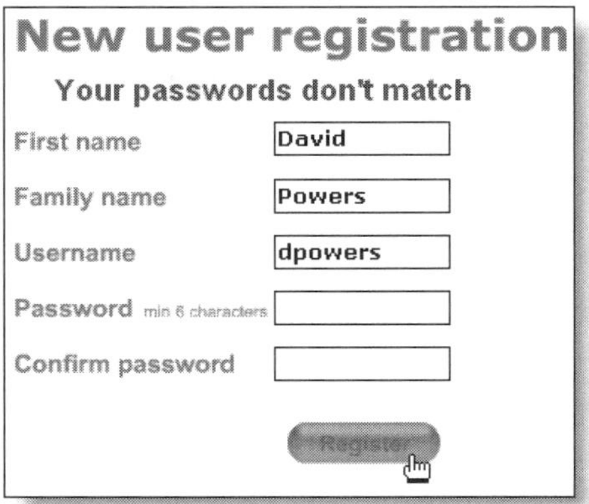

5. As you learned back in Chapter 2, using quotes or apostrophes in the middle of PHP strings can cause problems because the PHP parser has no way of knowing whether you intend the quote to be interpreted as part of the string or as a matching closing

quote. This also causes problems with inserting data into a database. Many PHP installations get around this by using a setting in php.ini called magic_quotes_gpc, which automatically inserts an escape backslash in front of single or double quotes in the GET and POST arrays. You cannot always rely on this being switched on, so place the following code in register.php immediately after the opening PHP tag (so it's *above* the existing code):

```
if (!get_magic_quotes_gpc()) {
  foreach($_POST as $key=>$value) {
    $temp = addslashes($value);
    $_POST[$key] = $temp;
    }
  }
```

This checks the value of magic_quotes_gpc on the server. If it's set to Off, the value of each element in the POST array is passed to addslashes(), which escapes all quotes. The value has to be saved in a temporary variable before being reassigned to the POST array because foreach loops always work on a copy of an array, not the original (see the section "Changing array values" in Appendix A for further details). If magic_quotes_gpc is set to On, the POST array is left unchanged, as the quotes will have been automatically escaped.

> *If you use this code at the start of every PHP script that handles data insertion into a database, you will avoid the danger of scripts breaking if moved to a server that employs a different policy toward* magic_quotes_gpc.

6. Save the amended version of register.php and test your movie again. This time, use a name that contains an apostrophe, and see what happens in the Output panel. You should get a result similar to Figure 8-21.

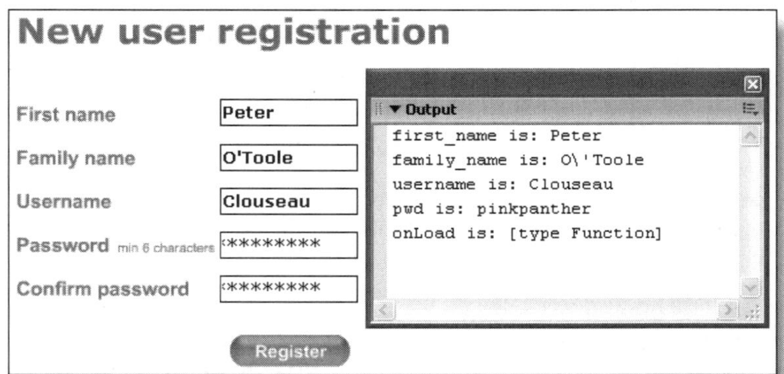

Figure 8-21. Quotes and apostrophes need to be escaped before they can be safely stored in a database.

7. Now that you know the data is being correctly transferred, it's finally time to communicate with the database. Change the content of register.php as follows (the original loop in step 2 is no longer needed, so the script is shown in its entirety here with new elements highlighted in bold):

```
<?php
// include the Database classes
require_once('../classes/database.php');

// escape quotes and apostrophes if magic_quotes_gpc off
if (!get_magic_quotes_gpc()) {
  foreach($_POST as $key=>$value) {
    $temp = addslashes($value);
    $_POST[$key] = $temp;
    }
  }

// create a Database instance and check username
$db = new Database('localhost','flashadmin','fortytwo','phpflash');
$sql = 'SELECT username FROM users
        WHERE username = "'.$_POST['username'].'"';
$result = $db->query($sql);
$numrows = $result->num_rows;

// if username already in use, send back error message
if ($numrows > 0) {
  $duplicate = 'Duplicate username. Please choose another.';
  echo 'duplicate=y&message='.urlencode($duplicate);
  }
?>
```

The script starts by including the external Database class file you created in Chapter 6. Don't forget, you should have chosen the appropriate set of classes for the versions of PHP and MySQL on your system, and changed the name to database.php. All the class files should be kept in the phpflash/classes folder, and the actual scripts are available in the download files for Chapter 6.

The contents of the POST array are then processed by the loop created in step 5 to escape any quotes or apostrophes. An instance of the Database class is formed on line 14 and assigned to the variable $db. Because $db will be used later to insert new records, you need to use the flashadmin username and password, and connect to the phpflash database.

Let's take a close look at the next two lines, which prepare a SQL query:

```
$sql = 'SELECT username FROM users
        WHERE username = "'.$_POST['username'].'"';
```

It's a SELECT query, so it's looking for existing records. The first half is quite straightforward: it's looking for entries in the username column of the users table. The second half is a WHERE clause; this qualifies a search by narrowing it down to records that match specified conditions.

As it stands, the WHERE clause looks rather horrendous. It's easier to understand if you replace the POST array variable with a real example:

```
WHERE username = "dpowers"
```

An important point to grasp here is that the username column is a string type (VARCHAR). When you insert a string value into a SQL query, it must be enclosed in quotes. The whole SQL query is built up from a string in single quotes (highlighted in gray), concatenated with a variable from the POST array. So the double quotes are treated as a literal part of the string assigned to the $sql variable.

```
$sql = 'SELECT username FROM users WHERE username = "'.$_POST['username'].'"';
```

Variable inserted into string by concatenation operators

Getting the sequence of quotes right when building SQL queries is one of the most difficult parts of working with PHP and MySQL (and other combinations of server-side languages and databases). If you find you're having difficulties getting the results you expect from a query, it's often a good idea to use echo to display the contents of the query being sent to MySQL (various debugging techniques for PHP and MySQL are discussed in Appendix A).

There's a major difference in the way SQL uses the equal sign (=). A WHERE clause can be regarded as the SQL equivalent of if in both PHP and ActionScript—it tests a condition or series of conditions. However, whereas both PHP and ActionScript require two equal signs (==) to test for equality, SQL uses just one. When working with all three languages, it's easy to get mixed up, so this is one of the first things you should check for if your scripts fail or produce unexpected results.

Once the query has been built, it's submitted to MySQL using the query() method of the Database class, and the number of results is captured using the num_rows property. If num_rows is more than zero, that means the username is already in use, so a conditional statement is used to send an error message back to Flash. The message contains two variables: duplicate, which is given a value of y, and message, which is a URL-encoded explanation of the problem.

8. Back in Flash, amend the showResult() function like this to handle the error message:

```
function showResult():Void {
  if (this.duplicate == "y") {
    error_txt.text = this.message;
    username_txt.text = "";
    Selection.setFocus(username_txt);
  }
}
```

The `if` statement checks whether `duplicate` has been set to y and displays the error message.

9. Test your Flash movie again. Make sure you use the same username as you did when creating your first entry with phpMyAdmin. I used dpowers, which already exists in my `users` table, so I got an error message as shown. The username is cleared from the input field, but all other input is left untouched—a good way to keep users happy. Equally important, you have prevented duplicate information from being entered into your database. You're now ready to enter information that passes all your tests, confident in the knowledge that it meets your basic criteria.

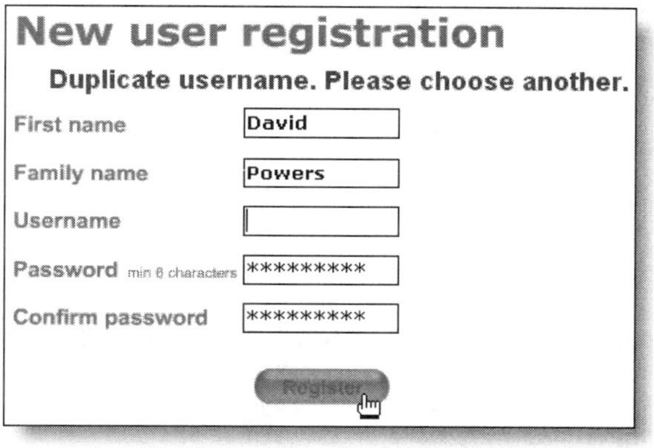

New user registration
Duplicate username. Please choose another.
First name David
Family name Powers
Username
Password min 6 characters *********
Confirm password *********
Register

10. Amend the final block of code in `register.php` as follows (the new code is highlighted in bold):

```
// if username already in use, send back error message
if ($numrows > 0) {
  $duplicate = 'Duplicate username. Please choose another.';
  echo 'duplicate=y&message'.urlencode($duplicate);
  }
else { // insert the data into the users table
  $sql = 'INSERT INTO users (first_name,family_name,username,pwd)
          VALUES ("'.$_POST['first_name'].'",
          "'.$_POST['family_name'].'","'.$_POST['username'].'",
          "'.sha1($_POST['pwd']).'")';
  $result = $db->query($sql);
  if ($result) {
    $created = 'Account created for '.$_POST['username'];
    echo 'duplicate=n&message='.urlencode($created);
    }
  }
?>
```

The `else` statement contains the code that inserts the data into the database, which will be executed if no duplicate entry is found. You already have an instance of the

Database class ($db), so all you need to do is create a new SQL query and capture the result. The values held in the $sql and $result variables in step 7 are no longer required, so it is perfectly safe to overwrite them.

The INSERT query looks complex, but the underlying syntax is actually quite simple:

```
INSERT INTO tablename (columns)
VALUES (values in same order as columns)
```

The first set of parentheses contains a comma-delimited list of the column names. All are included, except user_id, which will be automatically incremented to the next available number. The second set of parentheses contains the values you want to insert in each column, also as a comma-delimited list. Because all the columns are string types, the values need to be in quotes. This means you have to exercise great care to get the matching quotes and concatenation operators in the right places.

The final value to be inserted in the users table is the password. This needs to be encrypted, so it is passed to the sha1() function as the SQL query is built:

```
sha1($_POST['pwd'])
```

Although sha1() *is not available in MySQL 3.23, there is no problem using it in this PHP script, because the encryption takes place before passing the data to MySQL. As far as MySQL is concerned, it's just an ordinary string. As long as you delete any records made with phpMyAdmin, you can use* sha1() *to control your passwords. If you are using MySQL 3.23 and want to create records in phpMyAdmin (for instance, if that's the most convenient setup provided by your hosting company), use the* md5() *function instead.* md5() *is an older standard that performs a similar type of encryption, and it is available in both PHP and MySQL. You use* sha1() *and* md5() *in exactly the same way.*

Once the SQL query has been built, it is executed using the query() method of the Database class. If the insert operation is successful, duplicate is set to n and a URL-encoded message is sent to the Flash movie reporting that an account has been created for the username submitted. If there is any problem with the database, the Database class will automatically issue an error message.

11. Before you can conduct your final test, you just need to amend the showResult() function in the Flash movie so that it can handle the new variables sent from register.php. In Flash, change the function like this:

```
function showResult():Void {
  // this function displays the response from the PHP script
  if (this.error != undefined) {
    // if the Database class generates an error, display error message
    error_txt.text = this.error;
    // once error message has been displayed, unset showResult.error
    this.error = undefined;
  } else if (this.duplicate == "y") {
    // if username already used, show message and clear username field
```

```
      error_txt.text = this.message;
      username_txt.text = "";
      Selection.setFocus(username_txt);
    } else if (this.duplicate == "n") {
      // display any message from the PHP script and clear all fields
      error_txt.text = this.message;
      firstname_txt.text = "";
      familyname_txt.text = "";
      username_txt.text = "";
      password_txt.text = "";
      confPwd_txt.text = "";
      Selection.setFocus(firstname_txt);
    }
  }
```

This series of conditional statements simply displays the appropriate message in the error_txt message field and clears other input fields as necessary. The only one that requires special explanation is the first. The error variable will only be generated by the Database class if there's a problem with the database connection or query, so you need to check whether it has been defined. If it has, it displays the diagnostic message from the database. (For a public site, you would probably want to replace this with something more user-friendly, such as "Database unavailable; please try later.") After the error message from the Database class has been displayed, it's important to set the showResult.error property to undefined; otherwise, this first part of the conditional statement will always evaluate to true, even after the problem has been cleared (at least until the movie is reloaded).

12. Now, the moment of truth. Test the Flash movie again, this time using a different username. You should get a message like the one shown here. It tells you the name of the new user account and clears all the fields, ready for another user to be registered.

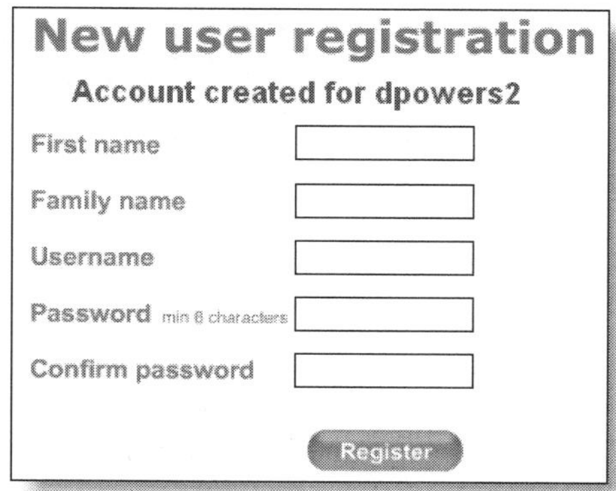

13. Open phpMyAdmin, and select the users table from the phpflash database. Click the Browse tab, and take a look at what your table now contains. It should be similar to the following screenshot:

←T→	user_id	first_name	family_name	username	pwd
	1	David	Powers	dpowers	fe228bd899980a7e23fd08082afddb74a467e467
	3	David	Powers	dpowers2	fe228bd899980a7e23fd08082afddb74a467e467

I deliberately used the same password to demonstrate that the PHP sha1() function produces exactly the same encryption as the equivalent MySQL function. Note, also, the user_id: although there are only two records in the database, user_id 2 is no longer used. I've said it before, but it's worth repeating: **a primary key must be unique, so once the related record is deleted, the number is never used again**.

What if it doesn't work?

Although this is quite a simple form, it's doing quite a lot by bringing together three technologies: ActionScript, PHP, and MySQL. Therefore, the potential for getting something wrong is quite high. That's why I've suggested testing everything each step of the way, and that's also why I've built in a series of error messages. You can check your code against the final versions in register_user04.fla and register.php in the download files for this chapter.

The most likely cause of your Flash form stumbling at the last hurdle is a parse error in your PHP. LoadVars can't interpret any error messages generated by PHP, so you may need to test the PHP script on its own to make sure it's working correctly.

The simple way to test register.php is to hard-code some test data into the top of the script, like this:

```
<?php
// include the Database classes
require_once('../classes/database.php');

$_POST['first_name'] = 'David';
$_POST['family_name'] = 'Powers';
$_POST['username'] = 'dpowers2';
$_POST['pwd'] = 'codeslave';

// escape quotes and apostrophes if magic_quotes_gpc off
```

This enables you to test your script directly in a browser without using Flash. If you get an error message like that shown in Figure 8-22, you need to go through your PHP syntax carefully, moving backward from the line number indicated in the error message. The arrow in Figure 8-23 shows where the cause of the error lies—it's a missing single quote toward the end of the code used to build the SQL query. Using a script editor that supports syntax coloring makes this particular error much easier to spot than if you're working in Notepad or TextEdit. (See Appendix A for a detailed explanation of how to interpret PHP error messages, as well as other advice on how to avoid and debug problems with your code.)

Don't forget: once you have debugged your PHP script, comment out or delete any hard-coded test variables and other code that might confuse your Flash movie. The only output from the PHP script should be the variables you want to send to LoadVars.

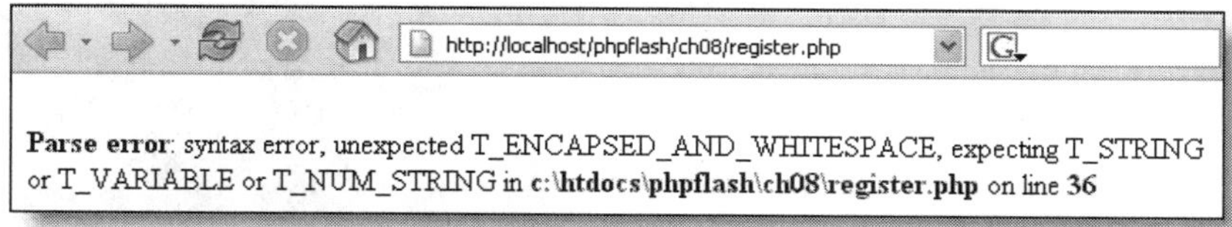

Figure 8-22. A syntax error in your PHP script is the most likely cause of failure.

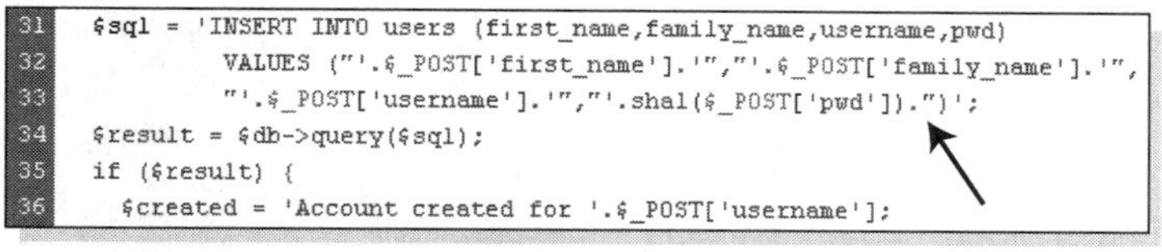

```
31 $sql = 'INSERT INTO users (first_name,family_name,username,pwd)
32          VALUES ("'.$_POST['first_name'].'","'.$_POST['family_name'].'",
33          "'.$_POST['username'].'","'.sha1($_POST['pwd']).'")';
34 $result = $db->query($sql);
35 if ($result) {
36   $created = 'Account created for '.$_POST['username'];
```

Figure 8-23. A missing single quote on line 33 caused the script to fail.

Time to take stock

It may come as a surprise how much effort it has taken to create what is essentially a simple online form. If you compare both scripts, you will see that the ActionScript is twice as long as the PHP code. This is more a reflection on what you have used them to do, rather than a comment on whether one is more efficient than the other. When working with a database, it's vital to make sure that any user input is validated as rigorously as possible. I could have chosen to use PHP checking routines instead of ActionScript to restrict the range of permitted characters in each field, but this would have been less efficient. The ActionScript carries out all the basic checks on the user's own computer before sending any data across the Internet to your server. This speeds up the process, reducing both user frustration and unnecessary load on the server. The only check carried out by PHP is for duplicate usernames, something that cannot be done locally. When you plan this sort of application, always split the task into its individual parts, and decide which is better carried out locally and which requires a round-trip to the server.

Now that you can enter new records in a database, you need to learn how to update them and delete them. It's also important to protect your administrative area from prying eyes. I'll show you how to do that in the next chapter, with PHP sessions. Then in Chapter 10, you'll tackle database maintenance with a simple content management system.

Chapter 9

PROTECTING YOUR DATA WITH SESSIONS

What this chapter covers:

- Examining what PHP sessions are and how they work
- Selectively restricting access to pages
- Building a login system
- Plugging a security gap with Flash movies

Now that you have a way of registering users, you can use the usernames and passwords stored in your database to control access to different parts of your site. You may, for instance, want to charge for access to premium content or prevent unauthorized people from seeing work that is still being developed for a client. Most important of all, you need to prevent outsiders from gaining access to your database maintenance area. An effective and easy way to do this is to use **PHP sessions**, which enable you to preserve information about individual visitors as they move from one page to another through your site. Although you'll use sessions in this chapter only as a method of restricting access, another important use of sessions is for building shopping carts, so you can apply the knowledge you gain here in many different ways.

Keeping track with PHP sessions

To understand the need for sessions and how they evolved, it's necessary to step back a moment and consider how the Web works. If you've been developing with Flash for some time, you'll be used to the concept of everything frequently being contained within a single movie or a series of interconnected movies. Although it may not be the optimal way to do it, you can even create an entire website in a single SWF file. With many Flash games or animations, clicking a button produces an immediate response because any timeline animations or ActionScript functions are all contained within the same unit (see Figure 9-1).

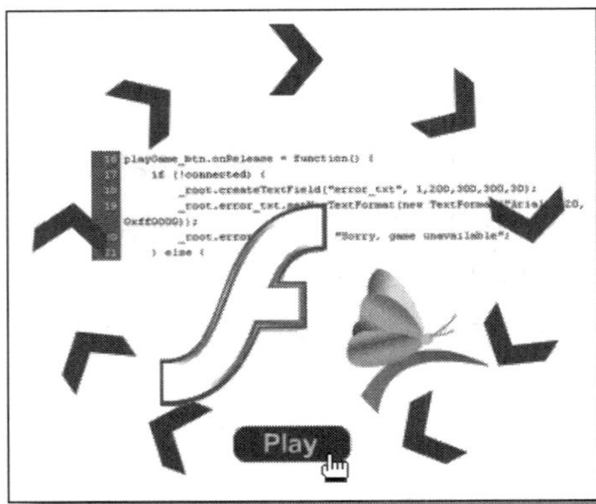

Figure 9-1. The interaction of buttons, animations, and ActionScript in a Flash movie frequently represents a self-contained world.

The Web is a stateless environment

The situation is quite different with traditional sites that use HTML or XHTML. When you visit a well-designed website, you should have a sense of continuity as the navigation system leads you from one part of the site to another. Apart from the delay in loading a new page, the feeling of cohesion should be no different from a Flash movie, but it's only an illusion. The reality is that each request to a web page is treated completely separately. Even each part of an individual page is stored and handled separately by the web server. For instance, a single request to the friends of ED homepage results in more than a dozen responses from the server (see Figure 9-2). A busy server handles hundreds (frequently thousands) of such requests every minute, zapping off files all over the world. Once a request has been handled, that's it. The server promptly forgets about it and moves on to the next task that comes along. In most circumstances, the server has no interest in which page you visited last or in where you go next. Even if the server logs the details of each request, such information is kept only for statistical and diagnostic purposes; the server makes no direct use of it. To use the technical expression, this is a **stateless environment**. What glues everything together is the system of IP addresses that identifies the computer originating each request, so that the web server knows where to send the response.

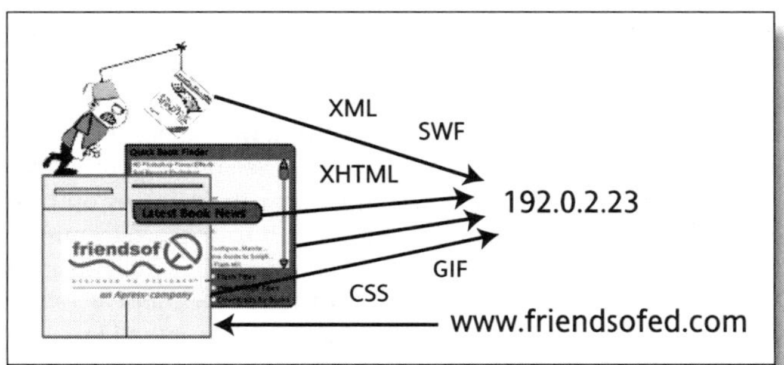

Figure 9-2. In an XHTML website, one request produces many responses. The server knows where to send material, but it normally does not keep track of individual visitors.

It all works remarkably well, and most of the time everything gets to its intended destination. The illusion of continuity is perfectly adequate when you surf most websites. The server knows where to send its responses, but it has no way of knowing whether those responses are always going to the same user. Many computers in schools, colleges, libraries, businesses, and Internet cafés are used by more than one person, presenting problems for a web application that needs to keep track of user information, such as during an e-commerce transaction or when restricting access to a particular part of a site.

This method of delivery highlights another major difference between a self-contained Flash movie and a traditional website: the life span of variables. A Flash movie, once downloaded, runs entirely on the visitor's computer (to use the technical term, it's a **client-side** application), so variables remain in local memory until needed. On the other hand, PHP runs on the remote server; in other words, it's a **server-side** language (see Figure 4-6 and the section "Understanding where PHP functions run" in Chapter 4). So all PHP variables remain in the remote server's memory only as long as it takes to process the script and send the result back to the client computer. Even if you call the same script over and over again, it is handled as a separate request each time, and the variables are initialized afresh.

- Flash variables are handled on the client side and have a life span determined only by the internal programming of the Flash movie. In that sense, they can be regarded as persistent.
- PHP variables are handled on the server side and are discarded as soon as the script finishes running. They are not persistent.

To get around these two problems of identifying a specific user and maintaining persistent information, PHP (in common with other server-side languages) offers **sessions**.

How sessions work

What a session does, in simple terms, is identify the client computer to the server. It does this by storing a unique identifier on both the server and the visitor's hard disk. The identifier is a random alphanumeric string. The following is an actual example from my own computer:

```
sess_e2595b837539e5df09b4b80806954a8e
```

PHP uses this identifier to allow the creation of special variables associated solely with the visitor or, to be strictly accurate, variables associated solely with the computer that initiated the session. Let's say I want to log on to one of my online databases (see Figure 9-3). I go to the login page, which is an ordinary online form. I enter my username and password, and click the Login button. This activates a PHP script to check my details. If everything is OK, the script starts a PHP session, and it creates the unique identifier on both my server and my local computer. It also creates three session variables and stores their values on the remote server only. The actual number of variables created is entirely up to the programmer, but you need to set at least one so that the value can be checked when making any requests to the server. In my case, the three variables contain my user ID, my access level, and a Unix timestamp indicating when the session started (timestamps are explained in Chapter 11).

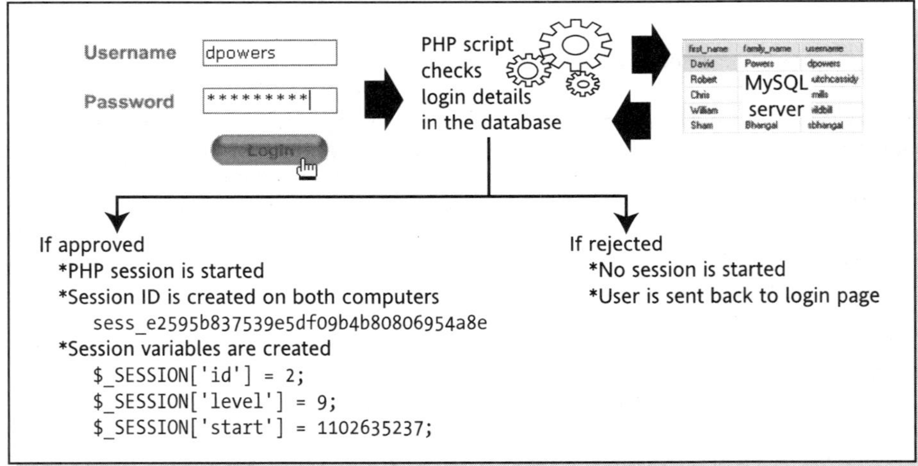

Figure 9-3. PHP initiates a session and creates session variables after a user successfully logs in.

The server now has a way of retrieving those variables even after the original PHP script has finished running. So, instead of lasting just milliseconds, the variables are now persistent in the same way as Flash variables. Every time I want to do something with my database, clicking a link or button launches a PHP script that begins by checking the session variables. If the session identifier (ID) on my computer doesn't match any of the session IDs on the server, a conditional clause terminates the script and sends me to the login page. If the level is set to 9, the visitor (me) is allowed to access all the administrative pages, giving me the ability to update records or add new items. If the level is anything lower than 9 (usually one of my clients), a conditional clause hides all the links to the administrative area, but allows the visitor to search the database and visit other restricted areas of the site. The reason for saving the visitor's ID as a session variable is that it lets me log who visits which page. The start time also lets me automatically end the session after a particular period of inactivity.

Session variables remain active until they're destroyed (typically by the visitor logging out) or until the browser is closed. Because web servers don't actively keep track of your movements, there's nothing to stop you from visiting other sites in the middle of a session. Those other websites will be totally unaware of the session relationship, but all the information stored in session variables will still be there when you come back (as long as the session is still active). That's why you can put something in a shopping cart on one site, go to another site and compare prices, and when you return to the original site the item in the shopping cart will still be there.

Once I log out of my database, the relationship that was maintained through the PHP session ceases to exist. Even if I try to get back to a restricted page that I had visited only a few moments before, the session variables will no longer be available to me, and the PHP script will deposit me back at the login page. This means I can safely use an Internet café to work on my database without worrying about the next customer gaining access to my files.

Although sessions play an important role in user authentication and e-commerce, they should not be confused with secure connections. Sessions provide a relatively secure method of establishing the identity of a client and server, but they don't use security certificates or an encrypted connection. Although sessions are perfectly adequate for shopping carts and most user authentication, you should not rely on them alone for credit card transactions or other highly sensitive data transfer. It is common to use sessions for the decision part of e-commerce, and then switch to an encrypted connection, using a protocol such as Secure Sockets Layer (SSL) for the actual transaction.

If you think this all this sounds similar to cookies, you're right. The main difference is that the session ID is stored on both your local hard disk and the remote server, so cookies normally have to be enabled on both computers for sessions to work. Many people are worried about personal information being stolen through cookies, so what sort of information is actually stored?

As already noted, the session ID is a random alphanumeric string. Nothing else is stored on the visitor's computer. All the important information is stored on the site's web server. Before that sends you into paroxysms of fear, let's take a look at the following session cookie from my own server:

```
id|s:1:"2";level|s:1:"9";start|i:1102635237;
```

These are the same three values as shown in Figure 9-3: `id`, `level`, and `start`. Admittedly, my aim is to reassure you, so I'm unlikely to show you anything alarming. Nevertheless, I'm not aware of any way for a remote server to store information in a session cookie without the visitor volunteering the information. You *can* use sessions with cookies disabled, but it's less secure—and since the whole idea is to improve security, it's not recommended.

The other important difference is that cookies are normally designed to persist between visits, whereas PHP sessions are destroyed automatically when the browser is closed. It's possible to create sessions that persist even after the browser is closed, but that's a more advanced subject, which you can read about in *Beginning PHP 5 and MySQL: From Novice to Professional* by W. Jason Gilmore (Apress, ISBN: 1-893115-51-8).

PHP session basics

So how do you create a session? Easy. Put the following command in every PHP page that you want to use in a session:

```
session_start();
```

This command should be called only once in each page, and it must be called before the PHP script generates any output, so the ideal position is immediately after the opening PHP tag. If you call `session_start()` more than once, your script will normally run without a problem, but it will generate a warning message that will prevent `LoadVars` from accessing your variables in Flash. If any output is generated before the call to `session_start()`, the command fails and the session won't be activated for that page. The scripts used in this book should present no problems on either score, but if you do find you're having difficulties with sessions, check the section titled "Headers already sent" in Appendix A.

You create a session variable by adding it to the `SESSION` superglobal array in the same way you would assign an ordinary variable. Say, for instance, you're passing a variable called `name` from a Flash movie, which will be received by the PHP script as `$_POST['name']`. To create a session variable called `user`, you assign it like this:

```
$_SESSION['user'] = $_POST['name'];
```

Because session variables are stored on the server, you should get rid of them as soon they are no longer required by your script or application. This is particularly important when you're logging out of a restricted area, because it is technically possible for a cracker to obtain the details of someone else's session. (Although if your server is so seriously compromised for a cracker to be able to do this, the prospect of someone hijacking a session is the least of your worries.) When you no longer have use for a particular session variable, unset it like this:

```
unset($_SESSION['user']);
```

To unset *all* session variables—for instance, when you're logging someone out—set the `SESSION` superglobal array to an empty array, like this:

```
$_SESSION = array();
```

> *Do not be tempted to try* `unset($_SESSION)` *as another method of unsetting all sessions variables. It works all right—but it's a little too effective. It not only clears the current session, but also prevents any further sessions from being stored.*

By itself, unsetting all the session variables effectively prevents any of the information from being reused, but you should also destroy the session with the following command:

```
session_destroy();
```

That way, the link between the two computers is broken, and there is no risk of an unauthorized person gaining access either to a restricted part of the site or to any information exchanged during the session. If you fail to destroy the session, the variables remain on the web server even after the visitor's browser is closed. Although this represents a theoretical security risk, it's not always possible to guarantee that a visitor will trigger the `session_destroy()` command. For instance, the visitor may forget to log out, or the session may be expired by a time limit built into your script. For that reason, you should never store sensitive information such as credit card numbers in a session variable.

That's about all there is to know about session commands (I told you it was easy).

> *You may find* `session_register()` *and* `session_unregister()` *in old scripts. These functions are now deprecated and will almost certainly fail in PHP 5. Replace them with* `$_SESSION['variable_name']` *and* `unset($_SESSION['variable_name'])`.

So much for the theory. Let's put sessions to work.

Using sessions to restrict access

PHP's primary role has always been with multipage websites. So, for PHP sessions to protect an area of your site, you need to do the same: use one web page as the gateway and another as the protected area. Unlike HTTP authentication (where the browser presents a standard dialog box asking for a username and password), PHP sessions gather information from forms that you design as an integral part of your site. PHP scripts handle the entire authentication process, and access is controlled on a page-by-page basis, rather than by giving access to an entire folder (or directory). This means you can present your visitors with a much more seamless experience, but at the same time, you also have to remember to apply security restrictions to every page that you want to keep private. Let's try a practical example.

The user registration application that you built in the previous chapter could be used for a variety of purposes, one of which is granting administrative rights over your database. In such circumstances, the last thing you would want is for anyone to be able to come along and create a username and password without having the authority to do so. Putting the registration form behind a security barrier is simple. It requires the following elements:

- A login form
- A PHP script to process the login and check the user's credentials
- A PHP script to restrict access to the registration form
- A logout button on the registration form
- A PHP script to process the logout and bring the PHP session to an end

Although that may sound like a lot, the amount of scripting involved is surprisingly small.

Creating the login form

As in the previous chapter, the design of the forms has been kept deliberately simple so that you can concentrate on the coding involved.

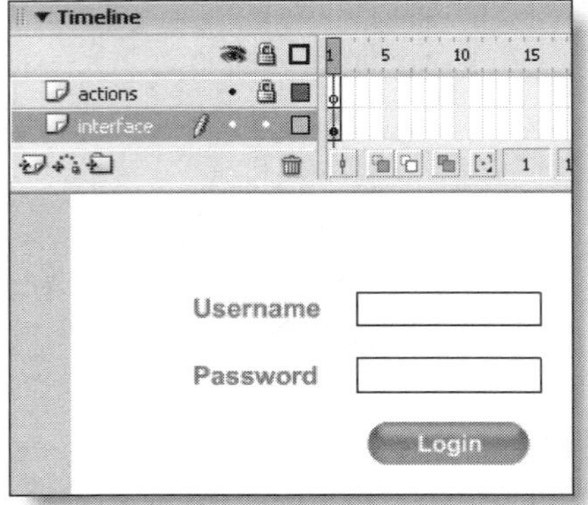

1. Create a new Flash document called `login.fla`. Alternatively, just use the version in the download files. It's such a simple file that I didn't create "before" and "after" versions. The timeline should have two layers: interface and actions. As always, the actions layer should be on top, and it's a good idea to lock it to prevent graphic elements from being placed on it by accident.

   On the interface layer, place two single-line text input fields and a button. Lay out the elements as shown here. The labels are just static text. As with the registration form in the previous chapter, a dynamic text field to display error messages will be added through ActionScript, so leave enough space for it above the elements on the stage.

2. Give the top input text field an instance name of username_txt and make sure it has a border around it by clicking the Show border around text icon in the Property inspector, as shown in the following screenshot.

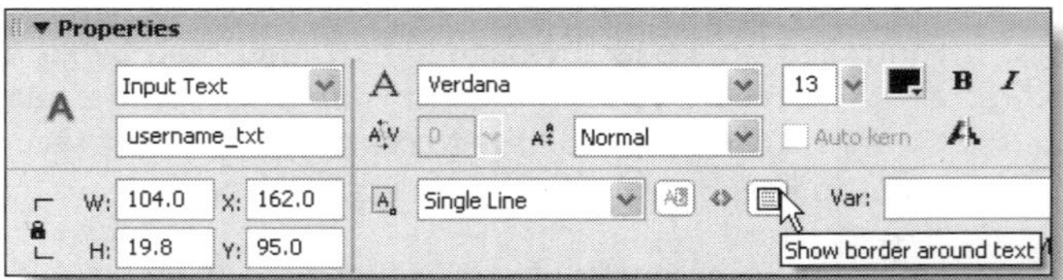

3. Give the bottom input text field an instance name of pwd_txt. Also give it a border, and set the line type drop-down menu to Password, as shown in the following image.

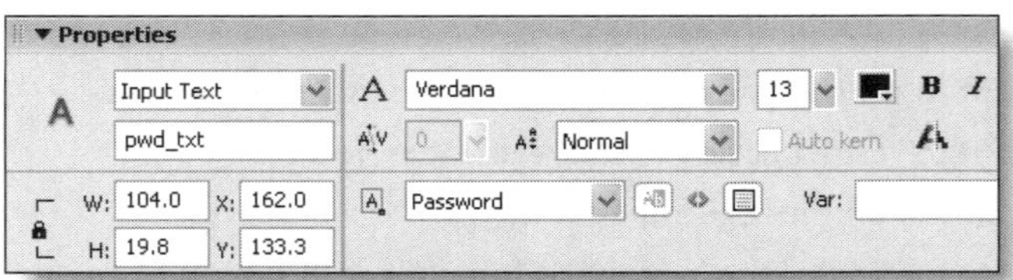

4. Give the button an instance name of login_btn.

5. Select the actions layer and open the Actions panel. The ActionScript is quite short—and very similar to that in the last chapter—so here it is in full with comments to explain what's happening:

```
function checkDetails():Void {
  // this gathers the form input and sends it to the PHP script
  // clear any error messages
  error_txt.text = "";
  loginDets.username = username_txt.text;
  loginDets.pwd = pwd_txt.text;
  loginDets.sendAndLoad("http://localhost/phpflash/ch09/
➥ process_login.php?ck="+new Date().getTime(), loginResponse);
}
function doLogin():Void {
  if (this.authenticated == "ok") {
    // if login details OK, load protected page
    getURL("http://localhost/phpflash/ch09/register_protected.php");
  } else {
    // otherwise display error message
    error_txt.text = "Sorry, access denied";
  }
}
// assign event handler to login button
login_btn.onRelease = checkDetails;
// create LoadVars instances to send and receive data
var loginDets:LoadVars = new LoadVars();
var loginResponse:LoadVars = new LoadVars();
loginResponse.onLoad = doLogin;
// set color for text input field borders
username_txt.borderColor = 0x377f7f;
pwd_txt.borderColor = 0x377f7f;
// initialize error message text area
this.createTextField("error_txt", 1, 70, 60, 400, 25);
// set the text format for the error message area and apply it
var errorFormat:TextFormat = new TextFormat();
errorFormat.bold = true;
errorFormat.color = 0xff0000;
errorFormat.font = "Arial,Helvetica,_sans";
errorFormat.size = 18;
error_txt.setNewTextFormat(errorFormat);
```

There are two functions and two instances of LoadVars. Although it would be perfectly acceptable in such a short script to use the same instance of LoadVars to handle both sending the data and receiving the response, I find using separate ones helps clarify the logic of my code and makes it easier to adapt if I want to make changes later. So loginDets will be used to send data to a PHP script called process_login.php (which you will create shortly), and loginResponse will handle the response.

The first function, checkDetails(), is assigned to the onRelease event handler of login_btn. It gathers the contents of the input text fields and assigns them to properties of loginDets before sending the data to the PHP script.

The second function, doLogin(), is assigned to the onLoad event handler of loginResponse, the instance of LoadVars that handles the response. The main thing to note about this function is that if the PHP script sends back a variable called authenticated with a value of ok, the global getUrl() function is used to load a page called register_protected.php.

Finally, the error message text field is initialized in exactly the same way as in the previous chapter, except that the position has been moved slightly.

6. Publish the movie so that you have both login.swf and login.html in your phpflash/ch09 folder. The quickest way to do this is to save login.fla in that folder, and then press *F12*. However, if you have been keeping your FLA files outside your server root, select File ➤ Publish Settings and change the default settings before clicking Publish.

Adapting the registration form

For this exercise, you can either make a copy of the Flash document you used in the previous chapter or work with the download files for this book. The files contain everything you need for this chapter.

1. Open register_user.fla from the last chapter and save it as register_protected.fla. Where you save the renamed FLA file depends on the policy you have adopted for your source files. I keep all my source files outside the web server root folder, but create a separate folder for each chapter. Also make a copy of register.php from phpflash/ch08 and save it in phpflash/ch09 as process_register.php. The PHP page must, of course, be within the server root for it to be processed correctly.

   Alternatively, use the download files for this chapter. If you plan to make the changes as you read along, use register_protected01.fla and process_register01.php. The final versions of these two pages are register_protected02.fla and process_register02.php.

2. Create a Log Out button and place it on the interface layer alongside the Register button. If you are using the download files, you can make a duplicate of the Basic button in the Library panel. Give it an instance name of logout_btn.

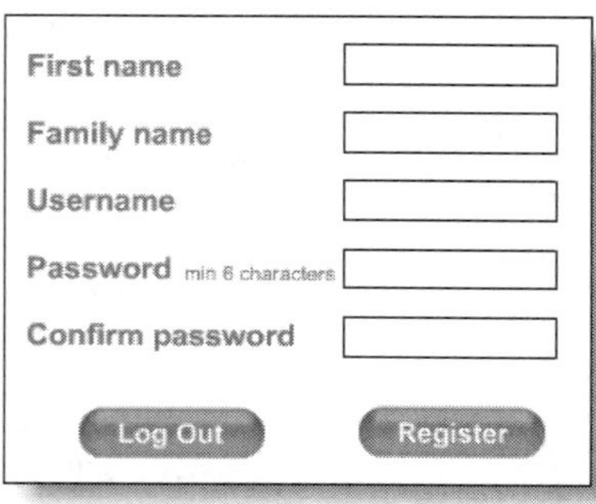

3. Select the actions layer and open the Actions panel. Change the target URL for userDets.sendAndLoad so that it will use process_register.php in the phpflash/ch09 folder instead of register.php in phpflash/ch08. You will find the code on about line 25 (the changes are highlighted in bold):

```
userDets.sendAndLoad("http://localhost/phpflash/ch09/
➥ process_register.php?ck="+new Date().getTime(), userRegistered);
```

4. The logout process will use a new instance of LoadVars called logoutSend. To keep your code in a logical order, declare it along with the existing instances of LoadVars as shown here:

```
72 register_btn.onRelease = registerUser;
73 var userDets:LoadVars = new LoadVars();
74 var userRegistered:LoadVars = new LoadVars();
75 var logoutSend:LoadVars = new LoadVars();
76 userRegistered.onLoad = showResult;
```

5. Insert the following script a few lines higher (about line 69), immediately after the end of the showResult() function:

```
logout_btn.onRelease = function() {
  // send logout request to PHP script
  logoutSend.logmeout = "done";
  logoutSend.sendAndLoad("http://localhost/phpflash/ch09/
➥ process_logout.php?ck=" + new Date().getTime(), userRegistered);
};
```

This assigns an anonymous function to the onRelease event of logout_btn. Figure 9-4 shows the process this initiates. It begins by assigning a value to the logmeout property of logoutSend. I have assigned it a value of done, but the actual value is unimportant; logmeout just needs to have a value of some sort. The sendAndLoad() method sends this single variable to another new PHP script called process_logout.php, which will unset the session variable used to authenticate users, and then destroy the session. The existing userRegistered instance of LoadVars is designated as the target to receive any data sent back.

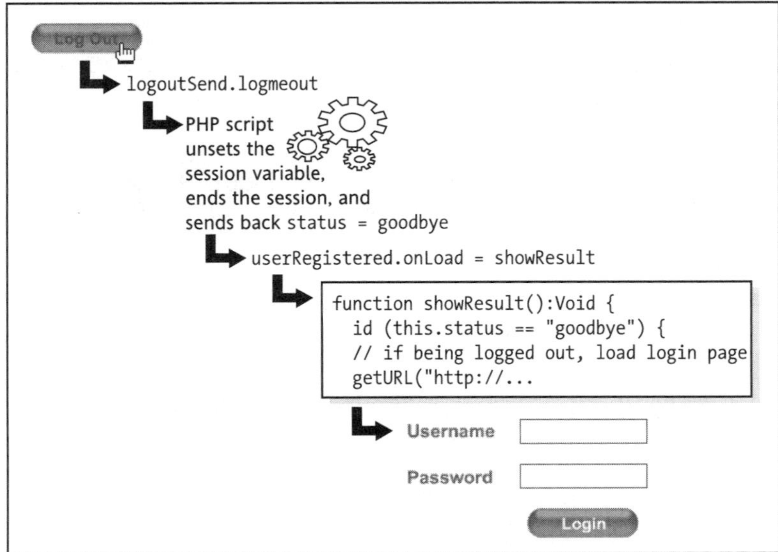

Figure 9-4. The chain of events triggered by clicking the Log Out button

6. The showResult() function (which begins on about line 46) is the onLoad event handler for userRegistered, so it needs to be amended to take account of the new data that will be sent by the PHP logout script. Change the first few lines of showResult() like this (the new code is in bold type):

```
function showResult():Void {
  // this function displays the response from the PHP script
  if (this.status == "goodbye") {
    // if being logged out, load login page
    getUrl("http://localhost/phpflash/ch09/login.html");
  } else if (this.error != undefined) {
```

   This completes the process shown in Figure 9-4. Whenever userRegistered receives a variable called status with a value of goodbye, it calls the global getUrl() function and loads the login page in place of the current one. So both this movie and the login one use the same technique: loading another page when trigged by the appropriate variable.

7. Publish the movie so that you have register_protected.swf and register_protected.html in phpflash/ch09. The web page that the SWF is embedded in will need to be renamed register_protected.php, but there is a danger of Flash overwriting any script you include in the page if you forget to uncheck the html option in the Publish Settings panel. I find it more convenient to leave the publish settings as they are and change the file extension from .html to .php by hand.

Putting it together with PHP

You now need to create the pages, process_login.php and process_logout.php, that drive the login system. In addition to these two new pages, a small amount of script must be added to the page used to display the user registration movie. All three completed scripts are available in the download files for this chapter.

1. Create a new PHP page called process_login.php in phpflash/ch09, and enter the following script. It is quite short, so here it is in full:

```
<?php
// check correct variables have been received through the POST array
if (isset($_POST['username']) && isset($_POST['pwd'])) {

  // initiate the session
  session_start();
  // include the Database classes
  require_once('../classes/database.php');

  // escape quotes and apostrophes if magic_quotes_gpc off
  if (!get_magic_quotes_gpc()) {
    foreach($_POST as $key=>$value) {
      $temp = addslashes($value);
      $_POST[$key] = $temp;
      }
    }
```

```
  // create a Database instance and check username and password
  $db = new Database('localhost','flashuser','deepthought','phpflash');
  $sql = 'SELECT * FROM users WHERE username = "'.$_POST['username'].'"
          AND pwd = "'.sha1($_POST['pwd']).'"';
  $result = $db->query($sql);

  // if a match is found, approve entry; otherwise reject
  if ($result->num_rows > 0) {
    $_SESSION['authenticated'] = $_POST['username'];
    echo 'authenticated=ok';
    }
  else {
    echo 'authenticated=getLost';
    }

  // close the database connection
  $db->close();
  }
?>
```

The whole script is wrapped in a conditional statement, which uses the function `isset()` to check whether the POST array contains values for username and pwd. Unless both values exist, the script will not run. This prevents anything from being displayed in a browser if the page is accessed accidentally.

The script inside the conditional statement begins with a call to `session_start()`; this is obligatory at the beginning of any page that uses sessions.

Eagle-eyed readers will notice that I have gone against my own advice at the beginning of the chapter and haven't placed `session_start()` *immediately after the opening PHP tag. This is because I don't want to start a session unless the conditions in the* `if` *clause are met. There is no point cluttering your server's hard disk with session cookies that are never going to be used. But I have placed the command right at the top of the script that will be using the session. I have also put it before the instruction to include the* `Database` *classes. This helps avoid a common problem with sessions and include files: a dreaded PHP error known as "Headers already sent." The problem and the solution are described in Appendix A.*

Next comes the instruction to include the `Database` classes, followed by a loop that checks that any quotes or apostrophes in your input text are correctly escaped. These should both be familiar to you from the previous chapter.

The second half of the script is what does the real work. To authenticate a user, you need to connect to the database and check whether there any records that contain both the username and password submitted. Because the password is stored in encrypted form, the password submitted by the user has to be similarly encrypted. If a matching record is found, the user is authenticated; otherwise, the attempted login is rejected.

Because this process requires only a SELECT query, the Database instance connects to the phpflash database as flashuser. The SQL query is similar to the one you used in the last chapter to check whether a specific username was already in use. Let's take a close look at this one, first as it appears in the script:

```
$sql = 'SELECT * FROM users WHERE username = "'.$_POST['username'].'"
        AND pwd = "'.sha1($_POST['pwd']).'"';
```

When I log in using codeslave as my password, the value held in $_POST['pwd'] is codeslave, but the variable is then passed to the sha1() function and encrypted. When the PHP variables are replaced by real input, the query looks like this:

```
$sql = 'SELECT * FROM users WHERE username = "dpowers"
        AND pwd = "fe228bd899980a7e23fd08082afddb74a467e467"';
```

The query tells the database to select all columns from the users table where the username column contains dpowers and the pwd column contains the encrypted version of codeslave. Both the username and pwd columns are text types, so the values must be in quotes. Also note the need to match single and double quotes correctly. The value assigned to $sql is a string, so it needs to be in quotes itself. I have used single quotes for the whole SQL query and double quotes for the values of the columns being searched.

The WHERE clause is testing for two conditions, so it will come as no surprise that the AND keyword means both conditions must be satisfied for a match to be made.

The result of the query is stored in $result. If your database has been properly maintained, the number of matching records should only ever be zero or one. However, as long as the num_rows property of $result is more than zero, you know there is at least one match. If a match is detected, the following code block creates a session variable called $_SESSION['authenticated'], assigns it the value held in $_POST['username'], and sends a variable called authenticated back to Flash with a value of ok. If no matches are found, no session variable is created, and the value of authenticated sent back to Flash is getLost.

```
if ($result->num_rows > 0) {
  $_SESSION['authenticated'] = $_POST['username'];
  echo 'authenticated=ok';
  }
else {
  echo 'authenticated=getLost';
  }
```

The final line of the script closes the database connection.

2. The logout script is very short. Create a PHP page called process_logout.php in phpflash/ch09 and enter the following code:

```
<?php
// verify correct variable received in POST array
if (isset($_POST['logmeout'])) {
  session_start();
```

```
  unset($_SESSION['authenticated']);
  session_destroy();
  echo 'logout=ok';
  }
?>
```

Again, the whole script is wrapped in a conditional statement that uses `isset()` to test for the existence of a POST variable called `logmeout`. Although the script in step 3 of the previous section set the value of `logmeout` to `done`, all that really matters is whether it has been set. Since `$_POST['logmeout']` will only come from a page or Flash movie that is requesting to be logged out, nothing will be displayed in a browser if anyone stumbles across this page by accident. As always with sessions, the page begins with a call to `session_start()`.

The next three lines unset the session variable `$_SESSION['authenticated']`, destroy the session, and send a variable called `logout` back to Flash with a value of `ok`.

3. Rename `register_protected.html` as `register_protected.php`.

If you are using Windows and you cannot see the filename extension, go back to Chapter 1 and follow the instructions in the section "Getting Windows to display filename extensions." Windows will present you with the warning message shown in the screenshot about the consequences of changing a filename extension. Just click Yes. You want the file to work as a PHP page in the future.

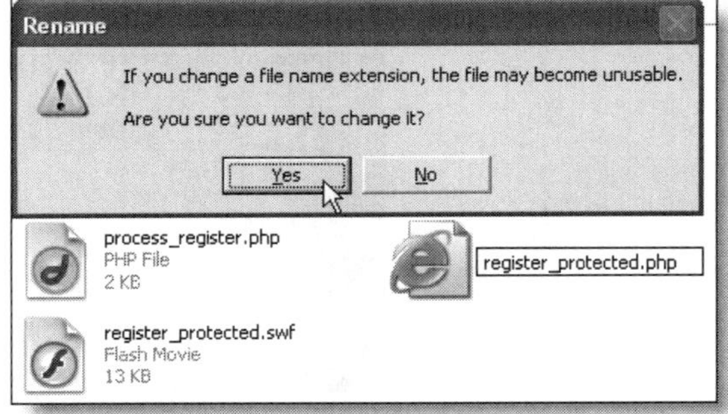

If you are using Mac OS X, the `.html` file extension should be visible in Finder. Click inside the filename, pause, and click again. You can then edit the filename extension. If the extension isn't visible in Finder, highlight the `register_protected` icon for a web page (the default for web pages is a Safari icon), *Ctrl*-click, and select Get Info from the contextual menu. Change the filename extension from .html to .php in the Name & Extension field, as shown, and press *Return*.

The Mac operating system will ask politely if you really want to make the change (none of the dire warnings that Windows users get). The answer is yes. Click Use .php and close the Info window.

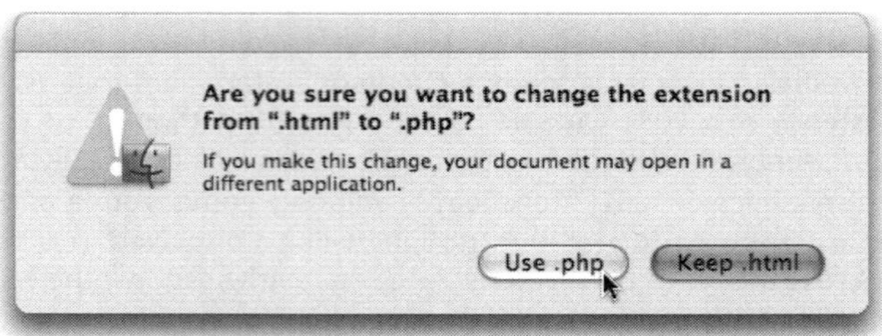

4. Open the renamed file (register_protected.php) in your script editor, and place your cursor on the first line, just in front of the XHTML Doctype. Insert a new line, and enter the PHP script shown in the following screenshot.

process_login.php process_logout.php register_protected.php

Code Split Design Title: Register new user

```
<?php session_start();
if (!isset($_SESSION['authenticated'])) {
  header('Location: http://localhost/phpflash/ch09/login.html');
  exit();
  }
?>
<!DOCTYPE html PUBLIC "-//W3C//DTD XHTML 1.0 Transitional//EN"
"http://www.w3.org/TR/xhtml1/DTD/xhtml1-transitional.dtd">
```

After the call to session_start(), a conditional statement checks whether $_SESSION['authenticated'] has been set. The isset() function is preceded by the negative operator (!), so the script is basically saying the following:

```
if $_SESSION['authenticated'] has not been set {
  redirect this request to login.html
  terminate this page
  }
```

In other words, if $_SESSION['authenticated'] doesn't exist, anyone trying to access the page won't be logged in and should be redirected to the login page. The redirect is performed by the following code:

```
header('Location: http://localhost/phpflash/ch09/login.html');
```

The PHP header() function can be used to send any HTTP header, *as long as* none of the body of a web page has yet been sent to the browser. If you attempt to use header() after the server has started sending any of the page content, you will get the "Headers already sent" error I mentioned earlier (see Appendix A for details). The HTTP header is passed to the function as a string. When you are redirecting a page, it is recommended that you give a full URL rather than just a relative address after Location:.

After sending the redirect header, you need to prevent the server from sending any further data by adding the command `exit()`. If you leave this out, the server will continue sending the rest of the code in the page. Consequently, the headers of the page will override the redirect and end up showing your secret page to all and sundry!

If `$_SESSION['authenticated']` *has* been set, the conditional statement containing the redirect is ignored, and your authenticated user can see the page.

5. Now it's time to put it to the test. Save all the pages you've been working on, and attempt to load `register_protected.php` into your browser. If you've scripted step 4 correctly, you should be taken directly to `login.html`. Some people like to display a message like Access denied when an unauthorized user attempts to view a protected page, but I think that can be counterproductive. There's a danger that a cracker will see it as a challenge. There's no guarantee that simply redirecting unauthorized users to the login screen will keep your site any safer, but at least it's not like a red rag to a bull.

   Type in your username and password, and click the Login button. I used codeslave as my password, but use whatever you registered earlier in the `users` table as your username and password.

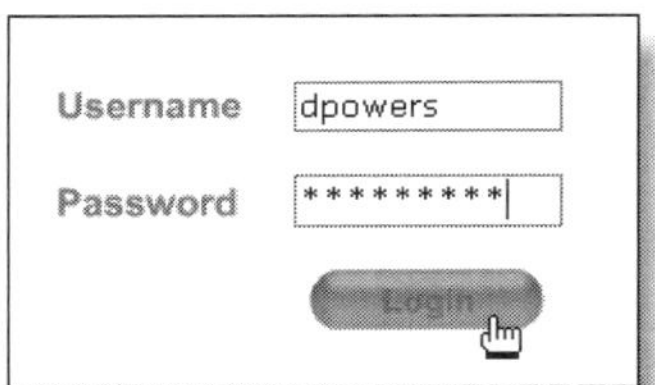

6. As long as you got your username and password correct, you should be taken to `register_protected.php` and your registration movie. Highlight the URL in the browser address bar and press *CTRL+C/⌘+C* to copy it to the clipboard. Click the Log Out button, and you should be taken back to `login.html`.

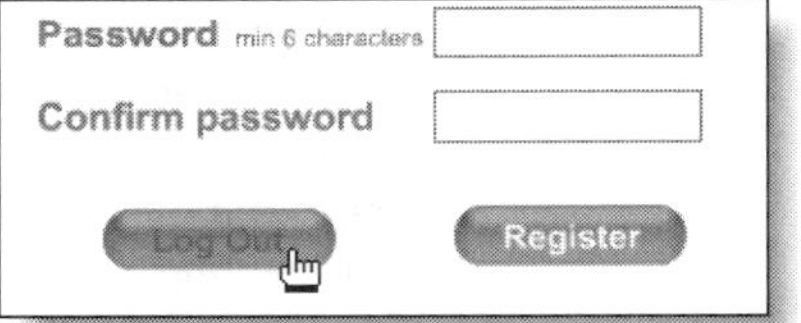

7. Try to get back into `register_protected.php` by pasting (*CTRL+V/⌘+V*) its URL in the browser address bar (type in the address if you forgot to copy it to the clipboard). Even though a session was created to let you in, the script in `process_logout.php` unset the session variable and destroyed the session. The only way you can get back into the page is to log in again. But there's still a gaping security hole in the system, which you need to plug. Let's deal with that next.

Plugging the security gap

PHP sessions work extremely well when used to protect ordinary web pages. As you saw, the few lines of script at the top of `register_protected.php` prevent the page from loading if the session variable hasn't been set. Unfortunately, that won't stop anyone from getting at your Flash movie.

1. Make sure that you have logged out of `register_protected.php` and cannot get back in by entering the URL in your browser's address bar.
2. Assuming you're using the file structure suggested in this book, type this URL in your address bar: http://localhost/phpflash/ch09/register_protected.swf (if you're on a Mac, type http://localhost/~*username*/phpflash/ch09/register_protected.swf). What you see in

your browser should give you pause for thought. As Figure 9-5 shows, protecting the web page that displays a Flash movie does nothing to stop people from accessing the movie itself if they know its URL.

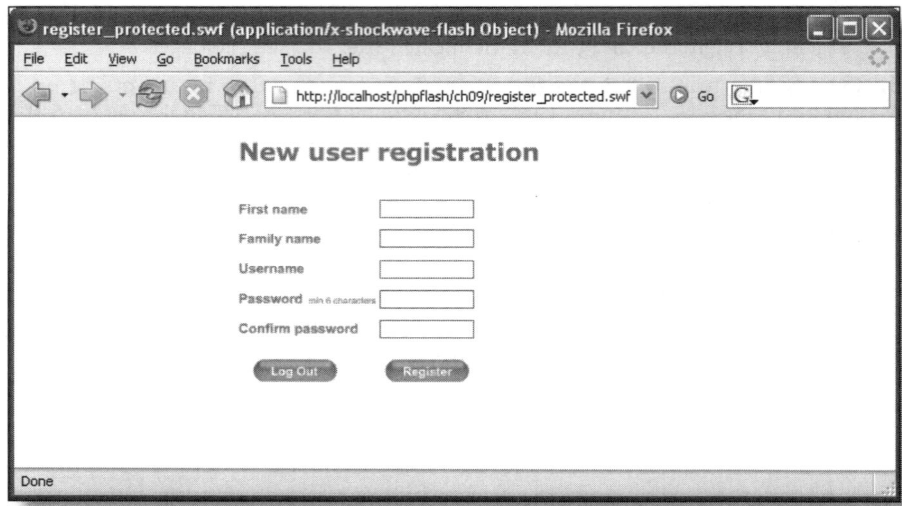

Figure 9-5. Just protecting the page that displays a Flash movie is not enough to prevent the movie itself from being accessed freely in a browser.

One commonly used technique to get around this sort of problem is known as **obfuscation**—that is, deliberately disguising the name of the SWF, even giving it a different filename extension. (The Flash Player takes no notice of filename extensions as long as all the other parameters are correct in the web page that is used to display it. So you could try to disguise your SWF as `daisy_the_dog.gif`, and it would still work correctly when embedded in a web page, but not if accessed directly.) PHP sessions offer a much better solution, but before I tell you what it is, let's take a quick look at the danger of an unprotected SWF.

3. Fill in the details of a new user and click the Register button. The new record will be entered into the database just as though you were properly logged in as an authorized user. The PHP sessions protection on the web page itself is totally worthless if a malicious user either knows or can guess the name of your Flash movie file! That's not to say there's no point in protecting the web page with sessions—every line of defense is important.

4. The solution is amazingly simple. Open `process_register.php`, the script used to enter the user details in the database. Change the opening lines so they look like this (the new code is highlighted in bold):

```
<?php
session_start();
if (!isset($_SESSION['authenticated'])) {
  echo 'status=goodbye';
  }
else {
```

```
// include the Database classes
require_once('../classes/database.php');
```

Then, right at the very bottom of the page, insert a closing curly brace. Effectively, this wraps the entire existing script in the else part of a conditional statement. When the Flash movie sends data to process_register.php, the script initiates a session and checks for the existence of $_SESSION['authenticated']. If the session variable hasn't been set, the script sends a variable called status with a value of goodbye back to Flash. This, you will remember, is the same key/value pair sent by process_logout.php. So, even if someone finds the URL to your SWF file, any attempt to enter unauthorized material in your database will be blocked. If the session variable has been set, of course, the original script will run as normal.

5. Save the amended version of process_register.php (it's in the download files as process_register02.php) and try entering another new record in the database. You should be quietly, but firmly sent back to the login page as soon as you click the Register button. A really determined cracker may still be able to find a way around this system, so it can't be recommended for hypersensitive information, but it's certainly far more effective than obfuscating the filename. Of course, if you obfuscate the filename as well, that add an extra level of security.

Other uses for sessions

The other main use of sessions is for shopping carts. The principle is exactly the same. Once you have given a visitor a session identity—by calling session_start()—you can store any details related with the session in the SESSION superglobal array. Any type of variable can be stored as a session variable, so a shopping cart can be constructed using a multidimensional array like this:

```
$_SESSION['cart']['item'][0]['title'] = 'Foundation PHP 5 for Flash';
$_SESSION['cart']['item'][0]['quantity'] = 5; // one for every room!
```

Using sessions for this sort of thing with Flash is perhaps less useful than it would be on an ordinary XHTML website, because a Flash movie can maintain persistent information in other ways, such as through the Flash SharedObject discussed in Chapter 7. Also, Flash movies can store variables in a persistent way even when a visitor moves from frame to frame.

Summary

This chapter has been a brief introduction to one of the main uses of PHP sessions: restricting access to web pages in a seamless fashion without the need to locate everything in a dedicated folder. Session variables can be used anywhere you have a need for maintaining continuity. Once a visitor has been given a session identity, session variables associated with that visitor's computer can be accessed by any PHP script until the variable is explicitly unset or the session is brought to an end. In the Flash context, the main value of sessions lies in user authentication in combination with a database.

Although sessions provide a simple and effective way of controlling access, they should not be confused with secure connections. They are not sufficient on their own for protecting hypersensitive information or financial transactions.

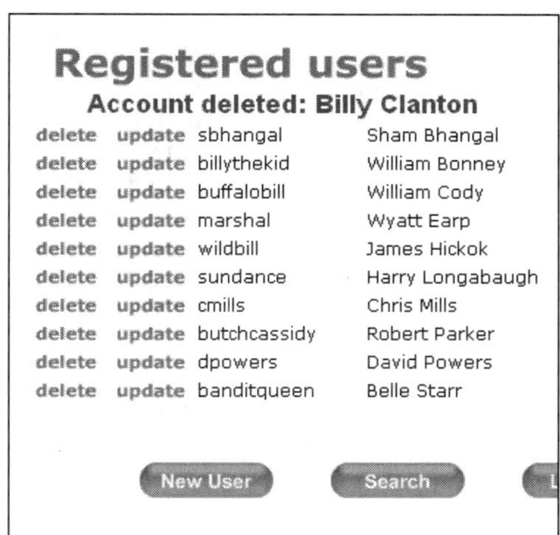

Chapter 10

KEEPING CONTROL WITH A CONTENT MANAGEMENT SYSTEM

What this chapter covers:

- Understanding the essential SQL quartet: INSERT, SELECT, UPDATE, and DELETE
- Planning a complex application
- Building the graphical interface for a CMS
- Displaying a full list of records in a database
- Searching for records according to variable criteria
- Updating and deleting existing records
- Adding a new column to a database table

There will come a time, sooner or later, when you will need to make changes to records in your database. Updates and deletions can be handled easily with phpMyAdmin, but phpMyAdmin is a tool for specialists. When you're building applications that will be used by nonspecialists, it's far preferable to create an intuitive interface that performs maintenance tasks at the click of one or two buttons. As a matter of fact, you wouldn't want to allow visitors to your website access to phpMyAdmin. You might, for instance, create a bulletin board where members can edit their own contributions, but giving them free rein with phpMyAdmin would be dangerous. By building a content management interface of your own, you can control exactly what others can do—and, more important, what they can't do.

Although there are many commands in SQL, four essential ones that you use all the time are `INSERT`, `SELECT`, `UPDATE`, and `DELETE`. With just these four commands, you can create a powerful content management system. To demonstrate how these commands are used, I'll show you how to adapt the registration form you built in Chapter 8. Even though it's just a one-table database, the principles you'll learn in this chapter are exactly the same as those you would apply to a much larger, more sophisticated system.

The four essential SQL commands

You've already met three of these commands, but I think it's useful to review them briefly again so you have a convenient place to look them up when you're not sure about something and need an easy reference. Each command has a large number of options; rather than confuse you by listing them all here, I'll concentrate on the most important ones.

SELECT

`SELECT` is used for retrieving records from one or more tables in a database. Its basic syntax is as follows:

```
SELECT [DISTINCT] select_list
FROM table_list
[WHERE where_expression]
[ORDER BY col_name | formula] [ASC | DESC]
[LIMIT [skip_count,] show_count]
```

Just to remind you how to read SQL syntax:

- Anything in uppercase is a SQL command (although you can write the command itself in lowercase, if you prefer, because Structured Query Language is case insensitive).
- Expressions in square brackets are optional.
- Lowercase italics represent variable input.
- A vertical pipe (|) separates alternatives.

The `DISTINCT` option tells the database you want to eliminate duplicate rows from the results. Ideally, you should design your database so that frequently duplicated data is stored in a separate table and referenced by a foreign key, but this is not always possible, or you may have inherited a single-table database. DISTINCT comes in handy in such circumstances. For instance, let's say you have a database of baseball players containing a single table called league, which contains three columns: player, team, and home_runs. To get a list of all the teams, you might use a query like this:

```
SELECT DISTINCT teams FROM league
```

The *select_list* is a comma-delimited list of columns that you want included in the result. To retrieve all columns, use an asterisk (*), for example:

```
SELECT player, home_runs FROM league /* gets just two columns */
SELECT * FROM league                 /* gets all columns */
```

> *As you might have guessed from the preceding examples, MySQL allows you to intersperse your SQL code with comments. You can use C-style comments, as just shown. Alternatively, anything from # to the end of a line is also regarded as a comment. This can be useful if you want to test the difference between two ways of writing your query—simply put C-style comments around the expression you want to exclude, and then remove them later. For instance,* `SELECT /* DISTINCT */ teams FROM league` *temporarily disables the* `DISTINCT` *option.*

The WHERE clause specifies any particular criteria you are looking for, and it can include comparison operators:

```
SELECT player, home_runs FROM league
WHERE team = 'RedSox'

SELECT player, home_runs FROM league
WHERE team = 'RedSox' AND home_runs > 5
```

ORDER BY specifies the sort order of the results. This can be specified as a single column, a comma-delimited list of columns, or an expression (such as RAND(), which was used to provide a random order in the Hangman game). The default sort order is ascending (a–z, 0–9), but you can specify DESC (descending) to reverse the order. This next example produces a list with the biggest hitters in alphabetical order, followed by the next biggest hitters, again in alphabetical order, and so on. (There's no need to specify ASC, because it's the default. However, it's often useful to do so when mixing sort orders so that the meaning of your query remains clear to you when you review it in several months' time.)

```
SELECT player, home_runs FROM league
ORDER BY home_runs DESC, player ASC
```

LIMIT stipulates the maximum number of records to return. If two numbers are given separated by a comma, the first tells the database how many rows to skip. For instance, LIMIT 10, 10 produces results 11 to 20. If fewer results exist than the limit specified, you get however many fall within the specified range. (You don't get a series of empty or undefined results to make up the number.) This can be useful for navigation through long lists of results.

Although you can choose as many or as few of the options as you like, they must come in the order indicated here. Chapter 12 will show you how to select records when more than one table is involved. For more details on SELECT, see http://dev.mysql.com/doc/mysql/en/SELECT.html.

INSERT

The INSERT command is used to add new records to a database. The general syntax is as follows:

```
INSERT [INTO] table_name (column_names) VALUES (values)
```

The word INTO is completely optional; it serves no function other than to make the command read a little more like human language. The column names and values are comma-delimited lists, and both must be in the same order. This has nothing to do with the order of columns when the table was originally created. You can use whichever order you like, but the database needs to know what it is!

The reason for this rather strange syntax is to allow you to insert more than one record at a time. Each subsequent record is in a separate set of parentheses, with each set separated by a comma:

```
INSERT numbers (x,y) VALUES (10,20),(20,30),(30,40),(40,50)
```

This is normally unnecessary with PHP, because multiple inserts are frequently performed using a loop. However, the application in Chapter 12 uses implode() to build a multiple INSERT query like this. If you find this syntax difficult to remember, you can use an alternative one, which you will see is very similar to UPDATE:

```
INSERT [INTO] table_name SET col_name = value [, col_name = value]
```

This can be used for only one record at a time:

```
INSERT numbers SET x = 10, y = 20
```

Any columns omitted from an INSERT query are set to their default value. **Never set an explicit value for the primary key where the column is set to auto_increment**; leave the column name out of the INSERT statement. For more details, see http://dev.mysql.com/doc/mysql/en/INSERT.html.

UPDATE

This command is used for changing existing records. The syntax is almost identical to the alternative INSERT syntax:

```
UPDATE [IGNORE] table_name SET col_name = value [, col_name = value]
[WHERE where_expression]
```

UPDATE generates an error and terminates the operation if you attempt to insert a duplicate value in a primary key column (primary keys, remember, *must* be unique). The IGNORE option instructs MySQL to abandon such attempts silently. While this sounds useful, you should never design a system where this is likely to happen.

The WHERE expression tells MySQL which record or records you want to update (or perhaps in the case of the following example, dream about).

```
UPDATE sales SET q2-2005 = 25000
WHERE title = 'Foundation PHP 5 for Flash'
```

For more details on UPDATE, see http://dev.mysql.com/doc/mysql/en/UPDATE.html.

DELETE

DELETE can be used to delete single records, multiple records, or the entire contents of a table, and it can even work on several tables at once. The general syntax for deleting from a single table is as follows:

```
DELETE FROM table_name [WHERE where_expression]
```

DELETE is totally unforgiving—there is no prompt to ask you to confirm the command, and once the data is deleted, it is gone *forever*. The only way to retrieve inadvertently deleted information is from a backup (see Appendix E).

```
DELETE FROM subscribers WHERE expiry_date < NOW()
```

Chapter 12 shows you how to delete records simultaneously from more than one table. For more details, see http://dev.mysql.com/doc/mysql/en/DELETE.html.

> *Although the* WHERE *clause is optional in both* UPDATE *and* DELETE, *you should be aware that if you leave* WHERE *out, the entire table is affected. This means that a careless slip with either of these commands could result in every single record being identical—or wiped out.*
>
> **You have been warned.**

Building a simple content management system

When working with databases, you need a system to help you manage the four essential SQL commands just outlined—in other words, you need a content management system. The project that follows performs these functions in an integrated way, but I don't want you to have any illusions: this is not a content management system with every bell and whistle (that could be the subject of a book on its own). The purpose is to show you how to handle the basic functions, so I've chosen to adapt the registration form you built in Chapter 8 and continued working on in the last chapter. Even though it's just a five-column, single-table database, the skills you'll learn from this project are equally applicable to a much more complex application.

To scale it up, the main changes you would need to make involve slightly more advanced SQL and the manipulation of a larger number of variables. In spite of its size, this project involves quite a lot of steps, so it's important to work out a plan of action.

Before you can make any changes to a record, you have to find it. There are two ways: select it from a list of all entries, or search for it. Once you've found the record, you need a means of selecting whether to update or delete it. In the former case, the existing details must be displayed in an editable form; in the latter case, it's a good idea to get the user to confirm the right record has been chosen before dispatching it to oblivion. So, the new elements you need are as follows:

- A search form
- A listing page
- Update and delete buttons
- An editing form
- A delete confirmation dialog box

Driving the whole application in the background is a combination of ActionScript and PHP, plus, of course, the SQL queries needed to interact with MySQL.

Building the content management interface

All the necessary files are available in the download files for this chapter. To start with, you need `register_management01.fla`, which you should rename `register_management.fla`.

If you prefer, you can continue working with the files from the last chapter. To do this, copy `register_protected.fla` and `login.fla` to wherever you are keeping your source files, and put them in a new folder for this chapter. Open each file in turn, highlight the actions layer, and open the Actions panel. Inside the Actions panel, click the Replace icon, and replace all instances of ch09 with ch10. Save `register_protected.fla` as `register_management.fla`, which is the file you will work with throughout the rest of the chapter. You no longer need `register_protected.fla`.

You should also copy `process_login.php`, `process_logout.php`, and `process_register.php` from the download files or from `phpflash/ch09` to `phpflash/ch10`.

If you want to get straight down to the coding side of things, skip ahead to the section titled "Scripting the application." The file `register_management02.fla` contains all the graphic elements that you will build in the next section. If you want to skip straight to the end already, you can find the finished version in `register_management12.fla`. Remember to rename it `register_management.fla` before you try it out.

Creating extra buttons and movie clip buttons

Most of the extra buttons required for the management interface are standard button symbols, but four of them will be displayed dynamically, so they need to be made as movie clips.

1. Take a look at Figure 10-1, which shows the changes you need to make from the original layout of the registration form in the last chapter. In addition to the drop-shadow background I have added for purely cosmetic purposes, the Log Out button has moved to the bottom right, and there are two new buttons, Search and List Users.

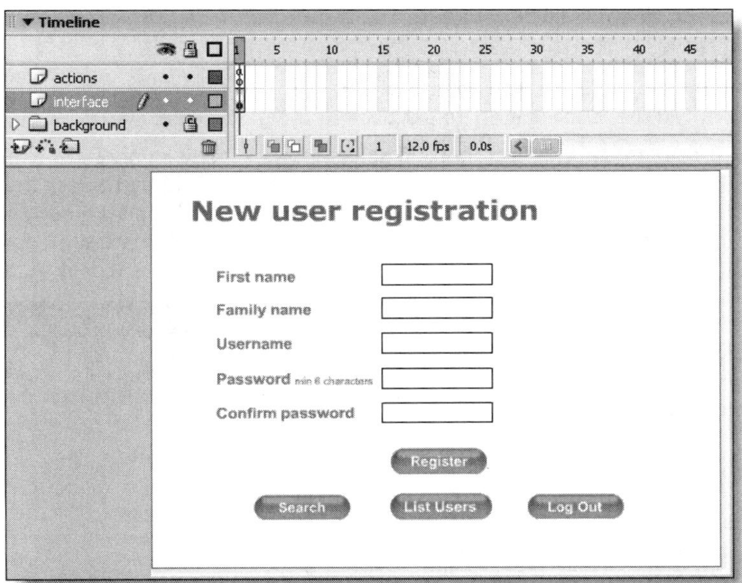

Figure 10-1. The first frame of the registration management system adds a Search button and a button to display a complete user list (List Users).

2. These are standard buttons made from the same Basic button symbol used for Register and Log Out. You need seven new ones in all: Cancel, Find, List Users, New User, OK, Search, and Update. Position the List Users and Search buttons on the stage as shown in Figure 10-1, and give them instance names of list_btn and search_btn, respectively. Leave the other buttons in the Library for the time being.

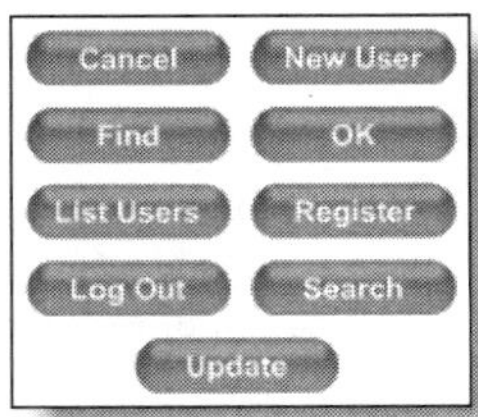

3. The remaining four buttons will be loaded into the movie dynamically at runtime. To load a symbol at runtime, the symbol needs to be a movie clip, but simply converting a regular button symbol won't work. Fortunately, it's quite simple to make movie clips that work exactly like buttons. The first step is to create a movie clip called hit_btn, which performs the same function as the hit state in a normal button. Select Insert ➤ New Symbol (*Ctrl+F8*/*⌘+F8*). In the dialog box that opens, type hit_btn in the Name field and select the Movie clip radio button. Click OK.

4. Inside the Edit Symbols window, rename Layer 1 as hit and draw a solid rectangle without any stroke. It doesn't matter what size you make the rectangle, because you will adjust it later for each button. The fill color is equally unimportant. This will be the hit area of your movie clip buttons.

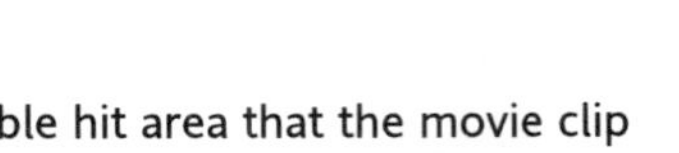

5. Still inside the hit_btn edit window, add a second layer called actions (above the hit layer) to the timeline. Select frame 1 on the actions layer, open the Actions panel, and insert the following ActionScript:

```
this._visible = false;
_parent.hitArea = this;
```

This turns the rectangle into an invisible hit area that the movie clip buttons can use. Click Stage 1 to get back to the main stage.

6. Now for the movie clip button itself. Select Insert ➤ New Symbol again. In the Create New Symbol dialog box, type delButton in the Name field and select the Movie clip radio button. This time, don't click OK, but reveal the Linkage section by selecting the Advanced option if it's not already open. Flash will automatically copy the name delButton into the Identifier field. The linkage identifier is used by ActionScript to select the right symbol to display at runtime. The identifier doesn't need to have the same name as movie clips in the Library, but since you need to use the identifier in your script, it's a lot easier to keep track of your movie assets if you have just one name for each symbol. If you prefer to use spaces in symbol names, remove any spaces from the linkage identifier and use camel case or underscores.

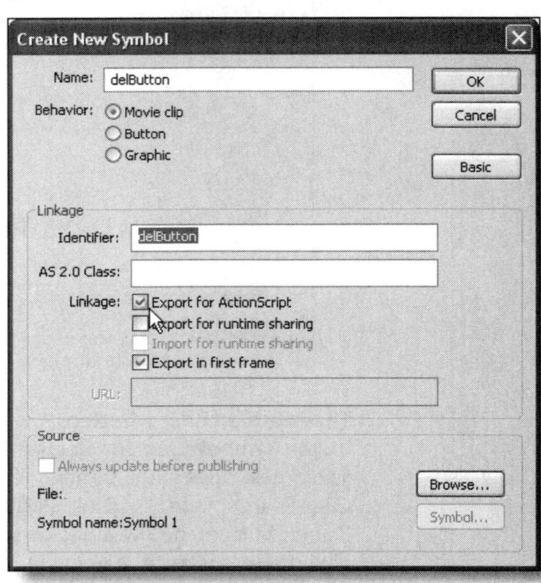

When compiling the SWF, Flash normally includes only those symbols that you have placed on the stage, so you need to select the Export for ActionScript check box. When you do this, Flash automatically checks the Export in first frame check box, which is exactly what you want. Make sure you set the options as shown here, and then click OK.

7. In the Edit Symbol window, you need three layers—text, labels, and actions—as shown alongside. Extend the timeline to frame 30 on all three layers. Select frame 1 on the text layer and create a static text field containing the word delete. I used Verdana 12pt bold and a text color of #377F7F. In the Property inspector, set the x and y coordinates of the text field to 0. This puts the registration point at the top-left corner of the button, which will make positioning it dynamically much easier. Insert a keyframe on frame 10. Select the text and give it a rollover color. I chose red to make it abundantly clear, although you may prefer something subtler. Do the same on frame 20 by inserting a keyframe and selecting a color for the button's down state.

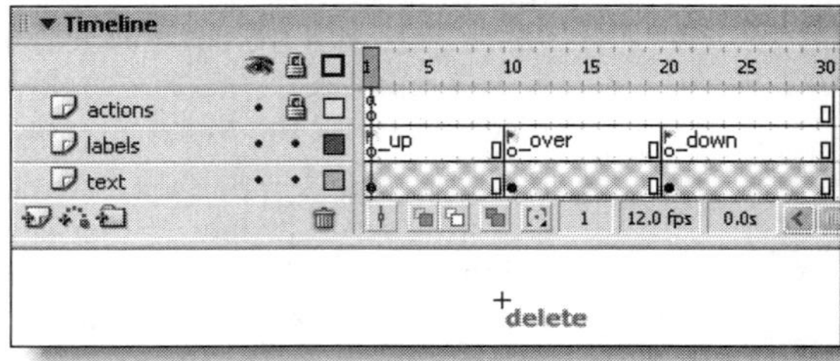

8. On the labels layer, insert keyframes on frames 10 and 20. Label the keyframes in the Property inspector _up, _over, and _down (all with a leading underscore), in that order. These are special names that will enable the movie clip to emulate the equivalent button states.

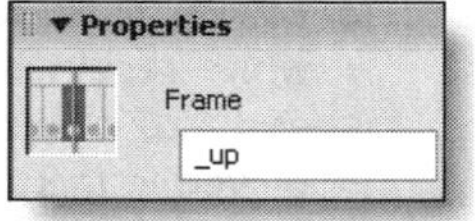

9. Select frame 1 on the actions layer and open the Actions panel. Type stop(); to prevent the movie clip from constantly looping through all three states.

10. Close the Actions panel and insert a new layer immediately below the text layer. Rename the new layer hit, and drag an instance of `hit_btn` onto the new layer. Resize it so that it just stretches beyond the text on the layer above, as shown in the screenshot. Make sure the x and y coordinates of top-left corner are both set to 0.

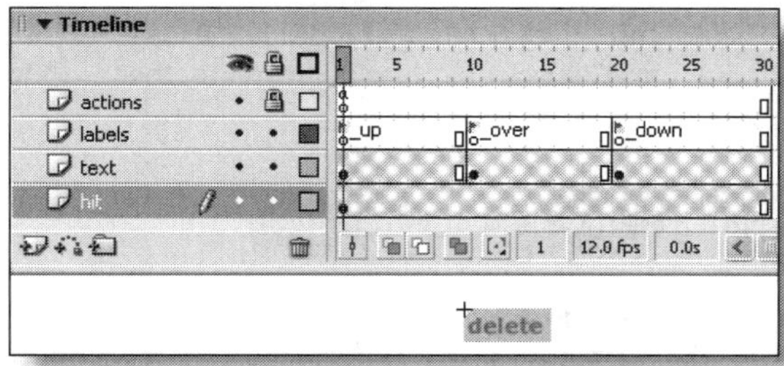

11. Click Scene 1 to return to the main stage. If you select delButton in the Library panel, you will still be able to see the hit_btn behind the text in the Preview panel. The same will happen if you drag an instance onto the stage. Don't worry, it will look fine if you test the movie, although the over and down states will not be active until a button event (such as `onRelease`) is added to the movie clip.

12. Repeat steps 6 to 11 to create three more movie clip buttons: nextButton, prevButton, and updButton. The first two will be used for navigation when the list of users stretches beyond a single page. The updButton movie clip will be used along with delButton to allow users to select the action they want to perform on a record. When completed, they should look similar to those shown here. (Figure 10-6 in the "Displaying the full list of users" section a little later in the chapter shows how they will be used in the completed application.)

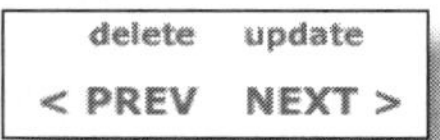

Creating the delete confirmation dialog box

Flash MX 2004 contains a version 2 `Window` component that could be used instead of a custom dialog box, but in view of the uncertainty about the future of version 2 components, I have decided to create a movie clip of my own, which is quick and simple to create.

1. Create a new movie clip symbol called confirmDel. Use the same name as linkage identifier and check the Export for ActionScript option.

2. For the background, create a series of nesting colored and white rectangles, the largest of which is 240 pixels wide and 120 pixels high. Because the dialog box will be displayed in the center of the stage, the symbol's registration point needs to be in the center, so set the x and y coordinates of the outer rectangle at -120 and -60.

3. Insert a separate text layer and lay it out as shown. The first two lines are static text fields. Beneath the second line, insert a dynamic text field and give it an instance name of delete_txt. In the Property inspector, make it a nonselectable, single-line field with no border. Set the text alignment to center.

4. Position the OK and Cancel buttons underneath the dynamic text field, and give them instance names of ok_btn and cancel_btn. Click Scene 1 and return to the main stage.

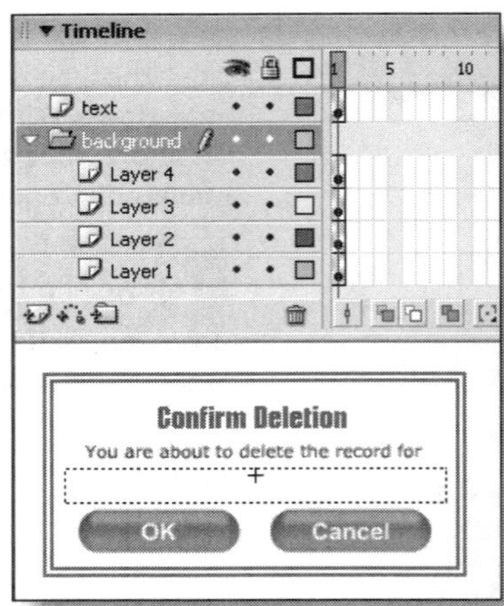

Laying out the individual frames for the interface

You now have all the assets needed to create the registration management system. Laying out the interface is simple. The first part of the interface—the registration form—is inherited from the movie created in Chapter 8. Three more frames are required, one each for the search form, the list of registered users (which will also display the search results), and the update page. With the exception of the page that displays the list, they are all based on the registration form. Since ActionScript means that Flash movies are no longer tied to the chronological order of the timeline, it makes sense to build the forms in the order that requires the least effort rather than in the order they will be seen by the user.

If you are using the download files or want to compare your own files, the starting point for this section is `register_management01.fla`, with the extra buttons on frame 1 laid out as shown in Figures 10-1 and 10-2. By the end of the section, the file will look like `register_management02.fla`. If you need any of the elements created in the previous two sections, get them from the Library in `register_management02.fla`.

1. Insert a new layer called labels above the interface layer. Extend all layers, including all the layers in the layer folder background, by entering blank keyframes (*F5*) in frame 40. Label frame 1 insertData.

2. Insert a keyframe (*F6*) in frame 10 of the interface layer and label the frame update.

3. You should now have a FLA file that looks like Figure 10-2. The update page requires only two minor changes. First, change the static text field at the top so that it reads Update existing user. Delete the Register button and replace it with the Update button symbol (make sure you use the regular button symbol labeled Update, not the updButton movie clip).

To avoid having to work out exactly where to locate the replacement button, right-click (CTRL-click) the existing button and select Swap Symbol from the contextual menu. A dialog box will appear that offers you a choice of all the other symbols in your Library. Select the one you want and click OK. If you use this technique, any existing instance name will be preserved, so you always need to remember to change it in the Property inspector afterward.

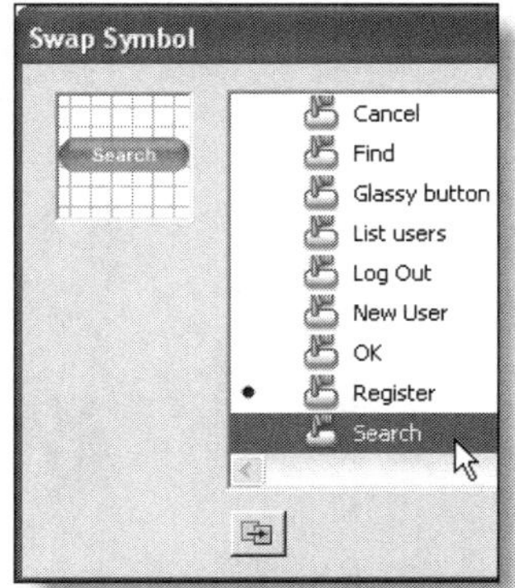

Give the new Update button an instance name of update_btn.

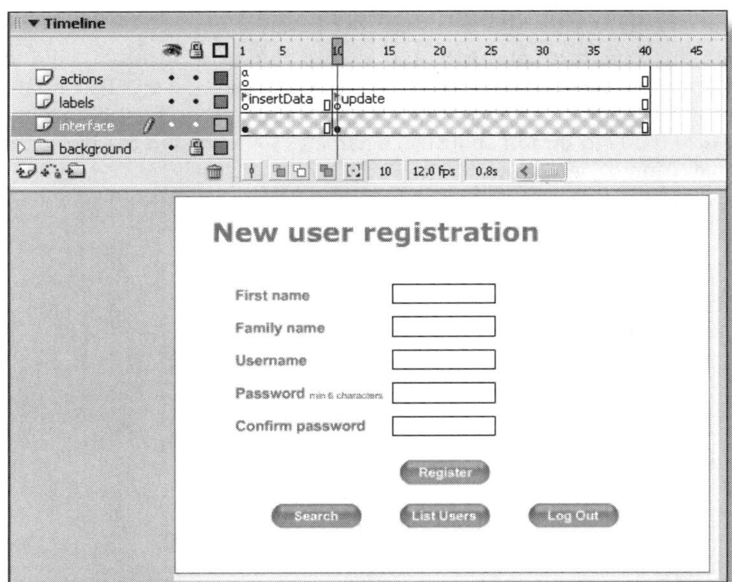

Figure 10-2. The individual frames of the management system are constructed by reusing existing elements.

4. Those are the only changes necessary to frame 10. Your interface on frame 10 should now look similar to Figure 10-3.
5. Select frame 20 on the interface layer and insert a new keyframe. Insert a keyframe on frame 20 of the labels layer and name it search.

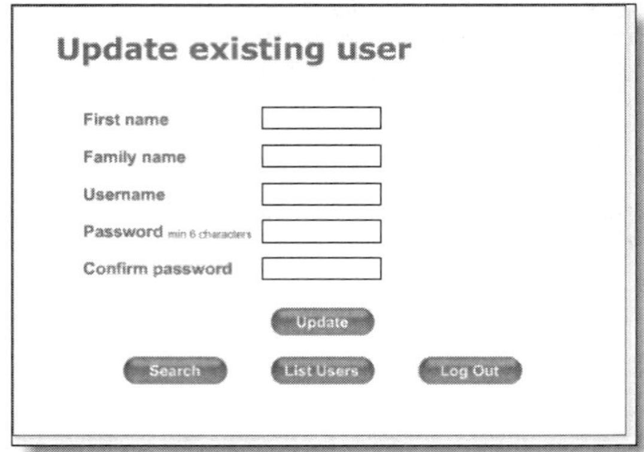

Figure 10-3. The update page requires the change of just the heading and one button.

6. Change the static text field at the top to read Find existing user. Delete the two password text input fields and the static text labeling them. Delete the Update and Search buttons; replace them with the Find and New User button symbols as shown in Figure 10-4. Give the Find button an instance name of find_btn and the New User button an instance name of new_btn.

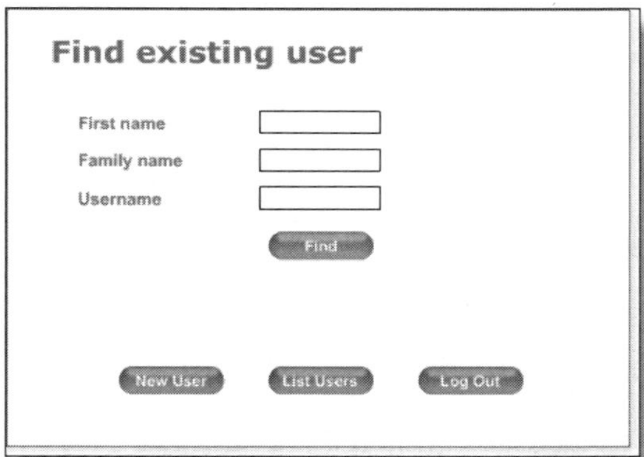

Figure 10-4. The search page follows the same pattern, preserving most of the existing structure.

7. Now for a bit of constructive destruction—the final frame of the interface. Select frame 30 on the interface layer and enter a keyframe. Enter a keyframe on the same frame of the labels layer and name it listUsers. Delete the remaining text input fields and their static text labels. Change the static text at the top to read Registered users, and replace the List Users button in the bottom row with the Search button. Give the Search button an instance name of search_btn. You should end up with something similar to Figure 10-5. Don't worry about the emptiness of the page; this is where a lot of dynamic text and buttons will appear.

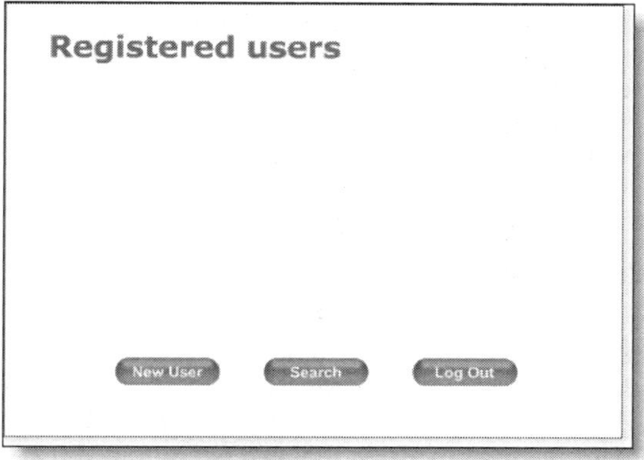

Figure 10-5. Most of the elements are removed from the final frame, because they will be replaced by results from the database.

That completes the graphical side of things. Now it's time to wire it all up with ActionScript, PHP, and MySQL.

Scripting the application

I've broken up this project into several stages so you can see how it progresses. Don't try to rush through everything at one sitting. There's nothing particularly difficult about what follows, but you should always bear in mind that you're combining three different technologies: ActionScript, PHP, and MySQL. When something goes wrong, it can be difficult to locate the problem. By testing everything thoroughly as you go along, you will not only get a better understanding of each technology, but also probably make fewer mistakes—and complete the project quicker in the end. I built several testing stages into the following instructions, but if you get stuck, read through Appendix A. If that still doesn't help, ask for help in the friends of ED forums (`www.friendsofed.com/forums`).

The approach I've taken roughly follows the line of development I pursued in developing this application. Building the interface first gave me a clear idea of my ultimate goal. I was then able to adapt the original scripts to work with this content management system. As you'll see in the next section, I built a skeleton PHP script with very little new code, but lots of comments indicating the new elements I needed. That gave me a clear view of how I needed to approach the ActionScript side of things. In the section "Transferring data with LoadVars," you'll see how each section of the skeleton PHP script has a counterpart in ActionScript. Once the basic structure was laid out, it was just a question of building and testing each section. Naturally, I discovered problems as I went along. I highlight some of these and then show you the way I worked around them.

The finished project contains more than 450 lines of new code, liberally sprinkled with comments, in addition to the existing scripts. It's a lot of typing (I know, I've done it several times!), so I've provided a complete set of download files showing the project at various stages of development. Consequently, you can pick up the project at several different places and just work on a small part at a time, if you wish.

Before you start, it's always a good idea to check that Apache, PHP, and MySQL are all working in harmony. The easiest way is to launch phpMyAdmin and see if it's listing your databases. If it is, you know that everything is running fine. If phpMyAdmin appears but can't list your databases, that probably means MySQL isn't running (see Chapter 6 for instructions on starting MySQL). If phpMyAdmin fails to launch, check that Apache is running (see Chapter 1 for startup instructions).

Building a multifunctional PHP script

By the time you finish, you will have created PHP scripts to perform more than half a dozen different tasks associated with registering and updating records in your database. Other books on PHP and Flash tend to ask you to create a separate PHP page for each task, filling your folders with lots of small scripts. I think it's more efficient to combine everything in one page because there are several common elements that can be usefully reused. What's more, it's easier to maintain. The first job is to adapt the existing PHP script so that it can be combined with those you'll build as you progress through the application.

Adapting the PHP registration script

The login script in `process_login.php` doesn't need any amendment, so I'm going to build all the new functionality into `process_register.php`, the script that currently inserts a new user into the database. To avoid confusion, I'll give the updated file a new name (`register_cms.php`) for use throughout this chapter. When complete, `register_cms.php` will control all the content management of the database—inserting new records, and updating and deleting existing ones. It will also incorporate the logout script from `process_logout.php`.

1. Make a copy of `process_register.php` and save it as `register_cms.php` in your `phpflash/ch10` folder. I chose this name to indicate that this is a content management system.
2. Open `register_cms.php` and delete the following code from the top of the script:

   ```
   session_start();
   if (!isset($_SESSION['authenticated'])) {
     echo 'status=goodbye';
     }
   else {
   ```

   Also remove the final closing brace immediately before the closing PHP tag. This removes the check for the session variable, which you don't want while testing the application. Otherwise, you would constantly need to make sure you're logged in. You'll restore this code at the end of the project, when you make the content management system secure.
3. Change the rest of the code in `register_cms.php` so that it looks like this (the new code is highlighted in bold; the entire listing is also in `register_cms01.php`):

   ```
   <?php
   // include the Database classes
   require_once('../classes/database.php');
   ```

```
// escape quotes and apostrophes if magic_quotes_gpc off
if (!get_magic_quotes_gpc()) {
  foreach($_POST as $key=>$value) {
    $temp = addslashes($value);
    $_POST[$key] = $temp;
    }
  }

// Register new user if "action" is set to "register" in POST array
if ($_POST['action'] == 'register') {
  // check whether anyone already has the same username
  $unique = checkDuplicate($_POST['username']);
  if ($unique) {
    $db = new Database('localhost','flashadmin','fortytwo','phpflash');
    $sql = 'INSERT INTO users (first_name,family_name,username,pwd)
       VALUES ("'.$_POST['first_name'].'","'.$_POST['family_name'].'",
       "'.$_POST['username'].'","'.sha1($_POST['pwd']).'")';
    $result = $db->query($sql);
    if ($result) {
      $created = 'Account created for ';
      $created .= stripslashes($_POST['first_name']).' '
➥ .stripslashes($_POST['family_name']);
      echo 'duplicate=n&message='.urlencode($created);
      }
    }
  }
elseif ($_POST['action'] == 'listAll') {
  // code for retrieving full list
  }
elseif ($_POST['action'] == 'find') {
  // code for search by name, etc.
  }
elseif ($_POST['action'] == 'getDetails') {
  // get user details for updating
  }
elseif ($_POST['action'] == 'doUpdate') {
  // update record
  }
elseif ($_POST['action'] == 'doDelete') {
  // delete record
  }
elseif ($_POST['action'] == 'logout') {
  // logout code goes here
  }

// Check for duplicate use of username
function checkDuplicate($username, $user_id = 0) {
  $db = new Database('localhost','flashuser','deepthought','phpflash');
  $sql = "SELECT username FROM users WHERE username = '$username'";
```

```
  // add to SQL if user_id supplied as argument
  if ($user_id > 0) {
    $sql .= " AND user_id != $user_id";
    }
  $result = $db->query($sql);
  $numrows = $result->num_rows;
  $db->close();

  // if username already in use, send back error message
  if ($numrows > 0) {
    $duplicate = 'Duplicate username. Please choose another.';
    echo 'duplicate=y&message='.urlencode($duplicate);
    exit();
    }
  else {
    return true;
    }
  }
?>
```

There are five important differences between this and the original script:

- The registration script is now enclosed in a conditional statement that checks the value of `$_POST['action']`. It must be set to `register` for the script to execute.
- The message returned by `$created` has been amended so that it will display the user's real name, rather than the username that has been registered in the database. Both names need to be passed to `stripslashes()` because they are still part of the POST array, and they may include apostrophes that have been escaped with a backslash.
- Six empty `elseif` code blocks have been added—one for each of the new actions that will be performed by different parts of the application. The final one will perform the logout procedure. Although the code for that already exists in `process_logout.php`, it will not be transferred until everything else has been completed, to avoid you being accidentally taken to the login page in the middle of testing part of the application.
- The check for a duplicate username has been moved into a separate function called `checkDuplicate()`.
- The `checkDuplicate()` function takes two arguments: the username and the `user_id` submitted in the POST array. The second argument is given a default value, making it optional.

This final change is probably the most significant. It means that the `checkDuplicate()` function can be reused later, when checking update requests. The only time a record can be allowed to have the same username as an existing one is when you're changing other details of the same record. Let's say, for instance, I've misspelled my own name as Poqers, but I want to keep the username `dpowers`. The original code will report that the username already exists and prevent me from making the change. The new function adds a further condition to the SQL query if a `user_id` is added to the arguments. Because automatically generated primary keys always begin at 1, it's perfectly safe to assign 0 as the default—any genuine second argument passed to the function will always be greater than 0. I'll come back to this issue when building the search page.

Transferring data with LoadVars

Every time data is transferred between the Flash movie and PHP and MySQL it will be done through an instance of LoadVars. In the original version of the registration form, three instances of LoadVars were created—one each for sending and receiving data related to new user registration, and one for sending logout instructions (the userRegistered instance of LoadVars was deliberately used to handle the logout response to prevent unauthorized users bypassing the authentication procedure through direct access to the SWF file). The changes made to the PHP code in the previous section mean that, in the future, you need only one instance of LoadVars to send data to your PHP script. Since this instance will always be used to query the database, I've decided to call it dbQuery. As long as the action property of dbQuery is set to the appropriate value, the PHP script will automatically know how to handle the incoming data.

The data coming back to the Flash movie needs to be handled differently, though. Each instance of LoadVars can be assigned only one onLoad event at a time, so it's far more convenient to create a separate instance to handle each type of data transfer. To make the final script easier to maintain, I decided to assign the onLoad event handler of each LoadVars instance to a named function (instead of using anonymous ones). Table 10-1 sets out what each of the actions will do, which instances of LoadVars will be used to send and receive data, and the named functions assigned to the onLoad event. Only two receiver instances (userRegistered and updateResult) are used more than once. This is because the logout process will be handled in the same way as in the previous chapter. Also, the update and delete processes have an almost identical outcome in the sense that they both update the database, although one results in the complete removal of a record.

Table 10-1. The LoadVars instances needed to handle each action in the registration management system

Action	Sender	Receiver	onLoad event handler	Description
register	dbQuery	userRegistered	showResult()	Checks that a new user has a unique username, and then registers the details in the database.
listAll	dbQuery	getUserList	fullList()	Retrieves a list of all records in the database.
find	dbQuery	searchDets	searchResult()	Retrieves a list of records based on search criteria.
getDetails	dbQuery	updateDets	recordFound()	Retrieves the details of all fields in a record to be updated.
doUpdate	dbQuery	updateResult	updateReport()	Updates a record providing it does not violate the principle of unique usernames, and then displays an amended list of records.

(Continued)

Table 10-1. The LoadVars instances needed to handle each action in the registration management system *(Continued)*

Action	Sender	Receiver	onLoad event handler	Description
doDelete	dbQuery	updateResult	updateReport()	Deletes a selected record, and then displays an amended list of records.
doLogout	dbQuery	userRegistered	showResult()	Logs out a registered user on request. Although logout on request will be handled by userRegistered, the onLoad event of each LoadVars instance will also forcibly log out any unauthorized user (through PHP checking for a session variable).

After declaring these new instances of LoadVars, you need to adapt the existing ActionScript to make sure the registration function still works. Because the finished application will have nearly 500 lines of code on frame 1, it's essential to organize your ActionScript in such a way that it's logical and easy to follow, and it adheres to the best practice of declaring ordinary functions first, followed by callbacks, any variables that need initializing, and finally any code that should run when the movie first loads.

The structure I have devised is as follows:

- Input checking functions (including checkPwd() from the original application)
- Interface display functions
- User registration functions (registerUser() and showResult() from the original application)
- Functions for listing users
- Search functions
- Update and delete functions
- Button callbacks
- Initialize variables

If you compare this list with Table 10-1, you will see the same logic applies to both the PHP and the ActionScript. Even though the process of building the script involves jumping from one part of the Actions panel to another, you should have no difficulty maintaining and adapting the finished script if you preserve this logic.

Adapting the registration ActionScript

1. Continue working with the same FLA document or use `register_management02.fla`. (The finished code for this section is in `register_management 03.fla`.) Now that the movie has more than one frame on the timeline, the first thing you need to do is prevent it from looping endlessly when testing. Select frame 1 on the actions layer, open the Actions panel, and put a `stop();` command at the bottom of the script. Pin the script so that you don't have to keep selecting the correct keyframe on the timeline.
2. Locate the following section and delete the `userDets` and `logoutSend` instances of `LoadVars` (shown here on lines 78 and 80):

```
78 var userDets:LoadVars = new LoadVars();
79 var userRegistered:LoadVars = new LoadVars();
80 var logoutSend:LoadVars = new LoadVars();
81 userRegistered.onLoad = showResult;
```

3. Add the new instances and event handlers like this:

```
// create LoadVars instances to communicate with PHP
var dbQuery:LoadVars = new LoadVars();
var userRegistered:LoadVars = new LoadVars();
var getUserList:LoadVars = new LoadVars();
var searchDets:LoadVars = new LoadVars();
var updateDets:LoadVars = new LoadVars();
var updateResult:LoadVars = new LoadVars();
// assign onLoad handlers for LoadVars
userRegistered.onLoad = showResult;
getUserList.onLoad = fullList;
searchDets.onLoad = searchResult;
updateDets.onLoad = recordFound;
updateResult.onLoad = updateReport;
```

4. Because `dbQuery` replaces the two instances of `LoadVars` you just deleted, you need to update all properties associated with them. Click the Replace icon at the top of the Actions panel and fill in the dialog box as shown here.

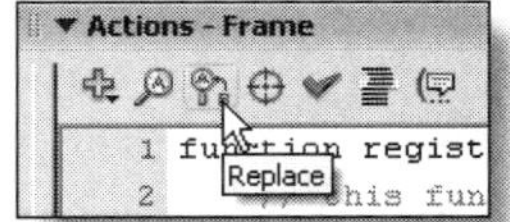

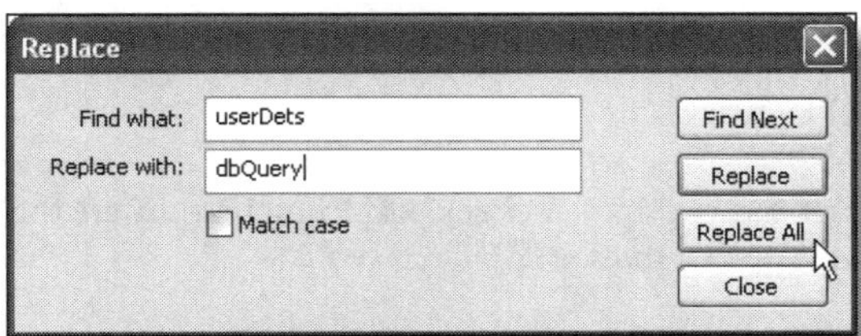

Click Replace All to replace all instances of `userDets`. A dialog box should appear reporting that Flash found and replaced five items.

5. Repeat the last step to replace all instances of logoutSend with dbQuery. Flash should report that it found and replaced two items.

6. To reflect the changes you made to the PHP script, you need to amend two lines in the registerUser() function around line 20 as follows:

```
if (checkPwd()) {
  dbQuery.action = "register";
  dbQuery.first_name = firstname_txt.text;
  dbQuery.family_name = familyname_txt.text;
  dbQuery.username = username_txt.text;
  dbQuery.pwd = password_txt.text;
  dbQuery.sendAndLoad("http://localhost/phpflash/ch10/
➥ register_cms.php?ck="+new Date().getTime(),userRegistered);
```

The first change creates the new dbQuery.action property; the other changes the URL used by dbQuery.sendAndLoad.

7. Test the movie and register a new user to make sure everything is working as before. At this stage, only the Register button will be working. The idea is to verify that registering a new user is still possible after making all these changes. If you encounter any problems, check your code against register_management03.fla and register_cms01.php.

Laying the groundwork for the new script

Once you have confirmed the registration process is still working with the new PHP script, you need to lay the groundwork for the rest of the scripting. Virtually all the ActionScript will go on frame 1; the only script required anywhere else in the Flash document will be to assign callback functions to the buttons on frames 10, 20, and 30. To make it easier to work with the script on frame 1, it's a good idea to build the same type of skeleton layout as you did with the register_cms.php. Continue with the same FLA file or use register_management03.fla. The finished code for this section is in register_management04.fla.

1. Locate the checkPwd() function. It should be around lines 33 through 46. Highlight the entire function and cut it to your clipboard (*Ctrl+X/⌘+X*). Scroll to the top of the Actions panel, insert a new line above registerUser(), and paste (*Ctrl+V/⌘+V*) checkPwd() onto line 1.

2. Insert a new line before the checkPwd() function and type the following comment:

```
/***********************
Input checking functions
************************/
```

3. Immediately after the end of the checkPwd() function, insert the following comments, which also serve as place markers:

```
/**************************
Interface display functions
***************************/
/**************************
User registration functions
***************************/
```

The beginning of your script should now look similar to this:

```
/************************
Input checking functions
************************/
function checkPwd():Boolean {
    // this function checks the length of the password
    // and checks that both input fields match
    if (password_txt.length<6) {
        error_txt.text = "Password must contain at least 6 characters";
        return false;
    }
    if (password_txt.text == confPwd_txt.text) {
        return true;
    } else {
        error_txt.text = "Your passwords don't match";
        return false;
    }
}
/**************************
Interface display functions
***************************/
/**************************
User registration functions
***************************/
function registerUser():Void {
    // this function gathers the input, validates it and
```

4. Scroll down to the end of the showResult() function (it should be around line 81), and insert the following place markers:

```
/**************************
Functions for listing users
***************************/
/***************
Search functions
****************/
/**************************
Update and delete functions
***************************/
/***************
Button callbacks
****************/
```

5. Immediately below this last place marker, you should see the following block of code:

```
94 logout_btn.onRelease = function() {
95     // send logout request to PHP script
96     dbQuery.logmeout = "done";
97     dbQuery.sendAndLoad(
"http://localhost/phpflash/ch10/process_logout.php?ck="+new Date().getTime
(), userRegistered);
98 };
```

This needs changing not only because of the amendments made to the PHP script, but also because the Log Out button, in common with several other buttons, is used on several different frames. Consequently, it's more efficient to define named functions for them rather than use anonymous ones. In other words, *instead* of using this style:

```
logout_btn.onRelease = function() {
  // this cannot be accessed from a different frame
};
```

Replace the existing anonymous function with the named function doLogout() as follows:

```
function doLogout():Void {
  // send logout request to PHP script
  dbQuery.action = "logout";
  dbQuery.sendAndLoad("http://localhost/phpflash/ch10/register_cms.php?
➥ ck="+new Date().getTime(), userRegistered);
}
```

This revised version sets the correct action property for dbQuery and changes the URL to which the data will be sent.

6. On the line immediately after the end of doLogout() (around line 99), you should find this:

```
register_btn.onRelease = registerUser;
```

This line assigns the registerUser() function to the Register button. Since there are several buttons now, it makes sense to put the function assignments all together, even though you haven't yet created the necessary callback functions, and to add a suitable comment/place marker. Amend the code like this:

```
/*******************
Initialize variables
********************/
// assign callbacks to buttons
register_btn.onRelease = registerUser;
search_btn.onRelease = gotoSearch;
list_btn.onRelease = listUsers;
logout_btn.onRelease = doLogout;
```

7. If you test the movie, the only button that will do anything at the moment is the Register button. Even though the Log Out button has a callback function assigned to its `onRelease` event, the new PHP script doesn't yet have any code for the `logout` action. It won't be long, though, before the whole application springs to life. If you want to check your code, use `register_management04.fla` and `register_cms01.php`.

That completes the changes to the original application as built in the previous chapter. You may be wondering at this stage why I've spent so much time adapting the previous application. Changing requirements are a fact of life when you're working with computer applications, and it's important to understand how to be able to adapt an existing project so that it meets new requirements. I could have created a complete content management system, and then removed the parts I planned to add later, and everything would have looked as though it fitted together perfectly like a jigsaw. By taking this approach, I hope to give you a more complete insight into application building.

Displaying the full list of users

This is the most complex part of the application—not because of any difficulty with obtaining a full list of records with PHP and MySQL (that's very simple), but because of the need to manipulate the data once it is received by the Flash movie. At the moment, if you click the List Users button, nothing will happen, but let's take a look at what we're aiming to achieve. Figure 10-6 shows how the list will look once the script is in place. All the delete, update, and navigation buttons, as well as the text fields, will be generated dynamically.

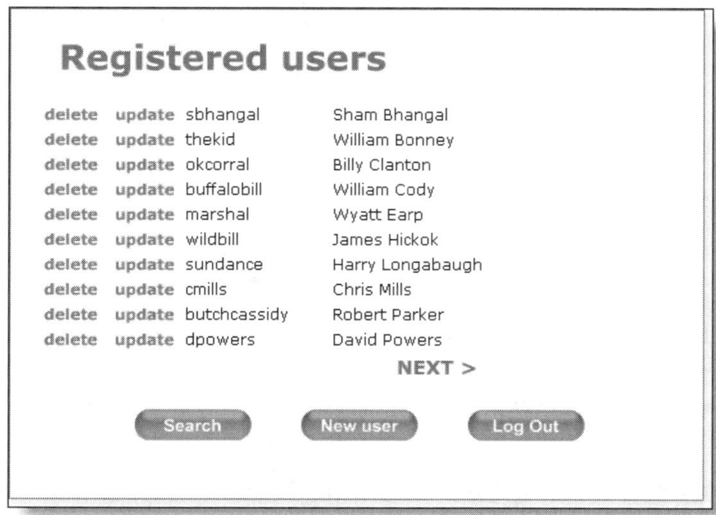

Figure 10-6. When completed, the final frame will display a list of users with options to delete or update their details.

To be of value, the list needs to respond immediately to any changes you make to records. Imagine that Wyatt Earp has just come back from the O.K. Corral. Billy Clanton has a bellyful of lead and no longer needs to be a registered user. As soon as his record is deleted, the list must be refreshed. Figure 10-7 shows that it's not just Billy Clanton gone; the NEXT navigation button has gone too, because Belle Starr is the last record in the database. Exactly why Chris, Sham, and I have ended up among a bunch of gunslingers and the Bandit Queen is something of a mystery. Perhaps the presence of Wyatt Earp indicates we're on the side of the good guys.

While I'm fantasizing about the Wild West, two of the names here raise an interesting problem. Wild Bill Hickok's real name was James Butler Hickock, and Butch Cassidy's real name was Robert Leroy Parker. Neither of them is ever referred to as James Hickok or Robert Parker; their middle name is always given. The rules laid down for the database in Chapter 8 stipulated no spaces in names, so there's no way to enter Butch Cassidy's full name, except perhaps as RobertLeroy or Leroy-Parker. For the purposes of this exercise, it's not a major disaster, but this is the type of issue you constantly have to struggle with when designing a database. Make sure the rules you set down don't lock you into situations you may later come to regret. Adding an optional column at a later stage is a lot easier than tidying up irregular data. I'll show you how to add the extra column at the end of the chapter.

Figure 10-7. The list and navigation buttons should be updated as soon as a record is deleted.

Before any delete or update operations can be performed, though, you first need a list of records in the database. So let's build that now.

Using PHP to get a full list of records from MySQL

Before you can display anything in Flash, you need to query the database and format the results in a way that Flash can understand. As in all previous examples, this requires a string of URL-encoded name/value pairs to be sent to a LoadVars instance.

1. Open register_cms.php or use register_cms01.php from the download files (the final code for this section is in register_cms02.php). Immediately after the opening PHP tag, type this:

```
$_POST['action'] = 'listAll';
```

   This code enables you to test the page in a browser without the need to use your Flash movie. It will be removed later.

2. On the next line, insert the following code:

```
// set sort order for results
$order = ' ORDER BY family_name, first_name, username';
```

   This code stores in a variable the sort order that will be used by the SQL query. You assign it to $order because the same order will eventually be used in more than one SQL query. This not only saves typing, but also makes it easier to change the order globally if you later change your mind. By declaring the variable outside any conditional statements or functions, you ensure it has global scope. *Make sure you leave a space* between the opening quote and ORDER. This is very important because it will be concatenated with another string variable; leaving out the space will cause your SQL query to fail.

3. Amend the first elseif block (it begins at about line 33) as follows (the new code is highlighted in bold):

```
elseif ($_POST['action'] == 'listAll') {
  // code for retrieving full list
  $sql = 'SELECT * FROM users'.$order;
  echo getUserList($sql);
  }
```

   The third line of this block concatenates the code in step 2 with a string to produce the full SQL query:

```
SELECT * FROM users ORDER BY family_name, first_name, username
```

   This tells the database to select everything in the users table, and to sort the results first by family_name, then by first_name, and finally by username. This avoids the need to do any sorting within the Flash movie.

   The final line within the elseif block passes the SQL query to a custom-built function called getUserList(), which you will now create, and outputs the result with echo.

4. Right down at the bottom of register_cms.php, insert the following function just before the closing PHP tag:

```
// gets a list of users
function getUserList($sql) {
  $db = new Database('localhost','flashuser','deepthought','phpflash');
  $result = $db->query($sql);
  $numrows = $result->num_rows;
  $userlist = "total=$numrows";
```

```
$counter = 0;
while ($row = $result->fetch_assoc()) {
  $userlist .= '&user_id'.$counter.'='.$row['user_id'];
  $userlist .= '&first_name'.$counter.'='.
➥ urlencode($row['first_name']);
  $userlist .= '&family_name'.$counter.'='.
➥ urlencode($row['family_name']);
  $userlist .= '&username'.$counter.'='.urlencode($row['username']);
  $counter++;
  }
$db->close();
return $userlist;
}
```

This is very similar to the code used to retrieve the word list in the Hangman game in Chapter 7. The main difference is that it has been turned into a function that takes a single parameter: a SQL query. You need to execute exactly the same code when returning the results of a search, so it makes sense to encapsulate it in a function.

The function creates a `Database` instance, submits the query, and loops through the results. `$userlist` stores the result as a URL-encoded string of name/value pairs. It begins with `total`, which reports the number of results found. A variable `$counter` is set to `0` and incremented at the end of each loop. `$counter` is used to identify each record by creating variables such as `user_id0`, `user_id1`, and so on.

The function then returns the entire string ready for transfer back to Flash.

> *Instead of using* `return` *inside the function and then immediately using* `echo` *to output the result, I could have used* `echo` *inside the function. In fact, that was how* `getUserList()` *was originally designed. I changed it to work like this because I also want to display an amended list after updating or deleting a record. This resulted in two calls to the remote server: one to make the change and the other to retrieve the amended list. While testing locally, there was no apparent delay, but you should avoid unnecessary round-trips to the server wherever possible. By returning the user list internally within the PHP script, the contents can be combined with the results of another operation and sent back together, saving bandwidth and speeding up the process.*

5. Save `register_cms.php` and load it into a browser. You should see output similar to that shown in Figure 10-8.

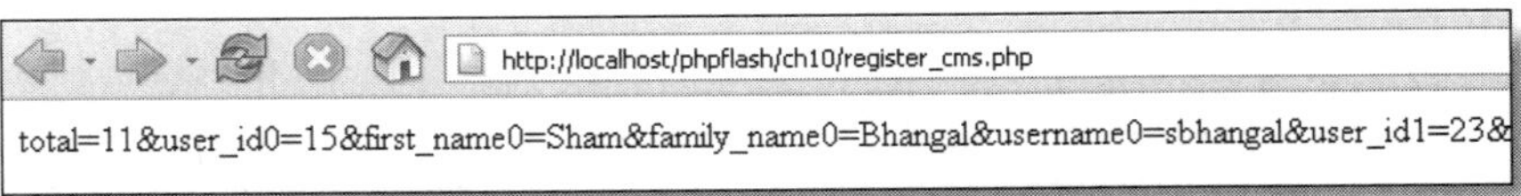

Figure 10-8. The output from the PHP script is formatted as a string of name/value pairs.

Check the output carefully. Make sure there are no gaps in the string. If there are, go back to the code in step 4 and remove whatever is causing the gaps. Although it looks tidier to put a space on either side of the equal signs or ampersands (&), it will cause your ActionScript to fail. Also make sure you don't get any PHP error messages, as they too will cause the application to break. (Check Appendix A for advice on the causes of PHP errors and how to deal with them.) I cannot stress enough how important it is to get the PHP side of things right. *If this part doesn't work, nothing does.*

Remove or comment out the testing code you entered in step 1:

```
$_POST['action'] = 'listAll';
```

If you forget to do this, your script will always default to displaying a full list of records!

Capturing the data in Flash

Now that the PHP script is in place, you need to build the ActionScript that will query the database and then display the results in the listUsers frame. Figure 10-9 outlines the steps involved.

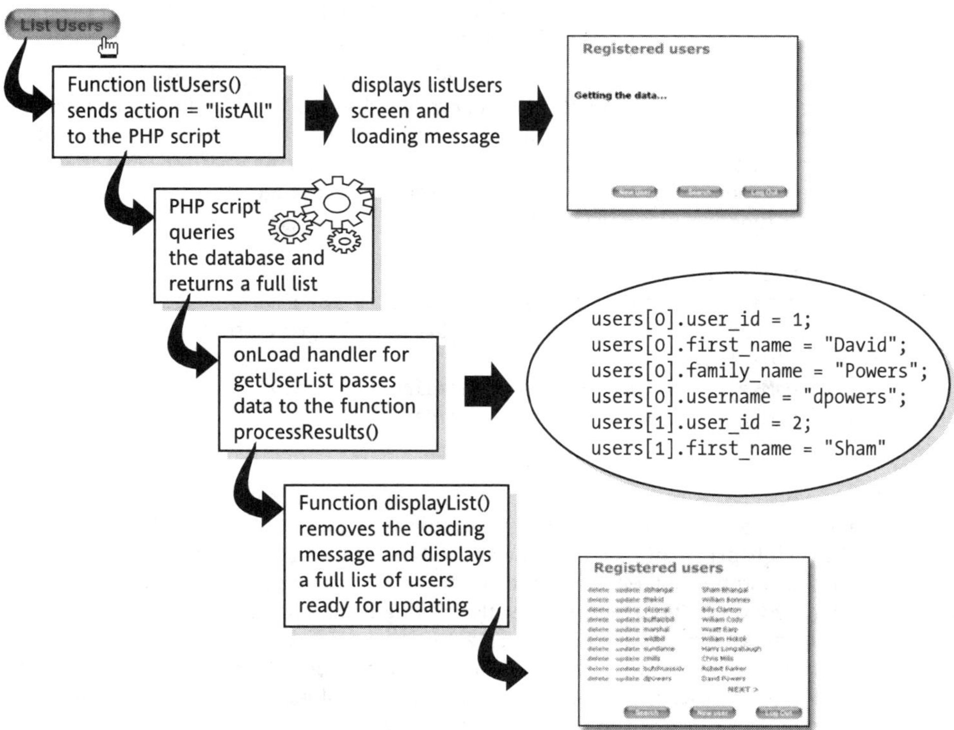

Figure 10-9. This is how the application retrieves and displays a full list of records in the database.

1. Continue working in the ActionScript on frame 1 of the same FLA document as before or use register_management04.fla. The final code for this section is in register_management07.fla (there are several intermediate files to help you check your progress if you are building this from scratch).

   Locate the place marker you created earlier for Functions for listing users (around lines 82–84). Immediately beneath the last line of the place marker, enter the following:

```
function listUsers():Void {
  // retrieve a list of all users, then go to listUsers frame
  dbQuery.action = "listAll";
  dbQuery.sendAndLoad("http://localhost/phpflash/ch10/
➥ register_cms.php?ck="+new Date().getTime(), getUserList);
  error_txt.text = "";
  gotoAndStop("listUsers");
  displayLoadingMsg();
}
```

   This is the function assigned to the List Users button. It sends instructions to the PHP script to retrieve a full list of users, clears the error_txt field of any messages, and sends the playhead to the listUsers frame, ready to receive and display the results.

   In this application, dbQuery will be used for all outgoing data. By setting the action property to listAll, the PHP script in register_cms.php will know to execute the code block in the action == 'listAll' conditional statement, which you created in the previous section. The target for the response is getUserList (see Table 10-1).

2. The final line of listUsers() makes a call to a new function, displayLoadingMsg(). Although both PHP and ActionScript will process the data quickly, there may be a delay in loading the results because of a slow Internet connection or heavy pressure on the web server. So it's a good idea to display a message informing visitors that the data is being retrieved. Scroll up to the place marker for Interface display functions and insert this function immediately after it (on around line 21):

```
function displayLoadingMsg():Void {
  // create and format text field to display loading message
  _root.createTextField("loadingMsg_txt", this.getNextHighestDepth(),
➥ 20, 120, 400, 60);
  loadingMsg_txt.setNewTextFormat(loadingMsgFormat);
  loadingMsg_txt.text = "Getting the data...";
}
```

   When you create a text field at runtime, you need to specify the depth at which the field is to be created. Rather than specify a particular depth, I have used the getNextHighestDepth() method introduced in Flash MX 2004. Not only is this easier, but it's also important with this sort of application, because text fields and movie clips will be loaded and unloaded frequently, making it difficult to predict where an object will appear in the depth stack. During testing, I discovered that failure to remove dynamically generated text fields and movie clips prevented me from accessing the text input fields on other frames. Dynamically generated objects are higher up in the depth stack than those created in the authoring environment. Consequently, hiding dynamically generated objects coats those on your stage with an invisible, but impenetrable barrier—rather like sealing your movie in plastic wrap! If you are using a version of Flash before MX 2004, or you need to support a version of Flash Player earlier than 7, you will need to keep track of any movie clips added dynamically at runtime by using a variable as a counter.

3. The loading message uses a TextFormat object called loadingMsgFormat. Declare this at the bottom of the ActionScript, just after the TextFormat object for the error message (around line 151):

```
// set text format for loading message
var loadingMsgFormat:TextFormat = new TextFormat();
loadingMsgFormat.bold = true;
loadingMsgFormat.font = "Verdana,Arial,Helvetica,_sans";
loadingMsgFormat.size = 18;
```

One thing to note about the font property of the TextFormat object here: specifying a list of alternative fonts has the same effect as in HTML or CSS—the movie will use the first font in the list that it can find on the user's computer. For this to work, there must be no gaps surrounding the commas between the font names, and you should always finish with one of Flash's default fonts (_sans, _serif, or _typewriter).

4. The onLoad event handler for getUserList is a function called fullList(). It's a very simple function that checks whether the data loads successfully. If the data does load successfully, the function passes the data captured by the getUserList instance of LoadVars to another function for processing. Enter the following immediately after the end of the listUsers() function (around line 99):

```
function fullList(success:Boolean):Void {
  // onLoad handler for getUserList
  if (!success) {
    loadingMsg_txt.text = "Sorry, database unavailable";
  } else {
    processResults(getUserList);
  }
}
```

The success parameter is a Boolean value (true or false) automatically available with a LoadVars.onLoad event that indicates whether the data loaded from the server was empty. It's not essential that you use this, but passing the success value as an argument to the function allows you to display an error message if you get nothing back. You should note, however, that "empty" means precisely that; if your PHP script generates an error message, the function will interpret it as though everything's hunky-dory—when it's not. Consequently, the Sorry, database unavailable message will appear only if there is genuinely no output from the server.

Is success equates to true, the function simply calls another function, processResults(), passing a single argument: getUserList, the name of the LoadVars instance containing the data that came back from the PHP script.

5. As I stated earlier, there are two ways of selecting a record that you want to update or delete: either from a full list or as the result of a search. Whichever method you use, the results that come back from the database will always consist of the same basic elements: the user_id, first_name, family_name, and username for each record found.

(Although the pwd column is retrieved by the database query, it is not sent back to Flash.) The only difference will be that a full list may contain a large number of records, whereas a search may produce only a handful or even none at all.

To be able to work with the database results inside Flash, it's necessary to convert them from the format shown in Figure 10-8 to an array. Each element of the array needs to represent an individual database record. So if you call the array users, you will end up with users[0], users[1], users[2], and so on. Then by converting each element into an object, it can be assigned individual properties relating to the value of each column in the database, like this:

```
users[0].user_id = 1;
users[0].first_name = "David";
users[0].family_name = "Powers";
users[0].username = "dpowers";
users[1].user_id = 2;
users[1].first_name = "Sham";
```

The users array will be accessed by several functions, so you need to declare it on the main timeline. Scroll toward the bottom of the ActionScript panel and declare it there, just below the assignment of onLoad handlers for LoadVars (around line 142):

```
// initialize variables
var users:Array = new Array();
```

6. Now scroll back up to the end of the fullList() function (about line 107), and insert the processResults() function. The full code is as follows:

```
function processResults(theTarget:LoadVars):Void {
  // process results of database query and filter into array
  // get number of results from "total" at beginning of PHP output
  var total:Number = theTarget.total;
  // display any error message returned by Database class
  if (theTarget.error != undefined) {
    loadingMsg_txt.text = theTarget.error;
    theTarget.error = undefined;
  } else if (total == 0) {
    // if total is zero, report no records found
    loadingMsg_txt.text = "No records found";
  } else {
    // remove the loading message and process results
    loadingMsg_txt.removeTextField();
    // clear any previous array
    users.length = 0;
    for (var i:Number = 0; i<total; i++) {
      // create a new object for each database record
      users[i] = new Object();
      // assign properties to object representing individual record
      users[i].user_id = theTarget["user_id"+i];
      users[i].first_name = theTarget["first_name"+i];
      users[i].family_name = theTarget["family_name"+i];
      users[i].username = theTarget["username"+i];
```

```
    }
    // display the list
    for (i = 0; i < users.length; i++) {
      for (var prop:String in users[i]) {
        trace("users["+i+"]."+prop+": "+users[i][prop]);
      }
    }
  }
}
```

The inline comments explain what happens at each stage inside the function. The LoadVars instance is referred to throughout by the local variable theTarget. This is because the same function will be used to process the results received by other instances of LoadVars.

The first half of the function deals with any problems that might occur during loading and changes the content of loadingMsg_txt accordingly. The only time the results will contain an error variable is if there is a problem with the Database class. After displaying the contents of the message, the error property of the LoadVars instance needs to be immediately reset to undefined; otherwise, the function will treat all future results as invalid. If everything is OK, the loading message text field is removed and the function processes the results ready for display.

The core of the function lies in the for loop, which filters the results from the name/value pairs output by the PHP script into an array of objects with properties equivalent to each column in the database (as described in the previous step). Just before the loop, any existing array is cleared; otherwise, new results would simply be tacked on the end of an ever-lengthening list.

7. Test the movie by pressing *Ctrl+Enter/⌘+Return*. Click the List Users button, and you should see all your records listed in the Output panel as shown in Figure 10-10. This is important confirmation that communication is being made properly between Flash, PHP, and MySQL, and that your data has been correctly filtered into an array of objects with the correct properties. It doesn't look pretty yet, but it will soon. If you have any problems, compare your code against register_management05.fla.

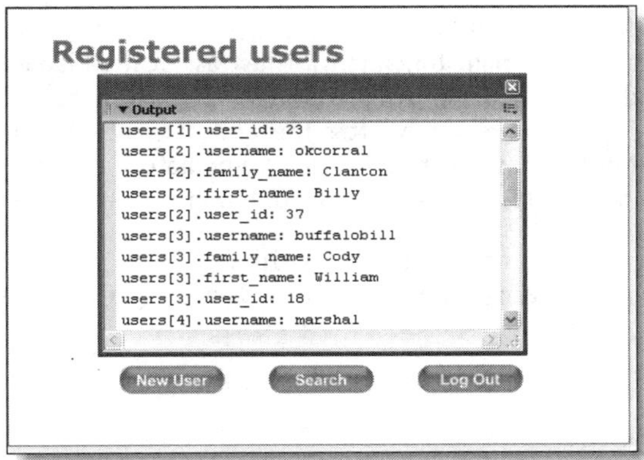

Figure 10-10. Checking the results of the getUserList.onLoad function confirms whether your data is suitably formatted to display.

8. Check also that the error message from the Database classes is working properly. Induce a deliberate error in register_cms.php by, for instance, misspelling your database password in the getUserList() function.

```
function getUserList($sql) {
  $db = new Database('localhost','flashuser','deepthught','phpflash');
  $result = $db->query($sql);
```

9. Save register_cms.php and test your movie again. None of the buttons work on the listUsers frame yet, so you will need to reload the movie in test mode to do this. You should now see an error message displayed as shown here. This is fine for local use, but you may want to display something less obvious on a public site.

Registered users

Couldn't connect flashuser to phpflash

10. Correct the deliberate mistake and resave register_cms.php, and then make sure your list displays correctly again in the Output panel. Constant testing is like the old joke about elections: unless you vote early and vote often, you won't get what you want. Frequent testing makes bug detection much less of a strain, particularly when you're mixing three technologies, as in this application.

11. Using trace to display output is fine for testing, but not for the finished product. Go back to the Actions panel, remove the double for loop at the end of the processReults() function (around lines 133–137), and amend your code so that the final section looks like this:

```
    // display the list
    displayList(0);
  }
}
```

This code calls a new function, displayList(), with a single parameter, which tells the function from which record to start displaying the list.

12. The displayList() function is quite long, so it will be easier to build it in parts. It makes uses of four variables (display, displayMax, prevList, and nextList) that need to be available on the main timeline, not just as local variables within the function. These are used to control the display as you navigate through the results, but since displayList() goes immediately after the end of processResults(), you'll declare them later, just before testing the function. Immediately after the final closing brace in step 11 (around line 136), insert the basic outline for displayList() as follows:

```
function displayList(start:Number):Void {
  // clear any existing display before displaying new results
  if (display > 0) {
    clearDisplay();
  }
  // if the array minus the start position is less than
  // the maximum, set display to the shorter number
  if (users.length - start < displayMax) {
```

```
    display = users.length - start;
  } else {
    // if the array is longer, set display to the maximum
    display = displayMax;
  }
  // set new start positions for previous and next pages
  prevList = start - displayMax;
  nextList = start + displayMax;
  // build the list and display it
  // code from step 13 goes here

  // display the navigation buttons
  // code from step 17 goes here
}
```

The start parameter taken by displayList() represents the number of the element in the users array at which the display should start. When displayList() is called from inside the processResults() function, you want the list to start with users[0].

The first thing displayList() does is check display, which represents the number of items currently being displayed. If it's greater than zero, a call is made to clearDisplay(). As its name suggests, this function clears the display of existing records to make way for the new list. (You will create this function a little later.)

Next, the function calculates how many items to display by using displayMax, which represents the maximum number of records to be displayed at any one time. It deducts the start position from the total length of the array. If the result is less than displayMax, display is set to the lower number; otherwise, it's set to the same value as displayMax. In other words, if the array has seven elements and the start position is 0, it is less than displayMax (10). On the other hand, if there are 12 elements in the array, it's longer than the maximum you want to show, so display will be set to 10.

```
            7    -    0   <      10
if (users.length - start < displayMax) {
   display = users.length - start;
} else {
   display = displayMax;
}                                  (display is 7)

               0          10
prevList = start - displayMax;  (prevList is -10)
nextList = start + displayMax;  (nextList is 10)
```

Finally, the value of prevList and nextList is calculated by subtracting or adding displayMax from start. These values give the start position required for navigating backward or forward through an array that contains more items than can be displayed at a time. As you can see from the sample calculation, this can result in a number beyond the range of the array (negative numbers, for instance, cannot be used as an array index). Further checks will prevent an error from occurring when prevList or nextList results in an out-of-range number.

13. Now for the part of the function that does all the hard work. It's a `for` loop that repeats as many times as determined by the value of `display`. Although it's long, it just goes through a series of statements that dynamically attach the delete and update movie clip buttons, position them, and give them properties that identify each button with an individual record. To make it easy to handle each movie clip within the loop, they are assigned to two temporary variables, `del_mc` and `upd_mc`.

Text fields are then positioned alongside and formatted, and the values held in the appropriate `username`, `first_name`, and `family_name` properties of the current `user` are assigned to the field's `text` property. Keeping track of everything are two iterator variables: `i` and `j`. `i` is used to keep count of the number of loops, while `j` adds the `start` position to the loop number.

Let's say there are 30 elements in the array, so all the records will be held in `users[0]` to `users[29]`. When the second page of records is being displayed, `i` will run from 0 to 9, but the value of `j` will be 10 to 19, so on the fourth pass, it will be able to access `users[13]`. The vertical coordinate of each element is similarly affected by the loop through storing the value in yPos. On the first iteration it will be 80, and it will increment by 20 each time, thus moving each row 20 pixels further down the screen. The inline comments should explain the rest of the code. Insert it at the point indicated inside the code you entered in step 12.

```
// build the list and display it
var yPos:Number;
for (var i:Number = 0; i < display; i++) {
  // set variables to reference array elements and y position
  var j:Number = start + i;
  yPos = 80 + (i * 20);
  // attach delButton and updButton movie clips
  var del_mc:MovieClip = _root.attachMovie("delButton","del"+i+"_mc",
➥ _root.getNextHighestDepth());
  var upd_mc:MovieClip = _root.attachMovie("updButton","upd"+i+"_mc",
➥ _root.getNextHighestDepth());
  del_mc._x = 25;
  upd_mc._x = 80;
  del_mc._y = upd_mc._y = yPos;
  // assign properties to the delete and update buttons
  // to identify which array element they refer to
  del_mc.theNum = upd_mc.theNum = j;
  // assign delete and update functions to each button
  del_mc.onRelease = deleteRecord;
  upd_mc.onRelease = updateRecord;
  // create, format, and populate text fields with details
  _root.createTextField("username"+i+"_txt",
➥_root.getNextHighestDepth(),135,yPos,120,20);
  _root.createTextField("details"+i+"_txt",
➥ _root.getNextHighestDepth(),250,yPos,280,20);
  _root["username"+i+"_txt"].setNewTextFormat(detailsFormat);
```

```
_root["details"+i+"_txt"].setNewTextFormat(detailsFormat);
_root["username"+i+"_txt"].text = users[j].username;
_root["details"+i+"_txt"].text = users[j].first_name +" "+
➥ users[j].family_name;
}
```

To avoid the need to type complex references such as `_root["username"+i+"_txt"]` *all the time, it is tempting to try to assign them to a temporary variable in the same way as you did with the movie clip buttons in this step. However, the following does not work:*

```
// causes a type mismatch
var user_txt:TextField = _root.createTextField("username"+i+"_txt",
➥_root.getNextHighestDepth(),135,yPos,120,20);
```

This is one of the cases where ActionScript 2.0 strict typing comes in handy. The compiler will report a type mismatch with the following error message: found Void where TextField is required. *If you want to assign a text field created at runtime to a variable, you must create the text field first, and then do the assignment, like this:*

```
_root.createTextField("username"+i+"_txt",
➥_root.getNextHighestDepth(),135,yPos,120,20);
var user_txt:TextField = _root["username"+i+"_txt"];
```

That's why I didn't bother with this block of code, but it would be worth doing if you intend to use a lot of properties of methods with a text field created at runtime.

14. Getting all the periods, quotes, and underscores in the right places can be tricky, so now is a good time to test everything and admire your handiwork. Before you can do so, you need to declare the four timeline variables used in `processResults()`. Scroll down toward the bottom of the Actions panel and put them with the other timeline variables (I put them starting on line 219, just after the `users` array was declared):

```
var display:Number = 0;
var displayMax:Number = 10;
var prevList:Number;
var nextList:Number;
```

Initial values are required for `display` and `displayMax`, but not for the other two. I set the value of `displayMax` to `10`, but if you have only a small number of records, you may want to use a smaller number so you can test the navigation system later.

15. While you're down at the bottom of the script, create a `TextFormat` object to make the text of the dynamically generated details look a bit smarter than the default Flash fonts. Add this code after the other `TextFormat` objects (I put it on line 245 after `loadingMsgFormat`):

```
// set text format for record details
var detailsFormat:TextFormat = new TextFormat();
detailsFormat.size = 12;
detailsFormat.font = "Verdana,Arial,Helvetica,_sans";
```

16. Test the movie and click the List Users button. You should see something like the screenshot alongside. Mouse over the buttons. They should display normal rollover behavior because they now have an onRelease button event attached to them. Nothing will happen when you click them (apart from showing the down state) because the functions have yet to be defined. Still, this is major progress. If you have any problems, compare your code against `register_management06.fla`.

Registered users

delete	update	sbhangal	Sham Bhangal
delete	update	thekid	William Bonney
delete	update	okcorral	Billy Clanton
delete	update	buffalobill	William Cody
delete	update	marshal	Wyatt Earp
delete	update	wildbill	James Hickok
delete	update	sundance	Harry Longabaugh
delete	update	cmills	Chris Mills
delete	update	butchcassidy	Robert Parker
delete	update	dpowers	David Powers

17. The final section of the `displayList()` function adds the navigation. Insert the following code at the point indicated in step 12 (around line 180):

```
// display the navigation buttons
// if start position greater than zero, display previous
if (start > 0) {
  _root.attachMovie("prevButton", "prev_mc",
➥ this.getNextHighestDepth());
  prev_mc._x = 25;
  prev_mc._y = yPos + 20;
  prev_mc.onRelease = function() {
    displayList(prevList);
  };
}
// if array has more items, display the next button
if (users.length - start > displayMax) {
  _root.attachMovie("nextButton", "next_mc",
➥ this.getNextHighestDepth());
  next_mc._x = 300;
  next_mc._y = yPos + 20;
  next_mc.onRelease = function() {
    displayList(nextList);
  };
}
```

This is outside the loop that displayed the main body of the list. It uses the same variables to calculate whether to display the previous and next buttons. If a button is required, it is loaded dynamically and given an instance name of either `prev_mc` or `next_mc`. Each button is assigned a callback function on its `onRelease` event. This simply calls the `displayList()` function using the `prevList` and `nextList` variables set earlier inside the function.

18. Test your movie now, and you should see something like Figure 10-6 at the beginning of this section. There at last! Well, not quite . . .

19. Make sure you have sufficient records in your database to trigger the display of the NEXT button (add some more records or change the value of displayMax). Now click the NEXT button. Oh dear, what a mess! As you can see from the image alongside, the old records have not disappeared, and the PREV button has landed in the middle of all the records. Some tidying up is in order.

20. If you cast your mind back to step 12, you will recall that the displayList() function begins with a call to clearDisplay(). That's what's missing. This fits into the categories you created at the beginning as an interface display function, so insert it immediately after the end of the displayLoadingMsg() function (around line 27):

```
function clearDisplay():Void {
  // remove the delete and update buttons and text fields
  for (var i:Number = 0; i < display; i++) {
    _root["del"+i+"_mc"].removeMovieClip();
    _root["upd"+i+"_mc"].removeMovieClip();
    _root["username"+i+"_txt"].removeTextField();
    _root["details"+i+"_txt"].removeTextField();
  }
  // remove the loadingMsg_txt text field if it's still there
  if (loadingMsg_txt != undefined) {
    loadingMsg_txt.removeTextField();
  }
  // remove the previous and next buttons
  prev_mc.removeMovieClip();
  next_mc.removeMovieClip();
  // clear the error message
  error_txt.text = "";
}
```

This shouldn't require any explanation beyond the inline comments. It's simply a housecleaning operation. Test your movie again, and it should work correctly.

The individual delete and update buttons are not yet active, but the main part of the movie is now complete. Take a well-earned break before moving on to the next stage. If you encounter any problems, compare your code against register_management_07.fla.

Searching for individual records

The purpose of the search function is to search for records based on all or any of three main criteria: the user's first name, family name, and/or username. For the search system to be really useful, users should be able to enter just part of a name and still get a list of matching records, as shown in Figure 10-11.

From the Flash point of view, the way a search works is almost identical to the way it displays a full list of registered users. The only difference is that, instead of sending an instruction to the PHP script to retrieve all records, it sends three variables containing the search criteria. The variables simply contain whatever the user enters in the three input fields shown in Figure 10-11. The only check on the contents of the fields will be to ensure that they're not all blank. All the hard work is left to PHP. When the search results come back from the PHP script, they're handled in exactly the same way as a full list by being handed to `processResults()`. Figure 10-12 outlines the steps involved.

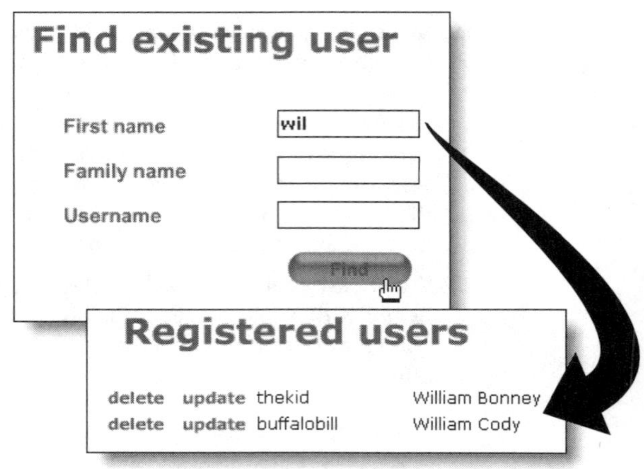

Figure 10-11. When you're searching for a record, even a partial name will bring up the appropriate results.

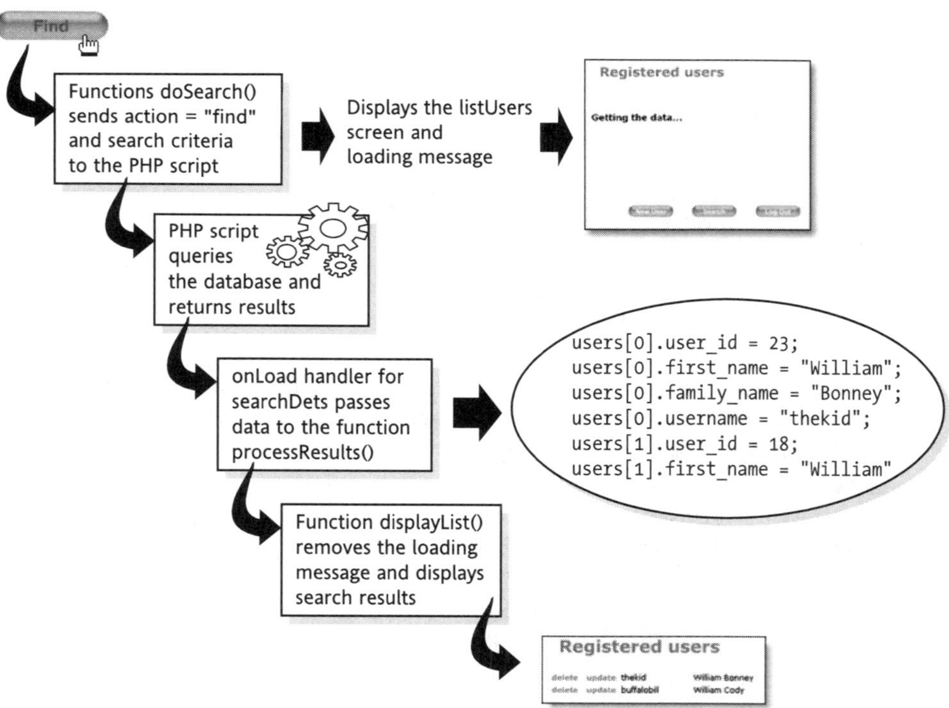

Figure 10-12. This is how the application processes a search and displays the results.

Scripting the search form

1. Continue with the file from the last section or use register_management_07.fla from the download files for this book. The final code for this section is in register_management08.fla. Select frame 20 on the actions layer and insert a keyframe. You need to enter only four lines of script, so there is no need to pin the Actions panel on frame 20, but make sure you put the script on the correct frame if you pinned frame 1 earlier.

2. There are four buttons on this frame that need to be wired up to their event handler functions. Add the following code on frame 20:

```
find_btn.onRelease = doSearch;
new_btn.onRelease = gotoRegister;
list_btn.onRelease = listUsers;
logout_btn.onRelease = doLogout;
```

   The last two functions already exist. You need to create doSearch(), which activates the search mechanism, and gotoRegister(), which activates the New User button. Both go with all the other main scripts on the first frame.

3. The doSearch() function gathers the input of the three text fields on the search frame, does a check to make sure they're not empty, and then sends the data to the PHP script. Switch back to the main script on frame 1 and enter the following code immediately after the Search functions place marker (around line 220):

```
function doSearch():Void {
  // checks the input fields
  // then uses the content as the basis for a search
  // initialize local variable
  var blankFields:Number = 0;
  // check number of blank fields
  for (var i:Number = 0; i < textFields.length ; i++) {
    var theField:TextField = _root[textFields[i]+"_txt"];
    if (isBlank(theField.text)) {
      // if blank, remove any empty spaces
      theField.text = "";
      blankFields++;
    }
  }
  // if all blank, display error message and terminate action
  if (blankFields == textFields.length) {
    error_txt.text = "You have not filled in any fields";
    Selection.setFocus("firstname_txt");
  } else {
    // if OK, send date to PHP, and go to listUsers frame
    dbQuery.action = "find";
    dbQuery.first_name = firstname_txt.text;
    dbQuery.family_name = familyname_txt.text;
    dbQuery.username = username_txt.text;
```

```
      dbQuery.sendAndLoad("http://localhost/phpflash/ch10/
➥ register_cms.php?ck="+new Date().getTime(),searchDets);
      error_txt.text = "";
      gotoAndStop("listUsers");
      displayLoadingMsg();
    }
  }
```

The inline comments should explain most of this function. The aim is to let users find records even if the fields are only partially filled in, so the first task is to find out if there is any usable input at all. Because the text input fields are on a different frame from the ActionScript that restricted the range of permissible characters, those restrictions no longer apply. One solution is to copy and paste the relevant ActionScript. Another is to adopt a more lenient attitude. The reason for blocking rogue characters on the registration form was to prevent bad data from being recorded in the database. On this occasion, the only person to suffer as a result of bad input will be the user. Still, it's useful to make sure there's at least something for the PHP script to work with.

The `for` loop uses the `textFields` variable to loop through the three text input fields. This is the same variable that was used in the original registration application, where it was declared as a local variable inside the `registerUser()` function, so it will need to be moved onto the main timeline. The loop uses a custom function called `isBlank()`, which you will create in step 5, to check how many fields are empty.

If all fields are blank, an error message is displayed without sending any data to the server; otherwise, the `dbQuery` instance of `LoadVars` is used to send the text field input to the PHP script. The target for the results is set to `searchDets`, and the playhead is sent to the `listUsers` frame—the same frame that was used to display the full list.

4. Locate the `textFields` variable declaration inside the `registerUser()` function. It's close to the beginning of the function around line 53, as shown here:

```
45 /**************************
46 User registration functions
47 **************************/
48 function registerUser():Void {
49     // this function gathers the input, validates it and
50     // transfers it to the PHP script for processing
51     // initialize variables
52     var validated:Boolean = true;
53     var textFields:Array = new Array("firstname", "familyname", "username");
```

Highlight the line and cut it (Edit ➤ Cut or *Ctrl+X*/*⌘+X*). Scroll down to the bottom of the ActionScript and paste (Edit ➤ Paste or *Ctrl+V*/*⌘+V*) the line at the end of the variables being initialized on the main timeline. The `textFields` array will now be accessible by both `registerUser()` and `doSearch()`.

5. The `isBlank()` function should go with the input-checking functions at the top of the script. I have placed it immediately after the `checkPwd()` function around line 18:

```
function isBlank(theInput:String):Boolean {
  for (var i:Number = 0; i < theInput.length; i++) {
    if (theInput.charAt(i) != " " && theInput.charAt(i) != "") {
      return false;
    }
  }
  return true;
}
```

The function uses the ActionScript `String.charAt()` method to examine each character of a string in turn. As soon as it encounters a character that is *neither* a blank space *nor* an empty string, it returns `false`. In other words, it will return `true` only if the string is entirely blank.

6. Although the search form is activated by the Find button, you need to be able to get to the search frame in the first place. You also need to wire up the New User button. Both functions simply clear any display and then move the playhead to the appropriate frame. Put the functions toward the bottom of the page in the `Button callbacks` section (around line 263):

```
function gotoSearch():Void {
  clearDisplay();
  gotoAndStop("search");
}
function gotoRegister():Void {
  clearDisplay();
  gotoAndStop("insertData");
}
```

The search function still needs the PHP script before you can use it. If you would like to check your ActionScript code so far, take a look at `register_management08.fla`.

Using PHP to find records based on variable search criteria

As was shown in Figure 10-9, you have no idea how many input fields will contain search criteria; it could be one, two, or three. You also have no idea whether the search criteria will be the full name or just the first few letters. It sounds like a tall order, but it can be accomplished in a dozen or so lines of PHP. Before adding the PHP code to `register_cms.php`, let's pause for a while to consider what is needed.

The SQL for finding records according to particular criteria is already familiar to you from the login project. It's a `WHERE` clause, which you can refine by using other keywords such as `AND` and `OR`. To assist with searches that use more vague criteria, SQL uses **pattern-matching operators**. Table 10-2 lists the main pattern-matching operators and wildcard characters used in MySQL.

Table 10-2. The main pattern-matching operators and wildcards used in MySQL

Operator/wildcard	Usage	Description
`LIKE`	`LIKE 'wil'`	Matches the exact string. This example will find records that match `wil`, but not `will` or `William`.
`NOT LIKE`	`NOT LIKE 'wil'`	Matches anything other than the exact string. This example matches `will`, `William`, and `David`, but not `wil`.
`%`	`LIKE 'wil%'`	Wildcard character that matches any characters (or none at all). This example matches `wil`, `will`, `William`, but not `swill` (to match all four, put `%` at the beginning of the pattern too).
`_`	`LIKE 'wil_'`	The underscore is a wildcard character that matches precisely one character. This example matches `wild`, `will`, and `wile`, but not `wil` or `William`.

Pattern matching in MySQL is case insensitive. To conduct a case-sensitive search, add the keyword `BINARY` *between* `LIKE` *and the string pattern. For instance,* `LIKE BINARY 'Wil%'` *will find* `William`*, but not* `will`*. You can perform more-sophisticated pattern matching with regexes and the* `REGEXP` *pattern-matching operator. For details, see the online documentation at* `http://dev.mysql.com/doc/mysql/en/Regexp.html`*. Also see* Regular Expression Recipes: A Problem-Solution Approach *by Nathan A. Good (Apress, ISBN: 1-59059-441-X).*

So, the SQL query used to find the results shown in Figure 10-11 needs to be

```
SELECT * FROM users WHERE first_name LIKE 'wil%'
```

Creating that query from the input is easy enough, but there's no way of knowing in advance that the only input will be in the `first_name` text field. It's quite possible that you might want to search for users whose first name begins with `wil` and whose usernames end with `bill`. For that, you would need this SQL:

```
SELECT * FROM users WHERE first_name
LIKE 'wil%' AND username LIKE '%bill'
```

Figure 10-13 shows the results of such a query. The problem is that there are so many imponderables. Again, part of the solution must involve you laying down the rules. You could add a variety of search options that would then be evaluated by your ActionScript and PHP. To keep things relatively simple—but still quite versatile—the rules I am going to adopt for this application are as follows:

- Searches can be conducted on the basis of *any* of the following in *any* combination:
  - First name
  - Family name
  - Username
- Searches will find records that contain the input text anywhere in the field being searched.

So the SQL that found the results in Figure 10-13 needs to be amended like this (the new code is highlighted in bold):

```
SELECT * FROM users WHERE first_name
LIKE '%wil%' AND username LIKE '%bill%'
```

Because the % wildcard matches any characters *or none*, the SQL statement still finds strings that begin with wil and end with bill. So, if Bill Gates signs up and picks the username billionaire, he would also come up in this search, depending on whether he enters Bill or William for his first name. (My lips remain firmly sealed as to whether he counts among the outlaws or good guys in the small but select group in this database.)

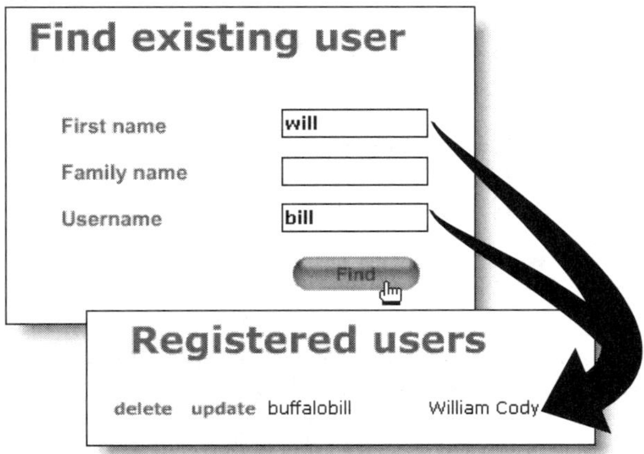

Figure 10-13. Using two search criteria narrows down the list of results.

Let's get back to scripting.

> *Remember, if you use* `register_cms02.php` *from the download files, you must remove or comment out* `$_POST['action'] = 'listAll';` *on line 2. This code was for testing only. If you leave it in, the script will not run correctly.*

1. Open register_cms.php or use register_cms02.php. The final code for this section is in register_cms03.php. Enter the following code *inside* the elseif clause that uses find as its action criterion (the block begins around line 37):

```
// code for search by name, etc.
// remove any leading or trailing blank spaces from input
$input['first_name'] = trim($_POST['first_name']);
$input['family_name'] = trim($_POST['family_name']);
$input['username'] = trim($_POST['username']);
```

Before you pass the contents of first_name, family_name, and username to the database, you need to remove any leading and trailing whitespace with the PHP trim() function. At the same time, the values are assigned to an associative array called $input.

Normally, it's bad coding practice to use a POST variable without first testing whether it has been set (using isset()), but there's no need to do it on this occasion, because the doSearch() function in the Flash movie automatically assigns a value to these three input fields—even if they're blank. That in turn creates a different problem: you need to weed out the empty values before creating the SQL query. That's easily done in the next step.

2. Input fields that are not blank will be used to build the part of the SQL query that contains the pattern comparison operators. You could do it with a long series of if... else statements or a switch() statement. It's much better, though, to use a loop. Insert the following code immediately after the code in the previous step:

```
// create an array of search parameters for use in SQL query
$searchParams = array();
$i = 0;
foreach ($input as $key => $value) {
  if (strlen($value) > 0) {
    $searchParams[$i] = $key.' LIKE "%'.$value.'%"';
    $i++;
    }
  }
```

First, an empty array called $searchParams is created, together with a counter, $i, set to 0. A foreach loop is ideal because it gives you the opportunity to separate the key and value of each element into temporary variables: $key and $value. There's nothing magic about these variable names—I could have used $sugar and $spice—but it makes sense to use names that reflect exactly what the code is doing.

Inside the loop, the length of $value is checked with strlen() (which you met in Chapter 4). If it's greater than zero, it must contain a search parameter, so its key and value are concatenated into a string that produces something like first_name LIKE "%wil%". Before the loop closes, the $i counter is incremented. This produces an indexed array of the search parameters.

3. There's still the tricky problem of how to get AND to join the search parameters to form valid SQL. Well, there's a clue for you—*join*. The PHP join() function (and its synonym implode()) works the same way as the ActionScript Array.join() method. Although it

defaults to a comma when joining elements of an array, you can specify *any* string. So by specifying AND with a space on either side, it's all done automatically for you. The final piece of code builds the SQL query using a string, the search parameters formatted by the join() function, and the sort order (which you earlier inserted at the top of register_cms.php). The query is then passed to the same getUserList() function as used for the full list. Put the following code immediately after that in step 2:

```
// create SQL query and concatenate with parameters and sort order
$sql = 'SELECT * FROM users WHERE '.join($searchParams,' AND ').$order;
// query database
echo getUserList($sql);
```

4. Save register_cms.php. Your code should now look the same as register_cms03.php. Proceed to the next section, where I'll show you how to display the search results.

Adding the ActionScript to display the search results

As I mentioned earlier, the search results are displayed in exactly the same way as the full list of registered users, so this step is simplicity itself.

1. Select the ActionScript on frame 1, and add the searchResult() function. Place it immediately after the doSearch() function (around line 257):

```
function searchResult(success:Boolean):Void {
  // onLoad event handler for searchDets
  // hands search result to processResults in preparation for display
  if (!success) {
    loadingMsg_txt.text = "Sorry, database unavailable";
  } else {
  processResults(searchDets);
  }
}
```

   This function is almost identical to fullList(). The only difference is that it specifies the searchDets instance of LoadVars as the argument passed to processResults().

2. Before you test the movie, it's a good idea to activate the buttons on the listUsers frame so you can return to both the search and insertData frames. Close the Actions panel and insert a keyframe on frame 30 of the actions layer. Open the Actions panel again, and insert the following code on frame 30:

```
search_btn.onRelease = gotoSearch;
new_btn.onRelease = gotoRegister;
```

   The associated functions have already been created, so this code simply assigns them to the relevant buttons on the listUsers frame.

3. You can now test the movie by clicking the Search button on the first frame. That will take you to the search form, where you can try a test search. Compare your code against register_management_09.fla if you encounter any problems.

Updating user details

Updating user details is a three-stage process. First, you need to find the user's record; then, you display the details in an editable form; and finally, you send the update instructions to the database. You have already completed the first stage, and you now have two ways of finding records: through a full list and through the search form. The next step is to activate the update buttons on the listUsers frame. Figure 10-14 shows the process that clicking an update button needs to accomplish.

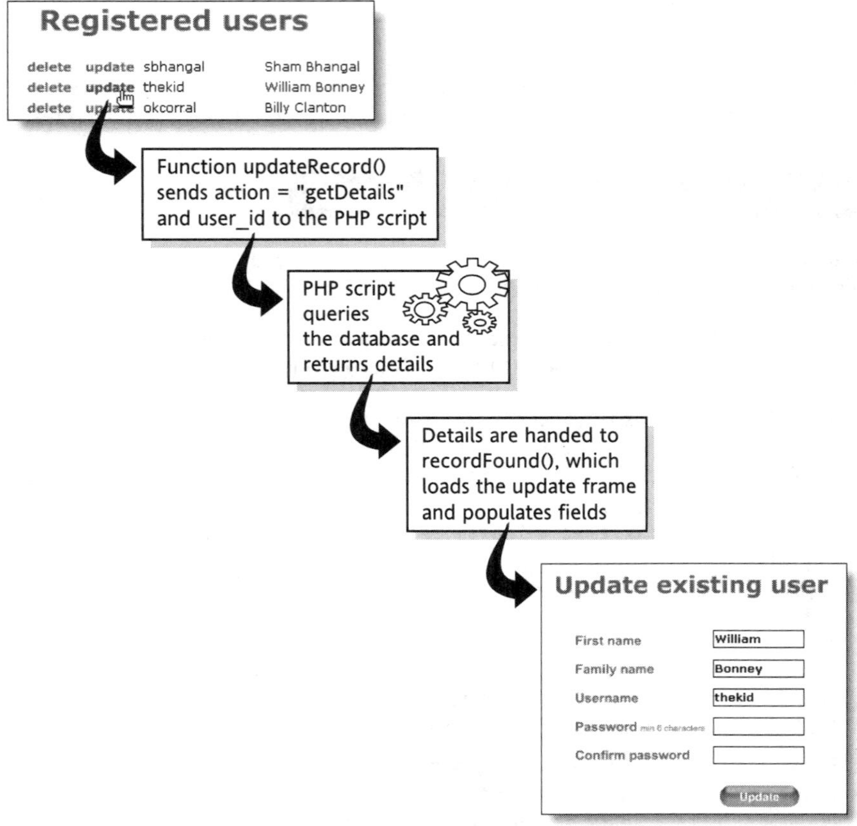

Figure 10-14. After locating a record, you need to display its details in an editable form before you can update it.

Although the buttons are identical, the `displayList()` function assigned each one a property, `theNum`, which identifies the record associated with it. By accessing this property, you can obtain the `user_id` of the record you want to update or delete.

Wiring up the update buttons

1. Continue with the same file as before. Alternatively, use `register_management_09.fla` from the download files for this chapter. The finished code for this section is in `register_management10.fla`. Open the Actions panel on frame 1 and locate the place marker for `Update and delete functions` (around lines 266–268). Insert the following code immediately after the marker:

```
function updateRecord():Void {
  trace("User_id: " + users[this.theNum]["user_id"]);
  trace("First_name: " + users[this.theNum]["first_name"]);
  trace("Family_name: " + users[this.theNum]["family_name"]);
  trace("Username: " + users[this.theNum]["username"]);
}
```

2. Test your movie and click the List Users button to bring up a full list. Select any of the records and click the update button. You should see all the details associated with the record in the Output panel as shown here. Do the same for the other records; the different data should be reflected in the Output panel.

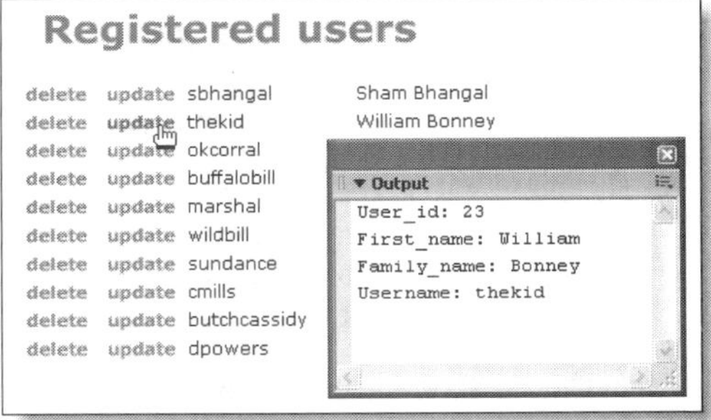

3. Now that you have confirmed that you are picking up the correct details, replace the `trace` statements with the actual code, as follows:

```
function updateRecord():Void {
  dbQuery.action = "getDetails";
  dbQuery.user_id = users[this.theNum]["user_id"];
  dbQuery.sendAndLoad("http://localhost/phpflash/ch10/
➥ register_cms.php?ck="+ newDate().getTime(),updateDets);
}
```

You can use the `this` keyword to identify `theNum` because `theNum` and `updateRecord()` are assigned dynamically to each movie clip button by `displayList()`. Consequently, `theNum` is automatically identified with the button, enabling you to pass the `user_id` for the required record to the PHP script. The value of `action` is set to `getUpdate`, and the target for the server's response is `updateDets`.

4. Before I show you the PHP code, insert the `onLoad` event handler for `updateDets`. Place it immediately after the end of `updateRecord()`:

```
function recordFound(success:Boolean):Void {
  // onLoad event handler for updateDets
  // captures details of selected record and displays in update frame
  if (!success) {
```

```
    error_txt.text = "Cannot load data. Please try later.";
  } else if (this.error != undefined) {
    error_txt.text = this.error;
    this.error = undefined;
  } else {
    clearDisplay();
    gotoAndStop("update");
    firstname_txt.text = this.first_name;
    familyname_txt.text = this.family_name;
    username_txt.text = this.username;
  }
}
```

This code handles the response from the PHP script; either displays an error message or clears the display; sends the playhead to the update frame; and displays the values of first_name, family_name, and username in the editable text fields on that frame.

5. At the moment, none of the buttons on the update frame have been activated, so close the Actions panel, select frame 10 on the actions layer, and insert a keyframe. Open the Actions panel and insert the following code on frame 10:

```
update_btn.onRelease = doUpdate;
search_btn.onRelease = gotoSearch;
list_btn.onRelease = listUsers;
logout_btn.onRelease = doLogout;
```

6. When a record is updated, you need to be sure that none of the rules laid down for original insertion is broken. So apply the same restrict properties to the text fields as on frame 1. Locate the following section of code on frame 1:

```
// set acceptable range of characters for input fields
firstname_txt.restrict = "a-zA-Z\\-'";
familyname_txt.restrict = "a-zA-Z\\-'";
username_txt.restrict = "a-zA-Z0-9";
password_txt.restrict = "\u0021-\u007E";
```

Copy and paste it onto frame 10 beneath the code in the previous step. The same rules will now apply on both frames.

7. Open register_cms.php (or use register_cms03.php) and insert the following code in the elseif clause where action is set to getUpdate (the block begins around line 57):

```
$sql = 'SELECT * FROM users WHERE user_id = '.$_POST['user_id'];
echo getDetails($sql);
```

This is a straightforward SQL query that retrieves the details for a particular record identified by user_id. It is handled by a custom PHP function, getDetails(), which is described in the next step.

8. Insert the getDetails() function at the bottom of the PHP page, just before the closing PHP tag:

```
// gets details for an individual record
function getDetails($sql) {
  $db = new Database('localhost','flashuser','deepthought','phpflash');
  $result = $db->query($sql);
  while ($row = $result->fetch_assoc()) {
    $details = 'user_id='.$row['user_id'];
    $details .= '&first_name='.urlencode($row['first_name']);
    $details .= '&family_name='.urlencode($row['family_name']);
    $details .= '&username='.urlencode($row['username']);
    $details .= '&pwd='.$row['pwd'];
    }
  $db->close();
  return $details;
  }
```

There is nothing new in this function. Listing it separately simply makes the code tidier. After retrieving the user's details from the database, it formats the result as a URL-encoded string of name/value pairs to be transferred to Flash—something you have done many times before in this book.

9. Save `register_cms.php` and test your movie. Either bring up a list of users or use the search feature, and then click the update button for one of them in the listUsers frame. Instead of seeing the details in the Output panel as in step 2, you should be taken to the update frame, and the details should be displayed in the editable text fields in the same way as shown in Figure 10-14. If you encounter any problems, check your code against `register_management10.fla` and `register_cms04.php`.

Finishing the update process: ActionScript

The final part of the update process is similar to registering a new user. The main difference is that the input fields have already been automatically populated with the existing data. The existing password is not displayed, because it is stored in a format that cannot be decrypted. Still, that does not present a problem—the update process allows users to keep their existing password or to set a new one.

Before a record can be updated, you need to check the username for duplicates, but there's a crucial difference from the way it was done for the original registration application in Chapter 8. Users must be able to keep their current username, but you need to prevent anyone else from choosing one that's already taken by someone else. Figure 10-15 shows the steps involved in the final stage of the update process.

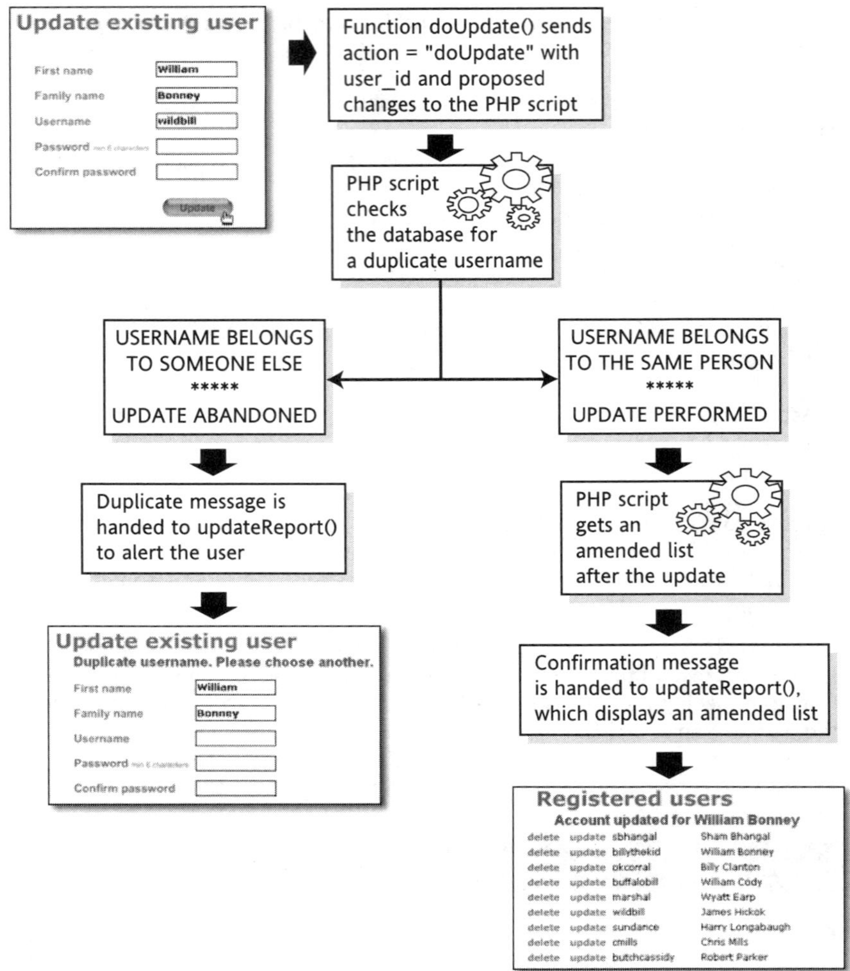

Figure 10-15. The final stage of the update process

1. Continue working with the same FLA document or use `register_management10.fla`. The finished code for this section is in `register_management11.fla`. Open the Actions panel on frame 1 of the actions layer.

2. The function assigned to the Update button, `doUpdate()`, needs to perform similar checks on the content of the input fields to those used in the registration application in Chapter 8. The checks on the first three fields are identical to the ones used earlier, so it makes sense to recycle the code. Locate the section of `registerUser()` highlighted in the following screenshot.

```
56 function registerUser():Void {
57     // this function gathers the input, validates it and
58     // transfers it to the PHP script for processing
59     // initialize variables
60     var validated:Boolean = true;
61     error_txt.text = "";
62     // check for invalid fields
63     for (var i = 0; i<textFields.length; i++) {
64         var theField:TextField = _root[textFields[i]+"_txt"];
65         if (theField.text.length<2) {
66             validated = false;
67             error_txt.text = "All fields must contain at least 2 characters";
68             Selection.setFocus(theField);
69             break;
70         }
71     }
72     // if valid, check password and send to PHP script
```

3. Once you have highlighted the code shown on lines 62 through 71 in the screenshot, cut (*Ctrl*+*X*/⌘+*X*) it to your clipboard.
4. Scroll up to the section marked `Input checking functions` and create an empty function called `validateFields()` just after the end of `isBlank()` (around line 26):

```
function validateFields():Boolean {

}
```

5. Place your cursor in between the curly braces of the empty function and paste (*Ctrl*+*V*/⌘+*V*) the code from step 4 inside.
6. Amend the code so that the function looks like this (new code appears in bold, and code that needs removing appears in strikethrough):

```
function validateFields():Boolean {
  // check for invalid fields
  for (var i = 0; i<textFields.length; i++) {
  var theField:TextField = _root[textFields[i]+"_txt"];
    if (theField.text.length<2) {
      validated = false;
      error_txt.text = "All fields must contain at least 2 characters";
      Selection.setFocus(theField);
      break;
      return false;
    }
  }
  return true;
}
```

7. Scroll back down to registerUsers() and amend the following lines (they will now be around line 72):

```
var validated:Boolean = true;
error_txt.text = "";
```

Reverse the order of the two lines and change the second one as shown here:

```
error_txt.text = "";
var validated:Boolean = validateFields();
```

The validateFields() function will now set validated to true or false, depending on the state of the input fields. You need to change the order to prevent any error message generated by the new function from being removed.

8. With that little diversion out of the way, you can now create the doUpdate() function, which sets in motion the next stage of the update process. It uses both validateFields() and checkPwd() before sending the data to the PHP script. However, there is an extra check on the password fields. If both are left empty, it is assumed the user wants to keep the existing one. Insert the function in the Update and delete functions section after recordFound() (around line 292):

```
function doUpdate():Void {
  // this function takes the data input on the update frame
  // and updates the selected record in the database
  // initialize
  error_txt.text = "";
  var validated:Boolean = validateFields();
  // if valid, check password and send to PHP script
  if (validated) {
    if (password_txt.text == "" && confPwd_txt.text == "") {
      // if both password fields empty, don't change existing password
      dbQuery.pwdChange = "noChange"
      dbQuery.canGo = "ok";
    } else if (checkPwd()) {
      // if password fields have input, and meet the checkPwd criteria
      // tell SQL to set new password
      dbQuery.pwdChange = "newPwd";
      dbQuery.pwd = password_txt.text;
      dbQuery.canGo = "ok";
    } else {
      // if password fields have input but don't match, halt update
      password_txt.text = confPwd_txt.text="";
      Selection.setFocus("password_txt");
      dbQuery.canGo = "ng";
    }
    if (dbQuery.canGo == "ok") {
      // if all tests OK, submit details to PHP/MySQL for updating
      dbQuery.action = "doUpdate";
      dbQuery.user_id = updateDets.user_id;
      dbQuery.first_name = firstname_txt.text;
      dbQuery.family_name = familyname_txt.text;
```

```
      dbQuery.username = username_txt.text;
      dbQuery.sendAndLoad("http://localhost/phpflash/ch10/
➥ register_cms.php?ck="+new Date().getTime(), updateResult);
    }
  }
}
```

By now, you should have little difficulty understanding the ActionScript with the help of the inline comments. If all the tests are passed, the action variable sent to the PHP script is doUpdate. The target for the result is the updateResult instance of LoadVars.

9. Let's create the onLoad event handler for updateResult before fixing the PHP code. Enter this into your ActionScript on frame 1, immediately after the code in the previous step:

```
function updateReport(success:Boolean):Void {
  // onLoad event handler for updateResult
  // reports if duplicate username requested
  // otherwise displays amended list of users
  if (!success) {
    error_txt.text = "Database not available. Please try later.";
  } else if (updateResult.duplicate == "n") {
    // the update succeeded, so display updated list on listUsers frame
    gotoAndStop("listUsers");
    processResults(updateResult);
    error_txt.text = this.message;
  } else if (updateResult.duplicate == "y") {
    // if the username is already in use by someone else, report error
    error_txt.text = updateResult.message;
    username_txt.text = "";
    Selection.setFocus(username_txt);
  }
}
```

If there is no problem with duplicate names, updateReport() sends the playhead to the listUsers frame and hands the data to processResults() to display an updated user list. It also displays a message confirming the name of the account that has been updated.

If there is a problem with duplicate names, it displays an appropriate error message and clears the username field, ready for the user to make a different choice. You can compare your code against register_management11.fla, but before it will work, you need to add the necessary PHP script to register_cms.php. You'll do that right now.

Finishing the update process: PHP

1. Open register_cms.php or use register_cms04.php. The finished code for this section is in register_cms05.php. Enter the following line of code in the elseif statement where action is set to doUpdate (the block begins around line 62):

```
$unique = checkDuplicate($_POST['username'], $_POST['user_id']);
```

This is where the change made to the `checkDuplicate()` function at the beginning of this project (in the section titled "Adapting the PHP registration script") finally comes into play. Take a look at the function declaration at the bottom of `register_cms.php` (it's also reproduced in Figure 10-16). The second argument ($user_id) is given a default value, which means it is optional. Since the default has been set to 0, and since MySQL always begins an `auto_increment` column at `1`, passing a `user_id` to `checkDuplicate()` will always trigger the first `if` statement inside the function (as indicated in Figure 10-16).

This adds `AND user_id != `*`user_id`* to the end of the SQL statement. So, if you take the example of William Bonney, whose `user_id` happens to be `23`, the entire SQL query will read as follows:

```
"SELECT username FROM users
WHERE username = 'thekid' AND user_id != 23"
```

The exclamation mark in front of the equal sign has exactly the same meaning in SQL as in ActionScript and PHP—it negates the expression. So, in other words, the SQL query is looking for any records *other* than William Bonney's that contain `thekid` as `username`. If you didn't do this, the `checkDuplicate()` function would always report that the username is already in use. Of course it is—it belongs to the original owner! You may wonder why it's worth bothering to check. Well, let's say Billy the Kid has an identity crisis and wants to call himself `wildbill`. The function would prevent him from doing so, because that username is already taken by James Hickok. (Historically speaking, William Bonney could have taken the other name for the last five years of his life because Wild Bill Hickok died first—but I think you get the drift of my meaning.)

```
// Check for duplicate use of username
function checkDuplicate($username, $user_id = 0) {
  $db = new Database('localhost','flashuser','deepthought','phpflash');
  $sql = "SELECT username FROM users WHERE username = '$username'";
  // add to SQL if user_id supplied as argument
  if ($user_id > 0) {
    $sql .= " AND user_id != $user_id";
    }
  $result = $db->query($sql);
  $numrows = $result->num_rows;
  $db->close();

  // if username already in use, send back error message
  if ($numrows > 0) {
    $duplicate = 'Duplicate username. Please choose another.';
    echo 'duplicate=y&message='.urlencode($duplicate);
    exit();
    }
  else {
    return true;
    }
  }
```


Figure 10-16. The optional second argument determines whether to include the user's own username in the search for duplicate records.

2. If the name is already in use by someone else, checkDuplicate() sends two variables back to Flash (duplicate=y and an error message) and terminates the operation by calling exit(), which stops a PHP script from running. Otherwise, it returns true, a value that is stored in $unique. You can now use that value to give the go-ahead to the rest of the update process. The code for that goes immediately after the single line of code you entered in step 1:

```
if ($unique) {
  $db = new Database('localhost','flashadmin','fortytwo','phpflash');
  $sql = 'UPDATE users SET first_name = "'.$_POST['first_name'].'",
          family_name = "'.$_POST['family_name'].'",
          username = "'.$_POST['username'].'"';
  if ($_POST['pwdChange'] == 'newPwd') {
    $sql .= ', pwd = "'.sha1($_POST['pwd']).'"';
  }
  $sql .= ' WHERE user_id = '.$_POST['user_id'];
  $db->query($sql);
  $db->close();
  $updated = 'Account updated for ';
  $updated .= stripslashes($_POST['first_name']).' '.
➥ stripslashes($_POST['family_name']);
  echo 'duplicate=n&message='.urlencode($updated);
  // display revised list
  $revisedList = 'SELECT * FROM users'.$order;
  echo $output .= '&'.getUserList($revisedList);
  }
```

This code builds and then executes the SQL query to update the record. An if clause inside this code block checks whether pwdChange has been set to newPwd. If it has, the new password is passed to the sha1() encryption function and added to the comma-delimited list of new values to be set. Next, a WHERE clause is added to the SQL query to tell MySQL which record it is you want to update. The update query is submitted to the database and a message is prepared that reports the successful update. (If the update fails, the error tests in the Database class will send an appropriate message.) Finally, a revised version of the complete list of users is retrieved and added to the list of variables sent to Flash. Doing the update and retrieving the amended list in a single operation like this saves an unnecessary round-trip to the server.

3. Save register_cms.php and test your Flash movie. Display a list of users and select one for updating. Everything should work fine, although you may need to slightly adjust the position of the error_txt text field if it's too close to the list of users. The code is around line 398. If you encounter any problems, check your files against register_cms05.php and register_management12.fla.

   As Figure 10-17 illustrates, changes should be reflected immediately in the list of users. If you want to double-check, take a look at the same database table in phpMyAdmin. Your Flash application is now working directly with the MySQL database and performing some of the same functionality. The important difference is that you have control over the changes that users can make to your database. You also have control over the way everything looks onscreen.

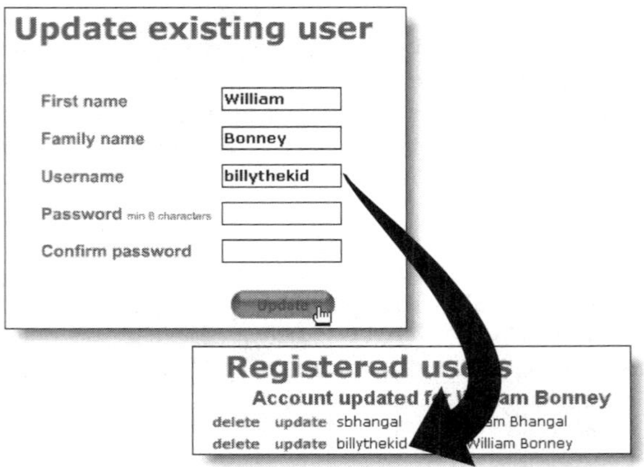

Figure 10-17. William Bonney got fed up just being called "thekid" and now has a more fitting name.

Deleting records

As I've already warned you, MySQL takes your instructions literally and doesn't ask twice. This makes for speed, but computer users have become used to the idea of always being asked to confirm they really want to delete something. So it makes sense to build that sort of safeguard into the delete mechanism. Figure 10-18 shows how the process works.

The delete movie clip buttons work in exactly the same way as the update ones by passing the user_id to the PHP script. The bulk of this section, therefore, deals with the confirmation mechanism.

1. Continue working with the same FLA file, or use register_management_11.fla from the download files for this chapter. The finished code for this section is in register_management12.fla. Open the Actions panel on frame 1 of the actions layer and enter the following code after doUpdate() (on around line 327):

```
function deleteRecord():Void {
  //initialize variables
  var j:Number = this.theNum;
  var theButton:MovieClip = this;
  // load the confirmation movie clip at very high depth
  _root.attachMovie("confirmDel","confirm_mc",10000);
  // center the confirmation movie clip
  confirm_mc._x = Stage.width/2;
  confirm_mc._y = Stage.height/2;
  // populate dynamic text in confirmation mc with user's name
  confirm_mc.delete_txt.setNewTextFormat(detailsFormat);
  confirm_mc.delete_txt.text = users[j].first_name +
➥ " " + users[j].family_name;
  // disable all other buttons
  toggleButtons();
  confirm_mc.cancel_btn.onRelease = function() {
    // remove confirmation mc and reactivate other buttons
```

```
    confirm_mc.removeMovieClip();
    toggleButtons();
    // reset the clicked delete button to its normal state
    theButton.gotoAndStop("_up");
  };
  confirm_mc.ok_btn.onRelease = function() {
    // delete code goes here
  };
}
```

First, the clicked delete button and its associated theNum property are assigned to new variables, theButton and j, to make them easier to handle inside two other functions that are nested inside this one. Then, the confirmation movie clip that you built all that time ago (remember?) is loaded and centered. Even though the movie clip will be on top of everything, any buttons still accessible by the mouse pointer will remain active, so a new function called toggleButtons() deactivates them.

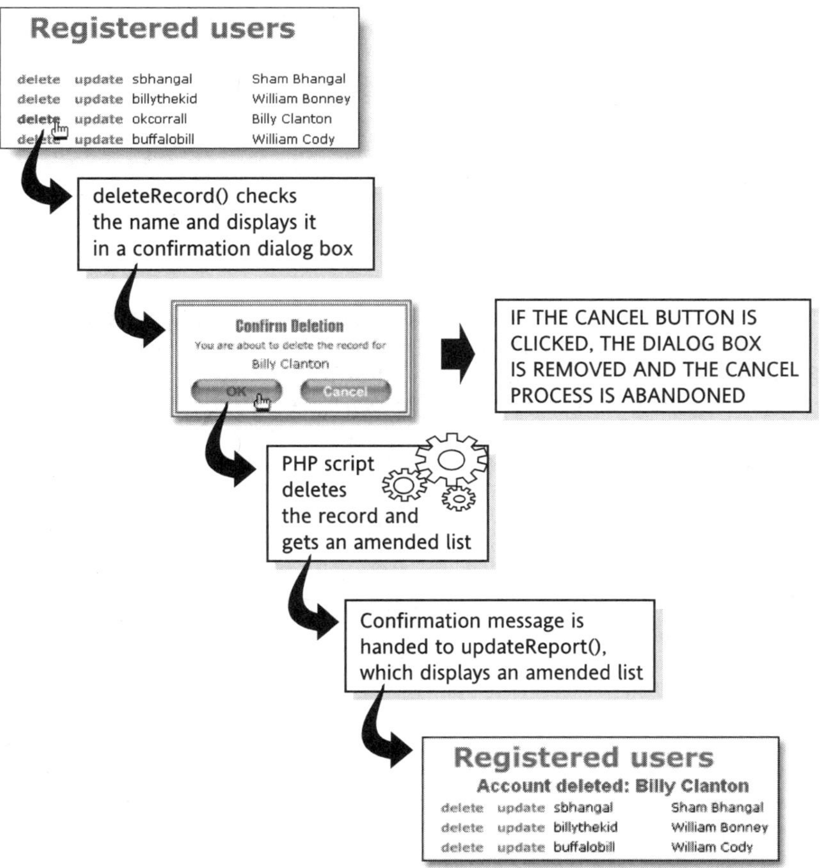

Figure 10-18. The chain of events to delete a record depends on confirmation by the user.

Finally come two nested callback functions to activate the Cancel and OK buttons on the confirmation movie clip. I've put them here, rather than on the movie clip itself, to keep all the code together for ease of maintenance. Using dot notation to specify the path to the buttons is a lot less hassle than burying everything on individual movie clips as many old-school Flash developers like to do.

Inside the `cancel_btn.onRelease` event handler, the other buttons are reactivated, and the delete button that you clicked is reset to its up state. It's not an ordinary button symbol, but a movie clip, so `gotoAndStop("_up")` prevents it from remaining in suspended animation on the _over frame.

I'll come back to the OK button in a short while.

2. Next, insert the `toggleButtons()` function in the `Interface display functions` section immediately after `clearDisplay()` (around line 65):

```
function toggleButtons() {
  for (var i:Number = 0; i < display; i++) {
    // define button names for current row
    var nextDel_mc:MovieClip = _root["del"+i+"_mc"];
    var nextUpd_mc:MovieClip = _root["upd"+i+"_mc"];
    // disable buttons on current row
    nextDel_mc.enabled = !nextDel_mc.enabled;
    nextUpd_mc.enabled = !nextUpd_mc.enabled;
  }
  search_btn.enabled = !search_btn.enabled;
  new_btn.enabled = !new_btn.enabled;
  logout_btn.enabled = !logout_btn.enabled;
}
```

This function uses a very simple technique, but it's one that had me racking my brain for hours when I first encountered it. The enabled property of a movie clip contains a Boolean value (`true` or `false`). So what this function does is say *`set the enabled property of this movie clip to the opposite of its current value`*. In other words, if the enabled property is `true`, set it to *`not true`* (`false`); if it's `false`, set it to *`not false`* (`true`). The loop toggles the values of all the update and delete buttons, while the last three lines toggle the buttons across the bottom of the frame.

> *When using this technique, make sure you don't confuse `= !` with `!=`. The former (as used here) means `set to the opposite of`, whereas the latter is a comparison operator (`not equal to`).*

3. Test the movie, display the full list of users, and click one of the delete buttons. The confirmation movie clip should appear onscreen, with the name of the person to be deleted in the center. (When you test in Flash, the confirmation dialog box will not be correctly centered on the stage. It should be positioned correctly when you finally test the movie in a browser.)

Try clicking any of the other buttons; they should have been disabled. The only two buttons still active are those in the confirmation movie clip, although OK won't do anything yet, because it still needs to be wired up. Click Cancel and everything should go back to normal.

4. Now put the delete code in ok_btn.onRelease function at the point indicated in step 1 (around line 362):

```
// send delete instructions to PHP script
dbQuery.action = "doDelete";
dbQuery.user_id = users[j].user_id;
dbQuery.who = confirm_mc.delete_txt.text;
dbQuery.sendAndLoad("http://localhost/phpflash/ch10/
➥ register_cms.php?ck="+ newDate().getTime(), updateResult);
// remove confirmation dialog box
confirm_mc.removeMovieClip();
// reactivate other buttons
toggleButtons();
```

There are two points to note here. First, dbQuery is assigned a property called who. This property contains the name of the person whose account is being deleted. It will be used to display a message confirming the deletion, so the text displayed in the confirm_mc movie clip fits this purpose exactly. The other point is that the target for dbQuery.sendAndLoad is set to updateResult, the same instance of LoadVars used to handle the results of an update. After the deletion, a revised list will be displayed in exactly the same way as after an update, so it makes sense to handle the result in the same way. The inline comments explain the rest of what's going on here, so let's move straight on to the PHP code.

5. Open register_cms.php (or use register_cms05.php) and enter the following code in the elseif clause where action is set to doDelete (the block begins around line 83):

```
$db = new Database('localhost','flashadmin','fortytwo','phpflash');
$sql = 'DELETE FROM users WHERE user_id = '.$_POST['user_id'];
$db->query($sql);
$db->close();
// display revised list
$revisedList = 'SELECT * FROM users'.$order;
$deleted = 'Account deleted: '.stripslashes($_POST['who']);
$output = 'duplicate=n&message='.urlencode($deleted);
echo $output .= '&'.getUserList($revisedList);
```

This is quite straightforward. First a DELETE query is executed, and then a fresh version of the user list is retrieved and sent back to Flash, together with a message confirming the deletion. This message uses the value contained in the who property sent by dbQuery. Because the onLoad handler for this is the same as for an update, the variables sent to Flash include the same duplicate and message variables. By setting duplicate to n (it's certainly not a duplicate!), updateReport() will handle the results in exactly the same way as an update. Although the record has been deleted, it's the database that has been updated, so it's perfectly logical to handle it this way.

6. Test the movie, bring up a list of users, and choose your victim to send to oblivion. If you test the movie in a browser, rather than in Flash, you should see the confirmation dialog box appear in the center of the movie, as shown here.

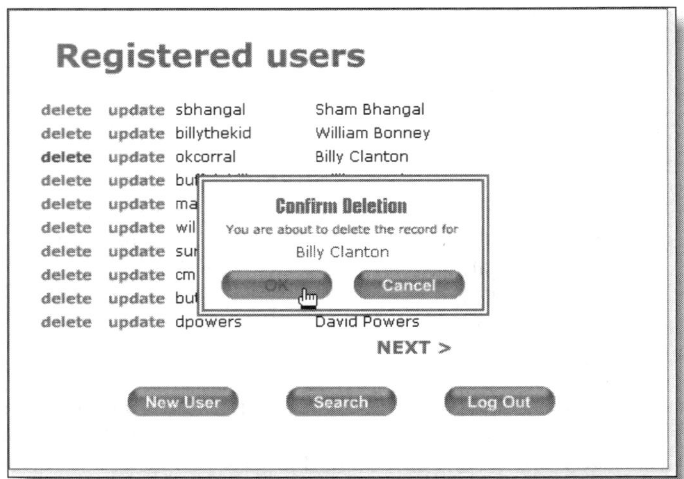

Congratulations, you're almost there. Again, if you have any problems, check your code against that in `register_management_12.fla` and `register_cms06.php`. All that remains to be done now is to make the content management system secure by reinstating the PHP session code.

Securing the content management system

Making the content management system secure is simply a matter of adapting the techniques used in the previous chapter.

Adding the login and logout procedures

You can use the `login.fla` file from Chapter 9, but not the SWF file, because it loads the wrong page.

1. If you haven't already done so, copy `login.fla` and `process_login.php` from `phpflash/ch09` to `phpflash/ch10`. The PHP file doesn't require any changes. The versions in the download files for this chapter contain the finished script.
2. Open `login.fla` and change the checkDetails() and doLogin() functions in the ActionScript on frame 1 of the actions layer as follows (the new code is highlighted in bold):

```
function checkDetails():Void {
  error_txt.text = "";
  loginDets.username = username_txt.text;
```

```
  loginDets.pwd = pwd_txt.text;
  loginDets.sendAndLoad("http://localhost/phpflash/ch10/
process_login.php?ck="+ new Date().getTime(), loginResponse);
};

// if login details OK, load protected page
// otherwise display error message
function doLogin():Void {
  if (this.authenticated == "ok") {
    getURL("http://localhost/phpflash/ch10/register_management.php");
  } else {
    error_txt.text = "Sorry, access denied";
  }
};
```

This code now points the login movie to the correct pages. Publish the HTML and SWF files to phpflash/ch10.

3. Publish the HTML and SWF files from register_management.fla to phpflash/ch10. If you have been using the download files, make sure you remove the number from the end of the filename before publishing.

4. Change register_management.html to register_management.php. Open the page in a script editor, and add the same PHP session script above the Doctype as you did in the previous chapter (but change the URL):

```
<?php session_start();
if (!isset($_SESSION['authenticated'])) {
  header('Location: http://localhost/phpflash/ch10/login.html');
  exit();
  }
?>
```

5. Open register_cms.php and add the following code in the final elseif clause where action is set to logout (the block begins around line 95):

```
unset($_SESSION['authenticated']);
session_destroy();
echo 'status=goodbye';
```

6. If you test your login and logout sequence now, you should be able to log into and out of the PHP page that contains the Flash movie, but you are still at risk from someone loading the SWF file directly into a browser. The solution is the same as before: put the following code at the very top of register_cms.php, immediately after the opening PHP tag.

```
session_start();
if (!isset($_SESSION['authenticated'])) {
  echo 'status=goodbye';
  }
else {
```

7. The matching closing curly brace (}) for the else clause goes immediately after the logout elseif clause as shown here. The reason it doesn't go at the bottom of the page is that checkDuplicate(), getUserList(), and getDetails() aren't part of the conditional statement. They're functions that need to be globally available within the script, so they must be kept outside other code blocks.

```
elseif ($_POST['action'] == 'logout') {
  // logout code goes here
  unset($_SESSION['authenticated']);
  session_destroy();
  echo 'status=goodbye';
  }
}
// Check for duplicate use of username
function checkDuplicate($username, $user_id = 0) {
```

Closing curly brace goes here

8. Save the amended version of register_cms.php (you can check it against register_cms07.php in the download files) and try to access the SWF directly. It will still load in the browser, but the check for the session variable will prevent you from entering new data into the database. As in the previous chapter, you'll be quietly deposited back at the login page. Attempts to search or list users won't result in expulsion, but you still won't be able to do anything because no data will be either sent to or received from the database. To make doubly sure of security, amend the beginning of all LoadVars.onLoad event handler functions like this:

```
if (!success) {
  error_txt.text = "Sorry, database not available.";
} else if (this.status == "goodbye") {
  getURL("http://localhost/phpflash/ch10/login.html");
} else...
```

Adding an extra column to a table

Even the best laid plans go awry, so it's useful to know that adding an extra column to a table is simple. What's usually not so simple is adapting the rest of your application to the change in database structure. There's also the problem of what to do about existing records—do you go back and update them all, or do you accept that they won't necessarily have the new information?

Adding a column for middle names

Earlier in the chapter, I promised to show you how to add an extra column to a table if, for instance, you want to have a separate place to record a person's middle name or initial. The easiest way is to do it in phpMyAdmin. The following instructions just give the basic outline of the process; the content management system itself won't be updated to reflect the additional column (although that's a project for you to work on independently).

1. Open phpMyAdmin and select the database and table to which you want to add an extra column. In this case, it would be the phpflash database and the users table.

2. Beneath the grid that displays the table structure is an option called Add new field, as shown here. (Remember that phpMyAdmin refers to columns as fields.)

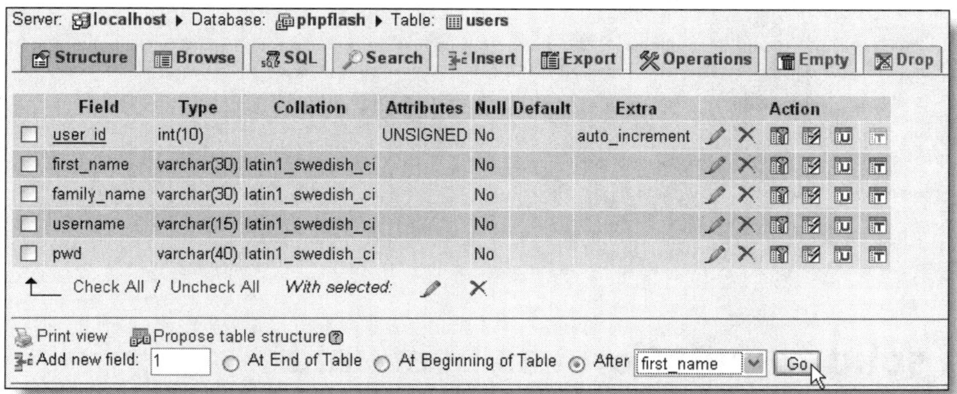

The input text field allows you to specify how many columns to add; the default is one. A set of radio buttons offers three choices of where to locate the new column: At End of Table, At Beginning of Table, or After [column_name] (to be chosen from a drop-down menu). After you have made your choice, click Go.

> *The position of a new table column is irrelevant as far as the database is concerned. The main reason for offering the choice is ease of maintenance. Particularly if you have a database table with many columns, it's a lot easier to group columns together in a logical order.*

3. The next screen allows you to set the name, data type, and other details for the new column. When adding a column to a table already populated with records, set the Null option to null. (The default in phpMyAdmin is not null.) This will allow that particular column to remain optional for existing and new records. When you have made your selections, click Save.

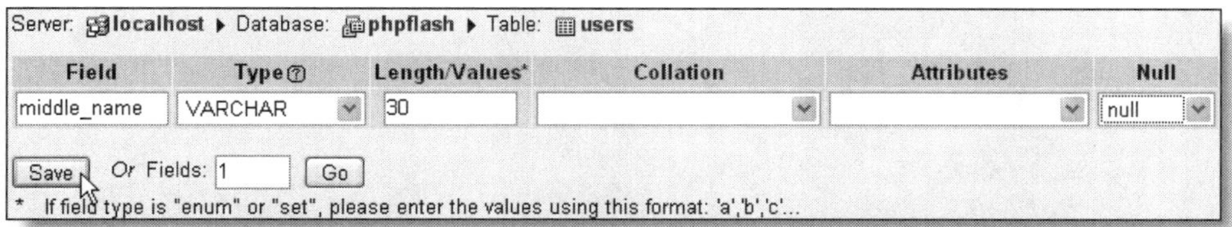

4. phpMyAdmin adds the new column and immediately displays an updated grid showing the new structure of the table. If you click the Browse tab, you will see that the value for `middle_name` on all existing records has been set to NULL.

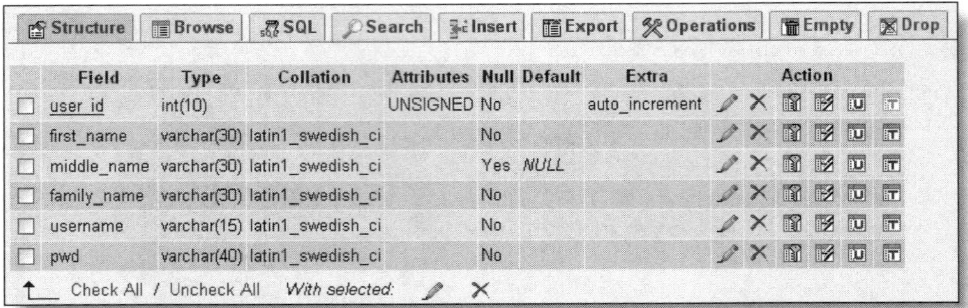

A solid foundation has been laid

This chapter covered a lot of ground, introducing you to the four basic tasks of working with a database. It may have seemed like a lot of work for such a simple table, but the principles of inserting, updating, and deleting records are common to every database no matter how large or small. You have also seen how to conduct a search based not just on a single field, but on flexible criteria. In the next chapter, you'll take a look at working with dates in PHP and MySQL, and build a Flash component to make your life easier when entering dates into database tables. Then, in the final chapter, you'll see how PHP 5 makes handling XML data easy, and you'll build a database project that uses more than one table.

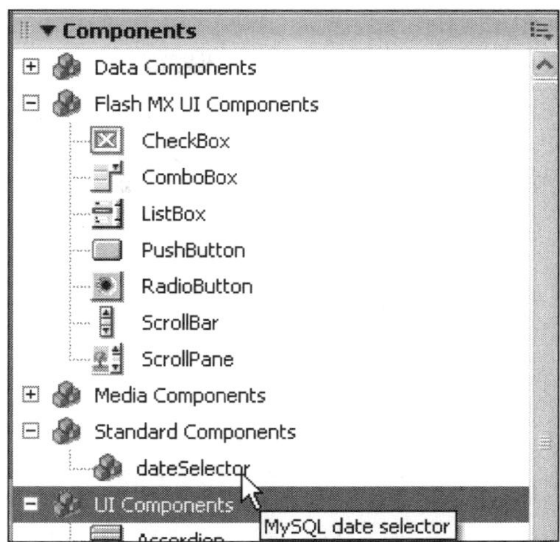

Chapter 11

WORKING WITH DATES

What this chapter covers:

- Using PHP to format dates in many ways
- Getting the right date format for MySQL
- Loading a table from a backup file
- Selecting database records by date
- Using subselects in SQL queries (MySQL 4.1 and above)
- Using aliases in SQL queries
- Building a date selector component in Flash

After the rigors of the last chapter, I thought you might appreciate a change of pace. Dates are an essential part of everyday life, but let's face it, they're not the easiest things to deal with when it comes to computers. First of all, a month can be from 28 to 31 days in length. Then, a week is seven days, but which is the first day of the week? In some cultures, it's Sunday; in others, it's Monday.

I can always remember the first line of the ancient rhyme "Thirty days hath September," but after that I begin to stumble. Many a month goes by when I forget to advance the date on my watch to keep pace with the rest of the world. Fortunately, I spend so much time in front of the computer screen that I can always check the date just by moving my mouse pointer over the time display.

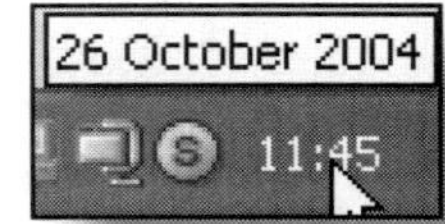

But look at the date style. It probably seems natural to you if you're from Europe, but for an American, the day and name of the month are in the wrong order. And that's not the only difference you might encounter. For example, I lived in Japan for many years, where the date is in a different order: year, month, day of the month. Even if you can't read Japanese kanji, the date taken from this Japanese news website should be recognizable as October 26, 2004.

2004年10月26日

Although the Windows and Mac operating systems take care of these differences automatically in their own displays, you're on your own when it comes to working with dates in Flash, PHP, and MySQL. To make things even worse, dates in ActionScript are strictly for geeks. January is month 0, and Sunday is weekday 0. It makes sense in computer terms, because all arrays start at 0, but it sure makes date calculations counterintuitive. PHP is for geeks of a different sort—it treats the months and weekdays in a more human-friendly way (most of the time, anyway), but has a bewildering variety of methods to format dates. MySQL is the most human-friendly of all, but it follows the same principle as Japanese dates: the year comes first, followed by the month and day of the month. This order has been chosen because it's the format laid down by ISO. It makes a lot of sense, particularly when combined with a time; a `DATETIME` column progresses naturally left to right from the largest unit (year) to the smallest (second).

This chapter aims to steer you through these complexities, and by the end of it, you will have built a handy date selector in Flash that formats user input dates ready for use in MySQL and also responds to dates passed to it directly from MySQL. I'll also show you how to turn it into a component, so that you can reuse it in your movies without having to rebuild it every time.

How ActionScript, PHP, and MySQL handle dates

Computers are great for number crunching, so they get around the problems of calculating human dates by converting them to a **timestamp**, doing any necessary calculations, and then converting them back again. A timestamp measures the time elapsed since what is known as the **Unix epoch**. All programming languages agree that the epoch is calculated from midnight UTC (GMT) on January 1, 1970. What they don't agree on is how to calculate it.

Navigating the minefield of incompatible timestamps

ActionScript adheres to the ECMAScript standard, which stipulates that dates and time must be measured to millisecond (one-thousandth of one second) precision for any instant of the 100 billion days either forward or backward from the Unix epoch. So ActionScript will not face a Y2K-type problem until the year 287586—probably sufficient for most of your needs!

PHP, on the other hand, calculates timestamps in whole seconds. Also, most systems use a 32-bit signed integer to handle PHP timestamps. This limits the effective range of dates that can be used for calculations in PHP from late December 1901 to early January 2038. This is a hardware issue, and it will apparently be solved for the next 292 billion years by moving to systems that store time values as 64-bit integers.

> *Timestamps prior to the Unix epoch are represented as negative integers. Some operating systems, notably Windows and some Linux distributions, do not support negative timestamps. Consequently, if you need to conduct date calculations outside of the 1970–2037 range, use ActionScript rather than PHP.*

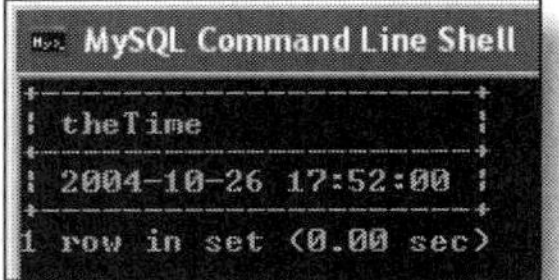

Just to make life really complicated, MySQL not only limits the range of its TIMESTAMP column type to dates between 1970 and 2037, but also uses a completely different method of calculation. In fact, it doesn't really calculate anything at all, as the screenshot alongside shows. In MySQL 4.1 and above, a TIMESTAMP column contains nothing more mysterious than the date and time in human-readable format. In previous versions of MySQL, the same timestamp would be presented as 20041026175200—exactly the same, only without the hyphens and colons for easier readability. Table 11-1 shows the timestamps that each language generated for the same time and date.

Table 11-1. Same time, same date, but very different timestamps

Actual time and date: 5:52 p.m., October 26, 2004

Language	Timestamp	Explanation
ActionScript	1098809520000	Number of milliseconds elapsed since midnight UTC on January 1, 1970
PHP	1098809520	Number of seconds elapsed since midnight UTC on January 1, 1970
MySQL 4.1	2004-10-26 17:52:00	Date and time in the format recommended by ISO
MySQL < 4.1	20041026175200	Same content as MySQL 4.1 and above, but formatted without any punctuation or spaces

As Table 11-1 shows, timestamps created by ActionScript, PHP, and MySQL are not interchangeable. You could, if you wanted to, use a PHP timestamp in ActionScript by multiplying it by 1,000, or an ActionScript timestamp in PHP after dividing it by 1,000. But there is no way a MySQL timestamp can be used in either PHP or ActionScript without first converting it to a format understood by that language. Figures 11-1 and 11-2 show what happens if you try to mix ActionScript and PHP timestamps without performing the necessary calculations.

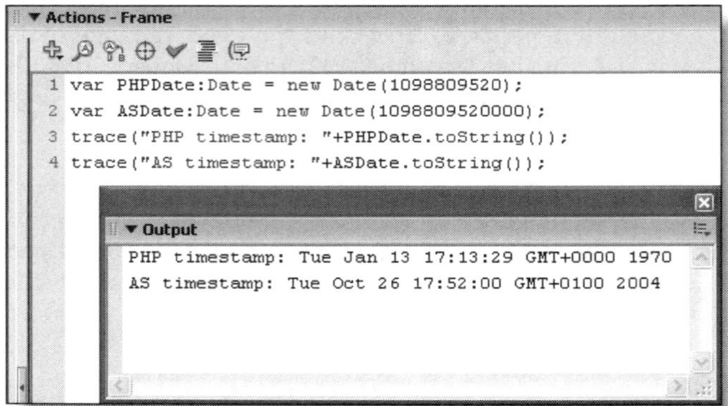

Figure 11-1. Using a PHP-generated timestamp in ActionScript produces a date more than 30 years off target.

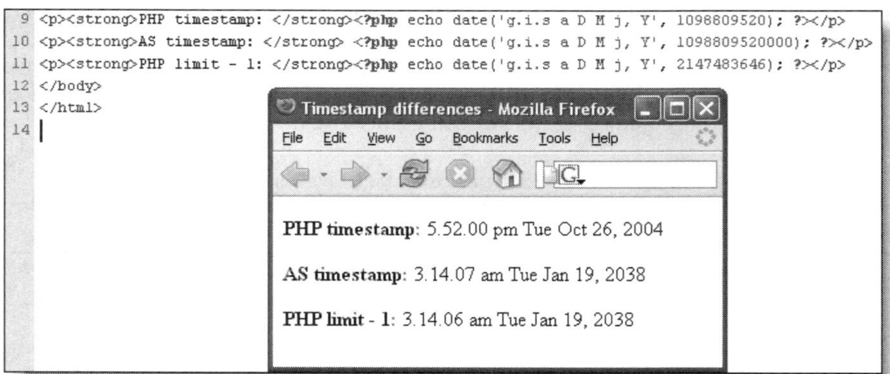

Figure 11-2. A current ActionScript timestamp always produces the same date in January 2038 when used in PHP.

A PHP-generated timestamp for October 26, 2004 is so small that ActionScript interprets it as January 13, 1970. On the other hand, an ActionScript-generated timestamp for a current date is so huge that it always produces the same date: 3:14:07 a.m. on January 19, 2038—the PHP limit. In fact, any ActionScript timestamp later than 8:31 p.m. on January 25, 1970, produces the same result.

The lesson from this is very simple:

- **Never use a raw timestamp from one language in another.**
- **Perform date calculations in a single language, and pass the result.**

Creating a timestamp

There are many reasons why you might want to create a timestamp, but the two most frequent are as follows:

- To get the current date and time. Although this may be stating the obvious, you never know in advance when a program will be run, so it's the equivalent of looking at your watch. As well as using the date and time to display onscreen, you can use them to record when something happens—for instance, when someone logs on to your site or when a record is inserted into a database.
- To calculate the number of days, weeks, or months between two dates.

An important point to remember about timestamps is that they represent a single point in time in the same way as a timekeeping system is used to clock employees in and out of the workplace. It's a common misconception that a `Date` object in ActionScript keeps track of the current time. It doesn't; it's a snapshot of the precise time at which it was created. PHP treats timestamps in the same way.

Getting the current date and time is easy in each language.

Creating a current timestamp in ActionScript

All you need to do is create a new `Date` object with no parameters, and assign it to a variable, like this:

```
var today:Date = new Date();
```

This creates a timestamp based on the current time on the user's computer, so it is only as accurate as the computer's clock. Once you have created a `Date` object, you can access a wide range of date and time parts through nearly 40 methods of the `Date` class. See Help ➤ ActionScript Dictionary in Flash for details. You will also see some of the main methods in use in the date selector application later in this chapter.

Creating a current timestamp in PHP

Getting a current timestamp is equally easy, but PHP offers three different functions for doing it: `time()`, `mktime()`, and `gmmktime()`. The first two are identical when used for a current timestamp. Simply assign them to a variable like this:

```
$today = time();
$today = mktime();
```

Both create a timestamp based on the current time on the PHP server, *not* the user's computer.

To see what gmmktime() does, run the following code in an empty web page with a .php extension. The PHP is embedded in an XHTML table to make it easier to read in a browser, so you don't need PHP tags at the top and bottom (alternatively, use current_timestamps.php in this chapter's download files):

```
<table>
<tr><td><strong>mktime(): </strong></td>
<td><?php echo mktime(); ?></td></tr>
<tr><td><strong>gmmktime(): </strong></td>
<td><?php echo gmmktime(); ?></td></tr>
<tr><td><strong>Difference: </strong></td>
<td><?php echo gmmktime() - mktime(); ?>
</td></tr>
</table>
```

I ran the code in the dying days of what we in the UK laughingly call British Summer Time, when the clocks move one hour forward of GMT (UTC) and we pretend that summer has come. As you will see from the screenshot, the difference between the timestamp created by mktime() and gmmktime() was 3600—in other words, one hour. Depending on where you live and what time of the year you run the code, you will get a different result. If you are on the East Coast of the United States (and your computer time zone is set correctly), the final line should read 18000, or 21600 during Daylight Saving Time. Someone in Tokyo, however, should see -28800 at any time of the year.

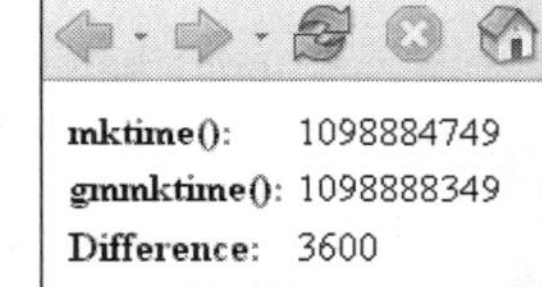

The purpose of gmmktime() is to create a timestamp based on the time at the prime meridian (0°), which runs through Greenwich, England. In the past, everyone used to call this Greenwich Mean Time (GMT; hence the PHP function's name), but the internationally recognized name has been changed to Coordinated Universal Time with the rather strange initials UTC, which match the name neither in English nor in French. (The International Bureau of Weights and Measures is located in France.) At least everyone agrees that UTC is the international time standard, and that's what really matters.

gmmktime() is extremely useful if you are running a website that needs to display times accurately. Say, for instance, you are based on the West Coast of the United States, but your remote server is in Florida. You can use calculations based on gmmktime() to display Pacific Standard Time (PST) accurately. ActionScript has a range of UTC-related methods, but they are much more cumbersome than gmmktime().

Creating a current timestamp in MySQL

Timestamps in MySQL are normally used for one thing only: recording the time a record was updated. You don't need to do anything to create a timestamp; as long as the column's type is set to TIMESTAMP—*and* it's the first TIMESTAMP column in the table—it will automatically be filled with the current date and time whenever a record is originally inserted or updated. The following exercise demonstrates how MySQL timestamps work.

Recording when a record was created in MySQL

Although you can use phpMyAdmin for this exercise, it's probably a lot easier to follow if you work directly through MySQL Monitor.

1. If you are using the Windows Essentials version of MySQL, you can launch MySQL Monitor from Start ➤ All Programs ➤ MySQL ➤ MySQL Server 4.1 ➤ MySQL Command Line Client. On a Mac, launch Terminal and type mysql -u root -p. On both systems, enter your MySQL root password when prompted.
2. Change to the phpflash database by typing use phpflash and pressing *Enter/Return*.
3. Create a new table called time_demo with the following SQL:

```
create table time_demo (
updated TIMESTAMP,
created TIMESTAMP,
val INT
);
```

   This creates a simple three-column table. The column type of the first two columns is TIMESTAMP, while the third column will hold only integers (whole numbers). Since this table is for demonstration purposes only, I haven't bothered with a primary key.

4. Insert some data with the following command:

```
INSERT INTO time_demo (val) VALUES (6);
```

   By specifying only the val column, MySQL will automatically fill the other two columns with the default values.

5. To see what values MySQL has used, type

```
SELECT * FROM time_demo;
```

   If you are using MySQL 4.1, you should see something similar to the left screenshot in Figure 11-3. If you are using an earlier version of MySQL, the result will look similar to the screenshot on the right. The MySQL 4.1 display is easier to read, but both versions contain essentially the same information: the real date, rather than a value based on the time elapsed since the beginning of 1970.

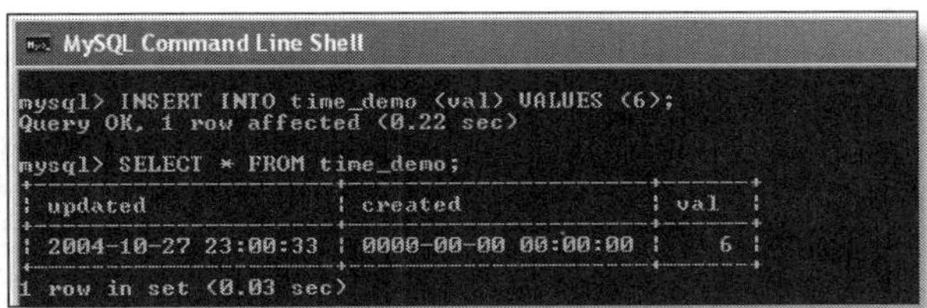

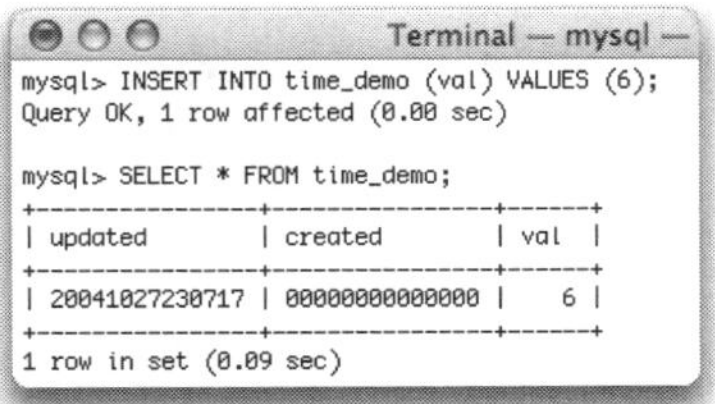

Figure 11-3. A TIMESTAMP column is much easier to read in MySQL 4.1 (left) than in earlier versions (right).

The important thing to note here is that the first TIMESTAMP column was automatically filled with a valid timestamp, but the second one was not. This is actually extremely useful, as you will see shortly.

> *Eagle-eyed readers will notice that the title bar in the left image in Figure 11-3 and some other Windows screenshots in this chapter says* MySQL Command Line Shell, *rather than* MySQL Command Line Client. *The name was changed with the release of MySQL 4.1.8 in December 2004, but the function is identical.*

6. Create another entry by using the following command:

```
INSERT INTO time_demo (created, val) VALUES (NOW(), 7);
```

This time, the first TIMESTAMP column (updated) is still given no value, but the MySQL function NOW() is used to set the value for the second one (created). As you might expect, NOW() returns the current date and time.

7. To see the effect, run the same SQL query as in step 5:

```
SELECT * FROM time_demo;
```

You should see something like this:

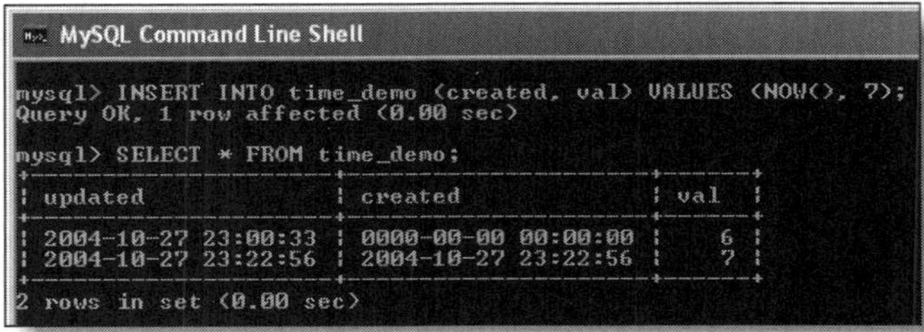

This time both TIMESTAMP columns contain the same value. You may wonder what's so special about that, but the point is that only the first TIMESTAMP column in a table is automatically filled. Any subsequent ones must be given a specific value. The significance of this should become clear in the next step.

8. Update the val column like this:

```
UPDATE time_demo SET val = 4 WHERE val = 7;
```

9. Select all results again with the same query as in steps 5 and 7. The result should look similar to this:

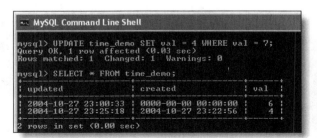

```
MySQL Command Line Shell
mysql> UPDATE time_demo SET val = 4 WHERE val = 7;
Query OK, 1 row affected (0.03 sec)
Rows matched: 1  Changed: 1  Warnings: 0

mysql> SELECT * FROM time_demo;
+---------------------+---------------------+------+
| updated             | created             | val  |
+---------------------+---------------------+------+
| 2004-10-27 23:00:33 | 0000-00-00 00:00:00 |    6 |
| 2004-10-27 23:25:18 | 2004-10-27 23:22:56 |    4 |
+---------------------+---------------------+------+
2 rows in set (0.00 sec)
```

Compare the updated and created times. The first TIMESTAMP column now has a different value from the second one. Only the first TIMESTAMP column in any table is ever automatically updated. So now you have a way of knowing both when a record was originally created and when it was most recently updated—use two TIMESTAMP columns, and set the value of the second one to NOW() only with the original INSERT command. Thereafter, there is no need to set a value for either column.

Moreover, the data is stored in a form that is very easy to handle. You can either present it as is, or use PHP or ActionScript string manipulation to configure the date to your preference. For instance, in PHP you could use the explode() function twice to extract the date parts, like this:

```
// first split the date and time on the space
// the date will be stored in $temp[0]
$temp = explode(' ', $MySQLTimestamp);

// then split the date on the hyphens
// year becomes $date[0]; month is $date[1]; date is $date[2]
$date = explode('-', $temp[0]);
```

This is particularly handy, because PHP treats months in the same way humans do. In this example, 10 means October, not November (as it would in ActionScript).

> *One word of caution about* TIMESTAMP *columns in MySQL: at least one value in a record must be changed for the* TIMESTAMP *to be automatically updated. If an* UPDATE *query results in no change to a record, the* TIMESTAMP *remains unchanged.* TIMESTAMP *records when something was actually updated, not when an* UPDATE *query was issued.*

Creating a timestamp for a specific date

Although creating a current timestamp involves different methods or functions in ActionScript and PHP, the basic process is the same: call the appropriate method or function without any parameters. When it comes to creating a timestamp for a specific date (say, for instance, you want to do some calculations based on Christmas), there is a dramatic parting of the ways. Not only do ActionScript and PHP count months differently, but also the order of parameters is totally different.

ActionScript syntax Although ActionScript treats months in a counterintuitive way, the order of arguments passed to the Date object is easy to remember—largest unit first, smallest last:

```
new Date(year, month, day, hours, minutes, seconds, milliseconds)
```

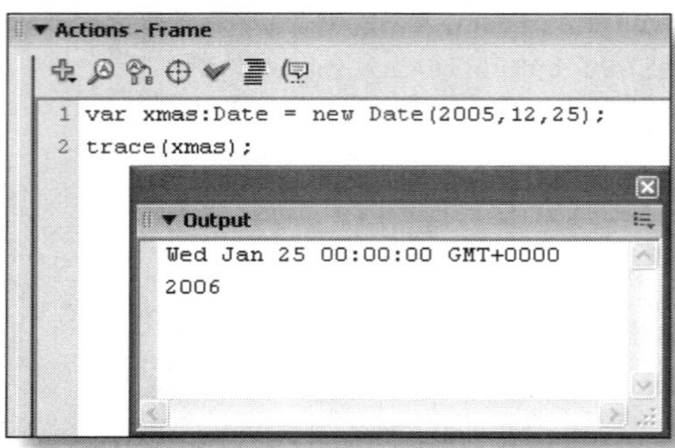

Figure 11-4. Pay insufficient attention to the scripting of ActionScript Date objects and you could end up celebrating Christmas in January!

The first two arguments (*year* and *month*) are required; all others are optional. All arguments must be integers.

Months are calculated from 0 to 11, but out-of-range numbers are also valid. The Date object simply calculates the correct timestamp by adding or subtracting the relevant number of units, so September 32 is treated as October 2. But it's a double-edged sword: if you enter 12 by mistake for December, you end up with a date in January of the following year, as shown in Figure 11-4. The Date object gives no warning of out-of-range input; everything is legal, including negative numbers.

PHP syntax PHP approaches timestamps in a more literal way—time first, date last—and it treats dates in the U.S. way. The time() function takes no arguments, and it cannot be used to create anything other than the current timestamp. Use mktime() or gmmktime() to create a timestamp for a specific date like this:

```
mktime(hours, minutes, seconds, month, day, year)
gmmktime(hours, minutes, seconds, month, day, year)
```

Although all arguments are optional from right to left, this syntax means you cannot omit the time, even if you just want a particular date. The normal practice is to set the time to 0 (midnight), like this:

```
$xmas = mktime(0,0,0,12,25,2005);
```

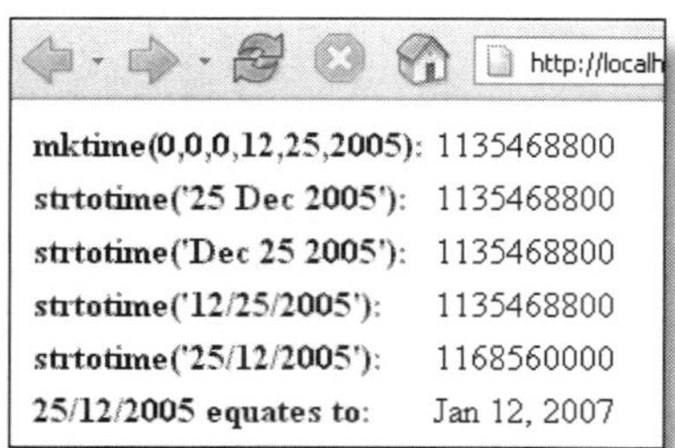

Figure 11-5. The PHP strtotime() function converts human-readable strings to timestamps.

Fortunately, PHP has a much more user-friendly way of doing things—at least, if you use English. The strtotime() function takes an ordinary English string and converts it to a timestamp. As Figure 11-5 shows, the timestamp created from a variety of strings is exactly the same as the one created by mktime(). The important thing to note is that strtotime() accepts the month and date in either *month-day* or *day-month* order, as long as the month is spelled out. When the date is given in numbers, it must follow the U.S. *month-day-year* order. The last two lines in Figure 11-5 demonstrate that PHP also accepts out-of-range numbers, treating month 25 as January of the year after next. (You can find the code in xmas.php in the download files for this chapter.)

The strtotime() function in PHP is extremely useful, and I strongly recommend you experiment with it. It accepts not only dates, but also other time-related expressions, for example:

```
$twelvedays = strtotime('+ 12 days');
```

The preceding code will give you a timestamp for the current time and date, 12 days from now. strtotime() also takes a timestamp as an optional, second parameter:

```
$xmas = strtotime('25 Dec 2005');
$twelvedays = strtotime('+ 12 days', $xmas);
echo date('j M Y', $twelvedays); // displays 6 Jan 2006
```

PHP timestamps on their own can only be used for behind-the-scenes calculations. To make any sense of them, you have to turn them back into human-readable form, as in the final line of the preceding example. That's the subject of the next section, but before we move on to that, a quick word about MySQL.

MySQL syntax Because MySQL timestamps represent the date in human-readable format, their only real purpose is to indicate when a record was created or updated. To record any other date or time, you should use one of the other date and time column types described in Chapter 8. When storing a date in MySQL, always use the format YYYY-MM-DD.

Formatting dates in PHP

PHP provides two functions to format dates: date() and strftime(). At first sight, they look rather daunting, but they are very powerful and not all that difficult to use. Both functions work the same way. They accept two arguments: a string that acts as the formatting template for the date, and a timestamp (optional). If the timestamp is omitted, the function returns the current date and/or time. So in the final example in the previous section, 'j M Y' indicated the format required, and $twelvedays was the timestamp.

Why two functions? Although both do essentially the same thing, date() is strictly monolingual—it always displays month and weekday names in English. On the other hand, strftime() is multilingual. It automatically renders month and weekday names in the correct language for the server's default locale. Figure 11-6 shows the difference between date() and strftime() on a page that has been made to simulate a French Canadian locale. The code on the left of the figure was used to generate the date and time displays alongside. (The code is also in date_formats.php in the download files for this chapter.)

Figure 11-6. Even on a non-English system, date() always displays dates in English, whereas strftime() uses the correct local expressions.

You can also change the language display used by `strftime()` *temporarily by invoking the* `setlocale()` *function. This can be extremely useful. For instance, a site in the United States geared toward a Hispanic audience would certainly find it very convenient to be able to change locale on the fly. The required parameters depend on the server's operating system. The PHP documentation at* `www.php.net/manual/en/function.setlocale.php` *has some useful links for finding the correct locale string. On Mac OS X, you can find a list of all supported locales by issuing the following command in Terminal:* ls /usr/share/locale.

Table 11-2 lists the most commonly used format specifiers. Although it appears that `strftime()` has fewer options, it does, in fact, have rather more than `date()`. Some of them are extremely useful shortcuts, but unfortunately, Windows supports only a limited range. Cross-platform support for `date()` is much stronger, so I recommend you use `date()` unless you have a particular need for the multilingual features offered by `strftime()`.

Note that the specifiers in Table 11-2 marked with an asterisk are not supported by Windows.

Table 11-2. The most common date and time format specifiers

Category	date()	strftime()	Format	Example
Year	Y	%Y	Four digits	2005
	y	%y	Two digits	05
Month	m	%m	Displayed as number, with leading zero	01-12
	n		Displayed as number, no leading zero	1-12
	M	%b	Month name abbreviated	Jan, Feb
	F	%B	Month name in full	January, February
Date	d	%d	Day of month, with leading zero	01-31
	j	%e*	Day of month, no leading zero	1-31
	S		English ordinal suffix (use with j)	st, nd, rd, th

(Continued)

Table 11-2. The most common date and time format specifiers *(Continued)*

Category	date()	strftime()	Format	Example
Weekday	`D`	`%a`	Weekday name, abbreviated	Mon, Tue
	`l`	`%A`	Weekday name in full (note that the specifier for `date()` is a lowercase "L")	Monday, Tuesday
Hour	`g`	`%l*`	12-hour format, no leading zero (note that the specifier for `strftime()` is a lowercase "L")	1-12
	`h`	`%I`	12-hour format, with leading zero (note that the specifier for `strftime()` is an uppercase "I")	01-12
	`G`	`%k*`	24-hour format, no leading zero	0-23
	`H`	`%H`	24-hour format, with leading zero	00-23
Minutes	`i`	`%M`	With leading zero	00-59
Seconds	`s`	`%S`	With leading zero	00-59
AM/PM	`a`		Lowercase	am, pm
	`A`	`%p`	Uppercase	AM, PM

Although these date format specifiers are difficult to remember (I always have to look them up!), they are extremely versatile, and make date formatting much easier than having to build your own arrays of month and weekday names in ActionScript. Any character included in the format string that PHP does not recognize is displayed literally. Consequently, you can use these specifiers to build whichever date format suits your needs. It is quite safe to use punctuation marks in both `date()` and `strftime()`, but you should avoid using letters in `date()` because of potential conflicts with specifiers. This is not an issue with `strftime()`, because all specifiers are prefixed by `%`. As a result, the `strftime()` example in Figure 11-6 uses `h` as a literal character to separate the hours and minutes. If you tried to do that with `date()`, it would display the hour instead. Table 11-3 shows some common examples of how the format specifiers work with `date()`.

> *Don't confuse the purpose of the PHP* `date()` *function with the* `Date` *object in ActionScript. The PHP* `date()` *function is used purely to format an existing date and time stored in a PHP timestamp, or the current date and time if used without a timestamp. Unlike the* `Date` *object in ActionScript, it can't be used to create a value suitable for use in other date and time calculations. For that, use* `time()`*,* `mktime()`*, or* `gmmktime()`*.*

Table 11-3. Typical examples of dates formatted with the PHP `date()` function

Code	Format	Display
`$jul4 = mktime(0,0,0,7,4,2005);`		
`date('n/j/Y', $jul4)`	M/D/YYYY	7/4/2005
`date('m/d/Y', $jul4)`	MM/DD/YYYY	07/04/2005
`date('j/n/Y', $jul4)`	D/M/YYYY	4/7/2005
`date('d/m/Y', $jul4)`	DD/MM/YYYY	04/07/2005
`date('Y-m-d', $jul4)`	YYYY-MM-DD	2005-07-04
`date('D, M j Y', $jul4)`	Abbreviated names	Mon, Jul 4 2005
`date('l, F jS Y', $jul4)`	Full names	Monday, July 4th 2005
`date('D, j M Y', $jul4)`	Abbreviated names	Mon, 4 Jul 2005
`date('l, jS F Y', $jul4)`	Full names	Monday, 4th July 2005

Working with dates in MySQL

As already noted, dates must always be formatted as `YYYY-MM-DD` for storage in MySQL. A little later in the chapter, you will build a simple Flash component that will automate the formatting for you. But first, it will be useful to take a look at some of the date and time functions available in MySQL. There are a lot of them, so I won't bombard you with everything. You can find the complete documentation at `http://dev.mysql.com/doc/mysql/en/Date_and_time_functions.html`.

The range of available functions further demonstrates the real power of a database like MySQL: not only can you retrieve the data you want, when you want, but also SQL empowers you to manipulate data, both when entering records into a database and when retrieving information already stored. You saw in Chapter 8 how the `SHA1()` function permanently encrypted the password as it was entered into the `users` table. Arguably more useful, though, is the ability to perform calculations on records inside the database without permanently affecting the underlying data. A good example of this is working with dates.

Using dates in calculations

Earlier in the chapter, you saw that the MySQL function `NOW()` creates a MySQL timestamp, which contains both the current date and time. The related function `CURDATE()` returns the current date without the time. If you still have MySQL Monitor open, you can see the values returned by both functions by typing the following commands:

```
SELECT NOW();
SELECT CURDATE();
```

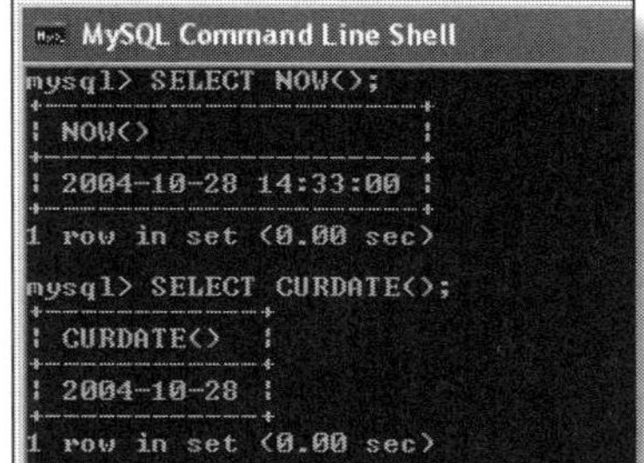

You should see the current date and time, followed by just the current date, as shown alongside.

Even though NOW() and CURDATE() are functions, they can also be passed to other functions. So, for instance, if you want to know what month it is, you could ask MySQL to tell you with the following command:

```
SELECT MONTHNAME(NOW());
```

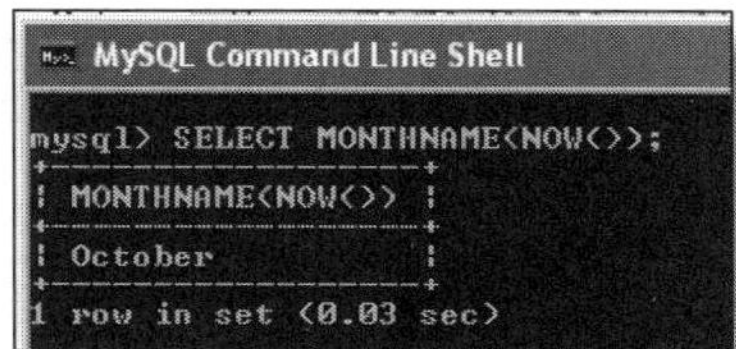

The result is fairly predictable—it displays the name of the current month, as shown.

As you may have gathered from these examples, you can use SELECT *to display the results of calculations onscreen in MySQL Monitor. It is of little practical value other than for testing when you are designing a SQL query. It also makes illustrating a book like this a lot easier!*

Table 11-4 shows some of the more useful date-part and time-part functions available in MySQL.

Table 11-4. Useful MySQL functions for extracting parts of dates and times

Function	Use
YEAR()	Extracts the year from a date as a four-digit number. The valid range is 1000 to 9999.
QUARTER()	Returns a number from 1 to 4, indicating the quarter of the year, with January to March being Quarter 1, and so on.
MONTH()	Extracts the month as a numeric value from 1 to 12.
MONTHNAME()	Extracts the month as a string (full month name).
DAYOFMONTH()	Extracts the day of the month as a numeric value from 1 to 31.
DAYNAME()	Extracts the weekday name (full weekday name).
HOUR()	Extracts the hour from a time or datetime value.
MINUTE()	Extracts the minutes from a time or datetime value.
SECOND()	Extracts the seconds from a time or datetime value.

One implication of this is that you could write SQL queries to format your dates, avoiding the need to do it in PHP, although it would probably be more efficient to use the MySQL DATE_FORMAT() function. Far more useful is the ability to use dates for extracting different sorts of information.

> DATE_FORMAT() *uses specifiers in a similar way to the PHP* date() *and* strftime() *functions. See* http://dev.mysql.com/doc/mysql/en/Date_and_time_functions.html#IDX1418.

Extracting records based on dates

I have created a simple database table called singers, which contains the names and birth dates of some of my favorite singers. You can either use the download files to create the same table or use a similar table of your own—anything that includes a DATE column type is fine.

1. Copy singers.sql from the download files for this chapter to the top level of your main C drive on Windows or your home folder on a Mac. It doesn't matter if MySQL Monitor is currently open, but if it is, you need to open a *new* Command Prompt or Terminal window to load the contents of singers.sql. You cannot use the Windows Essentials MySQL Command Line Client for the first three steps; it must be an ordinary Command Prompt window.
2. If you're using Windows Essentials 4.1.8 or later, and accepted the option to include the bin folder in your Windows PATH, skip to step 3. Mac users can also skip to step 3.

   If the MySQL bin folder is not in your Windows PATH, change directory to the bin folder. For Windows Essentials, type the following:

   ```
   cd \program files\mysql\mysql server 4.1\bin
   ```

   If you're running MySQL 3.23 or 4.0, use this command instead:

   ```
   cd \mysql\bin
   ```

3. Load the contents of singers.sql. In Windows, use the following command:

   ```
   mysql -u root -p phpflash < c:\singers.sql
   ```

   On a Mac, simply type

   ```
   mysql -u root -p phpflash < singers.sql
   ```

   Enter your MySQL root password when prompted. As long as singers.sql is in the location I suggested, the new table should be created and fully populated.

> *This is one method of restoring a database from a backup. If you open* `singers.sql` *in a text editor, you will see it contains all the necessary SQL commands to create the table and insert the records. It was created with a backup program called* `mysqldump`*, although I removed some of the* `mysql-dump` *commands to make the file compatible with older versions of MySQL. Backing up with* `mysqldump` *and restoring data are described in Appendix E.*

4. Launch MySQL Monitor (on Windows, you can use the MySQL Command Line Client from now on), and switch to the phpflash database by typing

```
use phpflash
```

5. First, take a look at the contents of the new table. Type

```
SELECT * FROM singers;
```

You should see the table shown here (the selection will give you a clue as to just how ancient I am):

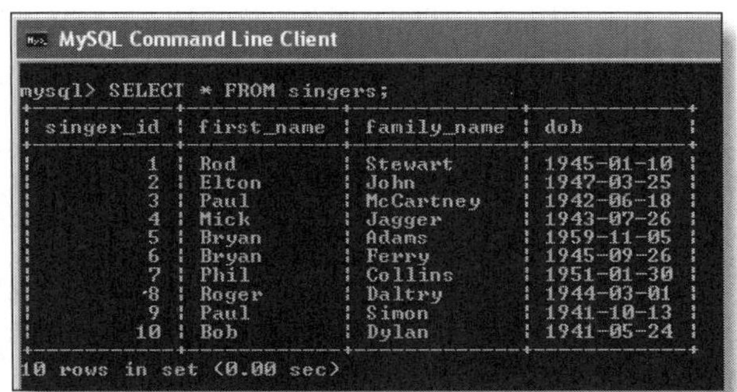

MySQL Command Line Client

```
mysql> SELECT * FROM singers;
+-----------+------------+-------------+------------+
| singer_id | first_name | family_name | dob        |
+-----------+------------+-------------+------------+
|         1 | Rod        | Stewart     | 1945-01-10 |
|         2 | Elton      | John        | 1947-03-25 |
|         3 | Paul       | McCartney   | 1942-06-18 |
|         4 | Mick       | Jagger      | 1943-07-26 |
|         5 | Bryan      | Adams       | 1959-11-05 |
|         6 | Bryan      | Ferry       | 1945-09-26 |
|         7 | Phil       | Collins     | 1951-01-30 |
|         8 | Roger      | Daltry      | 1944-03-01 |
|         9 | Paul       | Simon       | 1941-10-13 |
|        10 | Bob        | Dylan       | 1941-05-24 |
+-----------+------------+-------------+------------+
10 rows in set (0.00 sec)
```

The contents are fairly obvious: singer_id, first_name, family_name, and dob (date of birth). If you opened a separate Command Prompt to load the table, you can now safely close it, but keep MySQL Monitor open.

6. Now try the following SQL query:

```
SELECT first_name, family_name, dob FROM singers
WHERE MONTHNAME(dob) LIKE 'Jan%';
```

You should get the results shown: Rod Stewart and Phil Collins were both born in January.

MySQL Command Line Client

```
mysql> SELECT first_name, family_name, dob FROM singers
    -> WHERE MONTHNAME(dob) LIKE 'Jan%';
+------------+-------------+------------+
| first_name | family_name | dob        |
+------------+-------------+------------+
| Rod        | Stewart     | 1945-01-10 |
| Phil       | Collins     | 1951-01-30 |
+------------+-------------+------------+
2 rows in set (0.00 sec)

mysql> _
```

You would get the same result by rephrasing the query like this (note that the equality operator in SQL is a single equal sign, not a double one as in PHP and ActionScript):

```
SELECT first_name, family_name, dob FROM singers
WHERE MONTH(dob) = 1;
```

7. Rod Stewart was born in 1945. To see if anyone else in the list was born the same year, you could use the following query:

```
SELECT first_name, family_name, dob FROM singers
WHERE YEAR(dob) = 1945;
```

You would discover that Bryan Ferry was also born in 1945.

8. But what if you didn't know which year Rod Stewart was born in? With MySQL 4.1 and above, you could still find everyone born in the same year by using the following query:

```
SELECT first_name, family_name, dob FROM singers
WHERE YEAR(dob) = (SELECT YEAR(dob) FROM singers
WHERE first_name = 'Rod' AND family_name = 'Stewart');
```

This is an important addition to MySQL 4.1 called a **subquery** (or **subselect**). Basically, it's two SELECT queries in one. What happens is that MySQL first handles the subquery (and finds out the year Rod Stewart was born in), and then it uses the result to find everyone who was born in the same year. The subquery is enclosed in parentheses, so MySQL knows to treat it as a single entity.

> *Subqueries are not available in MySQL 3.23 or 4.0. To do this type of calculation in those versions of MySQL, you would normally have to do two separate queries, and store the result of the first in a PHP variable for use in the second query. To learn more about subqueries, see the online documentation at* `http://dev.mysql.com/doc/mysql/en/Subqueries.html`*. The documentation includes advice on how to rewrite subqueries to work with earlier versions of MySQL.*

9. Say you wanted to know who was born in spring and summer. A simple way of doing this would be to use QUARTER() as follows:

```
SELECT first_name, family_name, dob FROM singers
WHERE QUARTER(dob) IN (2,3);
```

This produces the following result:

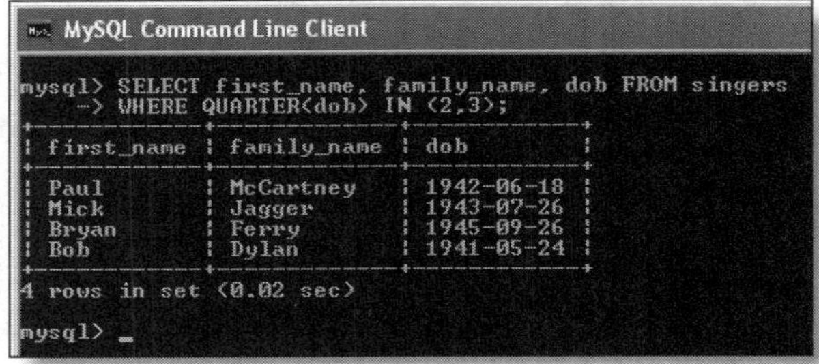

This introduces you to a new comparison operator, IN. Its meaning is very intuitive—it simply looks for at least one match in a comma-delimited list inside parentheses. QUARTER() returns a number from 1 to 4, indicating which quarter of the year a date falls in. The conditional clause—`WHERE QUARTER(dob) IN (2,3)`—is looking for records where the month falls in the second or third quarter. In other words, it will match any month between April and September inclusive.

That gives you just a brief glimpse of the way you can use MySQL date functions to retrieve data easily according to temporal criteria. With a little more calculation, you can also work out people's ages.

Calculating people's ages in MySQL

Calculating someone's age is a relatively simple calculation, but it's complicated by the fact that the result depends on whether that person's birthday has already passed. It makes a difference of one year to the calculation. A combination of date and string functions makes the calculation straightforward in MySQL. I'll continue using the `singers` table, so first let's work out the theory of what it is you need to ask the database.

1. In an ideal world, the query would be something like this:

   ```
   SELECT first_name, family_name, age FROM singers;
   ```

2. The problem is that you don't have an age column. Even if you did, it would need constant updating. The only answer is to calculate the result. You could do it in PHP, but MySQL can do the calculations for you quickly and efficiently. The solution is to devise a calculation that works out age and assign age to it as an alias. As the name suggests, an alias is just a way of giving a new identity to a piece of code, usually to make it easier to handle. An alias is identified by the keyword `AS`, so the ideal query from step 1 now becomes

   ```
   SELECT first_name, family_name, calculation AS age FROM singers;
   ```

3. So how do you calculate a person's age? The first part is easy: deduct the year of birth from the current year. `YEAR(CURDATE())` gives you the current year, and `YEAR(dob)` gives you the year of birth. So the query now looks like this:

   ```
   SELECT first_name, family_name,
   YEAR(CURDATE()) - YEAR(dob) AS age
   FROM singers;
   ```

4. If you test that in MySQL Monitor, you will get a result, as shown here:

   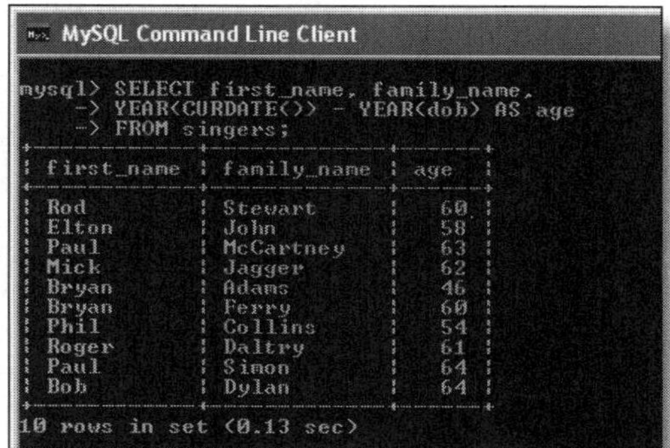

   As you can see, MySQL has used the alias as a new column name. That means you can use the alias age to access the results in PHP, and then send them on to your Flash movie. This is pretty satisfactory, except for one thing: depending on the time of year, some of the ages may be inaccurate. I ran this query in mid-January 2005, just before sending this book to the printer. If you look back at step 6 of the previous exercise, you'll see that the only two with birthdays in January are Rod Stewart and Phil Collins—and Phil's birthday is right at the end of the month.

5. If you conduct the calculation before the person's birthday, the figure in the age column will be one too many. Fortunately, a less-than comparison in MySQL evaluates to 1 if it's true and to 0 if it's false. So you need a way of comparing the month and date of birth with the current month and date. Working with the month and date separately would result in a complex calculation, but MySQL has a convenient string function called `RIGHT()`, which does the trick.

`RIGHT()` takes two parameters: a string, and the number of characters you want to select from the end of the string. `RIGHT('2004-10-28', 5)` returns `10-28`—in other words, the month and the date. `RIGHT('2005-01-01', 5)` also returns the month and date—they are always the last five characters of a date. This is where MySQL's insistence on leading zeros pays off. Now you can work out the birthday conundrum:

```
SELECT first_name, family_name,
(YEAR(CURDATE()) - YEAR(dob))
- (RIGHT(CURDATE(), 5) < RIGHT(dob, 5)) AS age
FROM singers;
```

The results you get will depend on the current date, but take a close look at the results after adding the third line to the SQL query:

Everybody except Rod Stewart is now a year younger, because their birthdays all come later in the year.

```
MySQL Command Line Client

mysql> SELECT first_name, family_name,
    -> (YEAR(CURDATE()) - YEAR(dob))
    -> - (RIGHT(CURDATE(), 5) < RIGHT(dob, 5)) AS age
    -> FROM singers;
+------------+-------------+------+
| first_name | family_name | age  |
+------------+-------------+------+
| Rod        | Stewart     |   60 |
| Elton      | John        |   57 |
| Paul       | McCartney   |   62 |
| Mick       | Jagger      |   61 |
| Bryan      | Adams       |   45 |
| Bryan      | Ferry       |   59 |
| Phil       | Collins     |   53 |
| Roger      | Daltry      |   60 |
| Paul       | Simon       |   63 |
| Bob        | Dylan       |   63 |
+------------+-------------+------+
10 rows in set (0.03 sec)
```

6. Of course, to make the results look a bit tidier, you can add an `ORDER BY` clause, using the dob column to order the singers with the oldest first:

```
MySQL Command Line Client

mysql> SELECT first_name, family_name,
    -> (YEAR(CURDATE()) - YEAR(dob))
    -> - (RIGHT(CURDATE(), 5) < RIGHT(dob, 5)) AS age
    -> FROM singers
    -> ORDER BY dob;
+------------+-------------+------+
| first_name | family_name | age  |
+------------+-------------+------+
| Bob        | Dylan       |   63 |
| Paul       | Simon       |   63 |
| Paul       | McCartney   |   62 |
| Mick       | Jagger      |   61 |
| Roger      | Daltry      |   60 |
| Rod        | Stewart     |   60 |
| Bryan      | Ferry       |   59 |
| Elton      | John        |   57 |
| Phil       | Collins     |   53 |
| Bryan      | Adams       |   45 |
+------------+-------------+------+
10 rows in set (0.01 sec)
```

Appropriately enough, Bob Dylan has come to the top of the list. The times, they may be a-changin', but the dates in the database remain fixed, and by using MySQL time calculations, you can always get a dynamic result from static data. Using a calculation like this in a SQL query and assigning it to an alias does not physically create a new column in your database table. The alias is stored in temporary memory only for as long as it takes to perform the calculation and return the result. When building a Flash/PHP application, you would store a query like this in your PHP script, so each time the query is run, **without changing a single line of code, every singer's age will automatically update on his birthday**.

Of course, calculating the ages of aging rock stars is nothing more than a bit of harmless fun. However, if you're creating an application that needs to calculate such things as retirement dates, maternity leave, and so on, this type of calculation becomes invaluable.

Finding and creating records based on temporal criteria

If you are running a news site, blog, or anything else with time-sensitive material, you may want to avoid displaying material that is more than, say, three months old. Equally, if you are running a subscription service, you may want to fix a future expiration or renewal date. MySQL can do that very easily with two related functions: `DATE_SUB()` and `DATE_ADD()`. The basic syntax for both functions is the same:

```
DATE_SUB(date, INTERVAL length period)
DATE_ADD(date, INTERVAL length period)
```

Both functions return a new *date* based on the date value passed as the first argument. `INTERVAL` is a fixed keyword, *`length`* indicates the length of the interval to be added or subtracted, and *`period`* indicates the type of timescale involved. It sounds complicated, but it is much easier to understand when you see an example.

Let's say you want to register a user's subscription to expire automatically in one year. As part of your `INSERT` statement, you could fix the value of an `expire_date` column as follows:

```
INSERT INTO users (expire_date, other_columns...)
VALUES (DATE_ADD(CURDATE(), INTERVAL 1 YEAR), other_values...)
```

`CURDATE()` gets the current date, and `INTERVAL 1 YEAR` adds one year—it couldn't be much simpler.

> *You may think the lack of a semicolon at the end of this example is a printing error. It's not. You only need a semicolon at the end of a SQL query when working directly in MySQL Monitor.*

You might also decide to send a renewal reminder to subscribers two months before their subscription runs out. To do that, you would use a query similar to this:

```
SELECT * FROM users
WHERE expire_date = DATE_SUB(expire_date, INTERVAL 2 MONTH)
```

The important thing to note here is that the *`period`* `MONTH` is fixed; you do not make it plural because *`length`* is greater than 1. Table 11-5 lists some of the main period values that can be used with `DATE_SUB()` and `DATE_ADD()`, as well as the expected format of *`length`*.

Table 11-5. The main interval types used with DATE_SUB() and DATE_ADD()

Period	Meaning	Length format
HOUR	Hours	Number
DAY	Days	Number
WEEK	Weeks	Number
MONTH	Months	Number
YEAR	Years	Number
DAY_HOUR	Days and hours	String ('DD hh')
YEAR_MONTH	Years and months	String ('YY-MM')

You can find the full list of available interval types and expected formats in the online documentation at http://dev.mysql.com/doc/mysql/en/Date_and_time_functions.html#IDX1416.

If you still have MySQL Monitor open, run the following SQL query to find out which of the golden oldies in the singers list is still younger than 60:

```
SELECT first_name, family_name FROM singers
WHERE DATE_ADD(dob, INTERVAL 60 YEAR) > CURDATE()
ORDER BY dob;
```

The calculation is simple: add 60 years to the date of birth, and see if the result is less than the current date. The query then uses the dob column to sort the results. The default for ORDER BY is ascending order (smallest number first), so the earlier someone was born, the higher he comes up the list. This is the result I got, although by the time you read this, Bryan Ferry and Elton John may no longer be on the list (but Jethro Tull got it wrong—you're *never* too old to rock 'n' roll).

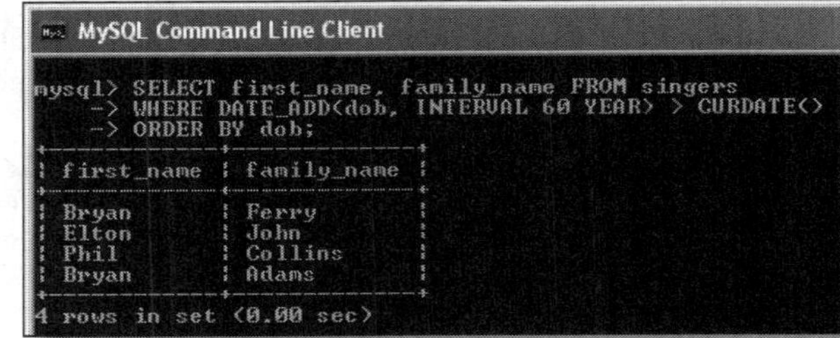

Again, this trip down memory lane is just to demonstrate how time calculations work in MySQL. The same principles can be applied to retrieving orders between certain dates, looking up hotel or airline bookings, and so on. The possibilities are limitless.

Handling dates in user input

One of the biggest problems with online applications is dealing with user input. When everything is under your own control, you can make sure that data to be input into a database and queries are formulated in the correct manner. However, to be truly interactive, most applications have to rely at some point or other on user input. The feedback form and user registration applications earlier in the book deployed various strategies to deal with text input and email addresses. You now need a strategy to cope with dates so that they are in the right format for presentation to MySQL, but the myriad formats used by humans make this a potential nightmare.

Formatting dates from text input

If you can rely on users adhering to a common format, such as MM/DD/YYYY, you can use ActionScript or PHP to convert the input to MySQL's required format, YYYY-MM-DD. For instance, the following ActionScript function would do it for you:

```
function date2MySQL(input:String):String {
  var theDate:Array = input.split("/");
  return theDate[2]+"-"+theDate[0]+"-"+theDate[1];
}
```

This function uses the String.split() method to convert the user input into an array, and it rearranges the year, month, and day elements in the right order with hyphens before returning the result. It's simple, and it works well, as shown here (you can test it for yourself with date2MySQL.fla in the download files for this chapter).

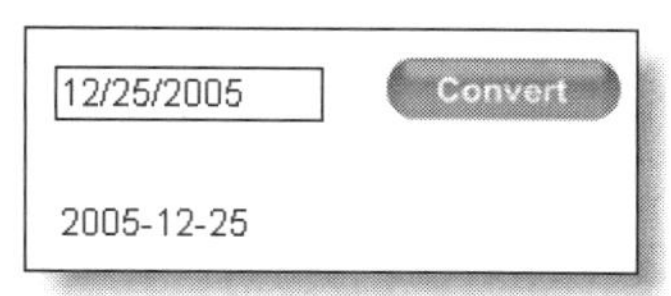

The problem is that it's impossible to guarantee users will adhere to the agreed format. Let's say a European enters the same date, but in the customary European format. The function still works, as shown, but it has now created an out-of-range value for the month. When this happens, MySQL does not assume a future date (which you wouldn't want anyway); it treats the date as 0000-00-00.

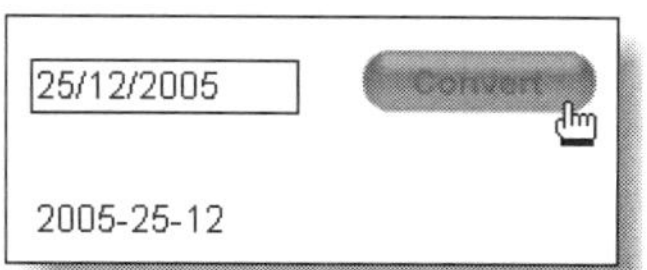

Another possibility is that an enthusiastic person knows you're using MySQL and tries to be "helpful" by using the MySQL format. You get an even more unusable result. So much for being helpful . . .

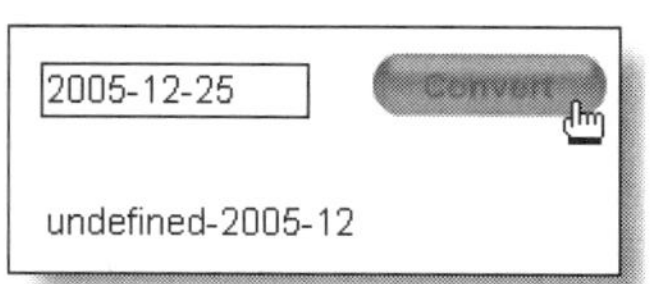

Of course, you could make the date2MySQL() function more robust by building in a series of conditional clauses to test the validity of the user input, but that involves a lot of coding. And even when you've finished, there's another problem: MySQL doesn't test dates for validity; it only tests whether the year, month, and date values are within the acceptable range. Consequently, February 29, 2003, or April 31, 2005, would be accepted without complaint, even though they are impossible dates. The Flash component that you will build shortly gets around this problem by using drop-down menus that are programmed to use only valid dates, but there may be times when you can't implement that sort of solution.

Checking a date's validity with PHP

Fortunately, PHP has a handy little function that checks the validity of dates. It's called checkdate() and it takes three arguments: *month*, *day*, and *year*—in that order. The arguments must be passed to the function as integers. Although PHP's loose typing means that strings will be automatically converted, PHP will generate a warning, which is likely to prevent any Flash movie from being able to retrieve any variables sent back through LoadVars.

In the download files for this chapter, you will find checkdate.fla and checkdate.php, which demonstrate how to use checkdate(). You need to save them in the phpflash/ch11 folder, because that's where the Flash movie will look for the PHP script. The Flash movie consists of an input text field called input_txt, a dynamic text field called output_txt to display the result, and a button called check_btn. The input is sent to the PHP script for checking. If the date is valid, it is formatted for MySQL and displayed in the Flash movie. You may notice in the screenshot alongside that there is no leading zero before the month. This is one area where MySQL allows a little flexibility. Even if you omit leading zeros on the month and date, MySQL will interpret the date correctly and add any necessary zeros when storing the record. Nevertheless, it's preferable to supply the correct format—a strategy that will be adopted in the final part of the chapter.

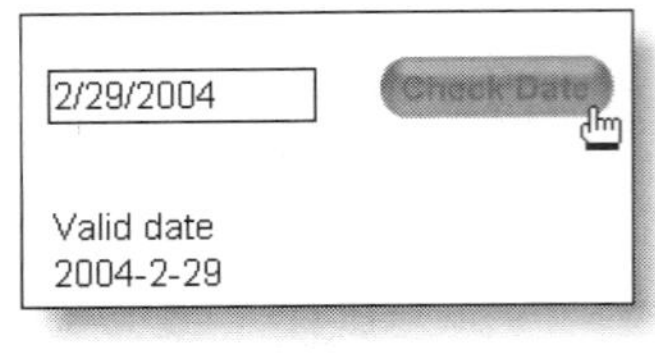

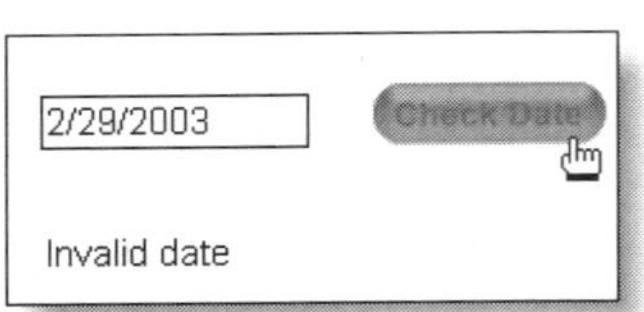

If the date is invalid, no formatting takes place, and a suitable message is displayed. The ActionScript and PHP code for both files is reproduced here for you to study.

ActionScript code for checkdate.fla

There is nothing new in this code. Everything is explained in the inline comments.

```
check_btn.onRelease = function() {
  // clear any previous result from the output text field
  output_txt.text = "";
  // send input text as "theDate" to PHP script for checking
  checkDate.theDate = input_txt.text;
  checkDate.sendAndLoad("http://localhost/phpflash/ch11/
➥ checkdate.php?ck="+ new Date().getTime(),phpResponse);
};
// initialize LoadVars instance to receive the response
var phpResponse:LoadVars = new LoadVars();
phpResponse.onLoad = function() {
  // display the results
  output_txt.text = this.output;
  // if PHP has formatted a valid date, display it
  if (this.formatted != undefined) {
    output_txt.text += "\n" + this.formatted;
  }
  // unset the formatted property to prevent display
  // when an invalid date is returned
  this.formatted = undefined;
};
// initialize LoadVars instance to send date to PHP script
var checkDate:LoadVars = new LoadVars();
```

PHP script for checkdate.php

The main points to look out for here are the way string values are cast to integers and then are passed to the checkdate() function. The relevant sections of code are highlighted in bold.

```
<?php
if (isset($_POST['theDate'])) {
  // split the date into component parts
  $theDate = explode('/',$_POST['theDate']);
  // each date part is a string so must first be cast to an integer
  // before it can be passed to the checkdate() function
  $month = (int) $theDate[0];
  $dayNum = (int) $theDate[1];
  $year = (int) $theDate[2];
  // initialize output string to send back to Flash
  $output = 'output=';
  // check the validity of the date
  // if valid, format for MySQL
  if (checkdate($month,$dayNum,$year)) {
    $output .= urlencode('Valid date');
    $output .= "&formatted=$year-$month-$dayNum";
    }
  else {
    $output .= urlencode('Invalid date');
    }
  // send result back to Flash
  echo $output;
  }
?>
```

The need to **cast** a variable from one type to another is a relatively rare occurrence in PHP. As in ActionScript, casting tells the script interpreter to treat a variable of one datatype as though it were of a different type. Casting is not permanent in either language, unless you assign the cast value to a variable, as has been done here. Consequently, each element of the $theDate array remains a string, but the values held in $month, $dayNum, and $year are integers.

The cast operators in PHP look rather strange. They are enclosed in parentheses and are simply placed in front of the variable to be cast, as shown in the preceding script. Table 11-6 lists the casting operators in PHP and their equivalents in ActionScript.

Table 11-6. Casting operators in PHP and ActionScript

PHP	ActionScript	Casts datatype to
(int)	Number()	Integer (ActionScript does not distinguish between integers and floating-point numbers)
(float)	Number()	Floating-point number (as above for ActionScript)
(string)	String()	String

(Continued)

Table 11-6. Casting operators in PHP and ActionScript *(Continued)*

PHP	ActionScript	Casts datatype to
(bool)	Boolean()	Boolean (true or false)
(array)		Array
(object)		Object

Although the ability to check dates with PHP is undoubtedly useful in many circumstances, the code in checkdate.fla and checkdate.php still has many failings. It involves a round-trip to the server to check the validity of the date, and it has no way of coping with the different ways users might insert dates. Rather than spend a lot of time refining it, I have a better idea: let's create a Flash component that creates only valid dates and formats them ready for MySQL.

Building a Flash date selector for MySQL

The concept of the date selector is quite simple. It is a set of combo boxes that allow users to select a date, which is then transformed into a string in MySQL YYYY-MM-DD format, ready to be inserted into a database or used in a SQL query. Creating combo boxes is easy. What makes this date selector special is that it will only permit users to select valid dates. It does this by changing the number of days displayed for each month, so 31 can never be selected together with April or September. It's also smart enough to know when to allow 29 days in February.

> *The* DateChooser *version 2 component in Flash MX 2004 Professional performs a similar task straight out of the box. Unfortunately, it's very difficult to scale, because it presents a full month at a time like a calendar. It's also available only in the Professional version. This date selector can be built with MX components that are freely available to all. Although the Flash MX UI components weren't included with Flash MX 2004, they can be downloaded free of charge from the Macromedia Exchange site (*www.macromedia.com/cfusion/exchange/index.cfm*) and installed into Flash using the Extension Manager.*

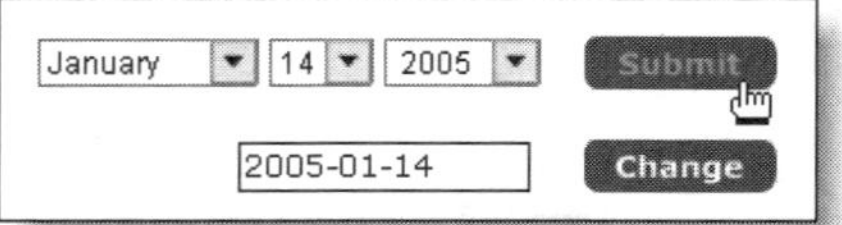

Let's first take a look at the finished component in a testing environment, so you can visualize what it is you're building. As you can see from the screenshot alongside, there are three combo boxes: one each for the month, day of the month and year. When the movie first loads, it automatically displays the current date. If you click the Submit button, the date is displayed in a dynamic text field in MySQL format. (Note that if you open the datehandler.fla file from the download files, the combo boxes will look all squashed on top of each other. This is deliberate. Just test the movie and everything will resize correctly.)

Of course, in a real application the date would be sent to a PHP script to interact with MySQL. The purpose of displaying it in a dynamic text field is to verify that the correct date is being formatted appropriately. The other reason for using a dynamic text field is so that you can change the date, click the Change button, and see the result reflected in the combo boxes. There are no checks on the input to the dynamic text field, because the purpose is to test how the date selector reacts to incoming data from MySQL. The assumption is that, if you have taken care to ensure that only valid dates are entered in the first place, you will be dealing only with valid output from your database.

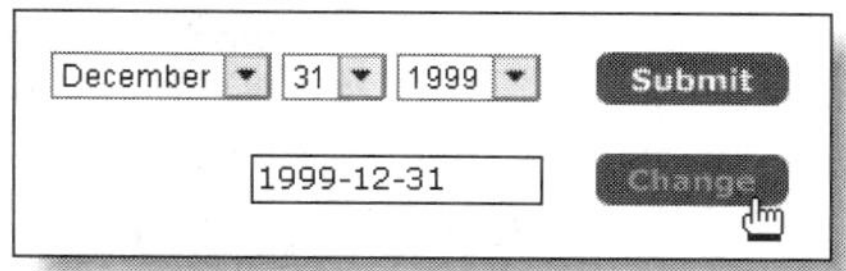

Now that you've seen what the goal is, let's get building. The component is built entirely in Flash and requires no PHP scripting, although the finished component is designed to send and receive data to MySQL through PHP.

Building the test environment

The test environment is very simple. It consists of two buttons and a dynamic text area.

1. Open a new Flash document and save it as `datehandler.fla`.
2. Place two buttons on the stage, one with an instance name of submit_btn and the other with an instance name of change_btn.
3. Insert a dynamic text field and give it an instance name of newDate_txt.
4. On the timeline, insert a new layer and name it actions. As always, the actions layer should be on top, and it's a good idea to lock it, to prevent accidentally placing graphic elements on it. Your document should look similar to Figure 11-7. You can also find it in the download files as `datehandler01.fla`.

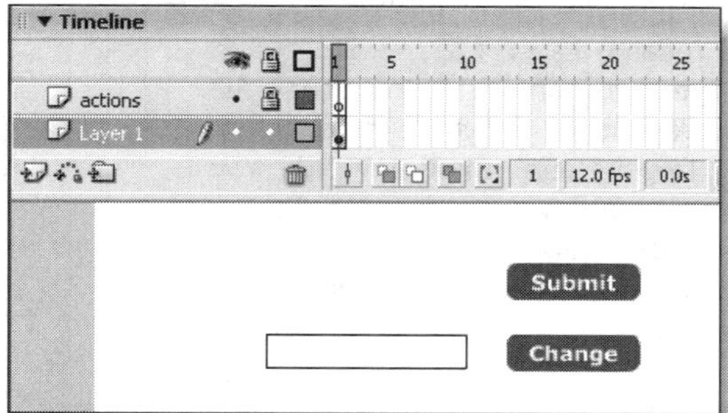

Figure 11-7. The testing environment for the date selector

Building the selector interface

For the selector interface, I decided to use the Flash MX combo box components as in previous applications, partly because they are lighter and easier to code than the version 2 components in MX 2004, and also because of anticipated changes to the version 2 architecture. Choose whichever components you find most convenient—the main functionality lies in the date-handling functions, not in the choice of Flash components.

1. Continue working with the previous file or open `datehandler01.fla` from the download files for this chapter. Choose Insert ➤ New Symbol (*CTRL+F8/⌘+F8*) and create a new movie clip symbol named dateSelector.

2. Open the Components panel (*CTRL+F7/⌘+F7*) and expand the Flash MX UI Components menu. Drag an instance of the `ComboBox` component into the Symbol editing window.

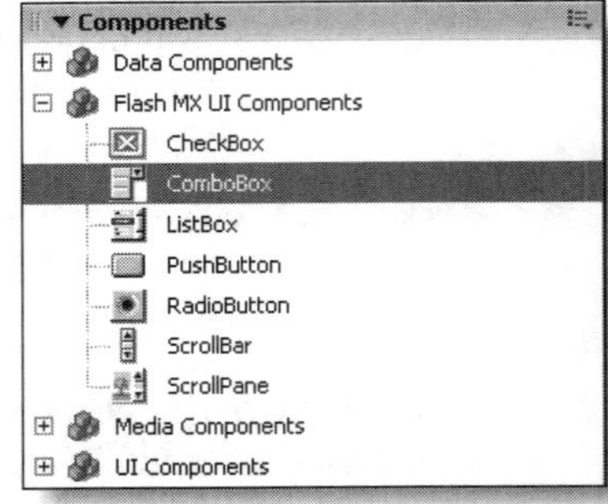

3. Use the Property inspector to position the component at X:0, Y:0. This will put the registration point of the new movie clip at the top left so that you can position it easily in any application. Give the combo box an instance name of month_cb.

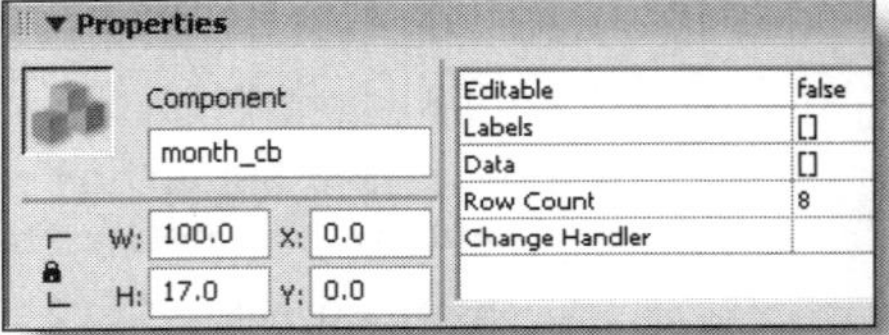

4. Drag two more `ComboBox` components into the Symbol editing window. Locate the first at X:90, Y:0, and give it an instance name of date_cb. This will make it overlap the first combo box, but that's not important, because ActionScript will later be used to adjust the widths. Locate the last combo box at X:135, Y:0, and give it an instance name of year_cb. It will also overlap the previous instance.

5. In the timeline, rename Layer 1 as combo boxes. Insert another layer and name it actions. Lock the actions layer. The layout in the Symbol editing window should look like the screenshot alongside. You can also compare your version with `datehandler02.fla` from the download files. Leave the Symbol editing window open, because that's where you'll continue working.

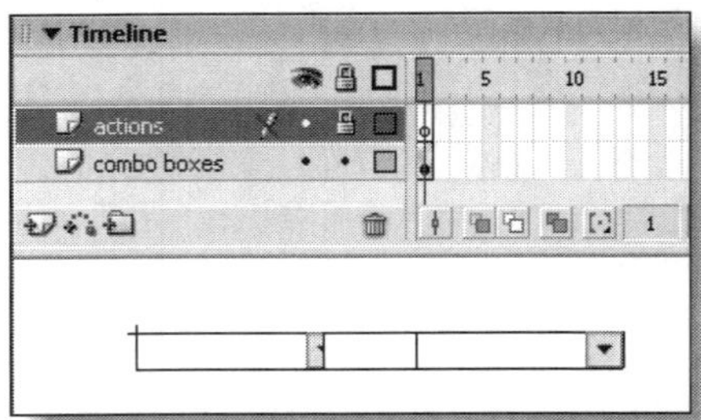

Scripting the date selector

The script needs to do the following things:

- Populate the combo boxes with the names of the months, the days in each month, and a range of years.
- Calculate how many days to display, depending on the selected month.
- Recognize when a leap year is selected, and change the number of days displayed in February accordingly.

- Set the month, day of the month, and year according to the current date when first loaded.
- Reset the month, day of the month, and year in response to external input.
- Output the date to the text field in MySQL YYYY-MM-DD format.
- Adjust the width of the combo boxes.

Because you are going to convert the movie clip into a Flash component, all the scripting will be done inside the dateSelector movie clip, and not on the main timeline.

1. With the dateSelector movie clip still in edit mode, highlight the actions layer and open the Actions panel (*F9*). Alternatively, open datehandler02.fla, open the Library panel (*CTRL+L*/*⌘+L*), and double-click the dateSelector movie clip to enter the edit window. If you don't want to type out all the code, open datehandler.fla instead and just read along.
2. First of all, you need to initialize some variables and populate the month_cb combo box so that you can monitor progress as you go along. Insert the following code in the Actions panel:

```
// initialize variables
var YEARS_BEFORE:Number = 2;
var YEARS_AFTER:Number = 8;
// get today's date and its constituent parts
var today:Date = new Date();
var thisMonth:Number = today.getMonth();
var thisDate:Number = today.getDate();
var thisYear:Number = today.getFullYear();
// populate the months combo box
var monthList:Array = new Array("January", "February", "March",
➥ "April", "May", "June", "July", "August", "September", "October",
➥ "November", "December");
for (var i = 0; i<monthList.length; i++) {
  month_cb.addItemAt(i, monthList[i], i+1);
}
// make year_cb editable
year_cb.setEditable(true);
// resize the combo boxes
month_cb.setSize(85);
date_cb.setSize(40);
year_cb.setSize(60);
```

   The inline comments explain what each section does, although the first two variables probably need a little more explanation. YEARS_BEFORE and YEARS_AFTER are constants that determine how many years to display in the year_cb combo box before and after the current year.

   The constituent parts of the current date are accessed using the getMonth(), getDate(), and getFullYear() methods of the Date object.

The loop to populate the months combo box uses the addItemAt() method, which takes three arguments:

- The position at which the item is to be added in the list
- The label that appears in the display
- The value of the item

By using the variable i as a counter, this creates a list in the combo box with January displayed in the first position (0), but with a value of 1 (i+1). This means that the months have the more human-understandable values of 1 through 12, ready for sending to MySQL. In other parts of the script, months will still need to be referred to using ActionScript's zero-based method of counting. This is perhaps one of the most difficult parts of working with dates: the need to go back and forth between the two counting systems.

The year_cb combo box is made editable, to enable users to enter a year outside the displayed range. The width of the combo boxes is reset by using the setSize() method, which takes just one argument for a ComboBox component: the width in pixels.

Pin the script in the Actions panel, because you will come back frequently to add more code.

3. Now that you have resized the combo boxes and you have some content in one of them, this is a good opportunity to see how things are going. Close the Actions panel and exit the Symbol editing window by clicking Scene 1 to return to the main stage. Drag an instance of the dateSelector from the Library and position it alongside the Submit button on Layer 1. As the screenshot shows, getting the right position visually is a little tricky, because Flash displays the last combo box at its full width of 100 pixels instead of the 60 pixels assigned by ActionScript. The total width of the date selector when it's displayed in a SWF will be 185 pixels, so place it 200 pixels or so to the left of the Submit button. Give the dateSelector movie clip an instance name of dateSelector_mc.

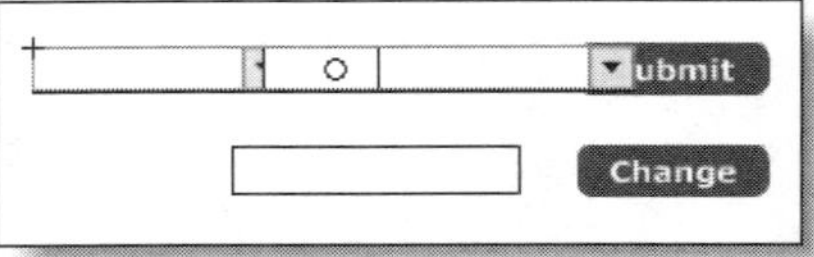

4. Test the movie, and you should see the combo boxes nicely slimmed down. If you click the arrow to the side of the months combo box, you will see that all 12 months have been displayed, with the names obtained from the monthList array.

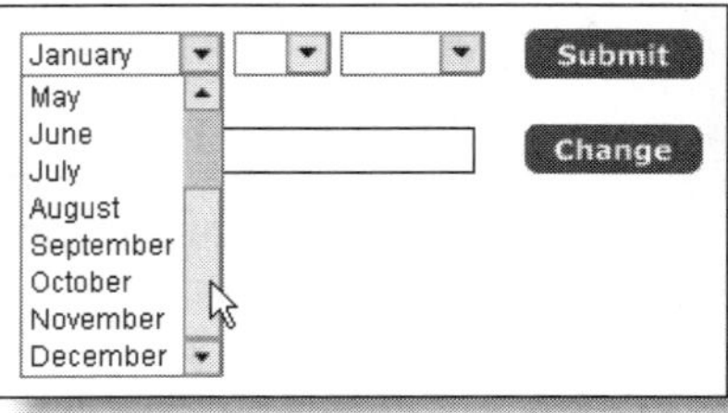

5. Back on the main stage, double-click the dateSelector_mc movie clip to enter edit mode. Open the Actions panel and make sure you're back in the script you entered in step 2 (it should open automatically on the same script if you pinned it earlier). Now it's time to start building some functions. Good ActionScript coding practice says these should come at the start of the script, so enter the following *above* the existing code:

```
function populateYear(yr:Number):Void {
  // this function populates the year combo box
  // initialize variables to set first year
  // and calculate number of years in range
```

```
  var startYear:Number;
  var numYears:Number;
  if (thisYear-yr>YEARS_BEFORE) {
    startYear = yr;
    numYears = thisYear-startYear+YEARS_AFTER;
  } else {
    startYear = thisYear-YEARS_BEFORE;
    if (yr>thisYear+YEARS_AFTER) {
      numYears = yr-thisYear+YEARS_BEFORE+1;
    } else {
      numYears = YEARS_BEFORE+YEARS_AFTER;
    }
  } // clear any existing display and
  // populate with the appropriate number of years
  year_cb.removeAll();
  for (var i:Number = 0; i<numYears; i++) {
    year_cb.addItemAt(i, startYear+i, startYear+i);
  }
  // set value to selected year
  year_cb.setValue(yr);
}
```

As its name suggests, populateYear() populates the year_cb combo box with a range of years. It takes one argument: a number representing the year to be displayed when the function is called. For a combo box to be of any use, it needs to display a range of values. The YEARS_BEFORE constant determines how many years before the current one should be displayed. I have chosen 2, but you can change this to suit your own needs. Because the year_cb has been made editable, users will be able to enter any year, so there is no need to have an extensive range. The constant YEARS_AFTER has been set at 8, giving an overall range of ten years.

The function begins by determining the first year of the range to display, as well as the total number of years in the range. If the year passed to the function is more than two years ago, it becomes the start of the range, identified by the variable startYear, and the total number of years to be displayed is the result of thisYear - startYear + YEARS_AFTER. So, if the year passed to the function is 1999, startYear will also be 1999. Deducting 1999 from thisYear calculates how many iterations are needed in addition to the eight for YEARS_AFTER. It doesn't matter when startYear is—the end of the range will always be the current year plus YEARS_AFTER. Similar calculations are made to work out the number of iterations required if the year passed to the function is within the current range or later. If the year passed to the function is later than the current range, it becomes the last year to be displayed. Otherwise, the standard range of YEARS_BEFORE + YEARS_AFTER is displayed.

Before the loop that populates the year_cb combo box is run, any existing range of years is deleted, to avoid displaying items from any previous list that may have been longer than the standard range.

Finally, the function uses the year passed to it as an argument to set the display in the combo box. The setValue() method is used rather than setSelectedIndex(), because year_cb is editable.

6. Making year_cb editable is more convenient, but it introduces the problem of invalid input. Unfortunately, the `restrict` property does not work with MX UI components, so it's necessary to build a custom function called `validateYear()`. The code goes immediately after the function you just entered.

```
function validateYear(yearInput:String):Boolean {
  // this checks the validity of input in the editable year combo box
  // first make sure only numerals are used
  for (var i:Number = 0; i<yearInput.length; i++) {
    if (yearInput.charCodeAt(i)<48 || yearInput.charCodeAt(i)>57) {
      return false;
    }
  }
  // then check to see if the year is within the MySQL range
  if (Number(yearInput)<1000 || Number(yearInput)>9999) {
    return false;
  } else {
    return true;
  }
}
```

This function takes a single argument, a string that is tested to see if it contains anything other than numbers 0 through 9. This is done by looping through every character and checking its character code with the `String.charCodeAt()` method—48 through 57 are the computer character codes for numbers. If the string contains only numbers, it's then tested to see whether it falls within MySQL's acceptable range of years. If the string fails either test, the function returns `false`; otherwise, it returns `true`.

7. It's a good idea to check everything's going OK, so add these three lines of code at the very bottom of your ActionScript:

```
// set current date
populateYear(thisYear);
month_cb.setSelectedIndex(thisMonth);
```

This code calls `populateYear()`, using the value stored in `thisYear`, one of the variables set in step 2, and the current month is displayed using `setSelectedIndex()`. The value of `thisMonth` will be 1 less than the current month (because ActionScript counts months from 0), but this is exactly what you want, because combo boxes also count items from 0. If you test the movie now, you should see the current month and year displayed, but the day of the month will still be empty. The year combo box should display a range of ten years.

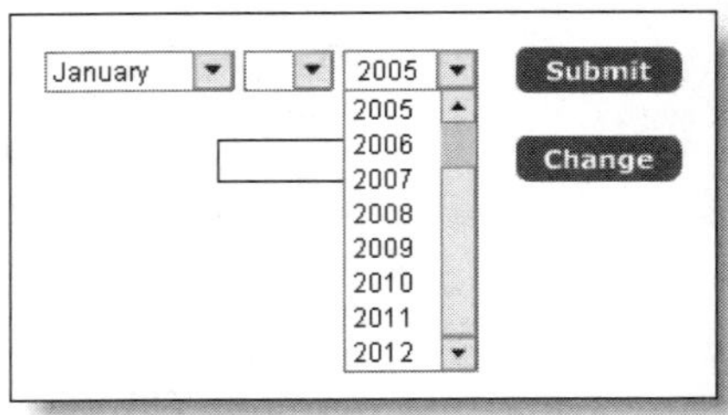

8. Let's get the day of the month sorted out now. Go back to the ActionScript you've been working in, and enter the following code immediately after the `validateYear()` function (around line 42):

```
function populateDate(selectedMonth:Number, selectedDay:Number):Void {
  // calculates how many days to display for the selected month
  var numDays:Number;
  switch (selectedMonth+1) {
  case 2 :
    numDays = calculateLeap();
    break;
  case 4 :
  case 6 :
  case 9 :
  case 11 :
    numDays = 30;
    break;
  default :
    numDays = 31;
  }
  // first clear existing display before populating combo box
  date_cb.removeAll();
  for (var i:Number = 0; i<numDays; i++) {
    date_cb.addItemAt(i, i+1, i+1);
  }
  // if month with fewer days selected, display last day of month
  if (selectedDay>numDays) {
    selectedDay = numDays;
  }
  // set selected day to display
  date_cb.setSelectedIndex(selectedDay-1);
}
```

This new function, `populateDate()`, takes two arguments: the selected month and the selected day. In ActionScript, the month is zero-based, but the date is the actual day of the month. Consequently, 1 is added to the month at the beginning of the function, and 1 is deducted from the date at the end to get the correct index number for the combo box.

The first half of the function is a `switch` statement that sets the number of days in the month. The only month that presents any problems is February, so that calculation is entrusted to a separate function, `calculateLeap()`, which is explained in the next step.

The second half of the function populates the combo box with the days of the month. It always clears any existing content; otherwise, you would still see 31 in November. The first 30 items would be repopulated from scratch, but unless you remove the thirty-first item, it will still be there. This is the same principle you applied earlier to the year combo box.

The last day of the month also causes a problem when you're changing an existing date. Let's say the display currently shows December 31. If you change the month to February, there are no longer 31 items in the list, so `setSelectedIndex()` would try to display a nonexistent item, and the date would jump back to 1. To prevent this from happening, `selectedDay` is reset to the last day of the month whenever the current selection is greater in number than there are days in the month.

9. The calculateLeap() function goes immediately after populateDate() (on about line 70):

```
function calculateLeap():Number {
  // gets year selected in year combo box
  // and calculates whether it's a leap year
  var selYear:Number = year_cb.getValue();
  if (selYear%400 == 0 || (selYear%4 == 0 && selYear%100 != 0)) {
    return 29;
  } else {
    return 28;
  }
}
```

This is a purely mathematical calculation. Leap years occur every four years on years that are wholly divisible by 4. The exception is that years divisible by 100 are not leap years unless they are also divisible by 400. (The year 2000 was a leap year, but 2100 won't be.) So the modulo operator is used first to check if the year is divisible by 400. If so, it's a leap year. If it fails that test, the second half of the conditional statement tests whether the year is divisible by 4, but not by 100. If it is, it's still a leap year. All other years are not. Simple!

10. The final function required for the display is a change handler called setDayNums(). This will be triggered every time the value in month_cb or year_cb is changed. It gets the index of the currently selected date and month, and passes them to populateDate(). Because it's a change handler, it's automatically passed a reference to the component that triggered it. If the _name property of the component is month_cb, populateDate() is always called, and it refreshes date_cb with the correct number of days in the month. If the _name property is year_cb, populateDate() is called only if the month currently displayed is February, because that's the only month that has a different number of days depending on the year. Note that February is identified as 1, because combo box lists are numbered from 0. Insert the following code immediately after calculateLeap() (around line 80):

```
function setDayNums(component):Void {
  // change handler for month_cb and year_cb
  // changes number of days whenever month is changed
  // or if year is changed while February selected
  var selDate:Number = date_cb.getSelectedIndex()+1;
  var selMonth:Number = month_cb.getSelectedIndex();
  if (component._name == "month_cb" || (component._name == "year_cb" &&
➥ selMonth == 1)) {
    populateDate(selMonth, selDate);
  }
}
```

11. To get the display working, you need to set the change handlers for the month and year combo boxes, and populate the current date. Amend the code at the bottom of your ActionScript as follows (the new code is highlighted in bold):

```
year_cb.setSize(60);
// set change handlers for month and year combo boxes
month_cb.setChangeHandler("setDayNums");
year_cb.setChangeHandler("setDayNums");
// set current date
populateYear(thisYear);
month_cb.setSelectedIndex(thisMonth);
populateDate(thisMonth, thisDate);
```

12. Save datehandler.fla and test the movie. The current date should display. Try changing the month and year, and check that each month displays the right number of days. Make sure you also test for leap year. Everything should be working fine, although the Submit and Change buttons have not yet been wired up.

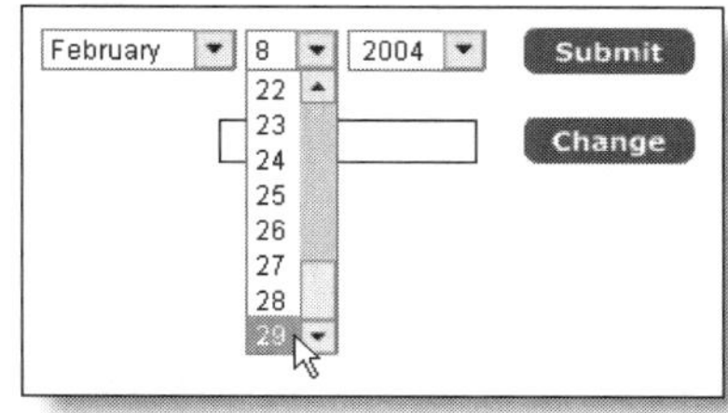

13. You now need two functions to get the date and to set it. Hmm, that sounds like good names for them: getTheDate() and setTheDate(). They are both quite straightforward, so here they are together (they go immediately after setDayNums() on about line 90):

```
function getTheDate():String {
  // this gets the date displayed in the date selector
  // and converts it to a string ready for MySQL
  // first, check the validity of user input in the year
  var yr:String = year_cb.getValue();
  if (!validateYear(yr)) {
    return;
  } else {
    // if the year is valid, get the other values
    // and add leading zeros to the month and day, if needed
    var mon:Number = month_cb.getSelectedIndex()+1;
    var dayOfMon:Number = date_cb.getValue();
    var theMonth:String = mon<10 ? "0"+String(mon) : String(mon);
    var theDay:String = dayOfMon<10 ? "0"+String(dayOfMon) :
➥ String(dayOfMon);
    // return the formatted string
    return yr+"-"+theMonth+"-"+theDay;
  }
}
function setTheDate(MySQLDate:String):Void {
  // this takes a MySQL formatted date, splits it into parts
  // and uses the parts to reset the date selector display
  var theDate:Array = MySQLDate.split("-");
  var theYear:Number = parseInt(theDate[0], 10);
  var theMonth:Number = parseInt(theDate[1], 10)-1;
  var dayIndex:Number = parseInt(theDate[2], 10);
  populateYear(theYear);
  populateDate(theMonth, dayIndex);
  month_cb.setSelectedIndex(theMonth);
}
```

The first function begins by getting the value of the year. Because this is an editable combo box, you need to validate the year by passing it to the validateYear() function created in step 6. If the content is invalid, the function returns nothing. This means that when you call the function, the date will be undefined, and you can use this to display an error message and prevent submission to your PHP script. The rest of the function assembles the values in each combo box and formats them as a string, which the function returns.

The second function, setTheDate(), takes a MySQL-formatted date, splits it into its component parts, and uses the same functions as before to set the combo box display to the new date. Because the incoming date is a string, parseInt() is used to convert the individual parts to numbers to prevent a datatype mismatch. Note that 1 is deducted from the month value, so that it conforms to ActionScript zero-based counting.

14. One final thing and you can test the date selector. You need to wire up the buttons in the test environment. Unpin your script, close the Actions panel, and return to the main timeline by clicking Scene 1. Highlight the actions layer on the main timeline and open the Actions panel. Enter the following code:

```
submit_btn.onRelease = function() {
  // gets the date from the date selector
  // and displays formatted result in newDate_txt
  var theDate = dateSelector_mc.getTheDate();
  newDate_txt.text = theDate;
};
change_btn.onRelease = function() {
  // resets the date selector using input from newDate_txt
  dateSelector_mc.setTheDate(newDate_txt.text);
};
```

Nothing new here—the callback functions access the getTheDate() and setTheDate() functions inside the dateSelector_mc movie clip.

15. Save datehandler.fla and test the movie. If you click the Submit button, the current date will appear in the dynamic text field correctly formatted for MySQL (see Figure 11-8). Make any changes to the date in the text field, click Change, and the new date will be displayed in the date selector, as shown in Figure 11-9. Also try changing the year combo box to an invalid value—when you click Submit, the text field will display undefined (see Figure 11-10). No similar checks are made on input into the dynamic text box, because the purpose of the date selector is to receive data from MySQL, so dates should be correctly formatted in a real environment.

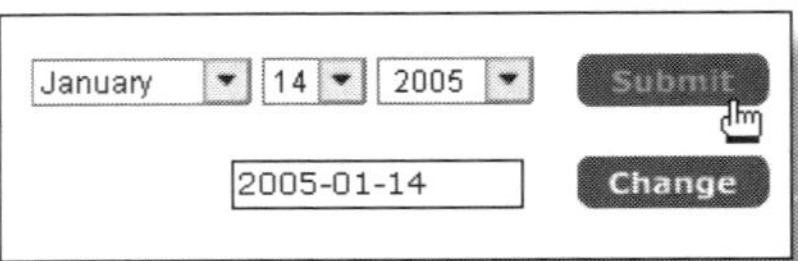

Figure 11-8. The current date is displayed in both the date selector and formatted for MySQL.

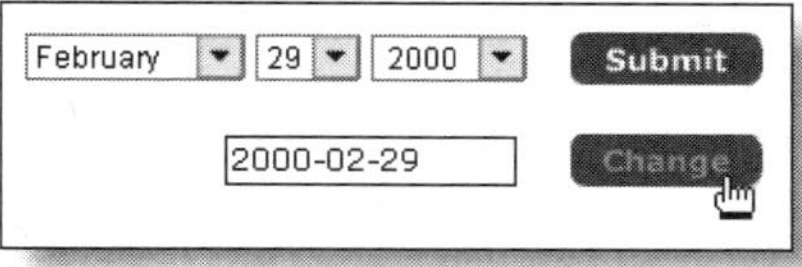

Figure 11-9. The display in the date selector updates when a new date is received.

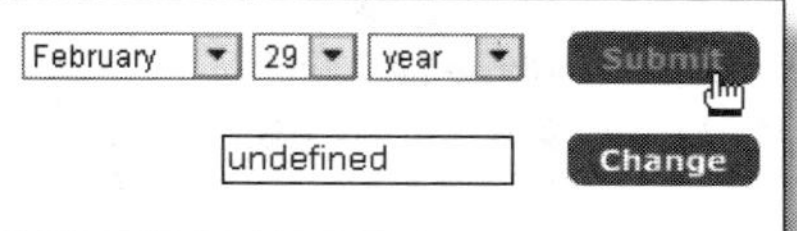

Figure 11-10. Any invalid input into the year combo box returns `undefined`.

16. Now, to make your date selector really useful, turn it into a component. In the Library panel, create a new folder called `dateSelector components`, and drag into it everything connected with the dateSelector except for the movie clip itself—the `ComboBox` and `ScrollBar` components, together with the `Component Skins` and `Core Assets - Developer Only` folders.

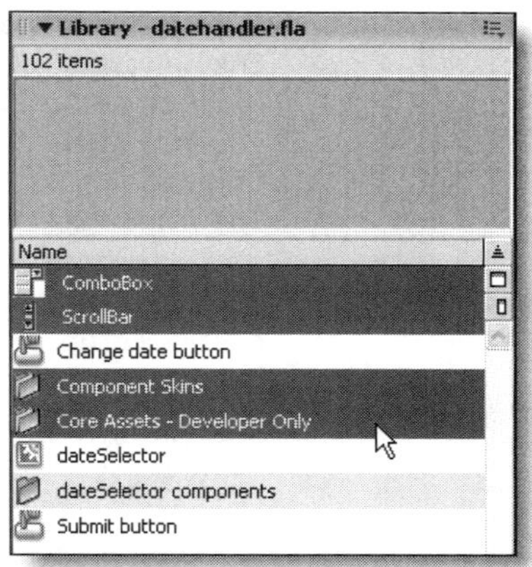

17. Highlight the dateSelector movie clip in the Library panel. Right-click (*CTRL*-click) and select Component Definition. In the dialog box that opens, check the Display in Components panel check box, and give your new component a Tool tip text of MySQL date selector. Click OK. The dateSelector can now be imported into any movie and used straight away by calling the `getTheDate()` and `setTheDate()` functions as in step 14.

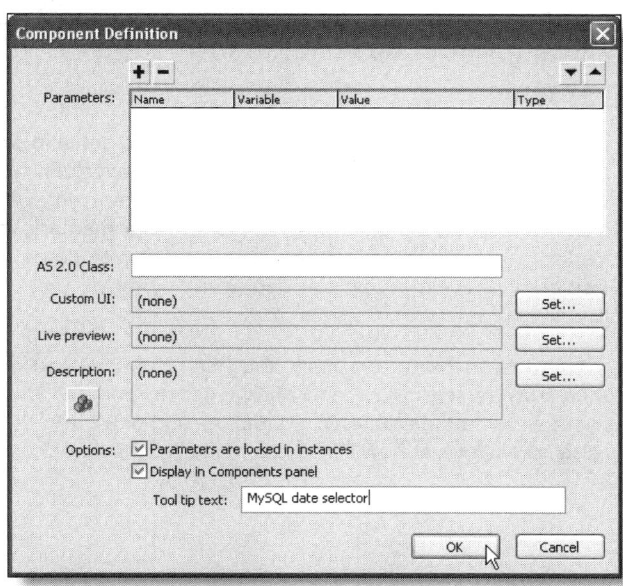

18. Although you can use the date selector component in any of your Flash documents, it won't automatically appear in your Components panel. You will need to import it from the Library of an existing document.

    To make it always available in the Components panel, you need to create a special compressed file known as a SWC file. You need Flash MX 2004 to do this, but it's very easy. Just highlight the component in the Library panel, and right-click (CTRL-click). Select Export SWC File from the contextual window and browse to a folder where you want to save the file. Give it a suitable name and click Save. I saved it as `MySQLDateSelector.swc` in the same folder as my FLA documents.

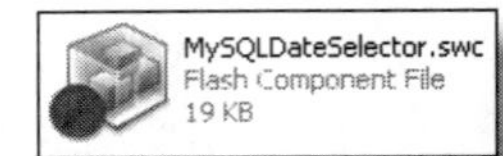

19. The SWC file needs to be copied to one of Flash's configuration folders. On Windows, the location is `C:\Program Files\Macromedia\Flash MX 2004\en\First Run\Components` (the en folder will have a different two-letter name if you are using a non-English version of Flash). On Mac OS X, it is `Macintosh HD:Applications:Macromedia Flash MX 2004:Configuration:Components`. The next time you run Flash, the component will be available in the Components panel in the Standard Components section. The name that appears in the Components panel is whatever you chose as the linkage identifier for the movie clip before turning it into a component. In this case, it's `dateSelector`.

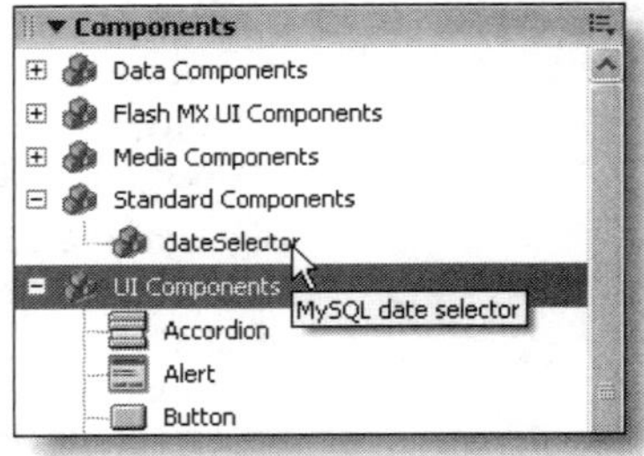

    Unfortunately, there is one minor drawback: there does not appear to be a way to export the Flash MX UI components together with your new `dateSelector` component. This means you need to drag an instance of the Flash MX ComboBox onto the stage as well. You can delete the Flash MX ComboBox immediately afterward, because all you need to do is import the elements that it uses into the document's Library. Once you have done this, the `dateSelector` component will work fine.

Nearly there

Working with dates can, at times, be confusing, but they are as essential in working with computers as they are in everyday life. PHP and MySQL offer some powerful ways of selecting and formatting dates. As you progress with database-driven development, you will likely find yourself coming back to this chapter on a regular basis to refresh your memory, as trying to take it all in at once is unrealistic. In addition to learning how to work with dates, you have built an extremely useful Flash component that you can deploy in any movie that uses dates in connection with MySQL.

You have just one more date to keep—the next, and final, chapter—and then you can consider yourself well and truly versed in PHP and MySQL. It's an in-depth case study, in which you'll learn how to work with multiple tables in a database, and delve into the mysteries of full and left joins. We'll also take a look at how PHP 5 can make light work of handling an XML file.

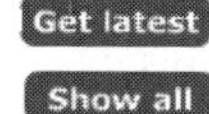

PHP5 for Flash
Want to create rich, inte
don't have the know-ho
shows you how to put t
web technologies - PHP
behind your Flash movie
PHP, MySQL,and Action
levels, and keeping you
The book is aimed at Fla
the Flash development environment, b
programming or database manageme
teaches you the core syntax of PHP an
relational database design. It's writte
tutorial, not only giving you hands-on
but also serving as a book that you'll

Chapter 12

WORKING WITH MULTIPLE TABLES AND XML

What this chapter covers:

- Using a database with more than one table
- Linking tables with foreign keys
- Using a lookup table
- Building the back-end of a database in XHTML and PHP
- Ensuring referential integrity
- Joining tables
- Finding incomplete matches with `LEFT JOIN`
- Deleting records simultaneously from multiple tables
- Parsing an XML feed with SimpleXML

As you've probably gathered by now, transferring data between Flash and an external source is easy. All that's necessary is to gather the variables in a format that the target application understands, and LoadVars does the rest. The complexity—and therefore the skill—lies in handling the data once it has been transferred. For Flash, you need good ActionScript skills, and for working with a database, you need a good knowledge of SQL and a server-side language—in our case, PHP.

All the databases you've worked with so far consist of just one table. For a simple project, that's often all you need, and working with single tables is a good way to learn the basics of MySQL and how to integrate a database with Flash. When you start storing more information, though, it's more efficient to create separate tables to prevent unnecessary duplication. In this final chapter, I'm going to raise your skills to the next level by showing you how to create the content management system (CMS) for a database of books that uses four tables.

Because this chapter represents a considerable step up, I want to devote most of it to working directly with PHP and SQL. Leaving Flash out of the equation, at least until the end, means you can concentrate on the core technology without the added layer of ActionScript. So, instead of building the forms in Flash, I use XHTML for the basic framework. It doesn't matter if you've never worked with XHTML forms—or even if you're a Flash designer who thinks XHTML is very old hat—the important thing to focus on is how PHP handles the data, performing all the necessary checks before inserting it into the database, or updating and deleting records.

As a bonus, you'll parse data from an external XML feed to update pricing information in the database directly. This used to be quite a complex operation, but a new feature in PHP 5 called SimpleXML lives up to its name—and it's certainly a lot easier than working with the ActionScript XML class.

Designing the table structure

It's rarely possible to predict all the uses a database will eventually have, but it's a good idea to think of things you may want to add at a later date, so that you don't tie yourself to a design that's going to be impossible to change.

Deciding the basic requirements

Since this is your first venture into working with multiple tables, let's keep the requirements simple, but realistic nevertheless. The finished application needs to be able to do the following:

- It should store details of individual books, including the title, the ISBN, the publisher, the names of all authors, a description, and pricing information.
- It should display a list of the most recently added titles, together with a line or two of description and a link to full details.
- The full details page should include an image of the book's cover.
- Visitors should be able to search for books by author, ISBN, or title.
- It should be possible to add book reviews and books from other publishers later.

Normalizing the tables

The requirements are similar to those for the multiple-table example in Chapter 8, but they need a little adaptation for this project. If you refer back to Figure 8-7, you will see a lookup table was used to create a link between the `users` and `publishers` tables, because each user had a relationship with more than one publisher and vice versa. This time, the publisher relationship is different. Each book can have only one publisher, so it's always a **one-to-one** (often represented as **1:1**) relationship. The complex relationship lies between authors and books. Sometimes, a book—like this one—has only one author. So that's a 1:1 relationship. However, I have written several books. In database terms, this is called a **one-to-many** (or **1:n**) relationship. Also, I co-authored some of the books with other writers, who—in turn—have written books separately from me. This is known as a **many-to-many** (or **n:m**) relationship. Figure 12-1 shows the different relationship types that will exist in the database.

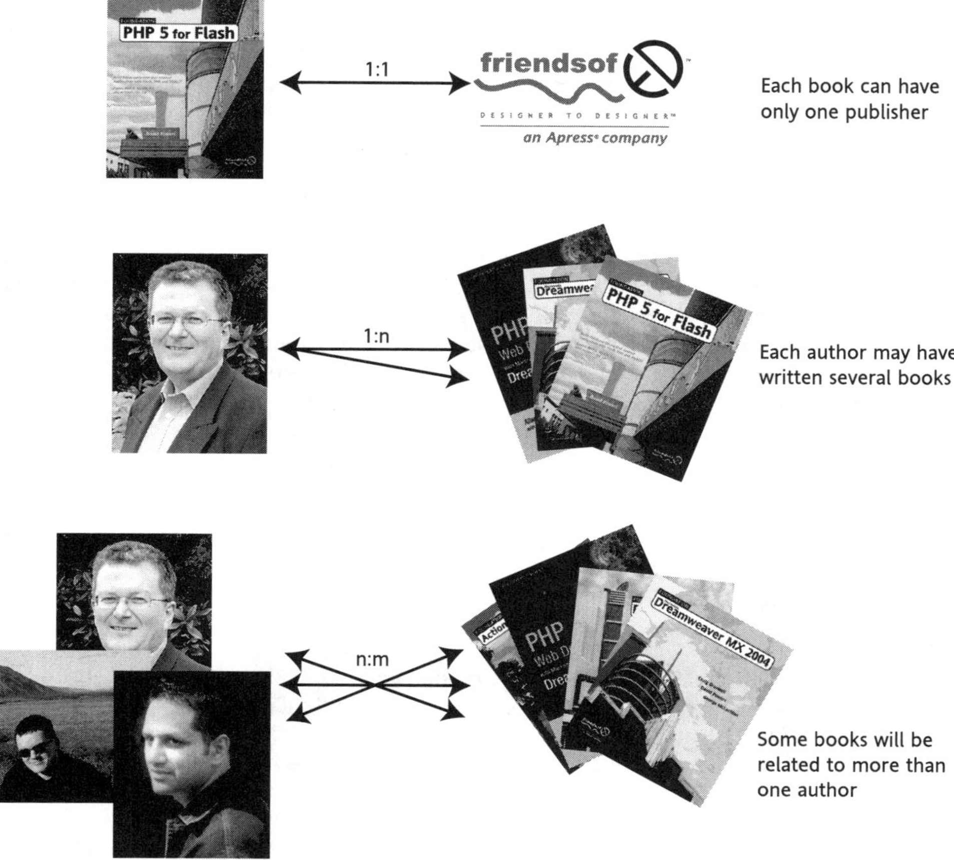

Figure 12-1. The database will have one-to-one, one-to-many, and many-to-many relationships.

Designing the books table

Surprising though it may seem, the complex relationship between authors and books means that the best way to build the books table is to leave out any reference to authors altogether. You could create columns for three authors and name them `author1`, `author2`, and `author3`. But that leaves you with the problem of what to do when there are more than three. Putting the authors in a completely separate table gets around this simply and efficiently. Table 12-1 shows how the books table might look with some sample data.

Table 12-1. A first attempt at designing the books table

book_id	isbn	title	publisher	image	description
1	1-59059-305-7	Foundation ActionScript for Flash MX 2004	friends of ED	1590593057.jpg	Inspirational.
2	1-893115-51-8	Beginning PHP 5 and MySQL	Apress	1893115518.jpg	Comprehensive.
3	1-59059-350-2	PHP Web Development with Dreamweaver MX 2004	Apress	1590593502.jpg	Stunning.
4	1-59059-466-5	Foundation PHP 5 for Flash	friends of ED	1590594665.jpg	Brilliant.

If you study Table 12-1, you will probably notice some redundancy straight away. For a start, the `publisher` column contains two instances of friends of ED and two of Apress. You may think it overkill to create a separate table for just two publishers, but one of the requirements was to add other publishers at a later stage. Even if no other publishers are ever added, creating a separate table and using a foreign key will get around the problem of misspelling. In fact, as you will see later, by putting the publisher in a separate table, the only time you will ever need to spell the name is when you first enter it into the database or subsequently update it.

You might also think that giving each book an ID in addition to its ISBN is redundant. Like a Social Security number, an ISBN must be unique, so it seems ideal as a primary key. Unfortunately, although an ISBN is always unique, it can change, as happened when Apress acquired the friends of ED imprint in 2003. What's more, the world is actually running out of ISBNs, so all of them are due to change before 2007 (see `www.isbn-international.org/en/download/implementation-guidelines-04.pdf`).

The redundancy with the ISBN lies elsewhere in the table. The ISBN (without hyphens) is used as the basis for the filename of each image. For an image to display in Flash, it must be a non-progressive JPG file. So, rather than type in all the details of the filename, you simply need to record whether or not an image exists. Most books will have a cover image, but you might want to list forthcoming titles, for which one doesn't yet exist. Most online bookstores omit the hyphens from ISBNs anyway, so you'll strip them out and just use an `ENUM` column to record "y" or "n" for the image (refer back to Chapter 8 if you need to refresh your memory about `ENUM` columns). This way, you can get either PHP or ActionScript to do all the hard work for you. When a book's record shows that an image exists, the script will add `.jpg` to the end of the ISBN. In the case that there's no image, you can either have a default "no cover available" image or use a conditional clause to change the page layout.

The requirements also call for pricing information. Since the price is unique to each book, this information could go either in the books table or in a separate prices table. If you're creating a site that does comparative pricing from many sources, a separate table would probably be preferable, but for the sake of this project, the prices will come from a single source, so you'll put them in the books table. With these changes, the structure of the books table will look like Table 12-2.

Table 12-2. The revised books table

book_id	pub_id	isbn	title	image	description	list_price	store_price
1	1	1590593057	Foundation ActionScript for Flash MX 2004	y	Inspirational.	$34.99	$23.09
2	2	1893115518	Beginning PHP 5 and MySQL	y	Comprehensive.	$39.99	$26.39
3	2	1590593502	PHP Web Development with Dreamweaver MX 2004	y	Stunning.	$39.99	$27.19
4	1	1590594665	Foundation PHP 5 for Flash	y	Brilliant.	$44.99	$29.70

You likely noticed that I moved the `pub_id` column immediately after `book_id`. This is because foreign key columns normally have to be declared at the start of a table. Even though support for foreign key constraints is not yet available on the default MySQL table type, putting the column here will save moving it later.

Even when MyISAM tables eventually offer support for foreign key constraints, just placing the column at the beginning of a table won't magically enforce their use. As with InnoDB tables, you'll need to set them up with the appropriate SQL commands (see `http://dev.mysql.com/doc/mysql/en/InnoDB_foreign_key_constraints.html`*).*

I did not add a column for each book's publication date, since I assumed that books will be entered into the database in the order they are published.

Designing the authors and publishers tables

There is very little to design here. The publishers table needs to consist of only two columns: the publisher's name and a unique ID. Similarly, the authors table needs only columns for first name and family name (for the sake of simplicity, I'm leaving out middle names or initials), and a unique ID.

Linking everything together with a lookup table

The primary keys of the books, authors, and publishers tables are the glue that links everything together. Searching a database for 1:1 and 1:n relationships is easy. The problem arises with n:m relationships. Trying to resolve them directly will have you going around in circles, like a dog chasing its own tail, but a lookup table simplifies matters by establishing 1:1 and 1:n relationships with the tables it joins.

Figure 12-2 shows how the lookup table simplifies the complex relationship between authors and books. Books 1, 2, and 4 are single-author books, so the lookup table contains just one record for each of them, linking each to the correct author. Book 3, however, was written by three co-authors. If you follow the links from the left of the figure, you will see a 1:n relationship between the books table and the lookup table, but following the links from the right, they all resolve to 1:1 relationships.

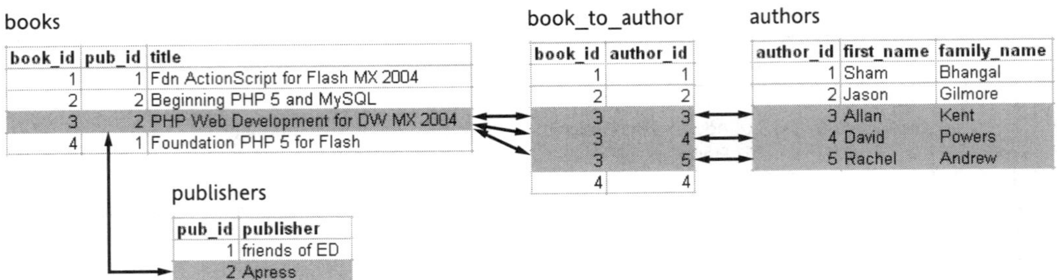

books

book_id	pub_id	title
1	1	Fdn ActionScript for Flash MX 2004
2	2	Beginning PHP 5 and MySQL
3	2	PHP Web Development for DW MX 2004
4	1	Foundation PHP 5 for Flash

book_to_author

book_id	author_id
1	1
2	2
3	3
3	4
3	5
4	4

authors

author_id	first_name	family_name
1	Sham	Bhangal
2	Jason	Gilmore
3	Allan	Kent
4	David	Powers
5	Rachel	Andrew

publishers

pub_id	publisher
1	friends of ED
2	Apress

Figure 12-2. A simplified view of the database, showing how the lookup table links multiple authors with a single book

Consequently, a search for *PHP Web Development with Dreamweaver MX 2004* will show all three authors' names, but a search of these four books for ones written by me would also bring up *Foundation PHP 5 for Flash*. The secret behind a lookup table is that every record is unique, and that when viewed from the correct perspective, it resolves to a 1:1 relationship with both tables. You ensure that each record in a lookup table is unique by declaring *both* columns as the table's primary key. I'll call this lookup table `book_to_author`.

Preparing to build the bookstore database

You've created all the tables you've worked with so far inside the `phpflash` database. Generally speaking, this isn't good practice; each database should be separate to avoid any conflicts between table and column names. It hasn't mattered because you've been working with single-table databases. Once you start working with multiple-table databases, the potential for confusion increases, so you'll build the application for this chapter in a new database called `bookstore`.

> *You can create as many databases as you like on your own computer, but if your hosting company limits the number of databases you are allowed to create, you may prefer to continue working with the* `phpflash` *database. Because all the table names are different, there should be no conflict. Just replace any reference to* `bookstore` *with* `phpflash`*. However, to use* `bookstore.sql` *in the download files, you will need to create the* `bookstore` *database on your own computer.*

Creating the database and granting user permissions

Normally, only the root user has authority to create a new database, and no one else can access it until the necessary permissions are set up. So those are the first tasks you need to attend to.

1. Launch phpMyAdmin. In the welcome screen, type bookstore in the Create new database field, leave Collation in its default position, and click Create.

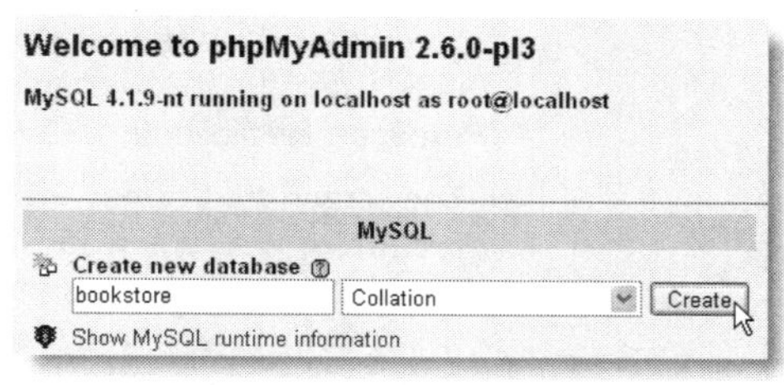

2. The screen that opens confirms that the bookstore database has been created and presents you with a form to create the first table. Rather than do that, let's first set up the user permissions. Click the localhost link at the top of the screen as shown in the image alongside.

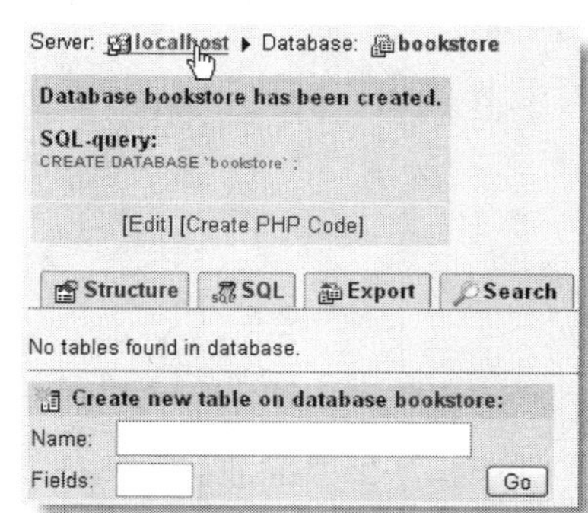

3. This will bring you back to the main welcome screen of phpMyAdmin. Click the Privileges link to access the area within phpMyAdmin that controls all user accounts and server privileges.

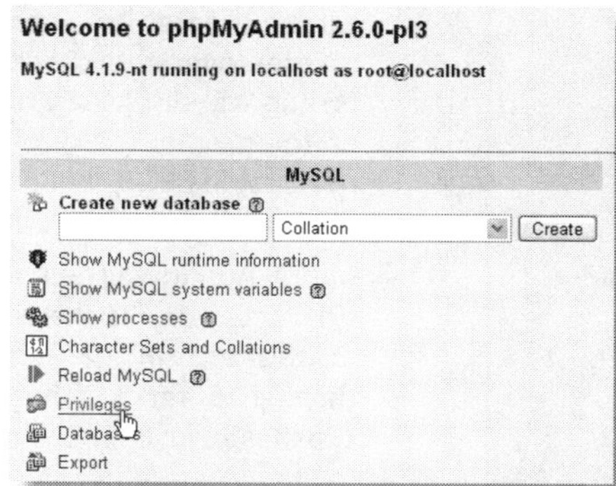

4. This will display a screen showing the users currently registered with the MySQL server. You will probably have just three users, as shown in Figure 12-3: flashadmin, flashuser, and root.

   As you can see from Figure 12-3, you can add new users or remove existing ones. Apart from providing fields to enter the username, hostname, and password, the screens for adding a new user are identical to those for changing the privileges of an existing one, so I'll just show you how to update `flashadmin` and `flashuser` to give them access to the new database.

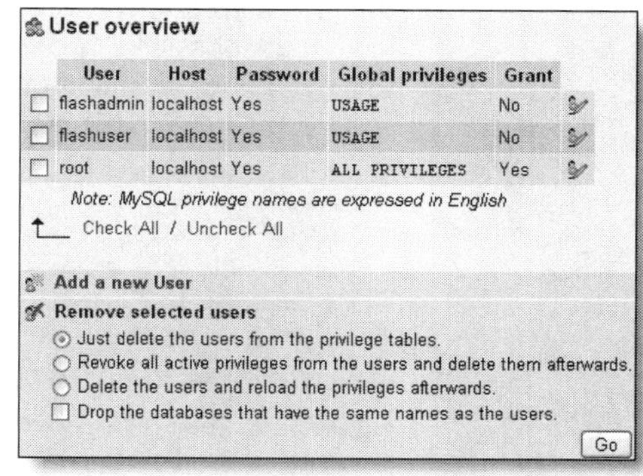

Figure 12-3. You can administer MySQL user privileges, and add or remove users within phpMyAdmin.

To edit an existing user's privileges, click the icon at the end of the row containing the user's details. It looks to me like a person holding a giant pencil. Begin by clicking the icon for flashadmin.

5. The screen that opens should show you the name of the user you are editing. The first section of the screen allows you to set **global** privileges—in other words, privileges on all databases (both existing and future ones) on the current server. Although this can be useful, it's generally safer to grant privileges only to specific databases, so scroll down until you find the section shown in the following screenshot:

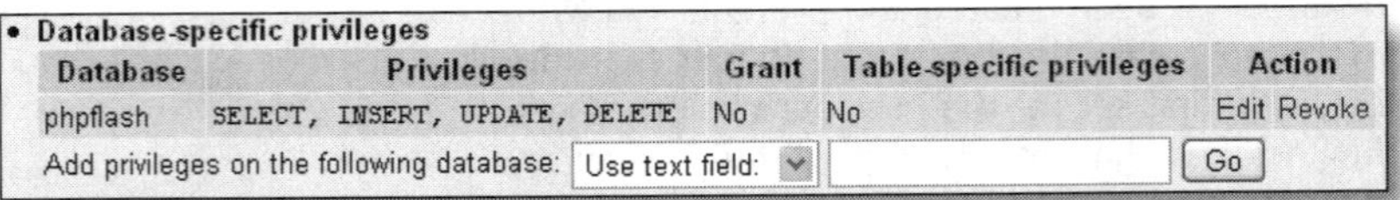

- Database-specific privileges

Database	Privileges	Grant	Table-specific privileges	Action
phpflash	SELECT, INSERT, UPDATE, DELETE	No	No	Edit Revoke
Add privileges on the following database:	Use text field:			Go

This table shows that `flashadmin` has SELECT, INSERT, UPDATE, and DELETE privileges on the phpflash database. Activate the drop-down menu that says Use text field to reveal a list of all databases on your server. Select bookstore, and the next screen should appear automatically. If it doesn't, click Go.

6. The next screen shows the various privileges that can be granted to a user. If you hover your mouse pointer over the check box next to each one, a tooltip will display a brief description of what each of them entails. Make sure you put check marks next to SELECT, INSERT, UPDATE, and DELETE. Then click Go.

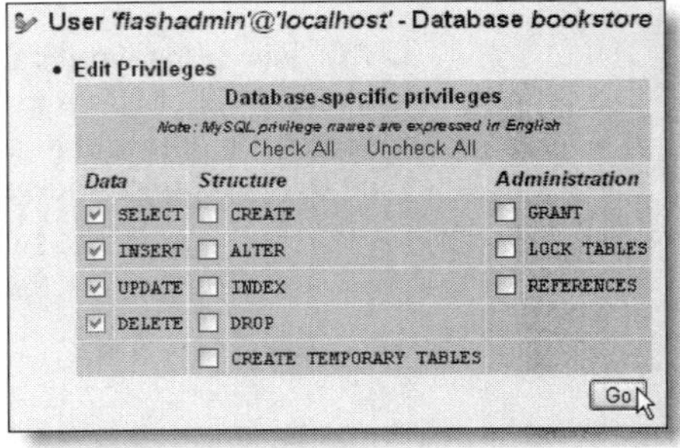

7. phpMyAdmin will tell you that it has updated the privileges for `flashadmin`. Click the Privileges tab at the top of the screen, and repeat steps 4 through 6 for `flashuser`. In the final step, give `flashuser` just SELECT privileges.

8. After you have edited both users, check that everything has been set correctly by clicking the Privileges tab. This will bring you back to the screen shown in Figure 12-3. Click the icon that looks like a person with a big pencil at the end of the row containing the details for flashadmin. In the screen that opens, scroll down to the Database-specific privileges table, and check that the details are the same as shown in Figure 12-4.

- Database-specific privileges

Database	Privileges	Grant	Table-specific privileges	Action
bookstore	SELECT, INSERT, UPDATE, DELETE	No	No	Edit Revoke
phpflash	SELECT, INSERT, UPDATE, DELETE	No	No	Edit Revoke
Add privileges on the following database:	Use text field:			Go

Figure 12-4. The privileges for `flashadmin` after adding the `bookstore` database

9. Repeat step 8 to check that the privileges for flashuser have been correctly updated. They should look like those shown in Figure 12-5.

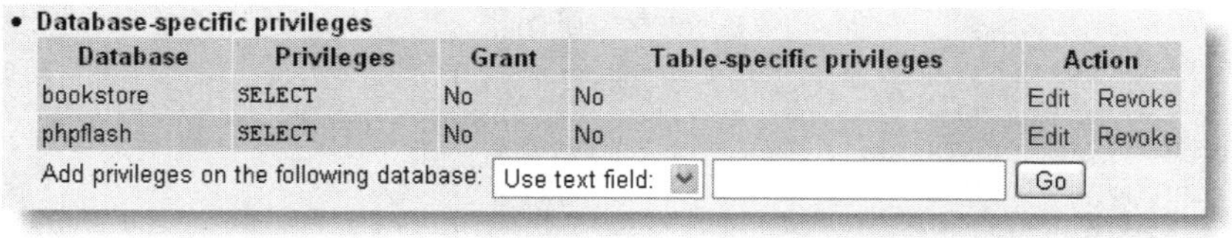

- Database-specific privileges

Database	Privileges	Grant	Table-specific privileges	Action	
bookstore	SELECT	No	No	Edit	Revoke
phpflash	SELECT	No	No	Edit	Revoke

Add privileges on the following database: Use text field: [ ] Go

Figure 12-5. The privileges for `flashuser` after adding the `bookstore` database

Getting an overview of the project

Because the CMS involves building a lot of pages, you may get a better idea of what you are aiming for if you take a look at the completed project to see how everything works.

Populating the database with test data

Even though the bookstore database is completely empty, the download files for this chapter contain three versions of a backup file that will not only build all the tables for you, but also populate the database with test data.

> *The `bookstore` database must first exist for the following instructions to work.*

1. If you have installed MySQL 4.1, use `bookstore.sql`. If you are using MySQL 4.0 or 3.23, use `bookstore_40.sql` or `bookstore_323.sql`, respectively (use the appropriate filename in the next step). Copy the file to the top level of your `C` drive (on Windows) or to your home folder (on Mac OS X).

2. Open a Windows Command Prompt (*not* the MySQL Command Line Client) or Terminal. If MySQL is not in your PATH, change directory to the MySQL `bin` folder. (This will be necessary only if you chose not to include MySQL in your PATH at the time of installation, or you are running a version of MySQL prior to 4.1.8. Refer back to Chapter 6 for details of the correct PATH for your operating system.) On Windows, enter the following command:

```
mysql -u root -p bookstore < c:\bookstore.sql
```

   On Mac OS X, use the following:

```
mysql -u root -p bookstore < bookstore.sql
```

3. Enter your MySQL root password when prompted. If all goes well, you will be returned to the command/shell prompt almost immediately. Load the `bookstore` database in phpMyAdmin, and you should see that it now contains four tables, as shown in Figure 12-6. Use the browse icon (immediately to the right of each table name) to view the test data.

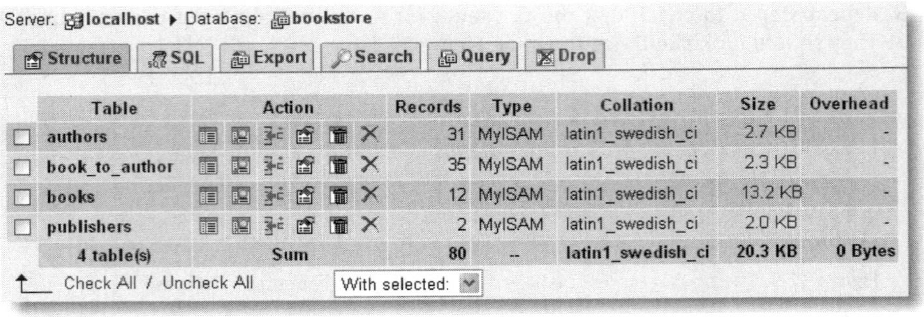

Server: localhost ▸ Database: bookstore

Structure | SQL | Export | Search | Query | Drop

	Table	Action	Records	Type	Collation	Size	Overhead
☐	authors		31	MyISAM	latin1_swedish_ci	2.7 KB	-
☐	book_to_author		35	MyISAM	latin1_swedish_ci	2.3 KB	-
☐	books		12	MyISAM	latin1_swedish_ci	13.2 KB	-
☐	publishers		2	MyISAM	latin1_swedish_ci	2.0 KB	-
	4 table(s)	Sum	80	--	latin1_swedish_ci	20.3 KB	0 Bytes

Check All / Uncheck All   With selected:

Figure 12-6. The `bookstore` database has been populated with four tables of test data from the SQL file.

Taking the CMS for a quick test-drive

The download files contain a folder called `cms` that contains all the finished files. Copy the entire folder to a new folder called `phpflash/cms`, and load `listbooks.php` into your browser. You should see a screen similar to Figure 12-7. This is the main interface used to display and edit books in the database. (You may also want to take a look at Figure 12-8 in the section titled "Deciding the basic structure" later in the chapter to see how all the pages interact with each other.)

Click each of the navigation buttons at the top of the screen and explore each of the pages to get a feel for how the CMS is laid out. Feel free to enter new authors' and publishers' names in the database. It doesn't matter if you make a mess of things, because it's only test material, and you can repopulate the database from the SQL file as many times as you like. By repeating the steps outlined in the previous section, you will always restore the data to its original state. Although the book details are genuine, the "store" prices are included purely for test purposes and shouldn't be regarded as a reliable guide to current prices.

Try deleting an author or publisher (the mechanism is identical to the Flash CMS in Chapter 10), and see what happens. Unless it's one of the names you added yourself, you won't be able to delete anyone, because they will still be associated with one or more books. Then return to the page shown in Figure 12-7, select a radio button next to one of the books, and click Edit book. Again, you'll see that the CMS works in exactly the same way as the one you built in Chapter 10. Then, with the list of books displayed, select the check box next to several titles, and make a note of some of the authors' names before you click Delete book(s). If you confirm that you want to go ahead with the deletion, the books will be permanently removed from the database. Now try deleting the author of one of the books you have just removed. If no more books are registered in that author's name, the deletion will go through this time. Even though the database uses MyISAM tables, which don't yet support foreign key constraints, the same functionality has been built into the CMS through a combination of PHP and MySQL.

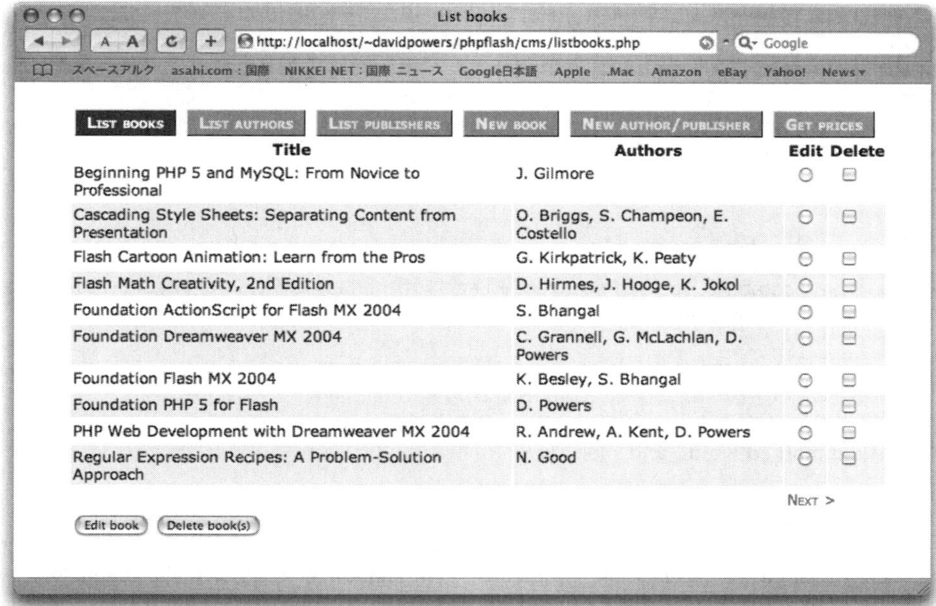

Figure 12-7. Viewing the contents of the bookstore database in `listbooks.php` of the CMS

Completing the database structure

Because the SQL file builds the table structure for you, this next section is optional. You can either continue to work with the test database, or drop the tables and build them again from scratch, using the instructions over the next few pages. The CMS itself involves a lot of coding, so you will probably be eager to get on with things. However, I recommend you read through the descriptions of the tables, because they explain why certain column types were chosen. Pay particular attention to the structure of the lookup table, since this is something you will need to understand when it comes to building a multiple-table database of your own.

If you do decide to rebuild the tables from scratch, load the bookstore database into phpMyAdmin, and click the Check All link beneath the grid that displays all four tables. Then select Drop from the drop-down menu as shown in the following image. (Don't select the Drop tab at the top of the screen—that will drop the entire database.)

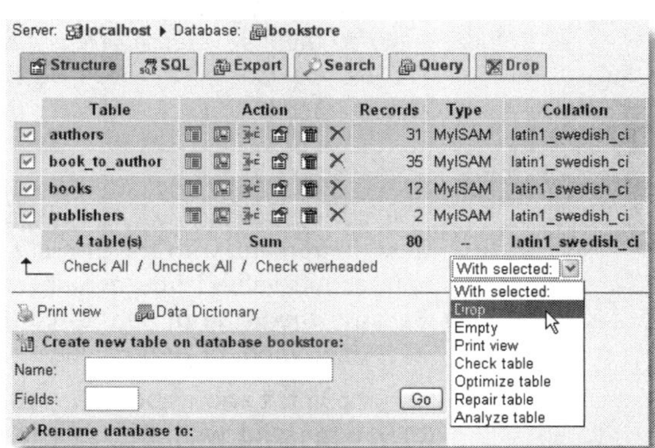

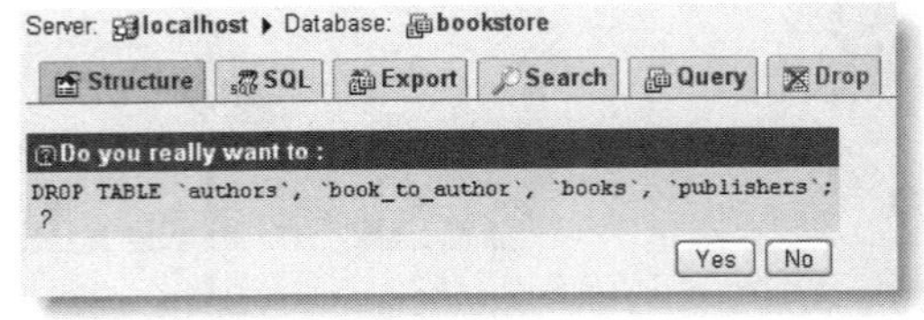

You will then be asked to confirm that you want to drop the four tables. Click Yes and they will be gone, but the database will still be there. Although you can create a new database quickly, doing it this way avoids the need to grant user permissions again, because when a database is dropped, all references to it disappear, including those in the permissions table.

Defining the books table

With an empty database, you can now rebuild each of the tables. The books table is the largest, as it contains eight columns.

1. With the `bookstore` database selected in phpMyAdmin, fill in the Create new table form as shown in the image alongside. Enter books in the Name field and 8 in the field marked Fields, and then click Go.
2. The next screen is where you define the column types for the books table. Table 12-3 lists the necessary settings. Collation has been left out, because it doesn't require setting unless you need to change the sort order of results (see the section "Choosing the right language settings" in Chapter 8). The Default column has also been left out, although you may want to add individual settings of your own.

> *Some developers find it useful to specify a default value for each column, in case they forget to fill in a particular field. When a column is set to* NOT NULL, *MySQL automatically sets the default for most text-related columns, including* VARCHAR, *to an empty string, which can be difficult to identify when debugging. Unfortunately, as noted in Chapter 8, the* TEXT *column type itself does not accept default values, so you cannot do this for the* `description` *column.*
>
> *There is little need to set a default for other* NOT NULL *column types, because the default for numbers and dates is automatically set to zero, and* ENUM *is set to the first value. There is never a point in setting a default for a column that has specifically been declared* NULL, *because declaring a column as* NULL *means you are happy for it to contain no value.*

The table's primary key is book_id, so this is the only column that should be set to auto_increment, with the primary key radio button selected. The next column, pub_id, will take its value from the `publishers` table and is used in this table as a foreign key. Because the value of pub_id comes from another table, you should *not* select either auto_increment or primary key.

Other points to note about the settings are that, even though ISBNs are called "numbers," they often end with "X," so you need to use a text-type column. With the hyphens removed, a valid ISBN will always be either 10 or 13 characters long, so VARCHAR with a length of 13 characters is sufficient.

Table 12-3. Settings for the column types in the books table

Field	Type	Length/ Values	Attributes	Null	Extra	Primary key
book_id	INT		UNSIGNED	not null	auto_increment	Selected
pub_id	INT		UNSIGNED	not null		
isbn	VARCHAR	13		not null		
title	VARCHAR	150		not null		
image	ENUM	'y','n'		not null		
description	TEXT			not null		
list_price	VARCHAR	10		null		
store_price	VARCHAR	10		null		

You need to specify the values for an `ENUM` column as a comma-delimited series of strings. In other words, each value must be in a separate pair of quotes. Make sure you don't put the comma inside the quotes.

Deciding the best column type for prices is tricky. As noted in Chapter 8, the `DECIMAL` column type is designed for currency values, but it is not the best choice for performing calculations. Ideally, you should convert all prices to the smallest unit of currency (such as cents or pence) and use an `INT` column. For the purposes of this case study, however, I have selected `VARCHAR` for the `list_price` and `store_price` columns, because they will be populated from an XML file that is based on the type of information you might get from an online bookstore. This type of file usually contains a currency symbol, such as the dollar sign, so a text-related column type is necessary.

When you've filled in all the fields, the screen should look like the following image. After you've checked that all the values are correct, click the Save button (it's at the bottom left of the screenshot).

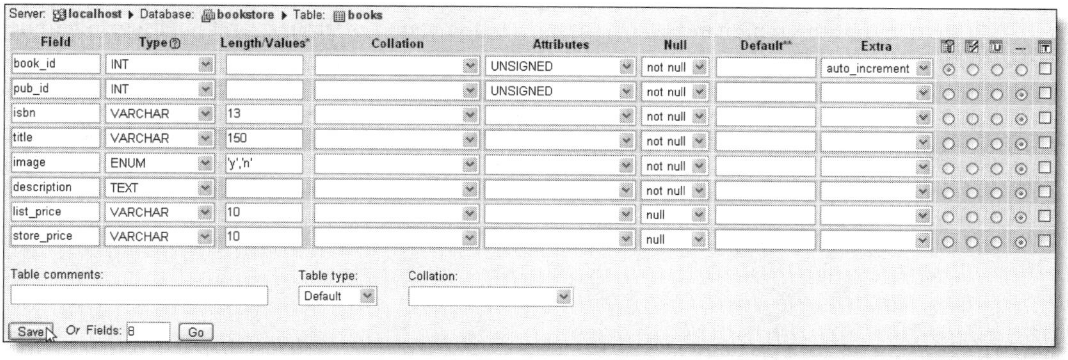

3. The next screen will show you the structure of your new table. It should look like this:

	Field	Type	Collation	Attributes	Null	Default	Extra	Action
☐	book_id	int(10)		UNSIGNED	No		auto_increment	
☐	pub_id	int(10)		UNSIGNED	No	0		
☐	isbn	varchar(13)	latin1_swedish_ci		No			
☐	title	varchar(150)	latin1_swedish_ci		No			
☐	image	enum('y', 'n')	latin1_swedish_ci		No			
☐	description	text	latin1_swedish_ci		No			
☐	list_price	varchar(10)	latin1_swedish_ci		Yes	*NULL*		
☐	store_price	varchar(10)	latin1_swedish_ci		Yes	*NULL*		

As you can see, the default for pub_id has automatically been set to 0, and the default for list_price and store_price has been set to NULL. No default is shown for book_id, but since it has been set to auto_increment, it will always take the next number available. Also, Collation for all the text-related columns has been set to the default for English (latin1_swedish_ci). I know it sounds strange, but the reason for this was explained in Chapter 8.

If there are any problems with your settings, phpMyAdmin will report an error and present you with the previous screen for you to correct. You can also make changes to any of the columns (or fields, as phpMyAdmin calls them) by clicking the pencil icon in the Action section.

> *If you decide that you have made a real mess of creating a table, it may be quicker to drop the table and start all over again. The* Drop *tab at the top right of the screen is context sensitive. If you have a table displayed, it drops the table; otherwise, it drops the entire database. Fortunately, phpMyAdmin always asks you to confirm your instruction, so you can cancel it if necessary.*

Defining the authors and publishers tables

These are both simple tables that contain just the names of authors and publishers identified by a primary key.

1. To create the next table, click bookstore either at the top of the screen or in the menu on the left side of the screen. This will take you to a screen with a Create new table form. Enter authors in the Name text box and 3 in the Fields text box. After clicking Go, define the column types for the `authors` table using the settings shown in the following screenshot and Table 12-4.

Server: localhost ▸ Database: bookstore ▸ Table: authors

Field	Type	Length/Values*	Collation	Attributes	Null	Default**	Extra
author_id	INT			UNSIGNED	not null		auto_increment
first_name	VARCHAR	30			not null		
family_name	VARCHAR	30			not null		

Table 12-4. Settings for column types in the authors table

Field	Type	Length/ Values	Attributes	Null	Extra	Primary key
author_id	INT		UNSIGNED	not null	auto_increment	Selected
first_name	VARCHAR	30		not null		
family_name	VARCHAR	30		not null		

Check that you have set the correct values, and then click Save.

2. Repeat the previous step to create the third table. Enter publishers in the Name field, and enter 2 in Fields. Use the settings shown in the following screenshot and Table 12-5 for the column types.

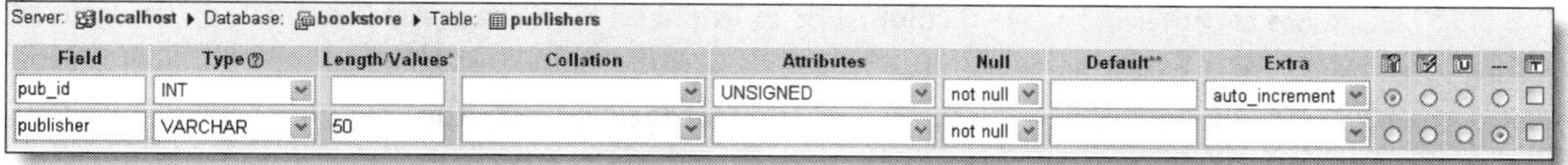

Table 12-5. Settings for column types in the publishers table

Field	Type	Length/ Values	Attributes	Null	Extra	Primary key
pub_id	INT		UNSIGNED	not null	auto_increment	Selected
publisher	VARCHAR	50		not null		

Creating the lookup table

The final table is the lookup table. It is created in the same way as the others, but the settings for the column types are unusual, because both columns will be used as a joint primary key.

1. In the Create new table form, enter book_to_author in the Name field, and enter 2 in Fields. For the column types, use the settings shown in the following screenshot and Table 12-6.

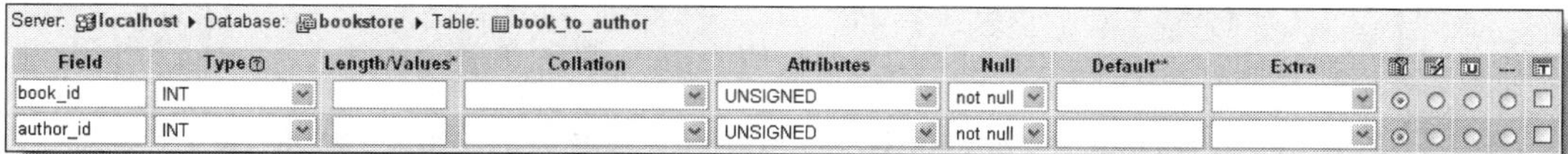

Table 12-6. Settings for column types in the book_to_author table

Field	Type	Length/ Values	Attributes	Null	Extra	Primary key
book_id	INT		UNSIGNED	not null		Selected
author_id	INT		UNSIGNED	not null		Selected

Although both columns are being used as the table's primary key, you should not select auto_increment. *The value in each column will be drawn from the primary keys of the* books *and* authors *tables, respectively.*

2. The structure of the lookup table is vitally important and—unlike other tables—should never be changed once you start entering data. So, after you create the book_to_author table, check the details of the table's index in the next screen that displays. It will be on the left side of the screen beneath the structure grid, and it should look like the screenshot alongside. It is important that both book_id and author_id are together in the Field column, as shown here. If you have made a mistake, re-create the primary key as explained in the following steps. Otherwise, skip to the next section.

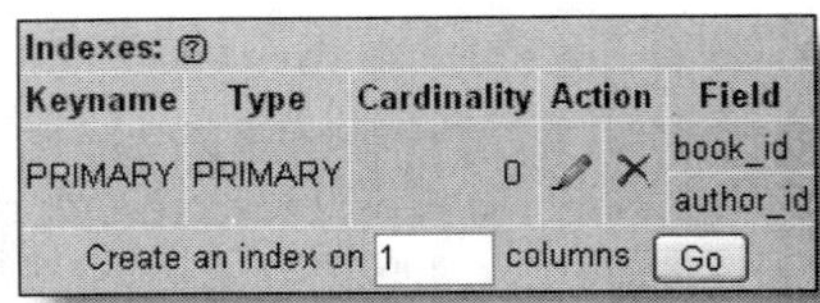

3. If book_id and author_id are not shown together, click the large X in the Action column shown in the screenshot in step 2, and confirm that you want to alter the table. The Indexes section will display a warning that no index has been defined. Enter 2 in the text input box immediately beneath the warning and click Go, as shown alongside.

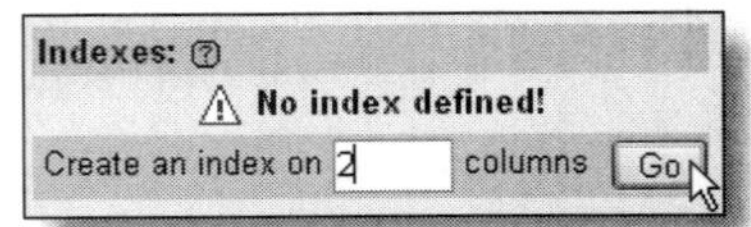

4. In the next screen, select book_id and author_id from the Field drop-down menus, as shown here. Leave all the other settings unchanged and click Save.

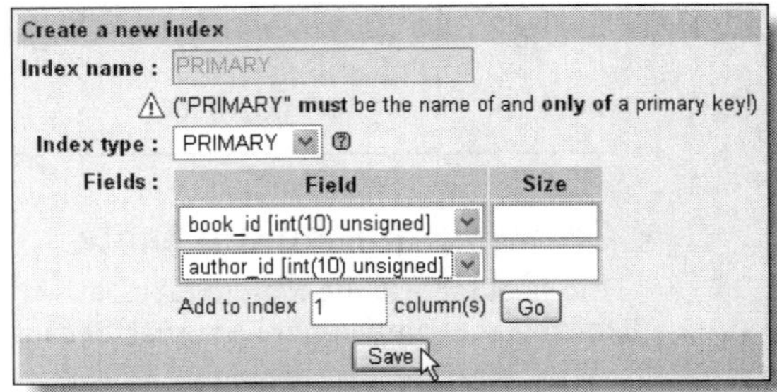

A table can have only one primary key. Although the lookup table seems to break this rule, it's the combination of the two columns that acts as the primary key. That's why you can't just add a second column to an existing primary key. You must always drop the existing primary key before you can change it. Changing the primary key of a table that already contains data is extremely unwise, so it's important to ensure you make the right choice before you start populating your database with valuable data.

You should now be able to see four tables in your database: authors, book_to_author, books, and publisher, exactly the same as in Figure 12-6. The only difference is that there is no data in the tables. You will add data soon after you start building the CMS.

Creating the content management system

After experimenting with the test database, you should now have a good idea of how the CMS prevents you from deleting authors' or publishers' names from the database if references to them still exist in other tables. The basic structure of the CMS is similar to the one you built in Flash in Chapter 10. The main difference is that, instead of just one table, this one works with four, and the way they interact requires considerable planning.

Deciding the basic structure

If you think back to Chapter 10, you needed a form to enter new details, a way to find existing records, a form to update existing records, and a way to delete records that are no longer required. Although there are four tables in the database, only three of them require a direct interface. The lookup table (book_to_author) will always be accessed through either the books table or the authors table. Also, the publishers and authors tables are so simple that they can safely be handled through the same interface. The following pages will, therefore, need to be created (Figure 12-8 shows how they all fit together):

- new_book.php: This is used to enter the details of new books, including both the names of the authors and publisher. Consequently, the underlying PHP and SQL will draw information from both the authors and publishers tables, as well as insert records into both the books table and the book_to_author lookup table. In other words, it accesses all four tables.
- new_auth_pub.php: This is used to enter the details of new authors and publishers.
- listbooks.php: This lists existing books so that their details can be edited or deleted.
- listauthors.php: This lists existing authors so that their details can be edited or deleted.
- listpub.php: This lists existing publishers so that their details can be edited or deleted.
- edit_book.php: This is based on new_book.php and is used to update book details.
- edit_auth_pub.php: This closely mirrors new_auth_pub.php, and is used to update the names of authors and publishers.
- del_book.php: This removes books from both the books and lookup tables.
- del_auth_pub.php: This checks whether any reference to an author or publisher still remains in the books or lookup table before deleting it.
- getprices.php: This gets pricing information from an XML file and inserts it into the books table.
- admin_funcs.php: This contains some common functions, including the menu to navigate around the CMS.
- admin.css: This is a stylesheet to take the rough edges off the look of the CMS.

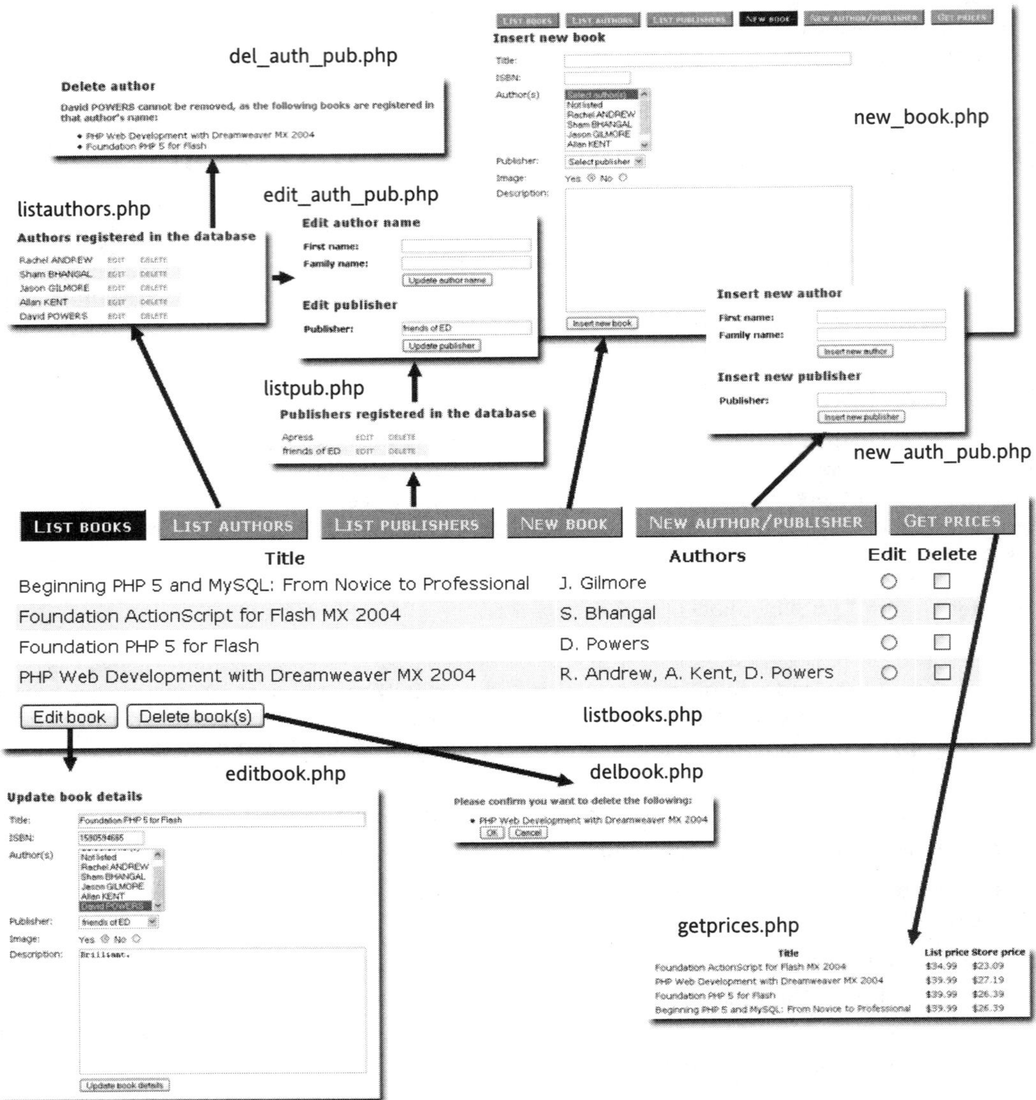

Figure 12-8. The CMS consists of ten interlinked PHP pages and a six-item navigation menu.

Yes, it's a lot of files—and a lot of coding, although you can build some pages quite quickly by copying an existing one and amending the underlying PHP and SQL. The best way to learn any programming language is to hand-code it yourself, but if you just want to read the explanation of what's happening with the finished files at your side, be my guest. Although all the files are essential to the CMS, the most important ones are `new_book.php`, `edit_book.php`, `del_auth_pub.php`, and `getprices.php`.

Building the basic forms in XHTML

As I mentioned before, PHP was originally developed to provide dynamic functionality to standard web pages using HTML or its successor, XHTML. The easiest way to build the CMS is to create the interface first in standard XHTML, and then add the PHP. The PHP will perform two basic functions:

- Validating the user input
- Interacting with the database to insert, update, or delete records

If you have a graphical XHTML editor, such as Dreamweaver or GoLive, or a text-based one, such as HomeSite or BBEdit, you can build the basic forms much more quickly than you can hand-code everything. Whichever method you choose, start by creating the stylesheet that will be attached to all pages. By using CSS, not only do you control all the styling centrally, but you also end up with much lighter code that is easier to integrate PHP into. Not to mention the fact that it's standards compliant, too.

> *If you plan to build the CMS yourself, save all the pages in* `phpflash/ch12` *to keep them separate from the completed test files. The download files contain all the pages at various stages of completion, so you can pick up the project at any stage or just read along while experimenting with the completed CMS. As in previous chapters, most files have a number at the end of the filename—for instance,* `new_book01.php`*. Always rename these files without the serial number (so, for example,* `new_book01.php` *becomes* `new_book.php`*).*

Create the stylesheet: admin.css

Copy the following code into a file named `admin.css` or use the file of the same name from the download files for this chapter. If you haven't worked with CSS before, this is simply a text file that will apply universal styles to any web page that it's attached to (normally using a `<link>` tag). It's the modern, standards-compliant way of applying styles, and it replaces `<font>` tags and other parts of HTML that have now been deprecated by the World Wide Web Consortium (W3C).

```
/* styles for main body and headings */
body {
  background:#FFF;
  font:85% Verdana,Arial,Helvetica,sans-serif;
  margin:25px auto 10px 50px;
}
h1 {color:#00478A; font-size:140%;}

/* styles for links */
a {font-variant:small-caps; text-decoration:none;}
a:link,a:visited {color:#696A21;}
a:hover,a:active {color:#692121; text-decoration:underline overline;}
```

```
/* table styles */
#booklist {width:95%;}
td {padding:2px 20px 2px 2px; vertical-align:top;}
td.ctr {padding:2px 10px;}
th.leftLabel {text-align:left; vertical-align:top; width:150px;}
tr.hilite {background:#F5F5DC;}
tr.nohilite {background:#FFF;}

/* width settings for text input boxes */
.mediumbox {width:200px;}
.narrowbox {width:100px;}
.widebox {width:450px;}
#description {height:200px; width:450px;}

/* style for warnings and alerts */
#alert {color:#F00; font-weight:bold; width:600px;}

/* styles for navigation menu */
#menu{margin:0;}
#menu a{
  background:#999;
  border:1px solid;
  border-color:#DDD #000 #000 #DDD;
  font-weight:bold;
  padding:3px 10px;
}
#menu a:link,#menu a:visited {color:#EEE;}
#menu a:hover,#menu a:active,
#uberlink a:link,#uberlink a:visited,
#uberlink a:hover,#uberlink a:active {
  background:#8B0000;
  color:#FFF;
  text-decoration:none;
}
#menu li {float:left; list-style-type:none; margin:0; padding:5px;}
#menu ul {margin:0; padding:0;}

/* this forces the rest of the page to sit below the menu */
#maincontent {clear:both; margin:30px 0;}
```

The stylesheet contains some basic comments to indicate what the styles are for, but I don't plan to go into any detailed explanation. To learn more about styling web pages with CSS, see Cascading Style Sheets: Separating Content from Presentation, *Second Edition by Owen Briggs, Steven Champeon, Eric Costello, and Matt Patterson (friends of ED, ISBN: 1-59059-231-X). Flash now supports a limited subset of CSS styles, so it's a subject that's likely to have increasing relevance to Flash development, too.*

The stylesheet will be attached to each of the pages in the CMS by the following <link> tag in the <head> of each XHTML page:

```
<link href="admin.css" rel="stylesheet" type="text/css" />
```

Insert new book framework

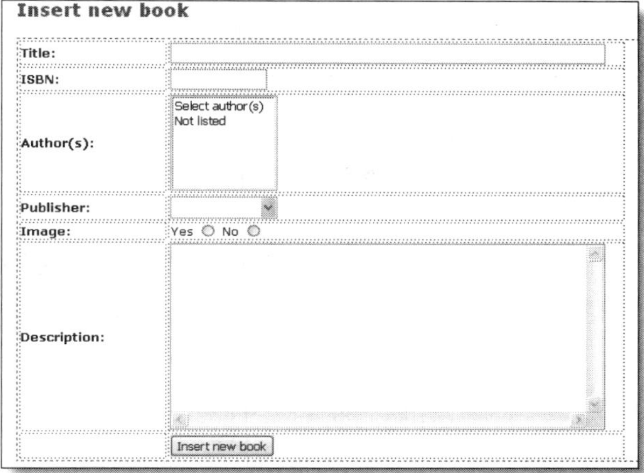

New books will be entered into the database using new_book.php. It consists of a form called bookDets, which contains a table with two columns and seven rows. Use the left column for labels and the right column for the form input elements. The screenshot here shows what the basic form looks like in Design view in Dreamweaver MX 2004.

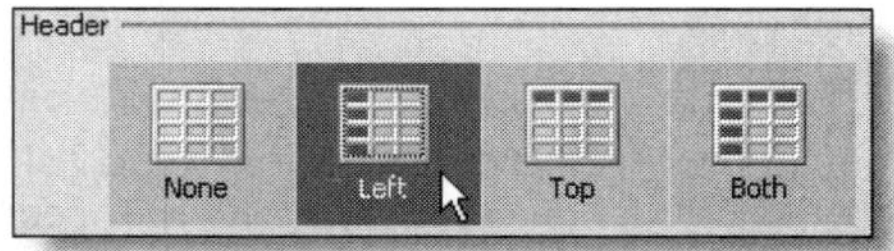

Table 12-7 describes the input elements that go alongside the XHTML label in each row of the table. The labels are all in <th> cells with a class of leftLabel. If you're not familiar with <th> cells, they're exactly the same as <td> table elements, except that they indicate a "table header." If you're using Dreamweaver MX 2004 to create the XHTML pages, select Header Left in the Table dialog box (as shown alongside), and Dreamweaver will automatically create the <th> tags for you. It will also insert scope="row" to indicate that the header applies to the row. I've removed the scope attribute because it's not necessary for anyone not using Dreamweaver, but there's no harm leaving it in.

Table 12-7. Settings for the input elements in new_book.php

Label	Form element	Type	Name/ID	Class	Notes
Title	input	text	title	widebox	
ISBN	input	text	isbn	narrowbox	
Author(s)	select		author		This is a multiple select element. Set size="6". Set the first option as the default selection.
Publisher	select		publisher		This is a single select element. Set the first option as the default selection.
Image	input	radio	image		Use two radio buttons. Set value="y" and value="n".

(Continued)

Table 12-7. Settings for the input elements in new_book.php *(Continued)*

Label	Form element	Type	Name/ID	Class	Notes
Description	textarea		description		An id selector in the stylesheet is used to set the size of this textarea element, so you must set id="description" as well as name="description".
	input	submit	Submit		Set value="Insert new book".

The full code for the XHTML structure of new_book.php follows. It is also available in the download files as new_book01.php.

> *Note that all the forms use the POST method, but the action attribute has been given no value. This is because the forms will subsequently be converted to PHP self-processing forms.*

```
<!DOCTYPE html PUBLIC "-//W3C//DTD XHTML 1.0 Transitional//EN"
"http://www.w3.org/TR/xhtml1/DTD/xhtml1-transitional.dtd">

<html xmlns="http://www.w3.org/1999/xhtml">
<head>
<meta http-equiv="Content-Type" content="text/html;
➥ charset=iso-8859-1" />
<title>Insert new book</title>
<link href="admin.css" rel="stylesheet" type="text/css" />
</head>
<body>
<div id="maincontent">
<h1>Insert new book</h1>
<form name="bookDets" id="bookDets" method="post" action="">
  <table>
    <tr>
      <th class="leftLabel">Title:</th>
      <td><input name="title" type="text" class="widebox" id="title"
➥ value="" /></td>
    </tr>
    <tr>
      <th class="leftLabel">ISBN:</th>
      <td><input name="isbn" type="text" class="narrowbox" id="isbn"
➥ value="" /></td>
    </tr>
    <tr>
```

```
    <th class="leftLabel">Author(s):</th>
    <td><select name="author" size="6" multiple="multiple"
➥ id="author">
        <option value="choose" selected="selected">Select
➥ author(s)</option>
        <option value="other">Not listed</option>
      </select></td>
  </tr>
  <tr>
    <th class="leftLabel">Publisher:</th>
    <td><select name="publisher" id="publisher">
      <option value="0" selected="selected">Select publisher</option>
      <option value="other">Not listed</option>
    </select></td>
  </tr>
  <tr>
    <th class="leftLabel">Image:</th>
    <td>Yes
      <input name="image" type="radio" value="y" />
      No
      <input name="image" type="radio" value="n" /></td>
  </tr>
  <tr>
    <th class="leftLabel">Description:</th>
    <td><textarea name="description" id="description"></textarea>
➥ </td>
  </tr>
  <tr>
    <th> </th>
    <td><input type="submit" name="Submit" value="Insert new
➥ book" /></td>
  </tr>
 </table>
</form>
</div>
</body>
</html>
```

The main points to note about this form are the two <select> tags. The first one (named author) is set to display six items and permits multiple selections. At the moment, it has just two options. The second (named publisher) permits only a single choice, and it currently has two options. The image alongside shows how they look in a browser. The rest of the options will be populated dynamically from the bookstore database using PHP.

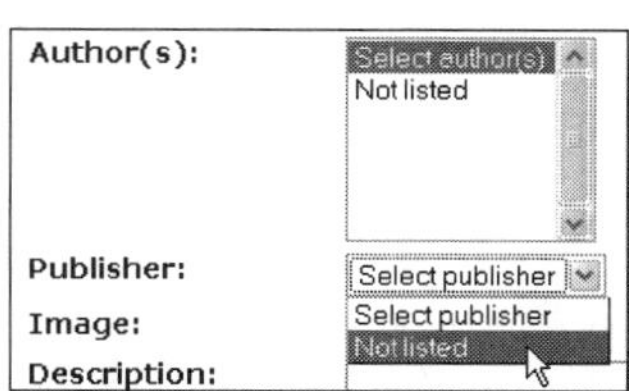

Insert new author or publisher framework

This page, called new_auth_pub.php, contains two XHTML forms: one for inserting the details of new authors and the other for new publishers. The form for authors, called authorDets, contains two text input elements called first_name and family_name, and a submit button labeled Insert new author. The form for publishers contains just one text input element called publisher and a submit button labeled Insert new publisher. The screenshot shows what the basic framework looks like in Dreamweaver's Design view.

The full code for the XHTML structure of new_auth_pub.php follows. It is also available in the download files as new_auth_pub01.php.

```
<!DOCTYPE html PUBLIC "-//W3C//DTD XHTML 1.0 Transitional//EN"
"http://www.w3.org/TR/xhtml1/DTD/xhtml1-transitional.dtd">
<html xmlns="http://www.w3.org/1999/xhtml">
<head>
<meta http-equiv="Content-Type" content="text/html;
➥ charset=iso-8859-1" />
<title>Insert authors and publishers</title>
<link href="admin.css" rel="stylesheet" type="text/css" />
</head>
<body>
<div id="maincontent">
  <h1>Insert new author</h1>
  <form name="authorDets" id="authorDets" method="post" action="">
    <table>
      <tr>
        <th class="leftLabel">First name: </th>
        <td><input name="first_name" type="text" id="first_name"
➥ class="mediumbox" /></td>
      </tr>
      <tr>
        <th class="leftLabel">Family name: </th>
        <td><input name="family_name" type="text" id="family_name"
➥ class="mediumbox"  /></td>
      </tr>
      <tr>
        <th> </th>
        <td><input name="insAuthor" type="submit" id="insAuthor"
➥ value="Insert new author" /></td>
      </tr>
    </table>
  </form>
  <h1>Insert new publisher</h1>
  <form name="publisherDets" id="publisherDets" method="post"
➥ action="">
```

```
      <table>
        <tr>
          <th class="leftLabel">Publisher:</th>
          <td><input name="publisher" type="text" id="publisher"
➥ class="mediumbox" /></td>
        </tr>
        <tr>
          <th> </th>
          <td><input name="insPublisher" type="submit" id="insPublisher"
➥ value="Insert new publisher" /></td>
        </tr>
      </table>
    </form>
</div>
</body>
</html>
```

List books framework

The underlying XHTML for the three pages that list books, authors, and publishers is simple, because PHP will be used to create most of the code when the details are retrieved from the database. You need only one table row for the details; everything else will be done by a `while` loop. The following is the basic XHTML code for `listbooks.php`. It is also available in the download files as `listbooks01.php`.

```
<!DOCTYPE html PUBLIC "-//W3C//DTD XHTML 1.0 Transitional//EN"
"http://www.w3.org/TR/xhtml1/DTD/xhtml1-transitional.dtd">
<html xmlns="http://www.w3.org/1999/xhtml">
<head>
<meta http-equiv="Content-Type" content="text/html;
➥ charset=iso-8859-1" />
<title>List books</title>
<link href="admin.css" rel="stylesheet" type="text/css" />
</head>
<body>
<div id="maincontent">
  <form name="list" id="list" method="post" action="">
    <table id="booklist">
      <tr>
        <th scope="col">Title</th>
        <th scope="col">Authors</th>
        <th scope="col">Edit</th>
        <th scope="col">Delete</th>
      </tr>
      <tr>
        <td colspan="4">No books listed </td>
      </tr>
      <tr class="hilite">
        <td> </td>
```

```
          <td> </td>
          <td class="ctr"><input name="book_id[]" type="radio"
➥ value="" /></td>
          <td class="ctr"><input name="delete[]" type="checkbox"
➥ value="" /></td>
        </tr>
        <tr>
          <td colspan="2"><a href="">Prev</a></td>
          <td colspan="2"><a href="">Next</a></td>
        </tr>
        <tr>
          <td colspan="4"><input name="editBook" type="submit"
➥ id="editBook" value="Edit book" />
            <input name="delBook" type="submit" id="delBook"
➥ value="Delete book(s)" /></td>
        </tr>
      </table>
    </form>
</div>
</body>
</html>
```

The important thing to note about this page is that the names for the radio button and check box (highlighted in bold) end with square brackets. This is because they will be enclosed in the while loop, so they need to be treated as an array. If you recall the discussion of arrays in Chapter 5, PHP automatically assigns the next available number as the key of an array if you use the square bracket notation without explicitly declaring a key.

List authors framework

This page doesn't contain an XHTML form. Instead, it makes use of a custom JavaScript function I created, which will trigger a dialog box (as shown alongside) asking you to confirm that you want to delete an author from the database. The following is the basic XHTML code and JavaScript for `listauthors.php`. It's also available as `listauthors01.php` in the download files.

```
<!DOCTYPE HTML PUBLIC "-//W3C//DTD HTML 4.01 Transitional//EN"
"http://www.w3.org/TR/html4/loose.dtd">
<html>
<head>
<meta http-equiv="Content-Type" content="text/html;
➥ charset=iso-8859-1">
<title>Authors registered</title>
<link href="admin.css" rel="stylesheet" type="text/css">
<script type="text/javascript">
function checkDel(who,id) {
  var msg = 'Are you sure you want to delete '+who+'?';
```

```
  if (confirm(msg))
    location.replace('del_auth_pub.php?name='+who+'&author_id='+id);
  }
</script>
</head>
<body>
<div id="maincontent">
<h1>Authors registered in the database</h1>
<table>
  <tr class="hilite">
    <td> </td>
    <td><a href="edit_auth_pub.php">edit</a></td>
    <td><a href="javascript:checkDel()">delete</a></td>
  </tr>
</table>
</div>
</body>
</html>
```

List publishers framework

This is identical to listauthors.php, with just three small differences. Save a copy of listauthors.php as listpub.php and change the JavaScript function as follows (the new code is highlighted in bold):

```
function checkDel(who,id) {
  var msg = 'Are you sure you want to delete '+who+'?';
  if (confirm(msg))
    location.replace('del_auth_pub.php?name='+who+'&pub_id='+id);
  }
```

The only other changes lie in the <title> and <h1> tags. Change them like this:

```
<title>Publishers registered</title>
<h1>Publishers registered in the database</h1>
```

You can find the full code in listpub01.php in the download files.

Delete book framework

This contains just a form called deleteBooks with two submit buttons called confDel and cancel, and a hidden <input> tag that will contain the book_id. Save the following code as del_book.php or use del_book01.php from the download files.

```
<!DOCTYPE html PUBLIC "-//W3C//DTD XHTML 1.0 Transitional//EN"
"http://www.w3.org/TR/xhtml1/DTD/xhtml1-transitional.dtd">
<html xmlns="http://www.w3.org/1999/xhtml">
<head>
```

```
<meta http-equiv="Content-Type" content="text/html;
➥ charset=iso-8859-1" />
<title>Delete book confirmation</title>
<link href="admin.css" rel="stylesheet" type="text/css" />
</head>
<body>
<form action="" method="post" name="deleteBooks" id="deleteBooks">
  <input name="confDel" type="submit" id="confDel" value="OK" />
  <input name="cancel" type="submit" id="cancel" value="Cancel" />
  <input name="book_id" type="hidden" id="book_id" value="" />
</form>
</body>
</html>
```

Delete author or publisher framework

This is a really minimalist page. All it contains at the moment are a couple of standard XHTML tags. Everything else will be added through PHP. Save the following code as `del_auth_pub.php` or use `del_auth_pub01.php` from the download files.

```
<!DOCTYPE HTML PUBLIC "-//W3C//DTD HTML 4.01 Transitional//EN"
"http://www.w3.org/TR/html4/loose.dtd">
<html>
<head>
<meta http-equiv="Content-Type" content="text/html;
➥ charset=iso-8859-1">
<title>Delete</title>
<link href="admin.css" rel="stylesheet" type="text/css">
</head>
<body>
<div id="maincontent">
  <h1>Delete</h1>
</div>
</body>
</html>
```

Get prices framework

This contains just a table with a single row of <th> cells. If you are using Dreamweaver, select Header Top in the Table dialog box. This will insert `scope="col"` in the <th> tags. I removed it, but there is no harm leaving it in. Save the following code as `getprices.php` or use `getprices01.php` from the download files.

```
<!DOCTYPE html PUBLIC "-//W3C//DTD XHTML 1.0 Transitional//EN"
"http://www.w3.org/TR/xhtml1/DTD/xhtml1-transitional.dtd">
<html xmlns="http://www.w3.org/1999/xhtml">
<head>
```

```
<meta http-equiv="Content-Type" content="text/html;
➥ charset=iso-8859-1" />
<title>Get book prices</title>
<link href="admin.css" rel="stylesheet" type="text/css" />
</head>
<body>
<div id="maincontent">
  <table>
    <tr>
      <thTitle</th>
      <th>List price</th>
      <thStore price</th>
    </tr>
  </table>
</div>
</body>
</html>
```

Building the navigation menu

The navigation menu is generated entirely by PHP, which creates an XHTML unordered list (<ul>) that is styled with CSS to look like a series of buttons across the top of each page. The inspiration for the menu and the original CSS came from Al Sparber, the CSS genius behind Project Seven (www.projectseven.com), the creators of some of the coolest extensions available for Dreamweaver. It's based on what Al calls the Uberlink menu. I won't go into all the details of the CSS (you can read about it from the original creator at www.projectseven.com/tutorials/css/uberlinks/index.htm), but one of the main ideas behind the Uberlink is to assign an id to the <li> tag of the current page to create a "you are here" down state to the button. What I have done is convert the design so that PHP does all the hard work of coding the Uberlink id automatically.

1. Create a new PHP page in phpflash/ch12 and call it admin_funcs.php. The finished code is in admin_funcs01.php in the download files. This is an include file that will be called from other pages, so unlike all the other PHP pages in this chapter, *it should not contain a Doctype or any other XHTML tags apart from those used in the following steps*. If you are using an XHTML editor that inserts the basic framework of tags automatically, strip them out before beginning. You should start with a completely blank page.

2. The menu is built using an associative array of six filenames and the label you want to appear in the associated button. Insert the following code into admin_funcs.php:

```
<?php
function insertMenu() {
  $pages = array('listbooks.php'    => 'List books',
                 'listauthors.php'  => 'List authors',
                 'listpub.php'      => 'List publishers',
                 'new_book.php'     => 'New book',
                 'new_auth_pub.php' => 'New author/publisher',
                 'getprices.php'    => 'Get prices');
```

3. When used in conjunction with XHTML, PHP is frequently interspersed among the XHTML tags and text. Anything between PHP opening and closing tags is interpreted by the PHP engine, while everything else is sent to the browser unchanged. The menu is built with XHTML tags, which you can create either by using echo or by embedding them directly in your code. You're going to do the latter, so—strange though it may seem—the next thing you put inside the insertMenu() function is a closing PHP tag, followed by two lines of XHTML, and then an opening PHP tag. Insert the following code immediately below the $pages array (indent it so that it lines up with the dollar sign of $pages):

```
?>
<div id="menu">
<ul>
<?php
```

The two lines between the closing and opening tags will be treated as ordinary XHTML. They create a <div> for the menu along with the opening <ul> tag. Doing it this way avoids the need to match opening and closing quotes around strings displayed by echo. There's also no need for semicolons at the end of each line.

4. The main part of the menu is created by a loop, which iterates through the $pages array. The following code goes immediately after the previous step.

```
foreach ($pages as $file => $listing) {
  echo '<li';
  if (strpos($_SERVER['SCRIPT_FILENAME'],$file)) {
    echo ' id="uberlink"><a href="javascript:;"';
    }
  else {
    echo '><a href="'.$file.'"';
    }
  echo '>'.$listing.'</a></li>';
  }
```

This basically loops through the $pages array, creating code like this:

```
<li><a href="listbooks.php">List books</a>
```

What's special about the loop is the test (highlighted in bold type) inside the conditional clause. It uses one of the PHP superglobal arrays, $_SERVER, to find the absolute path name of the current script. The insertMenu() function will be called by each individual page in the CMS, so this will check whether the path name of the file calling it includes the value held in $file. If it doesn't, strpos() (covered in Chapter 4) will return 0, which PHP interprets as false. Any other value is interpreted as true. So, if the path name and $file both include listbooks.php, the output sent to the browser will be as follows:

```
<li id="uberlink"><a href="javascript:;">List books</a>
```

In other words, it automatically inserts the id that will style the button in its down state, together with a JavaScript null link.

The $_SERVER superglobal array contains a lot of useful information about the web server that a PHP script is running on. You will use another of its constants shortly to turn all the XHTML forms into self-processing forms. For details of the $_SERVER superglobal array, see www.php.net/manual/en/reserved.variables.php#reserved.variables.server.

5. The final section of the insertMenu() function interpolates some more XHTML tags before the closing curly brace. It goes directly below the code in step 4.

```
?>
</ul>
</div>
<?php
}
```

6. After the function's closing curly brace, insert the closing PHP tag for admin_funcs.php. The full listing for the page, including opening and closing PHP tags, follows.

```
<?php
function insertMenu() {
  $pages = array('listbooks.php'     => 'List books',
                 'listauthors.php'   => 'List authors',
                 'listpub.php'       => 'List publishers',
                 'new_book.php'      => 'New book',
                 'new_auth_pub.php'  => 'New author/publisher',
                 'getprices.php'     => 'Get prices');
  ?>
  <div id="menu">
  <ul>
  <?php
  foreach ($pages as $file => $listing) {
    echo '<li';
    if (strpos($_SERVER['SCRIPT_FILENAME'],$file)) {
      echo ' id="uberlink"><a href="javascript:;"';
      }
    else {
      echo '><a href="'.$file.'"';
      }
    echo '>'.$listing.'</a></li>';
    }
  ?>
  </ul>
  </div>
  <?php
  }
?>
```

7. It may look strange as a function, but it works. To prove it, open each of the pages with an XHTML framework that you have created so far (there should be eight in all), and insert the following include command immediately *above* the Doctype (if necessary, switch to the interface that displays the underlying XHTML—it's called Code view in Dreamweaver):

```
<?php
require_once('admin_funcs.php');
?>
```

8. Immediately after the opening `<body>` tag in each page, insert a call to `insertMenu()` like this:

```
<?php insertMenu(); ?>
```

The following screenshot shows where I placed them (on lines 1 through 3 and on line 12) in `listbooks.php`.

```
1 <?php
2 require_once('admin_funcs.php');
3 ?>
4 <!DOCTYPE html PUBLIC "-//W3C//DTD XHTML 1.0 Transitional//EN"
"http://www.w3.org/TR/xhtml1/DTD/xhtml1-transitional.dtd">
5 <html xmlns="http://www.w3.org/1999/xhtml">
6 <head>
7 <meta http-equiv="Content-Type" content="text/html; charset=iso-8859-1" />
8 <title>List books</title>
9 <link href="admin.css" rel="stylesheet" type="text/css" />
10 </head>
11 <body>
12 <?php insertMenu(); ?>
13 <div id="maincontent">
```

9. Save all the pages and load `listbooks.php` into a browser. It should look like Figure 12-9. Click each of the buttons in the menu, and you should be taken to the relevant page. None of the forms will be functioning yet, and you will not be able to access `del_book.php` or `del_auth_pub.php` from the menu, but it's a good idea to make sure everything's working so far, because the next stage is to get down and dirty with PHP and SQL.

> *Make sure that there is no whitespace before the opening PHP tag or after the closing one in* `admin_funcs.php`*. This includes new lines, even if they have nothing on them. This is because the PHP* `header()` *function will be used to redirect some pages. This will fail and generate a "headers already sent" warning message if any whitespace is left outside the PHP tags. This problem is described in more detail in Appendix A.*

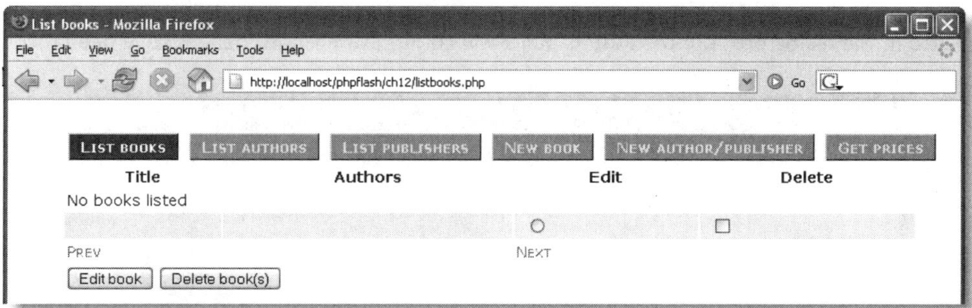

Figure 12-9. The menu is generated from a common function that automatically displays the button for the current page in its down state.

You may have noticed that two of the pages in the original list, `editbook.php` and `edit_auth_pub.php`, have not been created. This is because a lot of the PHP and SQL can be recycled from `new_book.php` and `new_auth_pub.php`, so they will be created much later.

Activating the forms with PHP

If you have worked with (X)HTML forms before, you will know that the opening `<form>` tag contains an attribute called `action`, which takes the address of the script that you want to process the form. Before server-side languages such as PHP became popular, this meant using a CGI script (usually written in Perl). Although a lot of nonprogrammers still rely on Perl scripts, you gain much greater flexibility and control by processing the data yourself. One nice feature with PHP is that you can create **self-processing forms**, where the script is embedded in the same page as the form. This has the advantage that if any of the data is rejected for any reason, you can display it again in the same form for the user to correct, in the same way as the Flash applications have done throughout this book. Forms that preserve the data in this way are normally referred to as **sticky**.

To turn all the forms in the CMS into self-processing forms, you need to set the `action` attribute in each one like this:

```
action="<?php $_SERVER['PHP_SELF']; ?>"
```

This tells the server that the same page is to be used to process the data in the form. Although you could simply type the actual name of the page between the quotes, `$_SERVER['PHP_SELF']` has the advantage that it's a constant value. Even if you change the name of the page, the form will remain self-processing.

The change needs to be made in the following files: `new_book.php`, `new_auth_pub.php` (in both forms), `listbooks.php`, and `del_book.php`. If you are using Dreamweaver and have defined a PHP site as described in the section "Setting up your work environment" in Chapter 1, you can do this in a single operation by selecting all four files in the Files panel (*F8*) and then choosing Edit ➤ Find and Replace (*Ctrl+F*/*⌘+F*). Fill in the dialog box as shown in the screenshot and click

Replace All. There won't normally be enough room for all of the selected filenames to be displayed in the dialog box, but the Results panel will confirm where the changes have been made.

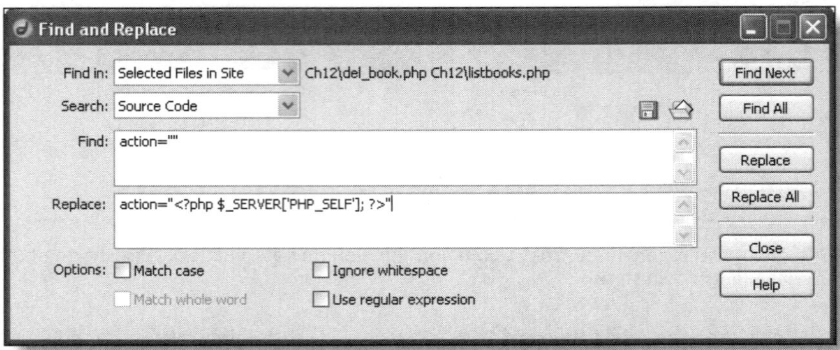

> *The rest of these instructions have been written from the viewpoint of working with a completely empty database. Although there is no problem if you decide to leave the test data from the download files in the tables, the order in which the CMS is built is dictated by the need to consider how to get information into the database in the first place. Because the* books *table uses the primary key from the* publishers *table as a foreign key, you must have records in the* publishers *table first. Otherwise, every single record in the* books *table would need to be updated later. Similarly, you need data in the* authors *table before you can start entering anything into the lookup table. So, even if you keep the test data, remember that the CMS had to be built first. Without it, the data could not have been created.*

Inserting new authors and publishers

The authors and publishers tables both have a simple structure and are not reliant on other tables, so let's start off by getting some information into them.

1. Open new_auth_pub.php, or use new_auth_pub02.php from the download files and change the action in both forms as described in the previous section. The finished code for this section is in new_auth_pub03.php.
2. Insert your cursor at the end of the include command for admin_funcs.php (it should be on line 2) and insert a new line before the closing PHP tag. Put the following code in the space you have just created:

```
if ($_POST) {
  // include Database classes
  require_once('../classes/database.php');
  // escape quotes and apostrophes if magic_quotes_gpc off
  if (!get_magic_quotes_gpc()) {
    foreach($_POST as $key=>$value) {
      $temp = addslashes($value);
      $_POST[$key] = $temp;
```

```
      }
    }
  // create Database instance
  $db=new Database('localhost','flashadmin','fortytwo','bookstore',0);
  // if the "Insert new author" button has been clicked
  if (array_key_exists('insAuthor', $_POST)) {
    // code for inserting author
    }
  // if the "Insert new publisher" button has been clicked
  elseif (array_key_exists('insPublisher', $_POST)) {
    // code for inserting publisher
    }
  // close database connection
  $db->close();
  }
```

The whole of this code block is enclosed in a conditional clause that checks whether the POST array has been set. This happens only when one of the submit buttons has been clicked. If that's the case, the Database classes will be included and a foreach loop escapes any single or double quotes in the data that has been submitted. After the loop, a Database instance is created and assigned to $db. You have seen all this code before, so there is nothing new so far.

Because there are two forms on the page, you need to know which one to process. This is done by the code highlighted in bold type, which checks whether insAuthor or insPublisher is in the POST array. These are the names of the submit buttons in the two forms. Only one button can be clicked at a time. When this happens, all the names and values are gathered from the form and sent in the POST array to the self-processing form. Since only the button that was clicked will be in the POST array, the script knows which block of code to execute.

3. Before inserting an author's name into the database, you need to perform the same check for duplicates as in the user registration application in Chapter 8. The code that handles this follows. It goes immediately after the code for inserting author comment (around line 18).

```
$first_name = $_POST['first_name'];
$family_name = $_POST['family_name'];
$checkName = "SELECT * FROM authors
              WHERE first_name = '$first_name'
              AND family_name = '$family_name'";
$result = $db->query($checkName);
if ($result->num_rows > 0) {
  $authorAlert = stripslashes($first_name).' ';
  $authorAlert .= stripslashes($family_name).' is already registered';
  }
```

The values from the first_name and family_name input fields are reassigned from the POST array to ordinary variables to make them easier to handle, and a SQL query is built from them. Because the first_name and family_name columns are of the VARCHAR type, the values need to be enclosed in quotes. By using ordinary variables, you can enclose them in single quotes, but build the entire query in double quotes so the values are automatically interpolated. If the SQL query returns more than zero rows, it means that the same name already exists in the database, so a warning message is created. When the warning message is built, the names are passed to the `stripslashes()` function to remove any backslashes that have been inserted to escape quotes or apostrophes. For instance, if you had entered O'Toole as a family name, the SQL query would include `family_name = 'O\'Toole'`. You need to remove that backslash before displaying it onscreen.

4. The code that creates `$authorAlert` is executed *only* if there is a duplicate entry. Consequently, if `$authorAlert` hasn't been set, you know that this is a new author and that you can enter the details in the database. The next block of code goes immediately after the code in step 3 (around line 28).

```
if (!isset($authorAlert)) {
  $insertAuthor = "INSERT INTO authors (first_name, family_name)
                   VALUES ('$first_name', '$family_name')";
  $result = $db->query($insertAuthor);
  if ($result) {
    $authorAlert = stripslashes($first_name).' ';
    $authorAlert .= stripslashes($family_name).' entered successfully';
    }
  }
```

This is fairly straightforward. The INSERT query is built using the `$first_name` and `$family_name` variables, it is submitted to the database, and a message is assigned to `$authorAlert`. Again, the names are passed to `stripslashes()` to remove any backslashes from escaped quotes or apostrophes.

The only check I've carried out on the input is to determine whether it's a duplicate entry. I'm assuming that use of a CMS for a database such as this will be restricted to bona-fide users. You can't always make such assumptions, and the more checks you build into your applications, the better. You could use either JavaScript form validation or PHP to check that only valid names are used (for instance, a regex could be used to limit input to a range of acceptable characters). I kept checks to a minimum here because I want to concentrate on working with multiple tables and techniques to ensure that referential integrity is maintained without using foreign key constraints.

5. The code for inserting a new publisher is identical in structure. The only difference is in the variable names and SQL queries that need to be built, so I'll just reproduce it here without comment. It goes immediately after the code for inserting publisher comment in step 2 (now around line 41).

```
$publisher = $_POST['publisher'];
$checkName = "SELECT * FROM publishers
              WHERE publisher = '$publisher'";
$result = $db->query($checkName);
if ($result->num_rows > 0) {
```

```
    $publisherAlert = stripslashes($publisher);
    $publisherAlert .= ' is already registered in the publishers table';
    }
  if (!isset($publisherAlert)) {
    $insertPublisher = "INSERT INTO publishers
                        SET publisher = '$publisher'";
    $result = $db->query($insertPublisher);
    if ($result) {
      $publisherAlert = stripslashes($publisher);
      $publisherAlert .= ' successfully entered in the publishers table';
      }
    }
```

6. You need to display the contents of the messages generated by the script. Place the following PHP immediately after the XHTML `Insert new author` heading (around line 74):

```
<h1>Insert new author</h1>
<?php
if (isset($authorAlert))
  echo '<p id="alert">'.$authorAlert.'</p>';
?>
```

A similar block goes after the `Insert new publisher` heading (around line 95):

```
<h1>Insert new publisher</h1>
<?php
if (isset($publisherAlert))
  echo '<p id="alert">'.$publisherAlert.'</p>';
?>
```

7. Save `new_auth_pub.php` and load it into a browser. If you need to start MySQL manually, do so, and then insert some authors' and publishers' names. Try entering the same name twice. Figure 12-10 shows the result when I entered my own name successfully for the first time, and then what happened when I tried to do it again.

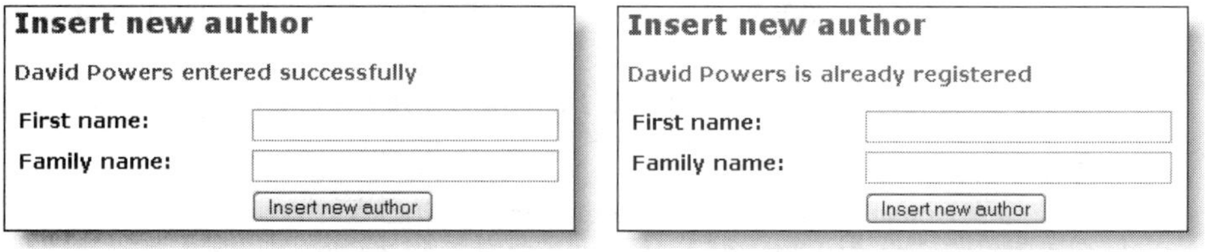

Figure 12-10. The CMS reports when a new author has been successfully registered (left), but it prevents you from entering the same name twice (right).

If you want to check that everything is working, take a look at the authors and publishers tables in phpMyAdmin after adding at least one author and one publisher through this page (although you can access `listauthors.php` and `listpub.php` from the navigation menu, they don't work yet). If you encounter any problems, check your code against `new_auth_pub03.php` in the download files.

Listing authors

Once you have confirmed that new_auth_pub.php is inserting authors' and publishers' details into your database, you can adapt the listauthors.php and listpub.php pages to do the same more conveniently within your CMS.

1. Open listauthors.php or use listauthors02.php from the download files. The completed code for this section is in listauthors03.php.
2. Place your cursor after the include command for admin_funcs.php (at the end of line 2) and insert some space before the closing PHP tag. Enter the following code:

```
require_once('../classes/database.php');
$db=new Database('localhost','flashuser','deepthought','bookstore',0);
$getAuthors = 'SELECT author_id,
              CONCAT(first_name," ",UPPER(family_name)) AS author
              FROM authors ORDER BY family_name, first_name';
$result = $db->query($getAuthors);
```

This includes the Databases classes and creates a connection to the bookstore database. The SELECT query uses two MySQL functions, CONCAT() and UPPER(), to format the first_name and family_name columns, and assigns them to author as an alias. You learned about the use of aliases in the previous chapter. What the functions do is fairly easy to guess from their names: UPPER() converts a string value to uppercase, and CONCAT() concatenates a comma-delimited list of values. So, by concatenating the value of first_name with a single space and the value of family_name converted to uppercase, and then assigning the result to author as an alias, this query produces results such as David POWERS, Sham BHANGAL, and so on. Finally, the results are sorted first by family_name, and then by first_name, so although David comes before Sham, the "B" of Bhangal takes precedence over the "P" of Powers.

3. Now comes the tricky bit (although it's the way PHP is used all the time in XHTML websites). The XHTML framework that you built earlier contains a table with just one row in it. You now need to build a loop to display the results of the SQL query in the right parts of the table. As you saw with the insertMenu() function, you can intersperse XHTML tags and plain text with dynamic output from PHP. Whatever appears between PHP tags is parsed by the PHP engine; everything outside them is treated as normal XHTML.

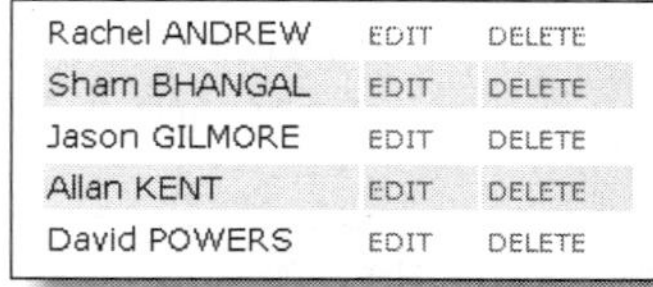

The first thing you need to do is create the loop. As you can see from the screenshot alongside, the list of authors consists of the author's name, followed by an EDIT link and a DELETE link, similar to the listUsers screen in the CMS built in Chapter 10. The structure of each row is always the same; the only things that change are the name and the author_id that will be used to activate the two links. The PHP code for the loop is placed just before the opening <tr> tag of the table row and just after the closing </tr> tag, like this (the new code is highlighted in bold type):

```
<table>
<?php
$i = 1;
while ($row = $result->fetch_assoc()) {
```

```
?>
  <tr class="hilite">
    <td> </td>
    <td><a href="edit_auth_pub.php">edit</a></td>
    <td><a href="javascript:checkDel()">delete</a></td>
  </tr>
<?php
  $i++;
  }
// close the database connection
$db->close();
?>
</table>
```

A counter ($i) is initialized just before the loop and incremented at the end of each iteration to enable each alternate row to be highlighted.

4. If you cast your mind back to Chapter 3, I said one of the uses of modulo was to determine whether a number is odd or even. If you use modulo division by 2 on any number, it will return 0 if the number is even or 1 if the number is odd. Since 0 is treated by PHP as false, the test if ($number % 2) returns false when $number is even. On the other hand, 1 is regarded as a positive result, meaning $number must be odd. By combining this with the conditional operator, you can change the class of alternate table rows from hilite to nohilite.

   Change the opening <tr> tag (line 6 in the code in the previous step) like this:

   ```
   <tr class="<?php echo $i%2 ? 'nohilite' : 'hilite'; ?>">
   ```

   When $i%2 equals 1, the PHP code will echo nohilite inside the double quotes of class="". In accordance with the stylesheet, this gives the table row a white background. Even rows will have a class of hilite, which is styled with a beige background.

5. In the next line of code, replace the   (nonbreaking space character) with the value of the author's name for the current row:

   ```
   <td><?php echo $row['author']; ?></td>
   ```

6. The next line of code contains an ordinary link to edit_auth_pub.php:

   ```
   <td><a href="edit_auth_pub.php">edit</a></td>
   ```

   This needs to be amended so that the link contains a query string that will identify the author you want to edit. Because the edit page will handle both authors and publishers (it will be based on the insert page new_auth_pub.php), the query string will carry three pieces of information: the name of the table that is being updated, the name of primary key (identified in the query string as type), and the primary key number. The first two pieces of information can be hard-coded in the query string, but the author_id needs to come from the current row of the database results. So, the final code for this line looks like this:

   ```
   <td><a href="edit_auth_pub.php?table=authors&type=author_id&num=
   ➥ <?php echo $row['author_id']; ?>">edit</a></td>
   ```

7. The final <td> element in the row contains a link that calls the JavaScript function checkDel(), which will be used to display a dialog box asking for confirmation of the deletion. The function takes two parameters: the author's name and author_id. As you can see from the screenshot alongside, the dialog box displays the author's name. To prevent any quotes or apostrophes from breaking the call to the function, the author's name must first be passed to addslashes(). Change line 9 of the code in step 3 like this:

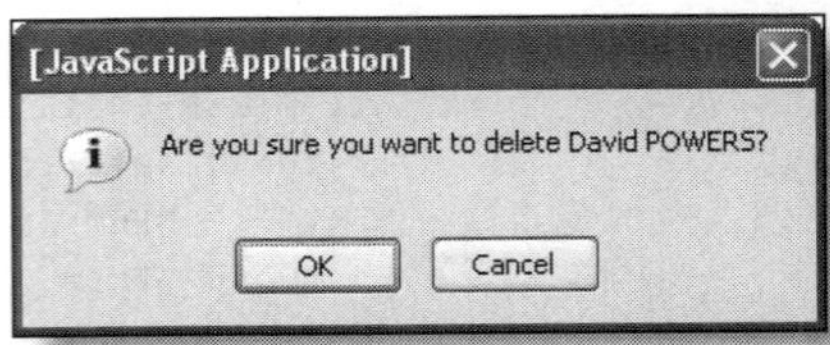


```
<td><a href="javascript:checkDel('<?php echo
➥ addslashes($row['author']); ?>',<?php echo $row['author_id']; ?>)">
➥ delete</a></td>
```

Although PHP allows you to break up code with whitespace, make sure that the code inside checkDel() doesn't include any hard returns; otherwise, the JavaScript will fail.

8. Save listauthors.php and view it in a browser. You should now see the full list of names that you have entered into the authors table. Test the DELETE links to make sure the confirmation dialog box appears. If you click OK, you'll be taken to the delete page, but nothing will happen. If you click the EDIT link, you'll get a "page not found" error because that page doesn't exist yet. If you have any problems, check your code against listauthors03.php.

Listing publishers

This page follows exactly the same pattern as listauthors.php, so no explanation will be given. Use your own version of listpub.php or listpub02.php from the download files, and amend it as described here. You can find the final code in listpub03.php.

1. Add the following block of code after the include call to admin_funcs.php above the Doctype:

```
require_once('../classes/database.php');
$db=new Database('localhost','flashuser','deepthought','bookstore',0);
$getPublishers = 'SELECT * FROM publishers ORDER BY publisher';
$result = $db->query($getPublishers);
```

2. Amend the table in the body of the page as follows:

```
<table>
<?php
$i = 1;
while ($row = $result->fetch_assoc()) {
?>
  <tr class="<?php echo $i%2 ? 'nohilite' : 'hilite'; ?>">
    <td><?php echo $row['publisher']; ?></td>
    <td><a href="edit_auth_pub.php?table=publishers&type=pub_id&num=
➥ <?php echo $row['pub_id']; ?>">edit</a></td>
```

```
    <td><a href="javascript:checkDel('<?php echo
➥ addslashes($row['publisher']); ?>',<?php echo $row['pub_id']; ?>)">
➥ delete</a></td>
  </tr>
<?php
  $i++;
  }
// close database connection
$db->close();
?>
</table>
```

3. Perform the same tests as on listauthors.php. Both pages should work in the same way. Check your code against listpub03.php if you have any problems.

Editing authors and publishers

All the forms in the CMS have their method attribute set to post, so all the data gathered from them is handed to the PHP scripts in the POST array. When we've sent data between PHP and Flash with LoadVars, this is the method we've always used. Forms built in XHTML, however, often use a **query string** attached to the end of the URL to transfer variables between pages. A query string contains one or more URL-encoded name/value pairs, and it's placed after a question mark at the end of the page's URL. You've probably noticed this sort of thing when using an online search engine, such as Google. The variables passed to a page in this manner are stored in the GET array, which is one of the PHP superglobal arrays discussed in Chapter 5. Because the query string is exposed in the browser's address bar, using the GET array to transfer variables is less secure than using the POST array. However, the fact that the two arrays are completely separate means you can exploit the differences and use the same page to do different things depending on whether the POST array has been set.

If you load listauthors.php into a browser and hover your cursor over the EDIT link alongside one of the authors' names, and then look at the browser status bar (at the bottom), you should see a query string attached to the URL for edit_auth_pub.php. Figure 12-11 shows that I have made a mistake in spelling Jason Gilmore's family name, so I need to edit it. The query string at the end of the URL looks like this:

```
?table=authors&type=author_id&num=3
```

This information will be available to PHP inside edit_auth_pub.php as if the following variables had been set:

```
$_GET['table'] = 'authors';
$_GET['type'] = 'author_id';
$_GET['num'] = 3;
```

Figure 12-11. The browser status bar displays a unique query string at the end of the URL, which instructs the edit page to display Jason Gilmore's details ready for correction.

The primary key numbers in the screenshots from this point onward will not necessarily be the same as the theoretical example in Tables 12-1 and 12-2 and in Figure 12-2 at the beginning of the chapter. The screenshots are taken from a live database, and some numbers may change as records are deleted and re-entered for test purposes.

This is why referential integrity is so important. The actual value of each primary key number is unimportant in itself, but the continuity of the relationships it maintains will determine the success or failure of the database. If the record associated with `author_id` *3 is deleted, all other records that contain a reference to it must also be deleted. If the same author is re-entered at a later stage, the* `author_id` *will be different, and there is no way of re-establishing the previous relationships.*

Adapting new_auth_pub.php to edit records

In the same way as the Flash-based CMS in Chapter 10 re-utilized a large part of the original user registration form, you can do the same with the page that is used to edit the details of authors and publishers. Most of the checks are the same, but the SQL needs to be altered so that it uses `UPDATE` rather than `INSERT`.

1. Open `new_auth_pub.php` and then save it as `edit_auth_pub.php`. Alternatively, use `edit_auth_pub01.php` from the download files. The finished code for this section is in `edit_auth_pub02.php`.
2. You now have an exact copy of the insert page for authors and publishers that can be adapted much more quickly than building all the PHP and SQL from scratch. The first thing you need to do is insert the code that will retrieve the details of the record that you want to edit. As just explained, the information will be passed to `edit_auth_pub.php` as a query string, so you need to extract the values from the `GET` array and use them to build a suitable SQL query.

   At the moment, the `Database` classes are included only if the `POST` array has been set. Begin by moving the include command outside the conditional statement at the top of the page. Find this code (it should begin on line 1):

   ```
   <?php
   require_once('admin_funcs.php');
   if ($_POST) {
     // include Database classes
     require_once('../classes/database.php');
   ```

   Change it like this:

   ```
   <?php
   require_once('admin_funcs.php');
   // include Database classes
   require_once('../classes/database.php');
   if ($_GET && !$_POST) {
     // get details of record to be edited
     }
   elseif ($_POST) {
   ```

This ensures that the Database classes will be available to all parts of the script, but that different code blocks will run depending on whether the POST array has been set. Since you need to have clicked one of the form buttons in the page for the POST array to be set, the second block of code will not run when you first access the page from either listauthors.php or listpub.php. Figure 12-12 shows the sequence of events.

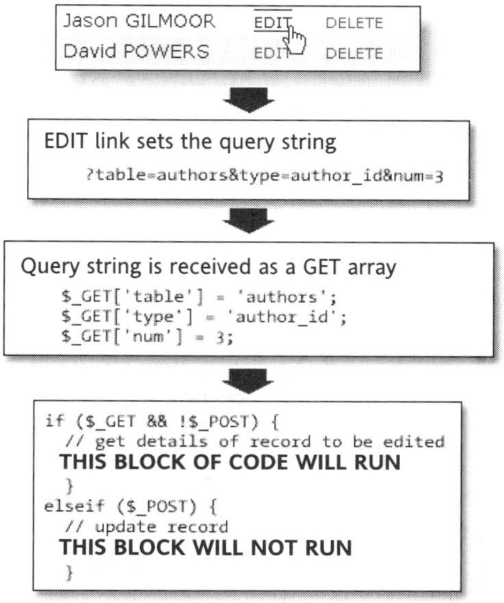

The first part of the conditional statement needs to specify explicitly that the POST array has not been set. This is because the action in PHP self-processing forms is set to $_SERVER['PHP_SELF'], which uses the current URL. The query string is regarded as an integral part of the URL, so it will be preserved, even after you click a form button to update the record being edited. So if ($_GET) on its own would always return true, and the second block of code would never be executed.

Jason GILMOOR EDIT DELETE
David POWERS EDIT DELETE

EDIT link sets the query string

?table=authors&type=author_id&num=3

Query string is received as a GET array

```
$_GET['table'] = 'authors';
$_GET['type'] = 'author_id';
$_GET['num'] = 3;
```

```
if ($_GET && !$_POST) {
  // get details of record to be edited
  THIS BLOCK OF CODE WILL RUN
  }
elseif ($_POST) {
  // update record
  THIS BLOCK WILL NOT RUN
  }
```

Figure 12-12. How edit_auth_pub.php knows which block of code to execute when accessed from listauthors.php

3. The code that goes inside the first set of curly braces builds a SELECT query from the contents of the GET array. Insert the following code after the get details of record to be edited comment:

```
$db=new Database('localhost','flashuser','deepthought','bookstore',0);
$getDets = 'SELECT * FROM '.$_GET['table'];
$getDets .= ' WHERE '.$_GET['type'].' = '.$_GET['num'];
echo $getDets;
```

4. Save edit_auth_pub.php and load listauthors.php into a browser. Click one of the EDIT links. edit_auth_pub.php should load into your browser and display the contents of the SELECT query at the top of the page, as shown in the screenshot here.

SELECT * FROM authors WHERE author_id = 3
LIST BOOKS LIST AUTHORS LIST PUBLISHERS

Make sure that the query is correctly formatted. The $getDets code contains spaces to separate the variables from the surrounding string. Forgetting to include the spaces and neglecting to include the necessary quotes are the main causes of SQL queries failing. You don't need any quotes here, because author_id is an INT (integer) column.

5. Click LIST PUBLISHERS and perform the same test with one of the publishers. You should see something like the screenshot here. This time, the SELECT query should contain publishers and pub_id.

SELECT * FROM publishers WHERE pub_id = 1
LIST BOOKS LIST AUTHORS LIST PUBLISHERS

6. Now that you know the SQL query is well formed, change the last line of code in step 3 like this:

```
$result = $db->query($getDets);
```

7. You need to extract the results of the query and display them in the appropriate input fields of the forms. Add the following line of code immediately after the line you just edited:

```
$row = $result->fetch_assoc();
```

There is no need for a loop because there will always be only one row of results.

8. To display the appropriate data for each input field, you need to add a value attribute to each one and echo the relevant result from the database. Scroll down to about line 90 and locate the following XHTML:

```
<td><input name="first_name" type="text" id="first_name"
➥ class="mediumbox" /></td>
```

Place your cursor after the closing quote of class="mediumbox" and press *Enter/Return* twice to enter two new lines. Move your cursor up to the blank line you just created and insert the following code:

```
value="<?php if (isset($row['first_name'])) echo
➥ $row['first_name']; ?>"
```

This is a simple conditional statement that will echo the value of $row['first_name'] inside the double quotes of value="". To see the effect, save edit_auth_pub.php, click LIST AUTHORS, and then click one of the EDIT links. You should see something like the screenshot—the author's first name has automatically been entered into the first input field. You now need to fix the other fields. There's also some onscreen text that needs changing. This is an update page, not one for entering new records.

9. Repeat step 8 for the family_name and publisher fields, using $row['family_name'] and $row['publisher']. Also amend the <h1> headings (around lines 81 and 106) to read Edit author name and Edit publisher.

10. When edit_auth_pub.php loads, it gets the author's or publisher's primary key from the GET array, but when you click one of the form buttons, all the amended information will be in the POST array. To make sure the right record is updated, you also need to include the primary key with the other POST variables. The way you do this with an XHTML form is to create a hidden field. Locate the following code (around line 101):

```
<th> </th>
<td><input name="insAuthor" type="submit" id="insAuthor" value="Insert
➥ new author" /></td>
```

Amend it like this:

```
<th><input name="author_id" type="hidden" id="author_id"
value="<?php if (isset($row['author_id'])) echo $row['author_id']; ?>"
/></th>
<td><input name="updateAuthor" type="submit" id="updateAuthor"
➥ value="Update author name" /></td>
```

The PHP code for the hidden field follows exactly the same pattern as the other input elements. The field is hidden only in the sense that it is not displayed directly in the browser, although you can see it if you view the underlying XHTML source code. Note also that the name and id attributes of the submit button have been changed. This will prevent the code in the POST block at the top of the page from being executed accidentally, because it still needs to be amended to handle updates, rather than insert new records.

11. Repeat step 10 with the final row of the publisherDets form (around lines 122–123), using **pub_id** instead of author_id, and **updatePublisher** instead of updateAuthor.

12. Now it's time to adapt the code in the POST block at the top of the page. This follows a similar pattern to that used in the Flash CMS in Chapter 10. Locate the comment around line 23 that reads if the "Insert new author" button has been clicked. Amend the comment and the following lines like this (the new code is highlighted in bold type):

```
// if the "Update author name" button has been clicked
if (array_key_exists('updateAuthor', $_POST)) {
  // code for updating author
  $first_name = $_POST['first_name'];
  $family_name = $_POST['family_name'];
  $author_id = $_POST['author_id'];
  $checkName = "SELECT * FROM authors
                WHERE first_name = '$first_name'
                AND family_name = '$family_name'
                AND author_id != $author_id";
  $result = $db->query($checkName);
  if ($result->num_rows > 0) {
    $authorAlert = "$first_name $family name is already registered";
    }
  if (!isset($authorAlert)) {
    $updateAuthor = "UPDATE authors SET first_name = '$first_name',
                     family_name = '$family_name'
                     WHERE author_id = $author_id";
    $result = $db->query($updateAuthor);
    if ($result) {
      $db->close();
      $author = urlencode("$first_name $family_name");
      header('Location: listauthors.php?author='.$author);
      }
    }
  }
```

As in Chapter 10, the check for duplicates must exclude the current record, so AND author_id != author_id is added to the end of the $checkname SQL query. If the name is not a duplicate, the UPDATE query is prepared and submitted to MySQL. If the update is successful, the author's name is assigned to $author and the header() function redirects the script to listauthors.php with the author's name added as a query string. You used the header() function in Chapter 9 to redirect unauthorized users away from your protected pages.

13. Save edit_auth_pub.php. Before you test it, open listauthors.php and add the following block of code immediately after the <h1> heading (around line 28):

```
<?php
if (isset($_GET['author']))
  echo '<p id="alert">'.stripslashes($_GET['author']).
➥ ' has been updated in the database</p>';
?>
```

This will display a message telling you that the author has been updated. The conditional statement ensures that it will run only when you have been redirected from the update page.

14. Save listauthors.php (the updated version is in listauthors04.php), select an author and click the EDIT link alongside, make some changes in edit_auth_pub.php, and click the Update author name button. If everything goes well, you should get the sort of result shown in Figure 12-13.

Figure 12-13. After the author's name has been corrected in edit_auth_pub.php (left), a list of the authors is displayed with a message informing you of the update (right).

15. If it doesn't work, the most likely cause of the problem will be in the SQL. Comment out the line that submits the UPDATE query to the database, and use echo to display the contents of $updateAuthor. Also compare your code with edit_auth_pub02.php.

16. Complete the page by amending the section of code that updates the publisher's details as shown here (the new code is highlighted in bold type):

```
elseif (array_key_exists('updatePublisher', $_POST)) {
  // code for updating publisher
  $publisher = $_POST['publisher'];
  $pub_id = $_POST['pub_id'];
  $checkName = "SELECT * FROM publishers
               WHERE publisher = '$publisher'
               AND pub_id != $pub_id";
  $result = $db->query($checkName);
```

```
if ($result->num_rows > 0) {
  $publisherAlert = "$publisher is already registered";
  }
if (!isset($publisherAlert)) {
  $updatePublisher = "UPDATE publishers SET publisher = '$publisher'
                      WHERE pub_id = $pub_id";
  $result = $db->query($updatePublisher);
  if ($result) {
    $db->close();
    header('Location: listpub.php?pub='.$publisher);
    }
  }
}
```

17. Repeat step 13 for listpub.php, replacing author with **publisher**. Check your code against edit_auth_pub02.php and listpub04.php.

The logical next step might seem to be to finish the content management for authors and publishers by adding the scripts to activate the DELETE links. However, it's important not to delete authors or publishers if any reference to them still exists in either the books table or the book_to_author table, which brings you to your first real encounter with multiple tables.

Inserting new books

The page that inserts new books into the bookstore database is the linchpin of the whole CMS. It draws details from the authors and publishers tables, and inserts records in the books table and book_to_author lookup table.

Populating the authors and publishers menus

If you click the NEW BOOK button in the navigation menu, you'll notice that the multiple-select menu for authors and the drop-down menu for publishers don't yet contain any selections. So the first job is to populate them.

1. Open new_book.php or use new_book02.php from the download files. The finished code for this section is in new_book03.php.
2. Amend the block of PHP code above the Doctype to include the Database classes and retrieve the records from the authors and publishers tables. The new code is highlighted in bold. It contains nothing you have not encountered before.

```
<?php
require_once('admin_funcs.php');
require_once('../classes/database.php');
// this code always runs, and gets lists of authors and publishers
$db=new Database('localhost','flashuser','deepthought','bookstore',0);
$getAuthors = 'SELECT author_id,
               CONCAT(first_name," ", UPPER(family_name)) AS author
               FROM authors
               ORDER BY family_name, first_name';
```

```
$authors = $db->query($getAuthors);
$getPublishers = 'SELECT * FROM publishers ORDER BY publisher';
$publishers = $db->query($getPublishers);
?>
```

3. Locate the code in the body of the page that creates the multiple-select menu for authors. It looks like this and should be around lines 37 through 40:

```
<td><select name="author" size="6" multiple="multiple" id="author">
  <option value="choose" selected="selected">Select author(s)</option>
  <option value="other">Not listed</option>
</select></td>
```

The name attribute of the <select> tag identifies the menu as author, but in this format PHP will recognize only the first item selected, so you need to add an empty pair of square brackets after author to tell PHP that it's an array.

Each <option> tag contains a value attribute that the form uses to identify selected items, and a label that goes between the opening and closing tags. To populate the menu with authors, you need to use a loop to create a new <option> tag for each author, assign the author_id to value, and place the author's name between the opening and closing tags.

Change the code so that it looks like this:

```
<td><select name="author[]" size="6" multiple="multiple" id="author">
   <option value="choose" selected="selected">Select author(s)</option>
   <option value="other">Not listed</option>
<?php
while ($row = $authors->fetch_assoc()) {
  echo '<option value="'.$row['author_id'].'">';
  echo $row['author'].'</option>';
  }
?>
</select></td>
```

4. Save new_book.php and click the Refresh button in your browser. The menu should populate with the names of authors, as shown in the screenshot alongside. View the source code of the page, and you should see the correct author_id values in the value attribute of each <option> tag.

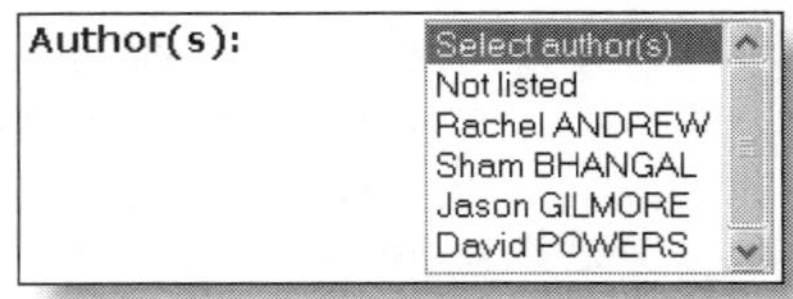

5. You now need to create a similar loop for the publisher drop-down menu. Because this menu permits only a single choice, do *not* add square brackets to the name attribute in the opening <select> tag. Just locate the closing </select> tag for the publisher drop-down menu (it should be around line 53), and insert the loop like this:

```
   <option value="other">Not listed</option>
<?php
while ($row = $publishers->fetch_assoc()) {
  echo '<option value="'.$row['pub_id'].'">';
```

```
    echo $row['publisher'].'</option>';
    }
  // close database connection
  $db->close();
  ?>
  </select></td>
```

6. Save new_book.php and click the Refresh button in your browser. Activate the drop-down menu, and you should now see a list of publishers, as shown in the screenshot alongside. Again, check in the browser's source code view to verify that the pub_id for each publisher is in the value attribute. Check your code against new_book03.php.

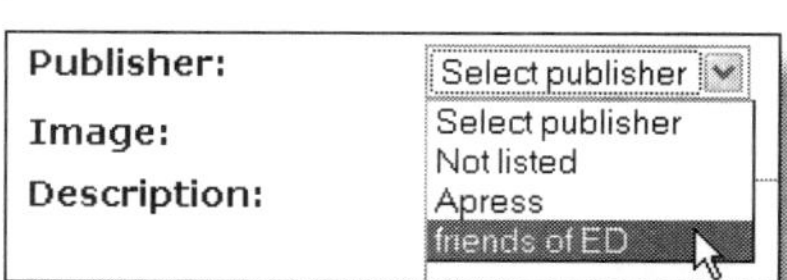

The code in the XHTML form now contains data from two of your database tables, which can be combined with user-input data to insert records into the books table and the book_to_author lookup table.

This answers the nagging question of how on earth you remember the value of a foreign key. You don't need to; you get the database to look it up for you. If you now edit the name of any author or publisher, all references to that author or publisher will automatically reflect that change. Pretty cool!

The select menus both contain an option for entering a book where the author or publisher is not yet listed, enabling you to come back later and update the record when the relevant information has been entered into the database.

Validating and inserting data

Before you can insert data into the books and book_to_author tables, you need to make sure it's valid and won't cause the SQL queries to fail.

1. Continue working with new_book.php or use new_book03.php from the download files. The completed code for this section is in new_book04.php.
2. The validation and insert code should be executed only if the submit button has been clicked, so it's enclosed in a conditional statement that checks whether the POST array has been set. The following code goes at the top of the page, just before the closing PHP tag in step 2 of the preceding section:

```
// this first block runs only if the form has been submitted
if ($_POST) {
  // check for empty fields
  foreach($_POST as $key=>$value) {
    // authors is a subarray, so skip
    if (is_array($value)) continue;
    $value = trim($value);
```

```
    if (empty($value)) {
      if ($key == 'isbn') {
        $error[] = 'ISBN is required';
        }
      // if no publisher selected, value is 0, considered empty by PHP
      elseif ($key == 'publisher') {
        $error[] = 'You must select a publisher';
        }
      else {
        $error[] = ucfirst($key).' is required';
        }
      }
    }
  // remove any hyphens from ISBN and check for valid length
  $_POST['isbn'] = str_replace('-','',$_POST['isbn']);
  if (strlen($_POST['isbn']) != 10) {
    if (strlen($_POST['isbn']) != 13) {
      $error[] = 'ISBNs have 10 or 13 characters (excluding hyphens)';
      }
    }
  // check that an author has been chosen
  if ($_POST['author'][0] == 'choose' && count($_POST['author']) < 2) {
    $error[] = 'Select at least one author, or choose "Not listed"';
    }
  // if all fields correctly filled, prepare to insert in database
  if (!isset($error)) {
    // final preparations for insertion
    }
  }
```

Although lengthy, this code simply trims any whitespace from each of the input fields in the POST array and checks if any of them are empty. One of the values in the POST array (`$_POST['author']`) is actually an array, which means it cannot be passed to `trim()`, so the continue keyword is used inside the foreach loop to skip any subarrays.

In the first set of checks, the ISBN is simply tested to see if it contains a value, but later a more specific test removes all the hyphens and rejects any ISBN that doesn't contain exactly 10 or 13 characters.

Because the menu for selecting authors permits multiple choices, the test on `$_POST['author']` assumes that the user might have left Select author still selected. So it checks that at least one other author has been selected.

Only if the input passes all of these tests will the final block of code be executed. At the moment, this contains nothing more than a comment because the insert code in itself is quite long.

3. Before I show you the insert code, it's a good idea to check that these tests are working. Scroll down to about line 60 and insert this code after the `<h1>` heading:

```
<h1>Insert new book</h1>
<?php
if (isset($error)) {
```

```
echo '<div id="alert"><p>Please correct the following:</p><ul>';
foreach ($error as $item) {
  echo "<li>$item</li>";
  }
echo '</ul></div>';
}
?>
```

4. Save new_book.php and test the warning messages. If you click the Insert new book button without filling in any fields, you should get a series of warning messages, as shown in the following screenshot.

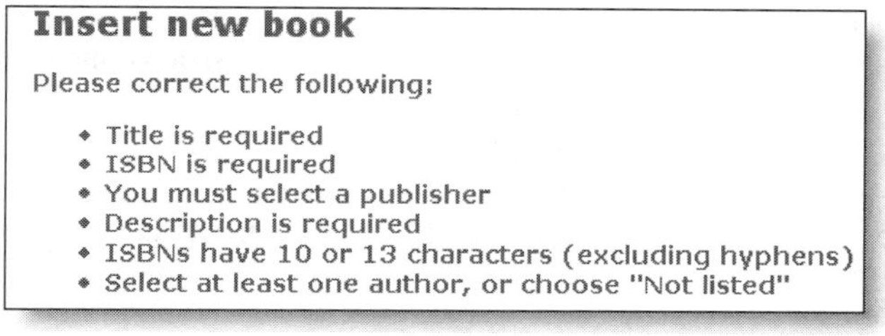

Insert new book

Please correct the following:

- Title is required
- ISBN is required
- You must select a publisher
- Description is required
- ISBNs have 10 or 13 characters (excluding hyphens)
- Select at least one author, or choose "Not listed"

5. Even though you've carried out some important checks on the validity of the data, you still need to establish that the ISBN isn't already registered in the database. However, I've decided to put this check inside the final block on the assumption that a duplicate ISBN is a genuine oversight, rather than simply the result of operator error. The following code goes immediately after the final comment in the code that you inserted in step 2 (around line 42):

```
// escape quotes and apostrophes if magic_quotes_gpc off
if (!get_magic_quotes_gpc()) {
  foreach($_POST as $key=>$value) {
    // skip author subarray
    if (is_array($value)) continue;
    $temp = addslashes($value);
    $_POST[$key] = $temp;
    }
  }
// create a Database instance, and set error reporting to plain text
$db = new Database('localhost','flashadmin','fortytwo','bookstore',0);
// first check that the same ISBN doesn't already exist
$checkISBN = 'SELECT isbn FROM books
              WHERE isbn = "'.$_POST['isbn'].'"';
$result = $db->query($checkISBN);
if ($result->num_rows > 0) {
  $error[] = 'A book with that ISBN already exists in the database';
  }
else {
  // if ISBN unique, insert book into books table
  // get the primary key of the record just inserted
```

```
// build array of book_id and author_id pairs, one for each author
// insert book_id/author_id pairs into lookup table
// if successful, redirect to confirmation page
}
```

The first section of this code is the loop you've used many times to escape quotes and apostrophes before inserting data into a database. It's slightly different this time to avoid problems with `$_POST['author']` being an array in its own right. As in step 2, any subarrays are skipped. Then a new `Database` instance is created, using `flashadmin`. This will replace the existing instance, which doesn't have the correct privileges to insert material into the `bookstore` database. A `SELECT` query checks that the ISBN isn't already registered. If all these tests are passed, it's finally OK to insert the book's details into the `books` and `book_to_author` tables. Although this appears a long, drawn-out process, such checks are necessary to make sure you record only valid data.

6. Although all the checks are complete, if the value of `$_POST['publisher']` has been set to `other`, it needs to be changed to `0`. The reason the form doesn't use zero in the first place is that zero is regarded by PHP as the same as "empty," whereas you want "other" to signify the deliberate choice of a publisher not currently listed in the database. The following code goes beneath the first comment in the final `else` clause of the code in step 5:

```
if ($_POST['publisher'] == 'other') $_POST['publisher'] = 0;
```

7. Now you can build the SQL query. It goes immediately after the previous line.

```
$insert = 'INSERT INTO books (title,isbn,pub_id,image,description)
          VALUES ("'.$_POST['title'].'","'.$_POST['isbn'].'",'.
          $_POST['publisher'].',"'.$_POST['image'].'",
          "'.$_POST['description'].'")';
echo $insert;
```

The query is straightforward, but it's one of those finger-twisting occasions when it's so easy to get quotes and commas mixed up. Save `new_book.php`, enter some book details, and click the Insert new book button. The contents of the SQL statement should be displayed at the top of the page, as shown in Figure 12-14.

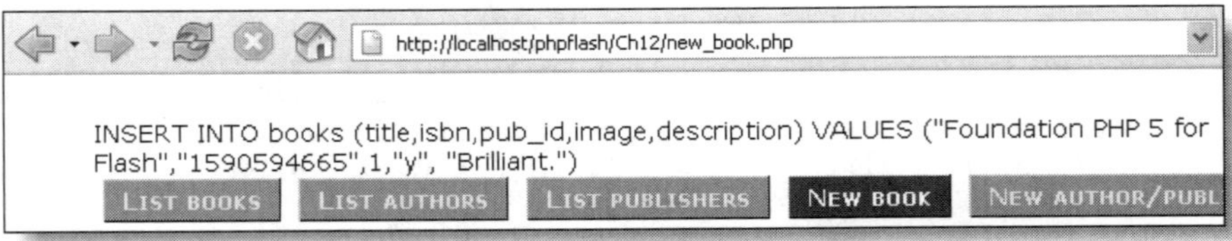

Figure 12-14. Using echo to display the contents of SQL queries is an important way of testing your code.

By displaying the contents of test queries like this, you can see immediately if you have left out a vital space between strings and variables, and whether you have commas and quotes in the right place. All the columns affected by this query—except `pub_id`—are text types, so each value apart from `pub_id` needs to be in quotes.

In American English, the normal typographical convention is to put commas and periods inside closing quotes. Don't do this when building SQL statements or arrays of strings in any computer language; the commas must go outside the quotes.

8. After testing your SQL code, amend the final line in step 7 like this to enter the data in the books table:

```
$result = $db->query($insert);
```

9. Next, you need to find the primary key of the record you just entered. You do this with the following code, which goes after the second comment in the else clause at the end of step 5 (around line 69):

```
$getBook_id = 'SELECT book_id FROM books
               WHERE isbn = "'.$_POST['isbn'].'"';
$result = $db->query($getBook_id);
$row = $result->fetch_assoc();
$book_id = $row['book_id'];
```

10. Now that you have the primary key of the book (book_id), you can begin to prepare the SQL query to insert it into the lookup table. If you look back at Figure 12-2, you will recall that each entry consists of a unique pair of the book_id and author_id. All the author_id values are held in the $_POST['author'] subarray. In addition to any authors registered in the database, two other values might have been selected: choose (if the default has remained selected for any reason) and other (if the author has not been listed in the database). The first value must be removed from the subarray with the following code, which goes immediately after the code in step 9:

```
// if "Select author(s)" still selected, remove it from the array
if ($_POST['author'][0] == 'choose') array_shift($_POST['author']);
```

This uses array_shift() (described in Chapter 5) to remove the first element of an array. To find out if other has been chosen, you can use the in_array() function, which takes two arguments: the array element you are looking for and an array. It returns true if the element is in the array. If it's there, it should now be the first element in the array, but just to make sure, it's safer to use array_search(), which takes the same arguments as in_array(), but returns the position of the element in the array. By combining these two functions, you can reset other to 0 like this (the code follows immediately after the code you just entered):

```
if (in_array('other',$_POST['author'])) {
  $i = array_search('other', $_POST['author']);
  $_POST['author'][$i] = 0;
  }
```

The reason you need a "not listed" author to have a value of 0 is so that you can list the book in the lookup table with an unknown author. If you don't do this, the book will fail to show up in searches that rely on the lookup table.

11. You now have all the necessary information to build the SQL to enter the primary key pairs into book_to_author. Whether there's just one author or twenty, the book_id will always be the single value in $book_id; the author_id values will be drawn from the amended $_POST['author'] array. The code to do this follows immediately after the code in step 10.

```
// build array of book_id and author_id pairs, one for each author
$values = array();
foreach ($_POST['author'] as $author_id) {
  $values[] = "($book_id, $author_id)";
}
// convert array to comma-delimited string
$values = implode(',',$values);
// insert book_id/author_id pairs into lookup table
$createLookup = 'INSERT INTO book_to_author (book_id, author_id)
                 VALUES '.$values;
$result = $db->query($createLookup);
// if successful, redirect to confirmation page
if ($result) {
  header('Location: listbooks.php?action=inserted&title='
➥ .$_POST['title']);
  }
```

Let's say the book_id returned by the SQL query in step 9 is 1, and the author_id array contains 1, 4, and 5. The INSERT statement generated by this code will be as follows:

```
INSERT INTO book_to_author (book_id,author_id)
VALUES (1,1),(1,4),(1,5)
```

12. Save new_book.php, load it into a browser, and enter the details of a book. If everything goes smoothly, you will be taken to listbooks.php. Don't worry that it says No books listed—you haven't coded that page yet. To confirm that your entry has been recorded, check the books table in phpMyAdmin. Click the Browse tab, and you should see something like this screenshot.

←T→	book_id	pub_id	isbn	title	image	description	list_price	store_price
☐ ✎ ✕	1	2	1590593502	PHP Web Development with Dreamweaver MX 2004	y	Stunning.	NULL	NULL

The list_price and store_price columns contain a NULL value, but all the other columns should contain the data from your form.

13. Now check the book_to_author table. Depending on the number of authors you selected, you should have one or more records that look something like the screenshot alongside.

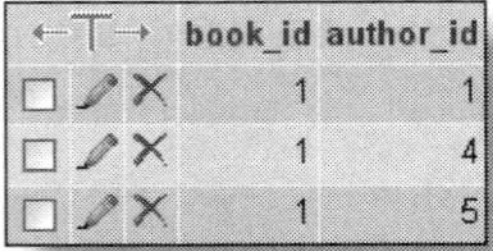

←T→	book_id	author_id
☐ ✎ ✕	1	1
☐ ✎ ✕	1	4
☐ ✎ ✕	1	5

14. If things didn't work, test the SQL in step 11 by using echo to display the query onscreen. Because the query relies on inserting a record into the books table and retrieving the book_id assigned to the new record, you will have to use phpMyAdmin to delete the record later. Otherwise, you will have a record in the books table that is not referenced in the lookup table. Finally, check all your code against new_book.04.php.

Making the input fields sticky

There's just one problem with new_book.php: if you make a mistake in one of the input fields, nothing gets inserted into the database. Worse still, everything you entered in the form is wiped out. It hasn't disappeared without a trace, though. If the details had been correct, they would have been retrieved from the POST array and inserted into the database. So if anything goes wrong, you need to get the details out of the POST array and redisplay them in the input fields. The technique to do so is exactly the same as you used in edit_auth_pub.php to display the details of a record to be edited. The only difference is that you use the POST array instead of the GET array.

1. Continue working with new_book.php or use new_book04.php from the download files. The completed code is in new_book05.php.
2. Locate the <input> tag for title (it should be around line 129), and insert the following code between the double quotes of the empty value="":

```
value="<?php if (isset($_POST['title'])) echo $_POST['title']; ?>"
```

3. Repeat step 2 for the ISBN field, using $_POST['isbn'].
4. The Description field is an XHTML <textarea>, which doesn't have a value attribute. Put the PHP code between the opening and closing <textarea> tags like this:

```
<textarea name="description" id="description">
<?php if (isset($_POST['description']))
  echo $_POST['description']; ?></textarea>
```

5. The menus for authors and publishers are slightly more complicated. XHTML <select> elements use selected="selected" to indicate a selected item. You want the first item to be selected automatically when the page first loads and the items selected by the user to remain selected if the POST array has been set. Once you have worked out the logic, the code is not difficult to understand. The authors menu takes multiple choices, so the logic is worked into the loop like this (the new code is shown in bold type):

```
<select name="author[]" size="6" multiple="multiple" id="author">
  <option value="choose"
  <?php
  if (!isset($_POST['author']) || (isset($_POST['author']) &&
➥ in_array('choose',$_POST['author']))) {
    echo 'selected="selected"'; } ?>
>Select author(s)</option>
<option value="other"
<?php
if (isset($_POST['author']) && $_POST['author'] == 'other')
```

```
echo 'selected="selected"'; ?>
>Not listed</option>
<?php
while ($row = $authors->fetch_assoc()) {
  echo '<option value="'.$row['author_id'].'"';
  if (isset($_POST['author']) && in_array($row['author_id'],
➥ $_POST['author'])) {
    echo 'selected="selected"';
}
  echo '>'.$row['author'].'</option>';
  }
?>
</select>
```

6. The drop-down menu for publishers is amended like this:

```
<select name="publisher" id="publisher">
  <option value="0"
  <?php if (isset($_POST['publisher']) && $_POST['publisher'] == '0')
    echo 'selected="selected"'; ?>>Select publisher</option>
  <option value="other"
<?php
if (isset($_POST['publisher']) && $_POST['publisher'] == 'other')
  echo 'selected="selected"'; ?>
  >Not listed</option>
  <?php
  while ($row = $publishers->fetch_assoc()) {
    echo '<option value="'.$row['pub_id'].'"';
    if (isset($_POST['publisher']) && $_POST['publisher'] ==
➥ $row['pub_id'])
      echo 'selected="selected"';
    echo '>'.$row['publisher'].'</option>';
    }
  // close database connection
  $db->close();
  ?>
</select>
```

7. XHTML radio buttons use checked="checked" to indicate which one has been selected. You want the Yes button to be selected by default, but the correct button to be selected when the POST array is set. The necessary changes are highlighted in bold type:

```
<input name="image" type="radio" value="y"
<?php
if (!$_POST || (isset($_POST['image']) && $_POST['image'] == 'y')) {
  echo 'checked="checked"';
  }?> />
  No
<input name="image" type="radio" value="n"
  <?php if (isset($_POST['image']) && $_POST['image'] == 'n')
echo 'checked="checked"';?> />
```

8. Check your final code against `new_book05.php`. Insert two or three more books in the database so you have some data to work on in the next section. You can use the examples in Table 12-2 or just make up your own.

Retrieving data from more than one table

It's taken a long time to get here, but you now have a relational database with foreign keys providing references to data held in separate tables. You've probably noticed that each table has been handled separately when you enter new data, but that's no longer necessary when you want to retrieve the information. So, how do you get it from more than one table?

The answer is to join them—not literally, but through a SQL query. There are several methods of joining tables, but I'm going to concentrate on the two most important: full joins and left joins. A **full join** (sometimes also called a **cross join**) joins each row of multiple tables to produce every possible combination. A **left join** (also called a **left outer join**) joins two tables, but also identifies rows in the left table that don't have a match in the right table. "Left" and "right" in this case refer to the order in which the tables appear in the SQL query. The first table named in a left join is regarded as being on the left (perfectly logical if you think about writing the query from left to right). For most queries, you will want a full join, but the left join will be invaluable when you're listing books that haven't yet been assigned an author in the `bookstore` database.

Avoiding ambiguous column references

Up to now, you haven't needed to worry about mixing up column names in your SQL queries because each column in a table must have a unique name and you have been dealing only with single tables. The bookstore database, however, uses the primary key from each table as a foreign key in other tables, so you need a way of distinguishing between `book_id` in the `books` table and `book_id` in the `book_to_author` table. The SQL solution to this problem will be very familiar to you from ActionScript—it uses dot notation. You identify a specific column by preceding it with its table name and joining the two with a dot or period. So, for example, you can identify the `book_id` columns in the `bookstore` database like this:

```
books.book_id
book_to_author.book_id
```

Dot notation is required only when a column reference is ambiguous. Some developers get around such ambiguity by giving foreign key columns a different name in each table. While this solves one problem, it creates another by making it difficult to recognize where the foreign key originally comes from.

Using a full join

Creating a full join between tables requires no special SQL vocabulary; it's all done with the humble comma. You just build the `SELECT` query in the same way as for a single table, except that you specify the tables that you want to draw the data from as a comma-delimited list. The best way to see it in action is to try it out.

Retrieving publishers' and authors' names

The following exercise assumes you have entered several books in the bookstore database using new_book.php.

1. Launch MySQL Monitor (see Chapter 6 for details, if you've forgotten how) and log on either as root or as flashuser. When you get the mysql prompt, select the bookstore database by typing use bookstore and then pressing *Enter/Return*.

2. Enter the following SQL query and execute it by pressing *Enter/Return*:

```
SELECT title, publisher
FROM books, publishers;
```

If you used the book titles listed in Table 12-2, you should get the result shown in Figure 12-15.

```
MySQL Command Line Client
Enter password: *******
Welcome to the MySQL monitor.  Commands end with ; or \g.
Your MySQL connection id is 51 to server version: 4.1.8-nt

Type 'help;' or '\h' for help. Type '\c' to clear the buffer.

mysql> use bookstore
Database changed
mysql> SELECT title, publisher
    -> FROM books, publishers;
+-----------------------------------------------------+-------------+
| title                                               | publisher   |
+-----------------------------------------------------+-------------+
| PHP Web Development with Dreamweaver MX 2004        | friends of ED |
| Foundation ActionScript for Flash MX 2004           | friends of ED |
| Beginning PHP 5 and MySQL: From Novice to Professional | friends of ED |
| Foundation PHP 5 for Flash                          | friends of ED |
| PHP Web Development with Dreamweaver MX 2004        | Apress      |
| Foundation ActionScript for Flash MX 2004           | Apress      |
| Beginning PHP 5 and MySQL: From Novice to Professional | Apress      |
| Foundation PHP 5 for Flash                          | Apress      |
+-----------------------------------------------------+-------------+
8 rows in set (0.00 sec)

mysql>
```

Figure 12-15. A SQL full join displays all possible combinations of the selected columns.

The title and publisher columns remain in their separate tables, but the SELECT statement produces a set of results that combine the two. I have just four books and two publishers registered in the bookstore database at the moment, so the full join produces 4×2 rows to show every possible combination. As it stands, this is not very useful. This is where the foreign key comes to your rescue. The books table uses the primary key of the publishers table (pub_id) as a foreign key for each record.

3. Add a WHERE clause so that the result is limited to rows where the pub_id in the books table matches the pub_id in the publishers table. Modify the previous SELECT query like this and run it again (don't forget that to save your tired fingers—and brain—you can use the arrow keys on your keyboard to display and amend previous commands):

```
SELECT title, publisher
FROM books, publishers
WHERE books.pub_id = publishers.pub_id;
```

You should now get a result like that shown in Figure 12-16. This is much more useful. Each book is now matched with its correct publisher.

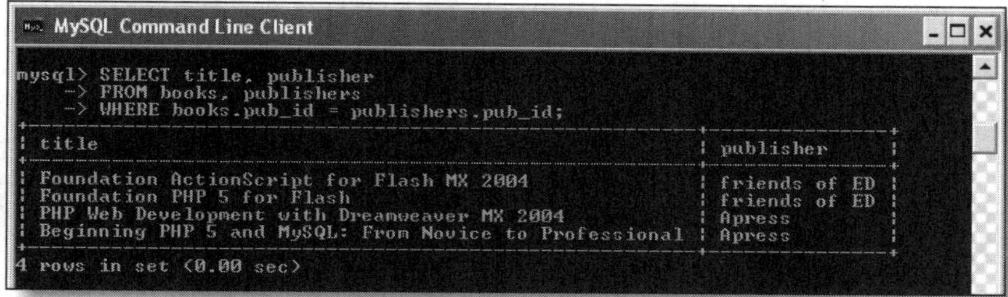

Figure 12-16. A WHERE clause restricts the results of the join to a meaningful set of matching records.

4. Now, if I edit the name of one of the publishers in the CMS and run the same query again, as you can see from Figure 12-17, all books previously listed with friends of ED as publisher become my friends instead. Only two books are affected on this occasion, but just imagine if you made a similar change to a record that is related to hundreds or thousands of others through a similar foreign key relationship.

Figure 12-17. Changing just one entry in the publishers table affects all related records.

5. Let's see what happens when you use a full join with the lookup table. Try the following SELECT query (I've used CONCAT to join the authors' names so that the result will display neatly inside MySQL Monitor):

```
SELECT title, CONCAT(first_name,' ',family_name) AS author
FROM books, authors, book_to_author
WHERE books.book_id = book_to_author.book_id
AND authors.author_id = book_to_author.author_id;
```

Note that the list of tables includes book_to_author, even though no data from the lookup table will be displayed; the comma-delimited list specifying the join must include *all tables referenced in the query*, not just those that will return data. This query matches each book_id and author_id pair in the lookup table with the corresponding rows in the books and authors tables, in exactly the same way as shown diagrammatically in Figure 12-2 at the beginning of the chapter. You can see the result in Figure 12-18.

Figure 12-18. A full join matches each of the authors individually with the titles of books the author has written.

As you can see, *PHP Web Development with Dreamweaver MX 2004* produces three separate records because it has three co-authors. You will use PHP to handle this later. The important point is that each author is now linked with the right book.

6. Sometimes, you will want to enter a book written by someone not yet listed in the authors table. It would be inconvenient if you always had to check that all the authors' names are registered first, so new_book.php allows you to use "Not listed" for an author's name. Let's put in a new book written by someone not already in the database. Figure 12-19 shows the data I entered. It doesn't matter what you enter, as long as you select only Not listed for the Author(s) field.

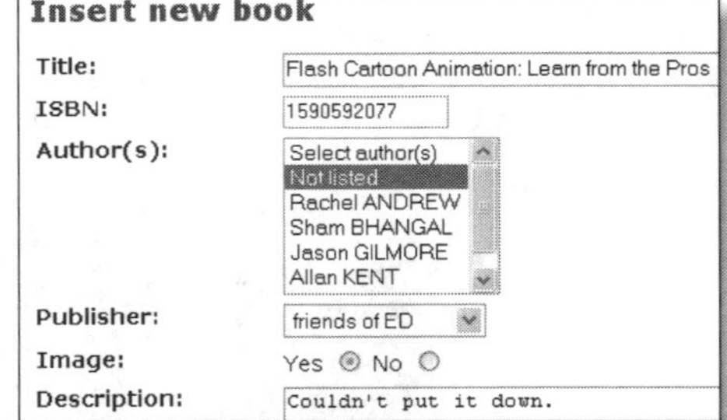

Figure 12-19. The authors of this book aren't yet recorded in the database, so Not listed has been chosen.

7. Run the same query as in step 5. The result should be the same as shown in Figure 12-18—*the new book doesn't show up*. Beginners often find the reason for this difficult to understand, but it's because a SELECT query will produce results only where *all* conditions are met. A quick check with phpMyAdmin shows that the new book has been properly recorded in the books table, and that it also has an entry in the book_to_author table. But as you can see from the screenshot alongside, the author_id has been set to 0. No one in the authors table has an author_id of 0, because auto_increment columns always begin at 1.

   One way to circumvent this problem is to create a record in the authors table with a dummy name. It's far better, though, to use a left join. Leave MySQL Monitor open, and I'll show you how in the next section.

Using a left join to find an incomplete match

In spite of its unusual name, a left join isn't difficult to use. What it does is produce the same set of results as a full join, but when there's no match for a row in the table(s) to the "left" of the join, the row is still included, but all the columns in the table to the "right" of the join are set to NULL. The syntax is as follows:

```
SELECT column_name(s) FROM first_table
LEFT JOIN second_table ON condition
```

If the condition is matching two columns of the same name (such as book_id), an alternative syntax can be used:

```
SELECT column_name(s) FROM first_table
LEFT JOIN second_table USING (column_name)
```

It's a lot easier to understand when you see it in action.

Retrieving books with no author

This is a continuation of the exercise in the previous section, and it assumes you have the necessary records in the bookstore database.

1. Amend the SELECT query in step 5 of the previous section to use a left join like this:

```
SELECT title, CONCAT(first_name,' ',family_name) AS author
FROM books, book_to_author
LEFT JOIN authors ON authors.author_id = book_to_author.author_id
WHERE books.book_id = book_to_author.book_id;
```

   This code performs a full join on books and book_to_author, but you know that there won't always be a match in the authors table. Consequently, authors is joined to the other tables with a left join that applies *only* to matches involving author_id. However, you know there will always be a match of book_id, so the final line uses a WHERE clause that applies to all three tables.

2. Run this query, and you should get a result similar to Figure 12-20. This time, the book without an author shows up, with a NULL value in the author column.

```
MySQL Command Line Client
mysql> SELECT title, CONCAT(first_name,' ',family_name) AS author
    -> FROM books, book_to_author
    -> LEFT JOIN authors ON authors.author_id = book_to_author.author_id
    -> WHERE books.book_id = book_to_author.book_id;
+------------------------------------------------------+----------------+
| title                                                | author         |
+------------------------------------------------------+----------------+
| PHP Web Development with Dreamweaver MX 2004         | David Powers   |
| PHP Web Development with Dreamweaver MX 2004         | Rachel Andrew  |
| PHP Web Development with Dreamweaver MX 2004         | Allan Kent     |
| Foundation ActionScript for Flash MX 2004            | Sham Bhangal   |
| Beginning PHP 5 and MySQL: From Novice to Professional | Jason Gilmore |
| Foundation PHP 5 for Flash                           | David Powers   |
| Flash Cartoon Animation: Learn from the Pros         | NULL           |
+------------------------------------------------------+----------------+
7 rows in set (0.00 sec)
```

Figure 12-20. Using a left join on the authors table enables you to find books even if they have not yet been assigned an author.

As you can see, the ON part of LEFT JOIN performs a similar role to a WHERE clause. However, the condition applied to a left join must be specified using ON. The only exception is when the columns being compared have the same name in all tables involved in the left join. Because the query in step 1 is performing a left join on two columns both called author_id, the SQL can be simplified like this:

```
SELECT title, CONCAT(first_name,' ',family_name) AS author
FROM books, book_to_author
LEFT JOIN authors USING (author_id)
WHERE books.book_id = book_to_author.book_id;
```

This will provide exactly the same result as shown in Figure 12-20, and it forms the basis of the main SQL used in listbooks.php, which is the next part of the CMS that you need to create.

Deciding which table to put on the right side of a left join takes a bit of practice. Experiment in MySQL Monitor with various combinations of the query used in this section, and see how they affect the results. When you're developing a new project or altering an existing one, it's always a good idea to use MySQL Monitor to test the results of your queries. Seeing the results "in the raw" shows you exactly what's happening and acts as an early warning system if your results are being distorted by a flaw in the logic of your PHP or ActionScript.

Completing the content management system

There are five more pages needed to complete the CMS: one each to list and edit books, two to perform delete operations, and one to update prices from an external XML source. A lot of the code uses techniques that you have seen before, so I have left much of the explanation to inline comments, and I will concentrate mainly on new techniques or particularly important points.

Managing existing book records

The way you manage records of books in the database follows the same principles as before: first display a list of existing records, and then choose the operation you want to carry out on them.

Listing books

The main features of listbooks.php are the SELECT query adapted from the preceding section, a loop to filter the results so that each book is associated with a list of authors, and a page navigation system.

Filtering the results

As Figure 12-17 shows, the results from a SELECT query will contain multiple references to any book associated with more than one author. You need to create a PHP loop to format the results in a more useable way.

1. Open listbooks.php or use listbooks02.php from the download files. The finished code for this section is in listbooks03.php.

2. Amend the opening block of PHP code above the Doctype to query the database and filter the results into three arrays, like this (the new code is in bold type):

```
<?php
require_once('admin_funcs.php');
require_once('../classes/database.php');
$db=new Database('localhost','flashuser','deepthought','bookstore',0);
// get details of books from database
$getbooks = 'SELECT books.book_id, title,
             CONCAT(LEFT(first_name,1),". ",family_name) AS author
             FROM books, book_to_author
             LEFT JOIN authors USING (author_id)
             WHERE books.book_id = book_to_author.book_id
             ORDER BY title, family_name';
$bookDets = $db->query($getbooks);
// if the result not empty, create arrays of book_id, title, and author
if ($bookDets->num_rows) {
  while ($row = $bookDets->fetch_assoc()) {
    $book_id[] = $row['book_id'];
    $title[] = $row['title'];
    $author[] = $row['author'];
    }
  }
echo '<pre>';
print_r($book_id);
print_r($title);
print_r($author);
echo '</pre>';
?>
```

The SELECT query in $getbooks is an adaptation of the LEFT JOIN example used in the preceding section. There are just two points to note about it. In the first line of the query, you must specify which table book_id is to be drawn from in the results, because both books and book_to_author have columns with the same name. The second line of the query uses the MySQL function LEFT() to extract just the first letter of each author's first name. LEFT() works the same way as RIGHT(), which you learned about in Chapter 11, except that it extracts characters from the beginning of a string. The same line uses CONCAT() to join the author's initial, followed by a period and a space, and family name. The result is assigned to author as an alias.

3. The result of the query is used to create three arrays, so it's a good idea to test that your code is working so far. The last five lines of code output the arrays to the browser for testing purposes. Save `listbooks.php` and load it into a browser. You should see a result like that shown in Figure 12-21.

   It's obvious from the first two arrays that the final three elements of each array all refer to the same book. Not only that—they are consecutive. This is because the SQL query specified that the results should be sorted first by title and then by the author's family name. If the sort order were reversed, the book_id results would be distributed randomly. Because they are together, a second loop can be used to filter the authors' names into a single string and to eliminate duplicate references to a particular title.

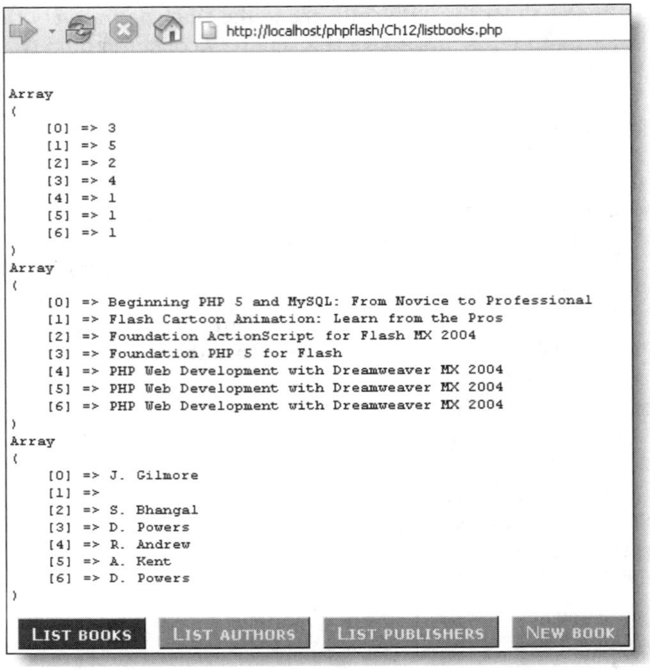

http://localhost/phpflash/Ch12/listbooks.php

```
Array
(
    [0] => 3
    [1] => 5
    [2] => 2
    [3] => 4
    [4] => 1
    [5] => 1
    [6] => 1
)
Array
(
    [0] => Beginning PHP 5 and MySQL: From Novice to Professional
    [1] => Flash Cartoon Animation: Learn from the Pros
    [2] => Foundation ActionScript for Flash MX 2004
    [3] => Foundation PHP 5 for Flash
    [4] => PHP Web Development with Dreamweaver MX 2004
    [5] => PHP Web Development with Dreamweaver MX 2004
    [6] => PHP Web Development with Dreamweaver MX 2004
)
Array
(
    [0] => J. Gilmore
    [1] =>
    [2] => S. Bhangal
    [3] => D. Powers
    [4] => R. Andrew
    [5] => A. Kent
    [6] => D. Powers
)
```

LIST BOOKS LIST AUTHORS LIST PUBLISHERS NEW BOOK

Figure 12-21. It's useful to check that you're getting the right data from the SQL query before formatting the results.

4. The second loop creates an indexed array called $book, which contains a separate element for each book. Each book element is an associative array containing the book's primary key and title, and a subarray of authors. So the book with three authors will end up like this:

```
$book[4]['book_id'] = 1;
$book[4]['title'] = 'PHP Web Development with Dreamweaver MX 2004';
$book[4]['author'][0] = 'R. Andrew';
$book[4]['author'][1] = 'A. Kent';
$book[4]['author'][2] = 'D. Powers';
```

The loop to create this array goes immediately after the first loop, still inside the conditional clause (around line 20). The surrounding code is shown so that you can see the exact position.

```
  $author[] = $row['author'];
  }
// find total number of elements in each array (all are same length)
$totalResults = count($book_id);
// initialize counter for 'author' subarray
$counter = 0;
// loop to create a single multidimensional array for each book
for ($i = 0, $k = 0; $k < $totalResults; $k++) {
```

```
    $book[$i]['book_id'] = $book_id[$k];
    $book[$i]['title'] = $title[$k];
    $book[$i]['author'][$counter++] = $author[$k];
    // if next $book_id is different, increment book counter
    // and reset author counter to zero
    if (($k < $totalResults-1) && ($book_id[$k+1] != $book_id[$k])) {
      $i++;
      $counter = 0;
      }
    }
  }
echo '<pre>';
print_r($book);
echo '</pre>';
```

The loop uses three counters: $k to keep track of the current iteration, $i to keep track of the current book, and $counter to keep track of the current book's subarray of authors. $k is incremented automatically for each iteration, but the conditional clause at the end of the loop determines how to handle the other counters. It works by comparing the value of the next element in the $book_id array ($book_id[$k+1]) with the value of the current element ($book_id[$k]). First of all, it needs to check that there *is* another element to compare with, so it makes sure that $k is less than $totalResults minus 1. If there is another element in the $book_id array, and it has the same value as the current one, it must be the same book, so the code inside the conditional statement is ignored. If the values are different, it's a different book, so $i is increased by 1, and $counter is reset to 0.

The print_r() command at the bottom of the code block has been changed to display only the new array.

5. Save listbooks.php and click the Refresh button in your browser. The new array should be displayed onscreen. Figure 12-22 shows the last two books in my set of results: one book that has just one author and the other with three authors.

```
[3] => Array
    (
        [book_id] => 4
        [title] => Foundation PHP 5 for Flash
        [author] => Array
            (
                [0] => D. Powers
            )

    )

[4] => Array
    (
        [book_id] => 1
        [title] => PHP Web Development with Dreamweaver MX 2004
        [author] => Array
            (
                [0] => R. Andrew
                [1] => A. Kent
                [2] => D. Powers
            )

    )
```

Figure 12-22. Each book has now been separated into an associative array, which becomes much easier to handle.

6. Once you have established that your code is working correctly, you can delete the final three lines of code in step 4 and display the results properly. The code to do this follows the same pattern as for all other pages and goes in the XHTML table from around line 56. The new code is highlighted in bold type.

```
<?php if (!isset($book)) { ?>
<tr><td colspan="4">No books listed</td></tr>
<?php }
    else {
    // get total number of items in $book array
    $display = count($book);
    // loop through array and display table row for each book
    for ($i = 0; $i < $display; $i++) { ?>
<tr class="<?php echo $i%2 ? 'hilite' : 'nohilite'; ?>">
   <td><?php echo $book[$i]['title'];?></td>
   <td><?php
    // extract first 3 authors and create comma-delimited string
    array_splice($book[$i]['author'],3);
    echo implode(', ',$book[$i]['author']);
    ?></td>
  <td class="ctr"><input name="book_id[]" type="radio"
➥ value="<?php echo $book[$i]['book_id']; ?>" /></td>
  <td class="ctr"><input name="delete[]" type="checkbox"
➥ value="<?php echo $book[$i]['book_id']; ?>" /></td>
</tr>
<?php } ?>
```

7. The closing curly brace in the final line of the previous step ends the for loop that displays the results, but you still need another curly brace to close the else clause that begins in the sixth line. Place it a few lines further down, after the row that displays the NEXT link, as shown here:

```
  <td colspan="2"><a href="">Next</a></td>
</tr>
<?php } ?>
```

8. Save `listbooks.php` and click the Refresh button in your browser. You should now have a nicely formatted display of books in the database as shown in the following screenshot.

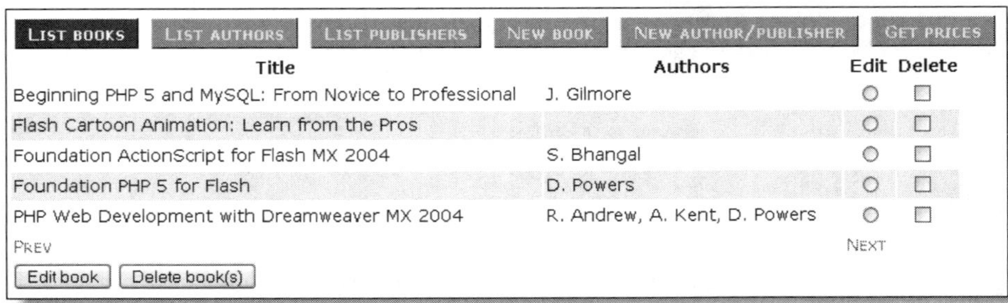

The PREV and NEXT links are not active yet, and the Edit and Delete options do not work properly, but everything is now beginning to take shape nicely.

9. Insert the following code right at the top of the page, immediately after the opening PHP tag. It will redirect the browser to the correct page with details of the book(s) that have been selected as a query string. You can edit only one book at a time, so just one `book_id` is sent to `editbook.php`, but a list of several books can be sent to `del_book.php` as a comma-delimited string.

```
if ($_POST && array_key_exists('editBook',$_POST)
➥ && !empty($_POST['book_id'])) {
  header('Location: editbook.php?book_id='.$_POST['book_id'][0]);
  }
elseif ($_POST && array_key_exists('delBook',$_POST)
➥ && !empty($_POST['delete'])) {
  header('Location: del_book.php?delete='.implode(',',
➥ $_POST['delete']));
  }
```

Before coding the edit and delete pages, the result navigation links remain to be activated. You'll do that next. Check your code so far against `listbooks03.php`.

Activating the result navigation links

This next section can be regarded as optional if you don't anticipate having a large number of records in the database. It performs the same task of navigating through a long sequence of results and displaying them on separate pages as the `displayList()` ActionScript function did in Chapter 10. This shows you how to achieve the same effect using PHP.

1. Continue working with `listbooks.php` or use `listbooks03.php` from the download files. The finished code is in `listbooks04.php`.

2. If you don't need a results navigation system, remove the following lines of code from `listbooks.php` (around lines 80 through 83):

```
<tr>
  <td colspan="2"><a href="">Prev</a></td>
  <td colspan="2"><a href="">Next</a></td>
</tr>
```

Otherwise, change them as shown here (the new code is in bold type):

```
<tr>
  <td colspan="2"><?php if ($start > 0) {
    echo '<a href="'.$_SERVER['PHP_SELF'].'?start='.($start-$max).'">';
    echo '&lt; Prev</a>'; } ?></td>
  <td colspan="2"><?php if (count($book) > ($start+$max)) {
    echo '<a href="'.$_SERVER['PHP_SELF'].'?start='.($start+$max).'">';
    echo 'Next &gt;</a>'; } ?></td>
</tr>
```

The conditional clauses determine whether to display the PREV and NEXT links on the basis of the values of $start and the total number of items in the $book array. < and > are simply XHTML entities that display angled brackets in place of left and right arrows. The links use $_SERVER['PHP_SELF'] to reload the same page together with a query string that uses the value of $start to indicate the number of the first record to be displayed.

3. All you need to do now is insert the code that controls the values of $start and $max. It goes just before the loop that displays the books. The inline comments explain how it works (the new code is shown in bold type).

```
<?php if (!isset($book)) { ?>
  <tr><td colspan="4">No books listed</td></tr>
<?php
  }
else { // if URL contains query string, use it to initialize $start
  if (isset($_GET['start'])) {
    $start = $_GET['start'];
    }
  else { // otherwise set $start to zero
    $start = 0;
    }
  // set value of maximum number of records to display
  $max = 10;
  if ($start+$max > count($book)) {
    // if $start + $max greater than total number of records
    // set the loop limit to the total number, otherwise $start + $max
    $display = count($book);
    }
  else {
    $display = $start+$max;
    }
  // initialize loop to begin from the value of $start
  for ($i = $start; $i < $display; $i++) { ?>
```

4. That completes the record navigation system. You can compare your code against listbooks04.php. To test the system with a small number of records in your database, change the value of $max temporarily to a low figure, such as 2.

Editing books

Books are selected for editing by clicking the Edit radio button alongside a book's details in listbooks.php and then clicking the Edit book button (as shown in Figure 12-23). The book_id is sent as a query string attached to the end of the URL, with the result that editbook.php opens with the existing details already filled in. Although the page contains a lot of code, most of it is exactly the same as new_book.php.

The most important thing to note is what happens to the lookup table. All existing entries for the selected book are deleted from the lookup table before new ones are inserted. This ensures that any changes to the authors are correctly recorded in the database. For instance, if you assign a book to someone by mistake, unless you delete the existing entries, the book will always show the wrong author in addition to any correct ones that have been added. Even if you make no changes to the authors, the existing records in the lookup table are deleted and then simply entered again.

This is the type of operation where support for transactions would be useful. Transactions treat a series of SQL queries as an integral unit that is executed only if all parts succeed, but they aren't yet supported on MyISAM tables. The only time this lack of support presents a problem is when you first test the final code. If you make a mistake in the SQL that inserts the new data in the lookup table, there's no way of getting back the records that have been deleted. (Just use phpMyAdmin to delete any books this happens to. That's what testing is all about—when you add a new feature to an application, always work with data that you're prepared to sacrifice if anything goes wrong.) As long as your SQL is correct, the sequence of queries should always succeed. Transactions take on a crucial importance only when dealing with unknown factors (such as there not being sufficient funds available to transfer from one account to another in a financial database).

1. Open `new_book.php` and save it as `editbook.php`. Alternatively, use `editbook01.php` from the download files. The finished code for this section is in `editbook03.php` (`editbook02.php` provides a halfway check for the changes you need to make to this important page).
2. Change the page `<title>` and `<h1>` heading to Edit book. Also change the final row of the table in the online form so that the update script knows which book to edit:

```
<tr>
  <td><input name="book_id" type="hidden" id="book_id" value="
  <?php if ($_GET) echo $book_id;
  elseif (isset($_POST['book_id'])) echo $_POST['book_id'];?>" /></td>
  <td><input type="submit" name="updateBook" value="Update book
➥ details" /></td>
</tr>
```

3. The code to retrieve the details of the book that is to be edited goes just before the block that runs only if the form has been submitted (around line 13). The existing lines immediately before and after this new code have been included to show you where it goes. The inline comments explain what the code does:

```
$publishers = $db->query($getPublishers);
// this block runs when the GET array has been set
// the book_id in the query string is used to get the book's details
if ($_GET && !$_POST) {
  $book_id = $_GET['book_id'];
  // get details of book from the books table
  $getDets = "SELECT title,isbn,pub_id,image,description
              FROM books WHERE book_id = $book_id";
  $bookDets = $db->query($getDets);
  // assign results to ordinary variables
  while ($row = $bookDets->fetch_assoc()) {
    $title = $row['title'];
    $isbn = $row['isbn'];
    $pub_id = $row['pub_id'];
```

```
    $image = $row['image'];
    $description = $row['description'];
    }
  // get list of authors from lookup table
  $getAuthors = "SELECT author_id FROM book_to_author
                WHERE book_id = $book_id";
  $author_ids = $db->query($getAuthors);
  // filter results into an array of authors
  while ($row = $author_ids->fetch_assoc()) {
    $authorList[] = $row['author_id'];
    }
  }
// this block runs only if the form has been submitted
if ($_POST) {
```

4. The details of the book now need to be displayed in the relevant input fields of the table. The code copied from new_book.php already does this when the POST array has been set. This code should be kept, because it's still needed in case a mistake is made in submitting the form. However, the code in step 3 will run only if the POST array *hasn't* been set. That means that you can check whether the variables assigned by the first while loop have been set. If they have, then you can display them. Amend the code for the Title input field (around line 153) like this:

```
<th class="leftLabel">Title:</th>
  <td><input name="title" type="text" class="widebox" id="title"
value="<?php if (isset($_POST['title'])) echo $_POST['title'];
  elseif (isset($title)) echo $title; ?>" /></td>
```

5. Repeat step 4 with $isbn and $description for the ISBN and Description input fields.

6. The select menu that lists the names of authors uses an array called $authorList created by the code in step 3. This shows how you incorporate it into the existing menu. The conditional statement in the fourth line may look the same as in new_book.php, but it's actually shorter, because one of the conditions (!isset($_POST['author'])) and a set of parentheses have been removed.

```
<select name="author[]" size="6" multiple="multiple" id="author">
  <option value="choose"
<?php
if (isset($_POST['author']) && in_array('choose',$_POST['author'])) {
  echo 'selected="selected"'; } ?>
>Select author(s)</option>
<option value="other"
<?php if (isset($authorList) && in_array(0,$authorList) ||
➥ (isset($_POST['author']) && $_POST['author'] == 'other'))
  echo 'selected="selected"'; ?>
>Not listed</option>
<?php while ($row = $authors->fetch_assoc()) {
  echo '<option value="'.$row['author_id'].'"';
```

```
  if ((isset($authorList) && in_array($row['author_id'],$authorList))
➥ || (isset($_POST['author']) && in_array($row['author_id'],
➥ $_POST['author']))) {
    echo 'selected="selected"';
    }
  echo '>'.$row['author'].'</option>';
  }
?>
</select>
```

7. The relevant section of the publishers drop-down menu that needs amending looks like this:

```
<option value="other"
<?php
if (isset($pub_id) && $pub_id == 0 || (isset($_POST['publisher']) &&
➥ $_POST['publisher'] == 'other')) echo 'selected="selected"'; ?>
>Not listed</option>
<?php
while ($row = $publishers->fetch_assoc()) {
  echo '<option value="'.$row['pub_id'].'"';
  if ((isset($pub_id) && $pub_id == $row['pub_id']) ||
➥ (isset($_POST['publisher']) && $_POST['publisher'] ==
➥ $row['pub_id']))
```

8. The radio buttons look like this:

```
<input name="image" type="radio" value="y"
<?php if ((isset($image) && $image == 'y') || (isset($_POST['image'])
➥ && $_POST['image'] == 'y')) {
  echo 'checked="checked"'; }?> />
No
<input name="image" type="radio" value="n"
<?php if ((isset($image) && $image == 'n') || (isset($_POST['image'])
➥ && $_POST['image'] == 'n')) echo 'checked="checked"';?> />
```

9. That completes the changes to the interface of editbook.php. This is a good opportunity to test that the page loads correctly and displays the details of the book you have selected. Save editbook.php, display a list of books, select the Edit radio button alongside one of the books, and click the Edit book button (see Figure 12-23). You should be taken to editbook.php, and all the details should be filled in automatically. In particular, make sure that the right names are being highlighted in the authors and publishers menus. If you have any problems, check your code against editbook02.php.

10. All that remains to do now is amend the code that does the actual updating of the database. Begin by amending the conditional clause that controls the code that runs only if the POST array has been set (it should be around line 39):

```
// this block runs only if the form has been submitted
if ($_POST && array_key_exists('updateBook',$_POST)) {
```

Figure 12-23. To edit one of the books, select the radio button alongside its details and click Edit book.

11. All the initial checks on the form are exactly the same as in new_book.php. The only one that needs changing is the SQL that checks for a duplicate ISBN (around line 84). As with all previous duplicate checks, you must exclude the item that is being updated, because it will always have the value that is being checked.

```
$checkISBN = 'SELECT isbn FROM books WHERE isbn = "'.$_POST['isbn'].'"
              AND book_id != '.$_POST['book_id'];
```

12. After the ISBN and all other tests have been done, the update sequence (from around line 91) looks like this (as always, the new code is in bold type):

```
// if ISBN unique, update book in books table
if ($_POST['publisher'] == 'other') $_POST['publisher'] = 0;
$update = 'UPDATE books
           SET title = "'.$_POST['title'].'",
           isbn = "'.$_POST['isbn'].'",
           pub_id = '.$_POST['publisher'].',
           image = "'.$_POST['image'].'",
           description = "'.$_POST['description'].'"
           WHERE book_id = '.$_POST['book_id'];
$result = $db->query($update);
// if "Select author(s)" still selected, remove it from the array
if ($_POST['author'][0] == 'select') array_shift($_POST['author']);
if (in_array('other',$_POST['author'])) {
  $i = array_search('other', $_POST['author']);
  $_POST['author'][$i] = 0;
  }
// build array of book_id and author_id pairs, one for each author
$values = array();
foreach ($_POST['author'] as $author_id) {
  $values[] = '('.$_POST['book_id'].", $author_id)";
  }
// convert array to comma-delimited string
$values = implode(',',$values);
// delete existing records for this book in lookup table
$deleteAuthors = 'DELETE FROM book_to_author
                  WHERE book_id = '.$_POST['book_id'];
```

```
$db->query($deleteAuthors);
// insert revised book_id/author_id pairs into lookup table
$createLookup = 'INSERT INTO book_to_author (book_id, author_id)
                 VALUES '.$values;
$result = $db->query($createLookup);
// if successful, redirect to confirmation page
if ($result) {
  $db->close();
  header('Location:listbooks.php?action=updated&title='
➥ .$_POST['title']);
  }
```

13. Save `editbook.php` and test it by selecting a book from `listbooks.php`. After editing the book, select it again, and you should see all your changes reflected in the edit page.

14. There's one last thing to complete the edit sequence. Open `listbooks.php` and add the following code immediately before the call to `insertMenu()` (around line 52):

```
<?php if (isset($_GET['action']) && isset($_GET['title'])) {
  echo '<p id="alert">'.stripslashes($_GET['title']).' has been ';
  echo $_GET['action'].' in the database.</p>';
  }
insertMenu(); ?>
```

This will display a message telling you when a book has been inserted or updated in the database. Check your code for `editbook.php` against `editbook03.php`. The updated version of `listbooks.php` is available as `listbooks05.php`.

Deleting records from more than one table

You have already studied the basic DELETE syntax in Chapter 10. It's very simple, and it works on one table at a time:

```
DELETE FROM table_name WHERE condition
```

If you are using MySQL 4.0 or higher, you can also delete records simultaneously from multiple tables. The syntax is similar, and it comes in two alternative forms. The first, which can be used in any version of MySQL 4.0 or higher, is a little strange. The basic pattern is

```
DELETE table_name [, table_name] FROM table_name [, table_name]
WHERE condition
```

Although this looks as though it's an instruction to delete the entire table, it's not. The first list of tables indicates the tables from which the records are to be deleted, while the second list indicates the tables used in the condition. So this, for example

```
DELETE t1, t2 FROM t1, t2, t3
WHERE t1.id = t2.id AND t2.id = t3.id
```

uses all three tables in determining which records to delete, but the deletions are done only from `t1` and `t2`.

A more intuitive syntax was introduced in MySQL 4.0.2. The pattern looks like this:

```
DELETE FROM table_name [, table_name] USING table_name [, table_name]
WHERE condition
```

So, the previous example can be rewritten in the following way:

```
DELETE FROM t1, t2 USING t1, t2, t3
WHERE t1.id = t2.id AND t2.id = t3.id
```

When deleting books from the CMS, you need to remove records from two tables, books and book_to_author, so the basic DELETE query in one operation looks like this:

```
DELETE FROM books, book_to_author USING books, book_to_author
WHERE books.book_id = $book_id
AND book_to_author.book_id = $book_id
```

Using a multiple-table delete would not be very efficient, though, if it limited you to deleting only one book at a time. Fortunately, this is an ideal situation in which to use the MySQL comparison operator, IN(), that you learned about in Chapter 11. It takes a comma-delimited sequence of quoted strings, or numbers (or a mixture of both), acting on every value in the same way as an array. So, by preparing the list of books to be deleted as a comma-delimited list of book_id values and assigning it to $books, you can do everything in one pass, like this:

```
DELETE FROM books, book_to_author USING books, book_to_author
WHERE books.book_id IN ($books)
AND book_to_author.book_id IN ($books)
```

Although the SQL required for the CMS uses a full join, there is nothing (apart, perhaps, from confidence) to prevent you from using a LEFT JOIN with a multiple-table delete. I adapted the LEFT JOIN from the SELECT query in listbooks.php like this to remove books with no matching author:

```
DELETE FROM books, book_to_author
USING books, book_to_author
LEFT JOIN authors USING (author_id)
WHERE books.book_id = book_to_author.book_id
AND authors.author_id IS NULL
```

As Figure 12-24 shows, the command resulted in two rows being affected: the listing for *Flash Cartoon Animation* in the books table and the corresponding record in book_to_author. You can see from the rerun of the SELECT query I used in Figure 12-20 that the book has indeed been eliminated from the database (although not from my bookshelf!).

This demonstrates an important use of LEFT JOIN: finding records that have no match. For listbooks.php, we want to display all records whether or not they have a match. However, by specifying IS NULL as the condition for the column to the right of LEFT JOIN, you can find only those that have no match. This can be useful for eliminating orphaned records, or for finding customers with no outstanding orders or unpaid bills.

```
mysql> DELETE FROM books, book_to_author
    -> USING books, book_to_author
    -> LEFT JOIN authors USING (author_id)
    -> WHERE books.book_id = book_to_author.book_id
    -> AND authors.author_id IS NULL;
Query OK, 2 rows affected (0.00 sec)

mysql> SELECT title, CONCAT(first_name,' ',family_name) AS author
    -> FROM books, book_to_author
    -> LEFT JOIN authors USING (author_id)
    -> WHERE books.book_id = book_to_author.book_id;
+--------------------------------------------------------------+----------------+
| title                                                        | author         |
+--------------------------------------------------------------+----------------+
| PHP Web Development with Dreamweaver MX 2004                 | David Powers   |
| PHP Web Development with Dreamweaver MX 2004                 | Rachel Andrew  |
| PHP Web Development with Dreamweaver MX 2004                 | Allan Kent     |
| Foundation ActionScript for Flash MX 2004                    | Sham Bhangal   |
| Beginning PHP 5 and MySQL: From Novice to Professional       | Jason Gilmore  |
| Foundation PHP 5 for Flash                                   | David Powers   |
+--------------------------------------------------------------+----------------+
6 rows in set (0.00 sec)

mysql> _
```

Figure 12-24. A multiple-table DELETE command can use LEFT JOIN to get rid of records that have no matches.

Maintaining referential integrity on deletion

Because your records are distributed across four tables, you need to make sure that you delete data in the right order. Figure 12-25 shows the 1:n relationships in a simplified representation of the bookstore database. Looked at from the perspective of the publishers table, Apress, for instance, has a relationship with both *Beginning PHP 5 and MySQL* and *PHP Web Development for Dreamweaver MX 2004*. If you remove Apress from the publishers table, those two books will be left with a pub_id that refers to a nonexistent publisher. But the reverse is not true; each book has a 1:1 relationship with its publisher. Removing a record from the books table has no impact on the publishers table. However, it does have an impact on the other two tables.

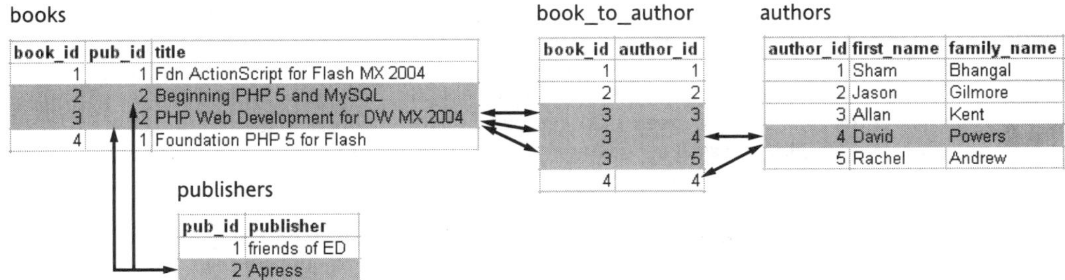

books

book_id	pub_id	title
1	1	Fdn ActionScript for Flash MX 2004
2	2	Beginning PHP 5 and MySQL
3	2	PHP Web Development for DW MX 2004
4	1	Foundation PHP 5 for Flash

book_to_author

book_id	author_id
1	1
2	2
3	3
3	4
3	5
4	4

authors

author_id	first_name	family_name
1	Sham	Bhangal
2	Jason	Gilmore
3	Allan	Kent
4	David	Powers
5	Rachel	Andrew

publishers

pub_id	publisher
1	friends of ED
2	Apress

Figure 12-25. The 1:n relationships in the database mean some records cannot be deleted without considering the impact on other tables.

Since the 1:1 relationship means you can remove a book without damaging the integrity of the publishers table, it's tempting to think the answer always lies in removing 1:1 relationships. But look at what would happen if you remove Rachel Andrew—there would still be a reference to her in the lookup table. In any case, not all relations between the authors table and the lookup table are 1:1. Two of my books are listed, so that's a 1:n relationship. If you remove my name, you need to delete not only both books linked to me, but also any references in the lookup table to the co-authors of one of those books. And that, of course, is the answer: as long as all references to a book are removed from the lookup table at the same time as the book is deleted, you don't need to delete anything from the authors table. It doesn't matter if an author is no longer associated with any books. You can still access the author's record in listauthors.php, and either delete it or leave it in the database for future use.

This may seem obvious with only four tables and a few records, but the interdependence of table relationships can be much more complex on a larger database, and it needs to be thought through carefully at the design stage.

Deleting books

Clicking Delete book(s) in listbooks.php sends a query string containing a comma-delimited list of book_id values to del_books.php, which lists the books and asks for confirmation. Unless the Cancel button is clicked, the deletion goes ahead without any further checks.

1. Open del_book.php or use del_book02.php from the download files. The completed code is in del_book03.php.
2. As with all self-processing forms, the page needs to know what action to take when it loads (or reloads) into a browser. There are three possible scenarios:
   - The page is accessed from listbooks.php with a request to delete one or more books. The titles of the books are displayed, the user is asked for confirmation, and the book_id values are stored in a hidden field ready for submission if the user clicks OK.
   - The user clicks OK. The script deletes the books and reports back.
   - The user clicks Cancel. The script returns the user to listbooks.php without deleting anything.

   The script that makes these decisions goes above the Doctype, and it looks like this:

```
<?php
require_once('admin_funcs.php');
require_once('../classes/database.php');
$db = new Database('localhost','flashadmin','fortytwo','bookstore',0);
// if OK button has been clicked, delete the books from the database
if ($_POST && array_key_exists('confDel',$_POST)) {
  $books = $_POST['book_id'];
  $titles = getTitles($db,$books);
  // multiple-table delete ** REQUIRES MySQL 4.0.2 OR HIGHER **
  $deleteBooks = "DELETE FROM books, book_to_author
                  USING books, book_to_author
                  WHERE books.book_id IN ($books)
                  AND book_to_author.book_id IN ($books)";
  $booksDeleted = $db->query($deleteBooks);
  }
// if Cancel button has been clicked, go to listbooks.php
elseif ($_POST && array_key_exists('cancel',$_POST)) {
  header('Location: listbooks.php');
  }
```

```
// if loaded from listbooks.php, get details of books to be deleted
elseif (isset($_GET['delete'])) {
  $books = $_GET['delete'];
  $titles = getTitles($db,$books);
  }
?>
```

The first thing you'll probably notice is that I've put the operation that needs to be run when the page first loads at the end of the sequence. This is because self-processing forms always use the current URL, which will contain the query string, thereby setting the GET array. If you put the GET block at the beginning of the conditional sequence, it will always run. However, the conditions set for the first two blocks are specific—they will run only if the right button has been clicked.

The getTitles() function is simply a convenient way of running the same block of code twice, which will be created in step 4. If you're running MySQL 4.0.2 or higher on both your local computer and remote server, you can skip straight there. If you are running a version of MySQL earlier than 4.0.2, read the next step first.

3. Multiple table deletes are not available in MySQL 3.23, which at the time of this writing is still in widespread use among hosting companies. If that affects you, split the delete operation into two queries as follows:

```
  $deleteBooks = "DELETE FROM books
                 WHERE book_id IN ($books)";
  $booksDeleted = $db->query($deleteBooks);
  $deleteLookup = "DELETE FROM book_to_author
                  WHERE book_id IN ($books)";
  $lookupDeleted = $db->query($deleteLookup);
}
// if Cancel button has been clicked, go to listbooks.php
```

4. The getTitles() function returns a result object that contains the titles of the books to be deleted. It takes two arguments: the Database instance and the comma-delimited list of book_id values. It's also needed in the script for deleting authors and publishers, so I put the function at the bottom of admin_funcs.php, which is automatically included in every page to create the menu. It's in the download files in admin_funcs02.php.

```
function getTitles($db,$books) {
  $getTitles = "SELECT title FROM books WHERE book_id IN ($books)";
  $result = $db->query($getTitles);
  return $result;
  }
```

5. The <body> section of the page is so short that I've reproduced it here in full, with the changes highlighted in bold type. Different messages are displayed, depending on whether the delete process has been completed, along with a list of the books scheduled for deletion. The hidden field at the bottom of the page stores the comma-delimited list of book_id values received from listbooks.php, telling the code in step 2 which books to delete.

```
<body>
<?php
insertMenu();
// if $booksDeleted is set, report that the books have been deleted
if (isset($booksDeleted)) {
  $alert = 'The following ';
  $alert .= $titles->num_rows > 1 ? 'titles were deleted:' :
➥ 'title was deleted:';
  }
// otherwise, display confirmation message
elseif (isset($_GET) && isset($titles)) {
  $alert = 'Please confirm you want to delete the following:';
  }
// in both cases, display a list of the titles (to be) deleted
echo "<p id='alert'>$alert</p><ul>";
while ($row = $titles->fetch_assoc()) {
  echo '<li>'.$row['title'].'</li>';
  }
?>
<form action="<?php $_SERVER['PHP_SELF'];?>" method="post"
➥ name="deleteBooks" id="deleteBooks">
  <input name="confDel" type="submit" id="confDel" value="OK" />
  <input name="cancel" type="submit" id="cancel" value="Cancel" />
  <input name="book_id" type="hidden" id="book_id"
➥ value="<?php echo $books;?>" />
</form>
</body>
```

6. Save del_book.php, bring up a list of books in listbooks.php your browser, select some for deletion, and click Delete book(s). You should see their titles displayed in del_book.php with a message asking you if you want to go ahead. As you can see in Figure 12-26, the book_id values have been passed to the page in the query string. If you view the source code of del_book.php, the same numbers should be in the value attribute of the hidden field at the bottom of the page. Test the page to make sure both the Cancel and OK buttons work as expected. Don't forget, though, that when you click OK, the books that have been selected will be permanently deleted from the database. It's necessary to sacrifice them to know that you've coded everything correctly. This is why it's important to test your code before you start working with vital data.

> *If you ever get yourself into a situation where you need to experiment with live data, always make a backup as described in Appendix E. You've already seen how easy it is to populate a database from a backup file, so there should never be any excuse for losing your records (unless, of course, you delete the backup, too!).*

Check your code against del_book03.php.

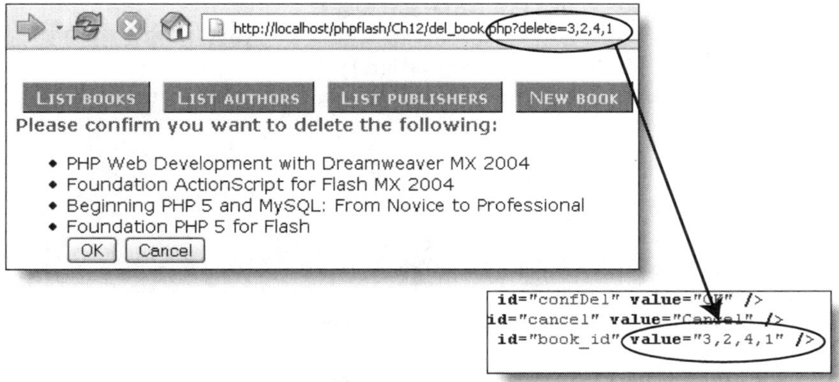

Figure 12-26. The book_id values passed in the query string are stored in the hidden field in readiness for the delete operation.

Deleting authors and publishers

Confirmation of the delete process is done by the JavaScript function in `listauthors.php` and `listpub.php`, so the script in `del_auth_pub.php` confines itself to checking whether referential integrity will be damaged. If there is a problem, the script halts and displays a list of dependent records; otherwise, it goes ahead with the deletion.

1. Open `del_auth_pub.php` or use `del_auth_pub02.php` from the download files. The finished code is in `del_auth_pub03.php`.

2. The block of PHP code above the Doctype checks whether any titles are still associated with the author or publisher. It does this by using the three values passed to the page in the query string: name, type, and either author_id or pub_id. The check is identical for both categories, except for the SQL query. I have created a custom function called checkExisting(), which will be described in the next step. First, amend the opening block of code like this (the inline comments explain what it does):

```
<?php
require_once('admin_funcs.php');
if (isset($_GET)) {
  require_once('../classes/database.php');
  $db=new Database('localhost','flashadmin','fortytwo','bookstore',0);
  if (!get_magic_quotes_gpc()) stripslashes($_GET['name']);
  // if query string includes author_id
  if (isset($_GET['author_id'])) {
    $author_id = $_GET['author_id'];
    // check whether author still listed in the lookup table
    $checkBooks = "SELECT book_id FROM book_to_author
                   WHERE author_id = $author_id";
    $titles = checkExisting($db,$checkBooks);
    // if no titles listed in lookup table, proceed with deletion
    if (empty($titles)) {
```

```
        $deleteAuthor = "DELETE FROM authors
                         WHERE author_id = $author_id";
        $result = $db->query($deleteAuthor);
        if ($result) $deleted = $_GET['name'].' has been removed from
➥ the authors table';
        }
      }
    // if query string includes pub_id
    elseif (isset($_GET['pub_id'])) {
      $pub_id = $_GET['pub_id'];
      // check whether published still listed in the books table
       $checkBooks = "SELECT book_id FROM books
                      WHERE pub_id = $pub_id";
       $titles = checkExisting($db,$checkBooks);
       // if no titles listed for that publisher, proceed with deletion
       if (empty($titles)) {
         $deletePublisher = "DELETE FROM publishers
                             WHERE pub_id = $pub_id";
         $result = $db->query($deletePublisher);
         if ($result) $deleted = $_GET['name'].' has been removed from
➥ the publishers table';
        }
      }
    // if author_id, $type is 'author'; otherwise, 'publisher'
    $type = isset($author_id) ? 'author' : 'publisher';
    }
?>
```

When designing a project like this, I normally concentrate on one aspect at a time, first handling the authors, and then copying and pasting the same script to adapt for the publishers. If you look at step 2, you will see the same pattern twice. This type of situation is often an ideal candidate to be turned into a function to save many lines of code. I did, in fact, seriously consider doing so, but decided that the time spent getting all the arguments and variables right was probably not worthwhile, and it could leave me with code that would not be as easy to understand in several months' time.

I did notice, however, that there were two sections of 20 lines or so that were virtually identical. So, I took them out and turned them into the `checkExisting()` function. I then noticed that they used several lines that were identical to a section in `del_book.php`. That's how I came to create `getTitles()`: even though it's only a couple of lines long, it's used in four places.

3. Open `admin_funcs.php` or use `admin_funcs02.php` (the final code is in `admin_funcs03.php`), and add the following code for the `checkExisting()` function. It's not important where you put the function, as long as it's not nested inside another function. However, since `checkExisting()` makes a call to `getTitles()`, the most logical place to put it is around line 29 above `getTitles()`.

```
function checkExisting($db,$sql) {
  // create an empty array to hold the titles
  $titles = array();
```

```
  // execute the SQL query and create an array of book_id values
  $result = $db->query($sql);
  if ($result->num_rows > 0) {
    while ($row = $result->fetch_assoc()) {
      $book_id[] = $row['book_id'];
      }
    // join the book_id values into a comma-delimited string
    $books = implode(',',$book_id);
    // pass to the getTitles function
    $result = getTitles($db,$books);
    // convert the result to an array of titles
    while ($row = $result->fetch_assoc()) {
      $titles[] = $row['title'];
      }
    }
  return $titles;
  }
```

The function uses the SQL query passed to it to return an array of titles (if any) still associated with an author or publisher. If it returns an empty array, the script in `del_auth_pub.php` knows it can go ahead with the deletion. If the array contains any elements, the `if (empty($titles))` test in steps 2 and 4 will fail, causing the delete operation to be abandoned and the reason to be displayed.

4. Amend the rest of `del_auth_pub.php` like this:

```
<!DOCTYPE HTML PUBLIC "-//W3C//DTD HTML 4.01 Transitional//EN"
"http://www.w3.org/TR/html4/loose.dtd">
<html>
<head>
<meta http-equiv="Content-Type" content="text/html;
➥ charset=iso-8859-1">
<title>Delete <?php echo $type; ?></title>
<link href="admin.css" rel="stylesheet" type="text/css">
</head>
<body>
<?php insertMenu(); ?>
<div id="maincontent">
<h1>Delete <?php echo $type; ?></h1>
<?php
// if $titles is not empty, the delete process has been abandoned
if (!empty($titles)) {
  // adjust message if only one book is in the list
  $book = count($titles) > 1 ? 'books are' : 'book is';
  echo '<p id="alert">'.$_GET['name']." cannot be removed, as the
➥ following $book registered in that {$type}'s name:</p><ul>";
  // display list of books still registered
  foreach ($titles as $title) {
    echo "<li>$title</li>";
    }
```

```
  echo '</ul>';
  }
// if delete operation completed, display confirmation message
elseif (isset($deleted)) {
  echo "<p>$deleted</p>";
  }
?>
</div>
</body>
</html>
```

Note the curly braces surrounding the third instance of $type. This is because there is no space between the variable and the string that follows it. Placing the variable inside braces instructs PHP to treat $type separately.

5. Save `del_auth_pub.php`, and select a publisher to delete from `listpub.php`. As long as the publisher has some books registered in the database, you should see a message similar to that shown in Figure 12-27. Delete a book, and then delete the author. If the author has no other books registered, you will get a message confirming the deletion. Check your code against `del_auth_pub03.php` and `admin_funcs03.php`.

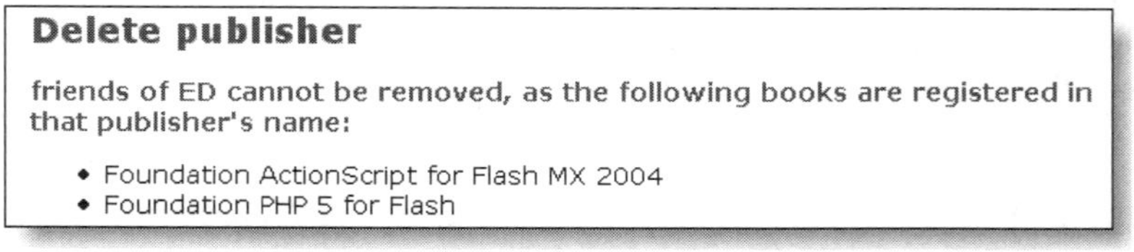

Delete publisher

friends of ED cannot be removed, as the following books are registered in that publisher's name:

- Foundation ActionScript for Flash MX 2004
- Foundation PHP 5 for Flash

Figure 12-27. Authors and publishers cannot be removed if any records are still dependent on them.

Updating multiple records

In the section "Using a full join," I showed you that when you change the name of a publisher, the change is immediately reflected in all results of books connected with that publisher ("friends of ED" in Figure 12-16 was replaced by "friends of David" in Figure 12-17). Remember that, while it may look as though all records in the books table were updated, the only change was to one field—the publisher's name in the `publishers` table. What caused all results to reflect the change was the primary key from the `publishers` table being used as a foreign key in the books table.

Now that you've seen how to do a selective delete of records from multiple tables, you may be wondering if you can do the same with updates. Say, for example, you discover that you have two entries in the `publishers` table for friends of ED: one as "friends of ED" and the other as "foED." Unfortunately, you can't change all instances of "foED" to "friends of ED" in a single operation, because that would involve using a subselect in an UPDATE query—something that MySQL doesn't yet support. However, MySQL does allow you to create **user-defined variables** in SQL queries. A user-defined variable acts in a similar way to an alias, in that it stores a value in temporary memory (usually until you close the connection with MySQL).

Updating multiple records with user-defined variables

To create a user-defined variable in MySQL, you use a variation of the SELECT statement. The variable name must begin with the @ symbol, and it is assigned by using a colon followed by an equal sign (:=). Figure 12-28 shows a sample set of records that use both "friends of ED" and "foED." The question is, how do you change all instances of "foED" to "friends of ED"?

```
MySQL Command Line Client
mysql> SELECT title, publisher
    -> FROM books, publishers
    -> WHERE books.pub_id = publishers.pub_id;
+------------------------------------------------------------+---------------+
| title                                                      | publisher     |
+------------------------------------------------------------+---------------+
| Foundation Dreamweaver MX 2004                             | friends of ED |
| Flash Cartoon Animation: Learn from the Pros               | friends of ED |
| Web Designer's Reference                                   | friends of ED |
| The Definitive Guide to MySQL, 2nd Edition                 | Apress        |
| Beginning PHP 5 and MySQL: From Novice to Professional     | Apress        |
| PHP Web Development with Dreamweaver MX 2004               | Apress        |
| Regular Expression Recipes: A Problem-Solution Approach    | Apress        |
| Foundation Flash MX 2004                                   | foED          |
| Foundation ActionScript for Flash MX 2004                  | foED          |
| Flash Math Creativity, 2nd Edition                         | foED          |
| Foundation PHP 5 for Flash                                 | foED          |
+------------------------------------------------------------+---------------+
11 rows in set (0.00 sec)
```

Figure 12-28. Two variations of the same publisher's name need to be merged.

The first step is to query the publishers table to find out the primary key of the two names you want to merge. Since the primary key is called pub_id, you need to create two variables to hold the value of the pub_id for "foED" and "friends of ED": @foED and @friends seem like reasonable choices. Figure 12-29 shows the necessary queries and the output that they produce. Although you don't need the output in the final step, it's a useful confirmation that your variables contain valid data.

```
MySQL Command Line Client
mysql> SELECT @foED := pub_id
    -> FROM publishers
    -> WHERE publisher = "foED";
+-----------------+
| @foED := pub_id |
+-----------------+
|               3 |
+-----------------+
1 row in set (0.00 sec)

mysql> SELECT @friends := pub_id
    -> FROM publishers
    -> WHERE publisher = "friends of ED";
+--------------------+
| @friends := pub_id |
+--------------------+
|                  1 |
+--------------------+
1 row in set (0.00 sec)
```

Figure 12-29. The values of the primary keys are assigned to user-defined variables.

Now that you have the value of both primary keys, all that's necessary is to use them to amend the books table. The UPDATE query looks like this:

```
UPDATE books SET pub_id = @friends
WHERE pub_id = @foED
```

If you then run the original query on the database, all the books previously listed as published by "foED" will have changed to "friends of ED" (as shown in Figure 12-30). You can now use the CMS to delete "foED" without destroying the integrity of your data. Although it involves working with MySQL Monitor, this is much quicker than finding and updating each book individually.

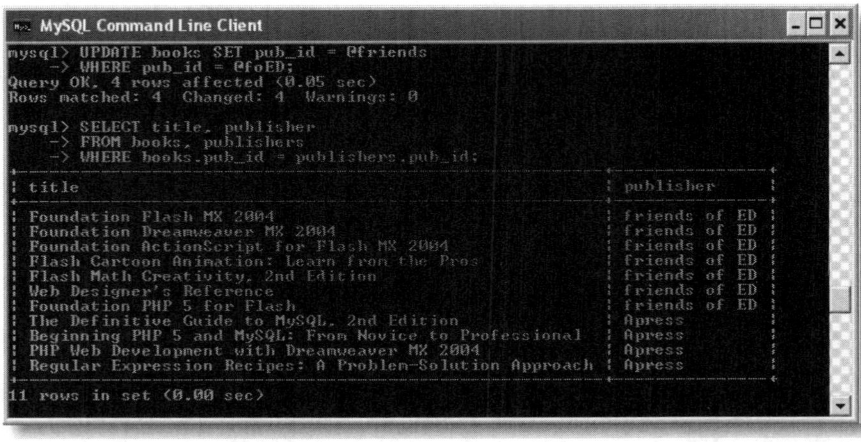

```
mysql> UPDATE books SET pub_id = @friends
    -> WHERE pub_id = @foED;
Query OK, 4 rows affected (0.05 sec)
Rows matched: 4  Changed: 4  Warnings: 0

mysql> SELECT title, publisher
    -> FROM books, publishers
    -> WHERE books.pub_id = publishers.pub_id;
+--------------------------------------------------------+---------------+
| title                                                  | publisher     |
+--------------------------------------------------------+---------------+
| Foundation Flash MX 2004                               | friends of ED |
| Foundation Dreamweaver MX 2004                         | friends of ED |
| Foundation ActionScript for Flash MX 2004              | friends of ED |
| Flash Cartoon Animation: Learn from the Pros           | friends of ED |
| Flash Math Creativity, 2nd Edition                     | friends of ED |
| Web Designer's Reference                               | friends of ED |
| Foundation PHP 5 for Flash                             | friends of ED |
| The Definitive Guide to MySQL, 2nd Edition             | Apress        |
| Beginning PHP 5 and MySQL: From Novice to Professional | Apress        |
| PHP Web Development with Dreamweaver MX 2004           | Apress        |
| Regular Expression Recipes: A Problem-Solution Approach | Apress       |
+--------------------------------------------------------+---------------+
11 rows in set (0.00 sec)
```

Figure 12-30. The user-defined variables allow you to perform a selective update on multiple records.

Using SimpleXML to parse an XML feed

XML is an amazingly simple concept that can be infuriatingly difficult to handle. That was certainly the case with the way PHP 4 handled XML. The tears of frustration induced by struggling with node values, and first children and siblings, now give way to tears of joy at how simple a task parsing an XML document has become with SimpleXML, which is new to PHP 5.

As its name suggests, SimpleXML is easy to use, but the (small) price you pay for this ease of use is that SimpleXML can be used only with documents where you know the format ahead of time. To load an XML document into a PHP script, pass the filename or URL to `simplexml_load_file()` and assign the result to a variable, like this:

```
$xml = simplexml_load_file('books.xml');
```

This creates an object that contains everything in the file. As long as you know the names of the elements you want to access, you can use a `foreach` loop to iterate through them using the `->` operator. You can also access any attributes using the `attributes()` method. The best way to describe SimpleXML is to show it to you in action.

Parsing an XML document

This exercise shows just a few of the basic methods available in SimpleXML. For a full description, see the online documentation at `www.php.net/manual/en/ref.simplexml.php`.

> *You must have PHP 5 installed to do this exercise. It will not run in PHP 4.*

1. Open your script editor and create an XML document called books.xml with the following code (it's also available in the download files):

```
<?xml version="1.0"?>
<Booklist>
   <Book>
      <Title>Foundation ActionScript for Flash MX 2004</Title>
      <Authors>
         <Author gender="male">Sham Bhangal</Author>
      </Authors>
   </Book>
   <Book>
      <Title>PHP Web Development with Dreamweaver MX 2004</Title>
      <Authors>
         <Author gender="female">Rachel Andrew</Author>
         <Author gender="male">Allan Kent</Author>
         <Author gender="male">David Powers</Author>
      </Authors>
   </Book>
</Booklist>
```

2. Create a PHP file in phpflash/ch12 called xmltest.php, and enter the following code to load the XML document and display its contents (or use xmltest1.php in the download files):

```
<?php
$xml = simplexml_load_file('books.xml');
foreach ($xml->Book as $book) {
  echo $book->Title.'<br />';
  foreach ($book->Authors->Author as $author) {
    echo $author.'<br />';
    }
  echo '<br />';
  }
?>
```

These nested foreach loops access each Book element as $xml->Book and assign it to the variable $book, so the child elements can then be accessed as $book->Title and the grandchildren elements as $book->Authors->Author.

3. Save both pages and load xmltest.php into a browser. You should get the result shown in the screenshot.

4. If you know that an element has a single attribute, you can access it with the attributes() method. Change line 6 in xmltest.php like this (xmltest2.php in the download files):

```
echo $author.' is '.$author->attributes().'<br />';
```

5. Save xmltest.php and click the Refresh button in your browser. You should now see is male or is female added to the name of each author. This is fine if there's just one attribute. To deal with more than one attribute, you need another foreach loop.

6. Amend the XML in books.xml to add a country attribute to each author like this:

```
<Author gender="male" country="UK">Sham Bhangal</Author>
```

   Allan Kent is the only one who lives elsewhere, so his entry should look like this:

```
<Author gender="male" country="South Africa">Allan Kent</Author>
```

7. Change the code in xmltest.php as follows (xmltest3.php in the download files):

```
<?php
$xml = simplexml_load_file('books.xml');
foreach ($xml->Book as $book) {
  foreach($book->Authors->Author as $author) {
    foreach ($author->attributes() as $key => $value) {
      if ($key == 'country') {
        echo "$author lives in $value <br />";
        }
      }
    }
  }
?>
```

8. Save xmltest.php and click Refresh in your browser. You should now see a list of the authors' names and the country each one lives in, as shown alongside.

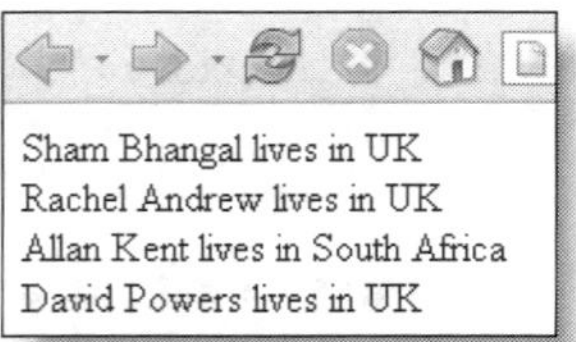

Sham Bhangal lives in UK
Rachel Andrew lives in UK
Allan Kent lives in South Africa
David Powers lives in UK

Although using SimpleXML involves a lot of looping to access the information you want, the ability to do so with ordinary variable names is much more intuitive than the normal way of parsing XML, which often involves iterating through anonymous nodes, children, and siblings.

Inserting prices from an XML feed

Some online bookstores, such as Amazon.com, provide free XML feeds that affiliates can use to incorporate pricing and other information in their own e-commerce sites. Access to such feeds requires registration for an affiliate account (this is usually free and will earn you commission on any sales). If you have such an account, you can try out the final page of the CMS with a live feed. Alternatively, you can simulate the same effect with an XML file on your local computer.

Creating getprices.php

This last section of the CMS is optional, and it requires PHP 5 to work since it relies on SimpleXML to parse pricing information from an XML file.

1. Copy `bookprices.xml` from the download files for this chapter and save it in `phpflash/ch12`. Open it and examine the format. It is very similar to `books.xml` in the previous exercise, except that the main document root is called Results and it contains more information. To save space, the following code shows only the details for this book:

```
<?xml version="1.0"?>
<Results>
   <Book>
      <ISBN>1590594665</ISBN>
      <BookTitle>Foundation PHP 5 For Flash</BookTitle>
      <Authors>
         <Author>David Powers</Author>
      </Authors>
      <Publisher>friends of ED</Publisher>
      <ListPrice>$44.99</ListPrice>
      <OurPrice>$29.70</OurPrice>
   </Book>
</Results>
```

An XML feed from an online bookstore often contains much more information about each book, but the pattern is likely to be similar. All you need to do is convert the XML data to a SimpleXML object and extract the information you want.

2. Open `getprices.php` or use `getprices02.php` from the download files (the final code is in `getprices03.php`), and add the following two lines to the PHP code block above the Doctype to include the Database classes and instantiate a Database object:

```
require_once('../classes/database.php');
$db = new Database('localhost','flashadmin','fortytwo','bookstore',0);
```

3. Insert the following code in the main body of `getprices.php`, just before the closing </table> tag (around line 22):

```
</tr>
<?php
if (!file_exists('bookprices.xml')) {
  echo '<tr><td colspan="3">Can\'t find XML feed</td></tr>';
  }
else {
  // load XML file as a SimpleXML object
  $xml = simplexml_load_file('bookprices.xml');
  // loop through each Book element to extract ListPrice, OurPrice, and
  // ISBN, and use the details to update the books table
  foreach ($xml->Book as $book) {
```

```
    $updatePrices = "UPDATE books SET list_price ='$book->ListPrice',
                     store_price = '$book->OurPrice'
                     WHERE isbn = '$book->ISBN'";
    $db->query($updatePrices);
    // get the price information from the books table
    $confirmUpdate = "SELECT title, list_price, store_price
                      FROM books WHERE isbn = '$book->ISBN'";
    $result = $db->query($confirmUpdate);
    // if that ISBN exists in the database, display the result
    if ($result->num_rows) {
      $row = $result->fetch_assoc();
      echo '<tr><td>'.$row['title'].'</td>
      echo '<td>'.$row['list_price'].'</td>';
      echo '<td>'.$row['store_price'].'</td></tr>';
      }
    }
  }
?>
</table>
```

This code begins by using the PHP function `file_exists()` to check that the XML file is accessible (`file_exists()` can be used with a URL or a local file). If there's a problem, it displays an error message; otherwise, it loads the data in `bookprices.xml` and converts it into a SimpleXML object. The code then loops through each Book element as in the previous exercise, but instead of displaying everything directly onscreen, it uses the data to build an UPDATE query. If an ISBN isn't in the database, nothing happens. Nothing is updated, but neither is an error generated.

After the UPDATE query, a SELECT query confirms the details have been recorded. If the ISBN isn't listed, `$result->num_rows` will return 0, so nothing is added to the table in `getprices.php`. The loop goes through the same process for each subsequent book.

4. Save `getprices.php` and click the Get Prices link in the CMS menu. You should see a list of the books in your database that have had pricing information added to them, as shown in Figure 12-31. It really is as simple as that!

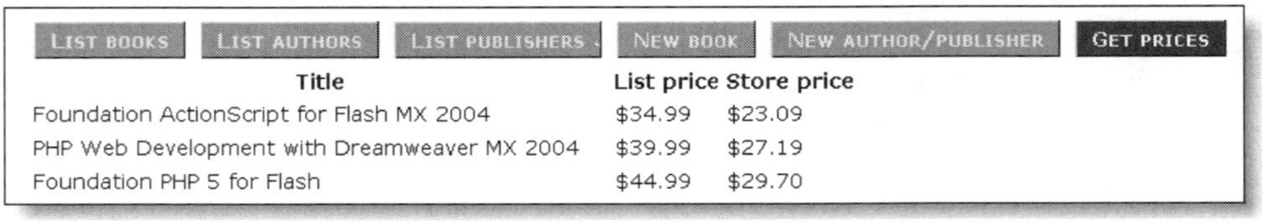

LIST BOOKS | LIST AUTHORS | LIST PUBLISHERS | NEW BOOK | NEW AUTHOR/PUBLISHER | GET PRICES

Title	List price	Store price
Foundation ActionScript for Flash MX 2004	$34.99	$23.09
PHP Web Development with Dreamweaver MX 2004	$39.99	$27.19
Foundation PHP 5 for Flash	$44.99	$29.70

Figure 12-31. The prices of books in the database have been updated from an XML feed.

When accessing an XML feed from an online bookstore, you normally have to send a list of the ISBN numbers that you want the details for. This is simply a matter of querying your database and using PHP to build a URL or query string in whatever format the feed provider requires. Some XML feeds provide prices complete with currency symbols, as has been done here.

That's why I chose VARCHAR as the column type for the prices. If you're running an e-commerce site, though, you may want to remove the currency symbol, convert the price to cents, and then store it as an integer. This will make calculations easier and faster. For instance, you could work out the percentage discount using the following formula:

```
$discount = round(($listPrice - $storePrice) / $listPrice * 100);
```

If you have been working with the test data in the database, all the prices will already be in the books *table. To verify that everything is working correctly, change some of the prices in* bookprices.xml*, or open MySQL Monitor, select the* bookstore *database (*use bookstore*), and type the following command:*

```
UPDATE books SET list_price = NULL, store_price = NULL;
```

Check in phpMyAdmin that the existing prices have gone, and then click GET PRICES *in the CMS. Because everything is on your local computer, the prices should be updated instantaneously.*

Securing your CMS

Once you have designed a CMS like this, you need to restrict access to it to prevent unauthorized people from altering your data. The simplest way of doing this is to use HTTP authentication (most hosting companies let you do this through a control panel). Since you're a PHP wizard by now, you should have little difficulty in adapting the login system from Chapter 9. Make sure you apply the authentication code to every page. You'll also need to add a logout button to the navigation menu.

Displaying the database contents in Flash

As I mentioned at the beginning of the chapter, I have deliberately kept the Flash side of this chapter to a minimum, in order to concentrate on the PHP and MySQL side of things. That has enabled us to cover some very important ground. Still, the chapter wouldn't be complete without showing you how to query the database from within Flash and transfer the data for display in a Flash movie. In keeping with the rest of the chapter, I intend to concentrate on the PHP and SQL needed, and leave the Flash wizardry up to your design and ActionScript skills.

Getting the database ready

After all the testing, the records in the bookstore database will probably need refreshing, either with the addition of some of your own material or by reloading the SQL file from the download files. Refer back to the section "Populating the database with test data" and reload bookstore.sql. The backup file will automatically overwrite any existing data and restore the database to the same condition as at the beginning of the chapter.

Communicating with the database through PHP

The PHP script queries the database in different ways, depending on the value of a single variable (action) received from the Flash movie. This follows the same principle as the CMS in Chapter 10. However, the major difference is that this application always uses a SELECT query, because all back-end administration is handled by the XHTML system created in the first part of this chapter. When the PHP script receives a request from the Flash movie, it uses the value of action to determine which SELECT query to execute, and then it loops through the results, formatting and creating name/value pairs ready to send back to Flash. Once the results are inside Flash, it's simply a matter of deciding how to display them.

The solution proposed here concentrates on the mechanics of getting the data from MySQL to Flash, and it is by no means the only way you could use the bookstore database. Once you have built the basic script, it should be easy to add extra functionality by creating new SQL queries that are executed in response to the value passed by action.

Building the SQL queries

The original specifications for this project stipulated that the site should display a list of the most recent additions to the database, and that it should be searchable by author, title, or ISBN. I think it would also be useful to get a full list of all entries. This breaks down easily into five values for action:

- **getLatest**: This will retrieve the five most recent additions to the database and display them with the most recent first.
- **fullList**: This will retrieve all books listed in the database, placing them in alphabetical order according to title.
- **byAuthor**: This will retrieve a list of all books written by a particular author. It will allow case-insensitive searches for partial names.
- **byTitle**: This will retrieve a list of all books, either by full title or by using a partial title.
- **byISBN**: This will retrieve details of a single book, based on its ISBN.

The specifications also stipulated that lists of books would show just a line or so of description, with a link to a full description. Because the database contains only a small number of books, I decided that the most efficient way is to use PHP string functions to create two versions of the description, and to send both to the Flash movie at the same time. This avoids the need for a round-trip to the server every time a user wants to see details of a book. The only time this is likely to create problems is with the full list, but this is easily overcome by creating a page navigation system to retrieve, say, 20 records at a time.

Let's start scripting:

1. Create a new PHP page called actions.php in phpflash/ch12 (the completed script is in a file of the same name in the download files for this chapter).
2. Insert the basic framework for the script as follows:

```
<?php
if (isset($_POST['action'])) {
  require_once('../classes/database.php');
```

```
  $db=new Database('localhost','flashuser','deepthought','bookstore');
  // this is common to all SQL queries
  $sql = 'SELECT books.book_id,title,publisher,isbn,description,
          list_price,store_price,image FROM books,publishers';
  // build rest of query based on action received from Flash
  switch($_POST['action']) {
    case 'getLatest':
    case 'fullList':
    case 'byAuthor':
    case 'byTitle':
    case 'byISBN':
    }
  // run the query and process the result
  // send the results back to Flash
  echo $output;
  }
// separate functions go here
?>
```

What makes this a relatively simple operation is that you always want the same information about each book, regardless of the nature of the query. Consequently, the first part of the SQL query is assigned to `$sql` outside a `switch` statement. In some queries, `book_id` will be ambiguous, so you need to qualify it as `books.book_id`.

3. The rest of each SQL query is determined by a `switch` statement. I'll describe the important points of each one in turn. The new code for each case is shown in bold type. First, `action` is set to `getLatest`:

```
case 'getLatest':
  $sql .=  ' WHERE books.pub_id = publishers.pub_id
           ORDER BY book_id DESC LIMIT 5';
  break;
```

As with each part of the `switch` statement, this code uses the combined concatenation operator (`.=`) to add the second half of the SQL query to the common first half. The important thing to note here is that a space is left in front of `WHERE`. If you don't do this, the combined query would include `publishersWHERE`, and fail. By using the `book_id` to sort books in descending order, you get the most recent first. If you want to retrieve more than five books, increase the number after `LIMIT`.

4. The next case retrieves details of all records in the database:

```
case 'fullList':
  $sql .= ' WHERE books.pub_id = publishers.pub_id
          ORDER BY title';
  break;
```

The only differences between this and `getLatest` are that results are sorted according to `title`, and `LIMIT` has not been set, so every record is included in the result.

If you are working with a larger database, you could create a page navigation system similar to the one in Chapter 10, and then retrieve, say, 20 records at a time by sending a variable called `start`. *All you need to do is add a* `LIMIT` *clause to* `fullList` *like this:*

```
case 'fullList':
  $sql .= ' WHERE books.pub_id = publishers.pub_id
          ORDER BY title LIMIT '.$_POST['start'].',20';
  break;
```

The value of `start` *would tell MySQL how many records to skip and then to retrieve the next 20. You could replace* `20` *with another variable, giving the user greater control over the way the database is used. The possibilities are limited only by your imagination and coding skills.*

5. Searching for details by author requires a much longer SQL query, because it needs to draw information from all four tables, as follows:

```
case 'byAuthor':
  $sql .= ',authors,book_to_author
          WHERE CONCAT(first_name," ",family_name)
          LIKE "%'.trim($_POST['searchFor']).'%"
          AND book_to_author.author_id = authors.author_id
          AND book_to_author.book_id = books.book_id
          AND books.pub_id = publishers.pub_id';
  break;
```

There is no need to leave a space at the beginning of the second half of the SQL query, because it begins with a comma. The `WHERE` clause begins by using `CONCAT()` to join the authors' first names and family names. Once combined, they are used to compare with the value of the search term. The search form in the Flash movie will have only one input field, so a common variable, `searchFor`, is used for all the search-based queries.

The value of `searchFor` is passed to the `trim()` function to remove any whitespace, and the percent signs on either side act as wildcards. This means that users can search not only for "Sham Bhangal," but also simply for "Bhan," and Sham's books will still come up. This type of search *won't*, however, find matches for "S. Bhangal" or for "Banghal." Building that sort of fuzzy search isn't impossible, but it involves a lot more scripting. Nevertheless, offering users a variety of methods of searching greatly improves usability.

6. Searching for books by title requires the following, much simpler query:

```
case 'byTitle':
  $sql .= ' WHERE title LIKE "%'.trim($_POST['searchFor']).'%"
          AND books.pub_id = publishers.pub_id';
  break;
```

Again, the search term is passed to `trim()` and surrounded by percent signs.

7. The final case involves searching by ISBN. The code needed is as follows:

```
case 'byISBN':
  $isbn = str_replace('-','',$_POST['searchFor']);
  $sql .= ' WHERE isbn = "'.trim($isbn).'"
          AND books.pub_id = publishers.pub_id';
```

This begins by using the same code as in new_book.php to strip any hyphens out of the ISBN, and then it completes the SQL query. Although I've passed the ISBN to trim(), I decided against using percent signs. If anyone is searching for a book by ISBN, it seems likely that they will either have the correct number or not at all. Because this is the last case in the switch statement, it doesn't need break at the end, although you should put it in if you plan to add further options later. This would avoid the likelihood of future errors (without break, any later code would be automatically executed as part of this case).

8. The code that runs the query and formats the output to be sent back to Flash follows a similar pattern to previous chapters and is explained through inline comments. It contains two custom-built functions, getAuthors() and shortDesc(), that will be explained in steps 9 and 10. The following code goes immediately after the closing curly brace of the switch statement.

```
// run the query and process the result
$result = $db->query($sql);
$numRows = $result->num_rows;
// begin the output string with number of results and action type
$output = "total={$numRows}&resultType=".$_POST['action'];
// create counter to identify related variables
$i=0;
while ($row = $result->fetch_assoc()) {
  foreach ($row as $key => $value) {
    // use the book_id to get a list of authors
    if ($key == 'book_id') {
      $output .= "&authors{$i}=".urlencode(getAuthors($db,$value));
      }
    // create a short version of the description
    elseif ($key == 'description') {
      $output .= "&short{$i}=".urlencode(shortDesc($value));
      }
    // create a variable made up of the array key and $i
    // and assign it the URL-encoded value
    $output .= "&{$key}{$i}=".urlencode($value);
    }
  // increment the counter for the variables to be sent to Flash
  $i++;
  }
  // send the results back to Flash
  echo $output;
  }
```

As you study the code, you will notice that several variables inside double-quoted strings are enclosed in curly braces. It's something I've mentioned before, but it's a technique that takes a little getting used to. It simply tells the PHP engine to treat what's inside the braces as a variable, even though there is no whitespace on either side. The output string sent to Flash must not contain any spaces, so without the curly braces, you would have to write this, for example:

```
$output .= '&'.$key.$i.'='.urlencode($value);
```

With the curly braces, it become this:

```
$output .= "&{$key}{$i}=".urlencode($value);
```

Omitting the period from concatenated strings is a frequent cause of mistakes, so you may find it helps to adopt this style when appropriate.

9. The first of the custom-made functions, `getAuthors()`, takes two arguments: a reference to the `Database` object and the primary key of the book. It uses these to find out which authors are associated with the book, and it builds a string to send back to the code in the previous step. There is nothing new in this code, although some of the decisions need explaining.

When building the test database, I decided to use *Flash Math Creativity* (friends of ED, ISBN: 1-59059-429-0) as one of the examples. Like a Cecil B. DeMille movie, it has a cast of thousands (well, all right, 15 authors). Not only that, one of them goes by the name Lifaros (just that—nothing else). The definition for the `authors` table doesn't allow empty fields, so I was faced with a dilemma: should I change the `first_name` column and remove the `NOT NULL` restriction? I felt that would create more problems than it solved, so I decided to enter NULL as the first name for anyone without one. This is perfectly valid, but it doesn't create a genuine `NULL` entry. Instead, it records "NULL" as a string. By testing for "NULL" at the beginning of the string, you can strip out the first five characters (including the space after "NULL"), leaving you with just the single name. Note that the test uses the identical operator (three equal signs), because you need to make sure the position of the string is zero, *not* anything else that equates to `false`.

I got around the problem of multiple authors by setting an arbitrary limit of three named authors. If there are more than three, the first two are named, and the string "and others" is added. The code for this function goes right at the bottom of `actions.php`.

```
// get a list of authors using the book_id
function getAuthors($db,$book_id) {
  $authorQuery = "SELECT CONCAT(first_name,' ',family_name) AS author
                  FROM authors,book_to_author
                  WHERE book_to_author.book_id = $book_id
                  AND authors.author_id = book_to_author.author_id
                  ORDER BY family_name";
  $authorResult = $db->query($authorQuery);
  while ($row = $authorResult->fetch_assoc()) {
    // remove first 5 characters from any result beginning with "NULL"
    if (strpos($row['author'],'NULL') === 0) {
      $authors[] = substr($row['author'],5);
```

```
      }
    else {
      $authors[] = $row['author'];
      }
    }
    if (!empty($authors)) {
      // if there are more than three authors, use the first two
      // and concatenate with "and others"
      if (count($authors) > 3) {
      array_splice($authors,2);
      return implode(', ',$authors).' and others';
      }
    // otherwise create a comma-delimited string of authors
    else {
      return implode(', ',$authors);
      }
    }
  else {
    return '';
    }
  }
```

In addition to Lifaros, other authors' names presented a variety of problems. Americans tend to use initials much more frequently than the British do, so Jason Gilmore is often listed as W. Jason Gilmore; and JD Hooge is always referred to as "JD" (without any periods between the initials). When creating the test data, I decided to lose initials, except in JD's case. I could have used "W. Jason" in the `first_name` column, but that might result in listing "W. Jason Gilmore" and "Jason Gilmore" as separate people. There is no right answer to these sorts of dilemmas, but you need to be aware of them when you plan a database and decide on policies to handle such situations.

10. The other custom-built function takes the description of each book and extracts the first sentence. Computer languages have no concept of what constitutes a sentence, so I used a `strpos()` to find the first period followed by a space. (Finding the first period on its own is no good, because it could be a decimal point, such as in ActionScript 2.0.) However, that on its own wasn't good enough, because some descriptions use question marks or exclamation marks. The solution is to use a PHP function called `strcspn()`, which takes two arguments: the string you want to search and another string that acts as a mask. It returns the length of the first string that doesn't contain any of the characters in the mask. In other words, the following code can be used to find the position of the first question mark or exclamation mark in `$description`:

```
$marks = strcspn($description, '?!');
```

The value of `$marks` will be either the position of the first question mark or exclamation mark, or—if neither is found—the length of the entire string. By comparing the values of `$marks` and the position of the first period followed by a space, you can be fairly confident that you will extract the first sentence unless it's an example sentence that contains code that uses any of these characters (but, hey, there's a limit to the amount of testing you can do for the average application). The shortDesc() function goes after the code in the previous step.

```
// extract the first sentence from the description value
function shortDesc($description) {
  // find the position of the first period followed by a space
  $period = strpos($description, '. ');
  // find the first question mark or exclamation mark
  $marks = strcspn($description, '?!');
  // use the lesser value to extract the first sentence
  if ($period && $period < $marks) {
    return substr($description,0,$period+1);
    }
  elseif ($period && $marks < $period) {
    return substr($description,0,$marks+1);
    }
  // if period has no value, return $description unchanged
  else {
    return $description;
    }
  }
```

Building the Flash interface

The Flash interface is very plain, and it was designed simply to show how a Flash application could be used to query the bookstore database and display the results. The finished FLA is available in the download files for this chapter as bookstore.fla. It contains just one frame and two layers: interface and actions. Figure 12-32 shows the various elements on the stage, all of which go on the interface layer. They consist of the following elements:

- Three buttons with instance names of latest_btn, showAll_btn, and go_btn.
- A multiline dynamic text field called mainText_txt. It has no border, but the text is selectable.
- An MX UI components scrollbar with an instance name of vSB, snapped to the right edge of mainText_txt. (Make sure the Snap to objects icon is highlighted in the Tools toolbar, if it fails to snap to the text field.)

- An MX UI ComboBox component with an instance name of search_cb. In the Parameters tab of the Property inspector, enter title,author,ISBN in the Labels field, and byTitle,byAuthor,byISBN in the Data field.
- A single-line input text field with an instance name of search_txt. The field has a border.

I made the stage 700×500 pixels. Most of it is taken up by the dynamic text field, mainText_txt. All the ActionScript goes on frame 1 of the actions layer.

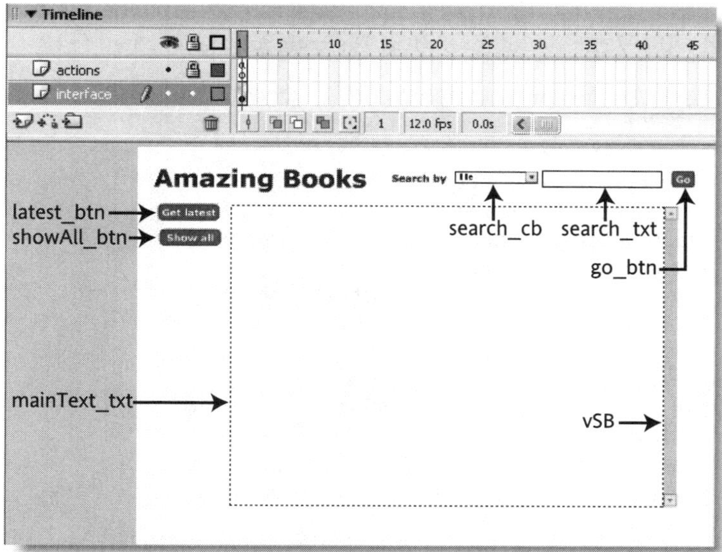

Figure 12-32. The Flash application uses just one frame to display the information in a variety of ways.

Creating the ActionScript to load results from the database

As explained earlier, the PHP script selects material from the database depending on one of five values for a variable called `action` that it receives from Flash. All the communication between Flash and the PHP script can be handled by two instances of `LoadVars`: one to send the data to `actions.php` (`dbQuery`) and another to receive the result (`recResult`). The ActionScript breaks down into four main sections:

- Database query and processing functions
- Display functions
- Button functions
- Main timeline variables and CSS styles

Rather than giving step-by-step instructions on how to build the script, I will present the code for each section in full and comment on the most important points. Each section of the script is liberally filled with inline comments, so you should have little difficulty in following it by this stage. The code is shown here in the same order as it appears in the Actions panel.

Querying the database and processing the results

This section consists of three functions. The first two, `queryDatabase()` and `processResult()`, are responsible for communication with the PHP script through the two instances of `LoadVars`. The third function, `buildBookArray()`, converts the stream of variables received from the PHP script and converts them into an array of objects called books with properties that can be easily accessed within ActionScript for display. The code for the functions follows:

```
/********************************************
Database query and result processing functions
********************************************/
function queryDatabase(action:String):Void {
  // this queries the database
  // action determines the type of query carried out by PHP
  dbQuery.action = action;
  dbQuery.sendAndLoad("http://localhost/phpflash/ch12/actions.php",
➥ recResult);
}
function processResult(success):Void {
  // this is the onLoad event handler for recResult
  var theText:String = "<body>";
  if (!success) {
    theText += "<title>Database unavailable. Please try later.
➥ </title>";
  } else {
    // pass recResult to buildBookArray()
    buildBookArray(this);
    // then build the list and display it
    theText += buildList();
  }
  theText += "</body>";
  //reset scroll position of dynamic text field and display text
  mainText_txt.scroll = 1;
  mainText_txt.text = theText;
  // show or hide the scrollbar, depending on length of text
  showHideSB();
}
function buildBookArray(theLoadVars:LoadVars):Void {
  // this builds the books array from the results
  // received by LoadVars
  currentResult = theLoadVars.resultType;
  var total:Number = theLoadVars.total;
  // clear any existing books array
  books.length = 0;
  // loop through the results assigning them to properties
  // of each book in the books array
  for (var i = 0; i<total; i++) {
    books[i] = new Object();
    books[i].title = theLoadVars["title"+i];
    books[i].authors = theLoadVars["authors"+i];
    books[i].publisher = theLoadVars["publisher"+i];
    books[i].short = theLoadVars["short"+i];
    books[i].description = theLoadVars["description"+i];
    books[i].isbn = theLoadVars["isbn"+i];
```

```
      books[i].listPrice = theLoadVars["list_price"+i];
      books[i].storePrice = theLoadVars["store_price"+i];
      if (theLoadVars["image"+i] == "y") {
        books[i].image = "http://localhost/phpflash/ch12/images/"+
➥ books[i].isbn+".jpg";
      }
    }
  }
```

The first function, queryDatabase(), takes a single parameter—a string that will be passed as the value of action to the PHP script. As the name suggests, it sends a query to the database.

The second function, processResult(), passes most of its work to other functions. Because it's the onLoad event handler for recResult, it can use the this keyword to pass recResult to buildBookArray(), which builds an array of objects called books. It then calls buildList() to build the HTML text that will be used to display the results within the movie. When the HTML has been created, it's assigned to the text property of mainText_txt, and showHideSB() determines whether a scrollbar is needed.

The third function, buildBookArray(), takes a single parameter, a LoadVars instance, and extracts all the variables received from PHP in a simple loop. It's similar in structure to the loop that was used to process the results from the database in Chapter 10.

Displaying the results

Four functions handle the display of the results. The first of them is buildList(), which is one of the functions called by processResult(). Before looking at the script, take a look at Figure 12-33, which shows how the results are displayed onscreen when the movie first loads.

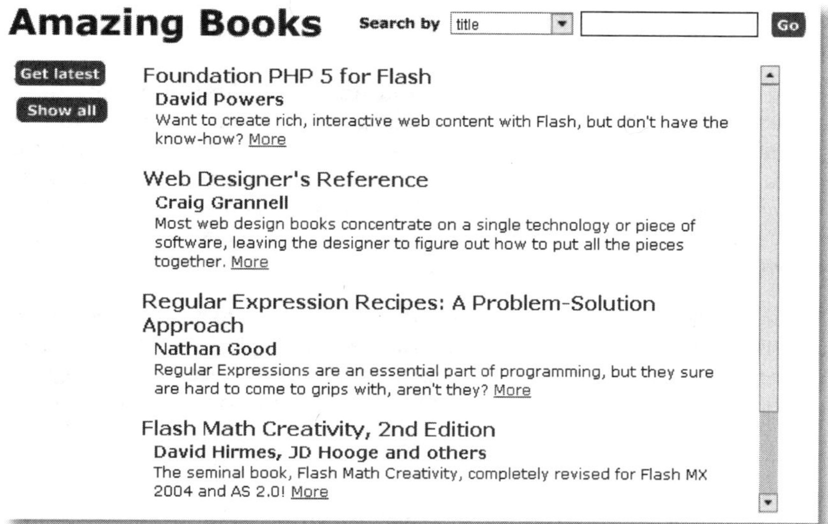

Figure 12-33. When the movie first loads, it displays a list of the five most recent additions to the database.

As you can see, four things are displayed for each book: the title, the name(s) of the author(s), the short description, and a link to further details. The buildList() function simply creates a string of HTML text by looping through the contents of the books array and concatenating the relevant properties of each book with the necessary HTML tags. Support for CSS in Flash Player 7 is limited to a small range of elements and style properties, but it lets you create your own tags, such as <authors>, rather like XML. The code for buildList() looks like this:

```
/****************
Display functions
****************/
function buildList():String {
  // this uses the books array to build the text
  // containing a list of results
  var theList:String = "";
  if (books.length == 0) {
    // if the books array is empty, there were no records
    theList += "<authors>No records found</authors>";
  } else {
    // display the short version of the books details
    // and add a link to display the full version
    for (var i = 0; i<books.length; i++) {
      theList += "<title>"+books[i].title+"</title>";
      theList += "<authors>"+books[i].authors+"</authors>";
      theList += "<p>"+books[i].short;
      // this link calls the showDetails() function
      theList += " <a href='asfunction:showDetails,"+i+"'>";
      theList += "More</a></p><br>";
    }
  }
  return theList;
}
```

The <a> tag uses asfunction instead of a URL to link to further details. This calls an ActionScript function within the Flash movie, instead of redirecting the user to an external web page. The code highlighted in bold shows how asfunction is used. The name of the function being called (in this case, showDetails()) is separated from asfunction by a colon. The parentheses after the function name are omitted, and any arguments passed to the function come after a comma. The argument in this case is i, the loop counter variable. In other words, showDetails() is passed the same number as the array key for the book.

The code for the showDetails() function is shown next. It simply builds an HTML string with the details of one book, and it takes advantage of the ability of Flash Player 7 to use the <img> tag. By setting a height and width for the images, Flash leaves a space for the image and wraps text around it. Of course, using it like this means that all images must be the same size.

If you are using Flash MX or need to support earlier versions of Flash Player, you need to load the images the traditional way with the `loadMovie()` *method. Because the images need to be embedded in a SWF, one way of loading them is to convert them all and store them as SWFs in the* `images` *folder. Alternatively, use* `createEmptyMovieClip()` *to load the image into, and use* `removeMovieClip()` *when the image is no longer required. You will also need to change the ActionScript to take account of this. The MX versions of the download files show how this is done.*

```
function showDetails(num:Number) {
  // this displays the details of an individual book
  var b:Object = books[num];
  var theText:String = "<body>";
  theText += "<title>"+b.title+"</title>";
  theText += "<authors>"+b.authors+"</authors>";
  theText += "<publisher>"+b.publisher+"</publisher>";
  theText += "<p>List price: "+b.listPrice;
  theText += " <op>Our price: "+b.storePrice+"</op></p>";
  theText += "<p>";
  if (b.image != undefined) {
    theText += "<img src='"+b.image+"' height='125' width='98'>";
  }
  theText += b.description+"</p>";
  theText += "</body>";
  //reset scroll position of dynamic text field and display text
  mainText_txt.scroll = 1;
  mainText_txt.text = theText;
  // show or hide the scrollbar, depending on length of text
  showHideSB();
}
```

Figure 12-34 shows how the details of a book look onscreen. By using the `text` property of `mainText_txt` all the time, there is no need for a function to clear the display; it's just the HTML text that's changed each time.

In an ordinary dynamic website, the browser would need to send another request to the server to display the list of books again. With Flash, though, all the details are still available as ActionScript variables, so the next function, `displayList()`, checks the value of the `action` passed to it against a timeline variable called `currentResult`. This is always set by `buildBookArray()` when it processes the result from the database. If `action` and `currentResult` have the same value, `displayList()` simply calls `buildList()` to redisplay the details in current memory. Otherwise, it passes `action` to `queryDatabase()` to get a new set of results. The callback functions for the buttons simply call `displayList()` with the appropriate `action` as the argument. The code for `displayList()` follows, together with two of the button callbacks and the function that shows and hides the scrollbar.

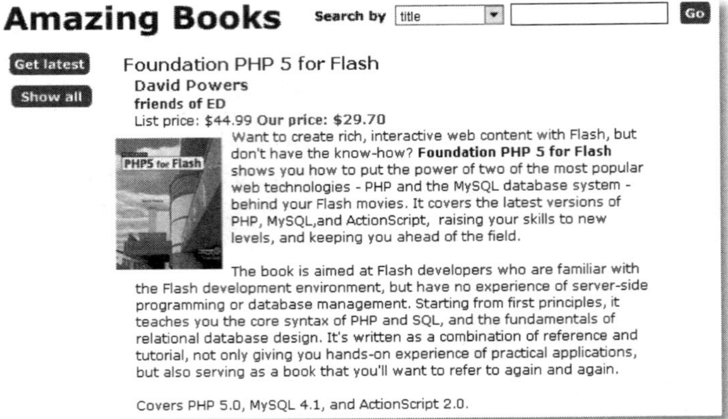

Figure 12-34. Details of individual books appear on the same screen, and the scrollbar disappears if it's no longer needed.

```
function displayList(action:String):Void {
  // this displays a list of results
  if (currentResult == action) {
    // if the currentResult is the same as action
    // that means the list is already in Flash's memory
    // so the list can be displayed immediately
    var theText:String = "<body>";
    theText += buildList();
    theText += "</body>";
    mainText_txt.text = theText;
    showHideSB();
  } else {
    // if not in current memory, query the database
    queryDatabase(action);
  }
}
function showHideSB():Void {
  // this checks the total height of the text
  // and shows/hides the scrollbar as required
  vSB._visible = mainText_txt.textHeight>mainText_txt._height ? true
➥ : false;
}
/***************
Button functions
***************/
latest_btn.onRelease = function() {
  displayList("getLatest");
};
showAll_btn.onRelease = function() {
  displayList("fullList");
};
```

Conducting searches

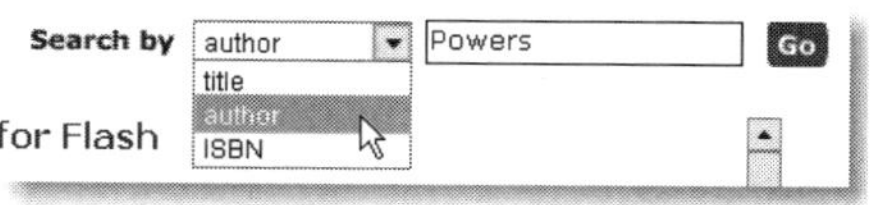

The search_cb combo box has three options: title, author, and ISBN. When you select one of the options, enter a search term in the input field, and click Go, the search is conducted in exactly the same way as all other actions. The only difference is that *two* variables are sent to actions.php: the contents of the search input field (search_txt) in addition to action.

The callback function for the Go button uses the getValue() method of the MX UI ComboBox component to find out which option has been selected. That's all there is to it. The code for the callback looks like this:

```
go_btn.onRelease = function() {
  // this sends details of a search to the PHP script
  dbQuery.action = search_cb.getValue();
  dbQuery.searchFor = search_txt.text;
  dbQuery.sendAndLoad("http://localhost/phpflash/ch12/
➥ actions.php", recResult);
};
```

> *Don't forget that the* localhost *address is for local testing only. When deploying your application on an Internet server, replace the* localhost *address with a relative or absolute address for* actions.php *on the server.*

Setting the main timeline variables

The rest of the ActionScript sets the main timeline variables and CSS styles. It looks like this:

```
// initialize variables
var dbQuery:LoadVars = new LoadVars();
var recResult:LoadVars = new LoadVars();
recResult.onLoad = processResult;
var currentResult:String;
var books:Array = new Array();
// set styles for the main text field
var styles = new TextField.StyleSheet();
styles.setStyle("body", {fontFamily:'Verdana, Arial, Helvetica,
➥ sans-serif', marginRight:'15px', color:'#000000'});
styles.setStyle("title", {fontSize:'16px', display:'block',
➥ fontWeight:'bold', marginLeft:'15px', marginTop:'20px',
➥ color:'#000066'});
styles.setStyle("authors", {fontSize:'14px', display:'block',
➥ fontWeight:'bold', marginLeft:'25px', color:'#000066'});
styles.setStyle("publisher", {fontSize:'12px', display:'block',
➥ fontWeight:'bold', marginLeft:'25px', color:'#000066'});
styles.setStyle("p", {fontSize:'12px', marginLeft:'25px'});
```

```
styles.setStyle("op", {fontWeight:'bold', color:'#FF0000'});
styles.setStyle("a:link", {textDecoration:'underline',
➥ color:'#1C0DCB'});
styles.setStyle("a:hover", {textDecoration:'underline',
➥ color:'#F5020C'});
mainText_txt.styleSheet = styles;
mainText_txt.html = true;
// get a list of the latest entries and display them
queryDatabase("getLatest");
```

The final line of the script makes a call to `queryDatabase()`, with the argument set to `getLatest`, so the movie will always display the latest five records on loading.

A long road traveled

So, here you are at the end of a long and sometimes exhausting journey, but I hope you have found it as exhilarating as I have. Working with PHP and MySQL can be frustrating at times, but that's not an indication that they're lacking in any way. All programming languages have their peculiarities, and ActionScript has certainly given me plenty of headaches, although that's less of a problem since the introduction of ActionScript 2.0, which has formalized the language to a great degree. The changes introduced in PHP 5 have also formalized the more advanced aspects of PHP, so it's fair to say that both languages are now approaching a more mature and stable level. Both will continue to evolve—meaning there will be more to learn, but also meaning enhanced functionality. The same is true of Flash and MySQL. The future for all of them looks bright.

I hope that what you've learned over the past few hundred pages not only alerted you to the differences between PHP and ActionScript, but also whetted your appetite for more knowledge. With the skills you learned, you should now be able to adapt many of the techniques to projects of your own. Whether you're developing games, an e-commerce site, or simply a personal site, the ability to team up the graphic and animation strengths of Flash with the power of a database and server-side functionality should inspire you to higher levels.

Thanks for staying the course, and happy coding.

mysql.connect_timeout	60	60
mysql.default_host	no value	no value
mysql.default_password	no value	no value
mysql.default_port	no value	no value
mysql.default_socket	no value	no value
mysql.default_user	no value	no value
mysql.max_links	Unlimited	Unlimited
mysql.max_persistent	Unlimited	Unlimited
mysql.trace_mode	Off	Off

mysqli

MysqlI Support	enabled
Client API version	4.1.7
MYSQLI_SOCKET	/tmp/mysql.sock

Directive	Local Value	Mas
mysqli.default_host	no value	no value
mysqli.default_port	3306	3306
mysqli.default_pw	no value	no value
mysqli.default_socket	no value	no value
mysqli.default_user	no value	no value

Appendix A

WHEN THINGS GO WRONG WITH PHP AND MYSQL

Throughout the book, I've tried to identify the most likely causes of problems, and I've suggested how to fix them. Learning a new computer language is rarely easy, and in this case you're dealing with at least two new languages: PHP 5 and the MySQL implementation of SQL. If you're also a beginner with ActionScript, that makes three new languages, so when things go wrong, a sense of despair can easily set in.

Don't worry. It's something even the world's greatest experts have experienced at one stage. The first thing to remember is to be patient. Computers work according to fixed rules and logic. Of course, software has bugs, but when you're first starting out, the cause of a script not working as expected is far more likely to be a mistake you've made, rather than a fundamental bug in the software. It's your bug, not the software's. Before you do major damage to either your forehead or keyboard by banging the two together, take a deep breath and try to work out where the problem may lie.

Flash automatically checks your ActionScript when compiling a SWF and reports any errors in the Output panel. You can also check whether you have made any mistakes in your script by clicking the Check Syntax button at the top of the Actions panel at any time (see the screenshot alongside). PHP and MySQL don't have that sort of luxury built in, so this appendix is intended to provide a little self-help for times when they don't respond the way you expect.

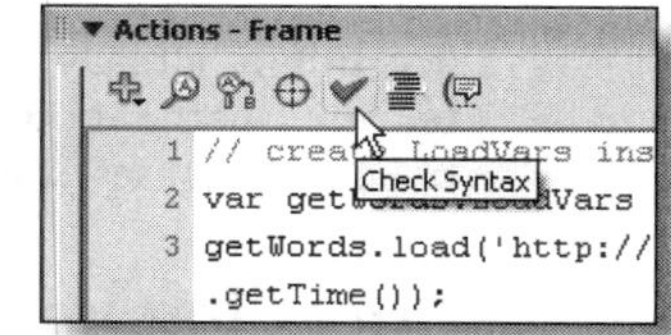

Most errors fall into one of the following categories:

- Syntax errors
- Runtime errors (both technical and caused by user input)
- Logic errors

This appendix assumes the most fundamental thing of all: that your computer and the necessary software are running normally. So, first a few words about what to do when nothing works.

Making sure everything is running correctly

As explained in Chapter 1, both PHP and MySQL rely on servers running in the background. If you set up everything as described in Chapters 1 and 6, the Apache and MySQL servers should start up automatically on most Windows and Mac computers. However, depending on your setup, you may need to start them manually.

If you have turned here for help before installing phpMyAdmin in Chapter 6, the first thing to do is check that Apache is running and serving PHP pages correctly. If the test page that you created in Chapter 1 (see Figures 1-9 and 1-13 for the Windows and Mac versions) displays correctly, that means Apache and PHP are running. If they don't display, but they have before, these are the most likely causes:

- Apache isn't running. Refer back to Chapter 1 for instructions on how to start Apache. The method differs depending on your operating system.
- You aren't storing your PHP files within the server root or one of its subfolders. If you followed the instructions in this book, this means `C:\htdocs` on Windows. On all Mac computers, it's `Macintosh HD:Users:`*`username`*`:Sites`. Refer to the section "Setting up your work environment" in Chapter 1 for an explanation.
- You aren't accessing the files through the correct URL. All PHP files must be served up through Apache, so you can't use the direct path name to the file. You should always use the URL. On Windows, this will be `http://localhost/` followed by the path from `C:\htdocs`. On a Mac, it will be `http://localhost/~`*`username`*`/` followed by the path from your `Sites` folder.
- You haven't given the files a `.php` extension. If you are using a text editor like Windows Notepad or TextEdit on the Mac, make sure it hasn't added `.txt` after the `.php`.
- You've saved your PHP files in Rich Text Format (RTF) or in a word processor, such as Microsoft Word or WordPerfect. PHP files must be saved in plain text.

If you have already installed phpMyAdmin, just launching the program is enough in itself to tell you whether both PHP and MySQL are working. If phpMyAdmin loads and displays details of your databases, it indicates that the servers are running normally.

Checking your PHP configuration

The test page that you created in Chapter 1 (`index.php`) displays all the configuration information about your PHP setup. Always display it if you need to check a setting or to find out whether a PHP extension is enabled. If you have installed phpMyAdmin, you can also display it by clicking the Show PHP information link on the phpMyAdmin welcome screen.

If you've set up your local computer according to the instructions in Chapter 1, everything should be correctly configured to run the scripts in this book. When things don't work as expected, load the configuration information, and check the settings in the Local Value column of the PHP Core section (close to the top of the page). The values recommended for this book are shown in Table A-1.

Table A-1. Recommended settings for PHP Core configuration on your local computer

Directive	Recommended setting for Local Value	Notes
`display_errors`	On	If this setting is turned off, you will not see any error messages generated by PHP.
`error_reporting`	2047	This is the value generated by a setting of `E_ALL` in `php.ini`. It shows all levels of error messages, except for `E_STRICT` (an option introduced in PHP 5 that is mainly of interest to advanced developers).
`extension_dir`	C:\php5\ext	This is required on Windows only. Make sure the version of PHP that you installed has a folder of this name and that it contains DLL files beginning with `php_`. In older versions of PHP, the same folder was called `extensions`.
`magic_quotes_gpc`	On or Off	This determines whether single and double quotes are automatically escaped in the `GET` and `POST` arrays. There is no "ideal" setting; it is normally on by default in Windows, but off in a Mac installation. The code in Chapters 2 and 8 shows how to handle this in a portable way.
`register_globals`	Off	This is an important security setting. Many hosting companies still leave this setting on, which can expose your website to attack. The coding practices adopted in this book will help keep your scripts secure, even if this setting is on.
`SMTP`	(See notes)	Windows users should set this to the SMTP server for their outgoing email; otherwise, they will not be able to test the feedback application in Chapter 2. No setting is required for the Mac, because email is automatically configured.

If you make changes to `php.ini`*, restart Apache, and find that the new settings are not reflected in the configuration information, it means you have two conflicting versions of* `php.ini` *on your system. To find out which one PHP is actually using, check the value shown in* Configuration File (php.ini) Path*. As shown in Figure A-1, it's near the top of the configuration page.*

If your configuration page shows a different location from the version of php.ini *that you have edited, consolidate all the changes in the version that PHP is using, and delete the one that is being ignored. This problem will normally arise only on Windows computers that have had a previous installation of PHP. Until the release of PHP 5, it was normal practice to save* `php.ini` *in the Windows system folder. This is no longer the recommended practice (see Chapter 1 for details about how to remove an old version and install everything in the currently recommended locations).*

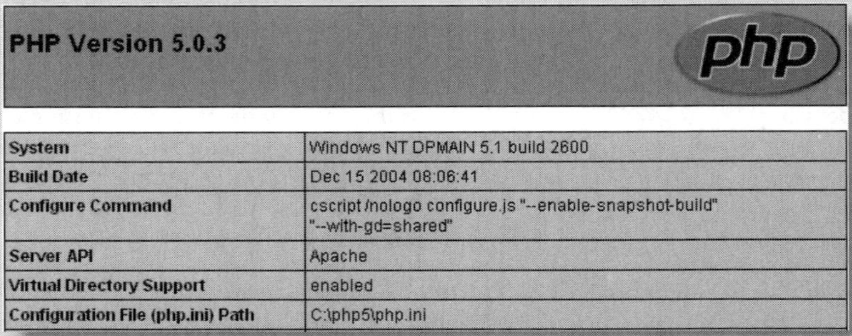

PHP Version 5.0.3 php

System	Windows NT DPMAIN 5.1 build 2600
Build Date	Dec 15 2004 08:06:41
Configure Command	cscript /nologo configure.js "--enable-snapshot-build" "--with-gd=shared"
Server API	Apache
Virtual Directory Support	enabled
Configuration File (php.ini) Path	C:\php5\php.ini

Figure A-1. The PHP configuration page is the first place you should check when PHP doesn't act the way you expect.

Even though you will probably have no control over the contents of `php.ini` on your hosting company's server, you should still familiarize yourself with how it's configured. If your hosting company offers phpMyAdmin, just click the Show PHP information link on the welcome screen. Alternatively, put the following code into a PHP file and upload it to your web server:

```
<?php
phpinfo();
?>
```

In addition to the PHP Core section, the configuration page also shows which extensions to PHP are enabled. They are listed in alphabetical order. As a minimum, you need `mysql`. To complete everything in this book, the following PHP extensions need to be enabled:

- `mysql`
- `mysqli` (requires PHP 5 and MySQL 4.1)
- `pcre`
- `session`
- SimpleXML (requires PHP 5)
- SQLite (standard with PHP 5, but may also be installed on earlier versions)

Troubleshooting your connection to MySQL

If you can't connect to MySQL, the following are the most likely causes on both Windows and Mac:

- The MySQL server isn't running. On Windows, this produces Error 2003. On a Mac, it's Error 2002. The solution is to start the server (see Chapter 6 for details).
- You've made a mistake in spelling your username or password. Both are case sensitive.
- The privilege settings haven't been updated after adding a new user. Launch MySQL Monitor (as described in Chapter 6), and type the following commands:

```
use mysql;
FLUSH PRIVILEGES;
```

  If you don't need to continue working in MySQL Monitor, you can close it immediately by typing exit.

For Windows only, the other most common cause of failure to connect to MySQL is forgetting to enable `php_mysql.dll` and `php_mysqli.dll` in `php.ini`. The instructions for enabling these DLL files are the section titled "Downloading and installing PHP" in Chapter 1. After making the necessary changes to `php.ini`, restart Apache and check your PHP configuration, as described in the previous section. The screenshot alongside shows a system with support for both the original MySQL and the Improved MySQL (`mysqli`) functions.

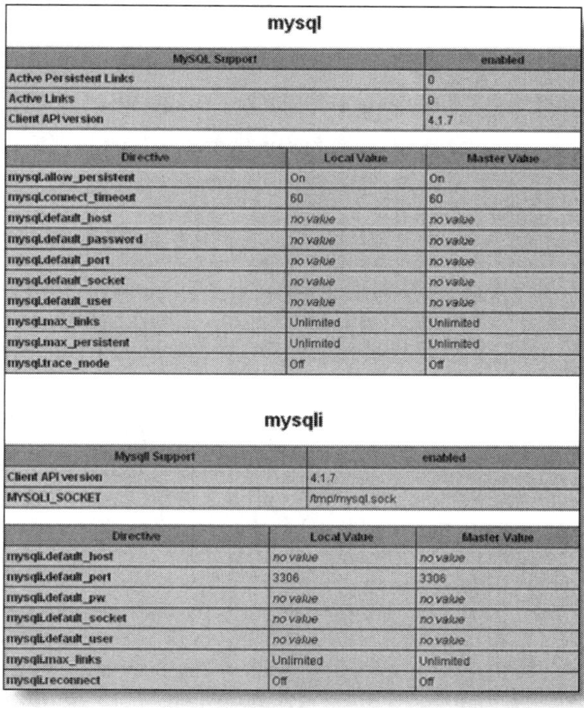

mysql

MySQL Support	enabled
Active Persistent Links	0
Active Links	0
Client API version	4.1.7

Directive	Local Value	Master Value
mysql.allow_persistent	On	On
mysql.connect_timeout	60	60
mysql.default_host	*no value*	*no value*
mysql.default_password	*no value*	*no value*
mysql.default_port	*no value*	*no value*
mysql.default_socket	*no value*	*no value*
mysql.default_user	*no value*	*no value*
mysql.max_links	Unlimited	Unlimited
mysql.max_persistent	Unlimited	Unlimited
mysql.trace_mode	Off	Off

mysqli

MysqlI Support	enabled
Client API version	4.1.7
MYSQLI_SOCKET	/tmp/mysql.sock

Directive	Local Value	Master Value
mysqli.default_host	*no value*	*no value*
mysqli.default_port	3306	3306
mysqli.default_pw	*no value*	*no value*
mysqli.default_socket	*no value*	*no value*
mysqli.default_user	*no value*	*no value*
mysqli.max_links	Unlimited	Unlimited
mysqli.reconnect	Off	Off

If mysql and mysqli fail to show up after you make the changes to `php.ini` and restart Apache, that means you either have conflicting versions of `php.ini`, as described in the previous section, or that PHP can't find the necessary DLL files. Check your setting for `extension_dir`, as described in Table A-1. Also make sure that the folder specified in `extension_dir` actually contains `php_mysql.dll` and `php_mysqli.dll`.

If these tests show everything is running correctly, your problem lies elsewhere. Read on.

Syntax errors

In human languages, **syntax** is the arrangement of words and phrases to create well-formed sentences. For a computer language like PHP, syntax is the set of rules that programmers must follow when creating statements to be processed by the computer. Unlike human languages, computer languages rarely permit any straying from the rules. Generally, if something is out of place or missing, the syntax is broken and everything stops.

The following are the most common causes of PHP syntax errors:

- Forgetting the opening and closing PHP tags
- Forgetting the semicolon at the end of statements
- Using incorrectly matched brackets or quotes
- Omitting the closing bracket or quotation mark of a pair
- Forgetting the concatenation operator when joining strings and variables
- Using the wrong symbol as concatenation operator (for example, + or & instead of a period)
- Forgetting to begin variables with the dollar sign
- Using an invalid variable name
- Misspelling the names of built-in PHP functions or classes
- Making a call to a nonexistent class or function

All these issues were covered in the section "The basic grammar of PHP" in Chapter 2, apart from the last two, which are basically common sense. Fortunately, if you do misspell a function or class, the error message generated by PHP will normally identify the problem in a way that is easy to understand. Other error messages, however, can be difficult to interpret unless you know how they are generated. First of all, though, you need to make sure you can see the messages.

What to do when confronted by a blank page

There's nothing more frustrating than developing a PHP script, leaning back and thinking "This will knock the socks off everyone," launching it in a browser—and all you get is a blank screen. It happened to me not so long ago, and I spent ages trying to find the fault in the logic of my script. If I had made a mistake in PHP syntax, I knew there would be an error message. Much head-banging later, I finally decided to look at `php.ini`, and there was the answer. I wasn't working on the computer I usually do all my development on, and `display_errors` had been set to `Off`. I changed the setting, restarted Apache, and reloaded my script. Immediately, an error message revealed I had made a silly typing mistake (a missing semicolon). You may hate error messages, but when things go wrong . . .

So if you get a blank page when loading a PHP page into a browser, first check your PHP configuration, as described earlier. Make sure you have the recommended settings for `display_errors` and `error_reporting`. If they are different, open `php.ini` and use the following settings (they are likely to be around line 280 or 350 depending on your version of `php.ini`):

```
error_reporting  =  E_ALL
display_errors = On
```

Make sure the commands you change are on a separate line that doesn't begin with a semicolon. If you still get a blank page after saving `php.ini` and restarting Apache, check that PHP is reading the correct version of `php.ini`. If it is reading the correct version, that means the fault lies either in the logic of your script, or—if you're querying a database—there are no records matching your criteria (which could also be a problem with the logic of your script). So, it's a good strategy to always devise a script that will produce some output, even if only to report that no records were found (for example, by returning a message that says, "Sorry, no matches."). I'll come back to logic errors later in this appendix. I'll also explain how to suppress error messages for individual scripts.

One other cause of a blank page when mixing PHP, MySQL, and Flash is failing to publish the SWF or publishing files to the wrong location. Check all your path names and that the files you think should be in a certain location are actually there.

Error messages and how to interpret them

Beginners are frequently confused when PHP reports an error on a line that appears to have nothing wrong with it. Sometimes, the line identified may be completely blank. More confusing is when PHP reports the problem on a line that doesn't exist, such as on line 1243 of a page that contains only 1242 lines of code. This is because PHP reports where it registers the existence of an error, not necessarily where the actual error lies. If it registers an error on the line after the end of a script, PHP is telling you there's a problem, but it has no idea where it is.

Although this may sound odd, Figure A-2 illustrates that Flash does exactly the same. If you look at the error message in the Output panel, you will see that it reports two errors: the first on line 5, and the second on line 142. But as you can see from the ActionScript in Figure A-2, the final command is on line 141; line 142 is blank. Moreover, it simply reports a syntax error, without identifying it. Where Flash has the advantage over PHP is that the first error message nails down the cause of the problem pretty accurately. It says

```
Line 5: Statement block must be terminated by '}'
  getWords.onLoad = function() {
```

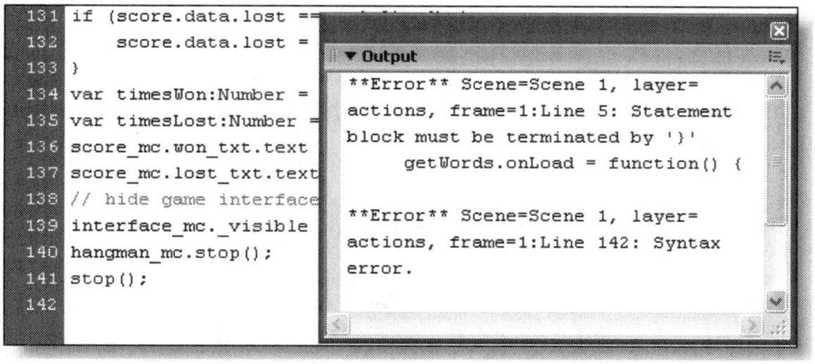

Figure A-2. The Flash Output panel reports errors both on line 5 and on the line following the end of the script.

If you look at Figure A-3, though, you will see there is no problem on line 5. The actual cause of the error is the closing curly brace that I deliberately removed from line 13 for the purposes of this demonstration. Where the Flash Output panel scores is that it identifies the block of code where the problem lies, and it usually tells you what the problem is—even if it doesn't pinpoint the precise location.

```
5  getWords.onLoad = function() {
6      if (this.error !== undefined) {
7          connected = false;
8      } else {
9          connected = true;
10         for (var i = 0; i<this.total; i++) {
11             wordList[i] = this["word"+i];
12             //trace("word"+i+": "+wordList[i]);
13
14     }
15 };
```

Figure A-3. The cause of the error is not on line 5 itself, but inside the function that begins on that line.

PHP error messages are nowhere near as helpful (but there is, after all, a big price difference between PHP and Flash). Still, they are a lot easier to understand if you realize how they work. The way the PHP engine deals with a script is in strict sequence. If it's happy with what you've written, it will continue merrily until it finds something it doesn't expect. Take a look at the following code from `temperature.php`, one of the test files in Chapter 3:

```
<?php
$value = 37;
$conversionType = 'cToF'; // Celsius to Fahrenheit
if ($conversionType == 'cToF') {
  $result = $value / 5 * 9 + 32;
  $resultUnit = ' degrees F';
else {
  $result = ($value - 32) / 9 * 5;
  $resultUnit = ' degrees C';
  }
echo $result.$resultUnit;
?>
```

If you have sharp eyes, you may spot the error straight away, but what do you think the error message produced by PHP will report? The answer is in Figure A-4.

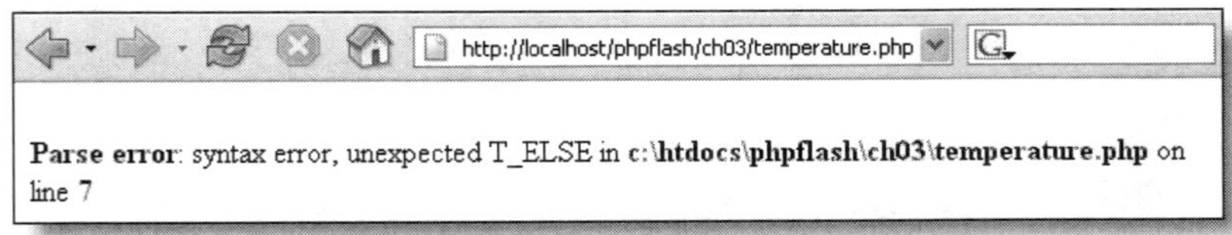

Figure A-4. PHP error messages report why the script failed, but often do not identify the cause of the problem.

This error message contains four useful pieces of information:

- It's a parse (syntax) error—there's something wrong with the code.
- T_ELSE was unexpected.
- The name of the file where the problem occurred. In this case, there's only one, but this information is vital if the problem lies in an include file or external class.
- The line where the unexpected behavior was found.

The key word in the last list item is "unexpected." PHP error messages tell you they've found something that shouldn't be there, but unlike the Flash Output panel, they don't go back and analyze the reason. Most error messages include something preceded by T_. Remove the T_, and that normally indicates what's being referred to. In this case, it's an unexpected `else` clause. Beginners normally scratch their heads wondering what on earth is wrong with their `else` clause, but they're looking in the wrong direction. The error message means that PHP didn't expect to find an `else` clause here. Therefore, the problem lies somewhere *before*, not in the `else` clause or after it.

Identify what's unexpected, and trace backward from it looking for anything missing or unusual.

In this case, what's missing is the closing curly brace from the `if` clause:

```
if ($conversionType == 'cToF') {
  $result = $value / 5 * 9 + 32;
  $resultUnit = ' degrees F';
  }
else {
  $result = ($value - 32) / 9 * 5;
  $resultUnit = ' degrees C';
  }
```

Another difference between PHP error messages and the Flash Output panel is that PHP is a firm believer in zero tolerance. Get one thing wrong, and it will give up straight away. PHP deals with only one error at a time. Don't write reams and reams of script, and expect it all to run perfectly the first time. Test each bit as you go along; otherwise, you'll always be looking for a needle in a haystack.

PHP categorizes errors as follows:

- **Parse errors**: These are mistakes of syntax: missing braces and semicolons, and mismatched quotes. They will prevent your script from working and produce no output other than the error message.
- **Notices**: These warn you about potential flaws in your script. They won't stop the PHP script from working, but they could prevent Flash `LoadVars` from receiving the data. You should always suppress the generation of notices, preferably by eliminating the flaws in your script or by using the techniques described later in this appendix.
- **Warnings**: These errors are more serious. They normally won't stop the script from working, but they're likely to have the same adverse effect on Flash receiving the output of your PHP page.

- **Fatal errors**: These kill your script stone dead. Typical causes are calls to nonexistent functions (is the name spelled right?) or classes (have you included the external file? Or, if it's a built-in class, has it been correctly enabled in your PHP installation?).

The best way to learn about PHP error messages is to take scripts that you know work (for instance, the download files from this book) and to remove one element at a time to see what type of error it generates. It may seem time consuming and frustrating, but learning by experience is usually far more productive than simple book learning.

Use a script editor to reduce syntax errors

There is no substitute for knowing the correct syntax, but using a dedicated script editor can help enormously. There are quite a few script editors that are suitable for working with PHP. Among the best that I have tried are TextPad (`www.textpad.com`) and SciTEFlash (`www.bomberstudios.com/sciteflash`), both for Windows, and BBEdit (`www.barebones.com`) for Mac OS X. They all have four important advantages over using an ordinary text editor, such as Notepad or TextEdit:

- **Syntax coloring**: This is an invaluable visual guide to understanding whether your code is well-formed. Script editors vary in the level of sophistication applied to syntax coloring, but most will highlight keywords, such as function names, conditional statements, and loop structures. They also help maintain matching pairs of single and double quotes by changing the color of text—if the closing quote is missing, all subsequent code is highlighted in the wrong color. Because most script editors work with a variety of programming languages, you normally have to select PHP from one of the program preferences or menu options to turn this option on. In SciTEFlash, it's on the Syntax menu; in BBEdit, select the Text Options icon and choose Language.
- **Line numbering**: The line numbers are not added to your script, but displayed alongside, as in the Flash Actions panel. When an error message tells you to look for a problem on line 379, this is not a luxury, but a total necessity.
- **Automatic indenting**: This is also something the Flash Actions panel does for you, although in a slightly different way from script editors. The Actions panel automatically indents your script on the next line following an opening curly brace. Script editors leave the indentation up to you, but automatically align each new line with the previous level of indentation. There are no hard and fast rules about code indentation, but keeping logical blocks together makes your scripts a lot easier to follow and troubleshoot.
- **Balancing braces**: One of the biggest challenges when scripting is making sure you have balanced opening and closing braces, brackets, and parentheses. The three script editors I have tested all offer a simple method of identifying the matching brace or highlighting the content in between braces, making it easy to spot the missing one that's causing your script to fall flat on its face. TextPad and SciTEFlash are a little weak in this area, but BBEdit is superb.

So which is my favorite script editor? None of them, actually—I use Dreamweaver MX 2004 for just about all my PHP scripting. The reason is that it offers something in addition to the four advantages just listed: auto-completion. When working in a PHP page in Code view, Dreamweaver MX 2004 has the same level of sophisticated code hinting and auto-completion as the Flash Actions panel. Its balance-braces feature is also as powerful as BBEdit's. If you have a copy of Dreamweaver as part of Studio MX/MX 2004, dust it off and give it a try. You don't have to learn the rest of the program to use it as a script editor.

If you don't have Dreamweaver, try SciTEFlash (free) or TextPad (not free, but you can try before you buy). On the Mac, BBEdit is the acknowledged industry leader. It's not cheap, but it's very powerful, and it supports a lot of scripting languages. You can also try it before you buy it.

Runtime errors

Runtime errors are problems that occur even when your script is syntactically perfect. Some you have control over; others are beyond your control. The following are typical causes of runtime errors:

- Using scripts or functions that aren't supported by your server
- Attempting division by zero
- Supplying incorrect or incomplete arguments to a function
- Making calls to undefined functions or classes (usually because of forgetting to include the external file where they are defined)
- Sending header information to the browser after the header has already been sent
- Being unable to read or write files because of incorrect permissions
- Being unable to connect to the database server
- Having database password problems
- Experiencing a network failure

Problems with server compatibility

As I've stated on several occasions throughout this book, your life as a developer would be a lot simpler if hosting companies upgraded PHP and MySQL as frequently as the software development teams. The move to PHP 5 and MySQL 4.1 introduces considerable changes that could cause code developed on your local computer to fail if you transfer it to a server that still uses older versions.

PHP 5 has been available as a stable version since July 2004, and MySQL 4.1 became a production release three months later. Judging from past experience, it can take hosting companies about a year before adopting this type of major upgrade. Some take even longer. Because of these problems, the code in this book has been designed to be as version neutral as possible, mainly through the use of the custom-built `Database` classes in Chapter 7. As long as you use the correct class files as described in that chapter, most scripts will work on any combination of server versions. I have noted in the text where a particular feature is available only in PHP 5 or MySQL 4.1.

Checking the versions your hosting company is running is easy. If phpMyAdmin is installed on your website, just launch it in a browser. The version number of MySQL is displayed immediately beneath the welcome message. The screenshot shows the MySQL version number as 4.1.7. The -nt after the version number indicates that it's running on a Windows server. On a Linux or Mac server, it will normally be followed by -standard. To find the PHP version, click the Show PHP information link on the right-hand side of the welcome page.

Welcome to phpMyAdmin 2.6.0-pl3

MySQL 4.1.7-nt running on localhost as root@localhost

If phpMyAdmin is not available, save the following code in a PHP page, upload it to your remote server, and view it in a browser:

```
<?php
$db = mysql_connect('localhost','username','password');
$result = mysql_query('SELECT VERSION()');
$row = mysql_fetch_row($result);
echo "<p>MySQL version is: $row[0]</p>";
echo '<p>PHP version is: '.phpversion().'</p>';
?>
```

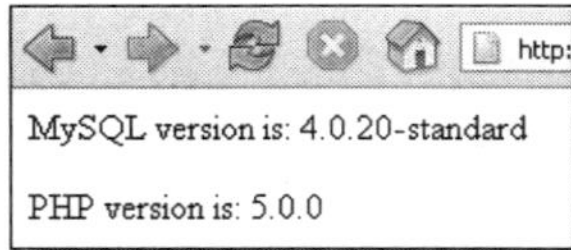

Replace *username* and *password* with your own username and password. This code (available in the download files as `getversion.php`) will run on all versions of PHP and MySQL, and display the version numbers of both, as shown in the screenshot alongside.

Problems with user input

All vital information should still be checked by PHP before any calculations are performed with it or it is input into a database. How you check user input, and precisely what you check it for, depends entirely on what you're planning to do with it, but some basic principles apply:

- Use a conditional structure, such as an `if... else` statement or `switch`, to test input.
- If the input matches your criteria, process it.
- If the input doesn't match your criteria, execute a separate block of code to display a custom error message.

The only way to make sure you cover all eventualities is to test, test, and test again. Also, make sure your tests include unexpected input.

"Headers already sent"

"Headers already sent" are words that send a shiver up the spine of most PHP programmers at some stage in their career. Seemingly perfect scripts send out this mysterious error message, and no end of head-banging ensues in the pursuit of the invisible cause, because that's what it is: invisible. If you've never encountered this problem, take my word for it, you will.

The problem usually arises when you're using header() to redirect a page, or when you're using sessions or cookies. Instead of working the way you expect, your syntactically perfect code produces the following message:

Warning: Cannot add header information - headers already sent

The solution is to make sure any header material generated by PHP comes at the very beginning of your page, before the opening <html> tag. If you have separate blocks of code surrounded by opening and closing PHP tags of their own, combine them into a single block of PHP, and make sure there is no whitespace preceding them. The PHP block *must* be the first thing the PHP engine encounters. Finally, if the problem persists, check all include files called by the problem page and remove any whitespace before or after the PHP tags.

This is probably the only time whitespace is likely to cause a problem with PHP, although the cause lies not with PHP, but with the way web servers handle headers. Only one set of HTTP headers can be sent to the browser. An attempt to send header material after any of the body is generated results in this error message. If you're using a script editor, a quick way to check for excess whitespace in include files is to look at the line numbers. If they extend beyond the closing PHP tag, you know there's whitespace that needs to be removed.

Controlling the output of error messages

Beginners often ask how they can get rid of error messages. The smug answer is, don't make mistakes. There are times, though, when you have no control over what happens. For instance, your database server might have crashed, or it might have been taken down by the administrator for routine maintenance. When that happens, a perfectly accurate script will fail. Note that I didn't say "a well-written script"—such scripts already take into account that sort of eventuality. The database classes in Chapter 7 handle such failure gracefully, and I showed you how to adapt them to "phone home" when there's a problem.

Still, it's useful to know how to prevent error messages from being output by a PHP script. The simplest way is to add the following line of code at the top of your script:

```
error_reporting(0);
```

That will kill all error messages stone dead. A more selective method is to use the **error-suppression operator** (@), which applies to a single expression. The following code opens a file on a Linux-type server and writes to it:

```
$transfer = fopen('/home/mydir/myfile', 'w');
```

If the correct permissions are not set, or if the disk is full, an error will be generated. You can place the error-suppression operator either directly in front of the expression likely to generate an error or at the beginning of the entire statement. Either of the following is acceptable:

```
$transfer = @ fopen('/home/mydir/myfile', 'w');
@ $transfer = fopen('/home/mydir/myfile', 'w');
```

Simply suppressing the error message is poor programming practice. You should always build in some form of check (usually through a conditional statement) to detect the failure of an operation that relies on resources beyond the control of your script. If using PHP as part of an XHTML page, you should at least display a message informing the user that the process couldn't be completed. When working with Flash, you need to send the error message back to your movie in a format that will be recognized by ActionScript, and build a suitable error routine into the Flash side of your application. You can find examples of how to do this throughout the book.

Logic errors

Errors of logic are probably the most insidious of all. The code is syntactically perfect, and no runtime errors occur, yet you get the completely wrong result. Causes of logic errors are infinite in variety, but some of the most common ones are as follows:

- Confusing the assignment (=) and equality (==) operators
- Infinite (endless) loops
- Loops that run without achieving any purpose
- Attempts to change array values with a `foreach` loop
- Functions with no return value
- Function arguments in the wrong order

Confusing the assignment and equality operators

Confusing the assignment and equality operators (see Chapters 2 and 3) is a common error that can lead to completely nonsensical results. The best way to explain the problem is with a practical example.

```
if ($guess = 5) {
  echo 'Bingo, correct!';
  }
else {
  echo 'Bad luck, try again';
  }
```

That conditional statement will *always* display Bingo, correct! The first line sets the value of $guess to 5. The `if` statement doesn't test the value; it checks whether the value has been successfully set. To test the value, the first line needs to be amended as follows:

```
if ($guess == 5) {
```

Make no mistake, this isn't a question of syntax. Syntax errors stop your pages dead; logic errors don't. That's why they're so dangerous.

Infinite loops

Loops (covered in Chapter 5) take a lot of the hard work out of processing data, but all good things, as they say, must come to an end. That's why a loop that doesn't come to an end is such a bad thing. It will not only fill the browser window with garbage, but also might tie up all your server's resources and freeze it or bring it crashing down. *Do not attempt to run the following code*!

```
$number = 1;
while ($number) {
  echo $number;
  $number++;
}
```

Loops must always have a condition to bring them to an end, as in the following example:

```
$number = 1;
while ($number <= 10) {
  echo $number;
  $number++;
  }
```

Useless loops

The converse of the infinite loop is one that runs but doesn't affect the code it's meant to control.

```
for ($i = 0; $i < 10; $i++);
{
echo $i.'<br />';
}
```

You might expect this code to display the numbers from 0 to 9. Instead, it displays 10 (and nothing else). The reason lies in the semicolon at the end of the first line. The for loop runs from 0 to 9, is terminated by the semicolon, and the echo command inside the braces then displays the next value of $i. All of this is perfectly correct, but almost certainly not what was intended. Semicolons are vital for ending statements, but in the wrong place they can terminate execution prematurely.

Remove the semicolon from the end of the first line, and the loop will perform as expected.

Changing array values

Loops are particularly suited to manipulating arrays, but you won't always get the result you're expecting. This is because foreach works on a copy of an array, while for works on the array itself. The following code and accompanying screenshot should make things clear:

```
<?php
$titles = array('PHP 5 for Flash', 'ActionScript for Flash MX 2004');
echo '<pre>';
echo '<h2>Using a foreach loop</h2>';
foreach ($titles as $title) {
  // amend array element and display to screen
  $title = 'Foundation '.$title;
  echo $title.'<br />';
  }
```

```
// display array contents after foreach loop
print_r($titles);
echo '<h2>Using a for loop</h2>';
for ($i = 0; $i < count($titles); $i++) {
  // amend array element and display to screen
  $titles[$i] = 'Foundation '.$titles[$i];
  echo $titles[$i].'<br />';
  }
// display array contents after for loop
print_r($titles);
echo '</pre>';
?>
```

```
http://localhost/phpflash/appA/arrays.php

Using a foreach loop

Foundation PHP 5 for Flash
Foundation ActionScript for Flash MX 2004
Array
(
    [0] => PHP 5 for Flash
    [1] => ActionScript for Flash MX 2004
)

Using a for loop

Foundation PHP 5 for Flash
Foundation ActionScript for Flash MX 2004
Array
(
    [0] => Foundation PHP 5 for Flash
    [1] => Foundation ActionScript for Flash MX 2004
)
```

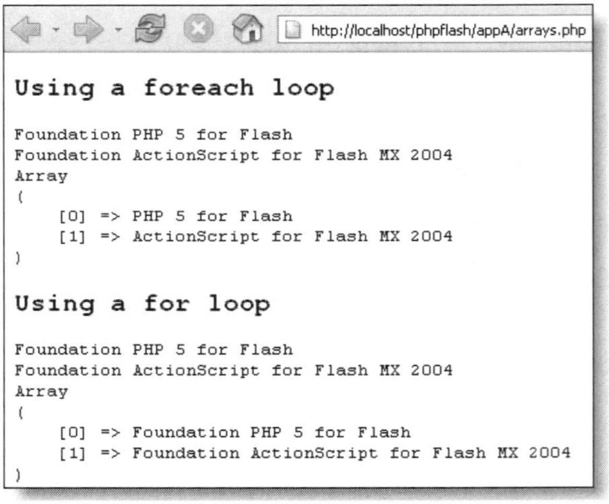

As the screenshot demonstrates, the change in value of each array element is temporary when using a `foreach` loop, whereas the change is permanent when using a `for` loop (see Chapter 5 to learn about `print_r()` and arrays).

Functions with no return value

PHP built-in functions will always return a value, but it's a common mistake for beginners to forget to return a value from their own custom-built functions. The following function takes two arguments—price and tax rate—to calculate the sales tax due on any item.

```
function salesTax($price,$taxRate) {
  $tax = $price*$taxRate/100;
  }
$taxDue = salesTax(100,17.5);
echo $taxDue;
```

This is just the type of logical error that will result in a blank page. The syntax is perfect, and the function itself works flawlessly every time. There's just one problem: the answer stays locked inside, and $taxDue has no value. You need to return the result of the calculation with the PHP keyword return.

```
function salesTax($price,$taxRate) {
  $tax = $price*$taxRate/100;
  return $tax;
  }
$taxDue = salesTax(100,17.5);
echo $taxDue;
```

This time, $taxDue will display the correct value (17.5).

Function arguments in the wrong order

Sometimes, it doesn't matter in which order you supply arguments to a function. Consider the salesTax() function in the previous section. The calculation inside the function produces the same result, regardless of whether you put the price or the tax rate first. *But this is a rare exception*. Amend the function slightly to calculate a tax-inclusive price, and see what happens.

```
function salesTax($price,$taxRate) {
  $total = $price + ($price*$taxRate/100);
  return $total;
  }
echo salesTax(500,8); // Displays 540
echo salesTax(8,500); // Displays 48
```

Scripts like this won't work, even though the function has all the necessary arguments, if the arguments are in the wrong order. The arguments supplied to a function do not need to use the same variable names as the function itself, but they do need to be in exactly the same order.

Giving variables meaningful names is a useful way of avoiding this type of error.

Debugging your code

One of the things I have tried to stress throughout the book is the importance of checking that your PHP scripts and SQL produce the results that you expect before you attempt to send the data to your Flash application. You should also always test that Flash and PHP are actually communicating with each other. To make sure your variables are being transferred from Flash, use the script in variable_checker.php from Chapter 2. Make sure your PHP script is not generating errors or warning messages, as these will prevent LoadVars from picking up the data correctly. Also use the List Variables option on the Debug menu in the Flash test environment to make sure your variables are being received by your movie.

It would be wonderful if we could all just sit down and write code that worked perfectly the first time, but let's admit it, few of us are superheroes like that. Even if you do become a top-level scripter, you need to check constantly that things work the way you expect them to. And boring though it may seem, the best way to check is to use one of the first tools you ever learned in PHP: the humble echo construct. In PHP terms, echo is the same faithful friend as trace in ActionScript. Whenever you convert a value using a function, it's a good idea to check the result by using echo to display it in your browser.

If you're used to working with ActionScript, that advice will seem almost like a statement of the obvious. What's less obvious, perhaps, is the value of displaying your SQL queries *before* they're run, so you know exactly what it is that PHP is sending to MySQL. Don't forget that most of the time your queries will be put together by PHP using variables that you can't normally see. Take this simple example:

```
$sql = "SELECT * FROM contacts WHERE first_name = $name";
```

The PHP syntax is fine, but this query will almost certainly produce no results, even if you have a million different names in the database. Why? Use echo to display the contents of the query, and it will show something like this:

SELECT * FROM contacts WHERE first_name = David

If you get a result like that, at least you know your variable is producing the right sort of output (if there's a mistake in the variable name, it could be empty). Unless you know SQL, the problem may not be immediately obvious, but it's the lack of quotes around David that will result in an empty set of results. David is a string (I admit I've been called plenty of things in my time, but never that!), and as such it needs to be quoted (yes, please). The correct way of writing the query is as follows:

```
$sql = "SELECT * FROM contacts WHERE first_name = '$name'";
```

Note that when storing a SQL query as a variable, you do **not** *need a semicolon inside the closing quotes. The semicolon required by MySQL Monitor is not an integral part of the query; it simply tells MySQL Monitor that you have finished and that the query is ready to run. When you use PHP to query the database directly, the semicolon is not required—although PHP still requires a semicolon after the closing quotes. I know it sounds confusing, but read it again slowly and look at the code.*

A useful debugging function

Although echo and print_r() are very useful for displaying the contents of variables and arrays when debugging PHP scripts, you need to remember what it is you're displaying in the browser. You also need to add some formatting so that your debugging information is displayed in an intelligible manner. To get around these problems, I created the following custom function called showVal():

```
function showVal($variable, $varDesc='') {
  // Test whether debugging has been turned on
  if ($_GET && $_GET['debug']) {

    // Check second argument, and format if present
    $varDesc = !empty($varDesc) ? " of $varDesc" : $varDesc;
```

```
    // If variable contains a non-empty array, display description
    if (is_array($variable) && count($variable) > 0) {
      echo '<p>Contents'.$varDesc.' - array with elements:<br />';

        // Loop through array to display both keys and values
        foreach ($variable as $key => $value) {
        echo $key.' => '.$value.'<br />';
        }
      echo '</p>'; // Close paragraph for each separate array
      }

    // If variable contains an empty array, display result
    elseif (is_array($variable) && count($variable) == 0) {
      echo '<p>Contents'.$varDesc.': empty array</p>';
      }

    // Code to display all other variables
    else {
      echo '<p>Contents'.$varDesc.": $variable</p>";
      }
    }
  }
```

I don’t intend to explain the inner workings of the function in detail—you can study the inline comments throughout the code—but I will show you how to use it.

Using the showVal() debugging function

You can find the code for this function in showval.php in the download files for this appendix. When using it with most of the PHP scripts in this book, you will need to hard-code some test variables into the top of your page. This is much easier than attempting to analyze incomplete data that may be received by a Flash application.

1. Copy and paste the showVal() function into the page you want to debug. It can go anywhere, as long as it is inside PHP tags. Alternatively, include it from an external file by inserting the following code at the top of your PHP page:

   ```
   require_once('showval.php');
   ```

   Amend the path to the showval.php file if it’s in a different folder.

2. Locate any variables in the page that you want to display. Insert a new line after any operation on the variable, and enter the following code:

   ```
   showVal($variableName, 'description of variable');
   ```

3. Do the same before any operation, if you want to compare the values before and after.

4. Save the page and load it into a browser. You should see no difference from the previous output. Now add the following to the end of the URL in the browser address bar, and reload the page:

```
?debug=1
```

5. All your instances of showVal() should now produce output. Figure A-5 shows the output of register_cms.php from Chapter 10. I hard-coded the following variables into the top of the page:

```
$_POST['action'] = 'find';
$_POST['first_name'] = 'wil';
$_POST['family_name'] = '';
$_POST['username'] = '';
```

This has the same effect as searching the database for names with "wil" in them. MySQL conducts case-insensitive searches, so this should produce two positive results. However, for demonstration purposes, I made a deliberate mistake in the SQL to prevent any records from being found. The fact that the final line produces a correctly formatted variable string to be sent to the Flash movie indicates that there's probably nothing wrong with the syntax of the PHP script.

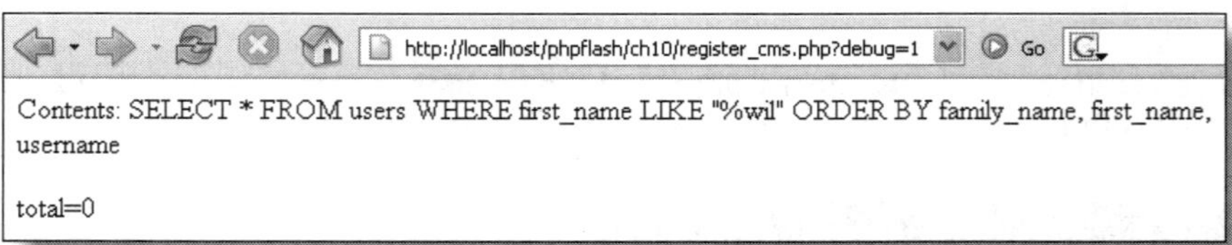

Figure A-5. Using showVal() to display the contents of a SQL query that's producing unexpected results

What's wrong is the logic of the SQL query. By using showVal() to display the query onscreen, you can see exactly what is being sent to MySQL. Here, the query is looking for records where the first_name column ends with wil—it won't find anything with wil in the middle or at the beginning of a name.

When you display the actual query onscreen like this, it becomes a lot easier to work out the cause of the problem. I deliberately took out the code to add the SQL wildcard character % after the letters being used as the search criterion. Figure A-6 shows the corrected output; as you can see from the string of variables at the bottom of the screenshot, everything is now working properly. To prevent the debug information from being output, you just need to remove the query string (?debug=1) from the end of the URL. Don't forget, of course, to remove the hard-coded variables after you've finished testing; otherwise, you'll always get the same results!

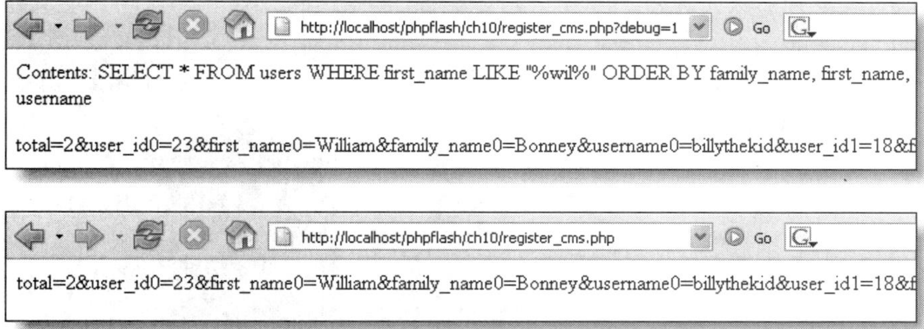

Figure A-6. After debugging, you can turn off the display by removing the query string at the end of the URL (bottom image).

Debugging is probably the least pleasant aspect of working with any programming language, but it's an essential skill. Not only will it help you avoid obvious errors, but also checking the values of variables as they are processed through your scripts will help you avoid any nasty gotchas lurking in the background.

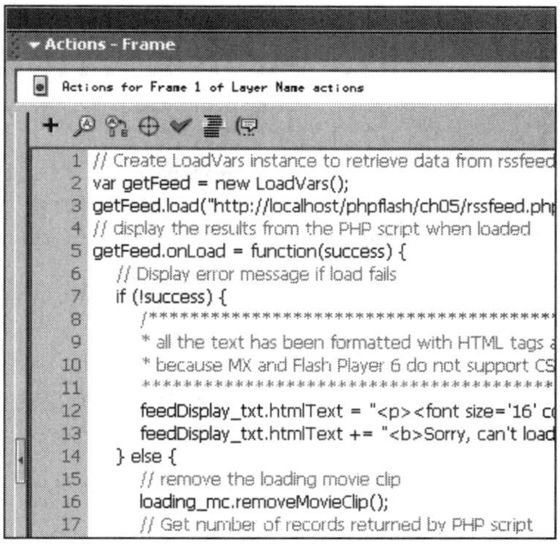

Appendix B

CONVERTING APPLICATIONS TO ACTIONSCRIPT 1.0

The release of Flash MX 2004 in September 2003 brought yet another upheaval to the Flash community, or at least to those members who had ventured into the geeky, but wonderful world of the Actions panel. ActionScript 2.0 was born, and the version used in Flash MX was retrospectively given a number of its own: ActionScript 1.0. Fortunately, the change was evolutionary, rather than revolutionary, so it means that converting the ActionScript 2.0 used throughout this book is a relatively painless process. It also means that anyone already familiar with ActionScript 1.0 can make the transition to ActionScript 2.0 with very little effort.

ActionScript 2.0 is now the standard, and although some changes are expected when the successor to Flash MX 2004 (codenamed 8Ball) is released, they will build on the standard, rather than tear it all up. So, if you have Flash MX 2004 or later but haven't yet made the leap to ActionScript 2.0, now is the time to do it. You *can* write ActionScript 1.0 in MX 2004, but the time you spend converting the scripts in this book could be used more profitably learning the new standard. The small amount of effort involved will be greatly repaid in code that is easier to debug and maintain.

This appendix is aimed mainly at readers who are working with Flash MX, which doesn't support ActionScript 2.0, and anyone obliged to support Flash Player 5 or earlier. Since only 3% of Flash installations don't support ActionScript 2.0, that's a very tiny target audience.

How ActionScript 2.0 differs from ActionScript 1.0

The changes to ActionScript 2.0 are designed to bring it in line with a proposed international standard known as ECMAScript 4, and to make it a fully object-oriented language. The differences can be broadly summarized as covering three main areas:

- The way custom classes are built
- Case sensitivity
- Strict (or static) datatyping

None of the applications in this book uses ActionScript classes, so you don't need to worry about the first area—at least as far as this book is concerned.

ActionScript 2.0 is case sensitive, so typing a variable name that uses camel case (such as `theClip`) entirely in lowercase will result in the script failing. ActionScript 1.0, on the other hand, is case insensitive, so `theclip` and `theClip` are treated the same. That means you can also safely ignore case sensitivity when converting any of the ActionScript in this book. Although you *can* do it, that doesn't necessarily mean that you *should* do it. In fact, it's a decidedly bad idea. PHP is case sensitive, so you need to make sure you use the correct combination of cases when handling any variables sent from Flash to your PHP scripts. It's also a sign of sloppy coding that will be difficult to debug and maintain.

Consequently, it's the third area—strict datatyping—that you need to concentrate on when converting ActionScript 2.0 to ActionScript 1.0.

Understanding ActionScript 2.0 datatyping

ActionScript, like other programming languages, has always had datatypes: arrays, strings, numbers, and so on. What's different about ActionScript 2.0 is that it's now recommended that you specify the datatype of all new variables when you first declare them. So, whereas in ActionScript 1.0, you might create a string like this:

```
bookTitle = "Foundation PHP 5 for Flash";
```

in ActionScript 2.0, the correct way is like this:

```
var bookTitle:String = "Foundation PHP 5 for Flash";
```

In other words, you should always use the `var` keyword and declare the variable's datatype immediately after the variable name, with a colon (and no spaces) between the two. The value of doing this is that Flash checks your code for type mismatches when compiling your movie and pinpoints any errors. It also means you don't have to build type-checking routines into many of your functions. Because `bookTitle` has been declared as a string, you can't accidentally assign a Boolean to it halfway through your script.

Datatyping is also recommended when declaring functions. Not only should all local variables be declared with a datatype, but also it's recommended to set the datatype of function parameters (arguments) and the function's return value, for example:

```
function isOverTen(theNum:Number):Boolean {
  if (theNum > 10) {
    return true;
  } else {
    return false;
  }
}
```

This tells the compiler that theNum must be a number and that the return value of the function is a Boolean. If you then try to pass bookTitle as an argument to isOverTen(), the movie won't compile.

```
// this generates an error
if (isOverTen(bookTitle)) {
```

The meaning of most datatypes is obvious. In addition to String, Number, Boolean, Date, Array, and so on, which are common to other programming languages, ActionScript 2.0 also has datatypes that are exclusive to Flash. These include MovieClip, LoadVars, TextField, and so on. If you've been working with Flash and ActionScript for any length of time, you're bound to be familiar with all of these. There's one datatype, though, that tends to confuse a lot of people. It's called Void, and it's used only with functions and class methods. It simply means that the function or method has no return value.

The idea is to encourage greater discipline when creating scripts. If you declare the datatype of a function as Void, and you later amend the function so that it returns a value, Flash will refuse to compile the movie—unless, of course, you also change the datatype to match the value being returned. Although this sounds like a nuisance, it actually saves you time. If you have assigned the wrong datatype or changed it halfway through the development process—without following the logic of the change throughout your script—your script is liable to fail anyway. The difference is that it will probably take you much longer to work out the problem for yourself than if you let the compiler do it for you.

Not everything can be assigned a datatype. If you try to declare a datatype for the property of an object, the movie will fail to compile. If you add Void as the datatype of an anonymous function, it won't cause the movie to fail to compile, but the Actions panel's Auto Format feature will silently remove it.

```
// before using Auto Format
messageSent.onLoad = function():Void {

// after Auto Format
messageSent.onLoad = function() {
```

Although datatyping involves a little more work when typing out a script, it soon becomes second nature, and Flash code hinting speeds up the process. Of course, if you don't have access to Flash MX 2004 or later, these benefits might seem rather academic. When building applications in Flash MX, you have to strip out all the datatyping. Pause a moment, though, before cursing the need to do this. Because the underlying syntax of ActionScript 2.0 (except for custom classes) is identical to ActionScript 1.0, reading code as it's presented in this book should give you a better idea of what's going on in a script. You can see at a glance whether a particular variable is being used as a string, number, or array. You can also see what type of value a function is likely to return.

Stripping out ActionScript 2.0 datatypes

All the code in the Flash MX version of the download files for this book has been converted to ActionScript 1.0 and provided in Flash MX format, so there is no need to hand-strip all the datatypes. When copying code from the book, all you need to do is omit the colons and datatypes after variable, parameter, or function declarations. Reproduced here is the code from the feedback form application in Chapter 2, with the datatyping highlighted in bold type (the inline comments have been removed for space reasons):

```
function checkForm():Boolean {
  var missing:Boolean = false;
  error1_txt.text = error2_txt.text = error3_txt.text = "";
  if (name_txt.text == "") {
    error1_txt.text = "Please enter your name";
    missing = true;
  }
  if (email_txt.text.indexOf("@") == -1) {
    error2_txt.text = "Please enter a valid email address";
    missing = true;
  }
  if (comments_txt.text == "") {
    error3_txt.text = "You have not entered any comments";
    missing = true;
  }
  return missing ? false : true;
}
function sendMessage():Void {
  var formOK:Boolean = checkForm();
  if (formOK) {
    message.from = name_txt.text;
    message.email = email_txt.text;
    message.snail = snail_txt.text;
    message.phone = phone_txt.text;
    message.comments = comments_txt.text;
    message.sendAndLoad("http://localhost/phpflash/ch02/
➥ feedback.php?ck="+new Date().getTime(), messageSent);
    // display message informing user that email is being sent
    gotoAndStop("sending");
  }
}
function backToForm():Void {
  gotoAndStop("theForm");
}
var dateDisplay:TextFormat = new TextFormat();
dateDisplay.font = "Georgia,Times,_serif";
theDate_txt.setNewTextFormat(dateDisplay);
theDate_txt.autoSize = "left";
var getDate:LoadVars = new LoadVars();
var message:LoadVars = new LoadVars();
```

```
var messageSent:LoadVars = new LoadVars();
getDate.load("http://localhost/phpflash/ch02/today2.php");
getDate.onLoad = function() {
  theDate_txt.text = this.theDate;
};
messageSent.onLoad = function() {
  if (this.sent == "OK") {
    gotoAndStop("acknowledge");
  } else {
    gotoAndStop("failure");
    failure_txt.text = this.reason;
  }
};
gotoAndStop("theForm");
```

To convert the preceding code, just remove the code in bold type. Once the code in bold has been removed, the remaining code works exactly the same in both ActionScript 1.0 and ActionScript 2.0. If you are an ActionScript 2.0 skeptic and have managed to read this far, I hope you will understand how little extra effort is required to include datatyping.

Applying depth dynamically at runtime

New versions bring new functionality, and one of the most useful in ActionScript 2.0 is the new `MovieClip` method `getNextHighestDepth()`. Movie clips and other elements on the same timeline must always be placed at a unique depth when loaded dynamically at runtime. It has always been a problem keeping track of the next available depth because loading an element into a depth that's already occupied results in the previous occupant being evicted. This new method solves that problem at a stroke, and I've used it in several applications.

If you are using Flash MX or need to support Flash Player 6, you need to use the traditional method of keeping track of dynamically loaded elements. Declare a variable as a counter and use the increment operator (++) to increase it by 1 each time a new depth is needed. If the application involves several frames, such as the content management system in Chapter 10, make sure the display is always cleared and the counter reset to its lowest number before moving to the next frame. If you want to keep particular depths free for specific elements, such as an error message text field, start the counter at least one number higher than the depth you want to reserve.

Styling HTML text

Flash Player 7 and Flash MX 2004 have greatly improved support for styling text with Cascading Style Sheets (CSS). The RSS aggregator application in Chapter 5 uses CSS to style the incoming feeds, and the content management system in Chapter 12 also uses CSS to display the database results. For Flash MX, use the `TextField.html` and `htmlText` properties. Flash supports a limited range of HTML tags, namely `<a>`, `<b>`, `<br>`, `<font>`, `<i>`, `<li>`, `<p>`, and `<textformat>`. For more details, see `http://livedocs.macromedia.com/flash/mx2004/main_7_2/00001040.html`. This link is for the Flash MX 2004 LiveDocs, but the details are essentially the same, except that MX 2004 and Flash Player 7 have added support `<img>` and `<span>`, which are not available in Flash Player 6.

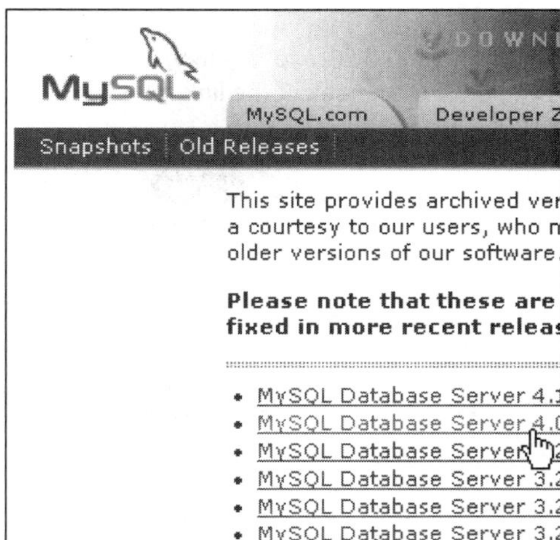

Appendix C

INSTALLING OLDER VERSIONS OF MYSQL ON WINDOWS

Bear in mind that everything included in this appendix refers to MySQL versions older than 4.1.

MySQL installation and configuration on Windows was greatly simplified with the release of MySQL 4.1.5 Windows Essentials. I recommend you choose the latest stable (Generally Available) version of MySQL for development on your local PC, but if your hosting company does not yet support MySQL 4.1, you may want to install an earlier version of MySQL. Before doing so, take a look at Appendix E, which shows how you can back up data from MySQL 4.1 to run on earlier versions of MySQL.

If you do decide you want to install an older version of MySQL on Windows, it's not difficult. A Windows installer takes care of the actual installation, but you have to do some manual configuration to set up a password for the root user (the main database administrator) and make the installation secure.

If you need to uninstall an older version of MySQL on either Windows or Mac OS X, see the instructions for upgrading MySQL in Appendix E.

Obtaining and installing an older version of MySQL

These instructions were tested with MySQL 4.0.21, but they should work with any version of MySQL as far back as 3.23.42 (the oldest Windows version of the 3.23.*x* series available for download from the MySQL website as of late 2004). File download sizes vary between 12MB and 25MB—the older the version, the smaller the file (because it has fewer features).

1. Go to the MySQL archives page at `http://downloads.mysql.com/archives.php`, and select the link for MySQL Database Server *x.x*, where *x.x* represents the version you want.

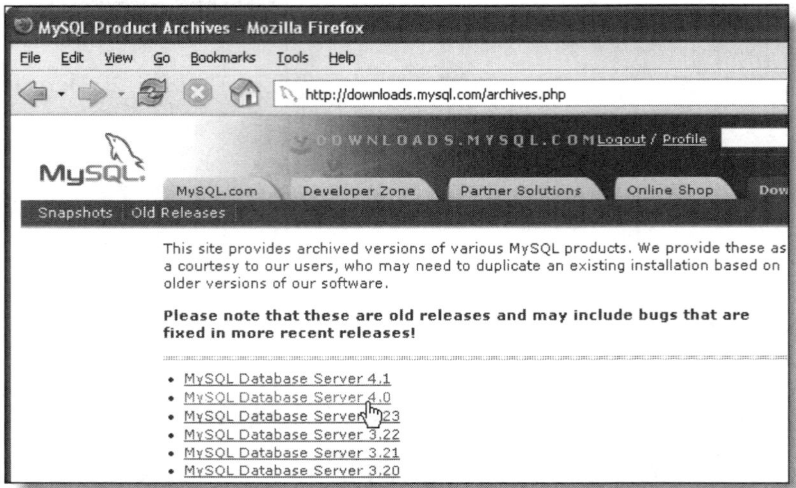

2. The page that opens is divided into two sections: Downloads by Version and Downloads by Platform. Scroll down to Downloads by Platform, and select the link for Microsoft Windows. Do *not* select Microsoft Windows Source, which is normally immediately above the link you want.

Software Downloads by Platform

- Source and other files (24 files)
- Linux (281 files)
- Linux RPM (272 files)
- Microsoft Windows Source (33 files)
- Microsoft Windows (40 files)
- Mac OS X (88 files)
- Mac OS X installer (25 files)
- Novell NetWare (24 files)
- Sun Solaris (224 files)
- QNX (27 files)
- FreeBSD (87 files)

3. The next page can be rather confusing, because Windows Source files are included among the binary files. Not only that, but version 3.23.58 and version 4.0.13 and above each display four choices. The one you want is normally (but not always) listed first. Place your mouse pointer over the link, and check what appears in the browser status bar. The file you need is called `mysql-`*x.x.x*`-win.zip`, where *x.x.x* represents the MySQL version number. Make sure you do not choose a file with `src` (source code only) or `noinstall` (does not include the Windows installer) in its name. If only two choices are displayed, choose the one marked Microsoft Windows.

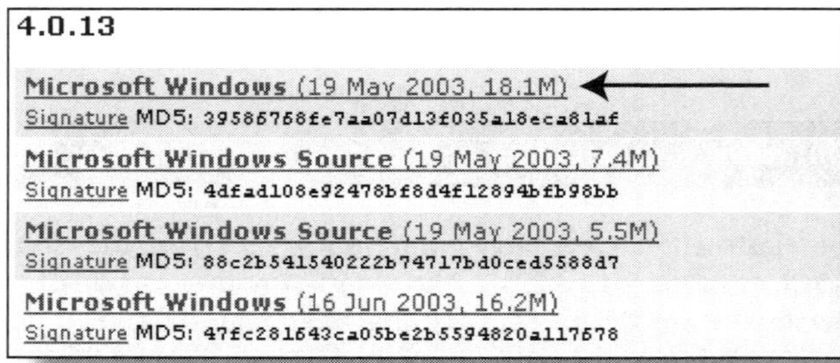

4. Download the file and extract the contents of the ZIP file to a temporary location. Open the unzipped folder and close all other applications. Double-click the SETUP.EXE icon in the unzipped folder. The Windows installer will begin the installation process and open a welcome dialog box, as shown. Click Next to continue.

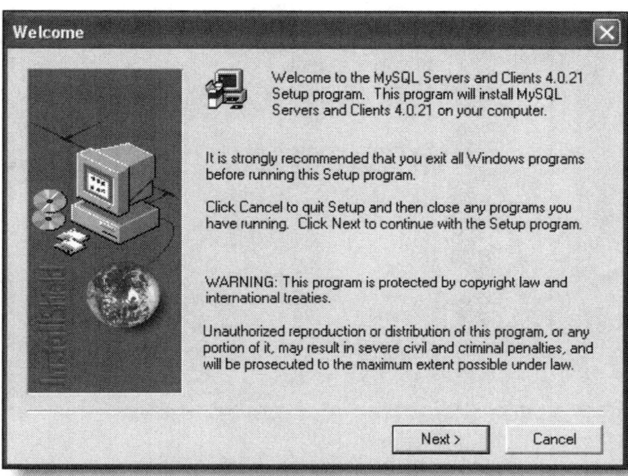

5. The next dialog box contains information about the configuration needed if you decide to install MySQL in a folder other than its default destination. I recommend that you accept the default later in the installation process, so these instructions do not apply. Click Next.

   If you later decide to move MySQL, details of the necessary steps can be found at `http://dev.mysql.com/doc/mysql/en/Windows_prepare_environment.html`.

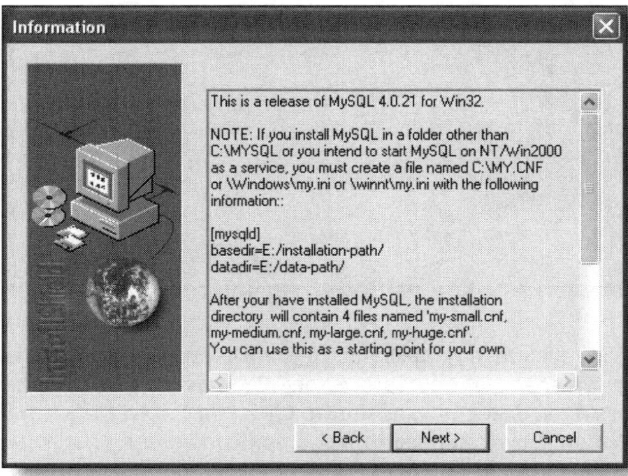

6. The next dialog box gives you the opportunity to change the installation destination. I recommend you accept the default (`C:\mysql`) and click Next.

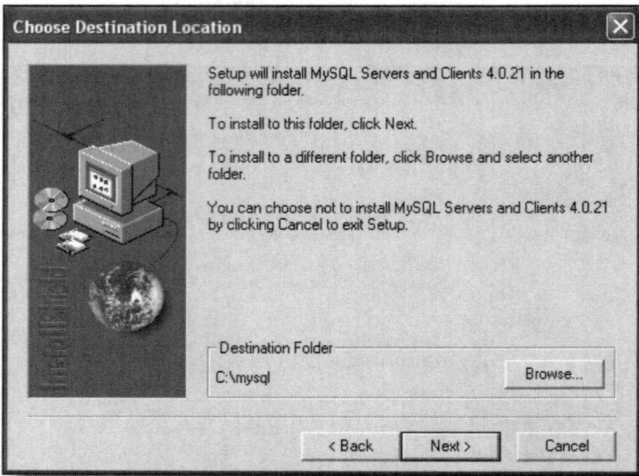

7. The next dialog box offers various options for installation. Accept the default (Typical) and click Next.

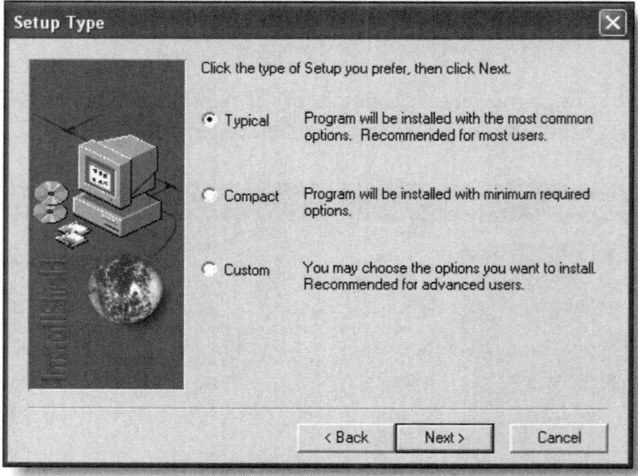

8. The actual installation now takes place, and it's normally quick—although this will depend on the speed of your processor. When everything's finished, you'll be presented with a final dialog box, as shown. Click Finish. MySQL is now installed on your Windows system. Now you need to test it and configure it to start up automatically in future.

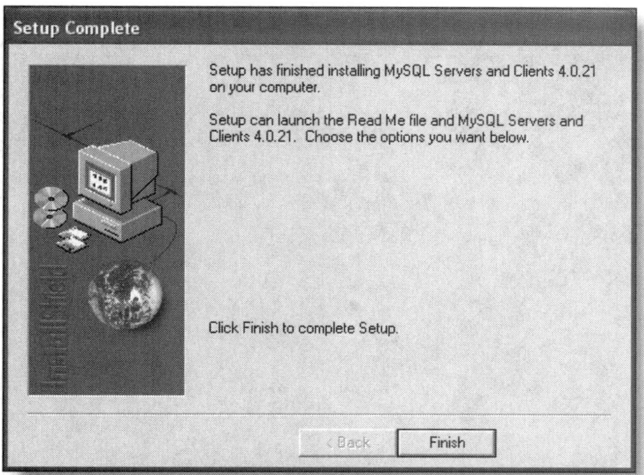

Testing the installation and configuring automatic startup

After the familiar luxury of a Windows installer, you now have to brace yourself for using the command line to communicate with programs. If this seems like an unnecessary throwback to the "bad old days of DOS," it's not. The vast majority of MySQL installations run on Linux or Unix machines, where the command line rules. It's not particularly difficult, and it has one great advantage: you get to see what the program is doing. When you work with databases, it's often necessary to test the results of your queries carefully. A graphic interface—or even a PHP script—can hide a lot of information. Working at the command prompt usually provides all the raw results of a database query, helping you to understand why some results are not what you expected.

1. After installing MySQL, you need to start the background process (or **daemon**, to use its correct technical name) that runs the MySQL database, `mysqld`. Open a Windows Command Prompt. Depending on your system, it is likely to be in Start ➤ All Programs ➤ Accessories ➤ Command Prompt. Alternatively, you can choose Run from the Start button, type cmd, and click OK.
2. Inside the Command Prompt window, type the following commands, each followed by *Enter* (all commands are followed by *Enter*, so I won't repeat this instruction every time):

```
cd c:\mysql\bin\
mysqld --console
```

3. As the daemon starts up, it will display various diagnostic messages. When the startup sequence ends, you should see output similar to the following screenshot.

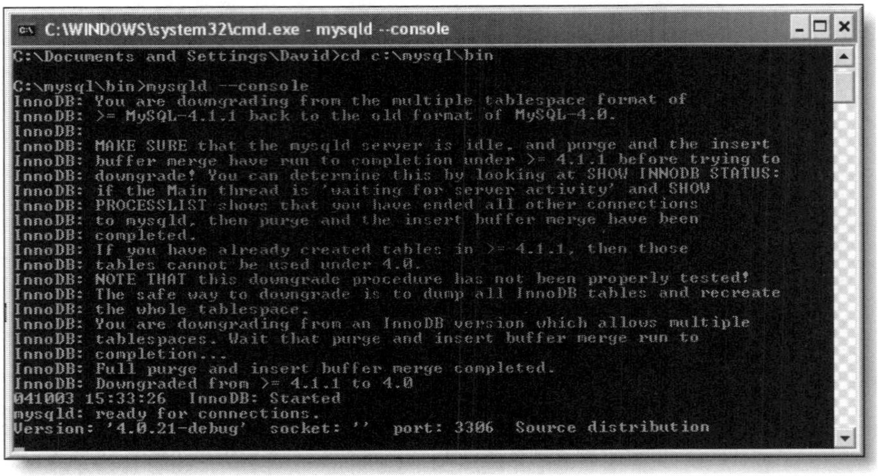

```
C:\WINDOWS\system32\cmd.exe - mysqld --console
C:\Documents and Settings\David>cd c:\mysql\bin

C:\mysql\bin>mysqld --console
InnoDB: You are downgrading from the multiple tablespace format of
InnoDB: >= MySQL-4.1.1 back to the old format of MySQL-4.0.
InnoDB:
InnoDB: MAKE SURE that the mysqld server is idle, and purge and the insert
InnoDB: buffer merge have run to completion under >= 4.1.1 before trying to
InnoDB: downgrade! You can determine this by looking at SHOW INNODB STATUS:
InnoDB: if the Main thread is 'waiting for server activity' and SHOW
InnoDB: PROCESSLIST shows that you have ended all other connections
InnoDB: to mysqld, then purge and the insert buffer merge have been
InnoDB: completed.
InnoDB: If you have already created tables in >= 4.1.1, then those
InnoDB: tables cannot be used under 4.0.
InnoDB: NOTE THAT this downgrade procedure has not been properly tested!
InnoDB: The safe way to downgrade is to dump all InnoDB tables and recreate
InnoDB: the whole tablespace.
InnoDB: You are downgrading from an InnoDB version which allows multiple
InnoDB: tablespaces. Wait that purge and insert buffer merge run to
InnoDB: completion...
InnoDB: Full purge and insert buffer merge completed.
InnoDB: Downgraded from >= 4.1.1 to 4.0
041003 15:33:26  InnoDB: Started
mysqld: ready for connections.
Version: '4.0.21-debug'  socket: ''  port: 3306  Source distribution
```

The output may differ greatly from what is shown here. The important thing to look for is the penultimate line:

mysqld: ready for connections.

If `mysqld` fails to start, use Explorer to navigate to the `C:\mysql\data` folder. Look for a file with an `.err` extension, and open it in Notepad. It's the MySQL error log, which should help troubleshoot the problem. If you can't solve it yourself, ask for help in the friends of ED online forums at `www.friendsofed.com/forums`.

If you are running a software firewall, such as Norton Internet Security, on your system, you will need to create appropriate security settings for MySQL and each of its component programs. The firewall will alert you each time it encounters a request from a program it doesn't recognize. The level of security you need to set will depend on a number of factors, including whether you have an external firewall blocking unauthorized access from the Internet. This is normally a one-time operation, although it may be necessary to reset permissions after upgrading.

4. If you're used to working at the Command Prompt, one thing you'll notice is that you aren't returned to the C:\> prompt after `mysqld` starts. That's because it's still running, and it will continue to do so until you either shut it down or turn off the computer. To shut down `mysqld`, open a second Command Prompt window (leaving the first one open), and type the following command:

```
c:\mysql\bin\mysqladmin -u root shutdown
```

If you're upgrading, and you've already set a root password for MySQL, use the following command instead:

```
c:\mysql\bin\mysqladmin -u root -p shutdown
```

Enter your root password when prompted.

5. Confirm that mysqld has closed down by returning to the first Command Prompt window. It should have displayed several lines reporting the shutdown and returned you to the C:\> prompt, as shown in the following screenshot.

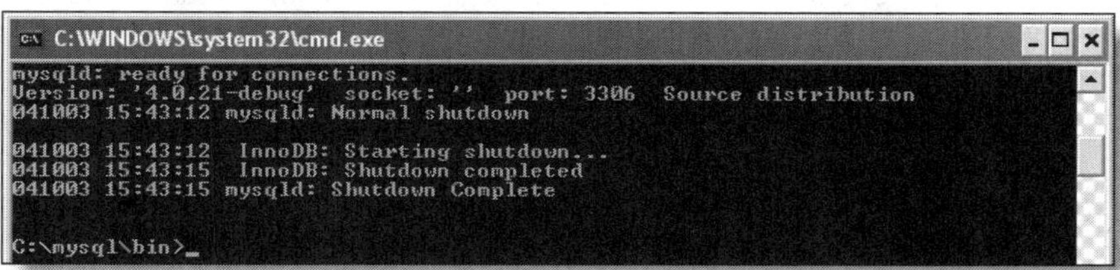

If anything goes wrong, run the checks suggested in the MySQL online documentation at `http://dev.mysql.com/doc/mysql/en/Windows_troubleshooting.html`. If you can't find the answer there, ask for help in the friends of ED forums.

6. If you're using Windows 98 or ME, you'll have to manually start MySQL every time you reboot your computer. Follow the instructions in Chapter 6 to start and stop MySQL manually.

7. Life is much simpler on NT versions of Windows, such as Windows 2000 and Windows XP. You can set up mysqld as a Windows service and basically forget about it. At the C:\> prompt, enter this command:

```
mysqld --install
```

If you get a message saying that mysqld is not recognized as an internal or external command, make sure you are in the correct directory by typing cd c:\mysql\bin.

8. You should see a message that says Service successfully installed. Now start mysqld by typing the following command:

```
net start mysql
```

Note that the command this time uses mysql, not mysqld.

9. This time, Windows should display a message saying The MySQL service was started successfully, before returning you to the C:\> prompt immediately. mysqld is now running in the background, and it will start up and shut down automatically whenever you boot or close down your computer.

10. If you need to stop mysqld for maintenance (or when upgrading to a new version), use the following command:

```
net stop mysql
```

11. If you ever want to remove mysqld as a Windows service, first stop it from running as described in the previous step, and then type the following command from the C:\mysql\bin directory:

```
mysqld --remove
```

Setting up the root user password and securing MySQL

A fresh installation of MySQL can be accessed by anybody, so you need to set a password immediately for the main administrative user (known as the **root** user) and to remove anonymous access. The root user has universal privileges in both the creative and destructive sense—even if you are the only person using the computer, leaving the root password unset is tempting fate.

1. Open a Command Prompt window. Change directory (folder) to the one that contains the main MySQL program files:

   ```
   cd c:\mysql\bin
   ```

2. Type the command to start MySQL Monitor:

   ```
   mysql -u root
   ```

   The command contains three elements:

   - **mysql**: The name of the program.
   - **-u**: This tells the program that you want to log in as a specified user.
   - **root**: The name of user.

3. You should see a welcome message like this:

   ```
   C:\WINDOWS\system32\cmd.exe - mysql -u root

   C:\mysql\bin>mysql -u root
   Welcome to the MySQL monitor.  Commands end with ; or \g.
   Your MySQL connection id is 1 to server version: 4.0.21-debug

   Type 'help;' or '\h' for help. Type '\c' to clear the buffer.

   mysql> _
   ```

4. The most common problem is to get an error message like the following one, instead.

   ```
   C:\WINDOWS\system32\cmd.exe

   C:\mysql\bin>mysql -u root
   ERROR 2003: Can't connect to MySQL server on 'localhost' (10061)

   C:\mysql\bin>_
   ```

   It means that mysqld is not running. If you have installed MySQL as a Windows service (as described in the previous section), restart the server by typing net start mysql. If you are using Windows 98 or ME, type mysqld.

5. As explained earlier, the root user has unlimited powers over database files, but you have just logged in without a password! That means anyone can get in and wreak havoc with

your files—a situation that needs rectifying immediately. Assuming you have logged in successfully as described in step 2, type the following command at the mysql> prompt:

```
use mysql
```

6. This tells MySQL you want to use the database called `mysql`. This database contains all the details of authorized users and the privileges they have to work on database files. You should see a message saying Database changed, which means MySQL is ready for you to work on the files controlling administrative privileges. Now enter the command to set a password for the root user. Substitute `myPassword` with the actual password you want to use. Also make sure you use quotes where indicated and finish the command with a semicolon.

```
UPDATE user SET password = PASSWORD('myPassword') WHERE user = 'root';
```

7. Next, remove anonymous access to MySQL:

```
DELETE FROM user WHERE user = '';
```

8. Tell MySQL to update the privileges table:

```
FLUSH PRIVILEGES;
```

The sequence of commands should produce a series of results like this:

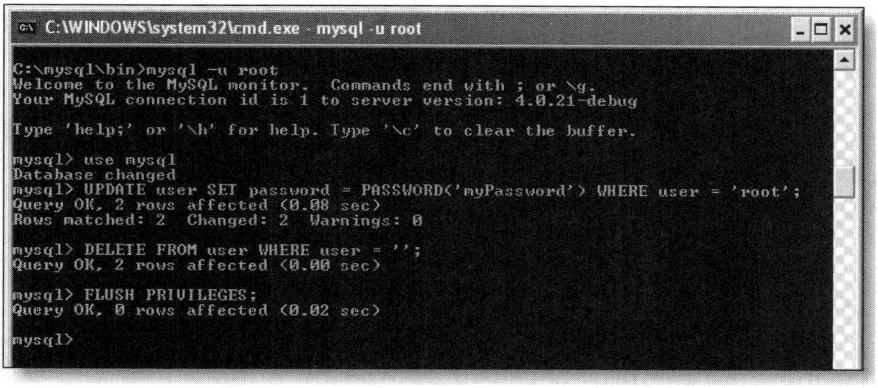

```
C:\WINDOWS\system32\cmd.exe - mysql -u root

C:\mysql\bin>mysql -u root
Welcome to the MySQL monitor.  Commands end with ; or \g.
Your MySQL connection id is 1 to server version: 4.0.21-debug

Type 'help;' or '\h' for help. Type '\c' to clear the buffer.

mysql> use mysql
Database changed
mysql> UPDATE user SET password = PASSWORD('myPassword') WHERE user = 'root';
Query OK, 2 rows affected (0.08 sec)
Rows matched: 2  Changed: 2  Warnings: 0

mysql> DELETE FROM user WHERE user = '';
Query OK, 2 rows affected (0.00 sec)

mysql> FLUSH PRIVILEGES;
Query OK, 0 rows affected (0.02 sec)

mysql>
```

9. To exit MySQL Monitor, simply type exit and press *Enter*.

10. Now try to log back in, using the same command as in step 2. MySQL won't let you in. Anonymous and password-free access has been removed. To get in this time, you need to tell MySQL that you want to use a password:

```
mysql -u root -p
```

11. When you press *Enter*, you will be prompted for your password. When you type it in, a series of asterisks will appear in place of the characters you type. As long as you type in the correct password, MySQL will let you back in. Congratulations, you now have a secure installation of MySQL.

word_id	english	japanese	furigana
3	beef	牛肉	ぎゅうにく
4	milk	牛乳	ぎゅうにゅう
1	park	公園	こうえん
8	work	仕事	しごと
9	university	大学	だいがく
6	clock	時計	とけい
2	beer	ビール	びーる
7	manga	漫画	まんが
5	baseball	野球	やきゅう

Appendix D

USING LANGUAGES OTHER THAN ENGLISH IN MYSQL

Fortunately, MySQL has made handling the world's languages relatively painless. A standard installation of MySQL is fully multilingual with support for more than 20 different encoding systems. So, even if you're running a default English installation of MySQL, you can support most languages without making any changes. I've been running a database in Japanese for many years on an English-language server. The addition of UTF-8 in version 4.1 means that MySQL now supports just about every living language in the world—and some dead ones too. If you want to store data in Hmong, Bugis, or Tamazight, you're out of luck: UTF-8 doesn't support them *yet*—but it will eventually.

How MySQL uses character sets

So, if it's not necessary to change the character set to support a language, what's the significance of being able to specify character sets in the first place? The answer—buried deep in the MySQL documentation—is that the specified character set controls just two things:

- The characters permitted in database, table, and column names
- The sort order of query results

Figure D-1 shows the effect of setting the default character set on a database to `sjis` (Japanese). Two of the column names have been specified in Japanese, and the one on the far right was used to perform a sort (using the SQL command `ORDER BY`).

Before you start thinking, "Wow, that's cool. How do I do that?" storing data that uses a particular character set and displaying it correctly are two completely separate issues. Figures D-1 and D-2 show two views of the same database on the same machine. Although the data can be correctly displayed through PHP, the underlying server environment is incapable of doing so. This makes it impossible to administer the database except through middleware, something that may not always be convenient or available. It is far safer to use only alphanumeric characters (A–Z, a–z, and 0–9) and the underscore in database, table, and column names.

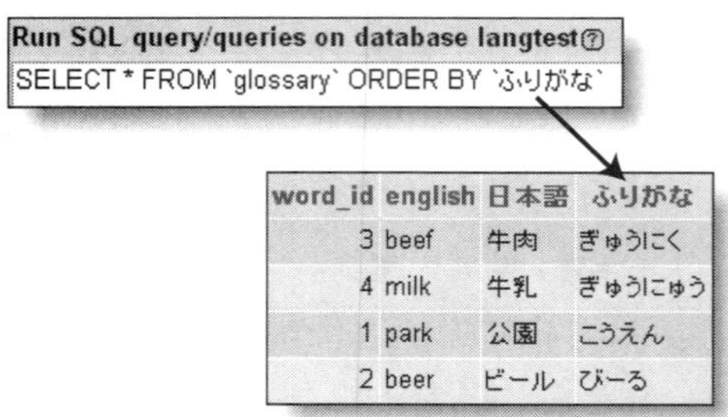

Run SQL query/queries on database langtest

SELECT * FROM `glossary` ORDER BY `ふりがな`

word_id	english	日本語	ふりがな
3	beef	牛肉	ぎゅうにく
4	milk	牛乳	ぎゅうにゅう
1	park	公園	こうえん
2	beer	ビール	びーる

Figure D-1. Setting the character set of a database allows you to use nonalphanumeric characters (in this case, Japanese) in table and column names.

```
MySQL Command Line Shell

mysql> use langtest
Database changed
mysql> SELECT * FROM glossary ORDER BY english;
+---------+---------+-----+--------+
| word_id | english | ??? | ????   |
+---------+---------+-----+--------+
|       3 | beef    | ??  | ?????  |
|       2 | beer    | ??? | ???    |
|       4 | milk    | ??  | ?????? |
|       1 | park    | ??  | ????   |
+---------+---------+-----+--------+
4 rows in set (0.00 sec)

mysql>
```

Figure D-2. Although MySQL supports a large number of character sets, you may not be able to view them correctly in MySQL Monitor.

Figures D-3 and D-4 show what happens when the same database is converted back to the default `latin1` character set, but with collation on the two Japanese columns set to `sjis_japanese_ci`. The Japanese text and sort order are still correct, but using alphanumeric characters for column names means that maintenance on the database can be done on any operating system—a much safer option.

word_id	english	japanese	furigana
3	beef	牛肉	ぎゅうにく
4	milk	牛乳	ぎゅうにゅう
1	park	公園	こうえん
2	beer	ビール	びーる

Figure D-3. Even with `latin1` as the default character set, MySQL stores and sorts Japanese correctly.

```
MySQL Command Line Shell

mysql> SELECT * FROM glossary ORDER BY furigana;
+---------+---------+----------+----------+
| word_id | english | japanese | furigana |
+---------+---------+----------+----------+
|       3 | beef    | ??       | ?????    |
|       4 | milk    | ??       | ??????   |
|       1 | park    | ??       | ????     |
|       2 | beer    | ???      | ???      |
+---------+---------+----------+----------+
4 rows in set (0.00 sec)

mysql>
```

Figure D-4. Using alphanumeric characters for table and column names makes maintenance easy, even though the contents of the table remain inaccessible.

> *You may have noticed that the SQL query used to sort these examples uses the fourth column (*furigana*), not* Japanese*. This is because computers cannot sort nonalphabetic languages like Japanese and Chinese in dictionary order. The* furigana *column uses the Japanese equivalent of an alphabet to represent each word phonetically, and it sorts the words into the correct Japanese order—*gyuniku, gyunyu, koen, biru.

The MySQL documentation on character sets is at `http://dev.mysql.com/doc/mysql/en/Charset.html`.

When you're working with languages other than English, Swedish, or Finnish in MySQL, it's **collation** that matters. In the vast majority of cases, there is no need to change character set, although phpMyAdmin does this for you automatically when you set collation.

Using phpMyAdmin to administer languages

When you launch phpMyAdmin in a browser (`http://localhost/phpMyAdmin/` on Windows; `http://localhost/~`*`username`*`/phpMyAdmin` on a Mac), you should see a screen similar to Figure D-5. (Installation instructions for phpMyAdmin were given in Chapter 6.) The main part of the screen is divided into two sections: MySQL and phpMyAdmin. The language options in the phpMyAdmin section on the right offer a choice of nearly 50 languages—these affect only the way phpMyAdmin displays onscreen instructions. To make changes to the way your database works, it's the choices in the MySQL section that you need to alter.

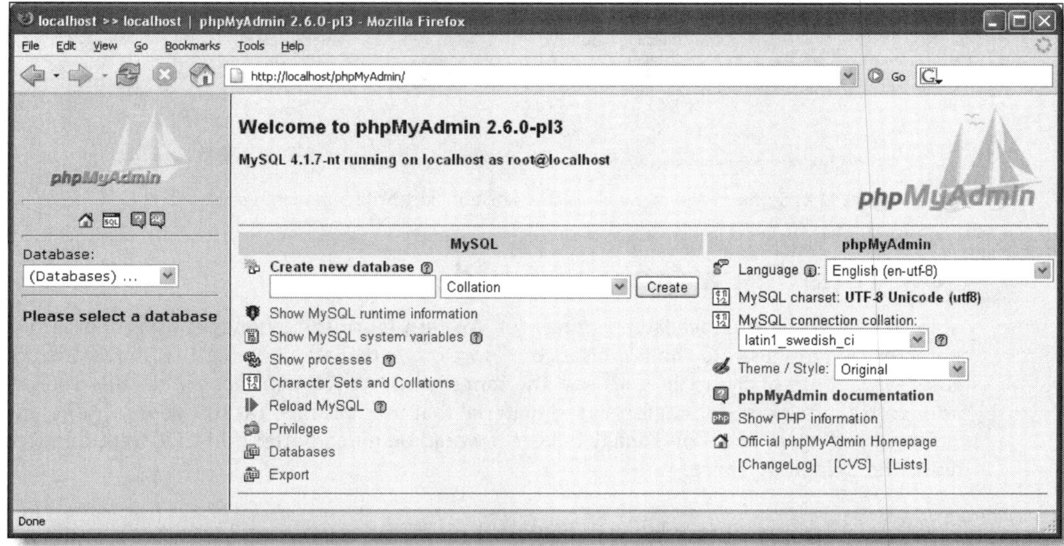

Figure D-5. When used with MySQL 4.1 or higher, phpMyAdmin displays options for specifying which language rules to use for sorting data.

You can see all the language options available on your version of MySQL by clicking Character Sets and Collations halfway down the list in the MySQL section. You should see a list similar to that shown in Figure D-6 (only the beginning of the list is shown here). The names of character sets are shown in bold at the beginning of each section of the table, with a description in italics in parentheses. Below each character set is a list of available collation options. Most Western European languages can be found under latin1, and most central European languages are under latin2 or latin7. To return to the main phpMyAdmin screen, click the Back button on your browser.

Character Sets and Collations

Collation	Description
	armscii8 *(ARMSCII-8 Armenian)*
armscii8_bin	Armenian, Binary
armscii8_general_ci	Armenian, case-insensitive
	ascii *(US ASCII)*
ascii_bin	West European (multilingual), Binary
ascii_general_ci	West European (multilingual), case-insensitive
	big5 *(Big5 Traditional Chinese)*
big5_bin	Traditional Chinese, Binary
big5_chinese_ci	Traditional Chinese, case-insensitive
	binary *(Binary pseudo charset)*
binary	Binary
	cp1250 *(Windows Central European)*
cp1250_bin	Central European (multilingual), Binary
cp1250_czech_cs	Czech, case-sensitive
cp1250_general_ci	Central European (multilingual), case-insensitive
	cp1251 *(Windows Cyrillic)*
cp1251_bin	Cyrillic (multilingual), Binary

Collation	Description
	latin2 *(ISO 8859-2 Central European)*
latin2_bin	Central European (multilingual), Binary
latin2_croatian_ci	Croatian, case-insensitive
latin2_czech_cs	Czech, case-sensitive
latin2_general_ci	Central European (multilingual), case-insensitive
latin2_hungarian_ci	Hungarian, case-insensitive
	latin5 *(ISO 8859-9 Turkish)*
latin5_bin	Turkish, Binary
latin5_turkish_ci	Turkish, case-insensitive
	latin7 *(ISO 8859-13 Baltic)*
latin7_bin	Baltic (multilingual), Binary
latin7_estonian_cs	Estonian, case-sensitive
latin7_general_ci	Baltic (multilingual), case-insensitive
latin7_general_cs	Baltic (multilingual), case-sensitive
	macce *(Mac Central European)*
macce_bin	Central European (multilingual), Binary
macce_general_ci	Central European (multilingual), case-insensitive

Figure D-6. Some of the many character sets and sort orders available in MySQL 4.1

How collation affects sort order

Table D-1 shows all the available settings for Western European languages using the `latin1` character set. To illustrate the importance of sort order (collation), Table D-2 shows the different ways some of the main ones sort the same items. As you can see, the default Swedish order sorts ü after x, so for English-based material that uses accents, `latin1_general_ci` is the preferred setting. In fact, I personally believe it would be much better if MySQL were to adopt this as the default in future.

Table D-1. Collation settings in MySQL for the `latin1` character set

Collation	Description
`latin1_bin`	Binary, follows the `latin1` encoding order (all uppercase letters come before lowercase ones: Z comes before a)
`latin1_danish_ci`	Danish/Norwegian, case insensitive
`latin1_general_ci`	Multilingual, case insensitive
`latin1_general_cs`	Multilingual, case sensitive

Collation	Description
latin1_german1_ci	German DIN-1, case insensitive
latin1_german2_ci	German DIN-2, case insensitive
latin1_spanish_ci	Modern Spanish, case insensitive
latin1_swedish_ci	Swedish/Finnish/English, case insensitive

Table D-2. Comparison of sort order produced by different collations

latin1_swedish_ci (default)	latin1_bin	latin_general_ci	latin_german1_ci	latin1_german2_ci
muffin	MX 2004	muffin	muffin	Müller
MX 2004	MySQL	Müller	Müller	muffin
Müller	Müller	MX 2004	MX 2004	MX 2004
MySQL	muffin	MySQL	MySQL	MySQL

Selecting the right sort order

Sort order (collation) can be set at four different levels:

- Server
- Database
- Table
- Column

Normally, you have no control over changes at the server level unless you are the server administrator. If you are, you should have no difficulty following the instructions in the MySQL online documentation at the URL shown earlier in this section. Specifying the sort order for the other three categories—both at time of creation and subsequently—is very easy in phpMyAdmin.

Setting the sort order for an entire database

When creating a new database, launch phpMyAdmin, and then follow these instructions:

1. Enter the name of the new database in the Create new database text field (see Figure D-5).

2. Click the arrow to the side of the Collation drop-down menu, and choose the appropriate sort order from the list that appears. Figure D-7 shows the settings for a new database that will use Spanish sort order.
3. Click the Create button (it's at the top-right of Figure D-7).

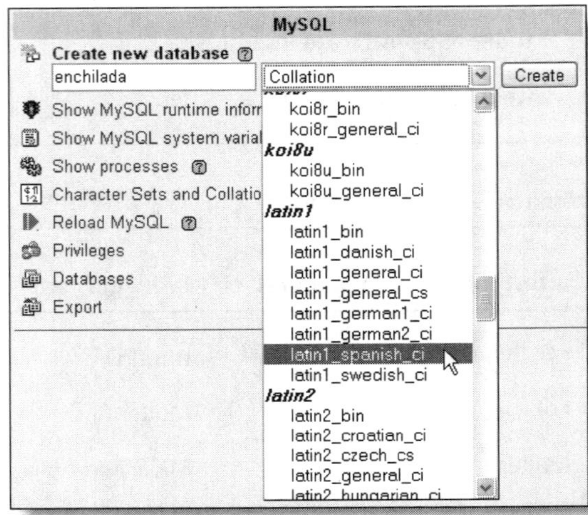

Figure D-7. Creating a new MySQL database that will use Spanish sort order

4. phpMyAdmin will create the database and display a screen as shown in Figure D-8. If you look at the bottom of the figure, you'll see that Collation for any new table is now automatically set to the Spanish sort order. Yes, you get the whole enchilada . . .

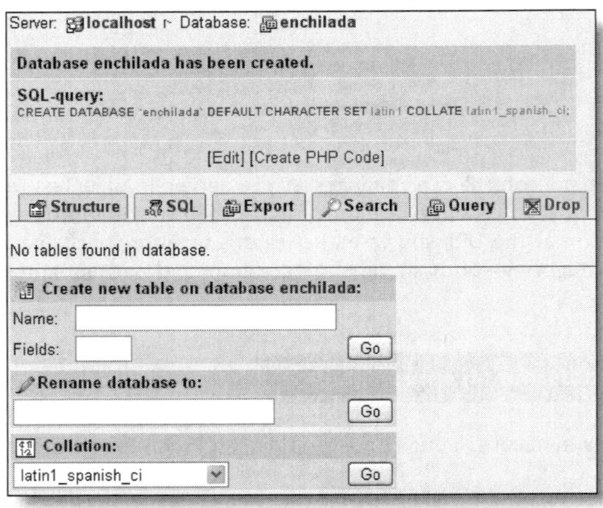

Figure D-8. Once the sort order has been set for the database, all tables automatically use the same setting.

5. If you need to change the sort order after a database has already been created, select the database in the drop-down menu on the left side of the main phpMyAdmin window, as shown in Figure D-9, and a screen similar to the bottom half of Figure D-8 will open. Select a new value for Collation, and click the Go button immediately to the right of the Collation drop-down menu (it's the last one in Figure D-8).

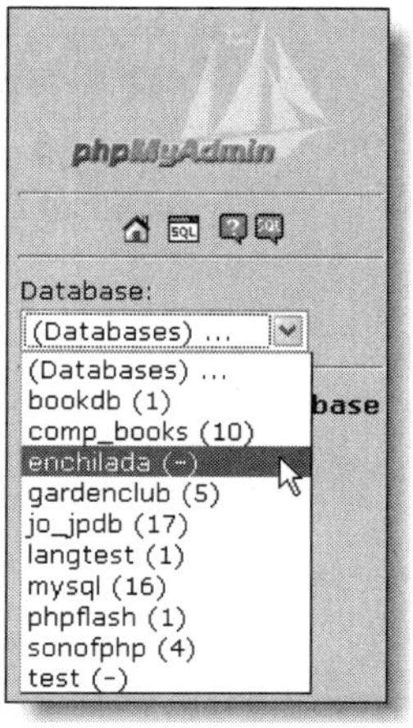

Figure D-9. Selecting a database in phpMyAdmin

Setting the sort order at the table level

Even if you have specified a particular sort order for a database, individual tables can have a different setting. The following instructions are for a new table. Instructions for changing the sort order of an existing table are given separately.

1. In phpMyAdmin, select the database you want to work with from the drop-down menu on the left-hand side of the screen, as shown in Figure D-9.

2. In the screen that opens, enter a name in the Name box, enter the number of columns the table is to have in Fields box, and click Go. Make sure you click the button marked Go alongside the Fields box, as shown in Figure D-10. If you attempt to change the Collation field at the same time, the new table will not be created, and you will end up changing the sort order for the entire database.

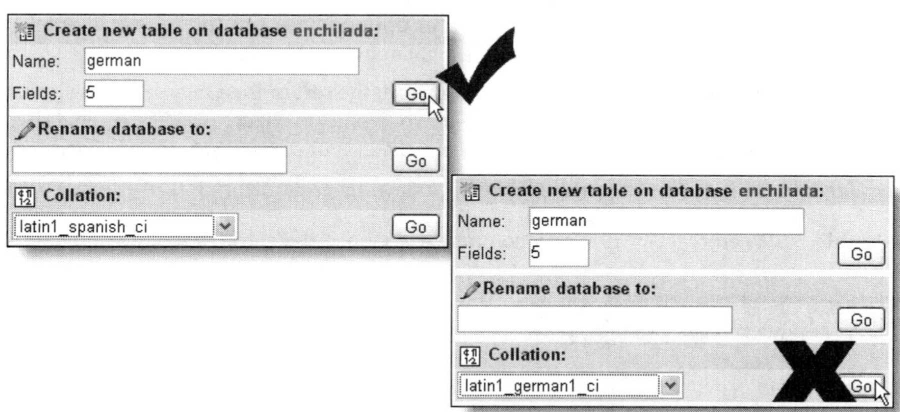

Figure D-10. Create a table before specifying its sort order; otherwise, you'll change the database default.

3. Follow the instructions in the next section.

Setting the sort order at the column level

If you leave the Collation option blank for a column, it will automatically use the character set and collation of its parent table.

1. When you first create a table, you will be presented with a screen like that shown in Figure D-11.

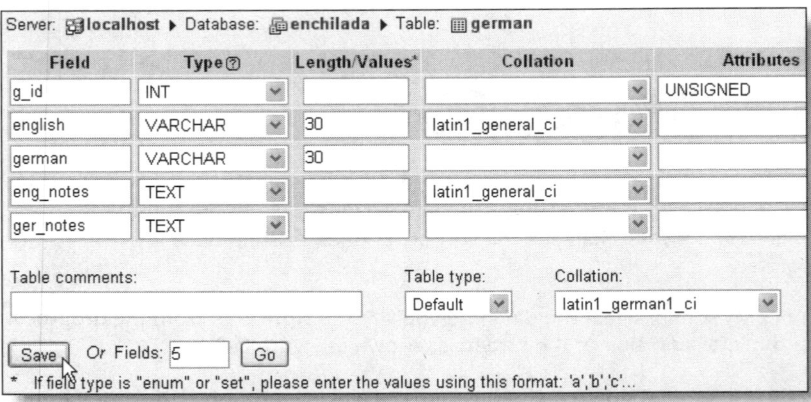

Figure D-11. The screen for specifying column settings has options for setting collation for the whole table or individual columns.

2. To specify the sort order for the whole table, select the required option from the Collation drop-down menu shown at the bottom right of Figure D-11. In this example, it has been set to latin1_german1_ci. If this option is not set, the table will automatically inherit the default character set and collation for the database.
3. To give individual columns a different setting from the rest of the table, select the required option from its related Collation drop-down menu. In Figure D-11, the English and Eng_notes columns (phpMyAdmin calls them "fields") have been set to latin1_general_ci.
4. When all settings have been specified, click Save (at the bottom left of Figure D-11).

Once a table has been created, any new columns will inherit the settings specified in step 2.

Changing the sort order of a table

Changing the sort order is mainly a question of finding your way through the phpMyAdmin interface.

1. If you don't already have the database open in phpMyAdmin, browse to it using the drop-down menu on the left of the screen, as shown in Figure D-9.

2. Once the database is open, phpMyAdmin will display a list of all tables in the database beneath the drop-down menu. Select the table you want to alter by clicking its name, as shown here.

3. To change the Collation setting for the entire table, click the Operations tab on the tabbed navigation at the top of the screen.

4. Change the Collation setting (it's close to the bottom of the screen), and click Go.

Changing the sort order of a column

The following instructions assume you already have the details of the table displayed in phpMyAdmin, as described in steps 1 and 2 of the previous section.

1. The main screen has a grid showing the main properties of each column in the table, as shown in Figure D-12. Put a check mark in the check box to the left of the name of each column you want to change, and then click the pencil-like icon beneath the grid.

   If you want to change just one column, you can also click the pencil-like icon in its associated row without the need to check any boxes.

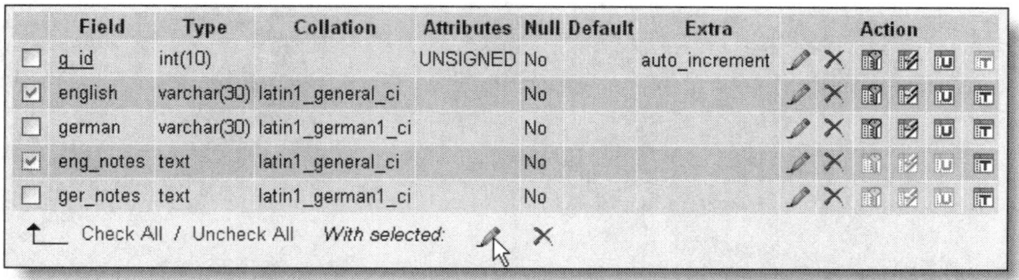

	Field	Type	Collation	Attributes	Null	Default	Extra	Action
☐	g_id	int(10)		UNSIGNED	No		auto_increment	
☑	english	varchar(30)	latin1_general_ci		No			
☐	german	varchar(30)	latin1_german1_ci		No			
☑	eng_notes	text	latin1_general_ci		No			
☐	ger_notes	text	latin1_german1_ci		No			

Check All / Uncheck All *With selected:*

Figure D-12. Select the columns you want to change in the main display grid, and click the pencil-like icon.

A screen will open, similar to the one used for setting column attributes when you first create a table (as shown in Figure D-11). Make any changes you want, and click Save.

Appendix E

ESSENTIAL MYSQL MAINTENANCE

I have been running MySQL for several years now, both on local Windows computers and a remote Linux server. More recently, I've also installed it on a Mac PowerBook running Mac OS X Panther. I'm not a professional database administrator, so I frequently leave MySQL running for months without doing any maintenance. I find it very stable; it basically looks after itself. There are, however, some essential maintenance chores that you need to be aware of. This appendix covers the following subjects:

- Backing up the database
- Performing backups compatible with earlier versions of MySQL
- Restoring from a backup
- Transferring a database to another server
- Upgrading and uninstalling MySQL
- Converting tables to InnoDB and back
- Repairing tables
- What to do when you forget your root password

This appendix is not intended to be an exhaustive survey of maintenance techniques. For the most up-to-date information, visit `http://dev.mysql.com/doc/mysql/en/Client-Side_Scripts.html`, the section of the online documentation that deals with MySQL client and utility programs.

Backing up your database

One of the most frequent questions I get asked is, "Where are my database files?" The reason people want to know is that they either want to copy their database or—if they're particularly prudent—create a backup. Copying the files directly is not always the best way to back up MySQL data. Still, for Windows users at least, knowing where the files are can be helpful. It's a different story on the Mac: the files are locked away from prying eyes.

Knowing where to find your data files

On a Windows machine, the data files are easy to find. If you installed the Windows Essentials version in the default location, the main data folder is `C:\Program Files\MySQL\MySQL Server 4.1\data`. Inside that folder you will find a file called whatever name you have given to your computer. If you look at Figure E-1, you will see that mine is called `DPMAIN.err`. The `.err` extension indicates that it's a logfile, and you may find more than one of them. A previous installation on my computer also had a file called `mysql.err`. (If you can't see the filename extensions, refer back to the section titled "Getting Windows to display filename extensions" in Chapter 1.) These are text files; right-click their icons and select either Notepad or WordPad to open them. The information they contain is rarely of value to the ordinary user, and it can sometimes be unnecessarily alarming. For instance, my logfile frequently says my InnoDB database *may* be corrupted, even though it's not. The Mac version of MySQL doesn't create logfiles. This is presumably to prevent clogging up disk space with files that most people never read, and that just grow and grow if they aren't deleted at regular intervals.

In addition to any ERR files are two InnoDB logfiles, `ib_logfile0` and `ib_logfile1`. Each of these is a cool 5MB, even if you have no InnoDB tables. If space is a problem on your hard disk, there is no point in just deleting them, because MySQL will create them again the next time the MySQL server starts up. To get rid of them permanently, check first that all your tables use the MyISAM format, and convert any that use InnoDB (instructions are at the end of this appendix). Once your data is secure, run the configuration wizard as described in "Configuring the MySQL server on Windows" in Chapter 6, and select Non-Transactional Database Only. After you have closed down the MySQL server, you can safely remove the InnoDB logfiles, and they will not reappear the next time the server is started.

If you chose the default location for InnoDB data file, you will also have a file called `ibdata1`. Even with no data stored in InnoDB tables, it will be 10MB. Although the InnoDB tables for all your databases are in this single file, do not copy it or move it. You should always use a utility like `mysqldump` (described in the next section) instead.

If MySQL server is running, you will have a PID file. This is a process ID file, and you should not delete it.

As you can see from Figure E-1, I have 11 more folders inside the `data` folder—one for each database on my system. If you take a peek inside the largest, which contains more than 10,000 records, you'll see the database folder contains 51 files totaling more than 13MB (see Figure E-2). There are 17 tables in the database, and because it uses the MyISAM format, each one consists of three files: an FRM file that contains the table definition, an MYD file that contains the data, and an MYI file that contains the indexes. InnoDB format databases don't have separate files for tables, just an FRM definition file. The data is stored in `ibdata1`, which acts as a virtual file system.

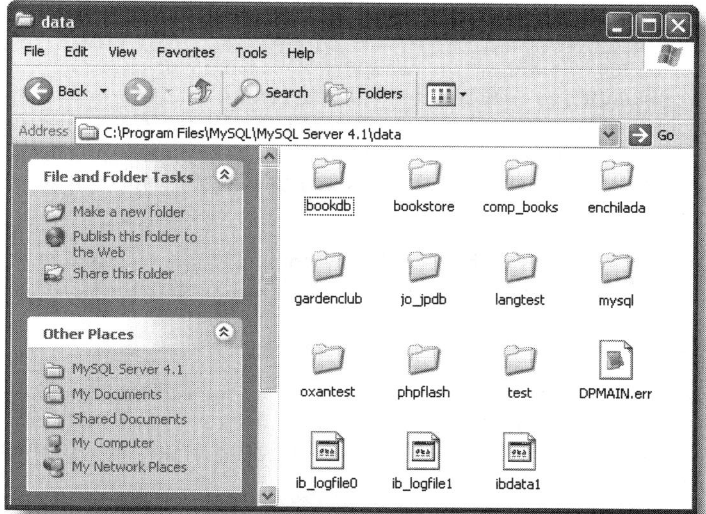

Figure E-1. On Windows, the MySQL data files are located within an easily accessible folder.

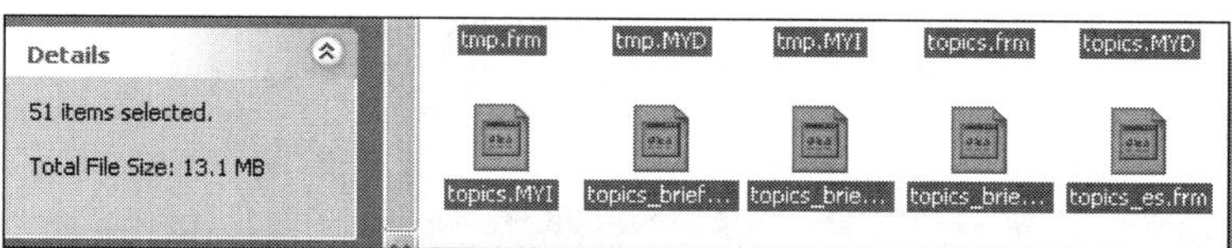

Figure E-2. In a MyISAM database, each table consists of three files.

The reason for showing you this is partly to satisfy the curiosity of anyone fascinated by this sort of thing but, more important, to try to convince you that building a large database on your local computer and then planning to upload it to your hosting company is a very poor strategy. My large database is an old backup copy that I use for testing purposes. The real version is on a remote server, and all maintenance is done through an online content management system.

Even though you can make a physical copy of the files in a database, you *must* stop the server before doing so. When copying the files to a new server, the recipient server must also be shut down. You can imagine the chaos if everyone on a cohosted server wanted to upload new database files every day. That's why content management systems, such as those demonstrated in Chapters 10 and 12, are so important.

The one time knowing where to find the physical data files comes in handy is when you are migrating to a new local computer. As long as your databases use only MyISAM tables, once you have closed down the MySQL server on both machines, you can copy the files to their new location, and be up and running in no time at all. On the other hand, it's probably just as quick to use the `mysqldump` utility, make a backup, and transfer the data to the new computer. If you're on a Mac, this is your only option, because the data files are locked away. It's also your only option with InnoDB. Fortunately, `mysqldump` is quick and easy to use.

Using mysqldump to back up your data

mysqldump creates a text file with all the necessary SQL commands to re-create an exact copy of your data. It can be used to copy selected tables, an entire database, or all databases on the same server. It also has the advantage that it doesn't require the server to be closed down. Moreover, the file that it creates is plain text, so you can use mysqldump to back up your data on one operating system and use the output file to replicate the data on a completely different system.

I'll give you precise instructions on how to use this command in a moment, but first let's take a look at the basic syntax. For most purposes, this is all you need:

```
mysqldump -u root -p db_name > db_name.sql
```

Replace db_name with the name of the actual database you want to back up. The > in the command instructs mysqldump to send the output to the destination immediately following. It's not obligatory to give the target file a .sql file extension, but it's a useful convention that helps remind you of the file's contents.

If you are using a version of MySQL prior to the 4.1 series, insert --opt after mysqldump, like this:

```
mysqldump --opt -u root -p db_name > db_name.sql
```

The --opt tells mysqldump to create a file that is optimized in speed and performance both for backup and for rebuilding the equivalent data elsewhere. This became the default in MySQL 4.1, so it is required only with older versions.

Backing up the phpflash database with mysqldump

The simplest way to show you how to use mysqldump is to do it with the phpflash database used throughout this book. All commands should be followed by *Enter/Return*. These instructions assume that Mac users have added MySQL to their PATH as instructed in Chapter 1.

1. In Windows, open a Command Prompt window (Start ➤ Run, type cmd in the Open field, and click OK). If you accepted the option to include the bin folder in your PATH when installing MySQL (Windows Essentials only), you should change directory to wherever you want to save the backup file. A convenient place is the top level of your C drive. Type cd C:\ and press *Enter*. Then skip to step 3.

   If the MySQL bin folder is not in your PATH, you must change directory to the folder. Depending on your version of MySQL, use one of the following:

   ```
   cd C:\Program Files\MySQL\MySQL Server 4.1\bin
   cd C:\mysql\bin
   ```

   Move to step 3.

2. On Mac OS X, open Terminal. If you have just opened a new instance of Terminal, you will automatically be in your home folder. Otherwise, return to your home folder by typing the following command:

   ```
   cd ~
   ```

3. If MySQL is included in your PATH, just type the following:

```
mysqldump -u root -p phpflash > phpflash.sql
```

This will create the backup at the top level of your C drive (Windows) or in your home folder (Mac).

If MySQL is not in your PATH, this will create the backup inside the MySQL bin folder. It's not a good idea to litter up your program files with backups, so you need to add a path in front of the backup filename. The simplest solution is to save the backup at the top level of your C drive like this:

```
mysqldump -u root -p phpflash > c:\phpflash.sql
```

4. Enter your MySQL root password when prompted. After a short while, you will be returned to the command/shell prompt. Unless there is a problem, you will see no output onscreen. In Windows, use Windows Explorer to navigate to the top level of the C drive. On the Mac, use Finder to navigate to your home folder. You should see phpflash.sql.

5. Use a text or script editor to open phpflash.sql. Figure E-3 shows the beginning of the file in BBEdit on a Mac. The important thing to note in Figure E-3 is line 5, which specifies the server version. In this case, it is 4.1.7-standard. You can use this file to restore or copy data to any MySQL server running the 4.1 series or higher. If you want to copy data to an older version of MySQL, see the upcoming section "Using mysqldump to copy to older versions of MySQL."

```
phpflash.sql
Last Saved: 19/12/04 11:55:39 am
File Path: ~/phpflash.sql
phpflash.sql

-- MySQL dump 10.8
--
-- Host: localhost    Database: phpflash
-- ------------------------------------------------------
-- Server version   4.1.7-standard

/*!40101 SET @OLD_CHARACTER_SET_CLIENT=@@CHARACTER_SET_CLIENT */;
/*!40101 SET @OLD_CHARACTER_SET_RESULTS=@@CHARACTER_SET_RESULTS */;
/*!40101 SET @OLD_COLLATION_CONNECTION=@@COLLATION_CONNECTION */;
/*!40101 SET NAMES utf8 */;
/*!40014 SET @OLD_UNIQUE_CHECKS=@@UNIQUE_CHECKS, UNIQUE_CHECKS=0 */;
/*!40014 SET @OLD_FOREIGN_KEY_CHECKS=@@FOREIGN_KEY_CHECKS, FOREIGN_KEY_CHECKS=0
*/;
/*!40101 SET @OLD_SQL_MODE=@@SQL_MODE, SQL_MODE="NO_AUTO_VALUE_ON_ZERO" */;

--
-- Table structure for table `wordlist`
--

DROP TABLE IF EXISTS `wordlist`;
CREATE TABLE `wordlist` (
  `word` varchar(30) default NULL
) ENGINE=MyISAM DEFAULT CHARSET=latin1;

--
-- Dumping data for table `wordlist`
--


/*!40000 ALTER TABLE `wordlist` DISABLE KEYS */;
LOCK TABLES `wordlist` WRITE;
INSERT INTO `wordlist` VALUES
('A'),('a'),('aback'),('abacus'),('abandon'),('abandoned'),('abandonment'),('
abashed'),('abate'),('abbey'),('abbr.'),('abbreviate'),('abbreviation'),('ABC'),
('ABC\'s'),('abdicate'),('abdication'),('abdomen'),('abdominal'),('abduct'),('
abduction'),('aberration'),('abet'),('abhor'),('abhorrence'),('abhorrent'),('
abide'),('abiding'),('ability'),('abject'),('ablaze'),('able'),('able-bodied'),(
'ably'),('abnormal'),('abnormality'),('abnormally'),('aboard'),('abolish'),('
```

Figure E-3. The mysqldump utility creates a text file that automatically rebuilds your data wherever you want.

Using mysqldump for partial and multiple backups

If you have a particularly large database, it may be more convenient to back up individual tables. On the other hand, you may have several databases that you want to back up simultaneously. Both situations can be handled easily with `mysqldump`.

In all the following examples, I have omitted the path to the target file for the sake of simplicity. If you don't specify a path, `mysqldump` *will create the file in the current working directory (folder). You can specify the path either with a full path name or a relative one. Although* `mysqldump` *creates the target file automatically, it can only do so in a folder that already exists. A good idea is to create a folder called* `MySQLBackups`*. If you specify a path that contains spaces, the entire path name and target file must be enclosed in quotes, for example:*

```
mysqldump -u root -p phpflash > "c:\MySQL Backups\phpflash.sql"
```

Partial backups To back up one or more tables from a single database, add the table name(s) in a space-delimited list after the database name. For instance, to back up the users table from phpflash, use the following command:

```
mysqldump -u root -p phpflash users > users.sql
```

To back up the users and the singers tables, use this command:

```
mysqldump -u root -p phpflash users singers > twotables.sql
```

Multiple backups To back up more than one database at a time, use the --databases option, followed by a space-delimited list of the databases you want to copy. To back up two databases called phpflash and books, use the following:

```
mysqldump -u root -p --databases phpflash books > db_backup.sql
```

If you want to back up all your databases in one operation, use the following command:

```
mysqldump -u root -p --all-databases > my_dbs.sql
```

Naming backup files

As noted earlier, the .sql filename extension is purely a convenient convention. It is not a file type recognized by any operating system. If you already have a backup file with the same name in the target location, mysqldump will automatically overwrite it—without warning. Often, this is what you want. However, you may want to keep backups of your data at different stages for archiving purposes. The simple way of naming them in an easily recognizable way is to add the date to the end of the filename. If you use the MySQL date format, they will also be in the correct order when you display a file list, for instance:

```
my_dbs.sql.2004-09-01
my_dbs.sql.2004-10-01
my_dbs.sql.2004-11-01
my_dbs.sql.2004-12-01
my_dbs.sql.2005-01-01
```

Using mysqldump to copy to older versions of MySQL

In the same way as a file created on Flash MX 2004 is not backward compatible with Flash MX, unless specifically saved in MX format, data backed up with mysqldump can be restored or copied only to a version of MySQL from the same series or higher. So you can use mysqldump files created on MySQL 4.1 to move data to MySQL 5.0, but the same file cannot move data to MySQL 4.0 or 3.23.

Fortunately, since MySQL 4.1.0, mysqldump has the equivalent of a “Save As” option. To create a backup file compatible with MySQL 3.23, use the following command:

```
mysqldump --compatible=mysql323 -u root -p db_name > db_name.sql
```

To create a backup file compatible with MySQL 4.0, use the following command:

```
mysqldump --compatible=mysql40 -u root -p db_name > db_name.sql
```

This feature is not available in versions of MySQL prior to the 4.1 series.

The MySQL documentation says that `--opt` shouldn't be used to create backup files that are to be reloaded into "a very old MySQL server," but it doesn't specify how old that means. Since `--opt` is now the default, insert `--skip-opt` after `mysqldump` in the preceding commands if you experience problems loading data into an older version of MySQL.

Restoring from a backup

This is even simpler than using `mysqldump`. The procedure varies slightly depending on what you actually backed up.

Restoring to a single database

If you used `mysqldump` to back up a single database or part of a database (such as one or more tables), the target database must exist before you can restore the data. If the database no longer exists, you need to create it, either using MySQL Monitor or phpMyAdmin. Say, for instance, your `phpflash` database no longer exists. Launch MySQL Monitor and issue the following commands:

```
create database phpflash;
exit;
```

The second command closes MySQL Monitor, because you need to be at the command line/shell prompt to perform the restore operation.

As long as the target database exists, issue the following command (change directory to the MySQL `bin` folder first, if necessary):

```
mysql -u root -p database_name < backup_file
```

Enter your MySQL root password when prompted. That's all there is to it. As with `mysqldump`, you need to provide the path name to the backup file, and if there are any spaces in the path name or filename, the entire location needs to be in quotes.

Restoring multiple databases

The backup file created by `mysqldump` contains all the necessary information to create the databases if they no longer exist, so all you need to do is issue the following command (after changing to the MySQL `bin` folder, if necessary):

```
mysql -u root -p < backup_file
```

Enter your MySQL root password when prompted. The databases will be automatically created and restored to their condition at the time of the backup. The same provisions regarding the path name of the backup file apply as to when working with `mysqldump`.

Transferring a database to another server

In theory, this is very simple. First of all, remember that a file created with `mysqldump` can be used only to copy a database to a MySQL server running the same version of MySQL or higher. So, if you're running MySQL 4.1.8 locally and your host is running MySQL 4.0.22 or MySQL 3.23.38 (some still are!), you must use the `--compatible` option described earlier. If, on the other hand, your version number is the same or lower than your host's, everything should be fine.

You simply need to create a backup using `mysqldump`, copy the backup file to the other server using FTP or a network connection, and then use the restoration method described in the previous section. I've done it on several occasions with no fuss or bother, but that's because I have the luxury of running a dedicated server, and I have full root access to MySQL at the command line.

If you are in a shared hosting environment, your host probably won't give you command-line access to MySQL. Most hosts do, however, offer facilities for clients to transfer existing databases from another server. The best advice I can offer is to ask your host and to use whatever utility they recommend.

If your host doesn't offer any facility for transferring a database, there is one other technique you can try as a last resort. Its success or failure will depend on the configuration of your host's server.

Using the PHP system() function to populate a database

PHP has a function called `system()` that executes an external program and displays the output. For security reasons, your host may restrict the directories that this function can access. If that's the case, this technique will almost certainly not work, but it may be worth trying if you have no alternative.

1. Create a backup of your database with `mysqldump` as described earlier.
2. Upload the backup file to your remote website.
3. Create a PHP page called `load_db.php` and insert the following code:

   ```
   <?php
   system('/usr/bin/mysql -u username --password=password database_name
   ➥ < backup.sql');
   ?>
   ```

   This assumes that your host's server is running on Linux, and that the MySQL program is in `/usr/bin` (another common location is `/usr/local/bin`). If the server is running on Windows, you will need to supply the correct path name to the MySQL `bin` folder, which may not be so easy to find out.

   As you can see, this is basically the same command as to restore from a backup on your own computer. The difference is that the password is supplied within the command, rather than in response to the server's request.
4. Upload `load_db.php` to the same folder on your website as the backup file.

5. Open a browser and enter the URL for `load_db.php`. Loading the page into the browser will run the script and attempt to execute the command. If you see no output, it probably means it has succeeded. Check in phpMyAdmin or whatever front-end your host provides to MySQL. If you get error messages, see if they give any clue as to what the problem might be.

   You may also need to add a hostname in the command. In between the password and database name, try the following:

   ```
   --host=localhost
   ```

   If that doesn't work, try

   ```
   --host=hostname
   ```

   If the script fails more than a couple of times, do *not* attempt to run it repeatedly, as the host may regard it as a hostile attack.

Upgrading and uninstalling MySQL

The process is different for Windows and Mac OS X. Make sure you read the relevant section for your operating system.

Upgrading and uninstalling MySQL on Windows

The default location for MySQL was changed in September 2004 with the release of MySQL 4.1.5, the first gamma version of Windows Essentials. All releases prior to that installed MySQL in `C:\mysql`. Since then, the default location has changed to `C:\Program Files\MySQL\MySQL Server 4.1`. As the folder name suggests, this is the default location for the 4.1 series only. It is planned to install MySQL 5.0 and later series into their own dedicated folders. This means the upgrade procedure depends on both your current version number and the version you intend to upgrade to.

Uninstalling MySQL is mainly done through Add or Remove Programs in the Windows Control Panel. The two main points to note are that you may need to remove MySQL as a Windows service before uninstalling, and that the uninstall process normally leaves data files untouched. So, if you need to leave a clean machine after you have finished with MySQL, you will need to delete the data files after the program has been removed. The details differ slightly for each series of MySQL and are described together with the upgrade instructions.

Upgrading from MySQL 3.23

Because of differences between the table structures, it isn't recommended to upgrade directly from MySQL 3.23 to MySQL 4.1 or higher. Instead, you should use MySQL 4.0 as a staging post. The only exception is if you don't want to preserve any existing data in your databases.

In either case, if MySQL has been installed as a service, you need to stop your existing installation of MySQL by opening a Command Prompt and typing net stop mysql. The uninstall process should leave the contents of C:\mysql\data untouched, but as a precaution, you should copy the entire contents of the data folder to a temporary location. Then remove the program by using Add or Remove Programs in the Windows Control Panel.

Follow the instructions in Appendix C to install the most recent version of MySQL 4.0. At the time of this writing, MySQL 4.0.23 was still listed by MySQL as being Generally Available, so there was no need to search for it in the archives, although this may change.

Once you have installed and started your new version, open MySQL Monitor and run the following command:

```
SOURCE C:\mysql\scripts\mysql_fix_privilege_tables.sql
```

You can safely ignore any Duplicate column name warnings that appear onscreen as the command runs. After running the script, stop the MySQL server and restart it. Your original data should be intact. If there are any problems, stop the server and copy the original data from the temporary folder. Restart the MySQL server, run the command, and restart the server again.

Upgrading from MySQL 4.0

The main issue when upgrading from MySQL 4.0 is the change in the default location of the data files. A simple way of handling this is to run mysqldump with the --all-databases option (see the section titled "Using mysqldump for partial and multiple backups" earlier in this appendix). Once the new installation is running, you can then use the technique described in the section "Restoring multiple databases," also earlier in this appendix.

The other important thing you have to do is remove MySQL as a Windows service on computers where it has been installed as such. **You must do this before uninstalling the MySQL program itself**. Open a Command Prompt window and type the following commands:

```
net stop mysql
cd \mysql\bin
mysqld --remove
```

Uninstall MySQL using Add or Remove Programs in the Control Panel. Then install MySQL 4.1 as described in Chapter 6. Restore your data files from the backup file. Once you have installed and started your new version, open MySQL Monitor and run the following command:

```
SOURCE C:\program files\mysql\mysql server 4.1\scripts\
➥ mysql_fix_privilege_tables.sql
```

You can safely ignore any Duplicate column name warnings that appear onscreen as the command runs. After you run the script, stop the MySQL server and restart it.

Upgrading MySQL 4.1

This applies to upgrading between point releases of the 4.1 series (such as upgrading from 4.1.5 to 4.1.8). As long as your existing installation of MySQL is version 4.1.5 or higher, the MySQL Installation Wizard performs server upgrades automatically. There is no need to remove the existing installation. The installation process automatically shuts down and removes the existing service before installing the new one. Data remains untouched.

Upgrading to MySQL 5.0 and beyond

Obviously, things may change, but the current plan is to install each future series in a dedicated folder of its own. So MySQL 5.0 will be in `C:\Program Files\MySQL\MySQL Server 5.0`, MySQL 5.1 will be in `MySQL Server 5.1`, and so on. This means you will need to back up all data with `mysqldump` and uninstall your previous version before upgrading. The uninstall wizard automatically stops MySQL and removes it as a Windows service. After you install the new version, restore your data from the backup file.

Upgrading and uninstalling MySQL on Mac OS X

Installing MySQL on Mac OS X is incredibly easy, thanks to the PKG files created by MySQL, but you can get a very nasty shock (as I did) if you don't plan your upgrades correctly. Most software comes with some sort of installation help file. In the case of MySQL, it's called `ReadMe.txt`, and it contains vital information, which you ignore at your peril.

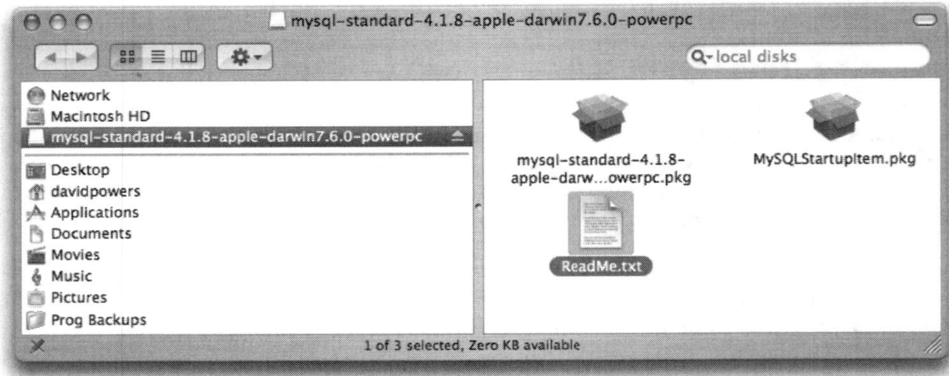

According to MySQL, the Mac OS X Installer "does not yet offer the functionality required to properly upgrade previously installed packages." What this means is that when you "upgrade" MySQL on Mac OS X, you are, in effect, installing a completely new version of MySQL that sits alongside the old version, and like bad neighbors, they never talk to each other. Apart from the old version taking up unnecessary disk space, that might not be so bad. The problem is that all your data is locked inside the old version.

The solution is simple: use `mysqldump` *with the* `--all-databases` *option to copy your data before upgrading.*

If you need to uninstall MySQL for any reason, follow the instructions from step 9 in the following section.

Backing up and upgrading on Mac OS X

The following instructions are based on the file that came with MySQL 4.1.8 in late December 2004, and they were correct at the time, but things may have changed by the time you read this. So I strongly recommend you resist the urge to double-click the PKG file icon for a few minutes, and check `ReadMe.txt` for any more recent information.

1. Open Terminal and make a backup of all your databases with the `--all-databases` option of `mysqldump`, as described in "Using mysqldump for partial and multiple backups" earlier in this appendix.
2. Stop the MySQL server by typing the following command:

   ```
   sudo mysqladmin -u root -p shutdown
   ```

3. When prompted for your password, enter your Mac password. You will then be prompted for another password. This time, enter your MySQL root password.
4. Install the new version of MySQL by double-clicking the PKG file icon from the upgrade that you have downloaded from the MySQL site. Follow the instructions onscreen.
5. When the installation has completed, restart MySQL. If you installed the `StartUpItem` as recommended in Chapter 1, restart MySQL by typing the following command:

   ```
   sudo /Library/StartUpItems/MySQLCOM/MySQLCOM start
   ```

   If you have an earlier version of the `StartUpItem`, the command is

   ```
   sudo /Library/StartUpItems/MySQL/MySQL start
   ```

   Enter your Mac password when prompted.
6. Launch MySQL Monitor by typing

   ```
   mysql -u root
   ```

   You don't need a root password, because this is a completely fresh installation of MySQL.
7. Reset your root password and remove anonymous access by typing the following series of commands:

   ```
   UPDATE user SET password = PASSWORD('root_password')
   WHERE user = 'root';
   DELETE FROM user WHERE user = '';
   FLUSH PRIVILEGES;
   exit;
   ```

8. Restore your data by issuing the following command:

   ```
   mysql -u root -p < backup_file
   ```

   Enter your root password when prompted. Your upgraded version of MySQL should now be working with all previous data in place.

9. Once you have checked that everything is working correctly, you can remove the old files to save disk space. (The rest of these instructions are optional if disk space is not an issue.) Type the following commands to change directory and list the files:

```
cd /usr/local
ls -l
```

10. You should see a list of files like that in the following screenshot. There are three references to `mysql`. The first contains ->, which indicates that it's a symbolic link. The actual name of the folder is `mysql-standard-4.1.8-apple-darwin7.6.0-powerpc`, which is a bit much to expect you to type out every time you want to access `mysql`. So, the symbolic link acts as an alias.

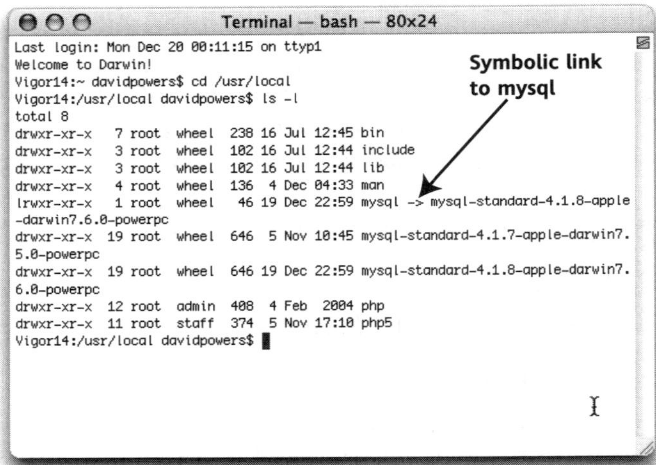

Immediately below are two more references to `mysql`. These contain the actual files. As you can see from the screenshot, the last one has the same number as the symbolic link. It was also created on December 19, so it is more recent than the middle one (which was created on November 5).

To remove the older files, type the following command (but don't press *Return* yet):

```
sudo rm -r
```

11. Use your cursor to highlight the folder name of the older version, as shown in the following screenshot. Make sure you have the full name, particularly as it's likely to run over two lines. *Ctrl*-click and select Paste Selection from the pop-up menu.

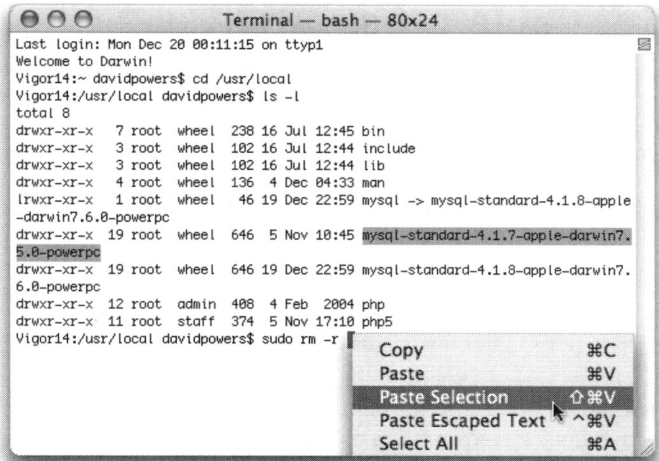

You should now have a line that looks like this (the actual folder name is likely to be slightly different, depending on when you installed your original version):

```
sudo rm -r mysql-standard-4.1.7-apple-darwin7.5.0-powerpc
```

12. Make sure the command is correct. Press *Return*. Enter your Mac password when prompted. That's it—the old files are gone. And when I say "gone," I really mean it. You cannot restore them from the Trash if you make a mistake.

13. One final bit of housekeeping: you should remove the old version from the `Package Receipts` directory. Change directory and list the contents by typing

```
cd /Library/Receipts
ls
```

14. The name of the package receipt you need to delete will be the same as in step 11, but with `.pkg` on the end. Remove it by typing this (substitute the correct name for the version on your computer):

```
sudo rm -r mysql-standard-4.1.7-apple-darwin7.5.0-powerpc.pkg
```

Press *Return*. If prompted, enter your Mac password.

Hopefully, by the time it comes for you to upgrade, the Mac OS X Installer will have overcome these problems. It's not a lot of work, but it's fiddly and very annoying if you forget to back up your databases first!

Converting table types

The default table type used by MySQL is MyISAM. It's fast, efficient, and very stable, but the 4.1 series doesn't support foreign key constraints or transactions. If you need either of these features, it's a simple operation to convert individual tables to the InnoDB table type. The easiest way to do it is in phpMyAdmin.

1. Launch phpMyAdmin and select a database from the drop-down menu on the left-hand side.
2. Select the table you want to convert by clicking its name in the list that appears on the left-hand side of the screen.
3. Click the Operations tab at the top of the main screen.
4. In the screen that opens, locate Table type, and select INNO DB from the drop-down menu. Click Go. As you can see from the screenshot, there is more than one Go button. The Operations screen contains many options, each with its own separate Go button. Always choose the button within the same section as the option you are changing. In the screenshot, the correct button is the upper one. The lower one is for Collation, but the details of that section are obscured by the drop-down menu.

5. When the conversion has been completed (usually a matter of seconds), the screen will refresh and report that the operation has been carried out. The table has been converted to InnoDB, and it will now support foreign key constraints and transactions. I have never known the operation to fail. If it does, it probably means that InnoDB support has been disabled on the server.

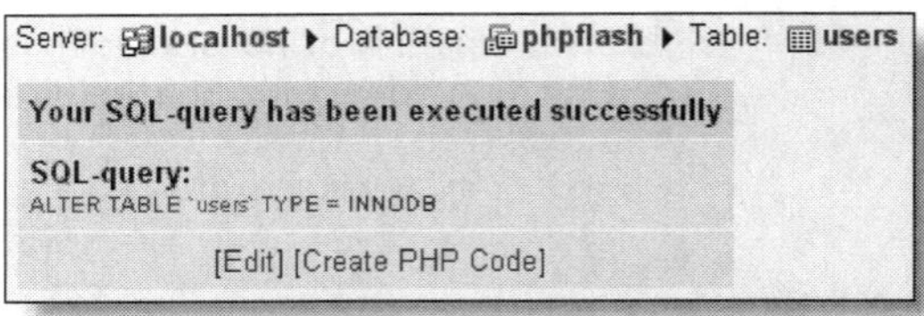

To convert an InnoDB table back to MyISAM, just select MyISAM from the drop-down menu in Step 4 and click Go.

Repairing tables

You should rarely need to repair a table. The only time it is likely to be necessary is if your MySQL server has not closed down properly, such as when the computer crashes. To check a table's integrity or carry out a repair, launch phpMyAdmin, select the database and table, and open the Operations screen as described in steps 1 through 3 of the previous section. The Table maintenance section on the right side of the screen displays the various checking and repair options appropriate to the type of table you are using. As Figure E-4 shows, there are more options for MyISAM tables than for InnoDB tables. This is because InnoDB tables perform an automatic recovery process when the server is restarted after a crash, although the success will depend on whether the files were damaged or corrupted.

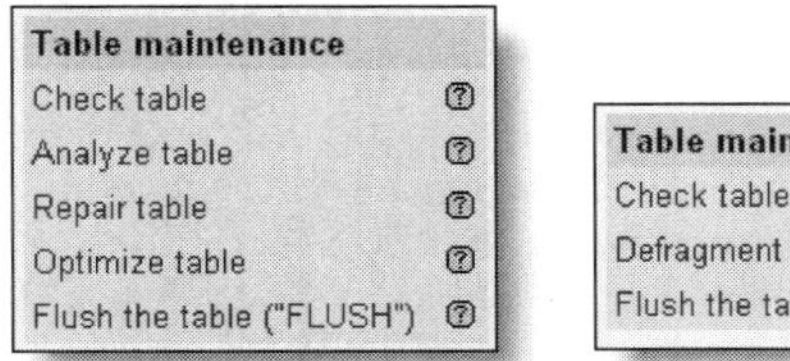

Figure E-4. The table maintenance options for MyISAM tables (left) and for InnoDB tables (right)

The meaning of most of the options is clear from their names, and if you need more information, clicking the question mark icon to the right of each option takes you to the relevant page of the MySQL online documentation. To run one of the maintenance options, just click the option name. Flush the table empties MySQL's internal caches. Because InnoDB stores all tables in a virtual file system, it may be necessary to defragment tables from time to time.

I haven't tested the ability of InnoDB to recover from crashes. So far, I've only needed to use Repair table on a MyISAM table once, and it did the job quickly and accurately. Where tables are damaged beyond repair, regardless of their type, the only solution is to restore them from a backup file as described earlier in this appendix. We all hope it will never happen to us, but it's wise to be prepared. If your databases are located on a hosting company server, check the company's backup policy or implement your own measures.

What to do if you forget your root password

Fortunately, it's not as catastrophic as it sounds. You can find the instructions for resetting the root password at `http://dev.mysql.com/doc/mysql/en/Resetting_permissions.html`. It's relatively straightforward on Windows. Mac OS X users should follow the instructions for Linux, but they will need to invoke superuser privileges through sudo, as explained in Chapter 1. Better still, don't forget your password!

> *The instructions in this book contain all the basic knowledge you need to work with MySQL, but it's a powerful database system with many options and features. To learn more about working with MySQL, consult* The Definitive Guide to MySQL, Second Edition *by Michael Kofler (Apress, ISBN: 1-59059-144-5).*

INDEX

(AS) stands for ActionScript.

Symbols

! negation operator 100
  testing for opposites 101
  using with empty() function 159
!= inequality operator 97
!== not identical operator 98
use in ActionScript 54
use in PHP comments 54
$_POST array
  passing information securely 198
&& logical AND operator 99
—compatible option (mysqldump) 675
.php filename extension 52
== equality operator 97
  testing for presence of zero 102
=== identical operator 98, 140
=> operator
  using with PHP array() construct 184
< less than operator 98
<= less than or equal to operator 98
<> inequality operator 97
> greater than operator 98
>= greater than or equal to operator 98
__construct() function, using 310
{} braces, use in PHP 55
  identifying position of character 141
  if . . . else statement 96
| | logical OR operator 99
?: conditional operator 70, 103, 155, 328–329

A

abs() function (PHP) 92, 153–154
action attribute (XHTML)
  <form> tags 545
actions layer, importance of locking 49
ActionScript
  arrays compared to PHP 188
  case conversion functions 136
  case sensitivity 57
  casting operators 497–498
  common heritage with PHP 7
  dates and times
    converting dates from text input to MySQL format 495
    measured in milliseconds 475
    timestamps, current 477
    timestamps, for specific date 481
  differences and similarities with PHP 8
  functions
    building custom functions 146
    deciding where to put functions 151
    functions remain in local memory 145
    variable scope 147–149
  locating in actions layer 49
  Math object 86
  regular expressions not supported 166
  substring methods 138
  trace 48
  version 2.0 compared to 1.0 642–645
ActionScript 1.0
  converting applications to 641–645
ActionScript 2.0
  applying depth dynamically at runtime 645
  understanding data types 642–643
addItemAt() method (AS)
  ComboBox component 502
addition operator (+) 87
addslashes() function (PHP) 552
  will not work on SQLite 339
administrator privileges (MySQL)
  named user 267, 520
  root user 250–251 (Windows), 259–261 (Mac)
AM/PM, formatting in PHP 485
AMFPHP (PHP remoting) development 5
anchors in regular expressions 167
AND keyword (MySQL) 400
and (logical AND operator in PHP) 99
Apache
  as daemon 7
  benefits of using 4
  configuring to work with PHP 21–24

installing on Windows 10–12, 14
Mac OS X
automatic starting on multiuser Mac 37
restarting from Terminal 38
starting Apache and testing PHP 26–28
versions 1.3 and 2 10
area conversion formulas 105
arithmetic operators 87
combining calculations with assignment 95
rules of precedence 95
array datatype (PHP and AS) 59
array manipulation functions (PHP)
ActionScript equivalent methods 201–202
add element(s) to end of array: array_push() 201
add element(s) at beginning of array: array_unshift() 202
extract part of array: array_slice() 203–204
join multiple arrays: array_merge() 201
remove and substitute elements: array_splice() 202, 205–206, 217
remove first element: array_shift() 202, 565
remove last element: array_pop() 201
reverse array order: array_reverse() 202
Array object (AS)
join() method 144, 450
length property 183, 188
PHP equivalents of methods and properties 201–202
toString() method 182
array search functions (PHP)
find array element and return key: array_search() 565
find if element exists in array: in_array() 565
array sort functions (PHP) 207–208
sort multiple arrays: array_multisort() 207, 218–221
array values (PHP), changing 633–634
arrays (PHP)
array length 188
PHP and ActionScript compared 188
associative arrays 184–185
mixing indexed and associative arrays 185–188
indexed arrays 181
examining contents of 182–184
manipulating arrays. *See* array manipulation functions
multidimensional arrays 179
nesting arrays 189–191
slicing and splicing 202–206
sorting arrays 206–208
superglobal arrays 198
ASP-style tags
nonstandard PHP tags 53
assignment operator (=)
combining calculations with assignment 95
confusing with equality operator 98, 632
using in PHP and ActionScript 86
associative arrays 180, 184–185
mixing indexed and associative arrays 185–188
automatic indenting
using script editors to reduce syntax errors 628

B

backslashes, removing 165
backup, database 668–674
naming files 673
balancing braces
using script editors to reduce syntax errors 628
BBEdit and reducing syntax errors 628
BEGIN keyword (SQLite) 340
BETWEEN min AND max comparison operator (MySQL) 331
BLOB (binary large object) column types 358
bookstore CMS case study
bookstore database
creating and granting user permissions 518–521
creating lookup table 527–529
deleting records from multiple tables 585–586
inserting prices from XML feed 598–601
maintaining referential integrity on deletion 587–594
managing existing book records 574–586
populating database with test data 521
securing CMS 601
updating multiple records 594
creating content management system 529
activating forms with PHP 545–569
deciding basic structure 529–545
displaying database contents in Flash 601
building Flash interface 608
building SQL queries 602–608
communicating with database through PHP 602
loading results from database 609–616
normalizing the tables 515
retrieving data from multiple tables
retrieving books with no author 573–574
retrieving publishers and authors names 570–572
Boolean datatype
PHP and ActionScript 59
braces, use in PHP 55
break keyword
breaking out of loops 195
using in switch statements 103
built-in functions
ActionScript compared to PHP 9

C

calculations 86
arithmetic operators 87
calculating people's ages in MySQL 491–492

combining calculations with assignment 95
operator precedence 93–94
PHP compared to ActionScript 86–87
PHP math functions 91–93
using in dates, MySQL 486–487
capacity conversion formulas 105
case conversion
PHP and ActionScript 135–137
case keyword (switch statement)
blocks of 160
grouping several instances together 156
using in switch statements 103
case sensitivity
ActionScript compared to PHP 8, 57
class names in PHP 57
case-sensitive searches. *See* character classes, PCRE functions in PHP, and string manipulation functions
Cascading Style Sheets. *See* CSS
casting operators
PHP and ActionScript 497–498
ceil() function (PHP) 92
CHAR column type (MySQL) 355
character classes (in regex) 168
and case-sensitive searches 168
charAt() method (AS) 138, 141
charCodeAt() method (AS) 504
checkdate() function (PHP) 495–497
chop() function (PHP) 164
class keyword (PHP and AS) 309
class names, case sensitivity in PHP 57
classes. *See* Database class, and PHP 5 classes
client-side application
Flash movies as 389
clients, and interaction with server 6
close() method
Database class 299
mysqli OO interface (PHP 5) 296–297
Codd, Edgar
relational database rules 351
collation (default sort order) 359, 658–665
columns, database
adding extra column to table 468–469
definition 350
MySQL column types explained 354–358
ComboBox component
addItemAt() method 502
getValue() method 615
setSize() method 502
commenting code in PHP 53–54
COMMIT keyword (SQLite) 340
comparison operators 97
using equality operator with if . . . else statement 98–99
table 97–98
CONCAT() function (MySQL)
used in SELECT statement 550, 571, 575
used in WHERE clause 604
concatenation operator
ActionScript compared to PHP 9, 62–63
ease of missing in PHP 78
joining strings together in PHP 62–63
conditional operator (?:) 103, 155
ActionScript and PHP 70
replacing with if . . . else conditional statement 328–329
conditional statements. *See* decision making
similarity in PHP and ActionScript 8
connect() method
Database class 299
mysqli OO interface (PHP 5) 295
constructor function (PHP 5 classes) 310–311
optional parameters 312
content management system (Flash interface) 411
adding extra column to a table 468–470
building Flash interface 412
creating buttons and movie clip buttons 412–415
delete confirmation dialog box 415–416
laying out individual frames for interface 416–418
elements required 412
scripting application 419–420
deleting records 462–466
displaying full list of users 429–443
multifunctional PHP script 420–422
searching for records 443–451
transferring data with LoadVars 423–429
updating user details 452–462
securing application 466–468
content management system (XHTML interface)
activating forms with PHP 545–569
building basic forms in XHTML 531–545
displaying database contents in Flash 601–616
inserting prices from XML feed 598–601
maintaining referential integrity on deletion 587–594
managing existing book records 574–586
retrieving books with no author 573–574
retrieving publishers' and authors' names 570–572
securing CMS 601
updating multiple records 594
continue keyword 317, 562
breaking out of loops 195
while loop 317
conversion specifications
printf() and sprintf() functions 133–135
cookies compared to Flash SharedObject 323
copyright notice, updating with PHP 51
cost, PHP, Apache and MySQL 4
count() function (PHP) 183, 193, 201, 213, 216

CREATE DATABASE command (MySQL) 266
Create New Symbol dialog box (Flash) 414
  Export for ActionScript check box 414
CREATE TABLE command (MySQL) 269
createEmptyMovieClip() method (AS) 613
cross-platform capability
  PHP, Apache and MySQL 4
CSS (Cascading Style Sheets)
  styling text in Flash 223, 227, 612, 615–6
  styling the bookstore CMS 531–533
CURDATE() function (MySQL) 493
  working with dates in MySQL 486–487
curly braces
  identifying position of character (PHP 5) 141
  if . . . else statement 96
  use in PHP 55
curly quotes
  removal from RSS feed 229–230

D

daemons
  Apache and MySQL as 7
data property
  Flash SharedObject 323, 326
Database class (custom PHP class)
  automatically email error messages 327–330
  changing content of error messages 327
  displaying contents of word list 306–308
  methods and property described 299
  PHP 4 version 304–305
  PHP 5/mysql version 302–303
  PHP 5/mysqli version 300–301
  testing error messages 438
  using num_rows property to test for duplicate records 380
database design
  choosing right language settings 358, 657–665
  column types 354
  default values and NULL 358
  flat-file databases 346
  relational databases 348–350
    normalizing data 350–352
database failures
  changing output of error messages 327
databases. *See* MySQL, and SQLite
  adding to Hangman game 263–264
  backup 668–674
  choosing right system 240–241
  communicating with PHP 291
  creating 264–267
  loading data from backup file 674
  loading data from external file 272–273
  reasons for choosing MySQL 234
database_mysql.php (PHP 5 custom classes)
  creating 302–304
  description 299
database_mysqli.php (PHP 5 custom classes)
  creating 300–302
  description 299
database_php4.php (PHP 4 custom classes)
  creating 304–305
  description 299
datatypes
  PHP and ActionScript 58–59
DATE column type (MySQL) 356
Date object (AS)
  accessing parts of current date 501
  creating timestamps 477
date() function (PHP) 51
  formatting dates 483
    examples 486
    specifiers 484–486
  updating copyright notice 51
dates
  formatting in PHP 483–486
  handling dates in user input
    building Flash date selector for MySQL 498–510
    checking validity of date with PHP 495–497
    formatting from text input 495
  handling with ActionScript, PHP and MySQL 474
  introduction 474
  MySQL format 356
DATETIME column type (MySQL) 356
DATE_ADD() function (MySQL)
  interval types used with 494
  temporal criteria 493–494
DATE_FORMAT() function (MySQL) 488
DATE_SUB() function (MySQL)
  interval types used with 494
  temporal criteria 493–494
DAYNAME() function (MySQL) 487
DAYOFMONTH() function (MySQL) 487
debugging code 635
  debugging function 636
dechex() function (PHP) 87, 92
DECIMAL column type (MySQL) 355
decimal numbers
  use of in PHP and ActionScript 86
decision making in PHP
  comparison operators 97–99
  conditional operator (?:) 103
  elseif statement 96
  if . . . else statement 96
    use of curly braces 96
  introduction 96
  switch statements 102–103

testing more than one condition 99
! negation operator 101
logical operators 99–100
xor exclusive OR operator 100
decrement operator (—) 87–88
default keyword (PHP)
use in switch statements 103
define() function (PHP)
declaring PHP constant 213
DELETE, MySQL administrator privilege 267
DELETE command (MySQL) 411
WHERE clause 411
deleting records
from multiple tables 585–586
from single tables 411
display_errors setting (php.ini) 624
PHP configuration 48
DISTINCT option (MySQL)
SELECT statement 408
division operator (/) 87
do . . . while loop
compared to while loop 195
double quotes in PHP 63
Dreamweaver MX 2004
advantages as PHP script editor 628–629
defining a PHP site 40–43
DROP DATABASE command (SQL) 265, 271

E

echo (PHP) 43, 47, 130–131
value in debugging code 380, 564, 576, 636
ECMAScript standard
ActionScript 2.0 compliance 7
ActionScript and dates 475
else statement 372, 381
elseif statement 96
empty() function (PHP) 102, 159
using with ! negation operator 159
encapsulation
introduced 292
ENCRYPT function (MySQL) 366
ENUM column type (MySQL) 357
equality operator
confusing with assignment operator (=) 632
equal sign (=)
used as equality operator in SQL 380
Error 2002
launching MySQL Monitor on a Mac 259–260
Error 2003
launching MySQL Monitor on Windows 258
error messages 625–626
controlling output of PHP runtime errors 631
Database class 308, 327
PHP categories 627
understanding SQL error messages 267
error_reporting setting (php.ini) 624
escape sequences, PHP 63
list of 64
escaping quotes
preparing data to insert into a MySQL database 377–378
using sqlite_escape_string() with SQLite 338–339
execute permission (Mac and *nix) 333
exit command (PHP) 265, 403
explode() function (PHP) 138, 143–144, 162, 481
Export for ActionScript check box (Flash)
Create New Symbol dialog box 414–415
external data sources
accessing 2
choosing right technology 2
communicating with 46
PHP, Apache and MySQL 4
interaction of 5
reasons for choosing 4

F

fatal error, PHP category of error message 628
fclose() function (PHP) 339
feedback form 64–68
coding back-end of interface 68–71
processing data and sending email with PHP 77–82
testing PHP is receiving the right variables 75–77
using LoadVars to gather and send variables 73–75
fine tuning 172–174
feof() function (PHP) 338
fetch_assoc() method
MyResult (PHP custom class) 299
mysqli OO interface 296
fetch_rss() method (MagpieRSS) 213
fgets() function (PHP) 338
fields, definition 350
FIELDS TERMINATED BY command (MySQL) 274
file handling functions (PHP)
close file: fclose() 339
confirm existence: file_exists() 600
detect end of file: feof() 338
open file: fopen() function 338
read from file: fgets() 338
filename extensions
enabling on Windows 10
file_exists() function (PHP) 600
final keyword (PHP 5 classes) 310
Flash
building date selector for MySQL 498–510
external data sources 2, 46
choosing right technology 2

interaction with PHP functions 146
movies
as client-side application 389
testing 50
PHP, Apache and MySQL, interaction of 5
problems with HTML entities 229–230
sending feedback from by email 64–82
SharedObject 323
FlashVars property
communicating with external data sources 46
flat-file databases 346–348
FLOAT column type (MySQL) 355
floating-point number datatype
PHP and ActionScript 59
floor() function (PHP) 92, 159
flush() method (Flash SharedObject) 323, 326
font. *See* text, styling in Flash
fopen() function (PHP) 338
for . . . in loops 374
compared to foreach loop 191
for loops 192–194
foreach loops
creating a transaction in SQLite 339
looping through arrays 191–192
nesting loops 197
working on both key and value at the same time 192
foreign keys 350–352
constraints to maintain referential integrity 352
support in MySQL table types 234, 238, 351, 353
using PHP to maintain referential integrity 587–594
FROM keyword (SQL)
SELECT query 315, 408
full joins in SQL 569
using 569–572
functions
arguments in wrong order 635
case sensitivity in PHP 57
creating custom functions 146–151
naming in PHP 56
optional parameters 312
return values 150–151, 634

G

getDate() method (AS) 501
getFullYear() method (AS) 501
getLocal() method (Flash SharedObject) 323
getMonth() method (AS) 501
getNextHighestDepth() method (AS) 434, 645
getUrl() function (AS) 398
getValue() method
ComboBox component 615
get_magic_quotes_gpc() function (PHP)
preparing data to insert into a MySQL database 377–378
removing backslashes from feedback form 172
global keyword (PHP) 149
gmmktime() function (PHP)
creating timestamps 477
for specific date 482
GRANT command (MySQL) 266

H

Hangman game
adding database 263–264
adding scoring system 324–326
building graphical elements 286
communicating with database using PHP 291
retrieving records from word list 294–298
creating database classes 298–305
creating word list database in SQLite 337–341
rewriting PHP script for SQLite 341, 343
downloading and installing word list 268–271
hanging man movie clip 287–289
interface movie clip 289–290
introduction 263
scoring mechanism with memory 322
setting different skill levels 330
word selection refinement
scripting Flash movie 318–322
word selection refinement 313–318
header() function (PHP) 402, 544, 558
runtime errors 631
hexadecimal numbers
use in PHP and ActionScript 86
hexdec() function (PHP) 87, 92
HOUR() function (MySQL) 487
hours, formatting in PHP 485
HTML tags, stripping 165
HTML text, styling in Flash MX 645

I

if . . . else statement 96, 155
as alternative to conditional operator (?:) 328–329
use of curly braces 96
using in combination with equality operator 98–99
IGNORE number LINES option (MySQL)
LOAD DATA INFILE command 275
IGNORE option (MySQL)
LOAD DATA INFILE command 273
implode() function (PHP) 138, 144, 450
equivalent of Array.join() 201
equivalent of Array.toString() 202
include statement (PHP)
including external files 213

include_once statement (PHP)
  including external files 213
increment operator (++) 87
indexed arrays 180
  examining contents of 182–184
  mixing indexed and associative arrays 185–188
indexOf() method (AS) 138, 140
infinite loops 632
InnoDB storage engine (MySQL) 353
  license 239
INSERT administrator privilege (MySQL) 267
INSERT command (MySQL) 339, 382, 410
  example 566
  INTO keyword 410
  setting value of TIMESTAMP column 481
  validating and inserting data 561–567
insertMenu() (custom-built PHP function) 542–544, 550
INT column type (MySQL) 355
integer datatype
  PHP and ActionScript 58
INTERVAL keyword (MySQL) 493
in_array() function (PHP) 565
isset() function (PHP) 102, 220, 399, 401
  using with negative operator (!) 402

J

join() function (PHP) 138, 144, 450–451
join() method (AS) 144, 450

K

krsort() function (PHP) 207–208
ksort() function (PHP) 187, 202, 207–208

L

languages
  administering with phpMyAdmin 275, 278, 659
    collation and sort order 359, 660
    selecting right sort order 661–664
lastIndexOf() method (AS) 138, 140
left joins (SQL) 569
  using 572–574
LEFT() function (MySQL)
  used in SELECT statement 575
length conversion formulas 105
length property (AS)
  String object 138
length property (AS)
  Array object 183, 188
LENGTH() function (MySQL) 315
LIMIT keyword (MySQL) 315
  SELECT statement 271, 409
line numbering
  using script editors to reduce syntax errors 628
literal characters in regex 168
LOAD DATA INFILE command (MySQL) 270–274
loadMovie() method (AS)
  loading images for older versions of Flash Player 613
loadVariables() (AS) 46, 73
loadVariablesNum() (AS) 46
LoadVars object (AS)
  checking correct variables received 225
  checking correct variables sent 75–77
  communicating with external data sources 46–48, 73–75
  compared to loadVariables() global function 73
  creating instance 50
  gathering and sending variables 73–75
  loading data in Flash 47–48
  onLoad event handler 73
  preventing the browser from caching old data 75
  sendAndLoad() method 75
LOCAL keyword (MySQL)
  adding to LOAD DATA INFILE command for Mac users 271
login system 393–405
logic errors
  changing array values 633–634
  common causes 632
  confusing assignment and equality operators 86, 98, 632
  function arguments in wrong order 635
  functions with no return value 634
  infinite loops 104–105, 632
  useless loops 633
logical operators 99–100
LONGBLOB column type (MySQL) 358
lookup table
  creating 527
  linking together with 517
loops
  breaking out of loops 195
  for loop 192–194
  infinite loops 104–105, 632
  looping through arrays with foreach 191–192
  nesting loops 196–198
  useless loops 633
  using for repetitive tasks 178, 180, 191
  while and do loops 194–195
loose typing
  PHP and ActionScript 8, 58
  tracking changes in variable types 59–61
ltrim() function (PHP) 164

M

Mac OS X
  Apache and PHP already installed 26
  automatic starting of Apache on multiuser Mac 37
  configuring PHP to display errors 36–37
  enabling PHP 31–33
  installing MySQL 33–34
  MySQL preference pane xvii–xix
  restarting Apache in Terminal 38
  starting Apache and testing PHP 26–28
  sudo (superuser privilege) 30-31
  Terminal 29–31
  upgrading MySQL 678–681
  uninstalling MySQL 680–681
  upgrading PHP 34–35
magic_quotes_gpc setting (php.ini) 165, 378
MagpieRSS parser 212
  installing 212
  merging two feeds 218–223
  parsing foED and Ablog RSS feeds 215–217
  testing 212–215
mail() function (PHP)
  processing data and sending email with PHP 77–81
  reporting database failures automatically 327–330
many-to-many relationships 515
math constants (PHP) 93
math functions (PHP) 91–93
Math object (AS)
  methods and properties matched by PHP 86
  round() method 90
max() function (PHP) 92
md5() function (PHP) 382
MEDIUMBLOB column type (MySQL) 358
metacharacters in regexes 168–169
methods (PHP)
  introduced 292
  setting for PHP 5 classes 312
metric conversion example 88–91
min() function (PHP) 92
MINUTE() function (MySQL) 487
minutes, formatting in PHP 485
mixed arrays
  sorting 187–188
mktime() function (PHP)
  creating timestamps 477
    for specific date 482
modularizing code with functions 144
  returning a value from a function 150–151
  variables and PHP and ActionScript functions 147–149
  where PHP functions run 145
  where to put PHP functions 151
modulo division operator (%) 87–88
month, formatting in PHP 484
MONTH() function (MySQL) 487
MONTHNAME() function (MySQL) 487
movie clip symbol, creating 415
multiconverter application 104
  area conversion 108
  capacity conversion 155–159
  conversion script described 105–107
  Flash interface
    building 110–127
    designing front-end 111–114
    initializing with ActionScript 114–116
    populating combo box 116–121
    reacting to changes in combo box 121–123
    sending data to PHP script and receiving
      result 123–126
  formatting main measurement units 152–155
  length conversion 109, 161–162
  temperature conversion 94, 109–110
  weight conversion 160–161
multidimensional arrays
  grouping similar items 179
  nesting arrays 189–191
multiple database backups
  using mysqldump 673
multiple database tables 513
  deleting records 585–586
  designing table structure 514
  normalizing the tables 515–518
  retrieving data from 569
    avoiding ambiguous column references 569
    using a full join 569–572
    using a left join to find incomplete match 572–574
  updating multiple records 594
    user-defined variables 595–596
multiplication operator (*) 87
MyISAM storage engine (MySQL) 353
MyResult (PHP custom class)
  fetch_assoc() method 299
  num_rows property 299
MySQL
  as daemon 7
  benefits of using 4
  building Flash date selector 498–510
  changing default table type on Windows
      Essentials 253–254
  column types 354
    storing binary data 357
    storing dates and times 356
    storing numbers 355
    storing predefined lists 357
    storing text 354
  communicating with PHP 292
  compared to SQLite 343
    choosing right database system 240–241
  configuring on Mac OS X 259, 261

creating database 263
creating timestamps 478–480
dates, working with 486
calculating people's ages 491–492
calculations 486–487
extracting records based on dates 488–490
temporal criteria 493–494
default values and NULL 358
functions for extracting parts of dates and times 487
installing older versions on Windows 647–650
setting up root user password and securing MySQL 654–655
testing and configuring automatic startup 651–653
installing on Mac OS X 33–34
installing on Windows 241–258
installing Windows Essentials version 243–245
keeping data files in central location 332
licenses 239
mysqli extension (PHP 5/MySQL 4.1 and higher) 292
pattern-matching operators and wildcards 448
reasons for using 234
shortcomings 234–235
SQL syntax
typographic conventions 272
starting and stopping manually on Windows 255
older versions of Windows 256
Windows NT4, 2000, XP and later 255–256
starting and stopping manually on Mac OS X 679
starting and stopping with preference pane on Mac OS X 10.3 xvii–xix
storage formats 353–54
strengths 236–237
upgrading on Mac OS X 678–679
upgrading to Windows Essentials 242
using foreign languages 358–359, 657–665
character sets 657–659
using via Terminal 34
using with graphical interface
MySQL Administrator and MySQL Query Browser 280–282
phpMyAdmin 275–280
versions 237–238
Windows, enabling relevant extension 18
MySQL Administrator 280–282
MySQL maintenance 667–683
backing up databases 668–674
copying to older versions of MySQL 673
location of data files 668–669
using mysqldump 670–674
converting table types 682
forgotten root password 683
repairing tables 682
restoring from a backup 674
transferring database to another server 675–676
upgrading and uninstalling on Mac OS X 678–681
upgrading and uninstalling on Windows 676–678
MySQL Monitor
ending your session 258
Error 2002 (Mac) 259–260
Error 2003 (Windows) 258
launching on Mac OS X 259–261
launching on Windows Essentials 257
other Windows installations 257
problems in viewing character sets 658
recording when a record was created in MySQL 479–480
working with 261–262
MySQL Query Browser 280–282
MySQL Server Instance Configuration Wizard
configuring MySQL server on Windows 246–253
mysqldump
backing up phpflash database 670–671
copying to older versions of MySQL 673
using for partial and multiple backups 672
using to back up data 670
mysqli OO interface
advantages and use 292

N

named users in MySQL 266–267
naming functions, PHP 56
case sensitivity 57
naming variables, PHP 55
case sensitivity 57
natcasesort() function (PHP) 207–208
natsort() function (PHP) 207–208
navigation menu
building 541–544
negative operator (!)
using with isset() function 402
nesting loops 196–198
new keyword
difference between AS and PHP when creating array 181
use with mysqli OO interface 295
use with PHP classes 306, 311
nonalphanumeric characters
using in MySQL 658
nonstandard PHP tags 53
normalization 515
NOT NULL values (SQL)
describing fields as 270
notices
PHP category of error messages 627
NOW() function (MySQL)
creating timestamp in MySQL 480–481
working with dates in MySQL 486–487

NULL datatype
  PHP and ActionScript 59
NULL values (MySQL)
  description 358
number_format() function (PHP) 89–90, 154
num_rows property
  MyResult custom class 299, 380
  mysqli OO interface 296

O

object datatype
  PHP and ActionScript 59
octal numbers
  use in PHP and ActionScript 86
one-to-many relationships 515
one-to-one relationships 515
onLoad event handler (AS)
  assigning to a function 376, 423–425
  using an anonymous function 50, 74
OOP (object-oriented programming)
  ActionScript compared to PHP 9
  classes and objects 292
operator precedence, testing 93–94
optional parameters in PHP functions 312
OPTIONALLY ENCLOSED BY option (MySQL)
  LOAD DATA INFILE command 274
or logical OR operator 100
ORDER BY clause (SQL) 316
  displaying peoples ages in MySQL 492
  SELECT statement syntax 408–409

P

parse errors
  PHP category of error messages 627
parseFloat() method (AS) 163
parseInt() method (AS) 163
partial database backups
  using mysqldump 673
PASSWORD function (MySQL) 360, 366
pattern-matching operators
  MySQL 448
PCRE (Perl-compatible regular expressions)
  list of principal quantifiers 169–170
  supported by PHP 166
PCRE functions in PHP 166
  find match: preg_match() 166, 316, 318, 342
  replace matching instances: preg_replace() 229
PHP
  adding to Windows startup procedure 19–21
  AMFPHP (open source Flash remoting) 5
  array functions with ActionScript equivalents 201–202
  arrays compared to ActionScript 188
  as server-side language 6, 145–146, 389
  basic grammar 52–64
    braces and semicolons 54
    case sensitivity 57
    commenting code 53–54
    file name extensions 52
    loose typing 58
    naming variables and functions 55–58
    PHP tags 53
    reserved words 56
    stringing words and variables together 62–63
    tracking changes in variable types 59–61
    whitespace 55
  benefits of using 4
  building custom functions 146
  calculating timestamps 475
  case conversion functions 136
  casting operators 497–498
  classes. *See* PHP 5 classes
  checking validity of date 495–497
  common heritage with ActionScript 7
  communicating with database 291
  configuration recommended for local computer 621
  configuring Apache to work with 21–24
  converting dates from text input to MySQL required format 495
  creating timestamps 477
    for specific date 482
  deciding where to put functions 151
  defining a PHP site in Dreamweaver MX 2004 40–43
  differences and similarities with ActionScript 8
  downloading and installing on Windows 14–19
  explanation of interaction with Flash movies 6
  finding records based on variable search criteria 448–451
  formatting dates 483
    specifiers 484–486
  functions and variable scope 147–149
  functions processed on remote server 145
  functions, setting optional parameters 312
  interaction of functions with Flash application 146
  Mac OS X
    configuring PHP to display errors 36–37
    enabling PHP 31–33
    starting Apache and testing PHP 26–28
    upgrading PHP 34–35
  POSIX and PCRE supported 166
  returning a value from a function 149–151
  string functions 138
  syntax errors 624
  upgrading on Windows 14
PHP 4 custom classes
  creating 304–305

PHP 5 classes 308–313
  accessing public methods 313
  building and using 308
  constructor function 310–311
  methods 312
  naming and declaring 309
  properties 309
  visibility of properties and methods 309–310
PHP 5/improved MySQL (mysqli) custom classes
  creating 300–302
PHP 5/MySQL custom classes
  creating 302–304
PHP and MySQL troubleshooting 619–639
  configuration problems 620
  logic errors 632–635
  MySQL connection 623
  runtime errors 629–632
  syntax errors 624–629
PHP Windows installer
  reasons for not using 14
php.ini
  files that can be used as basis of 16
phpinfo() 23–25 (Windows), 28–29 (Mac)
phpMyAdmin
  checking details of PHP and MySQL setup 293
  create new database 519
  create new table 524
  obtaining and installing 276–280
  setting user privileges 519
  using to administer languages 278, 659
    collation and sort order 278, 660
    selecting right sort order 661–665
plural() (custom-built PHP function) 156
  creating 152–154
POSIX regular expressions
  supported by PHP 166
post-colon syntax (AS) 69
pow() function (PHP) 92
preg_match() function (PHP) 166, 316, 318, 342
preg_replace() function (PHP) 229
primary keys 350–352
print (PHP) 131
printf() function (PHP) 133–135
print_r() function (PHP) 182, 186, 214, 220
  debugging code 636
private keyword (AS and PHP) 310
privileges, user (MySQL)
  setting in MySQL Monitor 266–268
  setting in phpMyAdmin 519–521
properties (PHP 5 classes)
  creating 309
  introduced 292
  visibility 309–310
protected keyword (PHP 5 classes) 310
public keyword (AS and PHP 5 classes) 310
  setting class methods 312
public methods
  accessing in PHP 5 classes 313

Q

quantifiers (PCRE) 169–170
QUARTER() function (MySQL) 487, 490
query() method
  Database custom classes 299
  mysqli OO interface 296
quotes, in PHP 63

R

rand() function (PHP) 93, 316
RANDOM(*) function (SQLite) 342
read permission (Mac and *nix) 333
read-only permission (Mac and *nix) 341
records, database
  definition 350
referential integrity
  foreign key constraints 352
  using PHP to maintain referential integrity 587–594
register_globals (php.ini)
  importance of 199
regular expressions
  anchors 167
  building 170–171
  not supported in ActionScript 166
  understanding basics 166–170
  using to identify patterns 166
relational databases 348–350
removeMovieClip() method (AS) 613
REPLACE option (MySQL)
  LOAD DATA INFILE command 273
require construct (PHP)
  including external files 213
require_once() construct (PHP)
  including external files 213
reserved words, PHP 56
resource datatype
  PHP and ActionScript 59
restrict property (AS)
  TextField class 375
return keyword (PHP) 153, 635
  returning a value from a function 150–151
RIGHT() function (MySQL)
  extracting month and day from a date 492
root password (MySQL)
  resetting forgotten password 683
  setting on Mac OS X 259–261
  setting in MySQL Windows Essentials 250–251

setting in previous Windows versions 654–655
round() function (PHP) 90, 93
rounding figures 91
round() method (AS Math object) 90
rsort() function (PHP) 207
RSS feed aggregator 209–230
deploying on Internet 230
displaying merged RSS feed in Flash 223–228
eliminating HTML entities 229–230
parsing RSS feed with MagpieRSS 212–223
rtrim() function (PHP) 164
runtime errors
controlling output of error messages 631
headers already sent 630
server compatibility 629
typical causes 629
user input 630

S

scientific notation
use in PHP and ActionScript 86
SciTEFlash (script editor)
reducing syntax errors 628
scope, variable 147–149
scoring system, adding to Hangman game 324–326
script editors, using to reduce syntax errors 628
<script> tag
nonstandard PHP tags 53
search form, scripting 444–451, 604–605, 615
SECOND() function (MySQL) 487
seconds, formatting in PHP 485
security
Apache servers and 4
securing the content management system 466–468
using PHP sessions for improved security 390–405
SELECT administrator privilege (MySQL) 267
SELECT statement (SQL) 400, 408
DISTINCT option 408
FROM keyword 315
LIMIT keyword 271, 409
ORDER BY clause 409
WHERE clause 315, 400, 409
<select> tags (XHTML) 535, 567
name attribute 560
self-processing forms 545
semicolons
use in PHP 54
sendAndLoad method (AS)
LoadVars object 75
preventing the browser from caching old data 75
server compatibility
runtime errors 629
server root 38
server-side language, PHP as 6, 145–146, 389
servers, explanation of interaction with client 6
SESSION superglobal array (PHP) 200, 392
sessions (PHP) 388–393
creating a session 392
destroying a session 392
introduction 388
other uses 405
restricting access 393
user registration application 393–405
session variables
creation 392
unsetting 392
web as stateless environment 388–389
workings of 390–391
session_destroy() command (PHP) 393
session_register() function, (PHP, deprecated) 393
session_start() command (PHP) 392
placement of 399
starting session 401
session_unregister() function (PHP, deprecated) 393
SET column type (MySQL) 357
setlocale() function (PHP)
changing language display 484
setSize() method
ComboBox component 502
sha1() function (PHP) 382
SharedObject (AS)
data property 326
flush() method 326
introduction 323
shell comments (PHP) 54
short tags
nonstandard PHP tags 53
show tables command (MySQL) 265
showVal() (custom-built PHP function)
debugging code 636
using 637–639
shuffle() function (PHP) 313
SimpleXML (PHP)
compared to ActionScript XML class 514
parsing an XML feed 596–598
simplexml_load_file() function (PHP) 596
single quotes in PHP 63
slice() method (AS) 142
SMTP setting for Windows 19
SOAP, connecting to web services 3
sort order, default (MySQL) 660–665
sort() function (PHP) 182, 187, 202, 207
sorting PHP arrays
multiple arrays 207, 218–221
PHP functions 206–208
split() function (PHP)
danger of confusion with ActionScript method 144

split() method (AS) 495
sprintf() function (PHP) 133–135, 154, 156, 162, 198
SQL, equal sign (=) used as equality operator 380
SQL commands
 CREATE DATABASE 266
 CREATE TABLE 269
 DELETE 411
 DROP DATABASE 265, 271
 GRANT 266
 INSERT 410
 SELECT 408
 UPDATE 410
SQL syntax 272
SQLite
 basics 331
 compared to MySQL 234, 239, 343
  choosing right database system 240–241
 creating word list database 337–341
 escaping quotes 339
 setting file permissions 333–335, 341
 setting up folder on Linux server 336–337
 setting up folder on Mac OS X 335–336
 shortcomings 240
 strengths 239
SQLiteDatabase class (PHP) 332
sqlite_escape_string() function (PHP)
 escaping quotes on SQLite 339
sqrt() function (PHP) 93
STARTING BY option (MySQL)
 LOAD DATA INFILE command 275
static keyword (AS and PHP) 310
storage formats (MySQL) 353–354
strcspn() function (PHP) 607
strftime() function (PHP) 51
 formatting dates 483
strict (static) typing
 ActionScript 8, 58, 642–643
 use in this book 69
string datatype
 PHP and ActionScript 59
string manipulation with PHP 130
 outputting strings
  changing case 135
  echo 130
  print 131
  printf() and sprintf() functions 133–135
  urlencode() function 132–133
 substrings 138
  converting strings into arrays and back 143–144
  extracting substring 142
  getting character at known position 141
  getting length of string 141
  getting position of character or substring 139–140
  replacing a substring 142–143
String object (AS)
 charCodeAt() method 504
 equivalent PHP functions 138
 split() method 495
string related functions (PHP)
 case-insensitive search for last instance of substring:
  strripos() (PHP 5) 138, 140
 case-insensitive search for substring: stripos() (PHP 5)
  138, 140
 case-sensitive search for last instance of substring:
  strrpos() 138, 140, 153
 case-sensitive search for substring: strpos()
  function 138–140, 154, 338, 607
 convert array to string: implode(), join() 138, 144, 450
 convert first letter to uppercase: ucfirst() 137, 198
 convert initial letters to uppercase: ucwords()
  function (PHP) 137
 convert to lowercase: strtolower() 137, 140
 convert to uppercase: strtoupper() 137, 198
 convert string to timestamp: strtotime() 482–485
 escape quotes with backslashes: addslashes() 552
 extract a substring: substr() 138, 142, 220
 find first instance of any character from a specified
  group: strcspn() 607
 length of string: strlen()138, 153, 315, 338
 remove backslashes: stripslashes() 165, 548
 remove whitespace. See whitespace
 replace all instances of substring: str_replace() 138,
  142–143
 replace first instance of substring: substr_replace() 138,
  142–143, 153
 split on specified substring and convert to array:
  explode() 138, 143–144, 162, 481
 strip HTML tags: strip_tags () 165
subqueries (MySQL 4.1) 490
substr() function 138, 142, 220
substrings, PHP and ActionScript 138
substr_replace() function 138, 142–143, 153
subtraction operator (-) 87
sudo (Mac OS X) 30-31
superglobal arrays (PHP) 198–200
superuser do. *See* sudo
Swap Symbol dialog box (Flash) 417
switch statement in PHP 102–103, 153, 155–157, 159–161
syntax coloring
 using script editors to reduce syntax errors 628
syntax errors 624
 blank pages 624
 error messages 625–627
system, checking details of PHP and MySQL setup 293
system() function (PHP)
 using to populate a database 675

T

Table dialog box (Dreamweaver MX 2004)
  Header Left option 533
  Header Top option 540
tables, database
  multiple tables 513
  show tables command 265
temperature conversion formulas 106, 109–110
Terminal (Mac OS X) 29–31
ternary operator (?:). *See* conditional operator
TEXT column type (MySQL) 355
TextArea components (Flash) 65
<textarea> tags (XHTML) 567
TextField restrict property (AS) 375
TextInput components 65
TextPad
  reducing syntax errors 628
text, styling in Flash
  CSS styles 223, 227, 612, 615–6
  TextFormat object 49, 371, 434–5, 440–441, 462
<th> tags (XHTML) 533
There's more than one way to do it 323
TIME column type (MySQL) 356
time() function (PHP)
  creating timestamps 477
TIMESTAMP columns (MySQL) 356
  caution when using 481
  creating timestamps in MySQL 478–480
timestamps
  ActionScript, MySQL and PHP 475
  creating
    in ActionScript 477
    in MySQL 478–480
      in PHP 477–478
  creating for specific date 481
    ActionScript syntax 481
    PHP syntax 482
  description 474
  incompatibility of 475–476
  Unix epoch 474
  uses 477
TINYBLOB column types (MySQL) 358
TMTOWTDI (There's more than one way to do it) 323
toLowerCase() method (AS) 137
toString() method (AS) 182
toUpperCase() method (AS) 137
trace (AS) 115–116, 225, 320, 372, 376, 438, 453
transactions, database 239, 339, 353, 581
  creating in SQLite 339
trigonometric functions (PHP) 93
trim() function (PHP) 164, 338, 562, 604–605
  whitespace characters removed by 165
type specifiers
  printf() and sprintf() functions 134–135

U

uasort() function (PHP) 207
ucfirst() function (PHP) 137, 198
ucwords() function (PHP) 137
uksort() function (PHP) 207
undefined datatype 102
Unix epoch (timestamps) 474
unset() function (PHP) 340
UPDATE administrator privilege (MySQL) 267
UPDATE command (SQL) 410, 558
  example 595
  WHERE clause 411
UPPER() function (MySQL) 550
URL encoding
  required format for data transfer to Flash 48
urlencode() function 47, 83, 132–133, 174
use (databasename) command (MySQL) 265
useless loops 633
user input
  removing backslashes 165
  runtime errors 630
  stripping HTML tags 165
  trimming leading and trailing whitespace 164
  using regular expressions to identify patterns 166
user privileges, database
  setting in MySQL Monitor 266–268
  setting in phpMyAdmin 520
user registration application 359–385
  database considerations 346
  registering users with MySQL 359–360
    creating an online registration form 368–370
    creating users table 360–364
    entering records in users table 364–368
    problem solving 384
    scripting registration form 370–376
    using PHP to communicate between Flash and MySQL 376–384
  restricting access
    adapting registration form 396–398
    creating login form 394–396
    plugging security gap 403–405
user-defined variables (MySQL)
  updating multiple records 595–596
usort() function (PHP) 207

V

VARCHAR column type (MySQL) 355
variable scope
  PHP and ActionScript functions 147–149
variables
  ActionScript compared to PHP 8
  case sensitivity in PHP 57
  naming in PHP 55

variable typing in AS and PHP 8
version numbers
Apache, checking version installed on Mac OS X 35
Apache, choosing the right version 10
checking details of PHP and MySQL setup 293
checking PHP version number 23–25 (Windows), 28–29 (Mac)
versions used in this book xvi
visibility of properties in PHP and AS classes 309–310

W

warnings, PHP category of error messages 627
web as stateless environment 388–389
web services
accessing external data sources 2
compared to Flash Remoting 3
weekdays, formatting in PHP 485
weight conversion formulas 106
WHERE clause (SQL) 379–380
AND keyword 400
DELETE command 411
SELECT statement 315, 400, 409
UPDATE command 411
while loop 194–195, 317
continue keyword 317
whitespace
trimming leading and trailing whitespace 164
use in PHP 55
wildcard characters (regex). *See* quantifiers
wildcards
MySQL 448
Windows
adding PHP to startup procedure 19–21
configuring Apache to work with PHP 21–24
displaying filename extensions 10
enabling MySQL 18
enabling SMTP (mail) relay 19
installing Apache 10–12, 14
installing MySQL Windows Essentials 244–245
installing older versions of MySQL 647–655
installing PHP 14–19
upgrading and uninstalling MySQL 676–678
upgrading PHP 14
word list
creating database in SQLite 337–341
displaying contents with classes 306–308
displaying first ten entries with MySQL Monitor 291
word selection refinement 313–318
work environment
setting up 38–40
write permission (Mac and *nix) 333

X

XHTML
building basic forms for bookstore CMS 531–545
stripping tags 165
XML
communicating with external data sources 46
connecting to web services 3
parsing with SimpleXML 598
XML class (AS)
compared to SimpleXML feature 514
XML document
parsing with SimpleXML 596–598
xor exclusive OR operator 100

Y

year, formatting in PHP 484
YEAR column type (MySQL) 356
YEAR() function (MySQL) 487
calculating people's ages in MySQL 491

friendsof
DESIGNER TO DESIGNER™
an Apress® company